DATE DUE

DEMCO 38-296

The Philosophy of Legal Reasoning

*A Collection of Essays by Philosophers
and Legal Scholars*

Series Editor

Scott Brewer
Harvard Law School

A GARLAND SERIES
READINGS IN PHILOSOPHY
ROBERT NOZICK, *ADVISOR*
HARVARD UNIVERSITY

Contents of the Series

Scientific Models of Legal Reasoning
Economics, Artificial Intelligence,
and the Physical Sciences

Edited with an introduction by

Scott Brewer
Harvard Law School

GARLAND PUBLISHING, INC.
A MEMBER OF THE TAYLOR & FRANCIS GROUP

New York & London
1998

R

Library of Congress Cataloging-in-Publication Data

Scientific models of legal reasoning : economics, artificial intelligence,
and the physical sciences / edited with an introduction by Scott
Brewer.
     p. cm. — (The philosophy of legal reasoning ; 5)
   Includes bibliographical references.
    ISBN 0-8153-2757-9 (v. 5 : alk. paper). — ISBN 0-8153-2654-8
(set : alk. paper)
    1. Law—Methodology. 2. Law—Interpretation and construction.
3. Reasoning. 4. Science—Methodology. 5. Artificial intelligence.
I. Brewer, Scott. II. Series.
K213.P494 1998
340'.1 s—dc21   98-5168
[340'.11]   CIP

Printed on acid-free, 250-year-life paper
Manufactured in the United States of America

Contents

Introduction

This five-volume set contains some of this century's most influential or thought-provoking articles on the subject of legal argument that have appeared in Anglo-American philosophy journals and law reviews. Legal decisions have long been a deeply significant part of the history and life of societies that aspire to satisfy some version of the "rule of law" ideal. These decisions—at least those rendered by a jurisdiction's most prominent courts—are also often accompanied by detailed publicly available statements of the arguments supporting those decisions. For these reasons, among many others, understanding the dynamics of legal argument is of vital interest not only to legal academics, judges, lawyers, and law students, but also to citizens who are subject to law and who vote, directly or indirectly, for the legislators, regulators, and judges who write and interpret laws.

Because of the importance to civil societies of legal decisons and the legal arguments offered to justify them, the subject of legal argument has long been closely studied by scholars and other analysts. These theorists have explicated and criticized the dynamics of legal argument from vastly different perspectives. It is thus not surprising that these theorists have reached strikingly different conclusions, with equally distinct concerns and emphases. Theorists of legal argument have, for example, maintained that legal argument is principally driven by *a priori* legal-cum-moral truths applied to individual cases by formal logical inferences, or that the driving force of legal argument is a more or less thinly veiled imposition of a judge's preferred social or economic policy, or that legal argument is or should be (theorists sometimes blur the line between the descriptive and the prescriptive in their analyses) the incessantly self-critical and self-correcting reasoned elaboration of legal rules and standards that transcend immediate partisan results, or that legal arguments offered by judges are little more than a mystificatory and would-be legitimating veneer covering such darker motives as race, class, or gender bias, or that legal argument is the interpretive effort by judges in the forum of principle to make the law the best it can be from a moral point of view, or is the decision of those legal officials who hold authoritative power by virtue of socially adopted rules.

This set of volumes represents all of the theories just encapsulated, and others as well. As the brief, and certainly incomplete, list in the foregoing paragraph suggests, theorists of legal argument produce what can seem a whelming welter of diverse explanations. Even so, the vast majority of theories of legal argument revolve around two central focal points—rather, perhaps, like the oval-shaped ellipse, which orbits around two fixed foci.

One focus is the role of different *modes of logical inference* in legal argument. There are four basic logical structures that operate in legal argument (indeed, it can be argued plausibly that these are the four that organize all arguments, in all intellectual domains): *deduction, induction, abduction,* and *analogy.* It may help the reader to have a few basic definitions of these terms at the outset—even though by no means all the theorists whose articles are included will use these terms in their analyses. First, the basic term 'argument.' The defining characteristic of *argument,* including legal argument, is the inference of a conclusion from one or more premises. As just noted, all arguments, including legal argument, deploy one or more of four principal and irreducible (though analogical inference is tricky in this regard) modes of logical inference: (i) *deductive inference,* in which the truth of the premises guarantees the truth of the conclusion as long as the conclusion is arrived at by an acceptable deductive inference rule; (ii) *inductive inference,* in which the truth of the premises cannot guarantee the truth of the conclusion, but when the premises are carefully chosen, their truth can warrant belief in the truth of the conclusion to greater or lesser degrees of probability; (iii) *abductive inference,* in which an explanatory hypothesis is inferred as the conclusion of an argument with two distinct types of premise: first, a proposition that describes some event or phenomenon that the abductive reasoner believes stands in need of *explanation,* and second, a proposition to the effect that, *if* the explanatory hypothesis that is inferred ("abducted") were in fact *true* or otherwise warranted, then the explanandum would be sufficiently explained for the reasoner's purposes; and (iv) *analogical inference,* in which a reasoner relies on particular examples to discover (indeed, to "abduce") a rule that states what are the relevant similarities or differences between a less well-known item (the "target" of the analogical inference) and a better known item (the "source" of the analogical inference). The other focal point of theories of legal argument is the role of various types of *norms* in legal argument, including *legal norms* (norms issued by proper legal authorities or endorsed by other social norms—the proper account of legal norms divides "legal positivists" and "natural law" theorists), *moral norms* (norms concerned with right and wrong), *epistemic norms* (norms concerned with true or otherwise warranted beliefs), *linguistic norms* (norms concerned with understanding the meaning of texts), and "instrumental" or "prudential" norms (those nonmoral norms that are "instrumental" to helping a reasoner achieve a goal he or she has chosen to pursue).

Even when they do not explicitly use this exact terminology of "logical inference," "deduction," "induction," "norm," and the like, in one way or another all of the articles in these volumes are within the intellectual gravitational orbit of these two focal points. One hastens to add that, far from being dry and remote "academic" exercises, the inquiries pursued by these articles touch on many of the most pressing and contentious issues in contemporary legal, moral, and political debate—as the list of conclusions of various theories of legal argument in the second paragraph of this introduction clearly indicates.

Several criteria have guided the selection of articles in this set. The broad impact of an article among scholars, judges, and lawyers was certainly a leading criterion, and a great many of the articles satisfy it. But that criterion was by no means the only one. Some of the articles in these volumes are fairly recent, and more time will be needed to assess their enduring impact on the worlds of legal thought and practice. It can be said fairly that even these more recent articles present fresh and thought-provoking claims and insights, worthy of being considered even if only to be ultimately rejected. The criterion of intellectually fertile provocation guided the selection of some of the older articles in the volumes (for example, some of those in volume one), which were chosen neither for fame nor influence but rather because they present an important perspective on an issue that—in this editor's opinion—has received far too little attention in twentieth-century American jurisprudence and legal education: the role of *deductive* inference in legal argument. Even though the role of one or more of the four basic logical inferences is a focus of theories of legal argument, generations of legal academics, judges, and lawyers have tended to ignore or understate the role of deductive inference, largely without understanding enough about what deductive inference is or the many very important ways in which it does guide legal argument. They have been led to this point largely because of the influentially expressed and often parroted sentiment of Justice Oliver Wendell Holmes Jr. and several of his followers, that "[t]he life of the law has not been logic: it has been experience."[1] By 'logic' Holmes meant deductive logic, and his maxim-al hyperbole has done much to encumber the proper understanding of the rational dynamics of legal argument. Several of the articles in these volumes were chosen to help readers rediscover and revivify this important issue and to see its importance for broader political and moral questions.

All in all, I am confident that the articles in these volumes will well repay the attentiveness of readers who wish to think seriously about the nature of significance of legal argument as a vital part of broader legal and political processes, as long as they bring reading minds that are fairly "braced with labor and invention."

Notes

[1]Oliver W. Holmes, *The Common Law*, ed. Mark DeWolfe Howe (Boston: Little, Brown, 1963) p.5.

[1]Oliver W. Holmes, *The Common Law* 1 ed. Mark DeWolfe Howe (?: ?, 1963).

Law and Scientific Method

By MORRIS RAPHAEL COHEN
Professor in the College of the City of New York.

[Address delivered at the Twenty-Fifth Annual Meeting of Association of American Law Schools, December 29, 1927.

IT WAS an English judge who once thanked God that the law of England was not a science. The sense of gratitude to God is often somewhat capricious; but there can be no doubt that the English bar has not only neglected the science of law but has felt a positive aversion for it. This was not overstated by the one who said that the very word "jurisprudence" was offensive to the nostrils of the English lawyer. Nor is this merely the English preference for muddling through. We must take into account the historic facts as to the relation between the English universities and the Inns of Court. As the universities would not teach English law, the business of preparing men for the well-organized profession of law fell into the hands of strictly professional corporations, whose traditions had little in common with the clerical and other-worldly traditions which prevailed in Oxford and Cambridge up to very recent days. And yet some part of the scientific spirit— something of the scholar's interest in history and respect for fact, and something of the spirit of detachment—did penetrate the English bar, partly through the separation of the barrister from the business of the solicitor and partly at least through the philologic studies which leaders of the bar pursued in the classical courses at the public schools and at Oxford and Cambridge. Certainly the old rules of pleading showed a highly refined logical technique.

Much more unfavorable for the development of any science of law have been the conditions in this country. Up to the last quarter of the nineteenth century, we had no real universities; and the practical demands on the service of lawyers was so great that any attempt to regulate their educational qualifications was resented by the public as an undue interference with the natural right of every enterprising citizen to choose and pursue his own calling. It is therefore not surprising that until very recently our law schools functioned practically as trade schools, and their connection with the colleges or universities was rather nominal. For men to make the teaching of law their major occupation is for us a new phenomenon, and I cannot help recalling the contemptuous references to the teachers of law which I heard at a meeting of a great State Bar Association not so long ago. To one who was neither a lawyer nor a teacher of law the vehemence of the contempt was rather amusing.

I venture to submit these trite observations to call your attention to the fact that despite the rapid expansion of our law schools in the last decade, and despite the increase of scientific interest in the law

1

as shown in our law reviews, we are still under tremendous pressure to prepare our students for practical success at the bar rather than to advance the science of the law. We may, when we view the situation abstractly, admit that ultimately the most practical thing that our law school can do for the community is to promote the science of law; but under pressure of immediate practicality we are loath to change the strictly professional curriculum. We fear to introduce theoretic studies as remote from immediately practical legal issues as are pathology in the school of medicine, physiological psychology in the school of education, or rational mechanics in the school of engineering. Men were undoubtedly successful physicians, teachers, and engineers, before the introduction of such studies, but no one doubts to-day their necessity to give men a liberal insight into their work. So men have been and will continue to be successful at the bar without direct attention to the science of the law. Indeed, if we were to judge by purely and immediately practical results, our present law school curriculum might be viewed as already too theoretical. A knowledge of the existing law, let us courageously admit, is not the sole, nor perhaps even the most important, condition for practical success at the bar. The art of properly manipulating judges, juries, and clients is at least as important, and yet does not, and rightly should not, receive the attention of the law school. The public interest which the university ought to serve is no more intimately connected with the personal success of the lawyer than with that of the modiste, the shoemaker, or the plumber. The primary object of the university as a public institution can only be the advancement of our legal institutions through the development of a liberal understanding or science of the law.

I.

If scientific method be a way of avoiding certain human pitfalls in the search for truth, then the law surely compares favorably in this respect with other human occupations. Court procedure to determine whether A and B did make a con-

tract, or whether C did commit a criminal act, shows a regard for orderly attainment of truth that compares very favorably with the procedure of a vestry board in determining the fitness of a minister, or of a college in selecting a professor or grading a student.

When we come, however, to the appellate work of higher courts, in which new public policies are decided under the guise of their legality or constitutionality, we find courts making all sorts of factual generalizations without adequate information. For the facilities of our courts for acquiring information as to actual conditions are very limited. They have to decide all sorts of complicated issues after a few hours of oral argument and briefs by lawyers. Are ten hours per day in the old type bakery a strain on the baker's health? Will a Workmen's Compensation Act, or minimum wage law, take away the property of the employer, or of the worker that receives less than the minimum of subsistence? It is not to the credit of any system that its chief exponents can put their amateurish opinions against those of physicians or economists who have given these questions careful scientific study. Yet the law cannot simply and uncritically accept all the opinions of economists or sociologists. After all, on many important points social scientists are not agreed among themselves; and intellectualists persist in claiming that the so-called social sciences do not demonstrate their results as rigorously as do the natural sciences. Much of what passes as social science is just exercise in technical vocabulary, or mere plausible impressionism, without any critical methods for testing data or accurately determining whether certain assumed results are really true. A good deal of psychology, normal and abnormal, is still in that condition. This, of course, is no argument for the law ignoring what experts in these fields have to say. But it should impress upon us the necessity for the law itself—in the persons of jurists, judges and advocates—having a trained sense of scientific method.

It was the great Poincaré who once said that, while physical scientists were busy solving their problems, social scientists

2

were busy discussing their methods. Making due allowance for Gallic wit, there is in this statement much to sober a too sanguine generation that expects heaven on earth as a result of a universal conversion to scientific method. A little critical reflection shows that the term "scientific method" is seldom used with a very definite meaning. If it denote the art of teaching men how to make discoveries in the sciences, we may well say that such an art is as unknown as the art of training great poets. Certainly we should expect little in this respect from books of logic, the authors of which have seldom made any contributions to science, and indeed often write from mere hearsay about it. Nor can we expect much from scientific specialists who occasionally take time off from their own work to write on scientific method in general. With some honorable exceptions their utterances are naturally as naive as that of the successful athlete or robust old man discussing general hygiene, or the successful man of affairs laying down the law as how to educate others to his level of attainment.

But, where the uncritical expect too much, wise men will not despise the little illumination which they can get. After all, experience shows that those who have received no training in a given field seldom, if ever, make discoveries in it. Knowledge of past achievement seems a most necessary condition for the advancement of any subject. But a creative capacity in any field is not developed by learning by rote, all its specific rules. Even if all of the latter could be acquired in a few years, at the end of the time there would be new rules. Effective scientific training enables men to handle new situations precisely because science seeks to get at the constant elements or laws which remain identical throughout the changes in a given field. It is, at any rate, by the possession of certain modes of analysis which reveal such constant or logical elements in the new situation that a scientifically trained man differs from the one who has merely routine knowledge. The latter, as habitual may be more sure in familiar situations, but it breaks down in novel situations.

II.

Whatever services scientific method is to render, it is reasonable to demand that it shall not hinder the growth of the science to which it ministers. But this is precisely what the method known as positivism or behaviorism does when it denies that there can be any normative branch of jurisprudence—that is, when it denies scientific character to questions as to what the law ought to be.

A superficial conception of science at the basis of what used to be called materialism, and is now called behaviorism, supposes that science can deal only with what actually is. But this is just nonsense. The actual has meaning for science only when judged in the light of some ideal. Indeed all mathematical and theoretic science deals with ideals and possibilities. Mankind at large, to be sure, happens to be interested in those theoretic sciences which find application in the actual world. But this does not deny the normative character of theoretic science. Positivists like Duguit and Ardigò, who insist that a science of the law should restrict itself to the law that is, generally fall into a crypto-idealism, that is, they set up some idealization of the actual law as the desirable state that ought to be. In the early stage of the historical school in this country many, like Langdell, Ames, and Gray, were inclined to set up the law of England at the end of the eighteenth century as the ideal of the common law. But no actual law is ever a complete system, as actual. it cannot be used to settle new issues without expanding it along the lines that seem desirable to the jurist. The law cannot avoid taking sides and committing itself as to whether it favors freer divorce, strict or liberal interpretation of the power of the state over private property, and as to similar issues. We are constantly faced with the question whether certain desirable remedies should be granted under circumstances that would mean a tremendous increase in the amount of litigation. What is this but a question of public policy?

The positivists justify their position by the contention that it is up to the Legis-

3

lature to determine the policy of the law, and that judges and jurists must simply obey it. But even if we ignore the part that judges and jurists play in making the law, we cannot ignore the fact that intelligent obedience requires a painstaking understanding of the purpose of the law. Even in military affairs, General Foch has taught us, discipline requires intelligent initiative in order to bring about conformity to the purpose of the superior command. Unintelligent obedience is always dangerous, even when the rules are most excellent (see the lamented Christy Matthewson on Inside Baseball).

We can thus see the one-sidedness of those who, like Ehrlich, tend to confuse the sociologic with the juristic point of view. The study of "living law" is a study of custom—a very important condition of law, but not a sufficient determinant of it. For actual practices may be contrary to the policy of the law. The law cannot accept everything as legal merely because it is the practice of a large number of people. Custom must meet certain criteria before the law will sanction it. It is doubtless of the utmost importance to know the actual conditions under which a legal rule is to be applied. But it cannot be too strongly insisted that the knowledge of such social conditions belongs to economics, or to some branch of descriptive social science. Law is a method of regulating social action, and the science of law has a content over and above that met in the knowledge of actual conditions.

At this point we may also dispose of the myth that scientific method is inductive—a myth which was originated largely by a famous lawyer, Francis Bacon, and which the case-system of teaching law has somewhat strengthened. But it is well to remember that Langdell like Bacon labored under a thoroughly rationalistic conception that not only was the number of legal principles very small, but that the number of cases was limited and could easily be manipulated to show all the possible principles. Few to-day profess this simple faith. The view that science can begin without anticipations of nature and proceed first of all to gather the facts, is nothing less than silly. For what facts are

we to gather as relevant for our inquiry? Indeed, to find out what are the facts is the very purpose of scientific investigation. It is an illusion to suppose that we can build up a legal system or science of the law by simply gathering all the cases together. For the very first question, What does the case stand for? involves a theoretic issue—namely, on what principle can the actual decision be supported, or from what principle can it be deduced. The notion that a single case or even a number of cases can by themselves prove a principle is of course the old fallacy of arguing from the affirmation of the consequent. If decisions in specific cases are either right or wrong, the question of principle is already involved.

This suggests certain considerations in regard to statistical methods in legal science. Theoretically, it might seem that every assumption of general fact that the law makes ought to be capable of being tested statistically. Thus, the assertion that the rigor of punishment acts as a deterrent of crime seems to involve the correlation of only two factors and ought to be tested statistically. The first difficulty, however, is one familiar to all students of social science—namely, the difficulty of isolating our factors. Groups of figures can show a correlation only on the assumption that all other factors balance each other or remain constant, an assumption which there is reason to believe is seldom true in social affairs. Other questions of fact involve unique elements not sufficiently numerous to be the subject of numerical methods. Thus, we cannot by statistical comparison of conditions in common and civil law countries really settle the question whether the principle of *stare decisis* does in fact make the law more certain. Too few instances and too many possible factors have to be considered to make the statistical results conclusive.

These difficulties are familiar enough, and, while they do not prevent statistical work in the social sciences, they certainly militate against the conclusiveness of the results obtained by such methods. In general, our statistical work depends upon the initial hypothesis which guides us in selecting the relevant facts and assigning a meaning to the possible correlations.

This brings us to the second limitation as to statistical methods in legal science, and that is that they are not applicable to purely juristic questions, to questions as to the meaning or validity of legal principles. In general, theories of value in economics, ethics, and politics cannot be discovered or established by statistical methods, though the latter may be used in the verification of factual generalizations.

The fact that questions of value have to be dealt by dialectical rather than statistical methods puts a limitation on the use of history for juristic purposes. History is undoubtedly a method of extending our experience. It helps us to eliminate vicious rationalism, the tendency typified by Blackstone of finding false reasons for actual legal rules. Yet, by itself, history cannot establish standards of value or of what is desirable in the law. In fact, the same sets of historical facts teach different lessons to those who have different biases as to what is desirable. It is customary to have historical introductions to all sorts of practical discussions; but generally they are like the chaplain's prayer which opens a political convention, graceful and altogether unexceptionable, but subsequent proceedings are not determined by them.

Moreover, in the reaction against Blackstonian rationalism, legal history has recently fallen into the inverse fallacy. I refer to the method of explaining old rules as mere survivals. No one doubts that many rules continue their existence after they have outlived their original function. But it is also true that many rules formerly useful, and now no longer so, have died. Is it not likely then that those that have survived may have done so because of a greater social vitality in serving some actual social need? This seems to me to hold with regard to the unusual liability of the common carrier. The latter is not adequately explained as a mere survival. It survived because of its utility.

Finally, if history is not to be a blind enslavement of the living present to the dead past, we must always be on guard as to what past rules are no longer suitable, and this requires, not only a knowledge of past facts, but also an understanding of the needs of the present as of the past. This involves a theory of social needs or ends which the law ought to serve.

III.

If at this point any of you accuse me of still believing in the old classical deductive methods—so discredited in the minds of modernistic illuminati—I must enter a plea of confession and avoidance. I admit faith in the hypothetico-deductive method, but I deny that it has ever been justly discredited. On the contrary, the method of beginning with hypotheses and deducing conclusions and then comparing these conclusions with the factual world, seems to me still the essence of sound scientific method. The prejudice against deduction is inspired by the abuse of that method on the part of those deficient in knowledge. Such abuse, however, is inherent in all human methods.

Stated positively, deduction has three functions in scientific method which ought to be rather obvious in the field of law:

First. It enables us to develop the implications of propositions and thus find out their true meaning. Knowledge grows most rapidly when we can properly utilize previous knowledge. Those who know make the most discoveries.

Second. Deduction helps to make our assumptions explicit and this makes possible a critical attitude towards them, and

Third. Deduction enables us to deal, not only with the actual, but with the possible. It thus liberates us to explore the field of possibility where there are to be found many things better than the actual.

Let me say a word about the second of these services. I say we begin always with hypothesis or assumptions. For the most part, however, it never occurs to us that we are making assumptions. We think we are starting with obvious truths. But propositions seem to us self-evident simply because it has never occurred to us to doubt them. It is, however, the business of scientific method to doubt all that pretends to be self-evident—e. g., that all property must have an owner, that no one can acquire rights by committing wrongs, that the maxim caveat emptor is necessary to encourage commerce, etc. The classic example of this are the axioms of Euclid which for over two thousand years were accepted as indubitable. Modern geometry has discovered new regions of investigation by learning to look at these axioms as assumptions. The same is true of the axioms of Newtonian mechanics.

Recently a distinguished economist has shown that a rational economic science can be built up on assumption contrary to those prevailing among orthodox economists. It would not be difficult to show that most of the principles appealed to as self-evident in legal discussion might easily be denied and their contrary shown to be just as plausible.

This does not mean universal skepticism, but only the recognition of the fact that as human beings we start, not with absolute certainties, but with hypotheses or guesses suggested generally by tradition and previous knowledge, but not on that account necessarily free from error. Scientific methodology has no objection to traditional views as such, except to warn us that, as traditional views are fallible, the only way of getting at the truth is to treat them as among a number of possible views and compare them with others. This process may lead us in the end to maintain the established views as the best. We may even contend that that which has stood the test of long experience has much to commend it. But, even when the traditional view is accepted a critical, logical examination of it refines it and thus enables us to eliminate irrelevant and unfortunate excrescences on it.

True it is that we do not actually reason in syllogisms. Yet law must try to assume the form of a deductive system:

First. To be as consistent as possible. The fact that, like other human institutions, the law does not always succeed in being consistent, is no argument against its trying to be so. The fact that we do not always succeed in attaining health is not an argument for being satisfied with disease. The admission that death will overtake us is no reason against seeking to prolong life.

Second. A deductive system which enables us to derive many legal rules from a few principles makes the law more certain, so that people can better know their rights. You cannot pass from past decisions to future ones without making assumptions. From the statement that a court has ruled so and so in certain cases nothing follows except in so far as the new cases are assumed to be like the old ones. But this likeness depends upon our logical analysis of classes of cases.

Third. The law cannot admit that it has abandoned the effort at consistency. We must remember that the law always defeats the expectation of at least one party in every lawsuit. To maintain its prestige, in spite of that, requires persistent and conspicuous effort at impartiality, so that even the defeated party will be impressed. This is most effectively promoted by genuine devotion to scientific method.

We cannot, however, leave this topic without considering the currently widespread distrust of logic and legal principles which the Germans denote by the word "Begriffsjurisprudenz." It was expressed long ago by Justice Holmes in the oft-quoted remark that experience not logic is the life of the law. As regards Justice Holmes himself, his remark is to be taken in the light of his own great scientific interests and achievements in the logical analysis of legal ideas and issues. But, as anti-intellectualism is so in vogue to-day, it is well to state boldly that experience or life without logic is stupid and brutish and supplies no guide for the good or civilized life.

What is experience? In its original sense, and the one which it still has to those uncorrupted by subjectivistic philosophy, experience denotes something personal that happens to us. Thus, we say we are fortunate in never having experienced the effects of ether or of certain diseases. In this sense, personal experience is obviously not an adequate basis on which to decide the policies of the law. But, if we generalize the term "experience" to include all that which has happened to human beings in general, and is likely to happen in the future, experience is certainly not something which is given in itself, but the very thing to be discovered by logical methods.

Certainly the experience of the past, or of the future, is not given to us, and it is by scientific study relying on the canons of logic that we reconstruct the past and predict the future.

Trust life rather than theory, say our modernists. But is it true that by mere living our problems are solved? Is not life full of illusions and frustrations? Life is the seat of all that is ugly as well as beautiful; of disease as well as health; of all that is vile and loathsome as well as of all that is inspiring. At all times it carries the seeds of death. The law like other institutions of civilization is organized to advance the good life, and what distinguishes that is not to be attained by abandoning our intelligence.

Law without concepts or rational ideas, law that is not logical, is like prescientific medicine—a hodge-podge of superstition, as has indeed been most of the world's common sense as distinguished from science.

To urge that judges, for instance, should rely on their experience or intuition in disregard of logically formulated principles is to urge sentimental anarchy. Men will generalize in spite of themselves. If they do it consciously in accordance with logical principles, they will do it more carefully and will be liberally tolerant to other possible generalizations. But those who distrust all logic think that they deal with facts when they are occupied with the product of their own grotesque theories.

Science, to be sure, is abstract. It tends to emphasize abstract considerations and deals with the definable classes rather than with the particular cases. But in doing so it forces us to see things from a wider point of view, and this tends to make us more just to the diversity of human interests. The air of unreality that science presents to the uninitiated is like the unreality which modern machinery presents to the old-fashioned artisan or those who cultivate the soil by hand.

Nor can we respect the metaphysical objection that life is changing but concepts are fixed. It is precisely because concepts are fixed in meaning that we can measure or determine the rate of change. Should the rules of arithmetic be changed whenever the volume of our business transactions is changed? Will even the change of our system of weights and measures require us to discard the multiplication table?

The real objection to conceptually mechanical jurisprudence is one against all human activity that is unintelligent. So-called strong judges, who decide to follow principles regardless of consequences, are simply too lazy to examine countervailing considerations and special circumstances which are relevant to the application of these principles. At best they are guilty of the fallacy of simplism, of supposing that the law always consists of theoretically simple cases, whereas the concrete cases actually before us are more complex because they generally involve many principles. This is the root of what is sound in the distinction between "law in books" and "law in action," and in the warning that the needs of life should not be sacrificed to the needs of the study.

From this point of view we can see reason for rejecting the extreme formalism of Stammler and of the school of Kelsen which seems to dominate contemporary European legal thought. There is a downright logical absurdity in Stammler's efforts to derive substantive rules of law from purely formal or logical principles —as absurd as to try to build a house with nothing but the rules of architecture. Nor can Kelsen establish by quasi mathematical methods positive rules of law that can be the rules of any actual jurisdiction. The analogy of mathematical physics which he, Felix Kaufman, and his other followers invoke, is really against them, since mathematical physics differs from pure mathematics precisely by making assumptions as to what exists—something which can never be derived from formal or pure mathematics.

In general, law is a specific type of existence and its specific nature cannot be deduced from something else. Kelsen's argument for a pure or unitary method would be sound if the law were the object of a pure and unitary science. But this cannot be, so long as the jurist has to deal with different kinds of problems, historical, psychological, logical, and ethical as well as mixed questions such as when we ask: What is it that courts do when they interpret a statute?

The law, and especially present American law, is desperately in need of a scientific elaboration. The old way of dealing with the law as a body of empirical rules has definitely broken down. *Stare decisis* means little in a changing society when for every new case the number of possible precedents is practically unwieldy. Without principles as guides, the body of precedents becomes an uncharted sea; and reliance on principles is worse than useless unless these principles receive critical scientific attention.

But if law is a fit subject for university study, it deserves to be studied, not merely for its practical consequences, but for the insight which it offers as to human life. Civilized life would be horribly impoverished if literature were devoted entirely to advertising or propaganda, even for righteous causes, or if the fine arts were used only for practical purposes rather than as ends in themselves enriching the enjoyment of life.

The theoretic study of the law is one of the ways in which we can attain a deeper and wider view of human existence, and that is good if anything is.

Supplementary Notes on a Program of Studies in Legal Method

I. Theory of Legal Concepts:

Cf. the work of Bierling, Pound, Hohfeld, and Kocourek.

Concepts are points of view offering perspectives.

As elements of the legal system they are artificial, but so are the letters of the alphabet which enable us to express enormously large number of words.

Concepts are of various degrees of definiteness, and one of the necessary tasks of a scientific legal system is to substitute more definite concepts for those having a large twilight zone; e. g., "twenty-one years" instead of "mentally mature."

2. Definitions in Legal Science:

Importance of legal definition not only to eliminate ambiguity, but also to eliminate penumbras of associated meanings which make for indefiniteness. Legal definitions are the bases of legal deduction.

3. Theoretic Divisions of Legal Science:

According to methods used.

Importance of distinguishing historical, sociologic, normative, and purely juristic problems as to the meaning of legal rules and their connection with each other in a system.

4. Importance of the Practical Divisions of the Law:

(1) The distinction between public and private law. Importance of Olney's remark (apropos of the Adair Case) that public issues should not be dealt with like those of a private horse deal.

(2) Commercial v. Private Civil Law.

The former emphasizes abstract value, while the latter attaches importance to specific things. Injury to human interests results from the failure to separate commercial law from that of human relations, such as are involved in labor cases.

Certainty, which is good in certain realms of business, is not good in public law when questions of justice are involved; e. g., a rule definitely depriving a man of his right to religious expression.

5. Critique of Legal Technique:

(1) Critique of axioms or first principles.

Abuse of legal maxims.

(2) Critique of legal hermeneutics.

Distinction between practical rules calculated to make the law workable and purely scientific rules of interpretation calculated to arrive at the real intention of the author.

Historic parallel between the rules of interpretation in religion and in law; e. g., in the Talmud and in the Canon Law. Grotius' reforms in both realms.

(3) Critique of the use of fictions.

(a) Different kinds of fictions.

Importance of language as a part of social life. Why the law must respect men's linguistic sensibilities as it does in various euphemisms, ceremonial expressions of public respect, etc. Inevitability of metaphors and the need of linguistic short-cuts.

(b) Atrocious confusion from failure to discriminate between facts or statements which are true and those which are only presumed to be so.

6. *The Theory of Interests Served by the Law:*

(1) How to find all these interests and not neglect some of them as is often done; e. g., in hastily granting injunctions.

(2) How to classify these interests.

(3) How to resolve conflicts of interests.

Can we accept Cardozo's heirarchy of the moral, the economic, and the æsthetic?

7. *Undue Influence of Concepts and Methods of Other Sciences* which have no real application to law except by analogy. Need for discriminating the specific characteristics of our own material.

(1) From physics we get such concepts as social forces, continuety, equilibrium, etc. Their application to law needs to be viewed more critically.

Action and reaction, for instance, are used in the Hegelian interpretation of legal history. But ideas in themselves do not react nor do they generate their opposites. Man's ideas change, not dialectically, but somewhat capriciously, like the changes of fashions. New analogies solicit our attention and these may come from entirely different realms; e. g., the influence of the biologic idea of natural selection on ethics and politics.

(2) From popular biology we get the vague concept of social evolution. but in what sense can we see a "law" of evolution in the legal field? Do legal institutions always and everywhere develop in the same way; e. g., are legal changes always from the simple to the complex?

(3) From recent physiology we get the vague notion of "behavior" which, if not synonymous with human conduct, means to eliminate questions of consciousness. Yet can questions of actual intention be eliminated from the law? Can we study the behavior of judges apart from the reasons or ideals which influence them? The danger of behaviorism is that it may draw our attention to purely physical changes and make us overlook intangible interests, such as respect for law, regard for justice, etc.

8. *Limits of Scientific Method:*

The pursuit of truth is not the only human interest. Other interests limit it; e. g., regard for human feelings or confidences as in the law of evidence.

The need of immediately economizing time and effort hinders the pursuit of truth.

While science can suspend judgment where adequate knowledge is wanting, the law is under the necessity of making immediate decisions.

RULES VERSUS STANDARDS:
AN ECONOMIC ANALYSIS

LOUIS KAPLOW†

This Article offers an economic analysis of the extent to which legal commands should be promulgated as rules or standards. Two dimensions of the problem are emphasized. First, the choice between rules and standards affects costs: Rules typically are more costly than standards to create, whereas standards tend to be more costly for individuals to interpret when deciding how to act and for an adjudicator to apply to past conduct. Second, when individuals can determine the application of rules to their contemplated acts more cheaply, conduct is more likely to reflect the content of previously promulgated rules than of standards that will be given content only after individuals act. The Article considers how these factors influence the manner in which rules and standards should be designed, and explores the circumstances in which rules or standards are likely to be preferable. The Article also addresses the level of detail with which laws should be formulated and applied, emphasizing how this question concerning the laws' relative simplicity or complexity can be distinguished from that of whether laws are given content ex ante *(rules) or ex* post *(standards). In so doing, it illuminates concerns about the over- and underinclusiveness of rules relative to standards.*

† Professor, Harvard Law School and Research Associate, National Bureau of Economic Research. I am grateful for comments from Lucian Bebchuk, James Boyle, Scott Brewer, David Charny, Erwin Chemerinsky, Stephen Choi, Richard Fallon, Marcel Kahan, Jeremy Paul, Richard Posner, Frederick Schauer, Steven Shavell, and participants in workshops at the University of Chicago, University of Connecticut, and Harvard University law schools.

11

TABLE OF CONTENTS

INTRODUCTION

This Article offers an economic analysis of the extent to which legal commands should be promulgated as rules or standards, a question that has received substantial attention from legal commentators.[1] Arguments about and definitions of rules and standards commonly emphasize the distinction between whether the law is given content *ex ante* or *ex post*.[2] For example, a rule

---

1. The two most substantial attempts to analyze the choice from an economic perspective are Colin S. Diver, *The Optimal Precision of Administrative Rules*, 93 YALE L.J. 65 (1983), and Isaac Ehrlich & Richard A. Posner, *An Economic Analysis of Legal Rulemaking*, 3 J. LEGAL STUD. 257 (1974). *See also* KENNETH C. DAVIS, DISCRETIONARY JUSTICE: A PRELIMINARY INQUIRY (1969); Anthony I. Ogus, *Quantitative Rules and Judicial Decision Making*, *in* THE ECONOMIC APPROACH TO LAW 210 (Paul Burrows & Cento G. Veljanovski eds., 1981). Other prominent discussions, often emphasizing definitions and jurisprudential concerns, include P.S. ATIYAH & ROBERT S. SUMMERS, FORM AND SUBSTANCE IN ANGLO-AMERICAN LAW: A COMPARATIVE STUDY IN LEGAL REASONING, LEGAL THEORY AND LEGAL INSTITUTIONS (1987); H.L.A. HART, THE CONCEPT OF LAW 126–31 (1961); HENRY M. HART & ALBERT M. SACKS, THE LEGAL PROCESS 155–58 (tent. ed. 1958); MARK KELMAN, A GUIDE TO CRITICAL LEGAL STUDIES 15–63 (1987); RICHARD A. POSNER, THE PROBLEMS OF JURISPRUDENCE 42–53 (1990); ROSCOE POUND, AN INTRODUCTION TO THE PHILOSOPHY OF LAW 115–23 (1922); FREDERICK SCHAUER, PLAYING BY THE RULES: A PHILOSOPHICAL EXAMINATION OF RULE-BASED DECISIONMAKING IN LAW AND IN LIFE (1991); ROBERTO UNGER, KNOWLEDGE AND POLITICS 88–100 (1975); Ronald M. Dworkin, *The Model of Rules*, 35 U. CHI. L. REV. 14, 22–29 (1967); Duncan Kennedy, *Form and Substance in Private Law Adjudication*, 89 HARV. L. REV. 1685 (1976); Roscoe Pound, *Hierarchy of Sources and Forms in Different Systems of Law*, 7 TUL. L. REV. 475, 482–87 (1933).

2. *See, e.g.*, HART, *supra* note 1, at 127–29; HART & SACKS, *supra* note 1, at 157

13

may entail an advance determination of what conduct is permissible, leaving only factual issues for the adjudicator. (A rule might prohibit "driving in excess of 55 miles per hour on expressways.") A standard may entail leaving both specification of what conduct is permissible and factual issues for the adjudicator. (A standard might prohibit "driving at an excessive speed on expressways."[3]) This Article will adopt such a definition, in which *the only distinction between rules and standards is the extent to which efforts to give content to the law are undertaken before or after individuals act.*[4] Other properties of rules and standards, including many emphasized in the jurisprudential literature, will be noted only in passing.[5]

("The wise draftsman . . . asks himself, how many of the details of this settlement ought to be postponed to another day, when the decisions can be more wisely and efficiently and perhaps more readily made?"). There is, however, substantial variation in the use of terminology and in the content of definitions, sometimes even by a single author. The choice of "rules" and "standards" as terms may contribute to the confusion. Outside the debate over formulation of the law, the terms are often used interchangeably. Dictionaries include as common meanings of "rule," "a standard of judgment" and "a regulating principle." WEBSTER'S NEW COLLEGIATE DICTIONARY 1012 (1977). Common meanings for "standard" include "something set up and established by authority as a rule for the measure of quantity, weight, extent, value, or quality." *Id.* at 1133. "Criterion" is listed as a synonym for both terms. Thus, one is not surprised when Ronald Dworkin uses "standards" to encompass both concepts as defined here, and uses "principles" in place of the more conventional "standards." *See* Dworkin, *supra* note 1, at 22–25. (I refer here to Dworkin's discussion of the rules and standards question, as distinct from much of his other jurisprudential work in which his use of the term "principles" plays a different role.) In this Article, I will attempt to minimize confusion by using the term "law" (and various derivatives) to refer generically to legal commands.

3. This example would not differ from that of the rule if all adjudicators held the view that an "excessive speed on expressways" was any speed "in excess of 55 miles per hour." Yet for purposes of this illustration, assume that the inquiry into "excessive speed" is relatively open-ended and requires real effort on the part of the decisionmaker in many cases. *See infra* Part II (a seemingly open-ended standard might be applied in a more straightforward fashion); Section III(B) (whether a law is a standard is determined by how it is understood rather than by the language in which it is formulated); subsection IV(B)(3) (government undertakes a study, publishing the results but not embodying them in a regulation).

4. In particular, as explored in Part II, this Article distinguishes the question of *when* a legal command is given content from *how much detail* is used in differentiating cases. Often, this latter dimension is expressly included. *See, e.g.,* Frederick Schauer, *Rules and the Rule of Law,* 14 HARV. J.L. & PUB. POL'Y 645, 650–51 (1991) ("Where the categories of decision are both large and opaque, the dimension of *ruleness* is greatest, and where the categories are narrow and more transparent to background justifications, the constraints of ruleness are minimized."). *But see* Ruth Gavison, *Comment: Legal Theory and the Role of Rules,* 14 HARV. J.L. & PUB. POL'Y 727, 747–48 (1991) (suggesting that only the strength of entrenchment and not breadth be incorporated in the concept of ruleness).

5. This Article will not address such issues as whether binding rules are possible,

The language of this Article will follow the common practice of referring to rules and standards as if one were comparing pure types, even though legal commands mix the two in varying degrees.[6] One can think of the choice between rules and standards

---

given the limits of language, or whether rules can be interpreted independently of their underlying justifications (which may be standards). *See generally* JOSEPH RAZ, PRACTICAL REASON AND NORMS 49–84 (1990); SCHAUER, *supra* note 1. Rather, the Article adopts the perspective—which I believe is amply defended in the relevant literature (and which one might have thought needed no defense)—that it often is meaningful to say that a law has been given some content *ex ante*, which the adjudicator should, could, and would take into account. *See, e.g.*, Frederick Schauer, *Rules and the Rule-Following Argument*, 3 CAN. J.L. & JURISPRUDENCE 187 (1990) [hereinafter Schauer, *Rules*]. Moreover, as many of the examples (such as the Internal Revenue Code and OSHA regulations) suggest, the realm in which this perspective is applicable to a great extent and is practically important is immense. See also the examples that Diver, *supra* note 1, explores in depth. (Perhaps it is the refusal to consider routine applications of the law that leads some, such as Pierre Schlag, *Rules and Standards*, 33 UCLA L. REV. 379, 400–18 (1985), to believe that considering the virtues and vices of rules and standards is a meaningless endeavor.) Sections II(A) and IV(A) touch on these jurisprudential concerns.

A concern related to whether rules can be binding is whether there is any content to a rule as long as a standard can trump the rule. When standards can be employed *ex post* to trump rules, the value of rules might be significantly eroded to the extent their purpose was primarily to constrain adjudicators' discretion for fear of abuse. *See infra* note 142 and accompanying text. But to the extent that adjudicators are faithful executors of legal commands, they would choose to use *ex ante* determinations to an appropriate extent. (In fact, pressures of time and cost would, as a practical matter, give them a great—perhaps an excessive—incentive to do so.) The focus in this Article is on the value of *ex ante* determinations, not on whether such determinations should be or can be made absolutely binding. *See, e.g.*, *infra* subsection IV(B)(3). The analysis emphasizes how laws—both rules and standards—will actually be applied and the relative difficulty of predicting their application. Thus, a law is "rule-like" if it in fact facilitates resolution of cases *ex post* and makes prediction easier *ex ante*, even if it expressly allows the adjudicator to create exceptions *ex post* (for example, with the suggestion that "these rules apply unless some other result is appropriate in light of the considerations motivating formulation of this law"). *See* SCHAUER, *supra* note 1, at 98–99 (even if the adjudicator is explicitly empowered to ignore the rule, it may produce many virtues of rules, although not that of allocating power to one other than the adjudicator). For discussions of the jurisprudence of presumptive rules, see, e.g., RAZ, *supra*, at 59–62; SCHAUER, *supra* note 1, at 108–11 (even "mere" rules of thumb may provide guidance); Schauer, *supra* note 4. On the related question of exceptions to rules, see Frederick Schauer, *Exceptions*, 58 U. CHI. L. REV. 871, 893–98 (1991).

The view that aspects of rules can usefully be analyzed while setting aside related issues of legal theory is not novel. *See, e.g.*, Gavison, *supra* note 4, at 730, 768–70 (concluding that "we should discuss the role of rules in law on its own merits, without trying to implicate general legal theory in the discussion," but noting similarities in scholars' use of theories of law and formal attributes of decisionmaking). In part, the separation is appropriate because many properties of rules (and standards), including much of what is explored in this Article, are not unique to *legal* rules, as distinct from rules followed in other realms of life. *See, e.g.*, SCHAUER, *supra* note 1; Schauer, *Precedent*, 39 STAN. L. REV. 571, 572, 602–03 (1987) [hereinafter Schauer, *Precedent*].

6. For example, a rule may determine which of two standards applies, or vice versa

as involving the extent to which a given aspect of a legal command should be resolved in advance or left to an enforcement authority to consider. Thus, advance determination of the appropriate speed on expressways under normal conditions, or even of the criteria that will be relevant in adjudicating reasonable speed (safety and the value of time, but not the brand of automobile or the particular driver's skill), are "rule-like" when compared to asking an adjudicator to attach whatever legal consequence seems appropriate in light of whatever norms and facts seem relevant.[7] Yet the same advance determination would be "standard-like" when compared to a precise advance determination of what constitutes normal conditions and what constitutes reasonable speed under various exceptional circumstances.

The analysis in Part I examines the relative desirability of *ex ante* versus *ex post* creation of the law in terms of legal costs and the extent to which individuals' behavior conforms to the law.[8] It focuses on an intentionally simple example—made more complex later—that is used to identify fundamental differences between rules and standards. The example has three stages: (1) A law is promulgated, either as a rule or as a standard. (2) Individuals decide how to act. Being imperfectly informed of the law's commands, they either act based on their best guess of the law, or they acquire legal advice, which allows them to act with knowledge of a rule or a prediction of the application of a standard. (3) After individuals act, an adjudicator determines how the governing law applies. Rules are more costly to promulgate than standards because rules involve advance determinations of the law's content, whereas standards are more costly for legal advisors to

---

(as when two rules arguably govern and some principle must be invoked to choose between the rules). Even focusing on a single step in reaching a legal conclusion, a particular law will have qualities of rules and of standards, with competing formulations differing in the degree to which they are rule- or standard-like. *See also infra* note 83. An important mixed type is the presumptive rule, in which a rule applies unless there appears to be sufficient reason not to apply it (and in which the decisionmaker does not first conduct a full inquiry to determine whether applying the rule is correct). *See* Gavison, *supra* note 4, at 750–52; *supra* note 5.

7. *Cf.* Thomas C. Arthur, *Workable Antitrust Law: The Statutory Approach to Antitrust*, 62 TUL. L. REV. 1163, 1225–28 (1988) (rejecting sharp dichotomy between rules and standards, instead advocating a middle position in which the legislature identifies goals and offers examples as guides for courts).

8. The analysis emphasizes how laws affect *ex ante* behavior rather than other goals, some of which are noted in Section III(E).

16

predict or enforcement authorities to apply because they require later determinations of the law's content.

To illustrate the analysis, consider the problem of regulating the disposal of hazardous substances. For chemicals used frequently in settings with common characteristics—such as dry cleaning and automotive fluids—a rule will tend to be desirable. If there will be many enforcement actions, the added cost from having resolved the issue on a wholesale basis at the promulgation stage will be outweighed by the benefit of having avoided additional costs repeatedly incurred in giving content to a standard on a retail basis.[9] Moreover, with regard to the countless acts of individuals subject to these laws, a rule will tend to be better as well. Because learning about a rule is cheaper, individuals may spend less in learning about the law, and may be better guided by a rule since the law's content can be more readily ascertained.

Contrast this result to that in the case of chemicals used rarely, and in settings that vary substantially. Designing a rule that accounts for every relevant contingency would be wasteful, as most would never arise. Although it might be more difficult and costly for an individual and an enforcement authority to apply a standard in a particular instance, such an application need be made only if its unique set of circumstances actually arises. Thus when frequency is low, a standard tends to be preferable.

Two features of this example are worth highlighting. First, the frequency of individual behavior and of adjudication is of central importance. Note in this regard that a law may still govern much behavior even though adjudications—which receive more emphasis in legal commentary—are rare, whether because most acts do not give rise to a lawsuit or because most cases are settled.[10] Laws in which the frequency of application in recurring fact scenarios is

---

9. Thus, when discussing presumptive rules, Gavison notes that requiring the decisionmaker to examine all relevant factors to determine whether a rule should apply would not make all cases difficult to decide but would "make all cases time-consuming, in ways that are extremely wasteful." Gavison, *supra* note 4, at 750; *see* HENRY J. FRIENDLY, THE FEDERAL ADMINISTRATIVE AGENCIES: THE NEED FOR BETTER DEFINITION OF STANDARDS 24 (1962); RAZ, *supra* note 5, at 59–60; SCHAUER, *supra* note 1, at 145–49 & n.14; *cf.* RICHARD A. POSNER, ECONOMIC ANALYSIS OF LAW § 20.4, at 547–48 (4th ed. 1992) (similar effect of precedent treated as a rule by subsequent decisionmakers); Schauer, *Precedent, supra* note 5, at 599 (same).

10. Isaac Ehrlich and Richard Posner have noted that costs of legal advice at the consultation stage may be greater than for advice in litigation. Ehrlich & Posner, *supra* note 1, at 270.

high include many traffic laws, aspects of the law of damages (how to value disability, loss of life, or lost profits), regulations governing health and safety, and provisions of the federal income tax (some of which apply to millions of individuals and billions of transactions). In contrast, some laws govern more heterogeneous behavior, in which each relevant type of act may be rare.[11] For example, the law of negligence applies to a wide array of complex accident scenarios, many of which are materially different from each other and, when considered in isolation, are unlikely to occur.[12]

Second, the advantage of rules at the stage involving individuals' behavior depends on whether individuals choose to acquire legal advice before they act. If the benefits of learning the law's content are substantial and the cost (whether of hiring legal experts or learning more on one's own) is not too great, individuals' behavior under both rules and standards will tend to conform to the law's commands. The advantage of rules in this case would be that the cost of learning the law is reduced. If, however, the cost of predicting standards is high, individuals will not choose to become as well informed about how standards would apply to their behavior. The advantage of rules in this case would be improved legal compliance. Thus, even if an enforcement authority were to give the same content (or "better" content) to a standard as might have been included in a rule, the rule might induce behavior that is more in accord with underlying norms.

After developing these ideas, the framework is extended in two ways. First, the analysis is reconsidered in light of the possibility that a standard might be converted into a rule through the creation of a precedent. Second, an inquiry is made into how much effort should and would be invested in promulgating and applying laws. It is noted, for example, that more should be spent on

---

11. Heterogeneity is emphasized because acts are only frequent in the relevant sense if the acts have enough in common that they should be treated in the same manner. Thus, negligence cases are frequent, although many types of negligence cases are not. *See infra* Section III(B); *cf.* Werner Z. Hirsch, *Reducing Law's Uncertainty and Complexity*, 21 UCLA L. REV. 1233, 1240–41 (1974) (discussing frequency versus heterogeneity in determining whether laws should be more precise so as to avoid uncertainty).

12. Roscoe Pound has stated that "no two cases of negligence have been alike or ever will be alike." POUND, *supra* note 1, at 142. It is less obvious whether the differences are typically of sufficient importance to justify an independent inquiry in each case or whether juries in fact respond to all conceivable subtle differences, issues explored in Part II.

determining the appropriate resolution of issues when a rule is designed once for many cases than when applying a standard (adjudication) or predicting the application of a standard (legal advice) in a single case. Finally, Part I concludes by observing that the problem of choosing between rules and standards can be viewed as one concerning how the government should acquire and disseminate information about the appropriate content of the law.

Part II seeks to illuminate the intersection between the debate over rules and standards (*ex ante* versus *ex post* creation of the law) and the debate over the appropriate degree of detail in legal commands. The focus is on the familiar suggestion that rules tend to be over- and underinclusive relative to standards.[13] This Part indicates that the suggestion is misleading because typically it implicitly compares a complex standard and a relatively simple rule, whereas both rules and standards can in fact be quite simple or highly detailed in their operation.

For rules, the potential variation in complexity is familiar, even if often ignored. A motor vehicle code could specify a single speed limit, a handful (one each for expressways, city streets, and alleys), or a plethora (identifying different types of roads, vehicles, weather conditions, traffic densities, and driver characteristics). For standards, this point has two important dimensions. Standards may admit few or many considerations in determining their application. A standard that one not drive at an excessive speed may allow only time and safety considerations or may also permit energy conservation considerations; it may deem relevant only road conditions or may also take into account vehicle types. There is, however, another important dimension that is commonly overlooked when analyzing standards: the level of detail *actually employed by*

---

13. *See, e.g.*, Ehrlich & Posner, *supra* note 1, at 268–70; Kennedy, *supra* note 1, at 1689, 1695; William H. Simon, *Legality, Bureaucracy, and Class in the Welfare System*, 92 YALE L.J. 1198, 1202, 1227 (1983). Coleman, in contrast, emphasizes that "rules are necessarily under- and over-inclusive *with respect to the sets of reasons that support or ground them*" (instead of in comparison to standards). Jules L. Coleman, *Rules and Social Facts*, 14 HARV. J. L. & PUB. POL'Y 703, 710 (1991); *see* SCHAUER, *supra* note 1, at 31–34, 50. Schauer describes rules as "entrenched generalizations likely to be under- and over-inclusive in particular cases," in contrast to "particularistic decisionmaking, which aims to optimize for each case and treats normative generalizations as only temporary and transparent approximations." Schauer, *supra* note 4, at 646; *see id.* at 648–49. As will be discussed further in Section I(D) and Part II, this sort of comparison, while not inherently misleading, is often understood in a manner that provides an inaccurate picture when considering how systems of rules and standards should or do operate.

the adjudicator. A standard that one not drive at excessive speed might well permit consideration of dozens of factors. But if ninety-nine out of a hundred juries make their decisions based on the same two or three factors, although the other factors are relevant in principle, the *de facto standard* might usefully be described as a rather simple one.[14]

Thus, there are simple and complex rules as well as simple and complex standards.[15] Moreover, as a matter of legal practice, it is not always the case that rule systems are simple compared to the standards that could be adopted in their place. Consider the federal income tax. It hardly seems plausible that a standard requiring individuals to pay "their appropriate share of the federal government's revenue needs," applied case by case,[16] would generate a more detailed law—one that took into account more factors, in more intricate ways—than the one embodied in the Internal Revenue Code and its accompanying regulations.

The conceptual distinction between the questions of how complex a law should be and whether any aspect of its detail is best determined *ex ante* or *ex post* has practical importance. For example, a complex standard might be preferred to a simple rule because of its complexity or because of the advantages of *ex post* formulation, or both. As a result, in some instances in which the complex standard is superior, it may be that complexity is better than simplicity, but a rule—a complex rule—would be preferable

---

14. *See* Stephen G. Gilles, *Rule-Based Negligence and the Regulation of Activity Levels*, 21 J. LEGAL STUD. 319, 321–27 (1992) (emphasizing rule-like elements of negligence and standard-like elements of strict liability). Juries may adopt a simple approach because the factors they can readily understand or that appear most salient are few in number. Alternatively, jury instructions may narrow their focus, *see, e.g.*, JOHN DICKINSON, ADMINISTRATIVE JUSTICE AND THE SUPREMACY OF LAW IN THE UNITED STATES 143 (1927) (giving examples involving notice of dishonor of negotiable instruments and due care in tort law), although in this case the standard may have been transformed into a rule to some extent.

15. Colin Diver offers an example with three formulations for a law determining who may pilot commercial aircraft: (1) No one over age 60; (2) No one who poses an unreasonable risk of accident; (3) No one who falls in any of a number of categories detailing combinations of values of variables that bear on accident risk. *See* Diver, *supra* note 1, at 69. In this example, (1) is a simple rule and (3) a complex rule. The standard is (2), which on its face appears complex, in that in principle it admits any consideration. Diver then notes the possibility that all those applying (2) understand it to mean anyone over 60, *see id.*, which would be a simple *de facto* standard.

16. And without the creation of precedents that would make the standard more rule-like. *See infra* Section I(C).

to a standard; or, it may be that a standard is better than a rule, but a simple standard would be preferable to a complex one.[17] For example, a standard (implicitly complex) that one dispose of toxic substances "appropriately" may be preferable to a rule that simply prohibits the dumping of petroleum byproducts into bodies of water. But, at least for substances frequently used in common settings—such as dry cleaning and automotive fluids—a complex rule detailing the appropriate manner of disposal for different substances may be even better. Part II discusses briefly the sort of analysis that is pertinent to a determination of the appropriate level of detail (for example, the extent to which different substances and contexts should be distinguished), noting how it differs from that in Part I (which concerns whether the appropriate manner of disposal should be determined in advance, or only after individuals act, in an adjudication).

Part III extends the framework in a number of ways. First, this Part considers the possibility that standards are more accessible to actors than rules are, contrary to the suggestion in Part I. Second, it examines why it is difficult to formulate some laws as rules, in the process elaborating on the definition of rules and standards and the notion of frequency of application emphasized in Part I. Third, it assesses further the consequences of individuals' acquiring legal advice. The relevant question involves whether the costs of advice are warranted by the benefits from the changes in individuals' behavior that result from their being better informed about the law. Fourth, it discusses risk aversion. Finally, it analyzes objectives of the law other than deterrence. For example, when legal remedies are nonmonetary (injunctions, incarceration), individuals' behavior after adjuducation is directly affected by the law, in addition to or instead of being affected *ex ante* in anticipation of how the law will apply (the focus of the previous discussion).

Part IV comments on the interpretation of the analysis. It considers briefly the relevance of the branch of government involved in the promulgation and application of law, the role of judge and jury, abuse of power, political influences on rule formulation, and the process by which precedent is created. It also notes

---

17. Conversely, if the simple rule were preferable to the complex standard, it would make a difference whether the benefit arose from simplicity, from *ex ante* formulation, or from both.

the ways in which rules and standards may change over time, and how laws regarding form (for example, formalities required in executing a will) and background laws (for example, laws providing contract remedies when parties do not specify one) may differ from laws regulating harm-producing behavior. Part V offers a brief conclusion.

I. *EX ANTE* VERSUS *EX POST* CREATION OF THE LAW

Section A offers a more precise statement, embodied in a simple illustration, of the three stages described in the Introduction. Section B analyzes how individuals might behave under rules and standards, assessing costs and benefits for each possibility. Section C describes how the analysis differs if standards are transformed into rules once they are applied, through the creation of precedents. Section D considers the fact that both individuals and architects of the legal system may choose how much effort will be devoted to predicting or giving content to legal commands. Section E comments on how the analysis of this Part suggests that the problem of creating the law can be interpreted as one involving the government's acquisition and dissemination of information.

A. *An Illustration*

The example involves three stages, as described in the Introduction. (1) The law is promulgated—that is, the government decides whether conduct will be governed by a rule or a standard. (2) Individuals make their choices. Since they are imperfectly informed, they first choose whether to acquire legal advice about the rule or standard. Next, they decide how to behave. (3) The law is enforced—that is, the rule or standard is applied. (A brief formal presentation of the example appears in the Appendix.)

1. *Law Promulgation.* The government enacts a law to regulate a harm-causing activity. It decides whether an aspect of the law is to be promulgated as a rule or as a standard. For example, it may use a rule to specify the level of damages to be awarded for a given harm, a standard of care, a list of prohibited acts, or the criteria an adjudicator should consider in making such determinations *ex post*. Alternatively, it may use a standard, thereby leaving any or all of such decisions for the enforcement authority.

22

The problem is that the ideal content of the law with respect to these issues is not immediately apparent.[18] Rather, some investigation and deliberation is required. It may be necessary to undertake an empirical analysis of the effect of a toxic chemical or to have some appropriate group deliberate about values (for example, how to value an invasion of privacy). To simplify the discussion, Sections A through C focus on the situation in which there is a given cost of determining the appropriate content of the law *ex ante*. Because of this cost, rules are more expensive to promulgate than standards.[19]

2. *Choices of Individuals.* Individuals are uncertain of the actual content of the law.[20] That is, they only have estimates of the content of a rule or of the content an enforcement authority would give to a standard. They may, however, acquire legal advice—whether from lawyers, through self-study, or by other means. Because a standard requires a prediction of how an enforcement authority will decide questions that are already answered in the case of a rule, advice about a standard is more costly.[21] Individuals can pursue one of two strategies. They can act based upon their best guess of the content of the law, or they can acquire advice and act based upon how the law actually would apply to their contemplated conduct.[22]

---

18. If it were, the issues addressed in this Article are of little significance, as the costs of promulgating and applying the law would be minimal. *See infra* Section III(A) (similarity of transparent standards to rules whose content is the same).

19. The analysis considers the case of a single jurisdiction. If another jurisdiction has already invested in promulgating a rule, which can simply be copied, there may be little additional cost in rules promulgation. Thus, jurisdictions might underinvest in (or delay) promulgation, attempting to free-ride on the investments of other jurisdictions. Projects designed to create model laws could mitigate this problem.

20. If individuals already know the content of the law, the situation is equivalent to one in which legal advice is costless. The analysis of subsection B(2) would be applicable (ignoring the advice cost differential). The possibility of transparent standards, *see infra* Section III(A), is essentially one involving costless advice.

21. *See, e.g.,* POSNER, *supra* note 1, at 44–45. The possibility that standards may be more accessible than rules is discussed in Section III(A).

22. The discussion considers the case in which there is no particular bias in uninformed individuals' estimates and their guesses are unaffected by whether there is a rule or a standard. (If one assumed, for example, that individuals made systematic errors with standards but not with rules, rules would appear better, but this advantage would have no obvious connection to the inherent features of rules and standards.) This is related to the supposition in subsection 3 that an enforcement authority will give a standard the same content that would have been given to a rule *ex ante*.

3. *Law Enforcement.* The enforcement authority determines the sanction, if any, that applies to individuals' conduct.[23] This process is costly, with the cost being greater if a standard governs because the adjudication will also require giving content to the standard.[24]

It should be emphasized that the "appropriate" content is taken to be the same *ex ante* and *ex post*,[25] which implies that both the law promulgator (with a rule) and the law enforcer (with a standard) are able to determine the appropriate content[26]—although the cost need not be the same when incurred *ex ante* or *ex post*.[27] The motivation for taking this view—an often unrealistic one for reasons explored later[28]—is to focus on certain inherent features of *ex ante* versus *ex post* creation of the law. Obviously, when one formulation more comports with underlying norms, it will be advantageous on that account. But, as will be seen, the nature of any such advantage cannot be assessed without first understanding the pure effects of *ex ante* versus *ex post* creation of the law. Also, as Section D emphasizes, the features of *ex ante* versus *ex post* creation explored in Sections B and C will be an important determinant of when rules or standards are likely to be given content more in accord with underlying norms.

---

23. "Enforcement authority" can be thought of as including the entire process by which laws are enforced, whether by private lawsuits or government prosecution. Thus, the costs encompass the total costs of this process, and the framework applies equally to civil and criminal cases resolved in courts (whether by judge or jury), as well as to administrative tribunals, arbitration, and the like. *See also infra* Sections IV(A)–(B).

24. *See also* SCHAUER, *supra* note 1, at 229–30 (noting how the effort under rules tends to be less even when rules are presumptive rather than absolute).

25. Most of the analysis only requires that enforcement tribunals give content to the standard in an unbiased manner. *See infra* note 124. The potential for inconsistent applications of standards is discussed in Section II(A). The possibility of changing circumstances is considered in Section IV(C).

26. For example, one might imagine that the same sort of inquiry would be conducted relying on the same experts or wise advisors. Note that a legislature promulgating a rule could, if it wished, impanel a jury of lay people and have lawyers present arguments to them, if it wished to enact popular understandings into law. Also, it could leave adjudication *ex post* to an expert panel consisting of the same individuals it would have consulted *ex ante* in promulgating a rule. *See infra* Section IV(A).

27. *See infra* Section D.

28. *See infra* Section D; Parts II–IV.

B. *Analysis*

The differences between rules and standards in this illustration depend on whether individuals will choose to acquire legal advice to guide their behavior. Individuals acting in their self-interest will acquire such advice only if its perceived value exceeds its perceived cost.

To determine the value of legal advice to individuals, it is necessary to compare how individuals would fare if they were uninformed with how they would fare if they were informed. Uninformed individuals act based on their best guess about how the law will apply to their contemplated conduct. Informed individuals act based on actual knowledge of the law. Thus, informed individuals might be deterred from conduct they would have undertaken if they had remained uninformed,[29] which can occur when they learn that such conduct is illegal or subject to a higher sanction than they otherwise would have expected. Or, informed individuals might choose to undertake acts they would have been deterred from committing if they had remained uninformed. Both possibilities are of value to individuals. The value of advice, then, is simply the value of each possibility weighted by the likelihood of its occurrence.[30] Note that, in this example, the value of advice is the same under both rules and standards, as uninformed individuals do not believe that the mode of formulation affects the substantive content of the law. In addition, informed individuals are afforded the same guidance under either formulation, because a standard will be given the same content as a rule would have had, and advice about the content of each formulation is equally good.

How, then, does the presence of a rule or a standard affect individuals' decisions whether to become informed? The value of advice is the same under both formulations, but the cost of advice differs. In particular, advice is more costly under a standard.[31]

---

29. "Deterrence" should be construed broadly here. It includes changing the level or type of an activity or the manner in which an activity is conducted.

30. Risk aversion is ignored to simplify the exposition. As the discussion in Section III(D) suggests, the results are similar when individuals are risk averse.

If individuals are mistaken in their view about the value of advice, the analysis in this Part would be largely unaffected. Misestimates of the value of advice are relevant primarily with regard to the relationship between the private and social values of advice, noted briefly in subsection 3 and explored further in Section III(C).

31. The possibility that advice is more costly with rules is explored in Section III(A).

Thus, there are three cases to consider:[32] (1) Individuals do not become informed either under a rule or under a standard, because the value of information is less than the cost of advice under both a rule and a standard. (2) Individuals become informed both under a rule and under a standard, because the value of information exceeds the cost of advice under both a rule and a standard. (3) Individuals become informed under a rule but not under a standard, because the cost of becoming informed is less under a rule than under a standard.

Before proceeding with the analysis, it is useful to state the criterion for evaluation employed here. The social objective is taken to be the maximization of benefits net of costs. Benefits are the net gain to individuals from their acts; costs include the harm caused by individuals' acts and legal costs—the costs of promulgating the law, the costs of legal advice sought by individuals, and the costs of enforcement proceedings.[33] The "appropriate" content embodied in a rule or that will be given to a standard by the enforcement authority provides the basis for assessing the weight to be given the benefits and harms of individuals' acts.[34]

1. *Individuals Do Not Become Informed Either Under a Rule or Under a Standard.* Because individuals do not become informed under either formulation of the law, information costs are not incurred. Moreover, uninformed individuals' behavior does not depend on whether a rule or standard prevails, so the benefits and harms of individuals' acts will be the same. Thus in this case, whether a rule or standard is preferable will depend solely on the differences in promulgation and enforcement costs.

The difference in promulgation costs favors standards, whereas that in enforcement costs favors rules. Which is greater depends on two factors. First, the cost differentials at the promulgation and enforcement stages need not be equal, for reasons to be explored

---

32. The discussion to follow will proceed as though a single case would apply to all individuals, for a particular law. More realistically, because individuals' available acts, opportunities to take precautions, knowledge of the law, and information costs will differ, each case might be relevant for some individuals.

33. Discounting for the passage of time is ignored. A higher discount rate tends to favor standards, which have a cost advantage at the first stage and disadvantages at the second and third stages.

34. That is, no independent standard of what constitutes good law is imposed. Rather, taking a stipulated set of objectives the law should embody, the analysis asks which formulation best implements them, taking into account legal costs.

in Section D. (It is often useful to think of a benchmark case in which these differentials are the same, adjusting the argument for cases in which they are not straightforward.)

Second, one must take into account the frequency with which the two types of costs will be incurred. Promulgation costs are incurred once. In contrast, enforcement costs may be incurred repeatedly or never.[35] On one hand, a law may apply to an activity that is undertaken by many individuals: some federal income tax provisions apply to millions of individuals and billions of transactions.[36] In such instances, rules tend to be preferable. Even if the promulgation cost differential significantly exceeds the enforcement cost differential in applying standards, rules may be much cheaper.[37] On the other hand, a law—or, as is often relevant, a particular component of a law, possibly a highly detailed one—may have a small likelihood of applying to any activity; consider the example of myriad unique accident scenarios. Then, standards tend to be preferable. Even if they are extremely costly to apply, the significant likelihood that the particular application will never arise may make standards much cheaper.[38]

---

35. The frequency with which enforcement costs are incurred may itself depend on whether there is a rule or a standard. *See also infra* note 41 (differing behavior under rules and standards, as in case 3, is another reason the frequency of enforcement actions may differ). If enforcement costs are indeed lower under rules, plaintiffs may be more likely to sue. (Plaintiffs also may have greater uncertainty about whether they have a viable case under standards, which could result in a change in the number and composition of cases: Some meritorious suits may not be brought and some suits that will fail might be brought.) The likelihood of litigation rather than settlement may also be affected. Lower litigation costs make litigation more likely under rules, but the greater predictability of outcomes makes litigation less likely. Some of these complications could be reflected in the measure of enforcement costs under each formulation. (For example, if litigation rather than settlement is more likely under standards, the enforcement costs under standards would simply be greater.) Factors affecting the frequency of litigation will affect both enforcement costs and compliance. (One could adjust damage awards or other aspects of the law to take this into account; for example, if fewer individuals would sue under standards due to higher litigation costs, one could have a more generous damages rule or less stringent proof requirements.)

36. The language of the discussion in the text suggests a finite number of repetitions, but the result is essentially the same if the number is infinite—as when the law will apply forever—and there is a sufficiently high discount rate on future costs and benefits.

37. This argument applies when the first adjudication does not create a precedent for future cases. *See infra* Section C.

38. This is in accord with the intuition that it is not worth providing with great care in advance for remote contingencies. *See also infra* Section III(B) (difficulty of formulating some laws as rules); note 78 (unforeseen contingencies covered in standards but not in rules); note 180 (example, involving fraud, of how a complex standard might result in

2. *Individuals Become Informed both Under a Rule and Under a Standard.* Informed individuals behave in the same manner whether a rule or standard prevails, so again the benefits and harms from individuals' acts will be the same. Thus in this case, whether a rule or standard is preferable will depend on the differences in promulgation and enforcement costs (as in case 1)—and also on the difference in the cost of advice.

The difference in the cost of advice, which favors rules, parallels the difference in enforcement costs. The first factor concerns the magnitude of the differential and how it compares with the other differentials. The second involves frequency. Few (if any) or many individuals may incur costs in becoming informed about a law to guide their conduct; the greater the number of individuals likely to become informed, the greater the likelihood of rules being preferable.

Note that the number of individuals who incur the cost of legal advice may greatly exceed the number who are subject to complete enforcement proceedings.[39] Some individuals who seek advice may choose not to commit acts subject to liability; others may commit acts that do not in fact cause harm (consider laws governing accidents); others may not be sued or prosecuted despite their liability; and most lawsuits are settled. Thus, even when advice is only moderately more costly under standards and enforcement proceedings are rare, there will be contexts in which the frequency with which advice is sought will make the advice cost differential decisive.[40]

---

little expenditure on enforcement).

39. Similarly, even if no enforcement proceeding would ever occur—and thus no adjudicator would ever have to apply the standard—the standard might suffer a substantial cost disadvantage.

40. A qualification is that the cost of legal advice may be decreasing over time. For example, a lawyer who has previously rendered advice on the same law would be able to offer advice to a subsequent client more cheaply. More generally, if a law governs a substantial amount of behavior, there may be conferences or publications through which information is disseminated among lawyers or to groups of clients. Nonetheless, it still seems plausible that the total costs will be greater as the number of acts increases, although this relationship need not have the simple linear form described here (in which a given cost of advice is multiplied by the number of individuals who acquire advice).

Related, there may be a public good aspect to legal advice. Those first to inquire about a problem, if billed for the full cost of researching the question, will pay a large amount, much of the benefit of which will flow to subsequent clients of the lawyer. If this occurred, there would be a disincentive to acquire advice initially. One way law firms

3. *Individuals Become Informed Under a Rule but Not Under a Standard.* In this case, unlike the first two, the manner of formulation affects whether individuals acquire advice and how they behave. Thus, a comparison of rules and standards requires that one consider all components of social welfare. The analysis of promulgation and enforcement costs is similar to that in the first two cases,[41] so the discussion here will focus on the remaining components.

Under a rule, but not under a standard, individuals acquire advice before they act. This is desirable in that behavior will be more in accord with legal norms,[42] but undesirable in that an ad-

---

might address this problem would be to bill the first client much less (writing off much of the time, or perhaps doing much of the research before the first client arrives, while attending conferences or reading material on legal developments) and bill subsequent clients more (billing a flat amount for a type of advice, or charging higher hourly rates for more knowledgeable attorneys, to recover costs previously incurred). Competition among lawyers complicates the story. (It may limit feasible pricing schemes, and it also results in duplication of effort.) To the extent a public good problem remains, government subsidy of information about the law might be appropriate. *See also infra* Section E (problem of choosing rules or standards viewed as one involving government acquisition and dissemination of information); Section III(C) (discussing possible divergences between the private and social values of legal advice). Of course, the government does to some extent perform such functions, as when publications are made available for free or sold at rates that do not reflect the cost of compiling the information (but only printing and distribution costs).

41. There is, however, a complication concerning the enforcement cost differential. In cases 1 and 2, that differential was weighted by the expected number of cases. Because individuals' behavior was the same under a rule and a standard in each case, the expected number of enforcement proceedings was the same. *But see supra* note 35 (suggesting that the difference in enforcement costs and information available to plaintiffs may result in a different number of enforcement proceedings). In case 3, however, the expected number of cases may differ. Recall that informed individuals may be deterred more or less from committing acts subject to legal sanctions, depending on what they learn. Thus, in some instances there might be more or fewer enforcement actions under rules. (There would be more when uninformed individuals were deterred from committing acts subject to modest sanctions—more modest than they anticipated—and fewer when uninformed individuals would have committed acts they would not have committed if they knew the actual legal consequences.) Thus, the weight to be given the frequency component with regard to enforcement costs may be higher or lower than otherwise. *See also infra* note 117 (how sanctions should reflect enforcement costs).

42. The view that advised individuals will behave better than uninformed ones, as evaluated by the law about which they receive advice, is commonplace, but should not be accepted uncritically. *See infra* Section III(C) (discussing the private versus social value of legal advice).

Another respect in which advised individuals may behave more in accord with the law concerns the effects of uncertainty under a negligence rule. *See infra* note 123 (dis-

ditional cost—the cost of advice—is incurred. In principle, the net could favor either rules or standards.[43] But more can be said. We know that individuals only acquire information when its benefits exceed its costs. Thus, the value of advice to individuals exceeds its cost. As a result, rules would be preferable on account of these components whenever the private value of advice—which takes into account both the benefit from the act itself and the legal sanction (if any) the individual expects to pay—equals the social value of advice. The discussion in Section III(C) identifies contexts in which this equation of private and social values of advice holds, and others in which it does not.[44]

To enter these components into the framework, recall that in case 2 the advice component involves multiplying the number of individuals who would seek advice by the differential in the cost of advice under rules and standards. In this case, the advice component instead involves multiplying the number of individuals who would seek advice by the differential between the social value of advice and the cost of advice under rules.

*   *   *

---

cussing the range of laws that should be seen as involving a negligence rule for present purposes). If, for example, there is uncertainty concerning what an adjudicator would deem to be due care, there may be a tendency for individuals to take care that is excessive relative to the expected due care requirement, although it is also possible that individuals would take less care than the expected due care requirement. *See, e.g.*, STEVEN SHAVELL, ECONOMIC ANALYSIS OF ACCIDENT LAW 79–83, 93–97 (1987); Richard Craswell & John E. Calfee, *Deterrence and Uncertain Legal Standards*, 2 J.L. ECON. & ORGANIZATION 279 (1986). The existence of a tendency toward excessive care depends, however, on how the causation requirement is applied. *See* Marcel Kahan, *Causation and Incentives to Take Care Under the Negligence Rule*, 18 J. LEGAL STUD. 427 (1989); *see also infra* note 125 (if uncertainty is resolved *ex ante* with some error, substituting a rule for a standard may make error more predictable and thus behavior may be worse).

43. In some contexts, it might be imagined that individuals are simply aware of the content of rules, so no cost is incurred, in which case the failure to become perfectly informed under standards implies an unambiguous loss. For example, the preference for rules in the context of substantive criminal law seems to reflect the view that rules will be known but standards may be applied in ways individuals would not anticipate. *See, e.g.*, Jonathan C. Carlson, *The Act Requirement and the Foundations of the Entrapment Defense*, 73 VA. L. REV. 1011, 1024 (1987).

44. If the private value of advice is less than its social value, the conclusion that rules are preferable with regard to the acquisition of advice also follows: The magnitude of the social gain with regard to these components would be even greater than suggested by private valuations. If the private value of advice exceeds its social value, the conclusion would be different only if the social value were sufficiently low that it were less than the cost of advice—which is possible.

In summary, the greater the frequency with which a legal command will apply, the more desirable rules tend to be relative to standards. This result arises because promulgation costs are borne only once, whereas efforts to comply with and action to enforce the law may occur rarely or often. Rules cost more to promulgate; standards cost more to enforce. With regard to compliance, rules' benefits arise from two sources: Individuals may spend less in learning the content of the law, and individuals may become better informed about rules than standards and thus better conform their behavior to the law.

C. *Precedent*

There is an additional aspect of enforcement activity that is important to the problem addressed in this Article: whether, under a standard, the enforcement authority's first adjudication constitutes a precedent for future enforcement proceedings. Section B examined the case of no precedent, in which the standard is totally unaltered by enforcement proceedings.[45] One can contrast the case in which the first enforcement proceeding essentially transforms the standard into a rule.[46] That is, in subsequent enforcement proceedings, courts simply apply the precedent rather than engaging in an inquiry concerning appropriate legal treatment—and access to this precedent costs no more than if the law had been promulgated as a rule in the first place. Similarly, legal advisors find it equally costly to consult a precedent as to consult a law initially promulgated as a rule, so that the costs of legal advice under a rule and a standard are equal once the precedent is established. (The discussion here focuses on polar cases for convenience.[47])

---

45. One can imagine a jury verdict that has no formal precedential value, is not evidence for future cases, and is not even accessible to legal advisors when researching a legal question.

46. *See, e.g.*, HART, *supra* note 1, at 129 ("Where the decisions of the court on such matters [regulated by standards] are regarded as precedents, their specification of the variable standard is very like the exercise of delegated rule-making power by an administrative body, though there are also obvious differences."); POSNER, *supra* note 9, § 20.1, at 539 ("[A]n accumulation of precedents dealing with the same question may create a rule of law having the same force as an explicit statutory rule."). For jurisprudential discussions of precedents as rules, see Larry Alexander, *Constrained by Precedent*, 63 S. CAL. L. REV. 1 (1989); Schauer, *Precedent, supra* note 5.

47. It is straightforward to adjust the analysis to account for intermediate cases—for example, when precedents and laws initially promulgated as rules are not equally accessible, or when only some of the activity governed by a standard is covered by the prece-

When the first adjudication does create a precedent, only the first enforcement proceeding and individuals' actions that precede the completion of that first proceeding need be considered, as subsequent events are identical under both rules and standards. Each of the three cases from Section B is now briefly reexamined.[48]

In case 1, in which individuals do not acquire legal advice under either rules or standards, the factor of repetition is removed. Because there will be only one enforcement proceeding in which costs differ, one compares the cost differential for one proceeding,[49] which favors rules, with the cost differential in promulgating the law, which favors standards. (Observe, however, that the cost of an enforcement proceeding under a standard may be higher when the result will be a precedent than when it will not.[50])

In case 2, in which individuals acquire legal advice under both rules and standards, the factor of repetition is removed for enforcement proceedings. But repetition may still be relevant with regard to individual behavior because many individuals may need to acquire advice before the precedent is established. (Reasons for this were noted in subsection B(2) and will be explored further in subsection IV(B)(1).)

Case 3 parallels the second. The factor of repetition remains present only for individual behavior before the precedent is established. As in the case of no precedent, the differential here favoring rules, for each individual, consists of the value of advice (which reflects changes in behavior to comply with the law) minus the cost of advice under rules.

In summary, if the first adjudication under a standard constitutes a precedent for future enforcement proceedings and thereby transforms the standard into a rule, the differences between pro-

---

dent. *See infra* subsection IV(B)(1). Such intermediate cases are believed to be important. Thus, arguments that civil law systems are superior to common law ones or that favor codifications, restatements, and other summaries of precedent are motivated by differences between the accessibility of precedents and statutes (or other compilations of the law). *See, e.g.*, Gregory E. Maggs, *Reducing the Costs of Statutory Ambiguity: Alternative Approaches and the Federal Courts Study Committee*, 29 HARV. J. ON LEGIS. 123, 126 & n.8 (1992).

48. The presentation in the Appendix examines each case with and without precedent.

49. This, however, must be discounted for the possibility that no enforcement proceeding would ever occur.

50. *See infra* subsection D(3).

mulgating the law as a rule and as a standard are diminished. But they are not eliminated. Frequency will still be an important dimension. If acts subject to the law are unlikely to arise, the possibility of saving the costs of giving content to the law tends to favor standards. If acts will be frequent, there may be substantial costs in the interim under standards—costs of advice or costs reflected in behavior that does not comply with the law—that are avoided under rules.

D. *The Degree of Effort Devoted to Rule Creation, Legal Advice, and Enforcement*

The discussion thus far has examined the situation in which the promulgation of a rule entailed a given additional cost and resulted in a determination of the "appropriate" content of the law. Similarly, both legal advice and enforcement under a standard involved a given additional cost and properly predicted or determined the law's content. Achieving complete and proper assessments is usually infeasible and, even if possible, unwise due to the cost involved. Rather, it generally would be sensible at each stage to determine how much additional cost to incur as a function of the benefits that result. This Section reconsiders each stage of the analysis in light of this consideration.[51] It also emphasizes factors that may influence the relative costs of inquiry at different stages.

1. *Law Promulgation.* Presumably, efforts to determine the appropriate content of the law are subject to diminishing returns. Further investigation and greater deliberation are almost always possible, but after a point would yield little improvement in the quality of the resulting law.[52] The value of effort in designing a rule depends on the frequency of behavior subject to the rule, for reasons explained in Section B. If the rule will govern the conduct of many individuals, most of whom will acquire advice about the

---

51. The problem of the optimal degree of investment in promulgating or applying rules or in seeking legal advice has, to my knowledge, received little attention. Most relevant is LOUIS KAPLOW & STEVEN SHAVELL, ACCURACY IN THE ASSESSMENT OF DAMAGES (Harvard Law School Program in Law and Economics Discussion Paper No. 116, 1992). This problem is related to the question of the optimal complexity of laws addressed in Section II(C).

52. The quality of the law can be understood as reflecting how closely it conforms to underlying norms or to the likelihood with which it conforms.

rule's content, it will be more important that the rule closely reflect the law's underlying norms. If the rule is unlikely to apply to many or any acts, or if individuals would not bother to consult it before acting, relatively little should be spent designing it.[53] Note that this result softens the disadvantage of rules in such instances by reducing the promulgation cost differential; at the same time it reduces the benefit of rules with regard to inducing individuals to behave in a socially optimal manner if the rules to which they will conform are less in accord with underlying norms.

    2. *Choices of Individuals.* The analysis for legal advice is similar. Because resources devoted to legal advice that determines the content of a rule or predicts the content of a standard will be subject to diminishing returns, individuals' decisions concerning legal advice involve questions of degree, rather than the all-or-nothing decision described in the example in Section B.

    Observe that when substantial expenditures will be made in designing a rule because it will apply to many individuals' conduct, the effort at the rule's promulgation stage will probably be greater than the effort an individual would choose to expend to have a lawyer predict the content of a standard, because the individual would be concerned only with the single instance of his own conduct. In this case, one might expect behavior to conform more closely to underlying norms under rules than under standards (even if more might actually be spent on legal advice under standards, due to the higher cost of prediction of standards compared to consultation of rules).[54] Conversely, if little effort is to be devoted to designing a rule because it might never apply, an individual subject to a standard might expend more effort (in predicting how the standard will be given content) once the event has actually arisen, suggesting better behavior under standards.[55] Thus, con-

---

    53. Of course, the more important the conduct subject to the law, the more should be spent at all stages for any given degree of frequency.

    54. The possibility that standards would be more accessible than rules, with the result that behavior conforms better under standards, is explored in Section III(A).

    55. These arguments abstract from possible differences in the cost of designing rules and predicting standards. One might imagine, for example, that the former is cheaper because the latter requires prediction, or that the latter is cheaper because one need only consider a single set of facts or because the facts are known to the individual but must be investigated by the government. Regardless, the dimension of frequency emphasized in the text will be important and will have the tendency suggested. *See also supra* note 40 (discussing public goods aspect of legal advice).

sidering variations in effort at this stage affects both the advice cost differential and the assessment of behavior under rules and standards.

3. *Law Enforcement.* Begin with the situation examined in Section B, in which the first application of a standard would not be a precedent for future cases. Then, the degree of effort that should be made in an enforcement proceeding to give content to a standard should reflect the fact that the determination will be relevant to one case.[56] Therefore, when a law applies to frequent conduct, less effort should be devoted to giving content to standards than when designing rules, suggesting that rules will give rise to behavior more in accord with underlying norms.[57] Conversely, when acts governed by a law (or a particular detail of a law) are unlikely to arise, more effort should be devoted to giving content to standards.

A number of important qualifications should be emphasized. First, how much effort should be spent giving content to a standard *ex post* in an enforcement proceeding depends importantly on the extent to which individuals would expend effort *ex ante* to predict how the standard would apply to their contemplated conduct. For example, if individuals would spend little to become informed, and thus would not be in a position to anticipate the actual content an adjudicator would supply, efforts devoted to more careful application of a standard would be wasted.[58] As a

---

56. The discussion emphasizes the effort that *should* be made. In the legal systems of the United States and some other countries, the effort in court adjudication is typically determined by a combination of the parties' expenditures on the case (which reflects private interests), *see* KAPLOW & SHAVELL, *supra* note 51, the overall workload of the court, whether the question is one of law or fact, and, with questions of law, the degree to which the judge(s) find the matter interesting or important. Only some of these factors are related to the socially appropriate level of effort, and even those factors may have only a modest connection.

57. Consider Schauer's suggestion that decisionmaking without rules is subject to errors arising from the adjudicator's lack of understanding. *See* SCHAUER, *supra* note 1, at 150. This view will be correct either when the sorts of individuals who are decisionmakers are less competent (perhaps because less expert) than those who design rules, *see infra* Section IV(A), or, as emphasized in this subsection, when the decisionmaking environment under standards involves less effort being applied.

58. If, regardless of the content given standards, individuals act based on gross estimates, an adjudicator might as well base its decision on such gross estimates. *See* KAPLOW & SHAVELL, *supra* note 51. Some elaboration of this issue appears in Section III(C). *See also infra* Section III(D) (discussing risk aversion).

related matter, if one wishes to induce individuals to become informed to some extent at the time they act, *ex post* expenditures will be necessary to ensure that an *ex ante* incentive to become informed exists. The more precise the adjudicator will be *ex post*, the more precise individuals will be induced to become *ex ante*. In this context, the value of a more accurate *ex post* adjudication lies in its *ex ante* effect on behavior.[59] Thus, the appropriate degree of effort in giving content to standards will reflect both that one actual case is involved (not many cases and not the mere possibility of a case) and that effort counts for the one case not in the abstract but rather to the extent it creates *ex ante* incentives for individuals to adjust their conduct.[60]

Second, the cost of inquiry into the appropriate content of the law need not be the same at the promulgation and enforcement stages. Most obviously, inquiry may be cheaper in an enforcement proceeding because only one set of facts need be considered,[61] or because the act itself provides information.[62] These factors would often be most important precisely when standards are more likely to be preferable generally—when acts governed by a law vary greatly in relevant characteristics, and each is unlikely to occur.[63]

---

59. *See also* Section III(E) (discussing objectives of the law other than the control of behavior *ex ante*).

60. In a single case, there is, of course, no *ex ante* effect on the actor's conduct from the actual *ex post* decision concerning effort in applying the standard. More broadly, however, the legal system will become known—to some extent generally and to some extent with regard to particular laws—for the degree to which it supplies content to standards in enforcement proceedings. The discussion in the text proceeds as though actual practice over time will determine perceptions. (To the extent that there are divergences, the effect on the analysis would be straightforward.)

61. For example, if a driver's speed was 100 miles per hour, one need not decide whether the ideal speed limit is 55 or 60 miles per hour.

62. *See, e.g., infra* note 78 (concerning events difficult to foresee); Section III(B). With technological uncertainty, the very fact of an accident or a pattern of harm may provide information that did not exist before the act was taken. (It need not provide such information: A substance may have been previously suspected to be carcinogenic, and the available tests may be no more reliable than previously.) Note that both of these factors seem more plausible with regard to fact scenarios than with regard to which norms are appropriate—that is, for example, whether only safety and time or also energy conservation should be considered in designing laws governing driving.

63. Of course, there may be acts that will arise frequently in the future about which little is known, as when there is a technological advance. When future frequency corresponds with past frequency, however, there will usually be substantial information available that can be consulted when designing a rule. Even when acts are new, if latency periods are not long, a rule designer might conduct tests to determine previously unknown effects. This would tend to be desirable if many such acts are expected to be

Note, however, that the lower cost of inquiry in applying a standard does not imply that the standard should always be applied more carefully on that account. If the application will govern only the single case or if it could not have been anticipated at the time the individual decided to act (perhaps because the consequences were not apparent until afterward),[64] there would be little value in using the newly available information, even if incorporating it into a decision is cheap. Also, in some cases inquiry may be cheaper when designing rules than when applying standards, due to economies of scale with regard to the former.[65]

Finally, consider the situation in which the application of a standard will produce a precedent. Then, the appropriate degree of effort in giving content to the standard at the enforcement stage is determined in much the same manner as for a rule at the promulgation stage.[66] Thus, whether a decision will constitute a precedent affects the degree of effort an adjudicator should expend in giving content to a standard. Also, note that this analysis bears upon when the creation of precedent is appropriate. If an initial decision to promulgate a law as a standard rather than as a rule is an appropriate judgment based on the relevant costs and benefits, rather than, say, a legislature's decision to delegate the question to the courts,[67] converting a standard to a rule via precedent would be sensible only if assessments of the relevant factors differed. These assessments might differ if, for example, the adjudicator

---

committed in the future. This may be one of many reasons that drug regulation requires tests prior to approval.

64. In contrast, if the facts that could not be readily or cheaply anticipated by the promulgator of a law are readily apparent to the actor, it is desirable that individuals anticipate that an adjudicator will take these facts into account. *See* Steven Shavell, *Liability and the Incentive to Obtain Information About Risk*, 21 J. LEGAL STUD. 259, 263–66 (1992).

65. *See infra* note 101.

66. A difference is that it is known with a standard that the case has arisen at least once. In addition, there are the differences noted previously concerning the cost of promulgation. Yet if the precedent will be confined to particular facts (for example, driving at 100 miles per hour is declared illegal without comment on driving 90 miles per hour), the precedent will be narrower than a rule (for example, one that sets the speed limit at 55 miles per hour)—in which case not as much effort would be appropriate (because the frequency with which the precedent will apply is lower). Presumably, this is relevant to courts' inclination, discussed in subsection IV(B)(1), to decide cases narrowly; they may have good information generated by the case with regard to the situation before them, but may have little information regarding other cases.

67. *See infra* Section IV(A); subsection IV(B)(1).

learns that a particular incident has indeed arisen and so might be able to assess the incident at lower cost than would have been possible *ex ante*.[68]

*   *   *

The foregoing considerations suggest that appropriately designed rules and standards will be imperfect and that individuals' behavior will imperfectly reflect the content of the law.[69] The preceding discussion casts further light on how imperfect rules and standards would be, the circumstances in which individual behavior will be better under one formulation or the other, and the magnitude of the cost differentials with regard to promulgating the law, obtaining legal advice, and enforcing the law.

This discussion speaks largely in an all-or-nothing manner: Should the law be promulgated as a rule or a standard, and how carefully designed and applied should either one be? Similar analysis applies to the question of how many factors should be included in a rule or a standard, as will be noted in the discussion of simplicity versus complexity in Part II. As a related matter, some aspects of a law—those likely to apply to many acts—are best included in a rule, whereas others—those unlikely to apply—are best left to a standard.[70]

---

68. Related, accumulated experience may change estimates of frequency or other factors. *See infra* note 160. Otherwise, as when the conduct subject to the law is frequent and the costs of determining the appropriate content of the law are unchanged, precedent is necessarily inferior for the reasons noted in Section C: In the interim, costs spent on legal advice may be higher, and conformity may be lower. *See infra* subsection IV(B)(1). Therefore, when events or technological changes decrease the costs of designing the law, it may be better to promulgate a rule at that time than to wait for a precedent reflecting the new information to be established.

69. As examined in Part II, commentators frequently note that the costs of *ex ante* rule creation may be great, with the result that imperfect, over- and underinclusive rules will be promulgated. Yet they assume that *ex post* it will be optimal to be more precise (even perfectly precise). (Compare the discussion in Section II(D) of whether rules or standards tend to be more detailed in operation.) In the absence of the sorts of factors discussed above, however, this result can arise only if the legal system inefficiently expends more *ex post* in making single applications of standards than it would expend *ex ante* in designing a rule that may be applicable to the behavior of many. If the system actually operates this way when it should not, standards are worse in operation than in principle. The additional accuracy *ex post*—which may not even be particularly valuable in governing behavior *ex ante*—is by assumption more costly than it is appropriate.

70. *See infra* Section III(B).

E. *Creation of the Law as Information Acquisition and Dissemination*

The analysis of this Part suggests that the problem of promulgating and applying rules and standards can be understood as one involving the government's acquisition and dissemination of information about the appropriate content of the law.[71] Whether a law should be given content *ex ante* or *ex post* involves determining whether information should be gathered and processed before or after individuals act.[72]

When the government promulgates a rule, it gathers information before individuals act and announces its findings.[73] As a result, the information is available to individuals when they act; individuals then may be guided by it and spared the expense of producing such information themselves.[74] In addition, the information is available to adjudicators, who realize similar advantages.

Whether the ideal time to acquire and disseminate information is *ex ante* or *ex post* depends, most importantly, on the frequency with which the information will be used. The savings from a single *ex ante* investigation will be great when the use of the results will be frequent, but will be negligible when the use of the results will be unlikely. Also, to the extent there are economies of scale in information acquisition, *ex ante* wholesale investments may be superior.[75] But if there are advantages in delay because information will be easier to acquire at the time individuals act or cases

---

71. *See also infra* note 196 (suggesting that government's choice between rules and standards may be illuminated by considering how complex private organizations formulate internal operating procedures). The term "information" is used here to include anything relevant to reaching a better decision, whether facts or understandings that can be improved through greater discussion and reflection.

72. Similarly, the question of how much effort to devote to rule-creation and to giving content to standards in enforcement proceedings involves determining the appropriate investment in information.

73. Whether the form of the announcement is legally binding in all of its particulars or is merely suggestive may be less important than whether the information is gathered and published. *See supra* note 5 (discussing whether binding rules are possible); *infra* Section III(B) (de-emphasizing the language of the law); subsection IV(B)(3) (noting that the government's conducting and publishing of a study on hazardous substances may have an effect similar to the adoption of a rule embodying the study's results).

74. *See also supra* note 40 (discussing public goods problem in private production of such information).

75. *See infra* note 101.

are adjudicated, *ex post* investments would tend to be preferable.[76]

II. RULES VERSUS STANDARDS AND COMPLEXITY: ON OVER- AND UNDERINCLUSIVENESS

This Part attempts to clarify understanding of the view that rules tend to be over- and underinclusive relative to standards, and more generally, the notion that differences between rules and standards typically involve differences of substance as well as of form. Section A offers a vocabulary for addressing this issue, one that allows the complexity of a legal command and the time at which it is given content (*ex ante* versus *ex post*) to be distinguished conceptually. Section B explains why this distinction is important. Section C briefly discusses how complexity ought to be analyzed. Section D concludes by commenting on whether there are reasons to expect standards to be applied in a systematically more or less detailed manner than rules.

A. *Distinguishing Complexity from the Choice Between Rules and Standards: Definitions*

It is useful to have a way to determine when rules and standards have the same content and thus the same degree of complexity. The following construction permits this. For any standard, consider the actual outcomes that would arise for all possible cases. Now, define the "rule equivalent to the standard" (or the "*de facto* standard") as that rule which attaches these same outcomes to these cases.[77] Thus, if a standard is compared to the rule equivalent to the standard, the content and level of detail are held constant. (For example, using the illustration in the Introduction, a standard that on its face admitted dozens of factors but in practice involved only two would be compared to a rule containing only those two factors.)

Note that nothing has been said about the practicality of the rule that would be equivalent to the standard, because it is merely

---

76. *See supra* subsection D(3).

77. One could also operate in the reverse direction and inquire into the "standard equivalent to the rule." Thus, as with the example in Part I, for a given rule one could imagine a standard that must be applied with the same level of detail, with the content of the standard to be determined by the same sort of investigation that determined the content of the rule.

an analytical construct that will demonstrate its usefulness in the discussion to follow.[78] One problem deserves brief attention: There may be inconsistency under a standard[79]—as one might expect, for example, when decision is by general jury verdict.[80] This could involve occasional aberrations or situations in which, say, a standard yielded one result half of the time and a different result the rest of the time.[81] Even for this extreme case, there ex-

---

78. One might object that the rule equivalent to the standard would be impossible, because not every contingency can be anticipated. *See* SCHAUER, *supra* note 1, at 83–84 (discussing the possibility that a rule might incorporate all relevant distinctions but still be vulnerable to the problem of unanticipated events). Because this construct is hypothetical to begin with, this is not decisive for the main argument that follows. (To establish it, one need not actually write what the rule equivalent to the standard would be.) Moreover, one can think of cases in which contingencies cannot be foreseen as those in which design of the relevant components of the rule would be prohibitively costly, rather than "impossible." Section I(D) examines the question of how much should be invested in designing rules. It is apparent that sufficiently remote contingencies that cannot be addressed except at high cost should not be included in rules in any event. If, as a result, the best rule would be less detailed than the rule equivalent to some particular standard, a comparison of the rule to the posited standard would require consideration of both differences in the level of detail (complexity) and differences between *ex ante* and *ex post* creation. This is precisely the sort of analysis advocated in the remainder of this Part. And, to be more concrete, such analysis suggests that the likelihood of important contingencies whose relevant contours cannot readily be anticipated when promulgating the law (but which would be understood by the time individuals subject to the law decide how to act) is a factor favoring the (implicitly) complex standard. Thus, there is nothing in the analytical construct offered in the text that is inconsistent with this sometimes important possibility. *See also infra* Section III(B) (concerning the difficulty of formulating some laws as rules).

There is also no necessary contradiction between this construct and the view that rules "are necessarily general rather than particular." Schauer, *supra* note 4, at 647, 649–51. Particularity is a matter of degree. Given the limits of language and a finite text, no feasible rule could ever be infinitely particular. Still, for all cases that might arise, one could in principle note the outcome and imagine the rule that stipulated such an outcome given all the particulars of the case. Moreover, as emphasized in this Part and in Section I(D), in practice standards will not and should not be applied in a manner that accounts for all conceivably relevant particulars.

79. There will be some inconsistency in practice under a rule as well, although generally less.

80. Other decisionmakers also can be quite inconsistent. For example, in a study of sentencing by district court judges in the Second Circuit, judges awarded widely disparate sentences in identical hypothetical cases. *See* ANTHONY PARTRIDGE & WILLIAM B. ELDRIDGE, THE SECOND CIRCUIT SENTENCING STUDY 5–11 (1974).

81. Such inconsistencies might reflect differences in the individual jurors selected, the parties' lawyers, or any number of other factors. One could specify these features of each case and simply make them part of the "rule equivalent to the standard." If the feature was normatively relevant, this would be appropriate. If not, presumably the simpler rule that ignored the factor would be superior on grounds of both its content and its simplicity.

ists an equivalent rule—a rule that specifies the two results as possibilities, with the actual result to be determined by the flip of a coin. Thus, the problem of inconsistency does not undermine the conceptual construction, which allows one to consider the desirability of *ex ante* versus *ex post* creation of the law, holding the content of the law constant. (Needless to say, in most contexts the randomized rule equivalent to the standard would be inferior to a rule that selected one of the two outcomes for all cases, or to a single, consistent compromise between the two outcomes.[82] Such a deterministic rule, in turn, would be superior to the hypothesized standard in this regard.)

B. *Distinguishing Complexity from the Choice Between Rules and Standards: Implications*

Using the construct of the rule equivalent to the standard, one can compare rules and standards of differing content (as they are applied) in two steps. First, one can compare the standard to an equivalent rule, using the analysis of Part I.[83] Second, one can compare this equivalent rule to the rule under consideration by analyzing their differences in details. (Alternatively, one could compare the rule to an equivalent standard and then compare this equivalent standard to the standard under consideration.)

Many discussions of rules versus standards combine—or confuse—these two concerns. In particular, simple rules are often

---

82. Consistency might be favored by considerations of risk aversion, fairness, or uncertainty that makes settlement before trial more difficult. The last reason is noted in Ehrlich & Posner, *supra* note 1, at 265.

83. The discussion of rules and standards in Part I focuses exclusively on the question of whether content is determined *ex ante* or *ex post*. Nothing depended on whether the comparison involved a simple rule and a simple standard or a complex rule and a complex standard. The analysis assumed only that the content, and thus level of detail, were held constant. For example, it may be that with a complex rule, the government must promulgate (stage one), a lawyer must consult (stage two), and a tribunal must apply (stage three) a detailed web of provisions, rather than, say, a simple statement of whether an act is prohibited. Likewise, with a complex standard, a web must be developed and applied *ex post* (stage three) and anticipated by lawyers (stage two). Presumably, each of these processes will involve a greater cost than with a simple rule or standard. Nonetheless, the relevant analysis would be the same. Of course, for a standard and corresponding rule, it may be that some details would better be promulgated in a rule and others left to an adjudicator using the formulation of a standard, rather than all being crafted in one mode, particularly because some details will concern frequently conducted activities and others infrequently occurring ones. *See supra* note 6 and accompanying text; *infra* Section III(B).

compared to complex standards; most commonly, it is asserted that rules tend to be over- and/or underinclusive relative to standards.[84] The reason for this suggested difference is that rules limit the range of permissible considerations whereas standards do not. Observe, however, that a rule cannot be over- or underinclusive relative to a standard if one is comparing the standard to the rule equivalent to the standard. Implicitly, therefore, commentators must be comparing a complex standard to a simple rule—that is, a rule simpler than the rule equivalent to the standard. Section D explores whether rule systems are indeed universally simpler than standards, as each formulation actually would be created and applied in practice. The focus here is on how one should compare rules and standards that indeed differ in complexity.

Whether a complex standard is preferable to a simple rule depends on the combined effects of complexity and promulgation of the law as a rule versus as a standard (*ex ante* versus *ex post* creation). When a complex standard is said to be preferable to a simple rule, it may be that complexity and use of a standard are both independently and unambiguously desirable.[85] But there are two additional possibilities.

First, it may be that a simple standard (one equivalent in content to the simple rule under consideration) is undesirable compared to the simple rule, whereas a complex standard is desirable. This suggests that the desirability of the complex standard arises from its complexity, not from its promulgation as a standard. In this case, a complex rule may[86] be even better than the com-

---

84. *See* sources cited *supra* note 13. The tendency to make this comparison has been noted in Schlag, *supra* note 5, at 423. Colin Diver indicates the possibility that a standard "may be under- or overinclusive in application, because its vagueness invites misinterpretation." Diver, *supra* note 1, at 73. This possibility may refer to the problem of inconsistency, discussed in Section A. To assume that this is the only manner in which a vague standard may be over- or underinclusive, however, is misleading. As Diver notes, *see id.* at 69, an open-ended standard may be interpreted in a simple manner. This, however, would be a "misinterpretation" only if it indeed were optimal to give it more precise content in practice. As the discussion in Section C indicates, this need not be the case.

85. Similarly, if the simple rule is preferable, it may be that simplicity and use of a rule are both desirable, or that only one dimension favors formulation as a simple rule.

86. This need not be the case, however, because of synergy. For example, designing the complex rule may be expensive and the likelihood of application for each of the detailed components may be sufficiently small that a complex standard is better, whereas the analogous balance is otherwise for the simple rule and simple standard—because the provisions would be rather general, applying to many actors.

plex standard.[87] Thus, requirements for handling different hazardous substances might better be promulgated as complex standards than as simple rules, which ignored important differences
among substances, but complex rules may be best of all (as noted
in the example in the Introduction).

Second, it may be that a complex rule is undesirable, but a
complex standard desirable. This suggests that the desirability of
the complex standard arises from its promulgation as a standard,
not its complexity. In this case, a simple standard—meaning one
that in practice is applied using little detail—should be considered.[88] For example, whether an exception to a town's requirement that people keep off the grass in the public square
should be made in the event that the President unexpectedly visits,
might best be left to a standard, because the event is so unlikely
to arise. Thus, a simple standard that considers only a few salient
factors might be preferable, since the expectation that an adjudicator would take into account myriad subtle factors *ex post* would be
unlikely to affect the crowd's behavior in any event.

C. *Analyzing the Problem of Over- and Underinclusiveness*

Comparing the desirability of a complex standard that is accordingly costly to apply with a rule that is sometimes over- and
underinclusive because of its simplicity raises two separate issues:
rules versus standards (*ex ante* versus *ex post* creation of the law),
already examined in Part I; and the appropriate level of detail,
which requires a separate analysis. In order to compare two rules
(or two standards) having different levels of detail, one needs a
framework for analyzing the effects of detail in laws. Because this
problem is not the primary focus of this Article and because it has

---

87. Unlike most other commentators, Colin Diver notes that when over- and
underinclusion is an important problem, it is optimal to employ either highly flexible formulas (complex standards) *or* intricate regulatory formulas (complex rules). *See* Diver, *supra* note 1, at 74–75.

88. Again, because of synergy, this implication need not follow. Thus, when there are
many possibilities, each unlikely to arise, a complex rule may be too expensive because
of promulgation costs and a simple standard may be of only modest benefit because it
does not respond to the range of possibilities, whereas a complex standard would be best
of all.

received attention in other work,[89] only a brief summary of basic principles is offered here.

To illustrate, consider what law should be promulgated to regulate a given set of activities—for example, the discharge of a certain class of chemicals. Most of the chemicals cause a known level of harm; the remainder of the chemicals are harmless. But it is not immediately apparent which of the chemicals are the harmful ones.

Compare two laws. A simple rule holds individuals discharging any of the chemicals in this class strictly liable for damages equal to the average harm (that is, the harm multiplied by the fraction of discharged chemicals that are harmful). A complex standard holds individuals "appropriately" responsible: An adjudicator will conduct an inquiry, the result being that those discharging chemicals that are actually harmful will be held strictly liable for damages equal to the level of harm caused, and those discharging harmless chemicals will not be held liable. Thus, the standard makes an *ex post*, case-by-case determination of which chemicals are harmful. The standard is complex compared to the rule, because the rule does not distinguish among chemicals in this class.

Observe that the simple rule is both over- and underinclusive compared to the more complex standard. The simple rule overdeters discharges of harmless chemicals covered by the law by subjecting them to positive liability. Some harmless discharges will therefore be deterred despite their desirability. The simple rule underdeters discharges of harmful chemicals covered by the law by subjecting them to liability for less than the actual harm they cause. Some harmful discharges will be made even though their benefit is less than the harm they cause.

To determine whether the simple rule or complex standard is superior, consider the differences in costs and behavior under the two laws. At the promulgation stage, there would be little difference. Although a rule is more costly to promulgate than a standard *of the same degree of complexity*, this rule is simple. There is no *ex ante* investigation to define which of the chemicals are harmful.

---

89. *See* LOUIS KAPLOW, A MODEL OF THE OPTIMAL COMPLEXITY OF RULES (Harvard Program in Law and Economics Discussion Paper No. 97, 1991). The analysis in that piece does not consider promulgation costs, although incorporating them would be straightforward.

At the stage concerned with individuals' behavior, one can identify two possibilities (or, two sets of individuals). First, individuals may not become informed with respect to the complex standard, because of the cost of determining whether the chemical they would discharge is harmful.[90] Suppose that they know only that the chemical they contemplate discharging is subject to the standard, which implies an expected liability equal to the average harm (which is precisely how they expect to be treated under the simple rule). In this instance, their behavior will be the same under both formulations of the law. At the enforcement stage, applying the complex standard will be more costly. But this will be a waste, because behavior will not be improved by avoiding over- and underinclusiveness. As a result, the simple rule would be superior. Achieving a better fit between the law and behavior is accomplished only if individuals are induced to conform their behavior to the legal norm.[91]

Second, consider individuals who do become informed with respect to the complex standard. They expend resources on advice and, upon learning whether their chemical is indeed harmful, may be induced (depending on what they learn) to behave differently. Suppose that this change in behavior is desirable, even when taking into account the cost of advice.[92] Then, with regard to the second stage, at which individuals' decisions are made, the complex standard will be superior to the simple rule.[93] At the enforcement stage, however, the complex standard will be more costly to employ. Thus, whether the simple rule or complex standard is superior depends on whether the benefits from the standard—which arise from its complexity—exceed the additional costs

---

90. For a discussion of the circumstances in which individuals would choose to become informed, see *id.*

91. Observe that it is plausible that a relatively simple rule would guide behavior *more* precisely than would a complex standard, as individuals might know all the modest content of the former but none of the potentially very detailed content of the latter. In this instance, the complex standard would be more over- and underinclusive *with regard to its effect on behavior* than the simple rule.

92. Because the legal regime imposes strict liability equal to harm actually caused, this adjustment in behavior will tend to be desirable, as explored in Section III(C).

93. This is the opposite of the result with case 3 in Part I. The reason is that, in the other case, individuals learned the content of the rule (but not of the standard) and conformed their behavior. Here, the simple rule has no content to guide behavior aside from what individuals already know, but the complex standard does and individuals learn its content.

of the standard—which arise from both its complexity and its promulgation as a standard.[94]

Consider the case in which the latter scenario prevails (individuals learn of how the complex standard would apply to their conduct) and the balance of factors is such that the complex standard is more desirable than the simple rule.[95] It still remains to ask whether the complex standard is more desirable than a complex rule—that is, one that determines in advance which chemicals are harmful. (Recall the hazardous substance illustration in Section B.) Such a complex rule would have higher promulgation costs than the complex standard, but lower advice costs and lower enforcement costs. This comparison between a complex rule and a complex standard is simply that between rules and standards, as presented in Part I. The components unique to the comparison between the simple rule and complex standard emphasized in this Section are those going to whether complexity is desirable.[96] Study of this example thus reinforces the view that comparing simple rules and complex standards consists of two operations: analyzing complexity and analyzing the desirability of giving content to the law *ex ante* versus *ex post*.

D. *Are Standards Systematically More Complex in Application than Rules?*

Sections A through C described the analytic difference between the dimensions of the time (*ex ante* versus *ex post*) at which the law is given content and complexity. This final Section casts into doubt commonly expressed beliefs concerning the relationship between these two dimensions in practice.

---

94. If it were not complex, there would be nothing to determine *ex post* other than what is required to apply the posited simple rule; if it were not a standard, the cost would have been incurred (once) at the promulgation stage.

95. Of course, if the complex standard is less desirable, it is still important to ask whether a complex rule might be superior to the simple rule.

96. It is apparent from the discussion how one would compare a simple rule and a complex rule. But one could equally apply the discussion to standards, which, if simple, invoke the principle of average harm for the class of activity but, if complex, invoke the principle of harm for the particular activity in the class. (For example, standards of "reasonableness" often are applied in an "objective" manner that looks to typical characteristics of a group of actors rather than to particular characteristics of the actor in a given case.)

Discussions often refer simply to rules and standards, indicating that the former tend to be over- and underinclusive. This characterization implicitly assumes that standards tend to be more complex than rules in the domains contemplated. This view may reflect that lawyers and legal academics are always able to imagine countless factors (arguments) that a decisionmaker might take into account if only it is permitted to do so. (Such imagining applies to rules as well, but standards are seen as allowing more room to maneuver.) This, however, is a romantic perspective, hardly a valid depiction of actual decisionmaking.[97]

As the Introduction noted, there are two fundamental problems with the assumption that standards inherently encompass more relevant considerations and thus achieve a better fit with underlying norms. First, standards need not admit all considerations.[98] (In contrast, a rule may contain provisions that depend on factors that are not admissible under a standard.) Second, even standards that admit broader consideration *ex post* may not operate in a more precise manner, as illustrated by the example in the Introduction in which juries consistently make their decisions based on the same two or three of dozens of relevant factors. One suspects that if automobile design or workplace health and safety requirements were left to juries under a reasonableness standard, juries might tend to focus on a handful of factors that are most salient and easiest to comprehend.[99] Thus, ignoring random error, the rule equivalent to the standard may depend on only a handful of factors and a simple weighting formula, nothing as complex as the analysis developed and the rules promulgated by auto safety regulators or OSHA. The same can be said with regard to the federal income tax, as noted in the Introduction.[100]

---

97. Some commentators emphasize that standards cannot simply be assumed to function without error. *See* Schauer, *supra* note 4, at 685–86 (decisionmakers unconstrained by rules will err, and this risk of error need not be less than that which would arise from faithful application of over- and underinclusive rules).

98. *Cf. id.* at 648 n.6 (distinguishing the case in which the decisionmaker consults a single background justification for a rule from that in which all possible justificatory norms may be considered).

99. Also, over time jury instructions may be developed that limit juries' focus. *See supra* note 14. Such instructions might be analogized to precedents (a form of rules), discussed in Section I(C) and subsection IV(B)(1).

100. An example that might be more familiar to many readers of this Article is the determination of financial aid. If financial aid is determined based on "need, all things considered," one might expect that case-by-case judgments would, in practice, ignore

There is a simple explanation, explored in Section I(D), for the fact that rule systems are often complex compared to the results that actually would arise under standards. Case-by-case creations (and re-creations) of complex formulas are expensive. When one economizes on that process, recognizing that the formula is to be used only once, it is sensible to oversimplify greatly, and thus to consider only the factors most likely to be important. When one makes a single pronouncement that will govern many (perhaps millions) of cases, it is worthwhile to undertake greater investigation into the relevance of additional factors and to expend more effort fine-tuning the weight accorded to each. Thus, when rules are to be applicable to frequent behavior with recurring characteristics, there is a systematic tendency for rule systems to be more complex than the content that would actually be given to standards covering the same activity. In contrast, when the behavior to be regulated by law is infrequent, or when each instance (no one very likely to occur) is unique in important ways, substantial *ex ante* analysis for each conceivable contingency would be a poor investment, whereas *ex post* determinations under standards are made with the knowledge that the scenario has indeed arisen. As emphasized in Part I, frequency is a central consideration determining the relative desirability of rules and standards. Here, we see that it is similarly relevant when considering the costs of employing more complex laws.[101]

---

many subtleties, overstating need in one case (because, for example, nontaxable sources of income are overlooked) and understating need in another case (because, for example, insufficient attention is given to how parents' other dependents dilute the parents' ability to pay). A complex rule scheme that is applied rather mechanically (at far less cost per case) may be much less over- and underinclusive than such case-by-case judgments would be.

101. There is also an important synergy between complexity and the choice of rules and standards (which implies that the optimal rule and optimal standard may differ in content). The degree of complexity affects frequency, in the sense used in this Article. *See infra* Section III(B). Consider the following example. There are 100 possible acts subject to a law, each with a 10% chance of ever arising. If complexity is of little value (that is, if the acts are rather similar, so little is lost by treating them identically), a rule may be cheaper: The promulgation cost differential is borne only once while the costs of interpretation by individuals and enforcers are expected to be borne 10 times (10% X 100). In contrast, if complexity is of great value and each of the 100 acts is really quite different, calling for different legal treatments, a standard may be cheaper: With a rule, 100 decisions must be made, whereas with a standard individuals and enforcers need only address the 10 acts that actually arise. This suggests that when complexity is important, frequency in the relevant sense will be less. Of course, if frequency is still sufficiently great, the relative benefit of rules may be even greater when complexity is important.

It is curious, therefore, that most commentators assume that standards tend to be complex in operation compared to the rules that might replace them, with little effort devoted to comparing standards that are simplistic in application with complex rule systems.[102] The main point to recognize is that there is no universal tendency for standards as they are actually applied to be more complex than rules that would plausibly be promulgated.[103] Thus, subsuming the benefits of complexity under the banner of standards or those of simplicity under the banner of rules not only obscures the analysis, as suggested in Section B, but does not correspond very well to the legal universe.

III. EXTENSIONS

A. *The Accessibility of Rules and Standards*

In Part I, it was suggested that individuals will find it cheaper to learn how rules would apply to their circumstances than to learn how standards would apply, because the former will have already been given content whereas the latter will require predicting the content that a later decisionmaker will provide. As a result, rules tend to be preferable with regard to individual behavior, because individuals will expend fewer resources learning about the law and will learn more under rules and thus behave more in accordance with the law. If, instead, it were cheaper to learn about standards, these aspects of the argument would be reversed. This Section considers the plausibility of the view that standards, rather than rules, would typically be more accessible. Ultimately, of

---

First, because the cost of learning about rules is less, it is more likely that behavior will reflect the law (which is more important when there are important differences among individuals' acts that the law takes into account). Second, there may be economies of scale in making the inquiries at the promulgation stage: Determining the appropriate treatment for each of the 100 possible acts may cost little more than for one act (because the same investigation may yield most of the relevant information). In that case, a rule would entail bearing the investigation cost—which may be unusually large with complex phenomena—once while the standard may require that it be borne 10 times in enforcement proceedings (and, possibly, additional times when individuals act).

102. Perhaps the bias arises because prior authors have been more familiar with laws such as the negligence rule for automobile accidents than with public regulatory regimes.

103. The question is meaningful only if one is considering a particular legal context—i.e., whether traffic laws should be formulated as rules or standards—rather than comparing the complexity of a rule in one area of law to that of a standard in another.

course, the question is empirical; whatever the correct answer is in a given context, the general framework of Part I could be applied.

In some instances, it might appear that a standard would be easier for individuals to apply because some cases will be obvious under the standard, whereas if the rule is complex, it may take some effort to verify that no exception applies. This construct implicitly assumes that, under a standard, modest effort would yield a rather confident (but probably not perfectly certain) prediction, whereas under a rule, either substantial effort would be expended to yield nearly complete certainty or little effort would be applied, leaving the individual with little idea of the governing law. But in most instances, these assumptions are inconsistent: The likely (if not certain) result will often be just as obvious under the complex rule as under the standard. For example, under a standard requiring safe driving, most drivers would readily anticipate that driving at night without headlights illuminated or parking in the middle of an intersection would be proscribed. At the same time, much unsafe driving behavior is currently prohibited by specific traffic regulations, most of which drivers have probably never read; surely, such drivers have no difficulty guessing, with high confidence, what these unseen rules require in most instances.

Individuals subject to a complex rule system will only make additional expenditures, to achieve higher confidence in their predictions, if the perceived value exceeds the perceived cost. But this can be true only if individuals are in fact materially uncertain about what the rules would say about their contemplated conduct.[104] For example, drivers of trucks that transport dangerous substances might check which roads or bridges are closed to such traffic. In precisely such instances, however, drivers probably will be uncertain about what content would be given to a standard that limited driving to "appropriate" routes.[105] And, if legal advice is

---

104. *Cf.* SCHAUER, *supra* note 1, at 139 (rules enhance predictability when actors cannot otherwise predict how an adjudicator would resolve the case because actors and adjudicators do not have common outlooks, but they do share common language).

105. Recall that the comparisons thus far deal with rules and standards that would have the same content if the same effort were applied in giving each content—that is, where the process producing the rule considers the same factors, giving them the same weight, as the process that will later give content to the standard.

A qualification arises when, because of the frequency of potential application, greater effort would be expended *ex ante* in designing a rule than *ex post* in applying a standard. In that case, there may be detailed distinctions made in the rule that would not be made in applying a standard. (This is precisely the instance noted in Section II(D), in

to be obtained in such a case, one would expect, as before, that rules could usually be predicted at lower cost than standards, precisely because more content has been provided in advance. Thus, with the rule, one would perhaps simply consult an official map. In contrast, under the standard, it would be necessary to ascertain the weight given to various factors by adjudicators and the actual circumstances of each route (such as population density, presence of groundwater, and the like).

The possibility that standards will be more accessible to individuals than rules might be rationalized on account of the differences in the institutions that give content to each.[106] The implicit scenario is one in which a legal command, if promulgated as a rule, will be given technical detail by lawyers or other relevant experts—whereas standards will be given content through decisions of lay juries, who will rely on common understandings (rather than on, say, expert testimony).[107] For the argument to work, it must further be assumed that the content given to standards by lay decisionmakers will diverge significantly from the content that experts would choose to give to rules. Otherwise, individuals guided by common understandings would be equally able to comply with the technical rules, as the preceding discussion explains.

This version of the argument has important shortcomings. First, these implicitly assumed features of rules and standards would involve choices that could be made differently. For example, if lay content were preferred for reasons of accessibility, but rules were preferred to avoid costs of repeated *ex post* decisionmaking, one could assemble a lay panel to design rules, just as expert

---

which rules are more complex than standards, as applied.) To the extent individuals subject to the more complex rule would not in fact expend the resources necessary to learn and thus adjust their behavior to the additional detail (or if the expenditures in learning the detail were not socially warranted), it would not be optimal *ex ante* to design so detailed a rule. This is the analysis of complexity, presented briefly in Section II(C), which was there distinguished from the issue of the appropriateness of giving content to the law *ex ante* versus *ex post*.

106. Institutional differences are considered further in Section IV(A).

107. *See, e.g.,* POSNER, *supra* note 1, at 47–48. Other institutional considerations suggest that rules might be more accessible to individuals. Representative legislative bodies or administrators subject to political pressure may be easier to predict than juries or other adjudicators, because of possible idiosyncrasies of the latter—concerning the decisionmakers themselves or the information that they will be given in a particular case—and their being subject to different influences.

testimony is used in adjudication when society wishes standards to be given content in a manner that incorporates relevant expertise.

Second, if experts would otherwise be appropriate when rules are promulgated, it must be because the content they will give to rules is *superior* to the *differing* content that would be supplied by lay decisionmakers *ex post*. This suggests that if standards would achieve greater conformity, the conformity is with commonly made mistakes rather than with underlying norms. (If the experts' results are indeed no better, but just different, then the accessibility argument disfavors relying on experts, not *ex ante* creation of the law.)

Finally, the scenario usually imagines that individuals will not seek advice to guide their behavior, which is plausible for the everyday activity of individuals that is unlikely to have significant legal consequences, but not for many other activities governed by legal commands. If expertise is indeed helpful in designing the law, and if the resulting law does differ importantly from lay understandings, then the tendency of technical rules to induce individuals to seek advice would be desirable. For example, suppose that in a regime covered by a standard that simply required appropriate disposal, most individuals dump most chemicals down the drain because they suspect a lay jury would find this action appropriate (from the point of view of unsophisticated actors, like themselves). Then, substituting detailed rules, indicating appropriate methods of disposal for those chemicals that are hazardous, may be helpful, as these individuals might then fear that they would be in violation of the law and be induced to seek advice before acting.[108]

B. *The Difficulty of Formulating Some Laws as Rules*

It would appear that some legal commands cannot plausibly be formulated as rules. For example, it may not be possible to

---

108. Observe that a similar result might follow if individuals knew that their liability would be adjudicated by experts, or by a lay jury instructed that the standard requires individuals to take technologically appropriate action and informed by the testimony of experts on the subject. This highlights the first point, that the desirability of expertise rather than lay instinct is, in principle, substantially separable from that of the choice between rules and standards. In practice, there may be an important connection for the reasons described in Section I(D): If a rule is to apply to many individuals' behavior, additional investment in design might be appropriate (so it might be worth investing substantially in expertise) compared to the situation employing standards. Or, if a circumstance is unlikely to arise, *ex ante* investment in expertise may not be warranted but, once the situation has arisen, it may be worthwhile to consult experts.

specify in a zoning ordinance which building designs are aesthetically inappropriate, but we may know them when we see them. Or we may be unable to specify in advance proper disposal techniques for all hazardous substances because we cannot foresee all potential hazards—whereas some hazards, and how best to address them, may become apparent when they arise.

Because of such factors, rules may seem not only to be inferior to standards, but an entirely infeasible option. Such limitations of rules, however, are already incorporated into the analysis. In particular, they are largely reflected in the frequency dimension emphasized in Part I, and also in the discussion of promulgation versus enforcement costs in Section I(D).[109] For example, the problem with building designs is that the possible permutations are many. The cost of making an advance ruling on millions of possibilities would be excessive, as few would ever arise in any event. It is not the case, however, that nothing can profitably be determined in advance. Size (square feet, height), building materials, distance from the street, and other characteristics could be articulated, leaving to some adjudicator the task of undertaking further review of submitted plans.

The choice between rules and standards is one of degree. Deciding solely on the relevant criteria in advance may save costs for both individual actors and adjudicators, while providing individuals some guidance. Also, adopting presumptions or ruling certain options in or out might be possible. The extent to which such approaches are desirable will depend on the anticipated frequency of behavior with the relevant common elements. The commonality aspect is worth emphasizing when defining frequency for the purposes of this Article. The law of negligence may cover millions of acts, but if most types have little in common with each other and are unlikely to arise, behavior at the relevant degree of detail is infrequent.[110] But if some particular type of act will arise even a dozen times, that may be sufficiently frequent to warrant an *ex ante* wholesale resolution of the problem.

Yet another limitation on the ability to formulate laws as rules involves limitations of language. Even if there is precise

---

109. The discussion in this section emphasizes frequency. The added cost of designing rules when events are difficult to anticipate is discussed in note 78.
110. This discussion highlights a synergy between the issue of complexity and the issue of when laws should be given content, as discussed in Part II. *See supra* note 101.

consensus on the meaning of, say, "vulgar behavior," it may be difficult to describe the set of behavior precisely and succinctly. As with the example involving aesthetic zoning, the problem may involve frequency, as the range of vulgar behavior is substantial.

If, however, the problem is simply that readily identifiable and recurring behavior is difficult to describe, using a rule may pose no difficulty with regard to the issues addressed in this Article. The rule could simply prohibit "vulgar behavior." As long as the relevant audience took this to refer to a familiar set of acts, an *ex ante* specification would have been made in the relevant sense.[111] That is, whether a law has been given content *ex ante* depends on whether information acquisition and processing that might require effort has been completed,[112] not on the *type of language* that best communicates the results of *ex ante* investigation and decisionmaking.[113] This Article has focused on the division of effort over time: A legal command is defined here to be rule-like to the extent that greater effort has been expended *ex ante*, rather than requiring such effort to be made *ex post*.[114] Thus, for a legal command prohibiting vulgar behavior to be viewed as a standard for present purposes, it would have to be understood that the command authorizes the adjudicator to make a *de novo* inquiry into what constitutes vulgar behavior, for only then would application of the standard be costly and difficult for individuals to predict. To the extent the domain of vulgar behavior would have been well understood, the decision to prohibit this category of activity, but not other activity raising similar concerns, should be seen as a rule.[115]

---

111. *See* Frederick Schauer, *Formalism*, 97 YALE L.J. 509, 512 n.8 (1988) (using the broadly worded university honor codes of the eighteenth and nineteenth centuries as an example of commonly understood precepts).

112. After all, even a precise rule—one prohibiting driving in excess of 55 miles per hour—requires some effort to interpret.

113. *See supra* Section I(E); *infra* subsection IV(B)(3); *cf.* ATIYAH & SUMMERS, *supra* note 1, at 81–83 (instances in which English laws appear less rule-like than American laws may still entail a more formal, predictable approach in England because of its more developed customary norms arising from the greater homogeneity of the British people and English judiciary); Sanford Levinson, *Some Reflections on the Posnerian Constitution*, 56 GEO. WASH. L. REV. 39, 40 n.2 (1987) (what may appear to an outsider as a rule might be understood by an insider as a standard, or vice versa).

114. *See supra* subsection I(A)(1) (emphasizing that the motivation for the problem is that the ideal content of the law is not immediately apparent); Section I(E).

115. A related limitation on formulating laws as rules may involve the reluctance to

C. The Private Versus Social Value of Legal Advice

Whenever individuals acquire legal advice, the question arises whether their decisions to do so are socially desirable. Answering this question involves comparing the effect of advice on behavior with the cost of advice. In subsection I(B)(3)—analyzing the case in which individuals would acquire advice under a rule but not under a standard—it was noted that the overall effect of obtaining advice is necessarily desirable if the private value of advice equals the social value of advice.[116] The reason for this result is that individuals only acquire advice when its private value exceeds its cost; so in this case, it must be that the social benefit of advice exceeds its cost.

In addition, the discussion in Section I(D) emphasized that individuals' decisions to acquire advice are a matter of degree. Individuals may, for example, choose to become more informed about rules because the cost of advice is cheaper. In such instances, their total expenditure on advice may be greater under rules or under standards. (Under standards, even when less advice is acquired, the cost for a given amount of advice is greater, so the total cost may be greater.) If expenditures are greater under standards, but individuals are more informed under rules—and more informed individuals act more in accord with underlying norms—the net effect of advice at this stage would tend to favor

---

draft precise legal commands except in simple "on/off" forms or as expressing linear relationships. For example, suppose that the ideal formula for the level of care depended on the variables x and y, so that there should be liability if and only if x^2y exceeds some particular level. After hearing (possibly expert) testimony, a factfinder might (approximately) reach correct conclusions under a standard. A rule could substitute if it indeed provided for liability as a function of the stated condition. But if the rule drafter were limited to having separate on/off tests for x and y, or possibly allowing x and y to be added, the best rule may lead to many poor results. Judgments of factfinders often may reflect (roughly) complex interactions of variables that we tend not to write in rules (except perhaps in the tax law and some other complex statutory or regulatory schemes). Related, judicial precedents and jury instructions tend toward simple formulations; when these are found unsatisfactory, multiple factor tests or commands to consider all the facts and circumstances are promulgated, often with little further guidance. See infra note 155. The option of a rule specifying a complex interaction does not usually receive serious attention. See generally Søren Bisgaard, Design of Standards and Regulations, 154 J. ROYAL STAT. SOC'Y 93 (1991) (ambiguity can often be reduced using statistical methods and concepts when laws are designed); Ogus, supra note 1 (discussing dichotomy between general and complex, precise rules, and the recent trend in judicial preference for generality).

116. See also supra note 44 (discussing the possibility that the private value of advice is greater than or less than its social value).

rules.[117] Determining whether the net effect at this stage favors rules or standards in other situations and quantifying the net effect requires that one examine the relationship between the private and social values of legal advice. Observe that if the private and social values of advice are equal, then whatever level of advice individuals acquire will be socially appropriate, producing benefits of advice in excess of the cost of advice—taking as given whether a rule or standard prevails. Moreover, to the extent the cost of advice is lower under rules than under standards, rules will necessarily be preferable on account of this factor.[118]

The subject of the social value of legal advice deserves and has received separate treatment.[119] A few themes will be noted here. First, there is an important instance in which the private and social values of advice will be equal: when individuals will be held liable for the full costs of any harm they cause.[120] Because an individual bears all the consequences of each act, it follows that advice guiding the choice among acts will have a value to the individual that reflects its social value.[121] Second, to the extent that the legal system does not provide liability equal to the actual harm of acts, there generally will be divergences between the private and social values of legal advice.[122] For example, under some circumstances the private value of advice will be socially excessive under a negligence rule, because individuals value escap-

---

117. Advice at this stage may affect total costs at the enforcement stage, because advice may affect the number of lawsuits that later occur. An optimal law of damages would take into account both the direct harm caused by acts and the enforcement costs, which can have the effect of internalizing this cost at the time individuals decide whether to acquire legal advice and how to act. *See* KAPLOW, *supra* note 89, at 8–9; *see also* A. Mitchell Polinsky & Steven Shavell, *Enforcement Costs and the Optimal Probability and Magnitude of Fines*, 35 J.L. & ECON. 133 (1992). If enforcement costs were thus internalized, individuals' decisions concerning the acquisition of information and level of care would be optimal. (Promulgation costs are sunk at the time individuals' decisions are made.) If there is an external effect on enforcement costs, it is not clear that it would tend to favor more or less advice, as advice may lead individuals to take actions that would result in fewer or more subsequent lawsuits. *See supra* note 41.

118. When social value is reflected in private demand, a reduction in the resource cost of supplying a good or service—here, legal advice—is desirable.

119. *See* Louis Kaplow & Steven Shavell, *Private Versus Socially Optimal Provision of Ex Ante Legal Advice*, 8 J.L. ECON. & ORGANIZATION 306 (1992).

120. *See also supra* note 117 (discussing subsequent enforcement costs as a component of the harm of an individual's act).

121. For a formal demonstration, see Kaplow & Shavell, *supra* note 119, at 308–09.

122. The examples that follow and others are analyzed in *id.* at 309–16.

ing liability entirely when they take due care, despite the fact that they nonetheless cause harm.[123] Third, to the extent there is legal error (for example, systematic misassessment of damages) that individuals can better anticipate with the aid of legal advice, the private value of advice may be socially excessive.[124] Moreover, in this instance, advice tends to be socially undesirable even without regard to its cost, because advice leads individuals to behave less in accord with underlying norms.[125]

If one adopts the view common (if often implicit) in discussions of rules and standards that greater knowledge of the law by individuals subject to it is desirable, the tendency for individuals to be more knowledgeable of rules because of the lower cost of advice about them would favor rules. Recognizing that the private and social values of advice need not be equal complicates the argument. Divergences between the private and social values of

---

123. The text speaks of a negligence rule, a term most commonly used in describing accident law. The concept, however, is more general. Any law in which liability only arises when care is unreasonable in some respect is a negligence regime for present purposes. *See id.* at 317. For further discussion of behavior when there is uncertainty regarding application of the negligence rule, see *supra* note 42.

124. The mere existence of error is not sufficient, as long as individuals (even with legal advice) expect the law to be applied properly, or if individuals do not expect there to be systematic biases in what enforcement tribunals will award.

125. The possibility that predictable legal error will lead to worse behavior might in some contexts favor standards over rules for the very reason that individuals will be unaware of the content of standards whereas they would become informed about rules. The scenario is as follows. Individuals know the true character of their acts (as they would be evaluated by an omniscient social authority), but the government—when promulgating rules or applying standards—cannot determine their true character. Rather, it makes random errors. If these errors will be made under a standard—and thus after individuals decide how to act—the actual error with regard to a particular type of behavior cannot be precisely predicted. But if an *ex ante* determination of the appropriate treatment of a particular act is made, any error will be knowable before individuals act, so it may lead them to act in an undesirable manner. This example illustrates how advice about error—whether error embodied in a rule or the prediction of error likely to be made in applying a standard—can be socially undesirable. It also suggests that errors under standards will be important with regard to behavior only to the extent individuals can anticipate the errors at the time they act, perhaps when aided by legal advice. *But see supra* note 42 (mere uncertainty under a negligence rule may adversely affect behavior). To the extent error will be anticipated, greater expenditures on *ex post* accuracy would be warranted. (This problem also creates a rationale for making errors difficult to predict—for example, by forbidding contact with jurors when interviews might reveal bases for decision unrelated to the underlying legal norms.) As noted in subsection I(D)(3), if behavior is frequent, greater investment in giving content to rules than to standards would be appropriate. This suggests that the problem of error may be greater under standards.

advice could favor either formulation relative to the balance of factors that otherwise would prevail.

D. *Risk Aversion*

Risk aversion is relevant to the analysis of rules and standards for two reasons.[126] First, individuals' behavior will reflect their risk preferences. The most important implication is that individuals will place a greater value on legal advice because advice reduces their uncertainty.[127] This suggests that it may be more valuable than otherwise for the cost of legal advice to be low, a factor favoring rules.

Second, when individuals are risk averse, their bearing of risk is socially undesirable. Because individuals tend to be less well informed concerning standards, they may bear more risk under standards, which would favor rules. Another consideration is that the precision with which laws are actually applied may affect the risk individuals bear. (For example, to the extent liability is designed to compensate uninsured victims, it is important that the compensation reflect actual losses.) This factor may favor standards, to the extent they can better take advantage of information available only *ex post*, or it may favor rules if less is invested in applying standards (because the investment will apply to only one case).[128]

---

126. Risk aversion is also relevant to Part II's discussion of complexity. More complex rules, which some individuals will not learn, might result in more risk being imposed. (Whether more risk is indeed imposed is formally ambiguous. *See* KAPLOW, *supra* note 89.) If more risk were imposed, simpler (and, as a result, more over- or underinclusive) laws—whether rules or standards—would tend to be favored.

127. This additional private value of advice is also a social value, because risk-bearing costs are social costs. Thus, the presence of risk aversion has no direct effect on whether there will be a divergence between the private and social values of legal advice, as discussed in Section C.

128. The appropriate investment in designing rules and applying standards may be determined in part by considerations of accurate compensation, in addition to the ability of the law to influence behavior, which has been the focus throughout. This might favor greater effort in giving content to the law (to fine-tune victim compensation) or less (because individuals will not be fully informed at the time they act or because the actual harm to a particular, unidentified victim cannot be predicted, so that fine-tuning *ex post* entails greater risk *ex ante* for those committing acts). See KAPLOW & SHAVELL, *supra* note 51, at 18–19.

E. *Objectives of the Law Other than Deterrence*

The analysis thus far has focused on the purpose and effect of law with regard to controlling behavior *ex ante*.[129] Individuals who anticipate the possibility of sanctions will adjust their behavior accordingly. This Section briefly notes the extent to which the analysis is applicable to other objectives of the law. The relevant objectives often depend on the nature of the sanction and on the type of legal proceeding.

The law uses not only monetary sanctions but also specific relief, such as injunctions in the civil context[130] and the incarceration of criminals. The anticipation of such nonmonetary sanctions obviously influences behavior *ex ante*, and to that extent the previous analysis is applicable. Because there are also *ex post* effects on behavior, however, the value of precision at the enforcement stage is greater than it otherwise would be. Thus, if extremely harmful activities are to be permanently enjoined or dangerous individuals are to be removed from society, it is valuable to invest resources to make accurate determinations in adjudication even if the enhanced accuracy does not affect *ex ante* behavior (because individuals would not invest in legal advice to a sufficient extent to refine their predictions). This favors both greater effort in designing rules and in giving content to standards.[131] And, whichever formulation results in a more accurate resolution of specific cases will tend to be favored.[132]

---

129. An exception is the argument in Section D that the outcome of enforcement proceedings will affect the extent to which actors and victims bear risk.

130. The effect of injunctions depends on how enforcement and bargaining actually operate. For example, if an injured party would negotiate for a payment in lieu of pursuing injunctive relief, the effect may be the same for present purposes as if the law provided for damages of that amount.

An important form of injunctive relief in which future conduct is a primary consideration is licensing. *See, e.g.,* Diver, *supra* note 1, at 79.

131. Considerations of *ex post* effects of laws are relevant when evaluating the law/equity distinction that was basic to Anglo-American law until developments in this century led to the currently often-held view that the distinction serves no social function. Because equitable remedies are nonmonetary, the appropriate proceeding for determining their application and the optimal content of governing legal commands is different from that for remedies at law—damages. Whether actual differences in legal and equitable proceedings historically or presently reflect this concern is another matter.

132. As noted previously, standards may provide more accurate resolutions because of information made available *ex post*, or less accurate resolutions because it is appropriate to invest less effort when the investment will be used in a single adjudication rather than in a rule that would apply to many cases and because economies of scale possible at the

Even when the law provides purely monetary relief, there may be objectives in addition to deterrence. As explored in the preceding Section, the compensation victims receive and the amounts injurers pay will be independently significant when individuals are risk averse. Accuracy of results will be of greater importance because it is desirable that victim compensation reflects actual losses,[133] while greater accuracy *ex post* is not obviously valuable for injurers.[134] As a related matter, some laws involve government transfers, such as Social Security payments to disabled workers. Here, accuracy is relevant primarily with regard to providing correct compensation.[135]

In addition to affecting future behavior and the ability of the legal system to achieve compensatory objectives, accurate outcomes may be viewed as an important determinant of the fairness of the legal system. If so, greater investment in the promulgation and application of laws may be warranted than otherwise and there would be an additional reason to prefer whichever mode of formulation tends to produce greater accuracy. Regardless of the weight generally thought appropriate to such fairness concerns, note that accuracy in the present context has an important characteristic distinguishing it from many others: Individuals may not anticipate the results. Recall that accuracy will not always influence *ex ante* behavior precisely because the ultimate application of laws may be too difficult to predict.[136] Even when standards provide more ac-

---

rule promulgation stage may be unavailable when standards are applied. *See supra* Section I(D); note 101; *see also supra* Section II(D) (rule systems may be more detailed than standards as actually applied).

133. To the extent compensation is motivated by risk aversion, monetary losses (with a possible adjustment for changes in the marginal value of money caused by the injury) rather than total losses would be relevant. *See* SHAVELL, *supra* note 42, at 228–31, 245–47.

134. Greater fine-tuning of damages to actual losses may increase the risk injurers bear without materially affecting their behavior. (Greater risk will deter, but the additional deterrence may be excessive and, if it is desirable, could be achieved, say, by increasing damages.)

135. The context of welfare payments is perhaps that in which accuracy has been most discussed, provoked by the Supreme Court's decision in Mathews v. Eldridge, 424 U.S. 319 (1976). *See, e.g.,* Jerry L. Mashaw, *The Supreme Court's Due Process Calculus for Administrative Adjudication in* Mathews v. Eldridge: *Three Factors in Search of a Theory of Value,* 44 U. CHI. L. REV. 28 (1976). The extent to which such determinations are to be governed by rules is one important element determining the ultimate accuracy of outcomes. *See, e.g.,* Diver, *supra* note 1, at 88–92. *See generally* JERRY L. MASHAW, BUREAUCRATIC JUSTICE: MANAGING SOCIAL SECURITY DISABILITY CLAIMS (1983).

136. *Cf.* Louis Kaplow & Steven Shavell, *Legal Advice About Information to Present*

curate resolutions of particular cases, individuals may not have effective notice of the result an adjudicator would reach and thus would be unable to act in light of it. Thus, even when rules will be less accurate in providing results that are appropriate to actual circumstances—which they often will not be[137]—they will tend to provide clearer notice than standards to individuals at the time they decide how to act.[138]

IV. FURTHER CONSIDERATIONS

This Part comments on additional issues relevant in comparing rules and standards. There is no attempt to be exhaustive or to analyze the issues in depth. (Many have been discussed elsewhere and most warrant further study.) Rather, the purpose is simply to note important factors that are related to the discussion in the preceding Parts.

A. *Promulgation and Enforcement of Law by Different Government Institutions*

The discussion thus far has suggested that the costs of promulgating and applying laws may differ for rules and standards. Reasons for such a difference that arise because rules are given content *ex ante* and standards *ex post* have been emphasized. Another reason that promulgation and enforcement costs, as well as the content of rules and standards, may differ is that different government institutions may be involved at the two stages.

Beginning with the most commonly assumed context, consider some of the differences between legislatures, which promulgate many laws, and courts, which often apply them. Legislatures may be better equipped to draw upon technical expertise than courts. Also, through the use of committees and staffs, legislatures may develop more expertise of their own. On the other hand, legisla-

---

in Litigation: Its Effects and Social Desirability, 102 HARV. L. REV. 565, 603 (1989) (discussing how legal advice in litigation may not align sanctions with individuals' *ex ante* understanding of the law because such advice affects sanctions in a manner individuals cannot anticipate).

137. *See supra* note 132 (factors determining whether rules or standards would be more accurate).

138. This may be more fair, as individuals are more able to comply with the actual content of the law, and more desirable in terms of the law's purposes to the extent that substantial compliance with imperfect rules yields better results than poor compliance with more nearly perfect standards.

tive agreement may be more difficult to achieve given the numbers of decisionmakers and the division of authority.[139] Courts, for better or worse, tend to rely on adversary proceedings in reaching conclusions. Also, courts tend to be driven by the concrete facts of a particular case, which may simplify judgment (one need not rely on imagination to anticipate contingencies) or may mislead the decisionmaker (as when the vividness of the instant case leads one to underemphasize other cases that might be subject to the same law[140] or when hindsight is not understood to be superior to foresight). Legislatures may be more politically responsive, which might make some value judgments more legitimate (because they are more representative of popular will) or more suspect (because they reflect the influence of unrepresentative interest groups).[141] Rules may be preferred to standards in order to limit discretion, thereby minimizing abuses of power.[142] Legislatures and courts may each be more sensitive to costs that they directly incur than to costs incurred by other institutions or by individuals, which may induce them to prefer an otherwise inappropriate formulation.[143]

---

139. *See, e.g.*, Ehrlich & Posner, *supra* note 1, at 267–68.

140. This problem is particularly important if a precedent is to be created. Related, relevant "legislative facts" may not be formally admissible in a particular controversy. This consideration is an important reason that judges are inclined to favor waiting before announcing precedents, formulating narrow ones, or simply deferring to the legislature. *See infra* subsection B(1); *see also supra* subsection I(D)(3) (when adjudication will govern only one case rather than many, it may be sensible to make a more superficial inquiry).

141. Concerning the latter, the content of a law or the mode of formulation may be designed to serve a well-organized group to the disadvantage of most citizens. Alternatively, a legislature may delegate authority (to agencies, as when it creates a commission and empowers it to promulgate regulations, or to courts, as when it enacts a standard) not because it deems delegation optimal in principle but because it wishes to avoid accountability. *See, e.g.*, Diver, *supra* note 1, at 106. Related, the discussion in subsection B(1) of courts' reluctance to establish precedents could reflect either a view as to what is proper or a desire to avoid taking responsibility.

142. *See, e.g.*, DAVIS, *supra* note 1; POSNER, *supra* note 1, at 44; SCHAUER, *supra* note 1, at 150–51, 158–62; Gavison, *supra* note 4, at 753–54. That is, it may be feared that courts, agencies, or other political actors will provide content to standards in improper ways. In contrast, if they were empowered simply to apply rules there would be less potential for such abuse because improper conduct could be more readily detected. *See, e.g.*, SCHAUER, *supra* note 1, at 150–55. *Cf.* RAZ, *supra* note 5, at 59–60 (rules may reduce risk of error because content is determined in time of tranquillity).

143. For example, legislatures may favor standards because the *ex post* costs are incurred by individuals and courts. (Often when legislatures fail to resolve an obvious ambiguity that ultimately will be resolved by courts establishing a rule—as in the failure to state a statute of limitations—one suspects that time pressures, a desire to transfer costs,

And the difficulty of learning about laws promulgated by legislatures may differ from those promulgated by courts (as when content is given to a standard through precedent) because of the manner in which legislative enactments and judicial opinions are written, published, and indexed.[144] An important caveat in considering these factors is that many are not inherent to the institution, but rather reflect particular choices that have been made. For example, courts could be specialized (as some, such as the tax court, are) or have expert staffs. Judges could be selected differently so that they would tend to be responsive to different forces.[145] Precedents could be established in a more rule-like fashion than is usually done. (Examples of such an approach include *Miranda*[146] and *Roe v. Wade*.[147]) On the other hand, some differences are intrinsic to the central question of this Article: whether the law is given content *ex ante* or *ex post*. Most notably, standards allow a decisionmaker to examine the concrete facts of a particular case.[148]

---

or a simple mistake is the explanation, rather than some intrinsic reason that a standard is preferable. *See* Maggs, *supra* note 47, at 142–51 (documenting and examining twenty recurring ambiguities in the drafting of statutes).) Courts, in turn, may favor rules to the extent that they reduce the courts' own future costs, or standards, because they save promulgation costs while many subsequent costs are borne by private parties (or different judges in future cases). Some agencies will be the adjudicators under their own laws, whether standards or rules, so they bear all the costs at stages one and three, although costs to individuals (stage two) are still external to them.

The choice of rules over standards also tends to reduce the costs borne by private parties. One implication is that lawsuits may be less costly, encouraging more potential plaintiffs to file. *See supra* note 35. Of course, public costs could be charged to private parties and private costs could be subsidized, so the incidence of costs is not an inherent feature of whether rules or standards govern. (Who bears costs may be relevant for incentive purposes aside from the effect on the likelihood of suits. For example, those developing new drugs must bear many of the costs of tests that are submitted to the government in determining whether to permit their sale; in this manner, the drug companies bear the full cost of their products.)

144. *See supra* note 47; *see also infra* note 162 (how prior judicial opinions guide a judicial decision).

145. There is in fact important variation in how judges are selected in different states (various forms of election and appointment) and across countries (for example, the use of career judiciaries, with various structures for promotion and retention).

146. Miranda v. Arizona, 384 U.S. 436 (1966).

147. 410 U.S. 113 (1973).

148. This difference, however, is less important than may first appear. A standard may be applied with the guidance of general studies of a problem and a rule may be designed with reference to a single occurrence that has been observed. Still, as described in subsection I(D)(3), standards have the advantage of access to concrete facts that may not have existed when a rule was created. Relatedly and more broadly, how rules and stan-

It should also be emphasized that the institutional possibilities are more varied than is suggested by the typical focus on legislatures and courts. First, rules are promulgated by all three branches of government. In addition to legislatures, courts create rules through precedents and executive agencies promulgate regulations and enforcement guidelines. Second, standards can be applied by many agents. Executive officials—often prosecutors—exercise prosecutorial discretion. Legislatures can override particular decisions and enact private legislation. And, within courts and other adjudicative bodies, standards can be interpreted by judges, juries, experts, or arbitrators.[149]

A consequence of these latter remarks is that many issues concerning the separation of powers, the operation of legislatures and government agencies, the exercise of prosecutorial power, and the rules of civil and criminal procedure, are importantly intertwined with the question of how a legal system can best give content to the law. Thus, in addition to asking whether a law should be promulgated as a rule or a standard, taking the institutional context as given, the present analysis is relevant to analyzing the reform of legal institutions. At a narrower level, an institution contemplating the enactment of a law may have choices as to which institutions (including itself) will design and apply the law.

B. *Precedent and Predictability*

Much of the analysis has been concerned with the ability of individuals and lawyers to predict the application of the law and of adjudicators to apply it. To the extent laws are promulgated as standards, predictability will be enhanced by precedent to the extent precedent transforms standards into rules.[150] This Section

---

dards are optimally designed and applied is influenced by their inherent difference with respect to timing, as discussed throughout Section I(D).

149. One effect of the choice of adjudicators concerns the predictability of their decisions by individuals and lawyers. One might suspect, for example, that juries (allegedly of one's peers) or arbitrators (if, for example, they are from the same industry as the actors) may be more predictable by individuals (without the aid of legal advice) than judges are. On the other hand, judges may be easier for lawyers to predict, which would tend to lower the cost and increase the accuracy of legal advice. *See also* Section III(A) (on the relative accessibility of rules and standards).

150. There also will be uncertainties concerning the application of rules that may be resolved through precedent—most notably involving boundary disputes—in which some condition determines which of two conflicting rules governs. As emphasized in the Intro-

offers further remarks on precedent and on other factors influencing how well a law's application can be predicted.[151]

1. *The Time Taken to Promulgate Precedents.*[152] As emphasized in Section I(C), the comparison of rules and standards in the case when standards become rules through precedent depends importantly on how many acts take place before the precedent is established, because individuals committing such acts will not be guided by the not-yet-established precedent.[153] Presumably, the longer the time, the more such acts there will be. In our legal system, this time period often is substantial. Time passes from when actions are taken to when lawsuits are adjudicated. Lawsuits often take years to reach a conclusion and usually settle beforehand. Many levels of appeal may have to be exhausted. Finally, courts often hesitate to make clear rulings that will cover a wide range of future cases.[154] Instead, they may avoid a ruling on jurisdictional or other grounds, make a narrow ruling,[155] state alternative grounds, fail to produce a clear majority opinion, or, with the

---

duction, rules are to some extent standard-like, and the difference is a matter of degree.

151. *See also supra* Section III(A) (on the relative accessibility of rules and standards); note 149 (on the predictability of adjudicators).

152. Precedent is usually discussed in the context of judicial decisionmaking, but the problem is similar for adjudication by administrative agencies. Agencies, however, have the additional tool of rulemaking. For a criticism of agencies' failure to promulgate rules, see FRIENDLY, *supra* note 9.

153. The discussion to follow usually takes precedent to be an all-or-nothing matter, as was done in Section I(C). The analysis applies directly to precedents that are incomplete—in covering only some behavior subject to the standard or in providing only partial guidance with respect to the behavior covered.

154. Some of these points are emphasized in Ehrlich & Posner, *supra* note 1, at 264.

155. The adoption of a multi-factor balancing test is broad to the extent it will apply to a category of cases but narrow in that each decision under the test—even if by the highest court in a jurisdiction—has little precedential value (assuming, as is usually the case, that the court refrains from stating the weight given to the factors). *See, e.g.,* Edward Yorio, *Federal Income Tax Rulemaking: An Economic Approach,* 51 FORD. L. REV. 1, 19–23 (1982).

Supreme Court, decline to grant certiorari.[156] Likewise, the scope for declaratory judgments tends to be narrow.[157]

As with the discussion of institutions in Section A, most of these features reflect choices rather than inherent features of a legal system.[158] The current choices often involve minimizing or postponing the establishment of precedents that will guide future activity.[159] The analysis here suggests that this involves a high cost, as behavior in the interim will not benefit from the guidance of whatever precedent might later be set. Also, in the interim additional costs will be incurred, both by the many who contemplate acts (in acquiring expensive, although only marginally helpful, advice) and in the many adversarial adjudications that arise, in which both parties and the court will expend resources determining how to give content to the standard.

To make the problem of delay in issuing precedent concrete, consider the following example, which considers only the cost of lawsuits (thus understating the benefit of an early determination). In the years before an issue is resolved by the creation of precedent, suppose there will be 1,000 adjudications concerning the contested issue that cost an average of $50,000 each—a total cost of $50,000,000. Is it likely that the later resolution will be better in some respect than an earlier determination by such an amount?[160]

---

156. For competing views on the virtue of delay in granting certiorari, see SAMUEL ESTREICHER & JOHN SEXTON, REDEFINING THE SUPREME COURT'S ROLE: A THEORY OF MANAGING THE FEDERAL JUDICIAL PROCESS 48, 50–52 (1986) (favoring percolation); Daniel J. Meador, *A Challenge to Judicial Architecture: Modifying the Regional Design of the U.S. Courts of Appeals*, 56 U. CHI. L. REV. 603, 633–34 (1989) (favoring prompt resolution of conflicts involving statutory interpretation).

When there are multiple jurisdictions (as with the many circuits in the federal system), there may arise conflicting precedents. Moreover, even after consistent precedents have emerged in a number of circuits, there will remain some uncertainty as to the others and, concomitantly, the possibility that the Supreme Court will grant certiorari in a subsequent case and reverse the circuit court precedents.

157. Article III limitations affect the availability of declaratory judgments and, through other doctrines, may increase the time before a precedent is established. These restrictive doctrines have often been criticized. *See, e.g.*, Evan T. Lee, *Deconstitutionalizing Justiciability: The Example of Mootness*, 105 HARV. L. REV. 603 (1992).

158. For example, some states and other countries allow the legislature to present constitutional questions to the highest court for an advance determination.

159. Not all participants in the system agree with such an approach. *See, e.g.*, Antonin Scalia, *The Rule of Law as a Law of Rules*, 56 U. CHI. L. REV. 1175, 1178–80 (1989); *cf.* DAVIS, *supra* note 1, at 109 (administrators often progress from discretion toward rules at a rate behind what their current understanding makes feasible).

160. It is commonly believed that waiting has its benefits, as the experience of prior

Might the resolution be even more satisfactory if a nontrivial portion of the $50,000,000 were spent in reaching a careful, but prompt resolution of the point?[161]

This example suggests that much of our legal system may be deficient in two respects. First, massive costs of delay in settling the law are regularly incurred. Second, costs devoted to resolving an issue are not channeled in a manner designed to produce the most informed possible result. Rather, there tends to be substantial duplication, with limited guidance to actors concerning their behavior in the interim.

2. *Predictability Without Precedent.* A related concern is with predictability short of precedent. Prior cases—both their outcomes and any written opinions—may reduce the costs and increase the accuracy of legal advice and adjudication even if no "binding precedent" is created.[162] The extent of such effects will depend on the manner in which the information produced by prior cases is made accessible. General verdicts by juries and rulings from the bench without opinion will provide limited guidance.[163]

---

cases will provide the basis for giving content to standards. *See, e.g.*, DAVIS, *supra* note 1, at 107–08; OLIVER W. HOLMES, JR., THE COMMON LAW 111–12 (1881); Ehrlich & Posner, *supra* note 1, at 266; *supra* note 156. The text does not question this assumption, the validity of which depends on the extent to which prior adjudications create a base of experience. (Many suits will not, as they will be settled, after significant expenditures on litigation; others will produce general verdicts but no written opinion. Also, the base of experience created may be biased. *See* Gillian K. Hadfield, *Bias in the Evolution of Legal Rules*, 80 GEO. L.J. 583 (1992).) Rather, the text asks whether waiting long periods of time so as to observe the particular cases that arise is the most sensible way to collect information, given that actions in the interim are left without more concrete and less costly guidance. (Other ways to collect information include studying actual or contemplated behavior that has not given rise to a lawsuit and been litigated to a final judgment. If one wanted experience, for example, with train accidents, existing data may be little enhanced by one court record of an adjudicated case, or even a half dozen, some years in the future. *See also supra* notes 63, 68.)

161. One could think of how many amicus briefs could be commissioned and examined and how many studies could be performed for even a small fraction of such an amount.

162. *Cf.* SCHAUER, *supra* note 1, at 174–81 (existence of a common law method of decisionmaking in which rules have no force in themselves but prior decisions provide guidance); *id.* at 182–83 (distinguishing precedent and learning from experience); *see also* Richard A. Posner, *An Economic Approach to Legal Procedure and Judicial Administration*, 2 J. LEGAL STUD. 399, 450 (1973) (suggesting that precedents involving "the compact and pointed statement communicated by [a] rule" may communicate accumulated experience to adjudicators more effectively than leaving them to extract prior experience on their own).

163. Litigators, however, will learn something from such a process. Of course, even a

This, too, reflects a choice in designing the system. Jurors could be asked to offer opinions or identify salient factors. Judges, especially as they develop experience, could make informative pronouncements.[164]

3. *Predictability Without Formally Articulated Rules.* The predictability of a law is determined by more than formal enactments, precedents, and even the results of past adjudications. As discussed in Section III(A), individuals' common knowledge will allow confident prediction in some contexts, even when precise official pronouncements are not consulted or do not exist.

Moreover, government action outside the formal lawmaking processes can provide important guidance for future behavior. For example, the government's undertaking and publishing the results of comprehensive studies of the hazards posed by various chemicals may have a substantial effect on their use even if the results are not embodied in a regulation or formally binding in a negligence suit or other legal proceeding.[165] If a regulatory agency undertook such an investigation, individuals might expect the agency to act on the results in setting its enforcement priorities and in adjudicating cases even if no rule was promulgated declaring the results to be binding.[166] Undertaking such efforts is rule-like in the sense used in this Article, because such efforts are an important aspect of giving content to the law in advance of individuals' actions.[167] Contrast this with a standard-like approach, in which the agency does not investigate the dangers posed by chemicals

---

very experienced litigator in most fields of law may have tried only a handful of cases to verdict, and the number of other relevant variables that may have affected the outcome in such cases will be relatively great. Exchanging stories, more formal conferences, and publications (by individual litigators and commercial services) all allow information to be pooled to a greater extent, although many of the factors that may have influenced a verdict will be lost in the process.

164. In some respects, the federal criminal sentencing guidelines reflect such an approach, although the guidelines are binding. The rules (with some standard-like aspects) are based in part on the prior experience of sentencing judges. *See* UNITED STATES SENTENCING COMMISSION, GUIDELINES MANUAL 1.2–1.4 (Nov. 1990).

165. *See, e.g.,* FED. R. EVID. 803(8) (hearsay consisting of public reports admissible); FRIENDLY, *supra* note 9, at 144–46 (advocating that agencies present data and make policy statements).

166. An agency may choose not to make the results binding so that it can also consider subsequent information. Nonetheless, substantial predictability would be possible, in contrast to the case in which no such comprehensive study had been undertaken.

167. *See supra* Section I(E).

until adjudicating the legality of a particular incident in which chemicals were discharged into a river. When a study is completed and published in advance, individuals may use it to guide their behavior and the agency may simply refer to it in an adjudication. When such a study is only to be made after-the-fact, individuals contemplating discharges of such chemicals would have to make their own investigations or act without knowledge of the actual dangers, and the agency would have to make an inquiry in each adjudication.

C. *Changing Rules and Standards over Time*

As available information, conditions, and perceived values change over time, so does the desired content of the law. In the present legal system, it is usually believed that standards are easier to keep up-to-date.[168] The reason is that standards are given content in a definitive way only when they are applied to particular conduct. Thus, a standard promulgated decades ago can be applied to conduct in the recent past using present understandings rather than those from an earlier era. In contrast, rules must be changed, which may require more effort.

The importance of changes in the law as well as the ease of change will vary greatly among fields. For example, it may be quite important to be able to change income tax rules quickly (as when there is a recession), and such laws are changed, often massively, with alarming frequency. In contrast, standards of due care or determinations of causation will reflect old understandings if rules governing expert testimony exclude new theories.[169]

Moreover, as with other institutional features, the ease of change is a matter of choice. Standards can be applied using either present or past understandings. (Note, for example, debates on questions of interpretation about the relevance of the original intent of the framers of the Constitution or of statutes.) For rules, the manner of evolution is also chosen. Legislatures were inten-

---

168. *See, e.g.*, POSNER, *supra* note 9, § 20.3, at 543; *see also* SCHAUER, *supra* note 1, at 140–42 (use of rules involves trade-off between enhancing the ability of individuals to rely and preserving the ability to adapt to a changing future); *cf.* Hirsch, *supra* note 11, at 1240–41 (identifying changing conditions as an element limiting the benefit of precise advance specification).

169. Book Note, *Rebel Without a Cause*, 105 HARV. L. REV. 935, 937–38 (1992) (reviewing PETER W. HUBER, GALILEO'S REVENGE: JUNK SCIENCE IN THE COURTROOM (1991)).

tionally devised to make changing laws difficult (absent rather broad agreement on the need for change). But within this institutional structure, a legislature can delegate rulemaking authority to an agency, so that rules may be changed more readily.[170] Also, some revision of rules is undertaken by courts,[171] and this practice could be much broader if it were thought desirable.[172] Precedents interpreting rules or giving content to standards can be respected more or less.[173] Changes in rules or the typical application of standards can be made prospective or retroactive to varying degrees.[174]

How readily laws may change or evolve will affect their predictability and, relatedly, the costs incurred when seeking legal advice or when adjudicators apply the law. The more room there is for argument about changed conditions, the more such argument will be offered, at greater cost and with less certainty in guiding behavior.[175] To the extent the actual legal system makes one formulation more subject to change than another, this difference will be relevant in choosing the optimal formulation.

---

170. *See, e.g.,* FRIENDLY, *supra* note 9, at 7; HART & SACKS, *supra* note 1, at 140; Erik H. Corwin, *Congressional Limits on Agency Discretion: A Case Study of the Hazardous and Solid Waste Amendments of 1984,* 29 HARV. J. ON LEGIS. 517, 521–22 (1992).

171. *See, e.g.,* GUIDO CALABRESI, A COMMON LAW FOR THE AGE OF STATUTES (1982); POSNER, *supra* note 1, at 46–47.

172. *See* CALABRESI, *supra* note 171.

173. For an empirical assessment of the degree to which reliance on prior decisions declines with the passage of time, see William M. Landes & Richard A. Posner, *Legal Precedent: A Theoretical and Empirical Analysis,* 19 J.L. & ECON. 249 (1976). It is familiar that an outmoded precedent may not be discarded for substantial periods of time, sometimes motivated by a desire to defer to the legislature or an administrative agency. If such issues were initially covered by a regularly reviewed statutory scheme or set of regulations, outmoded approaches may be discarded more quickly.

174. *See generally* Richard H. Fallon & Daniel J. Meltzer, *New Law, Non-Retroactivity, and Constitutional Remedies,* 104 HARV. L. REV. 1731 (1991); Louis Kaplow, *An Economic Analysis of Legal Transitions,* 99 HARV. L. REV. 509 (1986).

175. The discussion in the text should not be interpreted to suggest that such uncertainty is necessarily undesirable. To the extent uncertainty concerning application of the law reflects genuine uncertainty about the appropriate content of the law, the mixed signals provided by the legal system may constitute the appropriate guide for behavior. *Cf.* Kaplow, *supra* note 174, at 533–36 (noting the similarity between uncertainties deriving from the market and those due to government actions). There is more reason to doubt whether repeated expenditures at the enforcement stage on disputes over whether conditions have changed are justified by the social benefit of fine-tuning the law to current conditions.

D. *Laws Regarding Form and Background Laws*

This Article focuses on legal commands regulating harm-producing behavior. Although many points would continue to be relevant, a different analysis may be required for laws regarding form (for example, a requirement that there be two witnesses to the execution of a will for it to have legal effect)[176] and background laws (for example, that contract breach gives rise to liability for expectation damages, unless the contract stipulates to the contrary). Often, both types of laws are designed to facilitate rather than regulate behavior. Thus, what is best for the actors is deemed to be best for society.[177]

An important feature of laws regarding form is that they be cheaply accessible and precisely predictable.[178] If it were left to an adjudicator *ex post* to determine how many witnesses give one confidence in a document, the effect may simply be to induce actors to expend excessive resources on additional witnesses, because the cost of nullification is so great. On the other hand, because laws of form are often designed to prevent fraud,[179] which may be easier to commit if there are known rigid rules that a fraudulent actor can carefully circumvent, standards may be preferable in some contexts.[180] Such issues suggest that an appropriate

---

176. Some commentators have in fact distinguished the analysis of formality. *See, e.g.,* HART, *supra* note 1, at 130–31; Ehrlich & Posner, *supra* note 1, at 269–70; Kennedy, *supra* note 1, at 1697–701. For an extended discussion of rules versus standards in a context involving contract formalities, see Douglas G. Baird & Robert Weisberg, *Rules, Standards, and the Battle of the Forms: A Reassessment of § 2-207,* 68 VA. L. REV. 1217 (1982).

177. For contracts, it may simply be that there are no externalities. For wills or other gratuitous transfers, other parties will be affected, but a judgment may be made that it is best to allow donors to govern their own affairs. *See* Steven Shavell, *An Economic Analysis of Altruism and Deferred Gifts,* 20 J. LEGAL STUD. 401 (1991) (arguing that donors should be able to bind themselves to give gifts).

178. The relative accessibility of rules and standards is discussed in subsection I(A)(2) and Section III(A).

179. Familiar examples include the statute of frauds and parol evidence rule in contract law. *See generally* 3 SAMUEL WILLISTON, A TREATISE ON THE LAW OF CONTRACTS § 448 (statute of frauds); 4 *id.* § 631 (parol evidence).

180. For example, there are general prohibitions on fraud in contract law, and the federal income tax has quite open-ended standards (in addition to more particular rules) concerning sham transactions. *See, e.g.,* POSNER, *supra* note 1, at 56–60 (raising question of whether more detailed legislation and regulation or more *ex post* plugging of loopholes by courts is better course for federal taxation); *supra* note 125 (that rules are more predictable implies that errors in the law will be more predictable). Consider a complex standard that prohibits types of fraud or circumvention of parties' or legislatures' intent.

framework, taking into account effects on legitimate and fraudulent behavior, would differ from the one presented here. Yet, some factors will be the same. Most important is that laws of form often regulate extremely numerous acts and transactions, so the cost savings from *ex ante* creation of the law (rules) will be particularly significant.

Background laws raise different issues, and therefore would require that yet another framework be created. For example, an open-ended standard providing that ambiguity and incompleteness in contracts will be supplemented by courts *ex post* in the manner parties would have agreed to had they provided for the contingency has desirable properties. When parties contemplate entering into a contractual relationship, they have only a limited need to know how a court would fill gaps in their agreement,[181] as long as the court (or another designated decisionmaker) could be anticipated to act as they would wish.[182] The primary reason parties leave much unspecified is precisely to avoid the costs of specification. This cost savings would be nullified (or exceeded) if they invested in legal advice to inform themselves about how a court would provide for unspecified events. Thus, the calculus determining whether rules or standards are preferable would emphasize *ex*

Applying such a law in enforcement proceedings may often be costly. But if actors anticipated that such a law would be applied well (and if they knew rather well which acts were fraudulent or circumventions), they might be deterred from such activity. Then enforcement costs may not be incurred very often and costs of legal advice also may be modest if lawyers could predict with reasonable confidence that questionable schemes simply were not worth the bother. The problem is that, if it is not sufficiently clear *ex ante* or *ex post* which schemes are indeed improper, those engaged in possibly legitimate behavior may incur substantial legal costs to verify that their conduct is permissible or simply be deterred from committing desirable activity. Similarly, legitimate schemes may often be challenged in enforcement proceedings using such standards.

181. To determine what price is acceptable, they will care about the expected value of the contract, which will depend on how each contingency would be addressed. But a reasonably good approximation may be possible without a prediction of how each contingency would be resolved. If one party is more informed of the background rules, perhaps because it is sensible to be more knowledgeable when one enters into such transactions repeatedly, that party might have an advantage, which in turn may affect what the other party is willing to offer or may induce the other party to acquire additional advice to determine whether there might exist important background rules that would operate to its disadvantage.

182. *See* David Charny, *Hypothetical Bargains: The Normative Structure of Contract Interpretation*, 89 MICH. L. REV. 1815, 1819–23 (1991); David Charny, *Nonlegal Sanctions in Commercial Relationships*, 104 HARV. L. REV. 373, 444 (1990); Steven Shavell, *Damage Measures for Breach of Contract*, 11 BELL J. ECON. 466, 466–69 (1980).

ante promulgation costs and *ex post* enforcement costs, giving less attention to costs of advice by contracting parties because they often would not choose to acquire advice about such matters.[183]

E.	*Lawyers' Interest in How the Law Is Formulated*

The legal profession is not indifferent to how laws are designed. Since some of the promulgation costs and much of the costs of advice and enforcement consist of fees for lawyers' services, the profession as a whole has a general interest that tends to oppose that of society. Laws that induce individuals to seek advice more frequently or to seek advice having a higher cost,[184] or that increase the cost of litigation, will be favorable to the economic interest of lawyers.[185] Thus, while the bar will often have special expertise in evaluating many of the factors relevant to the design of laws, one must keep in mind that lawyers' advice on such matters may be tinged by self-interest.[186]

183.	If they had reason to believe that their preferences were atypical, and thus would not be reflected in the rules or in an adjudicator's application of the standard, they would want to include special provisions. But some advice may be necessary to have a sense of whether one's situation is likely to be atypical. Sometimes, however, it might be cheapest simply to include such provisions in the contract without incurring the cost to determine whether they are necessary. Thus, many contracts contain extensive boilerplate providing for the result an adjudicator would likely reach in any event.

184.	These factors oppose each other to some extent, because higher costs of advice tend to decrease the demand for it. It remains true, however, that there is a divergence of interests, because laws that maximize expenditures on legal advice are unlikely to be those that are socially best (particularly as expenditures on legal advice are a social cost, though a private benefit to the profession).

185.	*See, e.g.*, Ehrlich & Posner, *supra* note 1, at 271, 274 (emphasizing that lawyers may prefer judge-made law because precedents, which state rules implicitly, require more legal skill to master than statutes). *See generally* Michelle J. White, *Legal Complexity and Lawyers' Benefit from Litigation*, 12 INT'L REV. L. & ECON. 381 (1992).

186.	Any individual lawyer would have little interest in the formulation (unless there is extreme specialization), but lawyers often act as a group through professional associations. Lawyers may also have different interests depending on their past investments in learning rule systems or in predicting standards. *See supra* notes 40, 163. Finally, it is unethical for a lawyer (not representing a client) to advocate reforms in the profession's self-interest that are not believed to be in the public interest, *see* MODEL CODE OF PROFESSIONAL RESPONSIBILITY EC 8-4 (1980); MODEL RULES OF PROFESSIONAL CONDUCT Rule 6.4 (1989); however, lawyers' perceptions of the public interest may be influenced by their self-interest and the effect of ethical guidelines on such behavior is speculative in any event.

V. Conclusion

This Article provides an economic analysis of rules and standards, focusing on the extent to which the law should be given content before individuals act (rules), rather than waiting until afterward (standards). The problem motivating the choice is that giving appropriate content to the law often requires effort, whether in analyzing a problem, resolving value conflicts, or acquiring empirical knowledge. Undertaking such effort in advance involves additional costs, but results in savings when individuals must determine how the law applies to their contemplated conduct and when adjudicators must apply the law to past conduct.

The central factor influencing the desirability of rules and standards is the frequency with which a law will govern conduct.[187] If conduct will be frequent, the additional costs of designing rules—which are borne once—are likely to be exceeded by the savings realized each time the rule is applied. Thus, rules involve a wholesale approach to an information problem, that of determining the law's appropriate content.[188] Standards instead require adjudicators to undertake this effort, which may have to be done repeatedly (unless the standard is transformed into a rule through precedent[189]). And, regardless of whether adjudication will be frequent, many individuals contemplating behavior that may be subject to the law will find it more costly to comply with standards, because it generally is more difficult to predict the outcome of a future inquiry (by the adjudicator, into the law's content) than to examine the result of a past inquiry.[190] They must either spend more to be guided properly or act without as much guidance as under rules. Thus, when behavior subject to the relevant law is frequent, standards tend to be more costly and result in behavior that conforms less well to underlying norms.

If behavior subject to the law is infrequent, however, standards are likely to be preferable. Of particular relevance are laws for which behavior varies greatly, so that most relevant scenarios are unlikely ever to occur. Determining the appropriate content of the law for all such contingencies would be expensive, and most of

---

187. *See supra* Sections I(B), III(B).
188. *See supra* Section I(E).
189. *See supra* Section I(C); subsection IV(B)(1).
190. On the possibility that standards can be more accessible to individuals, see Section III(A).

the expense would be wasted. It would be preferable to wait until particular circumstances arise.

Some implications of this analysis run contrary to prevailing wisdom or suggest problems with common practices. Thus, it is usually said that standards result in more precise application of underlying norms because they can be applied to the particular facts of a case, in contrast to rules, which apply to the generality of cases. But if the cases are anticipated to arise frequently and have important recurring characteristics, rules will not only be preferable, but might be expected to be more precise.[191] In such instances, it is worth investing substantial effort to fine-tune a rule system. But, with standards, it may not be worth spending much effort to get precise results, because such efforts will be useful in resolving only a single case rather than many. Moreover, even in instances where standards would produce more accurate results in adjudication, rules may nevertheless produce behavior more in accord with underlying norms. The reason is simply that the rules, announced in advance, are more likely to influence actual behavior, whereas individuals may find it infeasible or too costly to predict how an adjudicator will apply a standard to their behavior. The discussion noted OSHA regulations and the tax code and regulations as examples of rule schemes likely to be far more precise in their application than the results one would expect to be produced by juries operating under a general standard.[192]

The analysis also is relevant to the processes by which laws are given content, including through precedent.[193] When a law will govern much behavior, there are substantial benefits to an early determination of its content. When legislators leave the details of law to courts (or to agencies that do not promptly issue regulations[194]), individuals may be left with little guidance for years or decades, while substantial legal costs are incurred both in providing advice to actors and in adjudicating disputes over unresolved questions. Similar costs are imposed when courts delay in promulgating precedents—whether by avoiding a decision or decid-

---

191. *See supra* subsection I(D)(3); Section II(D).

192. To be sure, individual jury verdicts under such a standard would be more varied due to inconsistencies. *See supra* Section II(A). But it is unlikely that any jury would go into such detail with respect to the factors giving rise to the content of these rule schemes.

193. *See supra* Section I(C); subsection IV(B)(1).

194. *See* FRIENDLY, *supra* note 9.

ing narrowly. Delay to a more convenient time, perhaps when there will be more experience, is considered a virtue. Whether the benefits are warranted by the interim legal costs receives little attention; costs involving individuals' attempts to comply with the law, in contrast to costs of adjudicated cases, receive even less. Moreover, when the law is finally given content, even in precedent-setting cases in the Supreme Court, the investment in reaching a correct decision is rarely in proportion to the magnitude of the stakes. And the investment is usually a trivial fraction of the total costs incurred in previous duplicative disputes over the same issue.

While the legal system, including the courts, is generally understood as a producer of law, basic considerations of efficient production—here, of an information product[195]—are foreign to most commentary on rules and standards.[196] Legal costs and the extent to which individuals will conform their behavior to the law are, to be sure, not the only relevant factors in choosing between rules and standards. They are, however, more significant than may first appear, because many of the institutional considerations usually thought to bear on the choice can be, and sometimes are, addressed separately from whether efforts to give content to the law are undertaken before or after individuals act.

---

195. *See supra* Section I(E).

196. It would be useful to compare the manner in which the laws of states are produced to that in which large corporations produce their own rules and standards for internal operations. While there are many important differences, the similarities are sufficiently great that the comparison should not be ignored.

APPENDIX

This Appendix formally presents an example of the kind analyzed in Part I. No attempt is made here to repeat the motivation, interpretation, or numerous caveats that appear in the body of the Article. For completeness, the presentation includes the case in which the first adjudication creates a precedent for subsequent enforcement proceedings, as described in Section I(C). In addition, the particular law that is chosen (strict liability, with damages equal to harm caused) is one for which the private and social values of legal advice are equal. (See the discussion in Section III(C).)

The Example

The government enacts a law subjecting a harm-causing activity to strict tort liability. Initially, the government does not know the level of harm h caused by this activity; it is believed that harm is distributed according to the density $f(\cdot)$ on $[0, \infty)$. It may promulgate a standard, which simply means that courts will determine h when individuals are sued. Or, it may promulgate a rule, which states the level of damages a court will award. In order to promulgate a rule, the government must first undertake an investigation, which determines the actual h.[197] The cost of promulgating the law is k_i, where $i = r, s$ (denoting "rule" and "standard"); $k_r > k_s$. Let $k = k_r - k_s$.

There are n identical risk-neutral individuals who engage in an activity that causes harm h with probability p. Individuals decide how much care to exercise; expenditures on care x reduce the probability of harm at a diminishing rate: $p'(x) < 0$, $p''(x) > 0$. Individuals do not know the level of damages a court will award; they know only the distribution $f(\cdot)$. Before choosing their level of care, they may obtain advice, which tells them what a court will award, at a cost of c_i, where $i = r, s$; $c_s > c_r$; and $c = c_s - c_r$. Individuals decide whether to acquire information and choose a level of care to minimize the sum of their cost of care, their expected liability costs, and the cost of information.

---

197. The example is more general than may first appear. Consider, for example, the possibility that h has two possible values, one of which is zero. Then, the inquiry is equivalent to determining which acts are harmful and thus subject to legal sanctions.

Individuals who cause harm pay damages equal to the actual value of *h*. The cost of an enforcement proceeding is e_i, where $i = r, s$; $e_s > e_r$; and $e = e_s - e_r$.

Finally, when there is a standard, the analysis will consider two possibilities concerning the first court determination of the actual level of *h*. First, it might be a precedent for future enforcement actions, in which event the situation thereafter will be as though a rule rather than a standard prevails. (That is, enforcement costs in the future will be e_r and future costs of information will be c_r.[198]) Second, it may not be a precedent, in which event the standard prevails indefinitely.

The social objective is the minimization of the sum of the cost of care, expected harm, and all legal costs—the costs of promulgating the law, individuals' expenditures to learn *h*, and the costs of enforcement proceedings.

Individuals' Behavior

If individuals act without becoming informed of the actual *h* (and thus the amount of damages a court will award), they will choose a level of care x_u ("u" for "uninformed") to minimize the sum of the cost of care and expected damage payments, so their expected total cost will be

$$(1) \quad C_u = x_u + p(x_u) \int_0^\infty hf(h)dh.$$

If they first acquire advice, they will learn the actual *h* and choose the level of care $x_i(h)$ ("i" for "informed") to minimize the sum of the cost of care and expected damage payments, and their expected total cost will be

$$(2) \quad C_i = \int_0^\infty [x_i(h) + p(x_i(h))h]f(h)dh.$$

Observe that the expressions for C_u and C_i measure both the private and social costs (aside from enforcement costs[199]) in each case for the familiar reason that strict liability requires individuals

---

198. It would be straightforward to consider the situation in which the precedential effect lowered subsequent enforcement costs but not individuals' information costs, or the converse, or that in which enforcement or information costs were reduced but not completely to the level under a rule. *See, e.g., infra* note 204.

199. *See supra* note 117.

to pay damages for all harm caused, and because, in this model, actual court awards will equal actual harm under both a rule and a standard. Thus, both the expected private and expected social values of information are given by the same expression:

(3) $I = C_u - C_i$.

It is apparent that I must be positive, because informed individuals are able to choose their level of care with knowledge of h.[200]

Individuals will choose to become informed whenever $I > c_i$.[201] Thus, there are three cases to consider: $I \leq c_r < c_s$; $c_r < c_s < I$; and $c_r < I \leq c_s$. In the first case, individuals do not become informed regardless of the formulation of the law; in the second, they become informed regardless of the formulation; and, in the third, they become informed if there is a rule but not if there is a standard.

Case 1: Individuals Do Not Become Informed Either Under a Rule or Under a Standard. Because uninformed individuals do not incur the costs c_i and take the same level of care x_u regardless of whether a rule or standard prevails, the only considerations pertinent to the relative efficiency of rules versus standards are promulgation costs k_i and enforcement costs e_i.

Precedent. If there will be at least one enforcement proceeding, a rule will be more expensive than a standard if and only if

(4) $k > e$.

That is, rules are more expensive when the cost of determining the actual h at the promulgation stage exceeds that of determining the actual h at the enforcement stage. To the extent that there is a significant probability that there would never be an enforcement proceeding under a standard, however, a standard would likely be less expensive.[202]

---

200. It is straightforward to show (from the first-order conditions when (1) and (2) are minimized with respect to the choice of x) that informed individuals choose a different level of care whenever h does not equal the mean of h—more (less) care when h is greater (less) than the mean of h.

201. Choice in cases of indifference are stipulated for convenience, without affecting the analysis. It is implicitly assumed that individuals either know whether a rule or standard prevails or that finding out the type of formulation is costless.

202. There will be at least one proceeding with probability $1 - (1 - p(x_u))^n$, which will

No precedent. The expected cost of a rule will exceed that for a standard if and only if

(5) $k > np(x_u)e$.

Using as a baseline the case in which $k = e$, the inequality (5) will hold when the expected number of suits, $np(x_u)$, is less than one.

Case 2: Individuals Become Informed both Under a Rule and Under a Standard. Because informed individuals take the same level of care, $x_i(h)$, regardless of whether a rule or standard prevails, the considerations pertinent to the relative efficiency of rules versus standards are promulgation costs k_i, information costs c_i, and enforcement costs e_i.

Precedent. If there will be at least one enforcement proceeding, a rule will be more expensive than a standard if and only if

(6) $k > \hbar c + e$,

where $\hbar$ is the expected number of individuals who act before the first enforcement proceeding.[203] Using as a baseline the case in which $k = e$, a standard will be more expensive than a rule by the amount $\hbar c$.[204] Observe that if there is never an enforcement proceeding, the standard saves the promulgation cost differential k, but it still may be more expensive because the information cost differential c will then be incurred n times.

No precedent. The expected cost of a rule will exceed that for a standard if and only if

(7) $k > nc + n\bar{p}e$,

where $\bar{p}$ denotes the expected probability of accidents when individuals are informed. (Recall that x_i is a function of h; hence, $\bar{p}$ is

---

almost equal 1 if n is sufficiently large.

203. Obviously, $\hbar$ is greater than or equal to one. The value of $\hbar$ will depend on the actual h, because the probability of harm depends on h when individuals are informed. When $p(x_i(h))$ is very small, $\hbar$ will be large and the cost differential noted in the text will be substantial.

204. If, after a precedent, there was still some additional information cost under a standard—because a precedent was more expensive to identify than a rule—there would be an added component of $n - \hbar$ times this differential.

the expectation of $p(x_i(h))$ over h.) Using as a baseline the case in which $k = e$, a necessary condition for (7) to hold is that the expected number of suits, $n\overline{p}$, is less than one. This is not sufficient, because any cost advantage of a standard would have to exceed nc, which can be very large even when $n\overline{p}$ is small. A rule can be more expensive than a standard only if the additional promulgation costs exceed each individual's information cost savings by a factor exceeding n.

Case 3: Individuals Become Informed Under a Rule but Not Under a Standard. This case differs from the first two because behavior is no longer the same under a rule and a standard. Under a rule, individuals spend c_r and choose the level of care $x_i(h)$. Under a standard, individuals make no expenditure on information and choose the level of care x_u, which in general results in a different probability of harm than when individuals are informed. The difference in effect on social welfare for each individual is simply $I - c_r$, because the expected social value of information (abstracting from enforcement costs) equals I. This captures both the difference in the level of expected harm and the difference in the level of care. Moreover, in case 3, it must be that $I > c_r$, so the effect on social welfare of each individual's behavior under a rule, including the information acquisition cost, is more desirable than under a standard.

Precedent. If there will be at least one enforcement proceeding, a rule will be more expensive than a standard if and only if

$$(8) \quad k > \hat{n}(I - c_r) + e.$$

Expression (8) is the same as expression (4) (for case 1, precedent) except that the term $\hat{n}(I - c_r)$, which is positive, appears on the right. Thus, when the benefit of information is sufficiently great that individuals acquire information under a rule (but not under a standard), the relative desirability of a rule is greater than when they do not. It is also useful to compare expression (8) with expression (6). The difference is that, with regard to the stage involving individual behavior, the benefit of rules in case 3 involves the improvement in behavior net of information costs, while in case 2 it involves the relative cost savings in becoming informed about rules rather than standards.

No precedent. The expected cost of a rule will exceed that for a standard if and only if

(9) $k > n(I - c_r) + n(p(x_u)e_s - \overline{p}e_r).$

The left side of (9) is the additional promulgation cost of a rule. The first component on the right side is the net benefit concerning behavior (the behavioral benefit I minus the cost of information c_r) for all individuals who act. The second component is the net enforcement cost difference, which is formally ambiguous because the relative magnitudes of $p(x_u)$ and $\overline{p}$ cannot be determined *a priori*. (Informed individuals take more care and thus cause harm less frequently when they learn that h is above average and take less care, causing harm more often, when they learn that h is below average.) If one considers the case in which these probabilities are equal, this second component favors rules in the same manner as in the prior two cases.[205]

---

205. *See also supra* note 117.

LEGAL PRECEDENT: A THEORETICAL AND EMPIRICAL ANALYSIS*

WILLIAM M. LANDES and RICHARD A. POSNER
University of Chicago Law School and
National Bureau of Economic Research

I. INTRODUCTION

IN a legal system such as ours, in which legislative bodies confine themselves for the most part to prescribing general norms of conduct rather than highly specific rules, the published decisions of courts and administrative agencies interpreting and applying the legislative enactments are important sources of the specific rules of law. When the parties to a legal dispute are unable to agree on the meaning of the governing statute as applied to their dispute, litigation may ensue in which that meaning will be an issue for the court to resolve. The court's resolution will define the specific requirements of the statute in the circumstances presented by the case and thus create (subject to a qualification noted below) a specific rule of legal obligation applicable to like circumstances.

The rules produced by the process of adjudication are distinctive in being implicit rather than explicit rules.[1] The rule promulgated by a decision is not the court's express statement, if any, of a rule; rather, it is the court's *hold-*

* The authors would like to thank Professor Benjamin Klein for his many helpful comments on an earlier draft. We also thank Marnie Berkowitz, Charles Haines, John Hancock, Philip Harris, Joan Meier, Brian McCollum, Douglas Otto, Andrew Rosenfield, and Pamela Trow for their research assistance in the preparation of this paper. Financial support was provided by the National Science Foundation through a grant to the National Bureau of Economic Research to support research in law and economics, and by the Law and Economics Program of the University of Chicago Law School. This is not an official National Bureau paper because it has not undergone the full critical review accorded Bureau studies, including approval by the Bureau's Board of Directors.

This is a revised draft of the paper prepared for the conference in honor of George Stigler. A pioneering figure in the application of economics to law, Professor Stigler is also a generous colleague to whom the authors of this paper are greatly indebted for inspiration and assistance in many ways over the years. This paper is dedicated to him with gratitude and affection.

After our article went to press, we discovered John Henry Merryman, The Authority of Authority, 6 Stan. L. Rev. 613 (1954) and his recently written and still unpublished sequel. Both of his papers apply citation analysis to the study of legal precedent and have several points in common with our analysis.

[1] See generally Edward H. Levi, An Introduction to Legal Reasoning 1-2 (1949); 1 Henry M. Hart, Jr. & Albert M. Sacks, The Legal Process: Basic Problems in the Making and Application of Law 138-39 (tent. ed. 1958).

ing, that is, the minimum rule (whether or not expressly articulated) necessary to explain the outcome of the case. The rule created by a single decision
will therefore tend to be extremely narrow in scope; a broader rule will
generally require a series of judicial decisions—a string of holdings—for it is
only from a series of decisions, each determining the legal significance of a
slightly different set of facts, that a rule applicable to a situation common or
general enough to be likely to recur in the future can be inferred.

A factor pushing in the same direction is that the authority of a rule
declared in a single decision is limited unless the rule is declared by a higher
court for the guidance of a lower one in the same jurisdiction. Especially in
appellate litigation, most of the judge-made rules urged on the court are
those of a coequal court, or those declared in the earlier decisions of the same
court; such rules have persuasive force, but are not binding. Where, however, the rule has been, as it were, solidified in a long line of decisions, the
authority of the rule is enhanced. The rule then represents the accumulated
experience of many judges responding to the arguments and evidence of
many lawyers and is therefore more likely to be followed in subsequent
cases.

The distinctive attributes of decisional rules are captured in the term that
the legal system uses to describe such rules: "precedents." In ordinary language, a precedent is something done in the past that is appealed to as a
reason for doing the same thing again. It is much the same in law. The
earlier decision provides a reason for deciding a subsequent similar case the
same way, and a series of related precedents may crystallize a rule having
almost the same force as a statutory rule. Accordingly, legal precedents are
more accurately described as inputs into the production of judge-made rules
of law than as the rules themselves; but this refinement will be ignored in
this paper to simplify the exposition.

The use of precedents to create rules of legal obligation has, to our knowledge, received little theoretical or empirical analysis.[2] This paper presents
and tests empirically an economic approach to legal precedent that is derived
mainly from the analysis of capital formation and investment. We treat the
body of legal precedents created by judicial decisions in prior periods as a
capital stock that yields a flow of information services which depreciates
over time as new conditions arise that were not foreseen by the framers of the

[2] However, legal precedent is discussed as a form of social capital having public-good characteristics in James M. Buchanan, The Limits of Liberty: Between Anarchy and Leviathan
(1974), especially in ch. 6, and some aspects of the economic theory of precedent are also
discussed in Isaac Ehrlich & Richard A. Posner, An Economic Analysis of Legal Rulemaking, 3
J. Leg. Studies 257 (1974), and in Richard A. Posner, An Economic Approach to Legal Procedure and Judicial Administration, 2 J. Leg. Studies 399, 448-51 (1973). Professors Lawrence
Friedman of Stanford Law School and Stanton Wheeler of Yale Law School, and their associates, are in the process of collecting a large sample of state appellate opinions which they
plan to use for an empirical study of precedents, though not within an economic framework.

existing precedents. New (and replacement) capital is created by investment in the production of precedents.

The basic data for the empirical analysis are case citations appearing in judicial opinions. An initial problem is that a case citation is not the same thing as a precedent. Sometimes a case is not cited as a precedent; an example is a citation of the decision of a lower court (or courts) in the same case. Our samples exclude this obvious nonprecedential citation and other, less obvious, ones.[3] In some instances, counting citations may result in underestimating the true number of precedents by excluding the precedent that is so effective in defining the requirements of the law that it prevents legal disputes from arising in the first place or, if they do arise, induces them to be settled without litigation. In the limit, such a "superprecedent" might never be cited in an appellate opinion yet have greater precedential significance than the most frequently cited cases. But such cases are probably rare. If a case is highly specific, it will hardly qualify as a "superprecedent"; by definition it will control only those infrequent cases that present virtually identical facts to those of the case in which it was originally announced. If it is highly general, and therefore more likely to be an important precedent, it is unlikely to decide—so clearly as to prevent disputes or litigation from arising—the specific form of the question presented in subsequent cases.

Citations by scientists and other scholars to scientific and scholarly books and articles (rather than by lawyers and judges to cases) have been studied extensively by historians of science, by sociologists, and by economists.[4] Scholarly citations, however, are not examples of the use of precedent. The normal function of the scholarly citation is not to adduce authority for a proposition but to give credit for prior original work, to refer the reader to corroborative or collateral findings by other scholars, and as a method of incorporating by reference relevant theorems, proofs, etc. Since the second and third functions of scholarly citation have counterparts in judicial citation, studies of scholarly citation may have relevance to understanding judicial citation, but the present paper does not explore the possible parallels between scholarly and judicial citation.

The idea of analyzing judicial citation practices for regularities that might refute or support hypotheses derived from capital theory will no doubt strike some lawyers, both practicing and academic, as a dubious undertaking. Not

---

[3] The research assistants who counted the citations in the opinions in our samples were instructed to exclude citations to lower-court decisions in the same case, "but see" and other citations indicating rejection of the cited case as a precedent, and multiple citations to the same case if cited on the same point.

[4] See, for example, Robert K. Merton, The Sociology of Science: Theoretical and Empirical Investigations 508-09, 514-15, 556 (1973), and references therein; Michael C. Lovell, The Production of Economic Literature: An Interpretation, 11 J. Econ. Lit. 27 (1973), and references therein; George J. Stigler & Claire Friedland, The Citation Practices of Doctorates in Economics, 83 J. Pol. Econ. 477 (1975).

only are many lawyers skeptical in general concerning the use of economic models and quantitative methods to study the legal system, but they assume that judges' citation practices are altogether too idiosyncratic to be illuminated by general theory and statistical aggregation. Whether a judicial opinion cites many cases or few, old cases or new, is, they believe, more a function of the judge's personal style, tastes, erudition, pedantry, etc. than of systematic characteristics of the legal process. Yet this seems improbable. The extensive research and writing that lawyers, judges, and law clerks devote to discovering, marshalling, enumerating, and explaining precedents are not costless undertakings, and would not be undertaken if precedent did not enter systematically into the decision of cases. However, the question whether or not the use of precedents is systematic does not have to be decided on *a priori* grounds; to the extent that judicial citation practices exhibit regularities explicable within a systematic analytical framework, a statistical analysis of precedent should reveal them.

The paper is organized as follows. Part II describes our case samples and presents tables summarizing the principal characteristics of the citations. The theoretical analysis is contained in Part III. There we formalize the capital-investment model, derive hypotheses, and discuss the production of precedents in the absence of an explicit market. Part IV develops techniques for using case citations to study precedents empirically and presents the results of our empirical analysis. The final part of this paper, Part V, suggests some areas of further research utilizing the approach developed here.

II. THE SAMPLES

Our first and principal source of data on precedents is a random sample of 658 decisions (a roughly one-in-ten sample) handed down by the federal courts of appeals during an approximately 18-month period beginning in January 1974 and ending in the summer of 1975. Each decision was classified by subject matter, and the number and age of citations to both earlier Supreme Court and other-court decisions were recorded. Two other data sources were also developed for this study: a random sample of 223 decisions (again an approximately one-in-ten sample) by the federal courts of appeals during 1960, and all of the decisions handed down by the Supreme Court during its 1974 term.

Table 1 presents a subject-matter breakdown of the decisions in our three data sets. The subject-matter classifications we employ are gross,[5] but this is unavoidable because of the limited number of cases included in our samples.

---

[5] Thus, the legal purist will be distressed at our placing admiralty cases in a category called "common law"; our purpose in doing so was to group together cases in which statutes have played a relatively small role as a source of legal rules. More refined classifications are used in our current research, not reported in this paper, which is based on a sample of about 7,000 federal court of appeals decisions.

TABLE 1
SAMPLES UTILIZED IN STUDY

Subject-matter Classification	Sample						Total Commenced	
	U.S. Courts of Appeals[1]				U.S. Supreme Court		U.S. Courts of Appeals[4]	
	1974-1975		1960		1974 Term[2]		1974	1960
	No.	(%)	No.	(%)	No.	(%)	(%)	(%)
Common Law	115	(17.5)	54	(24.2)	13	(8.3)	(12.8)	(23.6)
Torts and contracts	94	(14.3)	48	(21.5)	11	(7.3)		
Admiralty	21	(3.2)	6	(2.7)	2	(1.3)		
Economic Regulation	183	(27.8)	97	(43.5)	48	(30.8)	(20.7)	(33.2)
Tax	36	(5.5)	37	(16.6)	8	(5.1)		
Antitrust	12	(1.8)	4	(1.8)	8	(5.1)		
Labor	53	(8.1)	26	(11.7)	17	(10.9)		
Federal regulatory agencies, n.e.c.	50	(7.6)	10	(4.5)	13	(8.3)		
Patents, copyrights, and trade marks	32	(4.9)	20	(9.0)	2	(1.3)		
Civil Rights	47	(7.1)	2	(0.9)	13	(8.3)	(9.1)	(1.1)
Constitutional[3]	65	(9.9)	6	(2.7)	57	(36.5)		
Criminal[3]	239	(36.3)	50	(22.4)	37	(23.7)	(31.5)	(21.6)
Criminal (excl. const.)	193	(29.3)	46	(20.6)	12	(7.7)		
Bankruptcy	17	(2.6)	7	(3.1)	5	(3.2)	(1.7)	(3.1)
Military	11	(1.7)	5	(2.2)	2	(1.3)		
Land Condemnation	8	(1.2)	5	(2.2)	3	(1.9)	(1.1)	(2.5)
Not Classified	19	(2.9)	1	(0.4)	3	(1.9)	(23.1)	(14.9)
Total	658		223		156			

[1] "Memorandum" opinions—very short per curiam (unsigned) opinions that contain no citations—were omitted. Opinions of the U.S. Court of Claims and Court of Customs and Patent Appeals were included in the court of appeals samples.

[2] Summary affirmations (akin to memorandum opinions in the courts of appeals—see note 1 *supra*) were omitted.

[3] Criminal cases (including postconviction proceedings, which are technically civil proceedings) involving constitutional questions were counted in both the Constitutional and Criminal categories; but the second count was subtracted for purposes of computing the totals in the last row of the table.

Sources: F.2d (1960, 1974-75); U.S. (1974); and 1960, 1974 Admin. Office of the U.S. Courts. Ann. Rep.

Table 1 indicates the close comparability between the subject-matter distributions of our 1960 and 1974-1975 courts of appeals samples and those reported by the Administrative Office of the U.S. Courts for all cases commenced in the courts of appeals in fiscal years 1960 and 1974 respectively.[6]

To avoid confusion later on, the reader should be careful to distinguish between the *cases* in our three samples (hereafter "sample cases") and our measure of *precedents*. The sample cases presented in Table 1 are not the

[6] A comparison of *terminations* involving a written judicial opinion (our samples) to *commencements* is at best a crude one. Unfortunately, the subject-matter breakdown for terminations, and subsets of terminations such as terminations with a judicial opinion, are not reported by or available from the Administrative Office. Observe that the frequencies in our subject-matter classes tend to exceed the frequencies in the Administrative Office data because of the large proportion of unclassifiable cases in the Administrative Office data compared to our samples (for example, 23.1 per cent compared to 2.9 per cent in 1974, and 14.9 per cent compared to .4 per cent in 1960).

precedents that we studied; they are the source of our data on precedents. It is the citations in the sample cases that are the precedents (more precisely, the proxy for the precedents) used in the empirical analysis. Thus, we study Supreme Court precedents by analyzing the citations to Supreme Court decisions contained in both the courts of appeals and the Supreme Court sample cases, and court of appeals precedents by analyzing citations to court of appeals decisions in both the court of appeals and Supreme Court sample cases. This is not the only way to collect and analyze data on precedents. An alternative approach, not used in this study, is to trace the history of a case as a precedent by counting the citations to that case in later judicial opinions.[7]

Table 2 summarizes the data on precedents that we obtained from the three sets of sample cases. The average ages, standard errors, and numbers of citations are presented by subject-matter classes for each data set.[8] Within each subject-matter classification there is a further breakdown between citations to U.S. Supreme Court decisions and citations to other-court decisions. The reason for distinguishing empirically among subject matters, and between Supreme Court and other-court citations, is that our theory (developed in the next part of this paper) suggests that precedents will differ systematically both across subject-matter classes and between the Supreme Court and other courts, in particular the U.S. courts of appeals.[9]

[7] In a separate (and not completed) study we have classified some 400 Supreme Court decisions rendered in the Court's 1900, 1938 and 1958 terms by subject matter and then analyzed the survival rates of precedents by tracing the time path of the citations to each decision by the Supreme Court and by other courts.

[8] Only citations appearing in majority opinions are included in Table 2; citations appearing in concurring and dissenting opinions were also counted but are not utilized in the present study. A case cited more than once in an opinion was counted separately every time it was cited on a different issue; but, as previously noted, a case cited repeatedly for the same point was counted only once.

[9] However, a deficiency in our procedure (which will be remedied in subsequent studies) is the failure to distinguish within the category of other-court (that is, other than U.S. Supreme Court) citations between citations to U.S. court of appeals decisions and to other decisions (decisions of federal district courts, state courts, the Court of Claims, English courts, etc.). Still, our category of "other court" citations is a serviceable, if crude, proxy for U.S. court of appeals citations, because most other-court citations are, in fact, to U.S. court of appeals decisions. Thus, in a random sample of 261 citations appearing in volumes of the Federal Reporter, Second, for 1974 and 1975 (the source and period from which our 1974-1975 U.S. court of appeals sample was drawn), 74.7 per cent of the citations (excluding citations to the Supreme Court) were to U.S. court of appeals decisions.

However, the mean age of the court of appeals citations was only 5.8 years, compared to 14.5 years for the citations to other courts' decisions and 8.0 for both groups together (weighted). (This is somewhat lower than the mean age of other-court citations in our main 1974-1975 sample; see Table 2.) One reason why the mean age of the U.S. court of appeals citations is lower than that of the other non-U.S. Supreme Court citations appears to be that the courts of appeals are of comparatively recent creation (1891). The oldest citation to a court of appeals decision in our 261-citation sample discussed in the preceding paragraph is 50 years old, compared to 194 years for the oldest citation to another court's decision. If all citations in the sample of more than 50 years are reduced to 50 years, the mean age of the non-court of appeals citations in the sample falls from 14.5 to 10.5 years.

Two methods of calculating the age of citations are used in Table 2. The column labeled "unweighted" is the mean across decisions of the average age of the citations in each decision. The column labeled "weighted" is the average of all of the citations in the subject-matter class (that is, the average age of the citations in each decision weighted by the number of citations).[10] An example will help to clarify the difference between the unweighted and weighted method. In the 1974-1975 court of appeals sample, 492 cases cited Supreme Court precedents. For each of these 492 cases we calculated the mean age of citations to Supreme Court citations. The unweighted age (18.5 years in Table 2) is the average of the 492 means (that is, in effect each of the 492 case means is given a weight of one). The weighted average (19.1 years in Table 2) weights each of the 492 case means by the number of citations contained in that case, and is thus equivalent to the mean age of the 2,278 citations contained in the 492 sample cases.

Table 2 reveals some interesting regularities in the age of judicial citations. Citations to Supreme Court decisions regularly tend to be twice as old on average as citations to other courts' decisions—roughly, 20 years old compared to 10.[11] Of further interest is the similarity of the weighted and unweighted means and of the age distributions across subject-matter classes among the 1960 and 1974-1975 court of appeals samples and the 1974 Supreme Court sample. Another interesting statistic is the "half life," that is, median age, of a precedent. In the 1974-1975 court of appeals sample, half of the citations to Supreme Court and other-court decisions were less than 9.8 and 4.3 years old, respectively (compared to weighted means of 19.1 and 9.9 years). In the 1974 Supreme Court sample, the half lives of Supreme Court and other-court decisions were 13 and 5.4 years respectively (compared to weighted means of 25.8 and 15.7 years). The substantial skewness in the age distribution of citations is due in part, as we show later, to the growth over time in the production of precedents. But this cannot be the complete explanation because it does not account for the skewness in citations to the Supreme Court, where the production of precedents has remained relatively constant over time. Other explanatory variables are the obsolesence or depreciation of legal precedents, the generality or specificity of precedents, statutory activity, and other factors explored later.

---

[10] We also computed the ages of citations in a subsample limited to cases that cite *both* U.S. Supreme Court and other-court decisions, on the theory that cases citing only Supreme Court decisions might differ systematically from those citing only other courts' decisions and thus might distort a comparison of the mean ages of the citations in the respective types of decision. However, a comparison of the results of the subsample with Table 2 indicated that this refinement in the sampling method did not produce any marked change in results, so we did not utilize this subsample in our empirical analysis.

[11] We have not systematically tested the statistical significance of the differences in average age of citations across subject-matter classes, between citations to Supreme Court and other-court cases, etc. The standard errors are quite low, however, suggesting that most differences in means that we are interested in comparing are significant.

TABLE 2
AVERAGE AGE (IN YEARS) OF CITATIONS[1]

	U.S. Courts of Appeals, 1974-1975					
	Supreme Court			Other Courts		
Subject-Matter Classification	Age		No. per case	Age		No. per case
	w	u		w	u	
Total	19.1	18.5	4.630	9.9	8.8	9.197
	(.3)	(.7)	(.228)	(.1)	(.3)	(.360)
	[2278]	[492]		[5785]	[629]	
Common law	33.8	29.9	3.492	14.8	13.6	9.307
	(1.5)	(2.5)	(.385)	(.3)	(.9)	(.667)
	[213]		[61]	[1061]	[114]	
Torts and contracts	35.6	30.6	3.341	15.7	14.3	9.106
	(1.9)	(3.1)	(.457)	(.3)	(1.0)	(.663)
	[137]	[41]		[856]	[94]	
Admiralty	30.6	28.5	3.800	10.9	10.5	10.250
	(2.2)	(4.3)	(.720)	(.5)	(1.9)	(2.319)
	[76]	[20]		[205]	[20]	
Economic regulation	19.5	18.7	4.455	10.3	9.5	9.432
	(.5)	(1.3)	(.464)	(.2)	(.5)	(.720)
	[588]	[132]		[1660]	[176]	
Tax	26.1	21.5	2.538	15.1	12.7	9.818
	(1.6)	(2.7)	(.494)	(.4)	(1.3)	(1.478)
	[66]	[26]		[324]	[33]	
Antitrust	19.1	16.8	5.000	6.5	8.6	8.917
	(.9)	(2.9)	(1.183)	(.5)	(1.9)	(2.506)
	[50]	[10]		[107]	[12]	
Labor	14.9	14.3	4.133	8.3	8.0	8.327
	(.6)	(1.3)	(.515)	(.2)	(.7)	(1.079)
	[186]	[45]		[433]	[52]	
Other federal reg. agencies	19.2	15.9	7.059	8.0	7.0	10.851
	(.6)	(2.0)	(1.486)	(.2)	(.9)	(1.957)
	[240]	[34]		[510]	[47]	
Patents	30.7	33.1	2.706	13.2	12.5	8.938
	(3.5)	(6.6)	(.444)	(.4)	(1.5)	(1.148)
	[46]	[17]		[286]	[32]	
Civil rights	10.1	8.0	4.300	4.0	3.7	9.349
	(.5)	(1.4)	(.665)	(.1)	(.6)	(1.637)
	[172]	[40]		[402]	[43]	
Constitutional	12.6	10.8	8.000	5.5	4.4	8.158
	(.5)	(2.0)	(1.685)	(.4)	(.9)	(1.532)
	[136]	[17]		[155]	[19]	
Criminal (incl. const.)	16.2	16.0	4.946	8.0	6.2	9.057
	(.3)	(1.0)	(.378)	(.2)	(.4)	(.628)
	[999]	[202]		[2056]	[227]	
Criminal (excl. const.)	16.1	16.8	4.127	8.4	6.3	9.016
	(.5)	(1.2)	(.382)	(.2)	(.4)	(.737)
	[648]	[157]		[1650]	[183]	
Bankruptcy	37.4	37.9	1.750	14.7	19.6	9.118
	(4.8)	(7.3)	(.250)	(.8)	(2.8)	(1.749)
	[14]	[8]		[155]	[17]	
Military	11.1	17.1	5.167	6.0	5.3	7.455
	(1.4)	(2.9)	(2.272)	(.3)	(.9)	(1.337)
	[31]	[6]		[82]	[11]	
Land condemnation	50.2	39.2	7.500	22.9	21.4	7.625
	(2.4)	(8.8)	(1.832)	(2.4)	(7.5)	(1.224)
	[60]	[8]		[61]	[8]	

TABLE 2 (*Continued*)

Subject-Matter Classification	U.S. Courts of Appeals, 1960					
	Supreme Court			Other Courts		
	Age		No. per case	Age		No. per case
	w	u		w	u	
Total	22.5	20.3	3.654	14.8	11.8	8.486
	(.6)	(1.4)	(.350)	(.3)	(.7)	(.627)
	[497]	[136]		[1765]	[208]	
Common law	33.3	34.6	2.231	16.9	18.3	10.615
	(2.9)	(4.8)	(.256)	(.4)	(1.7)	(1.301)
	[58]	[26]		[552]	[52]	
Torts and	32.8	31.6	2.286	17.2	18.8	10.723
contracts	(3.0)	(4.9)	(.302)	(.4)	(1.8)	(1.433)
	[48]	[21]		[504]	[47]	
Admiralty	35.9	47.4	2.000	13.7	14.1	9.600
	(8.6)	(13.8)	(.447)	(.7)	(2.2)	(1.503)
	[10]	[5]		[48]	[5]	
Economic	19.8	16.1	4.164	15.2	10.5	9.091
regulation	(.7)	(1.4)	(.630)	(.5)	(1.0)	(1.108)
	[254]	[61]		[800]	[88]	
Tax	21.7	17.8	4.120	21.7	13.2	9.844
	(1.1)	(2.0)	(.851)	(1.1)	(2.0)	(2.124)
	[103]	[25]		[315]	[32]	
Antitrust	20.0	19.2	13.667	15.7	14.3	11.500
	(.4)	(2.6)	(9.207)	(.8)	(3.0)	(4.873)
	[41]	[3]		[46]	[4]	
Labor	15.7	13.1	3.158	7.2	6.7	10.800
	(1.5)	(2.2)	(.441)	(.2)	(.9)	(2.134)
	[60]	[19]		[270]	[25]	
Other federal	11.0	9.9	3.250	10.6	8.0	4.500
reg. agencies	(.9)	(2.1)	(1.436)	(1.3)	(2.8)	(1.452)
	[26]	[8]		[36]	[8]	
Patents	31.3	25.6	4.000	17.1	11.4	7.000
	(2.4)	(6.6)	(.966)	(.6)	(2.1)	(2.036)
	[24]	[6]		[133]	[19]	
Civil rights	19.3	15.8	1.500	7.1	6.2	8.000
	(7.2)	(10.8)	(.500)	(.9)	(3.7)	(2.000)
	[3]	[2]		[16]	[2]	
Constitutional	57.7	57.7	9.000	16.7	16.7	3.000
	(0.0)	(0.0)	(0.000)	(7.5)	(16.7)	(0.000)
	[9]	[1]		[6]	[2]	
Criminal (incl.	20.5	15.9	3.806	10.4	7.6	5.935
const.)	(1.0)	(2.1)	(.675)	(.4)	(1.0)	(.946)
	[137]	[36]		[273]	[46]	
Criminal (excl.	20.2	15.5	4.000	10.4	7.5	6.070
const.)	(1.0)	(2.1)	(.749)	(.4)	(1.1)	(1.005)
	[128]	[32]		[261]	[43]	
Bankruptcy	32.7	34.9	3.333	13.6	10.8	5.571
	(2.5)	(9.7)	(2.333)	(.6)	(2.3)	(1.510)
	[10]	[3]		[39]	[7]	
Military	8.2	9.4	1.667	11.3	6.1	6.800
	(1.5)	(2.3)	(.667)	(1.0)	(2.5)	(3.693)
	[5]	[3]		[34]	[5]	
Land	24.5	21.6	6.000	17.1	16.5	8.200
condemnation	(1.6)	(6.0)	(1.528)	(.8)	(2.4)	(1.855)
	[18]	[3]		[41]	[5]	

93

TABLE 2 (Continued)

	Supreme Court, 1974-1975					
	Supreme Court			Other Courts		
Subject-Matter Classification	Age		No. per case	Age		No. per case
	w	u		w	u	
Total	25.8	22.7	15.032	15.7	12.3	7.689
	(.3)	(1.3)	(1.012)	(.6)	(1.4)	(.694)
	[2345]	[156]		[938]	[122]	
Common law	35.4	27.9	12.000	26.5	20.1	11.500
	(1.2)	(4.9)	(2.334)	(2.2)	(9.8)	(4.070)
	[156]	[13]		[115]	[10]	
Torts and contracts	30.2	24.0	10.364	16.8	18.2	7.500
	(1.3)	(4.8)	(2.413)	(3.3)	(11.8)	(2.771)
	[114]	[11]		[60]	[8]	
Admiralty	49.5	49.9	21.000	37.2	27.5	27.500
	(.5)	(3.3)	(3.000)	(2.1)	(18.2)	(14.500)
	[42]	[2]		[55]	[2]	
Economic regulation	22.9	23.2	11.250	13.4	10.3	8.625
	(.6)	(2.1)	(1.029)	(.4)	(1.2)	(1.431)
	[540]	[48]		[345]	[40]	
Tax	40.7	36.2	9.375	12.1	10.5	11.500
	(2.1)	(6.4)	(2.420)	(.3)	(1.9)	(3.538)
	[75]	[8]		[69]	[6]	
Antitrust	18.3	22.1	12.000	20.7	13.3	7.000
	(1.1)	(5.6)	(2.163)	(2.6)	(6.7)	(2.168)
	[96]	[8]		[35]	[5]	
Labor	15.8	15.6	10.412	12.9	10.5	11.867
	(.6)	(2.2)	(1.269)	(.4)	(1.5)	(3.038)
	[177]	[17]		[178]	[15]	
Other federal reg. agencies	23.2	23.6	13.231	7.2	7.3	3.750
	(.7)	(3.4)	(2.790)	(.8)	(1.8)	(1.081)
	[172]	[13]		[45]	[12]	
Patents	38.2	36.9	10.000	23.8	18.7	9.000
	(.5)	(2.5)	(5.000)	(.6)	(5.7)	(8.000)
	[20]	[2]		[18]	[2]	
Civil rights	22.7	23.0	21.923	15.4	15.6	8.222
	(.5)	(2.8)	(3.857)	(1.8)	(6.2)	(1.786)
	[285]	[13]		[74]	[9]	
Constitutional	23.7	17.0	17.531	20.5	13.3	6.708
	(.7)	(3.0)	(2.826)	(2.2)	(3.9)	(1.256)
	[561]	[32]		[161]	[24]	
Criminal (incl. const.)	23.1	20.4	13.973	10.8	9.8	6.607
	(.6)	(2.7)	(1.943)	(.7)	(2.2)	(1.095)
	[517]	[37]		[185]	[28]	
Criminal (excl. const.)	29.4	20.9	7.500	10.9	8.6	7.167
	(1.8)	(5.6)	(2.076)	(1.2)	(2.9)	(1.266)
	[90]	[12]		[86]	[12]	
Bankruptcy	34.2	36.6	18.400	9.7	14.6	5.800
	(.7)	(5.2)	(10.829)	(2.0)	(6.5)	(1.530)
	[92]	[5]		[29]	[5]	
Military	30.5	30.8	23.000	9.8	6.8	5.500
	(.1)	(.4)	(12.000)	(.7)	(3.8)	(4.500)
	[46]	[2]		[11]	[2]	
Land condemnation	63.7	52.7	25.667	27.8	27.8	3.000
	(2.7)	(16.2)	(12.574)	(10.5)	(23.5)	(.000)
	[77]	[3]		[6]	[2]	

Notes: w = weighted average (see text for explanation). u = unweighted average (see text for explanation). No. per case = average number of citations per case.

[1] In each subject-matter class there are three numbers per column under the age columns: the top one is the mean age; the middle one (in parentheses) is the standard error of the mean; and the lowest one (in brackets) is either the number of citations (weighted columns) or number of cases with citations (unweighted columns).

[2] In the no.-per-case column there are two numbers per column: the top one is the mean number and the second one (in parentheses) is the standard error of the mean number.

The half life of citations in scholarly journals appears to be generally shorter than that of citations in judicial decisions—for example, 5.5 years in economic and in sociological articles and about four years in physics and biomedical research. [12] Another basis of comparison to scholarly citations is the number of citations per decision or article. Combining citations to both the Supreme Court and other courts, we find that the average number of citations per decision is 12.3 and 21 in the 1974-1975 court of appeals and in the Supreme Court samples, respectively. This compares to approximately 11 citations per article in leading economic journals, 18 in chemical journals, and four or five in medical journals. [13]

The data in Table 2 can be used to test a popular explanation of differences in average ages of citations: differences in the individual citation practices of judges. Arguably, whether a judge cites many or few cases is largely a matter of personal preference or taste for citing cases. One possibility is that the judge with little taste for citing cases will tend to cite only the most recent cases, either because he lacks information on the relevance of earlier decisions, wants to economize on his time, or believes that more recent ones tend to have greater precedential significance. By the same token, the judge with a taste for citing many cases will cite those same recent cases plus others less recent and hence the average age of his citations will be greater. Thus, if taste is the principal determinant of the number of citations, there should be a strong positive correlation between the number of citations per case and the average age of citations per case. We, of course, question the premise that citation practice is largely a matter of personal preference (and implicitly therefore not capable of being studied scientifically). The economist expects citation practices to be basically uniform across judges, just as he expects different business firms to pursue similar investment policies in the face of similar economic conditions. If a judge cites more cases, it is not because his taste for citations is different but because the case before him is different—perhaps it has more issues, or its issues are less clearly controlled by some precedent. Accordingly, we would not expect to find a strong positive relationship between the number of citations per opinion and their average age.

This issue can be illuminated by empirical analysis. A useful first step is to compare the weighted to the unweighted average ages in Table 2 since a positive correlation between average age and number of citations implies that the weighted method will yield a higher average age than the unweighted. [14] For all subject-matter categories taken together (the first row of Table

---

[12] See Michael C. Lovell, *supra* note 4, at 27.

[13] See *id.*

[14] Let C_i = number of citations per case, $\overline{C}$ = average number of citations per case, $\overline{A}_i$ = average age of citations per case, $\overline{A}$ = unweighted average age of citations ($= \sum_{i=1}^{n} \overline{A}_i/n$ where

2), the weighted exceeds the unweighted in all six possible comparisons. In our largest sample, however, the 1974-1975 U.S. court of appeals sample, the differences are slight—.6 years and 1.1 years for citations to Supreme Court and other-court decisions respectively. In the two smaller samples the differences are somewhat greater, averaging about three years.

A more powerful test of the importance of the number of citations on age (and thus a more powerful test of the "taste" hypothesis) is to estimate a regression of the form

$$\overline{A}_i = \alpha + \beta_1 C_i + \beta_j X_{ji} + u_i \tag{1}$$

where $\overline{A}_i$ is the average age of citations in the ith case, C_i the number of citations in the ith case, and X_{ji} a vector of subject-matter dummy variables. Equations $(3.1) - (3.6)$ in Table 3 present the results of simple regressions of $\overline{A}_i$ on C_i for Supreme Court and other-court citations for our three data sets. The regressions show that the number of citations does have a positive effect on the age of citations, but the effect is statistically significant in only four of the six equations, and the magnitude of the effect is small. For example, in the 1974-1975 sample of citations to the Supreme Court (I-SC) an approximate doubling in the number of citations in a decision, from the mean of 4.6 to 10, increases the mean age of citations by only about .6 years (from 19.1 to 19.7 years), and an increase in the number of citations to other courts (I-OC) from the mean of 9.2 to 20 increases the average age by only about 1.3 years (from 9.9 to 11.2 years). Even in the other two samples, the impact of the number of citations on the average age is small; for example, in sample II-SC, increasing the number of citations to Supreme Court cases from the mean of 15 to 30 would increase average age only from 25.8 to 30.2 years.[15] Although these results neither compel nor justify rejection of the "taste" hypothesis, they indicate it is a weak hypothesis. Not only is the magnitude of the effect of number on age of citations small, but the amount of variation in average age across cases that is explained by differences in the number of citations is negligible; the adjusted R^2's in Table 3 range from 0 to .07 in equations (3.1) to (3.6)

---

n = the number of cases), and $\overline{\overline{A}}$ = weighted average age of citations ($= \sum_{i=1}^{n} C_i \overline{A}_i / \sum_{i=1}^{n} C_i$ where $\sum_{i=1}^{n} C_i = n \cdot \overline{C}$). A positive correlation between C_i and $\overline{A}_i$ implies that

$$n \cdot \text{Cov}(C_i, \overline{A}_i) = \sum_{i=1}^{n} (\overline{A}_i - \overline{A})(C_i - \overline{C}) > 0$$

$$= \Sigma \overline{A}_i C_i - \frac{\Sigma \overline{A}_i \Sigma \overline{C}_i}{n} > 0.$$

Dividing by ΣC_i yields

$$\frac{n \cdot \text{Cov}(C_i \overline{A}_i)}{\Sigma C_i} = \overline{\overline{A}} - \overline{A} > 0.$$

[15] Observe that this implies that the first 15 citations in a case will have an average age of 25.8 years, and the next 15 an average age of 34.5 years in order to bring the average up to 30.2.

TABLE 3
AVERAGE-AGE REGRESSIONS

Equation Number	Sample	n	Constant	C_1	X_{jc}	R^2
3.1	I-SC	492	17.945	.110 (.750)	—	.00
3.2	I-OC	629	7.698	.122 (3.397)	—	.02
3.3	II-SC	156	18.326	.293 (2.905)	—	.05
3.4	II-OC	122	8.823	.450 (2.470)	—	.04
3.5	III-SC	136	18.460	.498 (1.418)	—	.01
3.6	III-OC	208	9.209	.311 (4.092)	—	.07
3.7	I-SC	492	29.430	.342 (2.439)	[8.89]	.18
3.8	I-OC	629	13.192	.123 (3.926)	[14.98]	.25

Notes:

1. Sample: 1 = 1974-1975 Courts of Appeals; II = 1974 Supreme Court; III = 1960 Court of Appeals; SC = citations to Supreme Court cases; OC = citations to other-court cases.

2. n = number of observations in regression.

3. t-statistics in parentheses.

4. F-statistic on set of dummy variables X_{jc} is in brackets.

Equations (3.7) to (3.8) add 14 dummy subject-matter variables to the 1974-1975 court of appeals regressions. Each variable takes the value 1 if the case involves the particular subject matter and 0 otherwise. This allows us to answer the question whether subject matter has a significant effect on average age if the number of citations is held constant. (Alternatively, equations (3.7) and (3.8) test the partial effect of numbers on age, holding subject-matter constant.) An F-test performed on the entire set of subject-matter variables indicates that differences in subject matter generate significant differences in the average age of citations.[16] This result tends to undermine the "taste" hypothesis, for there is no reason why preferences in citing cases should vary systematically across subject-matter areas. Moreover, the "taste" hypothesis supplies no rationale for separating the samples into citations to the Supreme Court and to other courts, and we suspect that if the samples were not separated in this way the observed positive effect of numbers on age would be even weaker than we found it to be. Although we have not estimated regressions based on a combination of these samples, the fact that citations to the Supreme Court tend to be older, yet fewer in number, than to other courts suggests that the positive effect of numbers on age would be even weaker if citations to the Supreme Court and to other courts were combined in the court of appeals regressions.

[16] The F-tests were 8.89 with 14 and 476 degrees of freedom for citations to the Supreme Court, and 14.98 with 14 and 613 degrees of freedom for citations to other courts. Both were significant at the .01 level.

97

In sum, there appear to be regularities in the citation data (for example, the difference between citations to the Supreme Court and to other courts, and the effect of subject matter) that are not explained by assumed differences in the individual citation preferences of judges. A more promising approach is to ignore differences in tastes or preferences and instead utilize an economic framework in which precedents are viewed as constituting a stock of legal capital subject to depreciation and the production of precedents is treated as a form of investment.

III. The Theoretical Framework: Legal Capital

This part of the paper develops a capital-investment approach for the analysis of legal precedent. We begin by formulating a model of optimal investment in the production of precedents, and then use this model to generate hypotheses concerning the rate of investment, the size of the capital stock and its rate of depreciation, and the interaction among these variables. Finally, we examine certain peculiarities in the precedent-production process that result from the seeming absence of market incentives on the part of participants in that process. Because of the novelty of our approach to legal precedent, we develop the theory in more detail than is necessary for the empirical analysis that follows. In particular, although the determinants of investment and the capital stock are discussed here, these variables are, with one exception, treated as exogenous in the empirical analysis. The main focus of that analysis is on measuring investment and the capital stock, and combining these measures with data on citations to estimate and test hypotheses concerning the depreciation of legal capital.

A. Some Definitions

Let L_t^i equal the stock of legal capital in a particular substantive area of the law (the ith area) in period t. The stock is defined as the set of precedents that have accumulated from judicial decisions in prior periods (t-1, t-2, etc.).[17] This stock generates a flow of services in period t that may be defined as bodies of information on the types of behavior that will be subject to civil and criminal sanctions and on the magnitude of these sanctions. One can write the stock of legal capital in period t as

$$L_t^i = I_{t-1}^i + (1-\delta^i)L_{t-1}^i \qquad (2)$$

where I_{t-1}^i is the gross investment (assumed to be nonnegative) in legal capital that takes place in period t-1, and δ^i is the depreciation rate (assumed to be constant) of legal capital during the interval t-1 to t.

For purposes of empirical estimation of legal capital, it is useful to express equation (2) as a function of investment and depreciation rates in all previous periods. By substituting for L_{t-1}^i, L_{t-2}^i, etc. we can rewrite equation (2) as

[17] To simplify exposition, we disregard the contributions to legal capital that are made by statutes, constitutional provisions, and administrative rulings and regulations.

$$L_t^i = I_{t-1}^i + (1-\delta^i)I_{t-2}^i + (1-\delta^i)^2 I_{t-3}^i + , . . , + (1-\delta^i)^{t-1} I_0^i \qquad (3)$$

where I_0^i is the investment in legal capital in the base period 0. Equation (3) illustrates the fundamental proposition that an investment in any period increases the stock of legal capital in all future periods, although the increments in the stock diminish with time due to the successive compounding of depreciation rates.

Although a precedent does not "wear out" in a physical sense, it depreciates in an economic sense because the value of its information content declines over time with changing circumstances.[18] Changes in social and economic conditions, in legislation, in judicial personnel, and in other parameters of legal action reduce the value of precedents as a source of legal doctrine. To illustrate, a decision involving a collision between two horse-drawn wagons is bound to lose some of its precedential value when wagons are replaced by cars and trucks, and a decision turning on the difference between "trespass" and "trespass on the case" may lose all of its precedential value when the common-law forms of action are abolished by statute. In general, passage of time reduces the flow of services of a precedent,[19] and this reduction represents the depreciation or obsolescence of legal capital.

The monetary equivalent of the information services generated by the stock of legal capital in the ith area in period t can be written as

$$V_t = V(L_t; N_t). \qquad (4)$$

(The subscript i is now suppressed for notational convenience.) We assume positive (namely, the greater the stock, the greater the total value of the information services) and diminishing returns to legal capital at each moment in time.[20] The services from a given stock will also be greater the greater is the number of users (N_t) of this type of legal capital. Since most activities involving two or more persons or firms are guided, in part, by the legal consequences of the activity, one might approximate N_t by the community's population, income, number of business transactions, number of

[18] This leaves open the question whether a 10 per cent depreciation rate, for example, implies that 10 per cent of last period's precedents "disappear" while 90 per cent survive in full, or whether the services yielded by each precedent decline on average by 10 per cent. This paper adopts the latter formulation because it encompasses both precedents that "disappear" (100 per cent decline) and those that decline partially in value.

[19] There are exceptions—a long-dormant precedent may acquire a new value because of a sudden upsurge in demand, as in the recent controversies over impeachment and executive privilege. The counterpart in the realm of physical capital is the abandoned machine restored to service because of a sudden increase in demand for its services.

[20] Conceivably, an increase in the stock beyond some level might produce conflicting precedents or so increase the difficulty of discriminating among nonconflicting ones as to reduce the amount of information about the expected outcome of legal disputes; either result would imply a negative value of the marginal product of legal capital. But we prefer to view these situations as reductions in the set of precedents (that is, negative investment) and hence in the capital stock, and thus rule out negative marginal products. Observe that the explicit replacement of an old by a new precedent (for example, when old decisions are overruled) is analytically distinguishable from a conflict between precedents, because the overruling can be viewed, sequentially, as the depreciation of the old precedent followed by investment in developing a new one.

firms, etc.[21] Our term "monetary equivalent" is simply a convenient index for measuring the value of the services (previously defined as information on the types of behavior subject to sanctions and on the magnitude of these sanctions) generated by legal capital.[22]

The source of investment in legal capital in period t-1 is the set of judicial decisions in that period that create precedents—mainly published appellate decisions. Although most legal disputes are terminated by out-of-court settlements, we ignore the contribution of settlements to legal capital since it is small; settlements, even when their terms are publicly disclosed, provide little information about the content of legal rules. Similarly, trials that occur only because of a disagreement over facts do not generate significant legal capital since the outcome of such a trial does not provide information about the content of legal rules. Since any legal issue decided on appeal—and any legal issues in cases that are not appealed—will have been decided either initially or finally at the trial level, trial decisions can be a source of legal capital, but the fraction of trials that generates precedents is small, so we are justified in limiting our empirical analysis to a sample of appellate decisions. (Of course, even at the appellate level, not all decisions contribute significantly to legal capital; an example of one that does not would be the decision of an appeal that involves only issues of the sufficiency of evidence.)

The creation of precedents through appellate decision-making consumes the (valuable) time of judges, attorneys, law clerks, court clerks, jurors, witnesses, and litigants, plus resources associated with the construction and maintenance of court houses, plus other scarce resources. Ignoring for the moment the underlying investment production function (discussed in subpart D), we can write investment costs in period t as

$$C_t = C(I_t) \qquad (5)$$

where the marginal cost of I_t is both positive (since increases in I_t require greater inputs) and nondecreasing.

B. Optimal Production of Precedents

An optimal investment policy would be one that maximized the present value (π) of the difference between the value of the flow of services and the

---

[21] The public-good aspect of legal capital is implicit in the formulation of equation (4). Since one person's use of precedents does not exclude another's use, V_t will rise as the number of users increases (that is, $\partial V_t/\partial N_t > 0$). If congestion eventually occurs as the number of users increases, then beyond some point $\partial V_t/\partial N_t^2 < 0$. In the development of our model we take as given the number of users.

[22] Although legal capital yields information, its value ultimately depends on the underlying behavior it promotes. If "value" is synonymous with "efficiency," then the more effectively legal precedents promote behavior consistent with efficient resource allocation, the greater will be their value. Precedents in fact differ greatly in the degree to which they affect efficiency, and some may actually reduce efficiency and hence should be assigned a negative value if value and efficiency are to be equated. But in this paper we ignore ultimate questions of value and assume that precedents are valuable insofar as they promote compliance with whatever legal norms the precedents are intended to implement.

costs of investment with respect to investment in each period, subject to the earlier conditions that $L_t = I_{t-1} + (1-\delta)L_{t-1}$, δ is constant and I_t is nonnegative.[23] This yields T first-order conditions (from t=0 to T−1) of the form

$$\frac{\partial \pi}{\partial I_t} = R_{t+1}V'_{t+1} + R_{t+2}V'_{t+2}(1-\delta) +$$

$$R_{t+3}V'_{t+3}(1-\delta)^2 + \ldots$$

$$+ R_T V'_T(1-\delta)^{T-t-1} - R_t C'_t = 0 \quad (6)$$

where R_{t+j} is the value (dollar equivalent) at the beginning of period 0 of the services of legal capital in periods t+j (i.e., $R_{t+j} = 1/(1+r)^{t+j}$, where the per-period discount rate, r, is assumed constant); V'_{t+j} is the value of the marginal product of the service of legal capital in t+j; and C'_t is the marginal cost of investment. The optimality condition in (6) represents the usual equality of marginal returns with marginal costs.

It is more convenient to represent the equilbrium condition in terms of the optimal stock of legal capital in period t+1. This is given by

$$V'_{t+1} = C'_t(r+\delta-\tilde{C}_t) \quad (7)$$

where $\tilde{C}_t$ is the percentage change in the marginal costs of investment from period t to t+1.[24] Equation (7), which states that in each period the capital stock is expanded until the undiscounted value of the marginal product in that period equals the marginal user cost of capital, has the advantage of allowing us to convert the multi-period flow equilibrium (equation (6)) into a single-period stock equilibrium. This is illustrated in Figure I, where we assume that the marginal cost of investment is constant and equal in each period (that is, $\tilde{C}_t = 0$), implying a single-period adjustment to any discrepancy between actual and desired capital stock. To illustrate, if the stock in t is below the equilibrium (or desired) stock in t+1 because, for example, a new statute is passed creating a demand for new legal capital or destroying old legal capital, then investment in period t will be sufficient to bring the stock up to its desired level in t+1. And if the variables in equation (7) remain constant thereafter, future investment will just offset depreciation and the capital stock will remain at its stationary desired level.

A fundamental implication of equation (7) and Figure I is that the stock of legal capital in any period will be greater, the greater the value of its marginal product and the lower its marginal user cost (that is, the lower $C'_t(r+\delta)$).

---

[23] Nonnegative gross investment results from the inability of the community to sell its legal capital. Although zero gross investment in a period is possible, we assume for mathematical convenience that the optimality conditions yield positive gross investment in every period.

[24] Equation (7) is derived by substituting $(1 - \delta)\partial\pi/\partial I_{t+1}$ (=0) into (6) and assuming that $\tilde{C}_t\delta \approx 0$. A similar expression for health capital is developed by Michael Grossman in his Demand for Health: A Theoretical and Empirical Investigation (Nat'l Bur. Econ. Res., occ. pap. no. 119, 1972), and Kenneth J. Arrow develops the general formula using continuous time in his paper Optimal Capital Policy with Irreversible Investment, in Value, Capital and Growth, Papers in Honour of Sir John Hicks 1-19 (J. N. Wolfe ed. 1968).

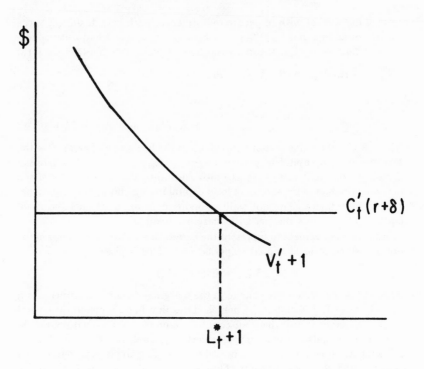

Figure I

Thus in areas of the law that affect more people, legal capital should be relatively more valuable and hence the optimal stock larger. However, the number of users of the legal capital (N_t in equation (4)) must be weighted by the value that users attach to the capital. Thus, a form of legal capital that has narrow applicability and hence a few users may still be relatively large if the users attach a higher value to this capital. Similarly, the per capita amount of legal capital should be greater in large than in small communities. This follows from the public-good aspect of legal capital. In the limiting case, the entire capital stock is received by each member of the community, and hence a larger community induces a shift in the demand curve in Figure I and a greater aggregate and per capita capital stock.

A related implication is that, assuming legislative activity tends to depreciate legal capital, then in those areas of the law where there is relatively greater statutory activity the depreciation rates of legal capital should be greater and the optimal stock of legal capital smaller.[25] The effect on gross

[25] This effect would be strengthened if legal capital and legislation are substitutable, in the

investment, however, is uncertain. Although a higher depreciation rate lowers the optimal stock, it also implies faster replacement of the (smaller) stock.[26] Observe, finally, that the stock of legal capital would tend to grow over time if, for example, N_t were growing over time, for the demand curve in Figure I would be shifting to the right (provided V'_{t+1} was a positive function of N_t), leading to a secular increase in the capital stock. And assuming a constant rate of growth of the capital stock and a constant δ, gross investment would grow at a rate equal to that of the capital stock.[27]

C. *Depreciation of Legal Capital*

The previous subpart considered the effect of different depreciation rates on investment and the capital stock but did not explore the forces that affect the depreciation rate itself. It is useful to extend that analysis in this direction since, as indicated earlier, it is possible to integrate data on investment and citations for the purpose of estimating depreciation rates on legal precedents by subject matter—estimates that we believe are interesting in themselves as well as necessary in order to test hypotheses derived from the capital-theory approach to legal precedent. What follows, therefore, is both the development of some testable hypotheses on depreciation and some further discussion of the interrelationship among depreciation, investment, and capital. We do not, however, explicitly incorporate depreciation as a decision variable in the formal model developed in the previous subpart and attempt to derive optimal depreciation rates. A preliminary attempt to do so indicated that such a modification would be exceedingly complicated and would not alter substantively the capital-investment framework used in the empirical analysis.

---

sense that on balance the value of the marginal product of legal capital was reduced by legislation. If they are complementary, legislation, though increasing the depreciation rate (and raising the cost of investment), would have an offsetting effect by increasing the demand for capital.

[26] To demonstrate this, we assume a stationary capital stock (that is, zero net investment). Since gross investment in period t equals δL_t, we have

$$\frac{\partial \ln I_t}{\partial \ln \delta} = 1 + \frac{\partial \ln L_t}{\partial \ln \delta} .$$

From equation (7) it follows that

$$\frac{\partial \ln I_t}{\partial \ln \delta} = 1 + \frac{C'_{t-1}\delta}{V''_t L_t} = 1 - e \cdot s$$

where $e = -(1/V''_t)(V'_t/L_t)$ (the elasticity of the demand curve) and $s = \delta/(r + \delta)$ (the share of depreciation in user cost). It follows that investment is more likely to increase with an increase in δ the smaller are e and s. This result would have to be modified if the capital stock were growing.

[27] Gross investment may be written

$$I_t = L_t(\tilde{L}_t + \delta)$$

where the rate of growth of the capital stock is $\tilde{L}_t = (L_{t+1} - L_t)/L_t \cong (\partial L_t/\partial t)/L_t$. This approxi-

1. *General Versus Specific Legal Capital.* Other things being equal, a precedent can be expected to depreciate more rapidly the narrower (more specific) it is in terms of the span of facts and issues that it covers. Conversely, the broader (more general) a precedent is, the slower should be its rate of depreciation. A general precedent is less likely to be rendered obsolete by a change in the social or legal environment in which the precedent is applied; for example, a decision laying down a broad principle of tort liability should retain its precedential force—be cited—for a longer period of time than one holding that railroads must station flagmen at certain crossings. A general precedent is like a machine that, being adaptable to a number of different uses, is less subject to technological obsolescence than one specialized to a particular industrial task, or it is like general human capital (for example, schooling), which tends to depreciate over the life cycle of an individual more slowly than investment in specific capital (for example, training specialized to a particular employer).

The distinction between general and specific legal capital implies that Supreme Court precedents will depreciate more slowly than those of other courts such as the federal courts of appeals. The Supreme Court is more selective than any other court in its choice of cases to review, due in major part to its more limited capacity compared to other courts, a tendency which is due in turn to society's evident reluctance to increase the number of Supreme Court Justices or take other measures that would enable the Supreme Court to increase its production of precedents. Thus, while the Supreme Court's output of precedents has remained constant for many years despite the enormous secular increase in the number of legal disputes within the Court's jurisdiction,[28] the appointment of additional judges to the federal courts of appeals has enabled those courts greatly to increase their output of precedents.[29] The more limited capacity of the Supreme Court compared to that of the courts of appeals has made the opportunity cost of developing new precedents and modifying old ones increase faster in the Supreme Court. That is why the Supreme Court has had to become relatively more selective over time in its choice of cases to review, and one might

---

mation allows us to ignore the one-period lag between investment and additions to the capital stock. Thus

$$\frac{\partial \ln I_t}{\partial t} = \frac{\partial \ln L_t}{\partial t} + \frac{\partial \ln(L_t + \delta)}{\partial t}$$

and $\partial \ln(\bar{L}_t + \delta)/\partial t$ equals zero by assumption.

[28] See Gerhard Casper & Richard A. Posner, A Study of the Supreme Court's Caseload, 3 J. Leg. Studies 339, at 340-41 (1974) (tab. 1 and fig. 1).

[29] The capacity of the federal appellate courts has not, however, grown at the same rate as the demand. The result has been not only an increase in court queues but also a decrease in the proportion of cases decided that are likely to produce precedents. Thus, while all cases tendered to the courts of appeals are (eventually) decided—the jurisdiction of these courts, unlike that of the Supreme Court, not being discretionary—an increasing number are being decided without creating a (significant) precedent, that is, without a written opinion. See *infra* Appendix B.

expect this selection to favor cases of greater generality[30] and hence more durability as precedents. This implies, incidentally, that, other things being equal, the depreciation rate of Supreme Court precedents should have declined over time relative to that of the courts of appeals.

In relying on the greater generality of Supreme Court precedents to predict that they will depreciate more slowly than court of appeals precedents, we may seem to be overlooking the obvious: Supreme Court precedents depreciate less rapidly than court of appeals precedents because, being more authoritative, they are more valuable. However, neither economic nor any other theory predicts that a capital good will depreciate more slowly because it is more valuable: modern weapons systems and computers are examples of expensive capital goods that depreciate rapidly (compared, say, to lathes). The initial value of a capital good does not dictate its rate of depreciation.

2. *Statutory Activity and Depreciation.* Precedents can be expected to depreciate more rapidly in areas of law in which there is considerable statutory activity, since a change in statutory law will tend to make precedents based on earlier statutory language obsolete. If we could reliably measure the levels of statutory activity across the various subject-matter areas in our sample, we could test this hypothesis rigorously. At this stage, only a casual empirical analysis of the hypothesis appears feasible. A further difficulty in testing this hypothesis arises from the possibility that the legal system will anticipate statutory activity. If statutory activity is anticipated in area A but not B, the courts may adapt by making their precedents in A more general and hence more adaptable, in which event the observed depreciation rate might not differ across areas that differed in statutory activity. Still another difficulty is that legislatures may pass statutes in areas where legal capital depreciates at a high rate precisely in order to compensate for the relative uncertainty in those areas. In such a case, statutory activity and depreciation would be positively correlated but the direction of causality would be reversed.

3. *Substantive Versus Procedural Citations.* We have attempted to disaggregate our 1974-1975 court of appeals sample into citations to substantive and to procedural issues by subject-matter classes. Since identical procedural issues can arise in different substantive areas, cases in different areas might cite many of the same cases on procedural questions. If so, one would expect less variation in depreciation rates of procedural precedents across subject-matter classes than of substantive precedents. The testing of this hypothesis, however, is hampered by the conceptual difficulty of distinguishing between "substantive" and "procedural" citations—for example, is the issue of damages in an antitrust case a substantive or a procedural question?

4. *Uncertainty, Litigation, and the Production of Precedents.* Suppose

---

[30] As urged by many of the Court's critics. See, for example, Henry M. Hart, Jr., The Supreme Court 1958 Term—Foreword: The Time Chart of the Justices, 73 Harv. L. Rev. 84, 96-100 (1959).

that the stock of legal capital, and hence the flow of information on the likely outcomes of potential legal disputes, were temporarily below the desired (long-run equilibrium) level. This might be due to new legislation or other unanticipated changes in economic or social conditions that rendered part of the existing capital stock obsolete. With the resulting increase in uncertainty, more disputes would arise, parties to a dispute would find it more difficult to forecast the outcome of litigation, and litigation would increase. The result would be a temporary increase in the production of precedents (investment) until the discrepancy between actual and desired capital was eliminated.[31] (This process is described in greater detail in the next subpart.) Alternatively, suppose depreciation were permanently higher in one subject-matter area of the law compared to another, with other factors held constant. Although the capital stock (and possibly gross investment) would be smaller in the area with higher depreciation, the ratio of investment to capital should be greater.[32] Thus, a higher observed depreciation rate, whether caused by temporary or permanent forces, should be associated with a greater investment-capital ratio.

This hypothesis can be tested in two possible ways. From estimates of depreciation, investment, and the capital stock by subject matter, the relationship between depreciation and the investment-capital ratio can readily be determined. A difficulty with this test is the limited number of subject-matter classes in our sample. An alternative test (not performed in this paper, however) would be to apply the depreciation rates calculated in this paper to other data sets containing more observations. Specifically, one could examine the trial-settlement ratios and appeal rates across the more than 90 U.S. district courts as a function of the average depreciation rate of the district's caseload and other variables such as the length of trial queues. Since higher depreciation is a measure of relative uncertainty, we should observe that, other things being equal, the higher the average depreciation rate of a district's caseload, the greater will be the proportion of trials in the district.

[31] The model developed in subpart B made the simplifying assumption of constant marginal costs of investment (see Figure 1). Thus, any discrepancy between the desired and actual capital stock would be eliminated in a single period (or instantaneously in a continuous-time model) by adjustments in investment. But if instead marginal cost is rising within a given period (and this is likely to be so, if only because the number of actual disputes capable of producing precedents is limited in each period), then discrepancies between actual and desired capital will tend to be eliminated gradually over several periods.

[32] We showed in note 26 supra that the effect of a higher depreciation rate on gross investment was uncertain. However, since $I_t/L_t = \delta$ for a stationary capital stock, a higher depreciation rate must be associated with a higher investment-capital ratio. If the capital stock were growing, then $I_t/L_t = \tilde{L}_t + \delta$ (see supra note 27). Here a higher depreciation would also be associated with a higher investment-capital ratio, provided there was not an offsetting decline in the growth rate ($\tilde{L}_t$) of the capital stock.

D. *The Production Function of Legal Precedents*

The actual production of legal precedents combines two basic inputs: (1) the resource inputs of the parties to legal disputes in litigating their disputes in the courts and (2) the inputs of judges in writing judicial opinions that will operate as precedents in future cases. A mysterious aspect of the production process is the apparent absence of market incentives. Consider first the production of precedents from the point of view of the disputants. The individual or firm that brings a case that becomes an important precedent—a *Hadley v. Baxendale* or a *Marbury v. Madison*—receives no "royalty" or other compensation from use of the case to decide subsequent cases. To be sure, some litigants (for example, railroads defending tort suits or the government prosecuting antitrust violations) anticipate the recurrence, in future litigation to which they will be parties, of the issues involved in the current litigation, and such litigants have an interest in the precedent produced by the litigation. But most litigants do not anticipate a recurrence of the same or even of similar issues in future litigation to which they will be parties, and from their standpoint the precedent produced by the current litigation is a worthless by-product of dispute resolution. This raises the question of how the demand for precedents shown in Figure I, a good that accrues primarily to the community as a whole rather than to individual litigants, can be translated into a private demand which will induce the private production of precedents.

The answer lies in an understanding of why litigation, as distinct from out-of-court settlement, ever occurs, given that normally it is costlier than settlement. Economic analysis suggests that, in general, litigation will occur only when the parties are unable to agree on the likely outcome of the litigation, and more particularly when one party (or both) significantly exaggerates the probability that it will prevail.[33] Thus the ratio of lawsuits to settlements is mainly a function of the amount of uncertainty, which leads to divergent estimates by the parties of the probable outcome of litigation. The amount of legal uncertainty[34] is, in turn, a function of the stock of legal rules, a stock in most areas of the law composed largely of precedents.

The ultimate dependence of the litigation rate on the stock of legal knowledge assures that at least one of the critical inputs into production of precedents, the litigants' research and advocacy, will respond in a manner at least roughly congruent with the social need for it. Absence or depletion of the relevant legal capital incites litigation, which produces precedents as a by-

---

[33] See John P. Gould, The Economics of Legal Conflicts, 2 J. Leg. Studies 279, 285, 288-90 (1973); William M. Landes, An Economic Analysis of the Courts, in Essays in the Economics of Crime and Punishment 164, 170-73 (Gary S. Becker & William M. Landes eds. 1974); Richard A. Posner, *supra* note 2, at 418-20, 422-26.

[34] We ignore, as irrelevant to the production of precedents, uncertainty purely over issues of fact, as distinct from legal issues, though factual uncertainty may also lead to litigation.

product and thereby builds up the stock. Suppose, for example, that a completely new statute has just been enacted. There are no precedents indicating how the statute is to be applied to a variety of specific disputes (we can assume that like most statutes this one is ambiguously or at least generally worded). Initially, therefore, there will be great uncertainty as to the practical meaning of the statute. The uncertainty will increase the private costs of negotiating out-of-court settlements of disputes resulting from attempts to apply the statute because the outcome of litigation over the meaning of the statute will be difficult to predict. Hence a good deal of litigation can be expected to occur and, as a by-product, precedents defining the precise meaning of the statute will be generated. As the stock of legal knowledge relating to the statute is built up, uncertainty will fall, and with it the amount of litigation and hence the production of additional precedents. But uncertainty will not be eliminated; as changing social or economic conditions generate new kinds of disputes over the application of the statute the stock of prior legal knowledge will depreciate, inducing litigation that will produce fresh precedents.

This analysis suggests how it has been possible for the Anglo-American legal system to rely, for almost a thousand years, on the uncompensated efforts of litigants to create most of the legal rules administered by the legal system. There are, to be sure, alternative methods of inducing the production of precedents. One is government subsidy. Since the end of the fee system of defraying judicial expenses, litigation has been (modestly) subsidized by having the expense of judicial personnel, court facilities, etc. defrayed by the taxpayer rather than by the litigants. Another possibility would be to give the litigants property rights in the precedents generated in any lawsuit to which they were parties. Just as a composer receives a royalty every time a song he has written is played on a radio station, so—in principle anyway—a litigant could be given a royalty every time that a case he had brought (or defended[35]) was cited in the brief or oral argument of a subsequent case.

Before appraising these alternatives, we must consider the incentives of the judges, the other critical input into the production of legal precedents, to participate in that production. The independence of the judiciary (especially of the federal judiciary, the focus of our attention in this paper) from the political branches of the government[36] makes it extremely difficult to model judicial behavior in economic terms; the outcome of a case seems unrelated to the judge's welfare. One approach is to posit that the independent judge derives utility by imposing his policy preferences on the community. This

[35] Presumably, defendants would be entitled to a share in the royalties only when the issue for which the case was cited had been raised by the defendant (rather than the plaintiff) in the original case by way of defense to the charge.

[36] See William M. Landes & Richard A. Posner, The Independent Judiciary in an Interest-Group Perspective, 18 J. Law & Econ. 875 (1975).

approach, which is broadly consistent with the ordinary assumptions of self-interested behavior employed in economic analysis, is helpful in explaining why a judge might want to create precedents rather than just resolve disputes: to the extent it is followed in subsequent decisions, the precedent will affect more behavior. Indeed, dispute resolution *as such* affects no behavior; it merely redistributes the losses created by some past incident, and those are sunk costs.

Less obviously perhaps, this approach may also explain why judges *follow* precedents. It is the practice of deciding in accordance with precedent that makes decisions operate as precedents. No matter how willful a judge is, he is likely to follow precedent to some extent, for if he did not the practice of decision according to precedent (*stare decisis,* the lawyers call it) would be undermined and the precedential significance of his own decisions thereby reduced. There is, to be sure, a potentially serious free-rider problem. The judge who disregards all precedents but his own may gain more utility in increased freedom to impose his personal preferences on the community than he loses by contributing to a general erosion of the principle of adherence to precedent. But the free-rider problem is held in check by the structure of appellate review. Usually there is one court, with relatively few members, which is supreme within any given jurisdiction. Its power to reverse the decisions of lower courts checks any tendencies on the part of lower-court judges to disregard precedent (reversal foils a judge's attempt to create his own precedent), and its own position in the judicial hierarchy checks its members' tendencies in that direction. If the U.S. Supreme Court refuses to accord precedential weight to earlier Supreme Court decisions, it thereby undermines the precedential weight of its own decisions. To be sure, the trade-off is a complicated one, and we would not expect—nor do we find— that the balance is always in favor of adherence to precedent. In particular, it would appear that judges whose decisions are not subject to reversal by a higher court will adhere to precedent less consistently than those judges whose decisions can be reversed. Our argument, however, is not that precedent is always adhered to, but that decision according to precedent will often constitute rational self-interested behavior of judges who personally disagree with the precedent in question.

If there is a judicial demand for legal advocacy that will assist courts in adhering to old and formulating new precedents, the litigants will supply such assistance even though their only interest is in resolving a dispute. However, although this point might seem to imply that the provision of subsidy or ASCAP-type royalties may not be necessary to prevent underproduction of precedents, it ignores the availability of substitute modes of dispute resolution—such as private arbitration—that do not involve the production of precedents and hence are less costly to the disputants. To avoid inefficient substitution away from the courts, a public subsidy of court litigation may be justified after all. (An alternative would be to tax private arbitration.) And since the identification of a case that will be an important precedent may be difficult or impossible to make in advance, a general subsidy of litigation may be more efficient than an attempt to subsidize just those litigants who is fact contribute to the production of precedents.

The question whether judges indeed follow the principle of *stare decisis* or decision according to precedent can be approached empirically by asking what a refusal to decide cases according to precedent would imply with regard to the citation practices of judges. (A preliminary question might be, if judges do not follow precedent why do they cite cases at all? The answer might be, to fool people into thinking they were following precedent. But we distrust explanations that assume persistent gullibility on the part of the community.) Such a practice would imply that the observed depreciation rate of precedents was zero: the judge who is indifferent to the precedential significance of the cases will tend to pick cases to cite from past years roughly in proportion to the amount of gross investment, implying (as we show in the next section) zero depreciation.[37]

A more plausible rival to the hypothesis that judges decide in accordance with precedent, giving due weight to depreciation, is that judges, in some courts and some periods, disregard the precedents established by their predecessors; they try to change the law to make it conform to their own views of public policy. This practice, sometimes called "judicial activism" and frequently associated with the "Warren Court" of the 1960s, does not imply an indifference to precedent as such, and hence does not imply a zero depreciation rate. Rather, it implies a desire on the part of the judges to replace the precedents of an earlier period with new, contrary precedents. Precisely what the citation practice of an activist court would be is unclear. The court might cite few cases; or it might reach back into the distant past for prececents, in which event the observed depreciation rate of the precedents *cited by it* might be low. Presumably, as the activist court produced more and more of its own precedents (namely, by deciding cases), the measured depreciation rate of precedents cited by it would rise, for it would tend to cite its own precedents, which would be recent, and not to cite (many) precedents of earlier judges. What seems unambiguous, however, is the impact of judicial activism on the depreciation rate of precedents cited in the decisions of a *lower* court. If the Warren Court was indeed an unusually activist one, then the depreciation rates of Supreme Court precedents should be lower in our sample of 1960 court of appeals cases (prior to the heyday of the Warren Court) than in our 1974-1975 court of appeals sample. The courts of appeals are bound by the precedents created by the Supreme Court and if the Warren Court destroyed much existing legal capital, replacing it with its own

---

[37] The same implication—a zero depreciation rate—could be derived from a seemingly opposite theory of judicial behavior: that judges are so blindly wedded to precedent that they don't realize that a precedent ever depreciates. But perhaps this is the same theory, in that it implies a rejection of (rational) adherence to precedent.

(necessarily recent) precedents, this would show up in an increase in the depreciation rate of Supreme Court precedents in the courts of appeals.

IV. EMPIRICAL ANALYSIS

A. *Specification of the Model*

There are two basic techniques for using the age distribution of citations to estimate rates of depreciation or obsolescence of legal capital. The first makes exclusive use of the mean of the age distribution. In its crudest form, the rate of depreciation is inferred solely from the reciprocal of the average age of citations; thus, the older the average age, the lower the depreciation rate. This procedure has a counterpart in the citation analyses of sociologists of science, where the age of citations to scholarly works is used to develop measures of the relative "hardness" of different scientific disciplines, the rate at which scientific knowledge diffuses, its rate of obsolescence, and other phenomena. The second technique we employ, a far more efficient one (as we show below), makes use of the entire frequency distribution of citations to earlier decisions, not just the mean. Using regression analysis, we are able to estimate depreciation rates and extend the empirical analysis to the determination of the forces affecting investment, depreciation, and capital, and the interrelationship among these variables.

1. *Average Age of Citations.* The reader will recall our earlier derivation of the stock of legal capital in equation (3). By utilizing the assumption of a constant nonnegative rate of growth of legal capital, equal to θ, which implies an identical constant rate of growth of gross investment,[38] we can transform equation (3) into

$$L_t = I_{t-1} \left[\frac{1}{(\delta + \gamma - \delta\gamma)} \right] \tag{8}$$

where $\gamma = \theta/(1+\theta)$ and the number of periods is sufficiently large so that $[(1-\delta)(1-\gamma)]^t \approx 0$. The proportion of precedents in this stock that are exactly one year old (I_{t-1}/L_t) equals $(\delta + \gamma - \delta\gamma)$; the proportion of two-year-old precedents (I_{t-2}/L_t) equals $(\delta + \gamma - \delta\gamma)(1-\delta)(1-\gamma)$; and, more generally, the proportion of precedents that are A_j years old is given by

$$f(A_j) = (\delta + \gamma - \delta\gamma)[(1-\delta)(1-\gamma)]^{j-1} \tag{9}$$

Now assume that we have a random sample of type i cases to be decided in period t and the stock of precedents relevant to these cases is given by equation (8). Since each proportion $f(A_j)$ can be interpreted as the probability of selecting a precedent that is A_j years old, the mathematical expectation or mean age of A_j is given by

$$E(A_j) = \sum_j f(A_j)A_j = (\delta + \gamma - \delta\gamma)[\sum_j A_j[(1-\delta)(1-\gamma)]^{j-1}], \tag{10}$$

[38] See note 27 *supra.*

111

which simplifies to

$$E(A_j) = \frac{1}{(\delta + \gamma - \delta\gamma)},\qquad(11)$$

assuming again that t is sufficiently large.

This result can be made clearer by an example. If today's capital stock contained some precedents that were one year old, some two years old, etc., and these precedents had been produced over time at a constant (nonnegative) growth rate of θ and had in turn depreciated at a constant rate of δ, then the mean age of precedents (citations) would be given by equation (11). Therefore, if one were able to estimate the growth rate and the average age, equation (11) could be used to calculate the depreciation rate. For example, a 10-year mean age and growth rate of 5 per cent per year would yield in the limit a 5.5 per cent depreciation rate. Finally, if either the depreciation rate or the growth rate were zero, equation (11) would simplify to $1/\gamma$ or $1/\delta$ respectively.

There are two drawbacks to this procedure for estimating depreciation rates. First, the assumption of a constant growth rate of investment—a convenient mathematical simplification—depends on the assumption that the legal system is on a long-run equilibrium growth path. For certain substantive areas of the law, the evidence strongly contradicts this assumption. Civil rights is the most obvious example. We have estimated that the production of precedents in the U.S. courts of appeals in the civil-rights area has been growing at an annual rate of 15.6 per cent since 1953 (the first year that civil rights cases were separately classified by the Administrative Office of the U.S. Courts). This is more than three times the average rate of precedent production in the courts of appeals.[39] Similarly, the civil-rights growth rate has been 7.3 per cent in the U.S. Supreme Court since 1948, compared to an overall (that is to say, all our subject-matter classes taken together) growth rate of 1.2 per cent. Changing social and economic conditions and their interaction with legislation over the last 25 years have induced a rapid increase in the demand for civil-rights precedents, but it would be highly questionable to assume that this is the long-run equilibrium growth in the demand for civil-rights precedents. Probably the growth in civil-rights precedents prior to the 1950's was closer to the overall growth rate of precedents in the courts of appeals and Supreme Court.[40]

A second drawback of this procedure is the absence of a measure of the standard error of the calculated depreciation rates. Although one can test the

[39] See the discussion and tables on investment in Appendix B, pp. 294-307 *infra*.

[40] One can respond crudely to the question of a nonconstant growth rate by deriving an expression for the mean age of citations in which age is expressed as a function of a single depreciation rate but two growth rates: a growth rate from the base period to period j and a growth rate from j to the current period, t. Given data on average and on the two growth rates (for example, the civil-rights growth rates before and after 1953), one can estimate the depreciation rate by an iterative procedure.

significance of differences in average ages of citations across subject-matter classes and between the Supreme Court and the courts of appeals, there is no readily available technique for testing the significance of differences in the depreciation rates themselves.

2. *The Age Distribution of Citations.* Let P_t^o denote the number of precedents produced t years ago (t = 0, 1, 2, . . . , T) that have survived to the current period 0, and C_t^o the number of citations in period 0 to judicial decisions t years ago. Assume that citations and precedents are related as follows:

$$P_t^o = kC_t^o \exp(u_t) \qquad (12)$$

where k is a proportionality factor between citations and precedents,[41] u_t is a random error term (for example, due to sampling errors in data collection), and $\exp(u_t)$ is e raised to the power u_t. The proportionality condition—the key assumption that allows one to use citations to study precedents—states that if, for example, we observe twice as many citations to decisions of X than 2X years ago, then twice as many precedents have survived into the present from the former than from the latter period. This example is also helpful in illustrating the implicit weighting scheme built into our empirical analysis. In recording the number of citations, our case readers made no distinction between two citations to a single case from t years ago and the citation of two such cases; in both instances the number of citations to t-years-old decisions would be two.[42] Thus, it is possible (though unlikely) that one would observe twice as many citations to decisions of X than to those of 2X years ago, yet the number of decisions actually cited in the two periods would be identical. Even so, one would not want to assign equal precedential significance to the surviving precedents from the two different time periods, and our method of counting citations weights decisions more heavily the more often they are cited. In our hypothetical example twice as many *equivalent* decisions (that is, decisions of equivalent precedential significance) would have survived from X- than from 2X-years-old decisions even though an equal number of cases from both periods continued being cited.[43] More generally, estimates of depreciation in our study are based on decisions of equal precedential significance where significance is assumed to be proportional to citations.

Let I_t^* equal the annual investment in precedent production that occurred t years ago, and assume that

[41] No substantive meaning can be attached to k, since it is a positive function of sample size; that is, the more cases in the sample, the more citations there will be and hence the greater k will be.

[42] However, we count only once multiple citations to an earlier decision if that decision is being cited for the same point in the same case. See note 3 *supra*.

[43] Not only is our method preferable to one that assigns equal weight to all prior cited decisions, but it greatly reduces the costs of data collection. Much more detailed information on citations must be kept in order to record citations in different sample cases to the same decision.

$$I_t^* = mI_t \exp(v_t), \tag{13}$$

where I_t equals our estimate of I_t^* based on a count of written opinions t years ago, m is a proportionality factor applicable to investment, and v_t is a random error term. The number of precedents that have survived from t years ago to period 0 equals investment in that earlier period discounted by the depreciation rate,[44] as in

$$P_t^0 = I_t^* \exp(-\delta t). \tag{14}$$

By making the appropriate substitutions, taking logs, and rearranging terms, our estimating equation becomes

$$\ln (C_t^0/I_t) = \alpha + \beta t + \epsilon_t \tag{15}$$

where α is a constant (equal to $\ln(m/k)$), β equals $-\delta$, and ϵ_t is a disturbance term assumed to be subject to first-order serial correlation (that is, $\epsilon_t = \rho\epsilon_{t-1} + e_t$ where ρ equals the serial correlation coefficient and e_t is a random disturbance term with mean zero). Since we have data on both the age distribution of citations and the annual number of written opinions, a simple regression (with an adjustment for serial correlation) of the log of the citation-investment ratio on time will yield an estimate of the depreciation rate.[45]

The regression method of estimating depreciation has several important advantages compared to that of the mean age. First, it enables a measure of the statistical significance of δ; this facilitates the testing of hypotheses. Second, there is no need to assume a steady-state equilibrium in which the capital stock and investment are growing at a constant rate. Third, equation (15) can be the foundation of a more complete estimation system for the determinants of depreciation and investment. A possible specification of this system in addition to equation (15) would include

$$\delta_t = \psi_1 + \psi_2 X_t + \epsilon_t' \tag{16}$$

$$I_t = \phi_1 + \phi_2\bar{\delta}_t + \phi_3 Y_t + \epsilon_t'' \tag{17}$$

where X_t is a vector of variables determining the depreciation rate in period t (possibly, turnover in judicial personnel and new legislation); Y_t is a vector of variables affecting the level of gross investment (possibly, changes in population, national income, legislation and the stock of legal capital); and $\bar{\delta}_t$ is an average of depreciation rates prior to t (since depreciation is expected to influence investment). We mention this more complete equation system, which is not estimated here but will be utilized in subsequent work on a

[44] For convenience we use a continuous time specification in the empirical analysis.

[45] Michael C. Lovell, *supra* note 4, employs a similar though less efficient regression technique to estimate the depreciation rate of economic knowledge. He estimates a regression of citations on time and then computes depreciation by subtracting an estimate of the growth rate of articles from the regression coefficients.

more comprehensive sample, because it shows clearly the interesting extensions that are possible when one integrates citation data into a regression framework.

B. *Depreciation-Rate and Capital-Stock Estimates*

1. *The Problem of Measuring Investment.* Before presenting our estimates of depreciation and of the capital stock of precedents, we discuss briefly how we measured investment. It might appear straightforward to measure the annual investment in the production of precedents—all one needs to know is the number of cases decided each year in the relevant court and subject-matter category. In fact, there are serious estimation problems.[46] The first is the problem of what to count as a precedent—all terminations, only contested terminations, all terminations in which an opinion is written, or only signed majority opinions (as distinct from per curiam and memorandum opinions)? Since only a decision in which an opinion is issued is likely to be cited in a subsequent decision, it is clearly appropriate to limit the pool of precedents to such decisions. Unfortunately, data on the number of written opinions are not published for the courts of appeals but must be tabulated by counting the opinions contained in the more than 800 volumes of the Federal Reporter.

Second, the available statistical data on subject matter are inadequate, and increasingly so the further back in time one goes. Subject-matter data are available for the Supreme Court back to 1930 but for the courts of appeals only since 1947 and only for cases commenced, not for cases terminated or for written opinions. If we assume that the distribution by subject matter of cases commenced in the courts of appeals is proportional to that of written opinions in those courts, then the distribution of written opinions by subject matter can be computed by multiplying the relevant proportion by our estimate of the total number of written opinions. But to obtain estimates of investment by subject matter in both the courts of appeals and the Supreme Court for years in which such data are not available a more arbitrary assumption must be made: that the distribution of opinions by subject matter in those years is equal to that of the earliest years for which such data are available. However, this assumption is not likely to create serious errors in our regression estimates of depreciation even though those estimates are generally based on a 100-year period: since our citation data have been aggregated for the early years, the number of *observations* for years prior to 1948 or 1930 is far fewer than the number of *years* between 1847 and 1930 or 1948.[47]

---

[46] Because it would burden the test unduly to recount our efforts in trying to deal with these problems, here we merely summarize the main problems and our solution to them. See Appendix B for a more detailed discussion of these problems as well as tables on investment.

[47] Our age distributions record the number of citations for each year from 1948 through 1973-1974 (a total of 25 observations); the average number of citations per year over 5-year

A further problem with our estimation procedure is the difficulty of matching citation and investment data by subject-matter classes. For example, our estimate of annual investment in civil-rights precedents is restricted to opinions in civil-rights cases, yet some citations in a sample civil-rights case may not be to prior civil-rights decisions but to decisions in other fields of law. Although this error is likely to understate actual investment within a subject-matter area, we have no reason to believe that it is systematically related to time. Hence the error would enter the residual term in equation (15), reducing the estimated R^2. The error is also likely to be relatively more important (and the R^2 lower), the more narrowly the subject-matter class is defined. This result is generally consistent with our findings in the empirical analysis.

2. *Depreciation-Rate Estimates.* Tables 4 and 5 present regression estimates derived from equation (15) of the depreciation rates by subject-matter classes of the precedents cited in our 1974-1975 court of appeals (Table 4) and Supreme Court (Table 5) samples.[48] Both ordinary-least-squares (OLS) and Cochrane-Orcutt generalized-least-squares (GLS) estimates are presented—the GLS method to deal with the assumed first-order serial correlation of the disturbance term. The estimated depreciation rates are nearly always positive, generally within a range of two to seven per cent per year, and most are statistically significant.[49] Several of our estimates, however, are based on a small number of cases, and though statistically significant are nevertheless unreliable.[50]

---

intervals from 1924-1948 (that is, a total of 5 observations); and the average number per year over 10-year intervals from 1874-1923 (that is, a total of 5 observations). Thus, only 6 of 35 observations in the regression analyses of citation data to the Supreme Court and 8 of 33 observations in the other-courts regression are for years in which investment data by subject matter are not directly available. There are only 33 observations in regressions of citation data to other courts because the U.S. courts of appeals were not established until 1892.

[48] Complete regression results appear in Appendix A, *infra.* The methods used in estimating depreciation rates in Tables 4 and 5 correspond to the unweighted method of estimating the age of citations. See p. 255 *supra.* Procedural and substantive citations were merged for purposes of making these estimates.

[49] In Table 4, δ is positive in 64 of 66 equations, statistically significant (.05 level) in 55, marginally significant (.10 level) in 5, and not significant in the remaining 6. In Table 5, δ is positive in all 22 equations, significant in 18, and marginally significant in 2 more. Of course, not all of these equations are independent (for example, the OLS and GLS equations, and the equations that aggregate several subject-matter classes into a larger class). The difference between the OLS and GLS estimates are for the most part negligible.

[50] Although the number of observations is typically 35 in regressions to Supreme Court precedents and 33 in regressions to other-court precedents, the number of sample cases that are the basis for the data need only be equal to one, for it is possible to estimate a regression on $\ln (C_i^2/I_i)$ using the citations contained in a single sample case. We of course do not expect the citations in a single case to yield a reliable estimate of δ, and in general the more sample cases in a subject-matter class the more reliable should be our estimate. In the Supreme Court sample, the number of cases in the detailed classes was often too small for us to make reliable estimates (for example, in citations to other-court cases there are only 2 admiralty, 6 tax, 5 antitrust, 2 patents, 5 bankruptcy and 2 land cases; see Table 2 for the number of cases in other categories). Even in the 1974-1975 court of appeals sample, the small numbers of cases in

TABLE 4
DEPRECIATION RATES, COURTS OF APPEALS, 1974-1975

Subject-Matter Classification	Citations to Other-Court Cases				Citations to Supreme Court Cases			
	S	n	Depreciation Rate Estimates		S	n	Depreciation Rate Estimates	
			OLS	GLS			OLS	GLS
All Classes	629	33	.052***	.042***	492	35	.042***	.038***
Common Law	114	33	.043***	.042***	61	35	.026**	.025**
Torts and Contracts	94	33	.040***	.040***	41	35	.018	.016
Admiralty	20	33	.065***	.063***	20	35	.031**	.030*
Economic Regulation	176	33	.067***	.062***	132	35	.055***	.055***
Tax	33	33	.054***	.052***	26	35	.059***	.059***
Antitrust	12	22	.157**	.142**	10	33	.021	.018
Labor	52	33	.118***	.118***	45	35	.053***	.053***
Other federal regulatory agencies	47	33	.086***	.085***	34	35	.029***	.036***
Patents	32	33	.033***	−.061*	17	34	.050***	.047***
Civil Rights	43	22	.320***	.331***	40	32	.029*	.036*
Constitutional (excl. criminal)					17	35	.049***	.049***
Criminal (All)	227	33	.050***	.043***	202	35	.026***	.024***
Criminal (const.)	44	33	.079***	.073***	45	35	.029**	.026*
Criminal (nonconst.)	183	33	.048***	.043***	157	35	.028***	.028***
Bankruptcy	17	33	.015	−.005	8	35	.022*	.024**
Land	8	33	.050***	.048	8	32	.011	.005

Notes:
1. ***—significant at .01 level in two-tail tests
   **—significant at .05 level in two-tail tests
   *—significant at .10 level in two-tail tests
2. OLS: ordinary least squares.
3. GLS: Cochrane-Oructt method of generalized least squares.
4. S: number of sample cases.
5. n: number of observations in OLS regression analysis.
6. For the complete regressions see Appendix A, *infra.*

TABLE 5
DEPRECIATION RATES, SUPREME COURT, 1974 TERM

	Citations to Other-Court Cases				Citations to Supreme Court Cases			
	S	n	Depreciation Rate Estimates		S	n	Depreciation Rate Estimates	
			OLS	GLS			OLS	GLS
All Classes	122	33	.039***	.030***	156	35	.033***	.030***
Common Law	10	33	.035*	.027	13	35	.024*	.021
Economic Regulation	40	33	.052***	.050***	48	35	.038***	.037***
Civil Rights	9	22	.186***	.191***	13	35	.022***	.022***
Constitutional (excl. crim.)					32	35	.033***	.031***
Criminal	28	33	.048**	.046**	37	35	.017***	.016**

Notes. See Table 4.

TABLE 6
CAPITAL-STOCK ESTIMATES

Subject-Matter	Depreciation Rate	Court of Appeals Precedents 1949-1973			1894-1973		
		L	ΣI	Ratio	L	ΣI	Ratio
All	.042	53,680	80,349	.67	63,839	141,188	.45
Common Law	.042	11,673	18,495	.63	14,402	34,902	.41
Economic Regulation	.062	12,794	24,620	.52	14,629	48,414	.30
Tax	.052	3,533	6,773	.52	4,560	15,859	.29
Antitrust	.142	366	971	.38	n.a.	n.a.	n.a.
Labor	.118	681	1,675	.41	708	3,999	.18
Other federal reg. agencies	.085	5,869	13,239	.44	6,212	23,540	.26
Patents	.033	1,307	1,963	.67	1,801	4,047	.45
Civil Rights	.331	769	2,783	.28	n.a.	n.a.	n.a.
Constitutional		n.a.	n.a.	n.a.	n.a.	n.a.	n.a.
Criminal	.043	21,792	30,805	.71	24,380	47,025	.52
Bankruptcy	.015	2,151	2,571	.84	4,104	6,343	.65
Land	.048	366	617	.59	479	1,472	.33

In our earlier discussion of the production function of precedents, we hypothesized that a court that gave no weight whatever to precedential significance in deciding a case and writing the opinion would act as if its choice of citations depended solely on the relative number of past opinions, and the citations by such a court would tend, therefore, to have a zero depreciation rate. Tables 4 and 5 enable us to reject this hypothesis and the theory of judicial decision-making that underlies it. We also suggested, however, as part of the rudimentary theory of judicial decision-making sketched in that discussion, that judges not constrained by the threat of reversal of their decisions by a higher court would tend to depart more frequently from deciding according to precedent than courts that were so constrained, and that this would show up in a lower depreciation rate of their citations (because they would be giving less weight to the recency of the precedents cited). Some evidence for this hypothesis is provided by a comparison between the depreciation rates in Tables 4 and 5. The depreciation rates of

antitrust (12 citing other-court cases and 10 citing the Supreme Court), bankruptcy (17 and 8) and land (8 and 8) suggest that the estimates of δ for these classes should be viewed cautiously. Notice also that the R^2's tend to be lower in these subject-matter classes; presumably, this is due to a greater amount of error in measuring the dependent variable.

The reason why, in Tables 4 and 5, the number of observations in the regression analysis was sometimes less than either 35 or 33 (for example, 22 in antitrust and civil rights in Table 4) is that in some years there were neither citations nor investment. For example, in the civil-rights area, there were no citations to cases and no (measured) investment before 1952. We excluded from the analysis any year when both citations and investment were zero, but if there were positive citations but zero investment, or positive investment but zero citations, then the year was included. In the former case we arbitrarily assumed that investment equaled 1, and in the latter case that the number of citations equaled .01.

TABLE 6 (*Continued*)

Subject-Matter	Depreciation Rate	Supreme Court Precedents 1949-1973			1874-1973		
		L	ΣI	Ratio	L	ΣI	Ratio
All	.038	1,373	2,104	.65	2,026	7,127	.28
Common Law	.025	163	234	.69	389	1,217	.32
Economic Regulation	.055	498	926	.54	658	3,596	.18
Tax	.059	75	153	.49	145	1,826	.08
Antitrust	.018	128	160	.80	180	290	.62
Labor	.053	129	240	.54	141	411	.34
Other federal reg. agencies	.036	229	345	.66	285	605	.46
Patents	.047	19	32	.59	51	481	.11
Civil Rights	.036	71	95	.75	78	150	.52
Constitutional	.049	709	1,106	.64	900	3,871	.23
Criminal	.024	618	801	.77	815	1,495	.55
Bankruptcy	.024	23	31	.75	130	478	.27
Land	.005	20	24	.83	122	249	.49

Notes:

1. The depreciation rates used in computing capital stock estimates are from the GLS regressions in Table 4, except for the court of appeals precedents in the patent and bankruptcy classes, where we used the OLS estimates because of the negative depreciation rates generated by the GLS method.

2. L = capital stock in the beginning of 1974.

3. ΣI = summation of investment unadjusted for depreciation.

4. n.a. = not available because no subject-matter breakdown was possible.

5. Antitrust and civil rights estimates for the court of appeals is for the period 1952-1973.

both Supreme Court and lower court precedents cited by the Supreme Court are almost uniformly lower than those cited by the courts of appeals. Of the ten possible comparisons from the GLS regressions (holding court and subject matter constant), nine depreciation rates are lower in the Supreme Court sample (Table 5) than the court of appeals sample (Table 4). This suggests that the Supreme Court pays less attention to recency (authority) in its citations than the courts of appeals—as we would expect since Supreme Court decisions cannot be reversed by a higher court.

3. *Capital-Stock Estimates.* Table 6 presents estimates of the stock of legal capital for precedents produced in the Supreme Court and in the courts of appeals (see equation (3)). Two estimates are given for each court. One is the capital stock of precedents produced in the period 1949 to 1973; the other is the stock produced in the longer period from 1874 (1894 for the courts of appeals) to 1973. The second estimate is the more comprehensive but is subject to substantially greater error because of the difficulty, noted earlier, of classifying very old cases by subject matter.

The precise interpretation of these numerical estimates is somewhat unclear. Since cases differ in their precedential significance, a pure count of cases or even one adjusted for depreciation does not reveal whether the capital stock of precedents is really larger in one subject-matter area than in another, or larger in the Supreme Court than in the courts of appeals. A more illuminating statistic, also shown in Table 6, is the ratio of the capital stock to accumulated investment (unadjusted for depreciation). This ratio tells us the proportion of precedents produced over a given period that have survived to 1974. For example, the ratio .63 for court of appeals common law precedents indicates that 63 per cent of these precedents produced in the period 1949-1973 have survived into 1974. This ratio can be meaningfully compared both across subject-matter classes and between courts. (For example, 67 per cent of common law precedents produced in the Supreme Court have survived into 1974 compared to 63 per cent for the courts of appeals.) Usually (but not always) a high depreciation rate will be associated with a low rate of survival of precedents.[51] To take an extreme example, a 33 per cent depreciation rate of civil rights precedents produced in the courts of appeals yields a 28 per cent survival rate of precedents produced between 1949 and 1973. As one might expect from the generally lower depreciation rates in the Supreme Court, the precedents produced in that court between 1949 and 1973 usually have a higher survival rate than those produced in the courts of appeals.[52] The differences in survival rates, however, are generally of relatively smaller magnitude than the differences in depreciation rates because of the more rapid growth in investment in recent years in the courts of appeals than in the Supreme Court.

C. Tests of Other Hypotheses

In this section, we present results of empirical tests of the remaining hypotheses developed earlier. These hypotheses concern (1) generality versus specificity of precedents, (2) effect of statutory activity, (3) procedural versus substantive precedents, (4) effects of uncertainty, and (5) Warren Court activism.

1. *General Versus Specific Legal Capital.* We hypothesized that Supreme Court precedents were more general than those of other courts (particularly the federal courts of appeals), and hence would depreciate more slowly. The results for the 1974-1975 courts of appeals sample in Table 4 are consistent with this hypothesis. The depreciation rate of Supreme Court citations is lower than that of other courts in 13 of the 16 possible comparisons using the GLS method. The major exception is federal taxation. The two other exceptions are the patent and bankruptcy classes, where we estimate negative depreciation rates from the GLS regressions (though a 95 per cent confidence interval includes positive depreciation rates for both classes) and positive rates from the OLS regressions. Incidentally, these are the only two negative depreciation estimates in our entire set of regressions.

[51] If high depreciation is offset by a rapid growth in investment, then the survival rate of precedents produced over a given period might be independent of the depreciation rate.

[52] Higher survival rates for Supreme Court precedents occur in most subject-matter classes but not in the "all" category.

The results from our sample of Supreme Court decisions are similar, but less marked—indeed, for all classes together, the Supreme Court and other-court depreciation rates are the same, using the GLS method. The explanation for the difference in this regard between the Supreme Court and court of appeals samples may be that, in general, decisions of other courts do not have substantial precedential significance in the Supreme Court and the Court may therefore be less concerned with their recency, which is an important attribute of a citation viewed as a precedent. This is consistent with our earlier attempt to explain the lower depreciation rates generally in the Supreme Court sample.

The hypothesis that Supreme Court precedents tend to be more general compared to other-court precedents can be tested indirectly by examining the *number* of citations per case to Supreme Court and other-court decisions. If Supreme Court precedents are indeed more general (implying that they cover more issues), then in a given opinion there should be fewer citations to Supreme Court than other-court decisions. The results for the court of appeals sample presented in Table 7 are consistent with this hypothesis; the

TABLE 7
AVERAGE NUMBER OF CITATIONS PER CASE, 1974-1975 COURT OF APPEALS
SAMPLE AND SUPREME COURT, 1974 TERM

	Court of Appeals Sample		Supreme Court Sample	
	Supreme Court Citations	Other-Court Citations	Supreme Court Citations	Other-Court Citations
All Classes	4.6	9.2	15.0	7.7
Common Law	3.5	9.3	12.0	11.5
Economic Regulation	4.4	9.4	11.3	8.6
Civil Rights	4.3	9.3	21.9	8.2
Criminal	4.9	9.1	14.0	6.6
Constitutional	8.0	8.2	17.5	6.7

Notes: See Table 2.

average number of Supreme Court citations is about half that of other-court citations in the broad subject-matter classes. Of further interest is the dramatic reversal of these ratios in the Supreme Court sample, which supports our earlier point that decisions of other courts may have little precedential significance in the Supreme Court. There is an interesting difference between the common law area and the other subject-matter areas in the Supreme Court sample: in the common law area the ratio of Supreme Court to other-court citations is 1.04 compared to a ratio of about 2 in the other subject-matter areas. The explanation may lie in the *Erie* decision, which gives other-court (especially state-court) decisions special precedential significance in federal litigation in the common law area.[53]

[53] Erie Railroad Co. v. Tompkins, 304 U.S. 64 (1938), held that in cases brought in federal

2. *Statutory Activity*. We hypothesized that the depreciation rates of legal precedents would be higher in areas of greater statutory change. Tables 4 and 5 provide modest support for this hypothesis. As expected, we find a lower-than-average depreciation rate in the common law area, one of limited statutory change, and a higher-than-average depreciation rate in the economic-regulation and civil-rights fields, both areas of substantial statutory activity. However, there are a number of anomalies, such as the very low depreciation rate of Supreme Court civil-rights precedents in the court of appeals sample (in contrast to a more than 30 per cent annual depreciation rate of other-court precedents), and the much higher depreciation rates of other-court precedents in antitrust (an area of realtively little statutory change over time) compared to tax (an area of great statutory change over time). The antitrust estimates, however, are probably not reliable because they are based on a small sample of cases. Thus, it is not surprising that the difference between the antitrust and tax depreciation rates is reversed for Supreme Court precedents.

There are two very serious problems in measuring the effect of statutory activity on the rate at which precedents obsolesce. The first is the difficulty of measuring statutory activity; simply counting the number of statutory enactments and amendments in an area is no measure of the relevant variable. The second problem is that measuring the effect of statutory activity on the depreciation rate requires that other facts be held constant, notably the depreciation caused by changes in judicial doctrine—an important factor in the antitrust area. Much more work must be done before the statutory-activity hypothesis can be considered either rejected or confirmed.

3. *Procedural Versus Substantive Precedents*. The theory suggests that the procedural precedents cited in cases within a particular subject-matter class should depreciate more slowly than the substantive precedents so cited. This is because the procedural precedent is more general or versatile—it could be used in another subject-matter area (for example, a case deciding a point of pleading in an antitrust case could be used to decide a similar point arising in a tax case). A major problem in testing this hypothesis is our complete lack of data on investment in producing procedural precedents. We can, however, test a weaker version of this hypothesis by comparing average ages. One should observe less variation in average ages across subject-matter classes for procedural than substantive citations because the former (at least in part) come from a common pool of precedents. The results of this comparison are presented in Table 8.

Table 8 provides little support for the hypothesis. There is no significant

---

courts only because of the diversity of citizenship of the parties, the courts had to apply substantive state law, including decisional law. Since most of the common law cases in our sample are diversity cases, the principally relevant precedents are state-law decisions, which are part of the "other court" category. We plan a more refined analysis of precedent in federal diversity cases in subsequent studies.

TABLE 8
MEAN AGES OF SUBSTANTIVE AND PROCEDURAL CITATIONS,
1974-1975 U.S. COURT OF APPEALS SAMPLE

	Supreme Court Citations		Other-Court Citations	
	Substantive	Procedural	Substantive	Procedural
Total	18.2	21.7	10.4	8.0
	[1724]	[554]	[4520]	[1265]
Common Law	31.3	38.2	16.0	9.9
	[186]	[78]	[846]	[215]
Torts and Contracts	32.1	39.7	17.0	10.3
	[74]	[63]	[691]	[165]
Admiralty	30.4	31.5	11.6	8.6
	[61]	[15]	[155]	[50]
Economic Regulation	20.0	17.4	10.5	9.3
	[461]	[127]	[1362]	[298]
Tax	26.5	24.0	15.4	11.2
	[55]	[11]	[303]	[21]
Antitrust	21.1	14.1	6.1	6.9
	[36]	[14]	[57]	[50]
Labor	14.3	17.5	7.9	10.5
	[150]	[36]	[368]	[65]
Other federal	20.0	15.5	7.9	8.2
reg. agencies	[193]	[47]	[399]	[111]
Patents	37.7	20.6	13.6	11.5
	[27]	[19]	[235]	[51]
Civil Rights	8.8	12.2	3.9	4.1
	[105]	[67]	[264]	[138]
Constitutional	15.0	16.6	5.6	6.9
	[393]	[94]	[443]	[118]
Criminal (non-	15.5	18.5	9.0	6.8
const.)	[500]	[148]	[1222]	[428]
Bankruptcy	40.4	29.8	15.3	9.4
	[10]	[4]	[140]	[15]
Land Condemnation	45.2	57.2	20.2	28.2
	[35]	[25]	[40]	[21]

Notes:

1. Mean ages are based on weighted method (see p. 255 supra).

2. In each subject-matter class there are two numbers per column: the top one is the mean age and the bottom one is the number of citations.

difference between the standard deviations of substantive and procedural mean ages across subject-matter classes.[54] Moreover, a regression analysis indicates that the age of substantive citations is a highly significant predictor of the age of procedural citations across subject-matter classes,[55] whereas

[54] The standard deviations across the 12 subject-matter classes are 11.6 and 13.1 years respectively for substantive and procedural citations to Supreme Court precedents, and 5.2 and 6.1 years respectively for substantive and procedural citations to other courts.

[55] The regression estimates are as follows

$$\text{Supreme Court Precedents: } Y_1 = 1.93 + .89X_1 \qquad R^2 = 60$$
$$(4.15)$$
$$\text{Other-Court Precedents: } Y_1 = .36 + .89X_1 \qquad R^2 = 53$$
$$(3.62)$$

123

the "common pool" hypothesis would suggest that ages of substantive citations would *not* be a significant predictor of ages of procedural citations.
There are reasons for doubting these tests rather than the hypothesis. First,
our case readers reported difficulty in classifying cases as procedural versus
substantive—a difficulty any lawyer will understand. Second, our impression is that most of the procedural procedents used in a particular substantive subject-matter area are precedents involving that area—that most procedural precedents are in practice, though not in principle, pretty much
limited in use to the substantive area in which they arose. This is partly an
aspect of the first point (many apparently procedural questions are in fact
influenced by the substantive context) and partly, perhaps, an aspect of
lawyers' research habits (they are more apt to be familiar with the procedural
decisions rendered in cases arising in the substantive areas in which they are
expert). No doubt there is a class of "pure" procedural cases that are of great
generality or versatility, but they may be too few to influence our statistical
results measurably. That, of course, is our rationale for combining substantive and procedural decisions in presenting the depreciation rates reported in
Tables 4 and 5.

4. *Depreciation and Investment.* We hypothesized that the higher the
depreciation rate of precedents, the more difficult it would be to forecast the
outcomes of legal disputes, and the greater the rate of investment in precedent production. One method of testing this hypothesis is to examine the
effect of differences in depreciation rates on the rate of investment across
subject-matter classes. Our estimating equation is of the form

$$\ln I_t^i/L_t^i = \beta_i + \beta_2 \delta^i + u^i \tag{18}$$

where I_t^i is the average annual investment in 1972 and 1973 in the ith
subject-matter class, L_t^i is the capital stock at the end of 1971 in each class,[56]
δ^i is the estimated depreciation rate from the GLS regressions on the 1974-
1975 court of appeals sample in Table 4,[57] and u^i is the disturbance term.
Since there are ten subject-matter classes in the courts of appeals and 11 in
the Supreme Court (the "constitutional" class forming an additional class)
there is a maximum of 21 observations in the regression analysis.

The results presented in Table 9 are consistent with the hypothesis that an

---

where Y_i = mean age of procedural citations in i^{th} subject-matter class, and X_i = mean age of
substantive citations in ith class. The number in parentheses is the t-statistic. There are 12
observations in each regression.

[56] In order to include the court of appeals civil-rights and antitrust classes in the regression
analysis (investment data for these two classes are available only since 1952) we estimated L_t^i
from annual investments over the 20-year period 1952-1971. When the Supreme Court is
analyzed separately, L_t^i can be computed over a 43-year period, 1929-1971, since investment
data for each class are available for this longer period.

[57] There are two exceptions. OLS estimates were used for the patent and bankruptcy precedents produced in the courts of appeals because the GLS method generated negative depreciation rates.

TABLE 9
WEIGHTED INVESTMENT REGRESSIONS

Court	Dependent Variable	n	α	δ	δ_{CA}	δ_{SC}	D	R^2
				Regression Coefficients (t-statistics)				
CA & SC	$\ln I_t/L_t$	21	-1.314		.745	.670	.127	.92
			(1.062)		(4.290)	(11.444)	(.229)	
CA & SC	$\ln I_t/L_t$	21	-1.125	.680			$-.818$	.92
			(1.011)	(13.130)			(.553)	
SC	$\ln I_t/L_{t_t}$	11	-1.870			.755		.88
			(.895)			(8.278)		

Symbols:
CA = U.S. Courts of Appeals
SC = Supreme Court,
I_t = average annual number of written opinions in 1972 and 1973,
L_t = capital stock at the end of 1971 computed from annual investment from 1952-1971 discounted by appropriate depreciation rate,
L_{t_t} = capital stock computed from annual investment from 1929-1971,
D = dummy variable that takes the value 1 for a court of appeals observation and 0 for a Supreme Court observation.

increase in depreciation leads to a positive adjustment in the rate of precedent production. The regression coefficients on the depreciation rates, which are positive and highly significant, indicate that a 10 per cent increase in depreciation is associated with approximately a 7 per cent increase in the rate of precedent production.[58] The elasticity estimate for the Supreme Court is unaffected by an expansion of the number of periods used to measure the capital stock (compare the first and third equations), and there is no significant difference between the Supreme Court and courts of appeals in either the responsiveness of investment to a change in depreciation (that is, the difference between the regression coefficients on δ_{CA} and δ_{SC} in the first equation is not significant) or the investment-capital ratio itself (that is, the coefficient on the dummy court variable is not significant).

There are, however, several potential problems with the analysis. First, there could be spurious positive correlation between I_t/L_t and δ. Since the depreciation rate is used to compute the capital stock, an increase in depreciation would lower the capital stock, giving rise to a positive regression coefficient in equation (18). As it turns out, spurious correlation is not a serious problem since the correlation between the depreciation rate and the capital stock for the 21 subject-matter classes is *positive* (.06) and not significant.[59] Other possible diffculties arise from the limited number of observa-

[58] Each observation in Table 9 was weighted by $\sqrt{C}$ where C is the number of sample cases used to estimate δ^1 in Table 4. Weighted regressions were estimated because the error in the estimated depreciation rates is likely to be a positive function of the number of sample cases. (See p. 280 *supra*.) Unweighted regressions, however, were also estimated, with little change in the results.

[59] For the Supreme Court, the unweighted correlations between δ and L_t are .09 and .04 (depending on whether L_t is computed from annual investment since 1952 or 1929), and for the

290 THE JOURNAL OF LAW AND ECONOMICS

tions in the regression analysis and our failure to include other variables that may affect the demand and supply of precedent production (a failure due in part to the difficulty of identifying variables that are specific to subject-matter classes).[60] Thus, our results should be viewed as preliminary evidence in support of the hypothesis that greater uncertainty about the outcome of legal disputes generates an increase in the rate of litigation and the production of precedents.

5. *Judicial Activism and the Warren Court.* Table 10 presents OLS and GLS depreciation rate estimates for the 1960 court of appeals sample.[61] To facilitate comparison with the 1974-1975 court of appeals sample, we have reproduced the relevant depreciation rates from that sample in columns (3) and (4) of Table 10. Although the sampling rates in the two court of appeals samples were both 10 per cent, the 1960 sample is considerably smaller (223 decisions compared to 653 in the 1974-1975 sample) because of the growth in annual precedent production between 1960 and 1975 and the fact that the 1974-1975 sample is based on approximately 1.5 years of opinions. As a result, fewer subject-matter areas are included in Table 10 because in many areas the 1960 sample lacked a sufficient number of cases to permit reliable estimates of depreciation. Another difference between the two samples is the virtual absence in 1960 of civil-rights and constitutional (both criminal and noncriminal) decisions and the corresponding (relative) reduction in the number of common law and economic regulation cases between 1960 and 1974-1975.

Before assessing the "judicial activism" hypothesis, two further points about the 1960 sample are worth mentioning. The first is that, in each of the subject-matter classes in the 1960 sample, Supreme Court precedents depreciate at a lower rate than other-court precedents. This finding is consistent with our detailed analysis of the 1974-1975 sample and our basic hypothesis that general rules will depreciate at a slower rate than more specific ones. The second point is the increase from 1960 to 1975 in the proportion of sample cases that cite Supreme Court decisions (see Table 11). For example, in the "all" class there is a statistically significant increase in the proportion of opinions citing the Supreme Court (.610 in 1960 compared to .748 in 1974-1975) while the proportion citing other courts remained approximately

courts of appeals the unweighted correlation is −.32. None of these correlation coefficients is significant.

[60] An alternative and promising approach would be to examine investment over time within a subject-matter area. The advantage is that one can identify variables (for example, the volume of business transactions, population changes, key legislation, judicial turnover, subsidies to litigants) that are likely to affect the demand and supply of precedent production. This approach would require one to estimate a depreciation rate that varied over time within a given subject-matter area. (For further discussion see p. 278 *supra*.)

[61] In most instances GLS estimates are unnecessary because first-order serial correlation is not present. Two exceptions are the all and labor classes in the citations to other courts. In one other regression—economic regulation in the citations to other courts—the Durbin-Watson test was inconclusive.

TABLE 10
DEPRECIATION RATES, U.S. COURTS OF APPEALS, 1960 AND 1974-1975 SAMPLES

| | S | n | 1960 Depreciation Rate Estimate | | 1974-1975 Depreciation Rate Estimate | | | |
			OLS (1)	GLS (2)	OLS (3)	GLS (4)	d_1 (3)-(1)	d_2 (4)-(2)
Citations to								
Other Courts								
All Classes	208	24	.049***	.042***	.052***	.042***	.003	.000
Common Law	52	24	.037***	.038***	.043***	.042***	.006	.004
Economic Regulation	88	24	.057***	.053***	.067***	.062***	.010	.009
Tax	32	24	.077***	.076***	.054***	.052***	−.023	−.024
Labor	25	24	.137***	.115***	.118***	.118***	−.019	.003
Criminal	46	24	.061***	.060***	.050***	.043***	−.011	−.017
Citations to								
Supreme Court								
All Classes	136	26	.036***	.035***	.042***	.038***	.006	.003
Common Law	26	26	.003	.002	.026***	.025***	.023	.007
Economic Regulation	61	26	.049***	.047***	.055***	.055***	.006	.008
Tax	25	26	.063***	.063***	.059***	.059***	−.004	−.004
Labor	19	26	.029	.028*	.053***	.053***	.024	.025
Criminal	36	26	.012	.010	.026***	.024***	.014	.014

Notes:

1. Complete regressions are presented in Appendix A.

2. ***—significant at .01 level in two-tail test
    **—significant at .05 level in two-tail test
    *—significant at .10 level in two-tail test

3. S = number of sample cases in 1960 sample.

4. n = number of observations in regression analysis.

5. Complete regression equations are presented in Appendix A.

unchanged (.933 in 1960 and .956 in 1974-1975). The three broad subject-matter classes—common law, economic regulation, and criminal—reveal a similar increase over time in the proportion of decisions citing the Supreme

TABLE 11
PROPORTION OF DECISIONS CITING SUPREME COURT AND OTHER-COURT PRECEDENTS,
1960 AND 1974-1975 U.S. COURT OF APPEALS SAMPLE

| | 1960 | | 1974-1975 | | | |
	Supreme Court (1)	Other Court (2)	Supreme Court (3)	Other Court (4)	d_1 (3)-(1)	d_2 (4)-(2)
All	.610	.933	.748	.956	.138	.023
Common Law	.481	.963	.530	.991	.049	.028
Economic Regulation	.629	.907	.721	.962	.092	.055
Tax	.676	.865	.722	.917	.046	.052
Labor	.731	.962	.849	.981	.118	.019
Criminal	.720	.920	.845	.950	.125	.030

Sources: See Tables 1 and 2.

Court.[62] These figures are superficially surprising. Assuming that the relative availability of Supreme Court compared to other-court precedents, which is determined in part by the relative number of decisions in these courts, influences citation behavior, then with the more rapid growth of precedent production in other courts relative to the Supreme Court since 1960, one might expect to observe a decline over time in the proportion of cases citing Supreme Court relative to those citing other-court precedents. The fact that the opposite effect is observed may reflect a growing authority or generality of Supreme Court precedents since 1960, which would increase the likelihood of their being cited.[63] This interpretation is consistent with our earlier point that the more limited capacity of the Supreme Court compared to the courts of appeals should lead the Supreme Court to become relatively more selective over time in its choice of cases to decide and thus to be choosing cases of greater generality today.

One test of judicial activism is a comparison of the depreciation rates of precedents before and after the period of supposed activism. Since judicial activism in the 1960s would imply an acceleration in the rate of replacement of the precedents created prior to the 1960s, we should observe a higher depreciation rate in the 1974-1975 court of appeals sample than in the 1960 sample if the Warren Court was indeed an unusually activist one. But the results in Table 10 provide only weak support for this hypothesis. There appears to be a slight tendency for depreciation rates of Supreme Court precedents to be higher in 1974-1975 than in 1960 (except in the tax area) but the differences are not significant. With respect to other-court precedents, the differences between the 1974-1975 and 1960 depreciation rates are more mixed and even smaller.

These results must be viewed as inconclusive. Our subject-matter classes may be too gross to detect changes in depreciation due to the Warren Court (for example, we were not able to make comparisons within the civil-rights area). Moreover, by 1974-1975 the reaction to the Warren Court associated with the emergence of a distinctive "Burger Court" may already have resulted in the resurrection of a number of precedents ignored by the Warren Court. In future work we hope to deal with these problems by expanding the number of cases in our samples and by including years between 1960 and 1974-1975.

V.   CONCLUSION AND SUGGESTIONS FOR FUTURE RESEARCH

The concept of precedent is at the heart of the way in which lawyers think about the legal system. And the results of the present study suggest that an

---

[62] The only significant increase, however, is in the criminal subject-matter class. Observe also that there were slight but statistically insignificant increases in the proportion of cases citing other-court decisions. In one class (tax) there was a greater increase from 1960 to 1974-1975 in the proportion of cases citing other courts than in the proportion citing the Supreme Court.

[63] This conclusion is of course a preliminary one. We have only examined two years and thus do not know whether the observed change reflects a persistent trend, as our explanation implies.

approach which treats legal precedents as a form of investment subject to the usual economic laws governing the formation and depreciation of capital may improve our understanding of precedent. But the present study is only preliminary. Future studies involving much larger samples will enable us both to utilize more information about each case and to study additional facets of legal capital. Eventually, we hope to compare the depreciation rates of judicial decisions with those of administrative-agency decisions, statutes, and constitutional provisions, to compare different courts, to examine citation practices in appellate briefs, and to examine the depreciation question from the "case history" as well as the "citation practice" standpoint.[64]

Of particular interest, we believe, would be a study of secular changes in depreciation rates. There is a widely held belief in the academic legal community that adherence to precedent has declined over time, particularly in the U.S. Supreme Court, partly perhaps as a result (or cause?) of the "legal realist" movement. The trend in depreciation rates may cast light on this question, as may a comparison of trends in different courts.

There are many other interesting areas of research on legal precedent, a few of which we shall mention briefly in closing:

1. The services produced by precedents, primarily in creating specific rules of legal obligation and thereby reducing the demand for litigation across subject-matter categories and over time, may, as suggested earlier, be important in explaining changes over time (or across states or federal judicial districts) in the volume of litigation.[65]

2. The measurement of precedential significance by counting citations may prove to hold the key to the problem of evaluating judicial output. For obvious reasons, the number of terminations, trials, or even judicial opinions does not measure the output of a judicial system in a socially interesting sense; the number of precedents—weighted by the significance of each precedent as measured by the number of times it is cited in subsequent decisions—may. A precedent-based measure of judicial output could be compared with the input measures used by the Administrative Office of the U.S. Courts in its "weighted caseload" studies, which measure the amount of judicial time allocable to various substantive and procedural classifications of judicial activity.[66] Precedential significance as a measure of judicial output might also be used to compare the importance of different courts as sources of law and even to evaluate individual judges.

3. The number of law clerks has risen sharply in relation to the number of judges in recent years, but we know of no systematic efforts to appraise the significance of this development. One hypothesis about law clerks which

[64] See p. 254 *supra*.

[65] Indeed, we first became interested in the possibility of studying legal precedents quantitatively as part of an ongoing study of the federal courts since 1874. That study is described briefly in Richard A. Posner, The Economic Approach to Law, 53 Texas L. Rev. 757, 769 (1975).

[66] See, for example, Federal Judicial Center, The 1969-70 Federal District Court Time Study (Statistical Reporting Service, U.S. Dep't of Agriculture, 1971).

could be tested using citation data would be that since law clerks (especially in the federal courts of appeals and Supreme Court) tend to be drawn from a relatively small number of "elite" law schools which employ highly uniform teaching methods and materials, judicial citation practices would tend to become more uniform—with respect to age and number of precedents—over time as law clerks played an increasingly large role in judicial research and opinion writing; and, further, that judicial citation practices would tend to be more uniform in the federal than in the state court system.

4. A comparison of citation practices in appellate briefs and judicial decisions may illuminate some of the fundamental characteristics of legal advocacy. Are there systematic differences between lawyer and judge citation practices? Are there systematic differences between the citation practices of the winning and losing lawyer? The answers to these questions may suggest the contours of an economic theory of legal advocacy.

5. The analysis of precedent may prove helpful in explaining observed characteristics of the legal profession. Current research by Peter Pashigian indicates that lawyers' earnings increase with age relative to those of other professionals. The explanation for this phenomenon may lie in the relatively low depreciation rates of legal precedent (see Tables 4-5). They imply that an important component of lawyers' capital—their knowledge of the substantive rules of law—obsolesces slowly, more slowly, we assume, than the essential knowledge of physicians, engineers, and other professionals. Therefore, when the lawyer reaches the point in his life cycle where additional investments in human capital would not be economical, due to the shortness of the period in which they would yield income, nonetheless his income may persist at a high level since his existing stock of capital will decline slowly. It would be consistent with this analysis to find that older judges cite on average older cases—but that study, too, we leave to the future.

APPENDIX A

The tables that follow contain the complete regression estimates of $\ln(C_t^q/I_t) = \alpha + \beta t + \epsilon_t$ where $\beta = -\delta$. (For convenience we present the coefficient for δ and not β.) Tables A1, A2, and A3 contain respectively the regression estimates for the 1974-1975 U.S. court of appeals sample, the 1974 U.S. Supreme Court term, and the 1960 U.S. court of appeals sample.

APPENDIX B

MEASURING INVESTMENT IN LEGAL PRECEDENT

As explained in the text, the correct measurement of the depreciation rates of legal precedents depends on knowing the number of precedents that are produced each

REGRESSION ESTIMATES: 1974-1975 COURT OF APPEALS SAMPLE

	s	n	Citations to Other Courts							
			OLS				GLS			
			α	δ	R^2	D.W.	α	δ	R^2	D.W.
All Classes	629	33	−2.573 (30.102)	.052 (16.869)	.90	.37	−2.919 (13.891)	.042 (8.020)	.97	2.90
Common Law	114	33	−2.737 (32.165)	.043 (14.057)	.86	1.05	−2.774 (19.114)	.042 (8.992)	.89	2.28
Torts and Contracts	94	33	−2.975 (36.678)	.040 (13.795)	.86	1.22	−2.978 (23.362)	.040 (9.499)	.88	2.15
Admiralty	20	33	−4.402 (13.102)	.065 (5.369)	.48	1.70	−4.480 (11.129)	.063 (4.504)	.47	1.99
Economic Regulation	176	33	−2.283 (20.213)	.067 (16.619)	.90	1.25	−2.412 (13.651)	.062 (10.624)	.91	1.94
Tax	33	33	−2.734 (16.856)	.054 (9.216)	.73	1.65	−2.783 (14.825)	.052 (7.908)	.72	1.84
Antitrust	12	22	−1.882 (2.120)	.157 (2.326)	.21	2.34	−2.063 (2.685)	.142 (2.449)	.22	1.90
Labor	52	33	−.434 (1.335)	.118 (10.136)	.77	1.79	−.417 (1.132)	.118 (9.181)	.77	1.93
Other federal regulatory agencies	47	33	−2.718 (17.882)	.086 (15.780)	.89	1.54	−2.761 (14.019)	.085 (12.597)	.89	2.09
Patents	32	33	−1.950 (6.645)	.033 (3.127)	.24	1.07	−4.648 (2.912)	−.061 (1.762)	.36	1.47
Civil Rights	43	22	−.652 (.879)	.320 (5.668)	.62	1.26	−.465 (.363)	.331 (3.619)	.65	1.49
Constitutional (excl. criminal)										
Criminal (All)	227	33	−2.801 (25.376)	.050 (12.518)	.83	.86	−3.002 (16.465)	.043 (7.462)	.89	2.66
Criminal (const.)	44	33	−4.786 (10.049)	.079 (4.623)	.41	1.67	−4.967 (8.987)	.073 (3.778)	.39	1.93
Criminal (nonconst.)	183	33	−2.996 (29.008)	.048 (12.859)	.84	1.03	−3.128 (19.983)	.043 (8.556)	.88	2.59
Bankruptcy	17	33	−3.399 (8.164)	.015 (.973)	.03	1.24	−3.791 (5.560)	−.005 (.212)	.12	1.73
Land	8	33	−3.255 (5.882)	.050 (2.529)	.17	1.07	−3.286 (3.449)	.048 (1.589)	.35	1.86

TABLE A1 (Continued)

			OLS (Citations to Supreme Court)				GLS			
	s	n	α	δ	R²	D.W.	α	δ	R²	D.W.
All Classes	492	35	.014 (.181)	.042 (18.333)	.91	.71	−.145 (.911)	.038 (9.878)	.95	2.03
Common Law	61	35	−.977 (2.660)	.026 (2.445)	.15	2.16	−1.027 (2.933)	.025 (2.478)	.15	2.03
Torts and contracts	41	35	−1.934 (4.276)	.018 (1.394)	.06	2.32	−2.027 (5.169)	.016 (1.435)	.07	2.01
Admiralty	20	35	−2.290 (4.261)	.031 (2.000)	.11	1.76	−2.308 (3.656)	.030 (1.715)	.12	2.00
Economic Regulation	132	35	−.202 (2.122)	.055 (20.042)	.92	1.61	−.217 (1.816)	.055 (16.427)	.92	1.83
Tax	26	35	−1.707 (3.414)	.059 (4.069)	.33	2.07	−1.699 (3.368)	.059 (4.084)	.33	2.03
Antitrust	10	33	−2.027 (3.611)	.021 (1.054)	.03	2.02	−2.132 (3.725)	.018 (.898)	.03	1.77
Labor	45	35	−.088 (.255)	.053 (5.298)	.46	1.63	−.099 (.228)	.053 (4.372)	.47	1.95
Other federal	34	35	−.503	.029	.37	1.02	−.411	.036	.48	1.69

Case type	s	n	OLS β₂ (const)	OLS β₄	R²	D.W.	GLS β₂ (const)	GLS β₄	R²	D.W.
regulatory agencies Patents	17	34	(2.189) −1.043 (1.959)	(4.361) .050 (3.284)	.25	2.05	(.963) −1.244 (2.388)	(3.283) .047 (3.163)	.22	2.02
Civil Rights	40	32	−.273 (.528)	.029 (1.841)	.10	1.66	−.379 (.582)	.036 (1.989)	.19	1.98
Constitutional (excl. criminal)	17	35	−1.864 (5.372)	.049 (4.933)	.42	2.22	−1.893 (5.957)	.049 (5.370)	.42	2.01
Criminal (all)	202	35	−.063 (.417)	.026 (5.933)	.52	.89	−.164 (.609)	.024 (3.559)	.65	1.79
Criminal (const.)	45	35	−1.708 (4.059)	.029 (2.345)	.14	1.72	−1.823 (3.707)	.026 (1.862)	.14	2.01
Criminal (nonconst.)	157	35	−.347 (2.334)	.028 (6.443)	.56	1.05	−.381 (1.544)	.028 (4.435)	.64	1.70
Bankruptcy	8	35	−3.689 (9.147)	.022 (1.887)	.10	2.13	−3.584 (9.462)	.024 (2.213)	.13	1.80
Land	8	32	−1.403 (2.585)	.011 (.754)	.02	1.47	−1.906 (2.756)	.005 (.243)	.04	1.80

Notes:

1. OLS: ordinary least squares.
2. GLS: Cochrane-Orcutt method of generalized least squares.
3. s: number of sample cases.
4. n: number of observations in OLS regression analysis.
5. D.W.: Durbin-Watson statistic.
6. t-statistics are in parentheses.
7. Estimated regression coefficient β_4 (see equation (15)) equals −8.

TABLE A2
REGRESSION ESTIMATES: 1974 SUPREME COURT TERM

	s	n	OLS				GLS			
			α	δ	R²	D.W.	α	δ	R²	D.W.
Citations to Other Courts										
All Classes	122	33	-4.570 (37.117)	.039 (8.745)	.71	.96	-4.769 (18.336)	.030 (3.789)	.77	2.00
Common Law	10	33	-6.026 (10.444)	.035 (1.699)	.09	1.33	-6.210 (7.288)	.027 (.954)	.17	2.06
Economic Regulation	40	33	-4.163 (26.143)	.052 (9.141)	.73	1.43	-4.200 (18.994)	.050 (6.653)	.74	1.82
Civil Rights	9	22	-3.461 (3.944)	.186 (2.779)	.28	2.93	-3.383 (5.799)	.191 (4.302)	.43	2.13
Criminal	28	33	-5.600 (11.259)	.048 (2.693)	.19	2.17	-5.669 (11.879)	.046 (2.704)	.18	2.02
Citations to Supreme Court										
All Classes	56	35	-.222 (2.094)	.033 (10.751)	.78	.89	-.331 (1.777)	.030 (6.381)	.84	2.11
Common Law	13	35	-1.615 (3.229)	.024 (1.688)	.08	1.60	-1.755 (2.807)	.021 (1.206)	.10	1.94
Economic Regulation	48	35	-.870 (2.842)	.038 (4.271)	.36	1.76	-.921 (2.584)	.037 (3.651)	.35	2.00
Civil Rights	13	35	.975 (5.488)	.022 (4.305)	.36	1.39	.994 (3.926)	.022 (3.244)	.42	1.94
Constitutional (noncriminal)	32	35	-1.147 (6.990)	.033 (6.857)	.59	1.49	-1.212 (5.811)	.031 (5.466)	.60	2.02
Criminal	37	35	.745 (5.005)	.017 (3.872)	.31	1.29	-.794 (3.652)	.016 (2.713)	.38	1.99

Notes: See Table A1.

TABLE A3
REGRESSION ESTIMATES: 1960 COURT OF APPEALS SAMPLE

	s	n	OLS				GLS			
			α	δ	R^2	D.W.	α	δ	R^2	D.W.
Citations to Other Courts										
All Classes	208	24	−3.085 (30.039)	.049 (12.437)	.88	.80	−3.235 (13.120)	.042 (5.666)	.92	1.87
Common Law	52	24	−3.112 (20.542)	.037 (6.349)	.65	1.91	−3.068 (19.276)	.038 (6.378)	.66	1.84
Economic Regulation	88	24	−2.863 (27.776)	.057 (14.511)	.91	1.27	−2.946 (18.201)	.053 (9.506)	.91	2.05
Tax	32	24	−2.592 (14.189)	.077 (11.144)	.85	1.83	−2.597 (15.141)	.076 (11.772)	.85	1.80
Labor	25	24	−.335 (1.297)	.137 (13.921)	.90	.89	−.725 (1.068)	.115 (5.750)	.93	1.65
Criminal	46	24	−3.502 (18.048)	.061 (8.212)	.75	2.12	−3.536 (18.500)	.060 (8.313)	.74	1.99
Citations to Supreme Court										
All Classes	136	26	−1.489 (17.461)	.036 (14.280)	.89	1.42	−1.541 (14.194)	.035 (11.568)	.90	1.83
Common Law	26	26	−3.555 (6.231)	.033 (.198)	.00	1.82	−3.811 (6.356)	−.002 (.106)	.00	1.57
Economic Regulation	61	26	−1.242 (10.140)	.049 (13.349)	.88	1.53	−1.279 (8.084)	.047 (10.562)	.88	1.73
Tax	25	26	−1.187 (2.971)	.063 (5.304)	.54	1.89	−1.172 (2.639)	.063 (4.906)	.53	1.94
Labor	19	26	−1.886 (3.127)	.029 (1.623)	.10	2.25	−1.949 (3.517)	.028 (1.722)	.10	1.99
Criminal	36	26	−2.242 (4.338)	.012 (.789)	.03	1.75	−2.357 (3.888)	.010 (.585)	.03	2.01

Notes: See notes to Table A1.

year. In this appendix we discuss how we derived estimates of the number of precedents.

Court of Appeals

We experimented with two methods of determining the growth of federal court of
appeals precedents. Method I involved use of data collected by the Administrative
Office of the U.S. Courts. Method II involved the use of data collected by our own
research assistants. For reasons to be explained, we used Method II as the basis for
deriving estimates of annual investment that were then used to calculate depreciation
rates for court of appeals precedents.

Method I. A fundamental problem in determining the number of precedent produced each year is translating *decisions* into precedents. As shown in Table B1, it
makes a great deal of difference whether we treat as precedents all terminations, only
contested terminations, only terminations where there is a (published) judicial opinion, or perhaps only some subset of the last. Since only a decision in which an opinion
is issued is likely to be cited in a subsequent decision, it seems clearly appropriate to
limit the pool of precedents to such decisions. But two questions remain: (1) Should
all opinions be counted as precedents, even though many per curiam opinions (that is,
opinions not signed by one of the judges) are extremely brief (sometimes only a
sentence announcing a bare conclusion)? And (2) what are we to do for years before
1966, when no statistics of opinions, signed or unsigned, were kept?

These questions turn out to be related. As shown in Table B1, the number of
signed opinions per court of appeals judge[67] was highly stable over the period (1966-
1974) for which the number of signed opinions is reported. (The average for the
period is 31.355 opinions per judge, and the standard deviation only 1.7938.) This
average can be used to project the number of signed opinions in earlier years from
available data on the number of judges per year, as we have done in the first column
of Table B2 ("Method I") back to 1892, the year in which the federal courts of appeals
were established; but there can be no certainty that the estimates are accurate for
periods remote from the 1966-1974 period on the basis of which the projections were
made. Moreover, the number of per curiam (unsigned) opinions per judge does not
possess a comparable stability. As shown in Table B1 there has been a dramatic
growth rate in the number of per curiam opinions since 1966 (20 per cent per year),
but it is unlikely that the growth rate was as high in earlier years, for which we have
no data.[68] Thus the data in Table B1 cannot be used to project the number of
unsigned opinions in earlier years.

There are several alternative methods of dealing with the per curiam opinions: (1)
Exclude them altogether on the grounds that they are (as we are about to see)

[67] There is a problem in measuring the number of judges, due to the fact that there is no
formal retirement of federal judges. At age 70 they become "senior judges," free to reduce their
workload, to zero if they like, without suffering any reduction in pay; but they also may if they
wish continue to hear cases, and most do so, to a greater or lesser extent. We translated number
of senior into number of active-judge equivalents by means of a regression equation based on
the ratio of the number of signed opinions written by senior judges to the number of signed
opinions written by active judges. The number of judges used in Table B1 to calculate the
number of signed opinions per judge is the sum of the active judges and the active-judge
equivalents in each year.

[68] An annual growth rate of 20 per cent would imply a total of only 27 per curiams in 1948,
almost certainly a gross underestimate (see note 69, *infra*).

TABLE B1
U.S. COURT OF APPEALS DECISIONS, 1966-1973

Year	Number								% Increase 1966-1973
	1966	1967	1968	1969	1970	1971	1972	1973	
Terminations	6,571	7,527	8,264	9,014	10,699	12,368	13,828	15,112	130%
Contested Terminations¹	4,087	4,468	4,668	5,121	6,139	7,606	8,537	9,618	135
Opinions	3,462	3,899	4,074	4,525	5,374	6,458	7,142	7,263	110
Signed	2,414	2,633	2,572	2,904	3,195	3,336	3,468	3,377	40
Per Curiam	1,048	1,266	1,502	1,621	2,179	3,122	3,674	3,886	271
Signed Per. Judge	29.4	30.5	28.4	32.0	33.7	33.1	33.0	31.7	
Signed Plus Unsigned Per Judge	42.2	45.1	45.0	49.8	56.7	64.0	68.0	68.1	

1. That is, terminations after oral argument or submission on briefs without argument.

Source: 1966-1973 Admin. Office of the U.S. Courts, Ann. Reps.

TABLE B2

ESTIMATED NUMBER OF OPINIONS, U.S. COURTS OF APPEALS, 1892-1974

Fiscal Year[1]	Method I		Our Subject-Matter Classes	Method II
	Signed	Signed and Signed Equivalents[2]		
1892	596	660		283
1893	596	660		578
1894	596	660		597
1895	627	694		683
1896	690	764		700
1897	690	764		563
1898	690	764		609
1899	690	764		687
1900	784	868		676
1901	784	868		688
1902	753	833		698
1903	815	902		685
1904	847	937		655
1905	847	937		698
1906	909	1006		817
1907	878	972		772
1908	909	1006		873
1909	909	1006		959
1910	909	1006		1029
1911	847	937		869
1912	815	902		1050
1913	847	937		1141
1914	972	1076		1167
1915	1003	1110		1368
1916	1003	1110		1250
1917	1035	1146		1256
1918	972	1076		1292
1919	1035	1146		978
1920	972	1076		1419
1921	1035	1146		1235
1922	1003	1110		1595
1923	1035	1146		1328
1924	1003	1110		1684
1925	909	1006		1644
1926	1035	1146		1908
1927	1035	1146		1403
1928	1066	1180		1674
1929	1066	1180		1798
1930	1223	1354		1816
1931	1223	1354		2006
1932	1160	1284		2292
1933	1160	1284		2000
1934	1254	1388		1587
1935	1286	1423		2295
1936	1254	1388		1825
1937	1286	1423		1673
1938	1411	1562		1803
1939	1411	1562		1892
1940	1542	1707		2306
1941	1546	1711		2078

TABLE B2 *(Continued)*

Fiscal Year[1]	Method I		Our Subject-Matter Classes	Method II
	Signed	Signed and Signed Equivalents[2]		
1942	1633	1807		2056
1943	1642	1817		1818
1944	1658	1835		1892
1945	1623	1796		1573
1946	1645	1821		1741
1947	1682	1862	1535	1951
1948	1678	1857	1331	1771
1949	1652	1828	1454	1929
1950	1773	1962	1738	2293
1951	1791	1982	1679	2278
1952	1755	1942	1751	2295
1953	1756	1944	2031	2447
1954	1809	2002	2120	2446
1955	1849	2046	2335	2704
1956	1832	2028	2726	3100
1957	1812	2006	2745	3154
1958	1880	2081	2708	3042
1959	1965	2175	2634	3077
1960	1972	2183	2866	3193
1961	1876	2076	N.A.	3257
1962	2280	2523	N.A.	3349
1963	2270	2512	N.A.	3575
1964	2320	2568	N.A.	3751
1965	2226	2463	3411	3767
1966	2414	2658	3647	4059
1967	2633	2928	4101	4544
1968	2572	2922	4161	4578
1969	2904	3282	4286	4765
1970	3195	3703	4820	5369
1971	3366	4064	5296	5957
1972	3468	4325	5235	5809
1973	3377	4284	4642	5172
1974			4255	4729

[1] Calendar year for Method II, 1947-1974.
[2] Term and method of computation explained in text.
Sources: Method I and Our Subject-Matter Classes: 1940-1973 Admin. Office of the U.S. Courts, Ann. Reps. Method II: see pp. 305-06 *infra*.

probably of much less precedential significance than signed opinions and that we have no satisfactory estimate of their number before 1966. (2) Estimate their number on the basis of the unrealistic assumption of a constant 20 per cent annual growth rate,[69] but appropriately weight them to reflect their lesser precedential significance.

[69] A partial check on the accuracy of using the 1966-1973 average growth rate of 20 per cent to estimate the number of unsigned opinions in earlier years is possible by using the samples of signed and unsigned opinions that we obtained for purposes of compiling Table B3 *infra*. The results, presented in the table below, suggest that this estimation procedure would grossly underestimate the number of unsigned in years prior to about 1964:

TABLE B3
COMPARATIVE PRECEDENTIAL VALUE OF SIGNED AND UNSIGNED
(PER CURIAM) U.S. COURT OF APPEALS OPINIONS

| | Signed opinions | | Unsigned opinions | | |
Period	(a) No. in sample	(b) Mean no. of citations[1]	(c) No. in sample	(d) Mean no. of citations[1]	Ratio of (d) to (b)
1959	147	2.850	104	.587	.206
1964a	156 ⎫	2.949 ⎫	62 ⎫	.935 ⎫	.317 ⎫
	⎬ 316	⎬ 2.943	⎬ 118	⎬ .763	⎬ .259
1964b	160 ⎭	2.938 ⎭	56 ⎭	.572 ⎭	.195 ⎭
1970	195	6.123	103	1.379	.225

[1] In first five years, in U.S. court of appeals decisions.
Sources: Vols. 268, 333, 334, and 428 F.2d; Shepard's Federal Citations.

(3) Use a better estimation procedure of the number of unsigned opinions, and as in (2) weight the estimate to reflect the lesser precedential significance of the unsigned. A possible procedure is to apply the 1966-1967 unsigned to signed ratio to our estimates of the number of signed opinions in 1892-1965, on the ground that the ratio seems not to have begun to increase until 1968 (see Table B2). The table in note 69 suggests that this produces more accurate estimates than method (2).

Table B3 presents the results of estimating the relative precedential significance of signed and of per curiam opinions by counting the number of citations to both groups in the five years after the opinion is issued.[70] Table B3 indicates that unsigned opinions have, as expected, substantially less precedential significance (as measured by the number of citations to them) than unsigned opinions. However, their precedential significance is not zero. By multiplying the number of per curiam opinions by the mean ratio of signed- to unsigned-opinion citations (.2333), we can translate per curiam opinions into "signed-opinion equivalents"; the results of this computation appear in Table B2 for the years 1966-1973. To obtain a rough estimate of court of appeals precedents *before* 1966, where precedents are measured by signed equivalents (that is, signed opinions plus weighted per curiams), we assume that the ratio of signed equivalents to signed opinions in 1892-1965 equaled its ratio in 1966-1967. We can thus derive two estimates for court of appeals precedents from 1892 to 1973: a

Estimated Ratios of Unsigned to Signed Opinions

Year	Actual (From Table B1)	20 Per Cent Method[1]	Alternative Method (No. 3)[2]	From Table B3
1959	n.a.	.13	.46	.71
1964	n.a.	.30	.46	.37
1970	.68	—	—	.53

[1] Number of unsigned opinions estimated on basis of assumption of 20% constant growth rate; number of signed is from Table B2.
[2] Number of unsigned assumed to be same fraction of signed as in 1966-1967; number of signed from Table B2.

[70] We drew two samples of 1964 cases because the first seemed to be an outlier compared to the 1959 and 1970 samples—an impression confirmed by the results of the second 1964 sample.

TABLE B4
NUMBER OF SIGNED OPINIONS, U.S. SUPREME COURT, 1927-1973 TERMS

Term	Total	Subject-Matter Classes[1]	Term	Total	Subject-Matter Classes[1]
1927	175		1951	90	75
1928	129		1952	110	78
1929	134		1953	88	59
1930	166	75	1954	81	66
1931	150	75	1955	94	75
1932	168	71	1956	113	86
1933	158	67	1957	119	95
1934	156	65	1958	112	93
1935	146	76	1959	105	92
1936	149	73	1960	118	86
1937	152	64	1961	96	64
1938	141	52	1962	114	87
1939	137	n.a.	1963	127	97
1940	165	n.a.	1964	114	89
1941	151	n.a.	1965	113	85
1942	147	n.a.	1966	119	98
1943	130	n.a.	1967	118	92
1944	156	n.a.	1968	120	95
1945	134	n.a.	1969	94	74
1946	142	n.a.	1970	112	79
1947	110	n.a.	1971	151	105
1948	124	77	1972	164	110
1949	98	75	1973	157	104
1950	98	74			

[1] Includes certain per curiam opinions, as explained in note 10.

Sources: Total: Letter from the office of the Clerk of the U.S. Supreme Court, 1975 (1927-1929 and 1939-1947); Our Subject-Matter Classes: Harv. L. Rev. (November issue) (1930-1938 and 1949-1973).

signed-opinion estimate, which probably underestimates the true growth rate because it excludes per curiam opinions; and a signed-equivalent estimate.[71]

Method II. We have reasonable confidence in estimates based on the procedure described above for the recent past. But for purposes of measuring depreciation rates, we need to be able to compute investment over a long period of time, and we lack confidence that projecting the number of opinions back to 1892 on the basis of the ratio of opinions to judges in the period 1966-1973 will produce estimates of sufficient accuracy for our purpose. Accordingly, we undertook to estimate from the court reports themselves (Federal Reporter and Federal Reporter, Second) the number of court of appeals opinions handed down each year since 1892. The resulting estimates, which appear in the columns headed Method II in Table B2, are probably more accurate for the period 1892-1965 than those based on Method I. Weaknesses of

[71] A further problem is that per curiams appear to depreciate at a more rapid rate than signed opinions. An analysis of the 1959 sample of courts of appeals opinions (see Table B3) reveals that the mean number of citations in 1965-1969 (six to 10 years after the decision) was 1.061 for the 147 signed opinions compared to .183 for the 104 per curiams or a ratio of unsigned to signed of .172. This is less than the ratio of .206 for the first five years after the opinion, suggesting a more rapid depreciation rate for per curiams. But we have not attempted to make any adjustment for the apparent differences in depreciation rates.

Method II are that it excludes memorandum opinions, which are very short per curiam opinions that have little, but not zero, precedential significance, and that it includes other per curiam opinions without separate indication of their number. Nonetheless, we have based our estimates of depreciation rates in the text on investment computed by means of Method II.

In estimating investment we must make an adjustment for the fact that our subject-matter classes comprise only a fraction—though a large one—of all decisions in the U.S. courts of appeals (see Table B2). For example, in 1973 our classes include 89.8 per cent of all cases commenced in those courts that year.[72] But of equal importance is the fact that the ratio of cases within our subject-matter classes to all court of appeals cases has been growing since 1947, when our subject-matter classes included only 78.7 per cent of all such cases. The method of adjustment for this factor was as follows. The total number of signed opinions in a given year (obtained by Method II) was multiplied by the ratio of cases commenced in our subject-matter classes to total commencements in the courts of appeals to yield an estimate of the number of signed opinions in a given year allocable to our subject-matter classes taken as a whole. We were then able to estimate the number of signed opinions in a given subject-matter class, for example common law, by taking the ratio of common law cases commenced to the total number of cases commenced in all our classes together and then multiplying this ratio by the total number of signed opinions. This procedure was repeated for each year back to 1947 (except for 1961-1964 when data by subject-matter classes were not available). Having no subject-matter breakdowns for the period prior to 1947, we assumed that the share of each subject-matter class in the total number of written opinions in the period 1892-1946 equaled its average share in the years 1947-1950.[73] Our estimates of investment by subject-matter classes should be viewed as first approximations only, because our assumption that the number of signed *opinions* per class is proportional to each class's share of total commencements is arbitrary. However, data on terminations by subject-matter class are unavailable from the Administrative Office of the U.S. Courts.

Supreme Court

Estimation of the number of precedents produced by the Supreme Court is more straightforward and requires fewer assumptions than the corresponding estimates for the courts of appeals. The *Harvard Law Review* has kept careful statistics since the 1930 term of the Supreme Court on signed opinions by various classifications, except for a gap from 1939 to 1947. These classifications were sufficiently detailed to enable us to reclassify the opinions into our subject-matter classes for each year covered by the *Review*'s statistics. We then assumed that the annual number of opinions by subject-matter class from 1874 to 1929 equaled the average per term from 1930 to

[72] Detailed subject-matter breakdowns are available only for commenced (not for decided) cases.

[73] Several additional adjustments were made in the "Method II" data in Table B2. Since those data are on a calendar-year basis while the subject-matter commenced data are on a fiscal-year basis, the former were first converted to a fiscal-year basis before obtaining the estimated number of written opinions per subject-matter class. However, our citation data are on a calendar-year basis. Thus, our estimates of investment by subject matter had to be reconverted to a calendar-year basis. The actual investment data by subject-matter class used in the regression analysis are available on request from the authors.

1948. (For the years 1939-1943, we used the average of 1938 and 1948, and for 1944-1947 we used the average of 1948 and 1949.) Table B4 presents both the number of signed opinions for our subject classes taken as a whole since 1930 and the total number of signed opinions per year since 1927.[74]

[74] Prior to 1927, when the full impact of the Judiciary Act was first felt, the Court's obligatory jurisdiction was a good deal broader, and in consequence it decided more cases, but presumably these were on average less important and so not readily comparable with its post-1927 output. See Gerhard Casper & Richard A. Posner, *supra* note 28, at 342-43.

In 1963 the editors of the Harvard Law Review began to include in the category of signed opinions certain per curiams that because of their length seem to be the equivalent of signed opinions; since such opinions are likely to have as much, or almost as much, precedential significance as signed opinions, they have been included in Table B4 for purposes of our subject-matter classifications. But in computing the total number of Supreme Court precedents, we excluded per curiam opinions because we have no information on them for the period before 1948. Between 1948 and 1974 they exhibited no growth. See Gerhard Casper & Richard A. Posner, The Workload of the Supreme Court, n. 17, at 75 (1976). If their growth was flat in the 1927-1948 period as well, then our exclusion of them would not affect our estimates of Supreme Court investment.

Note finally that the Supreme Court investment data are approximately on a fiscal-year basis, since the Court's terms (summer adjournment-summer adjournment) coincide roughly with fiscal years (July 1-June 30). Supreme Court investment data were converted to a calendar-year basis (for example, by defining the 1973 calendar year as the average of the 1973 and 1974 terms) to correspond to the citation data.

REFLECTIONS ON *TAXMAN*: AN EXPERIMENT IN ARTIFICIAL INTELLIGENCE AND LEGAL REASONING †

L. Thorne McCarty *

After introducing some basic techniques of semantic information processing developed in the field of artificial intelligence, Professor McCarty describes a computer program using such techniques which enables a computer to apply to certain fact situations concepts of the area of the taxation of corporate reorganizations. He considers both the present limitations of the program and ways in which it might feasibly be improved, and argues that if developed further by means of increasingly sophisticated techniques, it may prove of practical use to tax lawyers. The development of such computer models also has a dual theoretical purpose. It clarifies the structure of the area of law modeled, and the investigation of the limits of such models provides the foundation for a theory of the nature of legal concepts.

T HIS Article introduces a new approach to some of the classical problems of legal reasoning: What is the structure of a legal concept? What is the process by which legal concepts are transformed and modified? What are the arguments that lawyers characteristically make with respect to legal concepts? These are the kinds of questions that the Analytical Jurists once treated as essential, and the Realists dismissed as irrelevant; the kinds of questions that Cardozo ascribed to the Method of Philosophy in the judicial process, as opposed to the Method of Sociology.[1]

† Copyright 1977 by L. Thorne McCarty.

* Assistant Professor of Law, State University of New York at Buffalo. B.A. 1966, Yale University; J.D. 1969, Harvard University. The work on this project was begun while the author was a Law and Computer Fellow at the Stanford Law School, 1971–1973, and was supported at that time by a grant from the IBM Corporation; additional work was undertaken during a summer workshop at the Stanford Law School in 1975, which was also supported by a grant from the IBM Corporation. Computer time for the project was provided by the Stanford Artificial Intelligence Laboratory. The Article in its present form owes a great deal to the suggestions and comments of a number of individuals, including especially Richard S. Bell, Bruce G. Buchanan, Marc Galanter, David G. Hays, Thomas E. Headrick, Mary Kay Kane, Jonathan King, Ejan Mackaay, Philip Slayton, Colin Tapper, and George Williams. None of these individuals is responsible, of course, for any errors of fact or interpretation that remain. Special thanks are due, above all, to Associate Dean Joseph E. Leininger of the Stanford Law School, whose support and encouragement over the past few years made this Article possible.

[1] B. CARDOZO, THE NATURE OF THE JUDICIAL PROCESS (1921).

But my approach to these problems will be anything but classical. I will describe a computer program I have written which models certain aspects of the conceptual structures which occur in a specific area of the law, the taxation of corporate reorganizations, as set forth in subchapter C of chapter 1 of the Internal Revenue Code of 1954.[2] The program, dubbed mnemonically TAXMAN, is capable of performing a very rudimentary form of "legal reasoning": Given a "description" of the "facts" of a corporate reorganization case, it can develop an "analysis" of these facts in terms of several legal "concepts." I will describe in considerable detail how this program operates, what its limitations are, and how it might be revised and rewritten to achieve a somewhat higher level of sophistication.[3] By looking carefully at both the adequacies and inadequacies of a particular formal model of a particular area of the law, I hope eventually to provide some insights into the structure and dynamics of legal concepts generally.[4]

The present work also has a practical purpose. Despite its limitations, the TAXMAN system provides a number of tech-

---

[2] I.R.C. §§ 354–356, 358, 361–362, 368.

[3] The TAXMAN program was written in 1972–1973 and was first discussed in a paper presented at a workshop on Computer Applications to Legal Research and Analysis, Stanford Law School, April 28–29, 1972. McCarty, Interim Reports on the TAXMAN Project: An Experiment in Artificial Intelligence and Legal Reasoning, in *Artificial Intelligence Techniques in Legal Problem Solving* (June 1, 1973) (mimeo, Stanford Law School). The most extensive analysis of this unpublished paper appears in P. SLAYTON, ELECTRONIC LEGAL RETRIEVAL 18–19, 25 (Canadian Department of Communications, 1974); P. Slayton, Radical Computer Use in Law 67–68 (June 1974) (Draft Report prepared for the Canadian Department of Communications). Additional references to TAXMAN appear in Boyd, *Law in Computers and Computers in Law: A Lawyer's View of the State of the Art*, 14 ARIZ. L. REV. 267, 286–87 n.107 (1972); Bauer-Bernet, *Effect of Information Science on the Formation and Drafting of Law*, 14 JURIMETRICS J. 235, 248 n.14 (1974); Popp & Schlink, *JUDITH, A Computer Program to Advise Lawyers in Reasoning a Case*, 15 JURIMETRICS J. 303, 313–14 (1975). The present Article, however, contains the first full-length description of the program.

[4] The most important precursor to the present article is Buchanan & Headrick, *Some Speculation About Artificial Intelligence and Legal Reasoning*, 23 STAN. L. REV. 40 (1970), which urged that serious research be undertaken to apply computer science methods to legal problem-solving, and speculated that this research "could lead both to a greater understanding of the legal reasoning process and to the design of machine methods for performing parts of it," *id.* at 41. A more recent project along these lines is Meldman, A Preliminary Study in Computer-Aided Legal Analysis, Project MAC Report No. TR–157 (1975) (Ph.D. Dissertation, Mass. Inst. of Technology), which presents a detailed design of a program to assist in the analysis of a simple assault and battery case, but reports no actual implementation. *See also* Stamper, *The LEGOL Project and Language*, in PROCEEDINGS, DATAFAIR SYMPOSIUM, 1973, at 263 (British Computer Soc'y, London); Note, *A Computer Method for Legal Drafting Using Propositional Logic*, 53 TEX. L. REV. 965 (1975); Popp & Schlink, *supra* note 3.

niques that should be useful in automating the more mundane aspects of legal research and analysis. The existing systems for computer-aided research and analysis in the law depend either on an exhaustive search through the full text of a body of legal materials and a retrieval of documents by key-words or combinations of key-words,[5] or on a sequence of preprogrammed questions and answers about a legal problem that is designed to terminate in a legal conclusion, in much the same style as a program for computer-aided instruction.[6] The TAXMAN system, with its computer representations of actual legal concepts, suggests a more structured, more flexible, potentially more powerful alternative, although it remains to be seen how practical and efficient this alternative will be.[7] At the very least, the prospects seem promising enough to justify a substantial amount of additional research.

But whatever its practical applications, the TAXMAN system provides, I claim, an important tool for the development of our theories about legal reasoning. A great many of the classical jurisprudential problems are tied to problems about the uses of abstract concepts in the regulation of human affairs. Thus Dworkin to a large extent bases his analysis of judicial discretion on his "logical distinction" between "legal rules" and "legal principles";[8] Hart and Fuller devote a portion of their debate on legal positivism to a dispute about the "core," the "penumbra," and the "open texture" of legal concepts;[9] Levi describes the law as the prime example of a "moving classification system," and sees in this description an explanation for many of the perplexing characteristics of the legal process.[10] In these and other writings there are many illuminating examples and many valuable insights about the structure and dynamics of legal concepts. But taken as a whole, the jurisprudential literature is notoriously imprecise: the conceptual structures themselves are only vaguely defined and vaguely distinguished from one another; the dynamics of conceptual change appear only as suggestive metaphors.

The TAXMAN system adds a strong dose of precision and rigor to these discussions of linguistic and conceptual problems. Its critical task is to clarify the concepts of corporate reorganization law in such a way that they can be represented in

---

[5] *See* pp. 888–90 & notes 123–26 *infra.*

[6] *See* pp. 890–91 *infra.*

[7] *See* p. 888 *infra.*

[8] Dworkin, *The Model of Rules*, 35 U. CHI. L. REV. 14, 22–40 (1967).

[9] Hart, *Positivism and the Separation of Law and Morals*, 71 HARV. L. REV. 593, 606–15 (1958); Fuller, *Positivism and Fidelity to Law — A Reply to Professor Hart*, 71 HARV. L. REV. 630, 661–69 (1958).

[10] E. LEVI, AN INTRODUCTION TO LEGAL REASONING 1–7 (1949).

computer programs. This requires a degree of explicitness about the structure of these concepts that has never previously been attempted. When we describe concepts in this way, we implicitly articulate theories about them; when we run the computer programs that embody these concepts, we test out the implications of our theories. Used in this fashion, the computer is the most powerful tool for expressing formal theories and spinning out their consequences that has ever been devised.

We can see this point most clearly, I think, if we examine briefly the contemporary traditions in linguistics and cognitive psychology, two areas with obvious connections to the present work.[11] Both disciplines, in opposition to their behaviorist predecessors, posit abstract mental structures in order to explain basic linguistic and psychological facts. In linguistics, the proposed mental structures are syntactic and semantic in nature, and they purport to organize and explain our intuitions about the grammaticality of various sentences. In cognitive psychology, where the schools of thought are more varied and diffuse, the proposed structures may be perceptual schemata, or memory mechanisms, or devices for acquiring and abstracting concepts. But what is especially striking about the abstract structural models that appear in these disciplines today is the fact that they are so closely tied to computational structures, that is, to the kinds of structures that are most naturally represented by computer programs. There are many examples in the recent literature: semantic theories formulated and tested within a computer system that conducts a simple dialogue in English;[12] theories of associative memory written in the form of programs and validated by experimental data from human subjects.[13] In these areas at least, the computer program has proven itself to be one of the ideal modes of expression for linguistic and psychological ideas.

So too with TAXMAN. But one must proceed with sophis-

---

[11] I assume that most lawyers are generally aware of the revolutions wrought by Chomsky and others in linguistics and by Piaget and others in cognitive psychology, since their ideas have by now worked their way into the popular literature. For accessible introductions, see, *e.g.*, N. CHOMSKY, LANGUAGE AND MIND (1968); J. PIAGET, THE ORIGINS OF INTELLIGENCE IN CHILDREN (1952); U. NEISSER, COGNITIVE PSYCHOLOGY (1968).

[12] *See, e.g.*, T. WINOGRAD, UNDERSTANDING NATURAL LANGUAGE (1972); Schank, *Conceptual Dependency: A Theory of Natural Language Understanding*, 3 COGNITIVE PSYCH. 552 (1972); Woods, *Transition Network Grammars for Natural Language Analysis*, 13 COMM. OF THE ASS'N FOR COMPUTING MACH. 591 (1970).

[13] *See, e.g.*, D.A. NORMAN, D. RUMELHART, & THE LNR RESEARCH GROUP, EXPLORATIONS IN COGNITION (1975); J.R. ANDERSON & G. BOWER, HUMAN ASSOCIATIVE MEMORY (1973); Quillian, *Semantic Memory*, in SEMANTIC INFORMATION PROCESSING 227 (M. Minsky ed. 1968).

tication about the uses and abuses of formal models. A formal model is necessarily a simplification of reality. It omits details, by design, which in many contexts might be crucial; and so, by design, it will always be inadequate in some respects. And yet the simplification inherent in a formal model is also the source of its power and utility: it will often lead us to insights that would otherwise be obscured, overwhelmed by the complexity of our data. The unexpected consequences of our formulations may reveal surprising truths or, just as often, the inadequacy of the formulations themselves.[14] These unacceptable conclusions must not be ignored but must be exploited systematically for the insights they can yield.

This is the strategy I have attempted to follow. This Article thus explores the positive role of the TAXMAN system, pushing it to its limits. The formal model here comes from a branch of computer science devoted to the study of what is called *artificial intelligence*.[15] The model is designed to represent linguistic and conceptual information in ways that are arguably similar to the

---

[14] Chomsky has stated this point succinctly and accurately in the preface to his earlier work:

> Precisely constructed models for linguistic structure can play an important role, both negative and positive, in the process of discovery itself. By pushing a precise but inadequate formulation to an unacceptable conclusion, we can often expose the exact source of this inadequacy and, consequently, gain a deeper understanding of the linguistic data. More positively, a formalized theory may automatically provide solutions for many problems other than those for which it was explicitly designed. Obscure and intuition-bound notions can neither lead to absurd conclusions nor provide new and correct ones, and hence they fail to be useful in two important respects.

N. CHOMSKY, SYNTACTIC STRUCTURES 5 (1957).

[15] The field of artificial intelligence (often abbreviated "AI") is concerned with the problem of designing machines which exhibit some form of "intelligent" behavior. This includes machines which play chess, *see, e.g.*, Greenblatt, Eastlake, & Crocker, *The Greenblatt Chess Program*, in PROCEEDINGS OF THE FALL JOINT COMPUTER CONF., 1967, at 801 (Am. Fed'n of Information Processing Societies, Montvale, N.J.); prove mathematical theorems, *see, e.g.*, Bledsoe, Boyer, & Henneman, *Computer Proofs of Limit Theorems*, 3 ARTIFICIAL INTELLIGENCE 27 (1972); solve mass spectrometry problems in organic chemistry, *see, e.g.*, Buchanan, Sutherland, & Feigenbaum, *Rediscovering Some Problems of Artificial Intelligence in the Context of Organic Chemistry*, in 5 MACH. INTELLIGENCE 253 (B. Meltzer & D. Mitchie eds. 1970); and many others. The name "artificial intelligence" was chosen partly because of the provocative stance it takes on the question "Can a Machine Think?" that was raised in the early article by Turing, *Computing Machinery and Intelligence*, 59 MIND 433 (1950). On the unfortunate connotations of this choice of words, see H. SIMON, THE SCIENCES OF THE ARTIFICIAL 4 n.1 (1969). *See generally* COMPUTERS AND THOUGHT (E. Feigenbaum & J. Feldman eds. 1963); SEMANTIC INFORMATION PROCESSING (M. Minsky ed. 1968); REPRESENTATION AND MEANING (H. Simon & L. Siklossy eds. 1972). For a sharp critique, see J. WEIZENBAUM, COMPUTER POWER AND HUMAN REASON: FROM JUDGMENT TO CALCULATION (1976); H. DREYFUS, WHAT COMPUTERS CAN'T DO: A CRITICISM OF ARTIFICIAL REASON (1972).

representations of this kind of information in the human mind. The techniques used, sometimes referred to as techniques of *semantic information processing*,[16] are typical of the current applications of computer science to linguistics and cognitive psychology. The questions then are: How adequate is this paradigm? How adequately does it explain the familiar facts of legal reasoning? Specifically, how well does it handle the taxation of corporate reorganizations? It will become clear, I think, that the TAXMAN paradigm has considerable power but that it also has several serious deficiencies.[17]

The two Parts following this introduction are intended to provide the necessary background for anyone who knows nothing about either the legal or the technical foundations of the work. Part I thus presents an elementary introduction to the taxation of corporate reorganizations, and Part II presents an elementary introduction to the basic ideas of sematic information processing. With this background, Part III presents a description of the current implementation of TAXMAN, Part IV presents the actual performance of TAXMAN in analyzing a corporate reorganization case, and Part V outlines several extensions of the program which seem feasible within the present state of the art. A thorough exploration of these feasible extensions will help make clear the capabilities and limitations of the present approach.

I. SOME FUNDAMENTALS OF CORPORATE REORGANIZATION LAW

For an area of the law to be a suitable subject for a project like TAXMAN, it should possess both simplicity and complexity. The basic facts and concepts in the area should be simple enough for the application of the existing techniques of semantic information processing, allowing us to develop a working computer model

---

[16] *See, e.g.*, SEMANTIC INFORMATION PROCESSING (M. Minsky ed. 1968). I use the term here to indicate a subfield within the broader field of artificial intelligence, and to indicate also a general evolutionary trend in the field of artificial intelligence as a whole. As a subfield, semantic information processing is more closley tied to the work in linguistics and cognitive psychology, *supra* notes 12 and 13, than it is to the work on game-playing, theorem-proving, and problem-solving programs, *supra* note 15. But even within the game-playing programs themselves, the term indicates a shift in emphasis: the earlier programs were characterized primarily by their "heuristic search" techniques, while the later programs were increasingly characterized by their techniques for the "representation of knowledge." To see this shift in emphasis, compare the early articles collected in COMPUTERS AND THOUGHT (E. Feigenbaum & J. Feldman eds. 1968) with the articles collected in REPRESENTATION AND MEANING: EXPERIMENTS WITH INFORMATION PROCESSING SYSTEMS (H. Simon & L. Siklossy eds. 1972).

[17] In a future article I will discuss these deficiencies further and suggest some modifications. *See* pp. 892–93 *infra*.

in a reasonable amount of time. But at least some of these concepts should exhibit a richness and depth that cannot be captured in a trivial way, allowing us to push the current paradigm to its limits.

The taxation of corporate reorganizations is suitable in both respects. To convey briefly the basic ideas, I will use a simple hypothetical case.[18] Consider a New Jersey corporation which wishes to transfer its place of incorporation to Delaware. It chooses to do so by means of an "assets acquisition." It first sets up a new corporation in Delaware, then transfers all its assets to the Delaware corporation in exchange for all of the newly issued Delaware stock. The New Jersey stockholders then control a company which owns nothing but Delaware stock, and the New Jersey company operates the Delaware company as a wholly owned subsidiary. At this point, though, the old New Jersey company would probably be liquidated and the Delaware stock distributed pro rata to the New Jersey stockholders in exchange for their New Jersey stock.[19] This result would be fully equivalent to a direct reincorporation of the New Jersey company in Delaware.

If it were not for special provisions in the Internal Revenue Code, these transactions would produce a potential tax liability for both the stockholders and the corporation. The New Jersey stockholders would be taxed on the receipt of the Delaware stock, as on the receipt of any corporate distribution. If the Delaware stock were completely distributed and the New Jersey corporation completely liquidated, the stockholders would be taxed at capital gains rates on the appreciation of their investment, that is, on the difference between the market value of the Delaware shares received and the cost basis of their original shares in New Jersey.[20] In addition, the initial transfer of property to Delaware

---

[18] The hypothetical case that follows is based on United States v. Phellis, 257 U.S. 156 (1921), the earliest reorganization case. *Phellis* also appears in several subsequent sections of this Article. In using *Phellis* as a device for an introduction to corporate reorganization law, I have drawn heavily upon W. ANDREWS, FEDERAL INCOME TAXATION 126–58, 168–69, 757–844 (1969) [hereinafter cited as ANDREWS]; I have also drawn upon B. BITTKER & J. EUSTICE, FEDERAL INCOME TAXATION OF CORPORATIONS AND SHAREHOLDERS (3d ed. 1971) [hereinafter cited as BITTKER].

[19] Alternatively, and less likely, only a portion of the Delaware stock might be distributed in exchange for a portion of the New Jersey stock, while the New Jersey corporation itself remained in existence. The original stockholders would then control the Delaware company partly by direct ownership of its stock, and partly by indirect ownership through New Jersey.

[20] I.R.C. §§ 331(a)(1), 1001–1002, 1221–1222. The partial distribution in note 19 *supra* could result in even more burdensome tax consequences for the stockholders: unless qualifying as an "exchange" under § 302(b) or a "partial liquida-

would be viewed as a sale, and the New Jersey corporation would be taxed, at capital gains rates, on the value of the Delaware shares received less the cost basis of its transferred assets.

It could be argued, however, that these transactions have no economic significance beyond the change in the state of incorporation, and so should produce no tax consequences. In substance, the argument goes, there has been no sale or liquidation or distribution, but only the formal reshuffling of stock certificates: the stockholders retain the same interest in the same operating assets after the transactions as before.[21] The Internal Revenue Code adopts essentially this position in its provisions for tax-free corporate "reorganizations." Under section 354 of the Code, no gain or loss is recognized if "stock or securities in a corporation a party to a reorganization are, in pursuance of the plan of reorganization, exchanged solely for stock or securities" in a "corporation a party to the reorganization." Likewise, under section 361(a), no gain or loss is recognized if "a corporation a party to a reorganization exchanges property, in pursuance of the plan of reorganization, solely for stock or securities in another corporation a party to the reorganization." When a gain or loss goes unrecognized in a reorganization exchange, however, the basis of the property transferred is generally substituted for the basis of the property received,[22] thus making the unrecognized appreciation potentially taxable at a later date. The net effect of the recognition and basis provisions taken together, then, is not to eliminate the tax entirely, but to defer it until the reorganization related property is eventually sold in a nonreorganization exchange.

Since the recognition and basis provisions apply in full only to "reorganizations," that term is defined in elaborate detail in section 368(a). There are six types of reorganizations, known colloquially by the letter of the subsection in which they are defined. Type A, Type B, and Type C reorganizations are intended primarily for the combination of two separate corporations into

---

tion" under § 346, it would be treated as a "dividend" and included in ordinary gross income. I.R.C. §§ 301(a), (c), 302, 316–317, 331(a)(2), 346.

[21] This argument was originally made, and rejected, under a statute that contained no special reorganization provisions. *See* United States v. Phellis, 257 U.S. 156 (1921); Rockefeller v. United States, 257 U.S. 176 (1921); Cullinan v. Walker, 262 U.S. 134 (1923); Marr v. United States, 268 U.S. 536 (1925). *But see* Weiss v. Stearn, 265 U.S. 242 (1924).

[22] Under § 358, for example, the shareholders who receive stock or securities in the reorganization will carry their new certificates at the same basis as the old certificates they have given up, and the corporation which receives stock or securities in exchange for its property will carry the new certificates at the same basis as the transferred assets.

one, Type D reorganizations primarily for the division of one corporation into two, and Type E and Type F reorganizations for simple adjustments in capital structure, place of incorporation, etc., within a single ongoing corporation. Omitting some important detail, the six categories are: (A) "a statutory merger or consolidation"; [23] (B) "the acquisition by one corporation, in exchange solely for . . . its voting stock . . . , of stock of another corporation," if immediately thereafter the acquiring corporation has "control" of the acquired corporation; [24] (C) the acquisition by one corporation of "substantially all of the properties" of another corporation, again in exchange "solely for . . . voting stock" of the acquiring corporation; [25] (D) the transfer of assets by one corporation to another corporation of which the transferor immediately thereafter is in "control"; [26] (E) "a recapitalization"; [27] and (F) "a mere change in identity, form, or place of organization, however effected." [28] The concept of "control" is defined fairly mechanically as "the ownership of stock possessing at least 80 percent of the total combined voting power of all classes of stock entitled to vote and at least 80 percent of the total number of shares of all other classes of stock of the corporation." [29] The statute also delineates in detail the concept of "a party to a reorganization," [30] while the concept of a "plan of reorganization" is left conspicuously undefined.

Our New Jersey-Delaware hypothetical [31] clearly involves a Type F reorganization, but it fits the general pattern of two

---

[23] I.R.C. § 368(a)(1)(A). *See also* § 368(a)(2)(D) and (E), which provides additional rules for statutory mergers with a subsidiary corporation using stock of the subsidiary's parent, and which thus creates two hybrid reorganization patterns for "triangular mergers."

[24] I.R.C. § 368(a)(1)(B).

[25] I.R.C. § 368(a)(1)(C). *See also* § 368(a)(2)(B), which provides additional rules for the case in which the acquiring corporation exchanges "money or other property" in addition to voting stock.

[26] I.R.C. § 368(a)(1)(D). In order to qualify under § 368(a)(1)(D), however, the plan of reorganization must include a distribution of the transferee's stock or securities which qualifies under § 354, § 355, or § 356. But according to § 354(b)(1), § 354 does not apply to a Type D reorganization unless the transferee acquires "substantially all of the assets" of the transferor, and the transferor in turn distributes all of its properties (including those received in the reorganization) in what would effectively be a complete liquidation. Thus any putative Type D reorganization involving *less* than substantially all the assets of the transferor, or *less* than a complete liquidation of the transferor, would have to satisfy the requirements of § 355.

[27] I.R.C. § 368(a)(1)(E).

[28] I.R.C. § 368(a)(1)(F).

[29] I.R.C. § 368(c).

[30] I.R.C. § 368(b).

[31] *See* p. 843 *supra*.

other provisions as well. It could be viewed as an acquisition by the Delaware corporation of "substantially all of the properties" of the New Jersey corporation, a Type C reorganization. Or it could be viewed as a transfer of assets by the New Jersey corporation to the Delaware corporation, which New Jersey then "controls" by virtue of its ownership of all the newly issued Delaware stock, a Type D reorganization. In either case, if the overall transaction qualifies as a "reorganization," the receipt of Delaware stock by the New Jersey stockholders would be nontaxable under section 354, and the transfer of assets by the New Jersey corporation would be nontaxable under section 361.

Despite the apparent precision of these rules, the courts have intervened repeatedly throughout the history of the Code to deny a claimed reorganization status to transactions which have seemed inconsistent with their underlying purposes and assumptions. One early example is the doctrine of "continuity of interest" developed by the courts in a series of cases in the 1930's.[32] Prior to 1934, the predecessors of the Type B and Type C clauses lacked the requirement that a reorganization acquisition be made in exchange "solely for . . . voting stock" of the acquiring corporation and so applied, literally, to transactions which were outright sales. Suppose the New Jersey stockholders in our original hypothetical decide to sell out their company entirely to the DuPont corporation. They have New Jersey transfer all its assets to DuPont in exchange for DuPont's short-term notes, payable in two months; they then arrange the liquidation of New Jersey, receiving the notes as a liquidating dividend. Under the 1928 reorganization provisions these transactions would have qualified as a tax-free Type C reorganization,[33] with no tax to the New Jersey stockholders on receipt of the short-term securities, and no tax to the New Jersey corporation on the initial sale of its assets.

When a problem of this sort came to the Supreme Court in *Pinellas Ice & Cold Storage Co. v. Commissioner*,[34] however, the Court denied the claimed reorganization status. It held that a transaction in which the original owners retained no continuing interest in their transferred assets was, indeed, equivalent to a sale, and "to be within the exemption the seller must acquire an

---

[32] Cortland Specialty Co. v. Commissioner, 60 F.2d 937 (2d Cir. 1932), *cert. denied*, 288 U.S. 599 (1933); Pinellas Ice & Cold Storage Co. v. Commissioner, 287 U.S. 462 (1933); John A. Nelson Co. v. Helvering, 296 U.S. 374 (1935); Helvering v. Minnesota Tea Co., 296 U.S. 378 (1935); Helvering v. Watts, 296 U.S. 387 (1935); LeTulle v. Scofield, 308 U.S. 415 (1940).

[33] Revenue Act of 1928, ch. 852, § 112(i)(1)(A), 45 Stat. 791.

[34] 287 U.S. 462 (1933).

interest in the affairs of the purchasing company more definite than that incident to ownership of its short-term purchase-money notes." [35] Alternatively, the Court held that the transferred assets were not exchanged "solely for stock or securities in another corporation a party to the reorganization," under what is now section 361(a), since the notes "were not securities within the intendment of the act and were properly regarded as the equivalent of cash." [36] Today the transferor's continuity of interest in a Type B or Type C reorganization is assured by the "solely for . . . voting stock" requirement, but the term "stock or securities" is still defined only by judicial decision, and the "continuity of interest" doctrine remains important in other reorganization contexts.[37]

The celebrated case of *Gregory v. Helvering* [38] represents a more exotic example of a judicial refusal to apply the statutory language literally. Suppose our New Jersey corporation owns a block of General Motors stock which has appreciated substantially in value, and the New Jersey stockholders wish to sell the stock and realize a substantial profit. Since a direct distribution of the stock would be taxable at ordinary income rates, New Jersey embarks on the following plan of "reorganization." A new corporation is established in Delaware, and the General Motors stock is transferred to it in exchange for a controlling amount of newly issued Delaware stock, which is then distributed to the New Jersey stockholders. Under the 1928 statute, this transaction would have qualified as a Type D reorganization,[39] and neither the transfer of the General Motors stock nor the distribution of the Delaware stock would have been taxable. The Delaware corporation would then have been liquidated and the General Motors stock distributed to its stockholders. This liquidating distribution would normally have been taxable as a capital gain.[40] But while admitting that "the facts answer the dictionary definitions of each term used in the statutory definition,"[41] and that a taxpayer "may so arrange his affairs that his

---

[35] *Id.* at 470.

[36] *Id.* at 468–69.

[37] For example, it remains important for Type A and Type E reorganizations, where there is no statutory codification of a "continuity of interest" rule. *See* ANDREWS, *supra* note 18, at 810–15; BITTKER, *supra* note 18, ¶¶ 14.11, .12, .17.

[38] 293 U.S. 465 (1935), *aff'g* 69 F.2d 809 (2d Cir. 1934).

[39] Revenue Act of 1928, ch. 852, § 112(i)(1)(B), 45 Stat. 791. Under the current statute, though, the transaction would not satisfy the final clause of § 368(a)(1), *see* note 26 *supra*, which was intended to prevent a tax-free result in a case like *Gregory*.

[40] *See* I.R.C. § 331(a)(1).

[41] 69 F.2d 809, 810 (2d Cir. 1934).

taxes shall be as low as possible," [42] the Second Circuit and the Supreme Court denied the capital gains treatment in *Gregory*. According to the Supreme Court, "the whole undertaking, though conducted according to the terms of subdivision (B), was in fact an elaborate and devious form of conveyance masquerading as a corporate reorganization, and nothing else." [43]

The complex manipulations of *Helvering v. Elkhorn Coal Co.*[44] provide a similar example. Paraphrasing the facts again in terms of our hypothetical, we assume that New Jersey wishes to transfer some, but not all, of its assets to DuPont in a tax-free exchange. First, New Jersey transfers the assets it wishes to retain to a newly created Delaware corporation in a Type D reorganization, distributing the Delaware stock; second, New Jersey transfers all its remaining assets to DuPont in exchange for voting stock, claiming a Type C reorganization; finally, Delaware acquires all the outstanding New Jersey stock from the New Jersey stockholders in exchange for its own voting stock, a Type B reorganization. When Delaware subsequently liquidates New Jersey, the transaction is complete: the Delaware corporation has now stepped completely into the former position of the New Jersey corporation, retaining only the desired assets plus the stock from DuPont. Once again, under the 1928 statute, the definitions of a Type D, a Type C, and a Type B reorganization would have been satisfied.[45] But the Fourth Circuit in *Elkhorn* refused to find a tax-free reorganization. The transfer of assets to the newly created corporation, it said, served only to

---

[42] *Id.*

[43] The Court continued:

The rule which excludes from consideration the motive of tax avoidance is not pertinent to the situation, because the transaction upon its face lies outside the plain intent of the statute. To hold otherwise would be to exalt artifice above reality and to deprive the statutory provision in question of all serious purpose.

293 U.S. 465, 470 (1935). The principle developed in *Gregory* is known as the "business purpose" doctrine. It is restated in similar language in the Regulations under § 368: "A scheme, which involves an abrupt departure from normal reorganization procedure in connection with a transaction on which the imposition of tax is imminent, such as a mere device that puts on the form of a corporate reorganization as a disguise for concealing its real character, and the object and accomplishment of which is the consummation of a preconceived plan having no business or corporate purpose, is not a plan of reorganization," Treas. Reg. § 1.368-1(c) (1955).

[44] 95 F.2d 732 (4th Cir.), *cert. denied*, 305 U.S. 605 (1938).

[45] Revenue Act of 1928, ch. 852, § 112(i)(A),(B), 45 Stat. 791. In this case, unlike the earlier ones, the current statutory definitions of a Type D, a Type C, and a Type B reorganization might be satisfied as well. In particular, the requirements of § 368 (a)(1)(D) and § 355 could be satisfied if both the assets transferred and the assets retained constituted an "active trade or business." *See* BITTKER, *supra* note 18, ¶ 14.52.

strip these assets away temporarily in preparation for the contemplated Type C reorganization. Since this first step was "a mere shifting of charters,"[46] the subsequent step had only the appearance of being a transfer of "substantially all of the properties" of the transferor. In reality, only a portion of the assets of the old company was transferred, and the transaction would therefore be taxable as a sale. This is "not made a different result because reached by following a devious path."[47]

It should now be clear why this area of the law is ideally suited for a project like TAXMAN. Superimposed on a manageable foundation of manageable complexity is another system of concepts as unruly as any that can be found in the law, with all the classical dilemmas of legal reasoning: contrasts between "form" and "substance," between statutory "rules" and judicially created "principles,"[48] between "legal formality" and "substantive rationality."[49] It is perhaps no accident that two of the more quotable passages on the problems of legal interpretation have arisen in corporate tax cases. Holmes' famous metaphor — "[a] word is not a crystal, transparent and unchanged, it is the skin of a living thought" — appeared first in *Towne v. Eisner*,[50] the earliest stock dividend case. And the simile of Learned Hand — "the meaning of a sentence may be more than that of the separate words, as a melody is more than the notes" — appeared first in *Helvering v. Gregory*.[51] In a sense, the ultimate task for the TAXMAN project is to translate these metaphors and similes into something more precise and concrete.

But that is indeed an ultimate task. The current version of TAXMAN is capable only of classifying a given case under the statutory rules as a Type B, a Type C, or a Type D reorganization.[52] An extended version of TAXMAN would be capable of covering a much broader expanse of corporate tax law: the full treatment of the parties to a reorganization, including both the nonrecognition and basis provisions; the treatment of corporate distributions outside the reorganization context; etc.[53] But the

---

[46] 95 F.2d 732, 734 (4th Cir.), *cert. denied*, 305 U.S. 605 (1938).

[47] *Id.* at 738 (on rehearing) (quoting Minnesota Tea Co. v. Helvering, 302 U.S. 609, 613 (1938) (emphasis omitted)). The principle developed here is generally referred to as the "step transaction" doctrine.

[48] *See, e.g.*, Dworkin, *The Model of Rules*, 35 U. Chi. L. Rev. 14, 22–29 (1967).

[49] *See, e.g.*, Kennedy, *Form and Substance in Private Law Adjudication*, 89 Harv. L. Rev. 1685 (1976); Kennedy, *Legal Formality*, 2 J. Legal Stud. 351, 354–60, 391–98 (1973).

[50] 245 U.S. 418, 425 (1918).

[51] 69 F.2d 809, 810–11 (2d Cir. 1934), *aff'd*, 293 U.S. 465 (1935).

[52] *See* pp. 876–81 *infra*.

[53] *See* pp. 882–84 & notes 103–111 *infra*.

concepts of "continuity of interest," "business purpose," and "step transaction," developed initially in *Pinellas, Gregory,* and *Elkhorn Coal,* may very well be beyond the reach of these straightforward extensions of the program. If so, these cases and their successors will provide the material we need to push the current paradigm to its limits and to suggest modifications.

II. Some Fundamentals of Semantic Information Processing

To understand what the TAXMAN system can and cannot accomplish, and why, we need to understand some of the existing techniques of semantic information processing. The problem is to develop models of conceptual structures which are at least rough approximations of the conceptual structures developed by the human mind. In this Part, I will show how these conceptual structures can be represented and stored in computer memory, how they can be searched for and retrieved from computer memory, and how they can be manipulated to simulate some rudimentary patterns of human reasoning and inference.

In the past several years, much of the work on this problem has coalesced into the development of a family of programming languages designed especially for these purposes, and thus one of the best ways to analyze the current ideas in this branch of computer science is to study one of these programming languages in detail. In the exposition that follows, I will use a simplified version of the programming language in which TAXMAN is actually written,[54] which is itself one of the earliest members of the family. Despite this simplification,[55] the version of the language I will use

---

[54] TAXMAN is written primarily in a language called Micro-PLANNER, which is a subset of a (not fully implemented) language called PLANNER. *See* T. Winograd, *supra* note 12, at 23–25, 108–17; G. Sussman, T. Winograd, & E. Charniak, Micro-PLANNER Reference Manual, AI Memo No. 203 (Mass. Inst. of Technology, 1970); C. Hewitt, Description and Theoretical Analysis (Using Schemata) of PLANNER: A Language for Proving Theorems and Manipulating Models in a Robot, AI Memo No. 251 (Ph.D. Dissertation, Mass. Inst. of Technology, 1972). Micro-PLANNER itself is a high-level language written in a lower-level language called LISP, which has been one of the principal tools for artificial intelligence research for over a decade. *See* J. McCarthy, P. Abrahams, D. Edwards, T. Hart, & M. Levin, LISP 1.5 Programmer's Manual (1962); C. Weissman, LISP 1.5 Primer (1967). Portions of TAXMAN are also written directly in LISP.

[55] The expert reader will note that many of the technical developments since Micro-PLANNER are omitted from this account or relegated to qualifying footnotes. This seems to me justified on pedagogical grounds. For a comparative survey of PLANNER and related languages (CONNIVER, QA4, QLISP, etc.), see Bobrow & Raphael, *New Programming Languages for Artificial Intelligence Research,* 6 Computing Surveys 153 (1974).

exhibits most of the salient features, and most of the outstanding problems, of the current paradigm of semantic information processing.

The concepts we are concerned about, of course, are those of corporate reorganization law. We must express certain fundamental propositions about corporations: that a particular corporation exists; that it has issued certain classes of stock; that certain individuals or other corporations own various shares of that stock; that the ownership of these shares of stock has been transferred from time to time. Propositions of this sort function as the relatively concrete, relatively primitive facts upon which reorganization law is constructed. We must also express a range of concepts which function within reorganization law at a much higher level of abstraction: "stock distribution," for example, or the concept of "control," or the legal concept of a "tax-free reorganization" itself. In fact, a major portion of the task here is the representation of these various levels of conceptual abstraction and the connection of one such level to another.

I will begin with the simplest representational problems. Given a corporation named "New Jersey," we can express the proposition "New Jersey is a corporation" by storing in computer memory the simple *list* of two *words*: (CORPORATION NEW-JERSEY). This list is stored exactly as written, both words spelled out in full, and it is indexed in such a way that by specifying either of the words CORPORATION or NEW-JERSEY we can find the location of the list in memory and retrieve it. The conventions for interpreting such a list are similar to those of formal symbolic logic: the first word is a *predicate*; the remaining words designate *objects* to which the predicate is applied. If we also want to express the proposition that "Delaware is a corporation," we could do so by storing a second list (CORPORATION DELAWARE). Here, CORPORATION would be the same one-place predicate as before, with the same interpretation, but applied now to an object named DELAWARE. The indexing system could now be used to retrieve either (CORPORATION NEW-JERSEY), by specifying NEW-JERSEY, or (CORPORATION DELAWARE), by specifying DELAWARE, or both (CORPORATION NEW-JERSEY) and (CORPORATION DELAWARE) together, by specifying the word CORPORATION.[56]

---

[56] A list can be composed not only by stringing together a sequence of words (or atoms) like CORPORATION and NEW-JERSEY and enclosing them inside a pair of parentheses, but also by stringing together and parenthesizing a sequence of *sublists*, like (LIST (CORPORATION NEW-JERSEY) (CORPORATION DELAWARE)), and this nesting of lists and sublists can continue to an arbitrary depth.

For propositions of slightly greater complexity, we can select a representational convention on largely pragmatic grounds. Suppose we want to represent the simple fact that New Jersey, a corporation, has issued stock. Since it may be necessary to say something further about the particular stock that New Jersey has issued, that it was common stock, that it was worth so many dollars per share, etc., it will be helpful to have a symbol in computer memory to which we can attach these additional propositions. We should therefore construct a new object, S1, say, and introduce a new predicate, STOCK, with which to assert that the new object is a class of stock. We thus store two lists to represent our original proposition: (ISSUE NEW-JERSEY S1) and (STOCK S1). Later, if we wish to say that the stock issued by New Jersey is worth so many dollars per share, the previously stored information will tell us that S1 is a stock and that S1 is issued by New Jersey, so we need only store in computer memory the additional fact that S1 is worth so many dollars per share. This procedure illustrates one of the basic conventions of TAXMAN: that we *nominalize* the concepts of corporate reorganization law as much as possible. Whenever it is convenient to create a new conceptual object, we will do so, setting up an internal symbol like S1 to stand for the postulated entity.

Consider now how to represent a stockholder's ownership interest in some particular class of stock. One possibility is to translate a proposition like "Phellis owns New Jersey stock" into the list (OWN PHELLIS S1), where S1 again names the stock issued by New Jersey. But a number of other stockholders also own portions of S1; Phellis himself only owns a certain number of shares of S1. So we do not say that Phellis owns S1 directly, but rather that he owns some other entity called P1 which is itself a "share-of" or a "piece-of" S1. Thus the proposition here would be stored as two lists: (OWN PHELLIS P1) and (PIECE-OF P1 S1). It is then possible to talk separately about what Phellis owns and what other stockholders own, and to attach to Phellis' interest another proposition describing how many shares it represents. Nominalization, the introduction of the new entity, has enabled us again to expand a complex concept to fit a particular need. Should the present formalism later prove inadequate in some other context, it could be expanded once more. In principle, at least, this procedure could be repeated to whatever degree of complexity and density is useful.

By now I have developed enough semantic conventions to represent a moderately complicated cluster of facts. Consider

---

For a discussion of these syntactic conventions, see C. WEISSMAN, *supra* note 54, at 5–24.

the proposition "Phellis owns 100 shares of common stock issued by New Jersey." In the present formalism this factual cluster could be stored as:

    (CORPORATION NEW-JERSEY)
    (ISSUE NEW-JERSEY S1)
    (STOCK S1)
    (COMMON S1)
    (PIECE-OF P1 S1)
    (NSHARES P1 100)
    (OWN PHELLIS P1)

Notice how the objects in these lists are linked together in pairs by the predicates. PHELLIS and P1 are linked together by their appearance in the list with OWN; P1 and S1 are linked together by their appearance with PIECE-OF; NEW-JERSEY and S1 are linked together by ISSUE. Since these linkages can be represented in a diagram, as in Figure 1, the data structure here is generally referred to as a *semantic network*, a formalism that is often more convenient to understand and use than our initial disconnected lists. Both formalisms have an equivalent interpretation in the TAXMAN system, however. A list or network that is stored in the data base is taken to be "true." A list or network

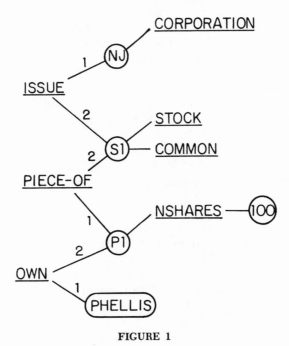

FIGURE 1

that is not stored in the data base, and thus not known to be true, is taken tentatively to be "false." The system can therefore be thought of as maintaining in its data base a "model" of the known "world" of corporations, stocks, stockholders, etc.

Let us now define some of the fundamental operations that the TAXMAN system ought to perform on the lists and networks in its data base in order to manipulate its "world model." I have already mentioned the simplest of these operations: at a minimum, we must be able to *store* a given list in memory, *retrieve* it from memory, and then, under some circumstances, *delete* it from memory again. The storage and deletion operations will be accomplished by the commands ASSERT and ERASE.[57] The command (ASSERT (CORPORATION NEW-JERSEY)) will call up a special program that stores and indexes the list (CORPORATION NEW-JERSEY), thus making it readily available for subsequent retrieval, or "true" in the "world" described by the data base. Similarly, the command (ERASE (CORPORATION NEW-JERSEY)) will remove the list (CORPORATION NEW-JERSEY) from memory, thus making it no longer available for retrieval, or "false" in that "world."

To retrieve a proposition from memory, a slightly more complicated GOAL command will be used. It is useful to distinguish several types of retrieval, depending on what information is to be retrieved and what information is available to guide the retrieval process. Thus, if we are considering the proposition (CORPORATION NEW-JERSEY) and want to know whether this proposition has already been asserted in the data base, the command (GOAL (CORPORATION NEW-JERSEY)) will provide the answer. The GOAL program will search the data base for the list (CORPORATION NEW-JERSEY) and, if successful, return T, otherwise NIL. Intuitively, the GOAL command tries to establish the "goal" of showing that the proposition "New Jersey is a corporation" is "true" in the given data base. This is the simplest form of retrieval: the straightforward verification that a particular assertion is present or absent in memory.

There are other retrieval possibilities, however. Suppose we wanted to find out whether there was an assertion in the data base about any corporation at all, whatever its name might be. We would then be asking whether a proposition of the form "x is a corporation," with "x" replaced by the name of a corporation, has been asserted in the data base, and this would be the case

---

[57] These ASSERT and ERASE commands (as well as some of the other operations in the discussion which follows, *e.g.*, GOAL, PROG, and THEOREM) are basic components of the Micro-PLANNER programming language.

if and only if a list of the form (CORPORATION X), with X replaced by the name of a corporation, appears in the data base. Accordingly, the command (GOAL (CORPORATION ?X)) [58] would search the data base for a list whose first element matched CORPORATION, as before, but, if the match succeeded, the variable X would be replaced by the second element of the list, the name of the matching corporation. For example, if (CORPORATION X) is matched to (CORPORATION NEW-JERSEY), X would be replaced by the name NEW-JERSEY. We also need some mechanism to handle the possibility that propositions about two or more corporations may appear simultaneously in the data base. The original GOAL commands were designed to search for only one matching list, and thus if the data base contained both (CORPORATION NEW-JERSEY) and (CORPORATION DELAWARE), the program would return whichever one it happened upon first. As an alternative, we could use a command like (FIND ALL (CORPORATION ?X)), which would return a list of all possible matches, in this case the list ((CORPORATION NEW-JERSEY) (CORPORATION DELAWARE)). [59]

The preceding analysis is still relatively simple, applying only to single lists taken one at a time. I have defined a *data base*, in which we can formally represent concepts, and a set of *operations* on this data base, enabling us to add new data structures to it, modify old ones in it, and retrieve information generally about the state of affairs it represents. I have also introduced implicitly the idea of *pattern-matching*: a major feature of the GOAL commands was their ability to match a partially specified pattern in the GOAL statement against the fully specified patterns stored in the data base.

The next important step is to design a program that can store and retrieve a somewhat larger chunk of data structure, such as a network of related propositions, by matching patterns of greater structural complexity than the single lists which have so far appeared in the GOAL commands. Consider the problem of making a simple logical deduction from a set of propositions stored in the data base. Suppose the data base contains a representation of the network of Figure 1, and suppose we wish to establish the truth of the proposition "Phellis is a stockholder of New-Jersey."

---

[58] Throughout this Article the prefix "?" will be used to indicate that the letter to which it is attached is a variable. Thus "?X" in this example indicates that "X" functions as a variable in the GOAL command. Any letter or word without the prefix, *e.g.*, P1, S1, PHELLIS, or NEW-JERSEY, is a constant.

[59] These simple examples do not exhaust all the retrieval possibilities. *See* Bobrow & Raphael, *supra* note 55, at 164–66.

There is no single proposition in the network that expresses directly the relationship between a corporation and its stockholders, but the stockholder relationship is expressed indirectly by the sequence of propositions involving ISSUE, STOCK, PIECE-OF, and OWN. What is needed, therefore, is a command to search for all four of these related propositions in succession. Since this command will have some of the characteristics of an ordinary sequential computer program, it will be given the name PROG and required to have the following form: (PROG <list of variables> <sequence of operations>).[60] But the PROG command will also have some important differences from the ordinary computer program.

To use the PROG command to establish the truth of the proposition "Phellis is a stockholder of New Jersey," we can write out the following expression:

```
(PROG  (S P)
   (GOAL   (ISSUE NEW-JERSEY ?S))
   (GOAL   (STOCK ?S))
   (GOAL   (PIECE-OF ?P ?S))
   (GOAL   (OWN PHELLIS ?P)))
```

Here the list (S P) is interpreted as a list of variables to be used in the computation, in the same way that X was used as a variable in the earlier example of a GOAL command. The list of four GOAL commands is then interpreted as a list of operations to be executed, one after another, so long at least as each GOAL command is successful in its search of the given network. Thus, the first thing the program does here is to execute the command (GOAL (ISSUE NEW-JERSEY ?S)). This command will succeed in the given network, and the variable S will be matched to the object S1. Next, the command (GOAL (STOCK ?S)) is executed: here, since S has already been replaced by S1, this second command amounts to a search for the constant list (STOCK S1), which also succeeds. The third GOAL command then becomes a search for a list to match (PIECE-OF ?P S1), where the original variable S has been replaced by the constant object S1. The search succeeds, and the variable P is matched to the object P1. Finally, the fourth GOAL command becomes a simple search for the list (OWN PHELLIS P1), which is also

---

[60] The angled brackets are used here to indicate in skeletal form the type of information which the command requires. The term "ordinary computer program" is used here to refer to the types of programming languages that most people are most familiar with: FORTRAN, BASIC, ALGOL, PL/I, etc. A subroutine in these languages contains a sequence of operations to be executed and a list of variables to be used while the subroutine is running. PROG is an "ordinary computer program" in this respect.

easily satisfied. The net result, therefore, is the successful execution of the original PROG command and so a successful search for the stockholder relationship.[61]

If the network were more complex, showing the New Jersey corporation with several stocks and bonds outstanding, and showing each of these stocks and bonds with several distinct stockholders and bondholders, the search might not proceed so simply. For example, it is possible that the first GOAL command would be satisfied by retrieving the list (ISSUE NEW-JERSEY S_7) and thus assigning to the variable S the value S_7. But it may then turn out that the object named S_7 is not a stock at all, but rather a bond, and so the subsequent search for (STOCK S_7) would fail. In such a case, the PROG command has the ability to *backtrack*: it would back up to the first GOAL command and search there for another match. If it then found the list (ISSUE NEW-JERSEY S_1) on this second turn, it would retrieve it, reassign S to the new object S_1, and proceed forward again to search for (STOCK S_1). Continuing in this manner, the program would eventually winnow out all the other incorrect matches, the wrong STOCKs, the wrong PIECEs, etc., until it arrived at a choice of S and P that would enable it to execute successfully the fourth command: (GOAL (OWN PHELLIS ?P)). The net result, again, would be the successful execution of the original PROG command.

To sum up: We want the program in this example to determine whether there are two objects satisfying the four propositions that make up the "stockholder" relation. To do this it must match the two variables and satisfy the four commands simultaneously, an essentially *parallel* task, but it accomplishes this result by a trial-and-error search, a *sequential* procedure.[62] This ability of the PROG command to find objects satisfying a sequence of propositions can be exploited further. In English we often use a *definite*

---

[61] Since all four of the GOAL statements must be satisfied in order to satisfy the PROG command, they can be thought of as being implicitly connected by a logical AND. Micro-PLANNER also provides for the explicit use of the other logical connectives: OR, NOT, and IF . . . THEN. It is thus possible to represent in a PROG command an arbitrarily complex proposition.

[62] The implementation of these search procedures in Micro-PLANNER has been sharply criticized, however. *See* Sussman & McDermott, *From PLANNER to CONNIVER — A Genetic Approach,* 1972 PROCEEDINGS OF THE FALL JOINT COMPUTER CONF. 1171 (Am. Fed'n of Information Processing Societies, Montvale, N.J.). Unrestricted backtracking can be highly inefficient if the PROG command is complex and the data base is large, since each new variable to be matched increases exponentially the length of the search. As an alternative, some of the more recent languages give the programmer explicit control over the order in which the search is to be carried out. *See, e.g.,* Bobrow & Raphael, *supra* note 55, at 156–58, 162–64.

description, such as "the New Jersey stock owned by Phellis," to single out an object about which we want to say something, as in "The value of the New Jersey stock owned by Phellis is $5000." We can make this assertion in TAXMAN with the following PROG command:

```
(PROG (S P)
    (GOAL (ISSUE NEW-JERSEY ?S))
    (GOAL (STOCK ?S))
    (GOAL (PIECE-OF ?P ?S))
    (GOAL (OWN PHELLIS ?P))
    (ASSERT (VALUE ?P 5000)))
```

As in the previous example, this program will first use a pattern-matching search to find an object P such that "New Jersey has issued S, S is a stock, P is a piece-of S, and Phellis owns P." In doing so it will replace P by P1, its name for that piece of stock, and then interpret the final command to be: (ASSERT (VALUE P1 5000)). The program thus represents quite naturally the assertion that "the value of the New Jersey stock owned by Phellis is $5000."

A far more significant application of the PROG pattern-matching capability, however, lies in the construction of a new concept out of a set of component concepts already present in a data structure, a simple form of conceptual *abstraction*. We have already seen how to express the proposition "Phellis is a stock-holder of New Jersey" in terms of the component concepts ISSUE, STOCK, PIECE-OF, and OWN, but we did this without developing a representation of the abstract concept of a STOCK-HOLDER itself. What we need now is a way to search for the STOCKHOLDER relationship as a high-level GOAL without having to specify all the lower-level searches through the data structure. This can be done by incorporating the basic mechanisms of the PROG command inside a structure called a THEOREM and having the following form: (THEOREM ABSTRACT < list of variables > < conceptual pattern > < sequence of operations >).

For example, using the THEOREM formalism, the STOCK-HOLDER relationship can be defined as follows:

```
(THEOREM ABSTRACT (O C S P)
    (STOCKHOLDER ?O ?C)
        (GOAL   (ISSUE ?C ?S))
        (GOAL   (STOCK ?S))
        (GOAL   (PIECE-OF ?P ?S))
        (GOAL   (OWN ?O ?P)))
```

Intuitively, the theorem states that the concept of a STOCK-HOLDER is abstractly equivalent to a particular pattern of the concepts ISSUE, STOCK, PIECE-OF, and OWN. Further, since the theorem incorporates the GOAL mechanisms of the PROG command, it shows how the relationship (STOCKHOLDER ?O ?C) can be established in any given network, for any objects O and C, by the familiar PROG pattern-matching process, assigning variables temporarily, backtracking, etc. The only difference between the use of this theorem and the use of the PROG command in our original example is the fact that the stockholder variable, O, and the corporation variable, C, can now be assigned initially to any objects we choose.

Suppose we wish to establish, as before, that "Phellis is a stockholder of New Jersey," but we know that the stockholder relationship has already been defined and stored in memory along with the usual factual network. We could then execute the command (GOAL (STOCKHOLDER PHELLIS NEW-JER-SEY) ABSTRACT). This command would first search the data base for a direct match with (STOCKHOLDER PHELLIS NEW-JERSEY), but the search would fail. Second, since the word ABSTRACT was present in the command, the program would search for an abstraction theorem with a final deduction which matched the list (STOCKHOLDER PHELLIS NEW-JERSEY), in this case retrieving the definition of STOCK-HOLDER with its matching pattern (STOCKHOLDER ?O ?C). The program would then assign to the variables O and C the values PHELLIS and NEW-JERSEY, respectively, and execute the four GOAL commands of the theorem as an ordinary PROG. The net result would be a successful determination that "Phellis is a stockholder of New Jersey," as before.[63] The other variations in the GOAL commands would operate analogously.[64]

---

[63] The use of the GOAL command together with the ABSTRACT theorem, as described in the text, is often referred to as a process of "pattern-directed function invocation," and it is generally considered to be one of the more important innovations of the PLANNER family of languages. *See* Bobrow & Raphael, *supra* note 55, at 159, 166–69, 170. The example in the text also illustrates what is referred to as the "procedural representation of knowledge," since the STOCK-HOLDER theorem there not only expresses an abstract equivalence between two conceptual structures, but also provides a concrete computer program for establishing that equivalence in a particular network. For a discussion of the arguments for and against these procedural representations, see Winograd, *Frame Representations and the Declarative/Procedural Controversy*, in REPRESENTATION AND UNDERSTANDING 185, 186–93 (D. Bobrow & A. Collins eds. 1975).

[64] For example, the command (GOAL (STOCKHOLDER ?O NEW-JERSEY) ABSTRACT) would apply the STOCKHOLDER definition with one variable assigned and one unassigned, and thus would eventually succeed by matching the unassigned variable O to one of New Jersey's stockholders, maybe Phellis, maybe

I have used the STOCKHOLDER definition in this example as a means of proceeding from the detailed level of the original network up to a less detailed, more abstract level expressing only a single general relationship between a corporation and its stockholders. But in many situations we may want to reverse the procedure. We may want to assert as a general proposition that "Phellis is a stockholder of New Jersey" without worrying about the detailed representation in terms of STOCKs, PIECEs, and OWNership relations, and yet have these concrete details available later for other purposes. In the TAXMAN system, these lower-level structures could be generated automatically by an *expansion* theorem:

(THEOREM   EXPAND (O C . . .)

(STOCKHOLDER ?O ?C)

<body of ASSERTions>)

which could be called into effect by a pattern-matching search from the command (ASSERT (STOCKHOLDER PHELLIS NEW-JERSEY) EXPAND).

I have been deliberately vague about the main body of this theorem, however, since the necessary details are more complex here than they were in the previous deductive use of the STOCK-HOLDER definition. Basically, the program should store the four assertions, (ISSUE NEW-JERSEY ?S), (STOCK ?S), (PIECE-OF ?P ?S), and (OWN PHELLIS ?P), which constitute the definitional expansion of (STOCKHOLDER PHELLIS NEW-JERSEY), but since the abstract STOCKHOLDER concept suppresses all information about the values of the variables S and P, there may be more than one concrete expansion possible. The program must therefore examine the context of whatever network already exists and make the best strategic choices possible.[65] Since any decisions made here could be contradicted by

---

someone else. Similarly, the command (FIND ALL (STOCKHOLDER ?O NEW-JERSEY) ABSTRACT) would locate and return a list of all of New Jersey's stockholders.

[65] If there have been no assertions at all stored yet about New Jersey stock, it would be reasonable to create a class of stock for Phellis to own shares of. If the existence of one class of stock has already been asserted, it may be reasonable to list Phellis as one of the owners. If two or more classes of stock are outstanding, however, the assertion is clearly ambiguous, and it may be best simply to note the ambiguity explicitly in the network. For a further discussion of the problems of expanding a relatively abstract concept to a more concrete level in a particular context, see Rieger, *Conceptual Memory and Inference*, in CONCEPTUAL INFORMATION PROCESSING 157 (R. Schank ed. 1975); Wilks, *A Preferential, Pattern-Seeking Semantics for Natural Language Inference*, 6 ARTIFICIAL INTELLIGENCE 53 (1975).

later assertions, the program should be capable of backing up later on to correct its mistakes.

The important point, though, is the basic process of abstracting and expanding concepts. There is not much power in a system that stores and retrieves single lists and single propositions. But as soon as the system can represent the relationship between two levels of conceptual abstraction, its power increases substantially. It is then possible to query the system at the higher level with a (GOAL <conceptual pattern> ABSTRACT) command, and have the lower-level searches carried out automatically; or state a fact at a higher level with an (ASSERT <conceptual pattern> EXPAND) command, and have the lower-level representations generated automatically. This process of conceptual abstraction can be extended to more than one level. The (GOAL (STOCKHOLDER ?O ?C) ABSTRACT) statement might thus appear as a component part of some other definition, and so at least two levels of data base searches could then be carried out automatically. Continuing in this way, an abstraction hierarchy of any desired complexity could be developed. Or multiple abstraction hierarchies could be developed, extending upwards from a common data base in different directions and for different purposes.

Perhaps even more interesting is the possibility of expanding the conceptual hierarchy downwards below the level of the concepts that have so far been treated as primitive. For example, the STOCK predicate has been used in this discussion as a basic, unanalyzed term, but it could itself be represented as an abstraction built up from a description of the rules governing the relationship between a STOCKHOLDER and a CORPORATION. A basic philosophy of the TAXMAN system is to treat concepts as primitives only provisionally, and only for certain purposes, and to retain the option of expanding them further in other contexts. In the current version of TAXMAN, however, STOCK is treated throughout as primitive.

The reader familiar with modern symbolic logic will have noted that there are strong similarities between these techniques for semantic information processing and the formalisms of the classical predicate calculus. Indeed, the power of TAXMAN to *represent* concepts in the data base is equivalent to that of the higher-order predicate calculus.[66] But since the *procedures* in

---

[66] *See generally* T. WINOGRAD, *supra* note 12, at 108–12; J.R. ANDERSON & G. BOWER, *supra* note 13, at 155–71; Sandewall, *Conversion of Predicate-Calculus Axioms, Viewed as Non-Deterministic Programs, to Corresponding Deterministic Programs,* PROCEEDINGS OF THE 3RD INT'L JOINT CONF. ON ARTIFICIAL INTELLIGENCE 230 (1973). For a rough idea of how this equivalence works, note that the

TAXMAN for the manipulation of these concepts have the flexibility of a general programming language, they are much more powerful than the proof procedures of symbolic logic. A programming language can express heuristic rules to guide the search for relevant theorems and propositions,[67] for example, or it can simulate in a natural way a dynamic change in the data base.[68] More important, it can function efficiently in an environment of structured complexity: because of the convention of pragmatic nominalization in TAXMAN, there tends to be a proliferation of objects in the data base, and conceptual definitions tend to be tied closely to these objects; the most important operations tend to be searches up and down the abstraction hierarchy for objects and concepts matching specified sets of definitional patterns, with the search process tightly controlled by the abstraction hierarchy itself. The techniques of semantic information processing are well designed for these purposes, but the formalisms of the predicate calculus are not.[69] Nevertheless, in assessing the adequacies and inadequacies of the TAXMAN paradigm, it should be kept in mind, for whatever limitations it may entail, that despite the additional power and flexibility of a general programming language, the representation of concepts in the current version of TAXMAN is still abstractly equivalent to the representation of concepts in the classical higher-order predicate calculus.[70]

STOCKHOLDER program, pp. 858-59 *supra*, could be represented in the (first-order) predicate calculus as follows:

$$(\forall O)\ (\forall C)\ ((\exists S)\ (\exists P)\ ((\text{ISSUE C S}) \ \& \ (\text{STOCK S}) \ \& \ (\text{PIECE-OF P S})\ \& \ (\text{OWN O P})) \supset (\text{STOCKHOLDER O C})).$$

See, e.g., I. COPI, SYMBOLIC LOGIC (1954).

[67] *See, e.g.,* Winograd, *supra note* 63, at 190-91. For an illustration in the TAXMAN system, although an imperfect one, see the discussion of the search procedures in the B-REORGANIZATION program, pp. 874-76 *infra*.

[68] *See, e.g.,* Winograd, *supra* note 63, at 189-90. For an illustration in the TAXMAN system, see the discussion of the TRANS assertion, pp. 866-67 *infra*.

[69] For a thorough and systematic discussion, see Minsky, *A Framework for Representing Knowledge*, in THE PSYCHOLOGY OF COMPUTER VISION 211 (P. Winston ed. 1975). Minsky argues that the theories of the more "logic-oriented" workers in artificial intelligence and cognitive psychology have been "too minute, local, and unstructured to account — either practically or phenomenologically — for the effectiveness of common sense thought," *id.* at 211, and then proposes a theory based on some larger and more highly structured entities called "frames." For an illustration in the TAXMAN system of a complex structure with some of the characteristics of Minsky's frames, see the discussion of the DISTRIBUTE concept, pp. 868-70 *infra*.

[70] There have been a number of attempts to apply formal symbolic logic to the analysis of legal concepts. Much of this work has focused on the most abstract legal concepts, "right," "duty," "privilege," etc., drawing on the important early analysis of Hohfeld, *Some Fundamental Legal Conceptions as Applied in Judicial*

III. Implementations

In this Part, I will show how the ideas of semantic information processing can, after further elaboration, be implemented in a computer program for the analysis of an actual case involving the taxation of corporate reorganizations.

There is a similarity between the preceding two sections which suggests how this might be done. The discussion in Part II emphasized the idea of a conceptual hierarchy, using the simple STOCKHOLDER example to show how the relationship between two or more levels of conceptual abstraction could be represented in computer data structures. The discussion in Part I of the taxation of corporate reorganizations revealed a similar hierarchy of abstractions. Our New Jersey-Delaware hypothetical and its variations were presented first in lower-level "factual" descriptions: transfers of stocks and assets, stock distributions and stock redemptions, and so on. The case was then analyzed in terms of several higher-level "legal" concepts: the concept of "control," [71] the various statutory concepts of a "reorganization," [72] and the judicial concepts of "continuity of interest," [73] "business purpose," [74] and "step transaction." [75] When the New Jersey-Delaware hypothetical was said to "fit the general pattern" of both a Type C and a Type D reorganiza-

---

Reasoning, 23 Yale L.J. 16 (1913). *See, e.g.*, Allen, *Formalizing Hohfeldian Analysis to Clarify the Multiple Senses of 'Legal Right': A Powerful Lens for the Electronic Age*, 48 S. Cal. L. Rev. 428 (1974); Anderson, *The Logic of Hohfeldian Propositions*, 33 U. Pitt. L. Rev. 29 (1971); Anderson, *The Logic of Norms*, 1 Logique et Analyse 84 (1958). None of this work has paid much attention to the problems of connecting these higher-level abstractions to the lower levels of the conceptual hierarchy, which is the major concern of the TAXMAN project. Another line of work in the legal literature has the disadvantage of using only the propositional calculus, which lacks the full expressive power of the predicate calculus. *See, e.g.*, Allen, *Symbolic Logic: A Razor-Edged Tool for Drafting and Interpreting Legal Documents*, 66 Yale L.J. 833 (1957); Allen & Orechkoff, *Toward a More Systematic Drafting and Interpreting of the Internal Revenue Code: Expenses, Losses and Bad Debts*, 25 U. Chi. L. Rev. 1 (1957). Popp & Schlink, *JUDITH: A Computer Program to Advise Lawyers in Reasoning a Case*, 15 Jurimetrics J. 303 (1975), and Note, *A Computer Method for Legal Drafting Using Propositional Logic*, 53 Tex. L. Rev. 965 (1975), are also based on the propositional calculus, and thus subject to the same comments.

[71] I.R.C. § 368(c); p. 845 *supra*.

[72] I.R.C. § 368(a); *see* pp. 844–45 *supra*.

[73] *See* Pinellas Ice & Cold Storage Co. v. Commissioner, 287 U.S. 462 (1933); Cortland Specialty Co. v. Commissioner, 60 F.2d 937 (2d Cir. 1932), *cert. denied*, 288 U.S. 599 (1933). *See* pp. 846–47 *supra*.

[74] *See* Gregory v. Helvering, 293 U.S. 465 (1935), *aff'g* 69 F.2d 809 (2d Cir. 1934); pp. 847–48 *supra*.

[75] *See* Helvering v. Elkhorn Coal Co., 95 F.2d 732 (4th Cir.), *cert. denied*, 305 U.S. 605 (1938); pp. 848–49 *supra*.

tion,[76] then, the analysis was similar to that of the simple STOCK-HOLDER program: a search through the abstraction hierarchy to match a conceptual structure at one level to one at another level.

The current version of TAXMAN takes advantage of the similarity to apply the semantic information processing treatment of conceptual hierarchies directly to corporate reorganization law. The TAXMAN system is capable of accepting a *description* of a corporate reorganization case at roughly the level of the statement of facts in an appellate opinion and then producing an *analysis* of the case at roughly the level of abstraction of the desired legal conclusion. In doing this, the program makes use of the *expansion* and *abstraction* mechanisms, respectively. In general, the descriptions are received at a slightly higher level of abstraction than the program requires, and the expansion mechanisms are used to rewrite these descriptions more concretely at a lower level. Once the descriptions are fully expanded, the abstraction mechanisms are used to apply to them, if possible, the higher-level legal concepts.

It would be a mistake to rely too heavily on this very general characterization of the TAXMAN system, however, for the performance of the system obviously depends on our ability to give a precise and programmable content to these mechanisms for the "description" and "analysis" of a corporate reorganization case. Unless the concepts of corporate reorganization law can, at least in principle, be incorporated into these description and analysis mechanisms, this general characterization is vacuous. It is therefore important to demonstrate that at least some of the concepts of corporate reorganization law *can* be represented within the current paradigm of semantic information processing, to show in some detail *how* they can be represented within this paradigm, and thus to show by inference how the existing program can be *extended* to handle problems of substantially greater complexity. The practical and theoretical limits of these extensions should then be evident.

The remainder of this Part is devoted primarily to these purposes. One of the claims I have made for the power of a programming language is that it can be used to modify a conceptual structure in various ways.[77] In Part III-A, I will show how the TAXMAN system makes use of this capability to represent an "event" as the modification of the description of a "state," and how these event descriptions can themselves be assembled into

---

[76] *See* pp. 845–46 *supra.*
[77] *See* p. 862 *supra.*

conceptual hierarchies to represent more complex events. In Part III-B, focusing on the concept of a "stock distribution," I will continue this analysis of complex event descriptions and also illustrate how the TAXMAN system can take advantage of repetition and redundancy in building an abstraction hierarchy. In Part III-C, finally, I will consider the implementation of the "reorganization" definition itself, showing how the pattern-matching process can be constructed and constrained, and indicating what effects these constraints might have.

A. *States and Events*

In order to talk about the facts of a corporate reorganization case, it is necessary to talk about corporate transactions, or corporate events, in addition to the static corporate structures of Part II. It is natural to think of an "event" of this sort as a transformation from one "state" to another. For example, the event described by the proposition "New Jersey issues a certain class of stock" could be viewed as a transformation from a state in which New Jersey has no such class of stock outstanding to a state in which it does. The TAXMAN system provides a simple way to implement these ideas in its mechanisms for *state descriptions* and *event descriptions*.

First, to capture the idea of a state description, the system allows the insertion of an optional extra variable at the end of a proposition to indicate that the proposition is true at a certain time: the proposition (ISSUE NEW-JERSEY S_1 T_4), for example, indicates that (ISSUE NEW-JERSEY S_1) is true at time T_4.[78] The network of all propositions in the data base that are true at a certain time can then be thought of as a description of the state of the "world" at that time.[79] With this data base available, the event descriptions play a dual role. As straightforward *representations* of events, the event descriptions have a hierarchical structure analogous to the structure of the state descriptions: certain simple events are taken as primitive, and more complex events are built up systematically from complex

---

[78] The same proposition without the final variable would indicate that (ISSUE NEW-JERSEY S_1) was true at all times during the period being described.

[79] For reasons of computational efficiency, the data base contains only one network, but each proposition in the network has attached to it a separate list describing the time periods during which it is "true," and the ASSERT, ERASE, and GOAL commands have been modified to check these listings of time-dependent truth values whenever necessary. To implement this I have rewritten the standard Micro-PLANNER interpreter for the ASSERT, ERASE, and GOAL commands. Other languages provide a general CONTEXT mechanism which allows the user to maintain more automatically these multiple state descriptions. *See, e.g.,* Bobrow & Raphael, *supra* note 55, at 161.

patterns of these primitives. But event descriptions also function as *programs* or *procedures* that actually carry out the transformation from one state description to another, rewriting the computer data structures to correspond symbolically to the transformation of states. For example, if the New Jersey corporation has no stock outstanding at a particular time, and if a subsequent event description represents the issuance by New Jersey of a certain class of stock, the TAXMAN system would interpret this event description as a program and write out a modified network for the subsequent time period in which a proposition of the form (ISSUE NEW-JERSEY ?S <time>) would be asserted as true.[80] Technically, the event description would be expanded by a command of the form (ASSERT <event> EXPAND), with the expansion theorem producing as its expansion the description of the modified state.

Using these mechanisms it is possible to write out the *history* of a corporate transaction. We first write out an initial state description, then write out a list of event descriptions, arranged in chronological order, and finally expand the event descriptions in order, thus producing a full sequence of modified state descriptions. In this way the TAXMAN system can have available in its data base information not only about current states and events, but about all prior states and events as well, an essential requirement for the application of the higher-level concepts of corporate reorganization law.

To see in greater detail how the event descriptions operate, let us examine the class of events involving the transfer of ownership from one individual to another, beginning with the primitive concept TRANS. For present purposes, the simplest event in the system will take the form (TRANS ?T ?P ?O ?R <time>), which is interpreted to mean "T transfers P from O to R at a certain time." The variable T represents the transferor; P represents the property being transferred; O is the former owner; and R is the new recipient. Or, more mnemonically, the proposition could be written as (TRANS <transferor> <property> <owner> <recipient> <time>).[81]

---

[80] In addition, any proposition not explicitly modified by the event description would be carried over unchanged into the modified state description network. The event descriptions thus produce only "incremental" changes in the state descriptions. For a discussion of these conventions, see T. WINOGRAD, *supra* note 12, at 116–17. For a general discussion of event descriptions, see Bruce, *Case Systems for Natural Language*, 6 ARTIFICIAL INTELLIGENCE 327, 331–33 (1975).

[81] Notice that TRANS refers here only to a transfer of "ownership," not to a transfer of "possession," or a transfer of "location," or any other sense of the word "transfer." In the system of Schank and his collaborators there are three basic TRANS events: "abstract transfer," "physical transfer," and "mental trans-

By definition, an expansion theorem for the TRANS proposition requires the modification of the ownership relationships from a prior to a subsequent state, and the essential aspects of the TRANS theorem could thus be written as follows:

(THEOREM EXPAND (T P O R TA TB)

(TRANS ?T ?P ?O ?R ?TB)

(IF   (GOAL   (OWN ?O ?P ?TA))
    THEN   (ERASE   (OWN ?O ?P ?TB))
           (ASSERT (OWN ?R ?P ?TB)))))

Suppose we wish to assert and expand the proposition "PHELLIS transfers the property P1 to DELAWARE," given the prior state description network of Figure 1. The desired event could be represented by the command (ASSERT (TRANS PHELLIS P1 PHELLIS DELAWARE <time>) EXPAND). Recall from the discussion in Part II how to trace through the effects of such a command: the basic TRANS proposition would be added to the factual data base first; then the TRANS theorem above would be retrieved and the variables matched; then the main body of the theorem would be executed with O as PHELLIS, P as P1, R as DELAWARE, and with TA and TB representing, respectively, the prior and subsequent states. In the execution of the theorem, the IF . . . THEN statement would carry out the main substantive operation: the IF clause would check to see if PHELLIS owned P1 in the prior state; if so, as in the present case, the THEN clause would proceed to erase PHELLIS' ownership and assert in the subsequent state description that DELAWARE now owned P1 instead. In short, stripping away the technical details, the TRANS assertion does exactly what we would expect: it changes the proposition (OWN PHELLIS P1) into the proposition (OWN DELAWARE P1), and writes out the modification in the subsequent state description network.

Once the basic TRANS operation is defined, it becomes possible to assemble some of the more complicated structures involving the transfer of property. One pattern of TRANS propositions that is particularly useful in corporate reorganization cases involves the transfer of only a portion of an individual's interest in a piece of property. Suppose we wish to assert the proposition "Phellis transfers 20 shares of the property P1 to Delaware." Intuitively, we could imagine that Phellis' interest in the property P1 is "split" into two "pieces," with only one

fer." Using these and several more "primitive actions," Schank is able to represent a surprising number of English verbs. Schank, *Conceptual Dependency Theory*, in CONCEPTUAL INFORMATION PROCESSING 22. 40–67 (R. Schank ed. 1975).

of these pieces transferred to Delaware. Thus the proposition could be represented as follows:

```
(PROG  (P)
   (ASSERT (NSHARES ?P 20))
   (ASSERT (SPLITPIECE ?P P1 <time>) EXPAND)
   (ASSERT (TRANS PHELLIS ?P PHELLIS DELA-
      WARE <time>) EXPAND))
```

In this example, SPLITPIECE is a special event description which creates a new piece of property, P, of size NSHARES = 20, and adjusts the ownership relationships in the networks so that Phellis owns both the original piece of stock, P1, reduced in size now by 20 shares, and the new piece, which can then be transferred. The final command, (ASSERT (TRANS PHELLIS ?P PHELLIS DELAWARE <time>) EXPAND), carries out the transfer of the 20-share piece of stock, as desired.

B. Description Mechanisms

To illustrate the construction of event descriptions of greater complexity than the TRANS assertion, I will analyze here the concept of a "stock distribution," a relatively abstract event, and show how the TAXMAN system can expand it downwards to a more concrete level.

Intuitively, a "distribution" of any kind consists of the splitting-up and piece-by-piece transfer of a certain "property" from its current "owner" to a certain "class of recipients." For example: "The New Jersey corporation distributes its Delaware common stock to its own common stockholders." Accordingly, a distribution could be represented at a relatively abstract level by a proposition of the form (DISTRIBUTE <transferor> <property> <owner> <class of recipients> <time>), where both the property transferred, e.g., "the Delaware common stock owned by New Jersey," and the class of recipients, e.g., "the common stockholders of New Jersey," could be represented by a definite description in the manner discussed earlier. At a more concrete level, a distribution could be represented by a sequence of particular transfers from one particular individual to another, or a sequence of particular TRANS assertions.

The TAXMAN system should be able to expand this concept from the first level down to the second. If P1 represents the total property to be distributed, then the distribution to any particular recipient, R1, could be represented by:

```
(ASSERT (SPLITPIECE ?P P1 <time>) EXPAND)
(ASSERT (TRANS <transferor> ?P <owner> R1
   <time>) EXPAND)
```

and the full distribution could be represented simply by repeating this partial transfer one time for each recipient. The expansion program for DISTRIBUTE, then, would simply examine the description of the class of recipients and, for each R that satisfied this description, generate an appropriate pair of SPLIT-PIECE-TRANS assertions, as above.[82] The result would be a list of concrete SPLITPIECE-TRANS events which could then be executed sequentially to generate a modified state description.

In a typical stock distribution, though, stock is transferred according to a formula, "two-shares-for-one," "pro rata," etc., which takes into account the proportionate ownership of the recipients in another security, and the TAXMAN system needs a mechanism to represent these concepts as well. At the concrete level of the SPLITPIECE-TRANS events we could use the NSHARES predicate to represent the number of shares of stock transferred to each recipient:

```
(ASSERT (NSHARES ?P  <number>))
(ASSERT (SPLITPIECE ?P Pı <time>) EXPAND)
(ASSERT (TRANS  <transferor>  ?P  <owner>  Rı
    <time>) EXPAND)
```

What we need, then, is a way to represent a proportionate stock distribution at a more abstract level, and a way to expand this abstraction into a sequence of concrete NSHARES-SPLIT-PIECE-TRANS assertions. To do this, the TAXMAN system takes advantage of the fact that we generally use a single description to define both the class of recipients of a stock distribution and the rule expressing the proportionality of the distribution. For example, if the recipients are defined as "the common stockholders of New Jersey," the distribution would typically be made in proportion to each recipient's ownership of "the common stock of New Jersey," or, more colloquially, the distribution would be made to the New Jersey common stockholders "with respect to their stock." Suppose we are describing an "n-shares-for-one" distribution. Then we could write out at the more abstract level

---

[82] The recipient class of "the common stockholders of New Jersey" would be represented, using the descriptions discussed in Part II, pp. 857–58 *supra*, by means of the pattern:

```
(GOAL (ISSUE NEW-JERSEY ?S))
(GOAL (STOCK ?S))
(GOAL (COMMON ?S))
(GOAL (PIECE-OF ?P ?S))
(GOAL (OWN ?R ?P))
```

The DISTRIBUTE program would simply match this pattern to the network; it would thereby FIND ALL the objects which match the variable R; and it would then write out a pair of SPLITPIECE-TRANS assertions for each object located.

a DISTRIBUTION-RULE that gives each recipient N shares of the distributed stock for each ONE share of the security with respect to which the distribution is made: (DISTRIBUTION-RULE <distribution> (N FOR ONE)). Since the expansion program for DISTRIBUTE examines the description of the recipient class to determine the names of the recipients in the SPLITPIECE-TRANS assertions, the expansion program for the DISTRIBUTION-RULE would simply examine this same description more thoroughly to determine how many shares of the defining security each recipient owned.[83] A simple arithmetical calculation would then provide the proper value of NSHARES.

Finally, if the distribution rule is "pro rata," (DISTRIBUTION-RULE <distribution> (PRORATA)), the expansion program could proceed by calculating the number N in the preceding (N FOR ONE) rule, and then applying the (N FOR ONE) rule as before. To do this, it would have to examine both the description of the recipient class and the description of the property to be distributed, for it would be necessary to compute the total number of shares involved in each description. This calculation, however, would clearly be manageable.

Notice how complex this conceptual hierarchy has become in what is still a fairly simple example. The structural "core" of the concept, the sequence of pairs of SPLITPIECE-TRANS assertions, is "modified" by the insertion of the appropriate NSHARES propositions, all of which have been generated by the expansion of a DISTRIBUTION-RULE. The DISTRIBUTION-RULE, in turn, may have been generated by the expansion of a still more abstract concept, such as PRORATA, describing the type of distribution in question. Finally, when the structural core and the prescribed modifications have all been assembled, they are themselves expanded to produce in the data base a modified state description network. It is this compression into a higher-level description of complex lower-level information which gives the conceptual hierarchy its power and flexibility, and it is the existence of recurrent patterns in the concept of a stock distribution itself which enables us to structure and stratify the hierarchy in this way.

---

[83] For example, when the DISTRIBUTE program matches the STOCKHOLDER pattern in note 82, *supra*, to the network to locate a recipient, R, it also locates the recipient's ownership interest, P, and so can easily determine the number of shares R owns. Of course, the recipient class might conceivably be defined as "the left-handed dentists in Atlantic City," in which case the search for the recipients might still succeed, given an appropriate data base, but the usual concept of a proportional stock distribution would be meaningless.

C. Analysis Mechanisms

I will now assume that the history of a corporate reorganization case has been stored in its expanded form in the data base,
and turn to the mechanisms that can analyze the case in terms
of the operative concepts of the Internal Revenue Code. The simplest example to start with is the concept of CONTROL. By
statute, CONTROL is defined as:

> the ownership of stock possessing at least 80 percent of the total
> combined voting power of all classes of stock entitled to vote
> and at least 80 percent of the total number of shares of all other
> classes of stock of the corporation.[84]

It should be clear why this concept is relatively easy to program
into the TAXMAN system: it is a concept applying only to a
single state description, has an algebraic formula at its core, and
is composed of essentially the same elements that entered into the
analysis of the concept of STOCKHOLDER.

Suppose that (CONTROL ?X ?Y <time>) is used to represent the proposition that "X controls Y" at a certain time.
A first step in the application of this concept would be to check
whether X owns any stock of Y at all. This could be accomplished most easily with the command (GOAL (STOCK-
HOLDER ?X ?Y <time>) ABSTRACT). If the state description passes this test, the CONTROL program must then determine the total stock ownership of X and compare this with the
total amount of stock issued by Y. The program must therefore
make an exhaustive search to locate all the stock issued by Y,
i.e.,

(GOAL (ISSUE ?Y ?S <time>))
(GOAL (STOCK ?S <time>))

and divide that stock into two classes depending on whether or
not the proposition (VOTING ?S <time>) is true. Then, for
each stock S, whether voting or nonvoting, the program would
locate the total ownership interest of X, *i.e.,*

(GOAL (PIECE-OF ?P ?S <time>))
(GOAL (OWN ?X ?P <time>))

and calculate the total number of votes or the total number of
shares, respectively, for each such P. Finally, sorting out the
S's and the P's and the votes and the shares, the two separate
calculations and comparisons of the "80 percent" figure would
be performed in a purely mechanical fashion.

---

[84] I.R.C. § 368(c).

For a more complex example, consider the concept of a B-REORGANIZATION. By statute, a Type B reorganization is defined as:

> the acquisition by one corporation, in exchange solely for all or a part of its voting stock (or in exchange solely for all or a part of the voting stock of a corporation which is in control of the acquiring corporation), of stock of another corporation if, immediately after the acquisition, the acquiring corporation has control of such other corporation (whether or not such acquiring corporation had control immediately before the acquisition).[85]

The representation of this complex concept must, like the representation of the DISTRIBUTE concept, build on the several lower levels of abstraction in the structure that makes it up. An acquisition seems to have the basic structure of an "exchange" or mutual "transfer" of property. More exactly, since it may consist of several exchanges, we can represent it by an expression of the form (ACQUISITION $<$list $<$exchange$>_i>$), where the subscript i indicates that the list may consist of one, two, or several members. An exchange, in turn, has the basic structure of a pair of "transfers," or rather, since an exchange may involve the mutual transfer of several objects, a pair of lists of transfers: (EXCHANGE $<$list $<$trans$>_j>$ $<$list $<$trans$>_j>$). Putting all this together, an acquisition could be represented as follows:

(ACQUISITION
  $<$list (EXCHANGE
    $<$list (TRANS ?T_1 ?P_1 ?O_1 ?R_1 $<$time$>$) . . . $>$
    $<$list (TRANS ?T_2 ?P_2 ?O_2 ?R_2 $<$time$>$) . . . $>$)
  . . . .$>$)

Consider now the problem of matching the ACQUISITION structure to the given network. Starting at the innermost level, the TRANS propositions would be matched with the command (GOAL (TRANS ?T ?P ?O ?R $<$time$>$) ABSTRACT). But the assignment of variables in this matching process cannot be entirely unconstrained. Since a pair of lists of TRANS propositions is intended to represent a mutual transfer, the recipient, R, of one transfer must be the same as the prior owner, O, of the other. To ensure this, the EXCHANGE program would require that within a single list of TRANS propositions, all the O's be identical and all the R's be identical; that the R_1's from the first member of a pair of lists be identical to the O_2's from the second member of the pair; and that the R_2's from the second be

---

[85] I.R.C. § 368(a)(1)(B).

identical to the O_1's from the first. Once the EXCHANGE structure is fully matched, then, the program obtains a single recipient, R_1 ($=O_2$), who has exchanged certain properties with another single recipient, R_2 ($=O_1$). By convention, we will take R_1, the recipient in the first list of TRANS propositions, to be the "acquirer" in the final ACQUISITION. If the ACQUISI-TION consists of multiple exchanges, so that there is more than one EXCHANGE to R_1, these exchanges would all be located and listed in the ACQUISITION structure; if not, the ACQUI-SITION structure would consist of only one EXCHANGE.

With the concept of an ACQUISITION represented in this way, it is now a relatively simple matter to represent the re-mainder of the B-REORGANIZATION definition: a B-RE-ORGANIZATION is just the result of imposing a further set of constraints on the ACQUISITION structure. One constraint is the statutory requirement that the acquisition be "by one corpo-ration," which means simply that R_1, the acquirer located by the ACQUISITION match, must be a corporation, or: (GOAL (CORPORATION R_1)). Another is the requirement that the acquisition be "of stock of another corporation," which means that each P_1 which is transferred to R_1 in the first list of TRANS propositions should be a PIECE-OF a STOCK which is ISSUEd by some other CORPORATION. A more crucial constraint is that the acquisition must be:

> in exchange solely for all or a part of [the acquiring corpora-tion's] voting stock (or in exchange solely for all or a part of the voting stock of a corporation which is in control of the acquiring corporation) . . . .

To apply this test, the B-REORGANIZATION program must locate all the P_2's in the second list of TRANS propositions, *i.e.*, all the properties transferred by R_1 ($=O_2$) "in exchange for" the P_1's, and determine that these P_2's are either (a) each a PIECE-OF a VOTING STOCK which is ISSUEd by R_1, or (b) each a PIECE-OF a VOTING STOCK which is ISSUEd by another CORPORATION in CONTROL of R_1. The ma-chinery necessary to implement this "solely for voting stock" re-quirement is already available and can simply be arranged in the appropriate patterns. Finally, consider the constraint that "immediately after the acquisition, the acquiring corporation has control of the acquired corporation." Again, the components of this test are all in place: the "time" of the acquisition has been recorded in the lists of TRANS propositions; the "acquiring corporation," R_1, has been previously identified, and the "ac-quired corporation" has been located in the course of the search for the issuer of the stock with piece P_1. We now need only add the specification: (GOAL (CONTROL <acquiring corporation> <acquired corporation> <time>) ABSTRACT).

For expository purposes I have been describing in the preceding paragraphs a particular sequence of operations: first the matching of the ACQUISITION concept to the network, then the imposition of the B-REORGANIZATION constraints. But in many situations this would be a highly inefficient procedure. For example, it would be highly inefficient for the program to locate first a large number of ACQUISITION structures and only then discover that these were not acquisitions of STOCK, or not even acquisitions by a CORPORATION. Instead, ideally, the B-REORGANIZATION constraints should be checked at the same time that the ACQUISITION structure is being matched. The current version of TAXMAN takes a step in this direction, in fact, by specifying a particular order in which the B-REORGANIZATION and ACQUISITION searches are to be performed. The program first searches for a relationship of CONTROL between two corporations and locates the earliest time at which this control exists; second, it searches backwards in time to locate the transfers of stock, if any, to the controlling corporation; third, for each such transfer of stock to the controlling corporation, it locates the transfers made in exchange and determines whether or not these are all solely for voting stock. If any of these initial decisions leads to a dead end, the program backs up to the appropriate point and starts the search over again from there.[86]

There are various substantive legal questions reflected in this choice of a search procedure. The problems of "creeping acquisitions,"[87] for example, are reflected in the structural ambiguities

---

[86] This procedure appears to be reasonably efficient in the great majority of situations we would expect to encounter. A more sophisticated version of the program, beyond the current capacity of TAXMAN, would be able to alter its search procedures as it goes along, depending on the specific information it is searching for and the specific knowledge it has already obtained.

[87] Prior to 1954, the Type B reorganization was defined as "the acquisition by one corporation . . . of at least 80 per centum of the voting stock and at least 80 per centum of the total number of shares of all other classes of stock of another corporation," Int. Rev. Code of 1939, ch. 1, § 112(g)(1)(B), 53 Stat. 40, and this language seemed to require that the entire 80 percent controlling interest in the acquired corporation be purchased in a single solely-for-voting-stock transaction, thus precluding the use of a Type B reorganization by a corporation that already owned more than 20 percent of the acquired corporation's shares. *See* Lutkins v. United States, 312 F.2d 803 (Ct. Cl.), *cert. denied*, 375 U.S. 825 (1963); Robert A. Pulfer, 43 B.T.A. 677 (1941), *aff'd per curiam*, 128 F.2d 742 (6th Cir. 1942). *But see* Charles A. Dana, 36 B.T.A. 97 (1937), *aff'd*, 103 F.2d 359 (3d Cir. 1939). The 1954 statute was intended to reverse this result by specifying only that the acquiring corporation have control "immediately after the ac-

of the B-REORGANIZATION concept as it has been described so far: first, the ACQUISITION structure is an open-ended list of EXCHANGE relationships, and it is unclear how far back into the past or forward into the future this list should be extended; second, the CONTROL relationship can exist over an extended period of time in the history of a corporate transaction, and the process of obtaining control can sometimes be a lengthy one. When we specify the order and scope of the search procedures for the ACQUISITION and CONTROL concepts, therefore, we determine which exchanges will be included in a qualifying B-REORGANIZATION. Actually, the current TAXMAN system does a rather poor job here, since it fails to embody accurately any of the current rules on these issues.[88] The important point, though, is that the current formalism reveals all the possibilities quite clearly, and thus provides a means of examining in concrete detail the possible solutions. A feasibly extended version of the TAXMAN system could contain further rules,

---

quisition . . . (whether or not such acquiring corporation had control immediately before the acquisition)." There were additional problems under the 1954 statute, however. Would a prior acquisition of stock for cash disqualify from reorganization treatment a subsequent acquisition made solely for voting stock? Conversely, would a prior acquisition of stock in exchange for voting stock qualify as part of a subsequent tax-free reorganization? The Treasury Regulations would ignore the prior acquisition for cash if it was clearly separate and occurred well before, *e.g.*, 16 years before, the claimed reorganization, and would include the prior acquisition for voting stock if it occurrred "in a series of transactions taking place over a relatively short period of time such as 12 months." Treas. Reg. § 1.368-2(c) (1960). *See generally* BITTKER, *supra* note 18, ¶ 14.33 to .34; Kanter, *Cash in a "B" Reorganization: Effect of Cash Purchases on "Creeping" Reorganization*, 19 TAX L. REV. 441 (1964); MacLean, *"Creeping Acquisitions,"* 21 TAX L. REV. 345 (1966).

[88] Most significantly, the current TAXMAN system contains no explicit provision for decomposing a sequence of exchanges into two or more separate acquisitions. Instead, the treatment of "creeping acquisitions" is left by default to the somewhat haphazard interaction of the ACQUISITION and CONTROL structures, according to the search procedure described in the text, pp. 871-74 *supra*. At first glance, this procedure might appear to implement the 1939 rather than the 1954 statute, *see* note 87 *supra*, since it seems to search only for acquisitions which precede the time of earliest control. But after first searching backwards from the earliest control relationship, the program can then search forward for any later control relationships which are themselves preceded by prior acquisitions, and in this way locate an entire sequence of qualifying Type B reorganizations, if such a sequence exists. This forward search will continue until the control relationship no longer exists, or until an exchange is made which is not solely for voting stock, a single mechanism for terminating the future extent of the ACQUISITION structure. It should be evident from this brief discussion that the problems of "creeping acquisitions" were not carefully thought out at the time the current TAXMAN system was designed, but it is not implausible to suggest that the problems of interpretation under the 1939 and the 1954 statutes have a similar origin: the unanticipated consequences of choosing a particular mode of expression for the "acquisition" of "control."

expressed in higher-level concepts, about "creeping acquisitions."[89]

IV. RESULTS

Let us now observe the TAXMAN system as it describes and analyzes an actual case involving the taxation of corporate reorganizations.[90] TAXMAN is an on-line real-time computer program, and the description mechanisms and analysis mechanisms correspond quite literally to the operations that can be performed by a user of the program typing at a terminal. The user types out a description of the case in the programming language we have been working with throughout,[91] starting with an initial state description and proceeding with a sequence of event descriptions.[92] The user then interrogates the system with the various GOAL commands to determine whether or not — and why or why not — the case fits the pattern of a Type B, a Type C, or a Type D reorganization.

I will use as an illustration *United States v. Phellis*,[93] one of the earliest reorganization cases, and the case upon which our original New Jersey-Delaware hypothetical was based. Since the original *Phellis* case was decided under a statute which con-

---

[89] At a minimum, these rules could incorporate the simple Treasury Regulation, *see* note 87 *supra*, to distinguish a single acquisition from two or more separate acquisitions.

[90] The TAXMAN system was programmed for and run on the PDP-10 computer at the Stanford Artificial Intelligence Laboratory. *See* notes * and 3, *supra*. The example of a corporate reorganization case that follows occupied a core image of approximately 40,000 words on that machine, of which approximately 20,000 words were available for the assertions and theorems necessary to describe and analyze the case. The abstraction and expansion theorems were expressed in approximately 450 lines of code in Micro-PLANNER and LISP, *see* note 54 *supra*; and the case description itself required slightly over 200 lines of code in addition. The illustrations in the text generally took less than 30 seconds to process, when the time-sharing system was lightly loaded. The Micro-PLANNER programming language is known to be slow and inefficient, however, *see, e.g.,* Sussman & McDermott, *supra* note 62, and a moderate increase in the complexity of the TAXMAN system would have produced a substantial degradation of performance. Complete listings of the program and a sample terminal session are available from the author upon request.

[91] *See* notes 54–55 *supra*. It is tedious to write case descriptions in the Micro-PLANNER programming language, and until this requirement can be relaxed a system like TAXMAN will be accessible only to a small number of specialists. For a discussion of the possibilities of incorporating a natural language capability into a system like TAXMAN, see pp. 886–88 *infra*.

[92] *See* p. 866 *supra*. The requirement that these event descriptions be written out in chronological order is a serious restriction. For a discussion of the possibilities of relaxing this requirement, see pp. 884–85 & notes 112–114 *infra*.

[93] 257 U.S. 156 (1921).

tained no provisions for a tax-free corporate reorganization, the TAXMAN system will make no attempt here to reproduce the original decision, but will instead attempt to analyze the case as it would be decided under the present Code. I have already pointed out some of the ways in which the TAXMAN analysis is imperfect and incomplete,[94] and these will be confirmed by the illustration; but the illustration should also suggest the potential power of the approach.

The following is a statement of the relevant facts in *United States v. Phellis*:

> Mr. Justice Pitney delivered the opinion of the court. The court below sustained the claim of C. W. Phellis for a refund of certain moneys paid by him under protest in discharge of an additional tax assessed against him for the year 1915, based upon alleged income equivalent to the market value of 500 shares of stock of a Delaware corporation called E. I. du Pont de Nemours & Company, received by him as a dividend upon his 250 shares of stock of the E. I. Du Pont de Nemours Powder Company, a New Jersey corporation. The United States appeals.
>
> From the findings of the Court of Claims, read in connection with claimant's petition, the following essential facts appear. In and prior to September, 1915, the New Jersey company had been engaged for many years in the business of manufacturing and selling explosives. Its funded debt and its capital stock at par values were as follows:

5% mortgage bonds	$ 1,230,000
4½% 30-year bonds	14,166,000
Preferred stock ($100 shares)	16,068,600
Common stock ($100 shares)	29,427,100
Total	$60,891,700

> . . . In that month a reorganization and financial adjustment of the business was resolved upon and carried into effect with the assent of a sufficient proportion of the stockholders, in which a new corporation was formed under the laws of Delaware with an authorized capital stock of $240,000,000 to consist in part of debenture stock bearing 6 per cent. cumulative dividends, in part of common stock; and to this new corporation all the assets and good-will of the New Jersey company were transferred as an entirety and as a going concern, as of October 1, 1915, at a valuation of $120,000,000, the new company assuming all the obligations of the old except its capital stock and funded debt. In payment of the consideration, the old company retained $1,484,100 in cash to be used in redemption of its outstanding 5% mortgage bonds, and received $59,661,700 par value in debenture stock of the new company (of which

---

[94] *See* pp. 875–76 & notes 88–89 *supra*.

$30,234,600 was to be used in taking up, share for share and dollar for dollar, the preferred stock of the old company and redeeming its 30-year bonds), and $58,854,200 par value of the common stock of the new company which was to be and was immediately distributed among the common stockholders of the old company as a dividend, paying them two shares of the new stock for each share they held in the old company. . . . Each holder of the New Jersey company's common stock (including claimant), retained his old stock . . . and the New Jersey corporation retained in its treasury 6 per cent. debenture stock of the Delaware corporation equivalent to the par value of its own outstanding common stock. . . . After the reorganization and the distribution of the stock of the Delaware corporation, the New Jersey corporation continued as a going concern, and still exists but, except for the redemption of its outstanding bonds, the exchange of debenture stock for its preferred stock, and the holding of debenture stock to an amount equivalent to its own outstanding common and the collection and disposition of dividends thereon, it has done no business. It is not, however, in process of liquidation. It has received as income upon the Delaware company's debenture stock held by it, dividends to the amount of 6% per annum, which it has paid out to its own stockholders including the claimant. . . . The fair market value of the stock of the Delaware corporation distributed as aforesaid was on October 1, 1915, $347.50 per share. The Commissioner of Internal Revenue held that the 500 shares of Delaware company stock acquired by claimant in the distribution was income of the value of $347.50 per share and assessed the additional tax accordingly. . . .[95]

Some of these facts could not be represented at all in the current TAXMAN system. For example, it is not possible to express the fact that the New Jersey company "had been engaged for many years in the business of manufacturing and selling explosives," or that the plan of reorganization was "carried into effect with the assent of a sufficient proportion of the stockholders." But it should also be clear that the operative facts of the case could indeed be represented in TAXMAN, using the basic description mechanisms we have examined so far. For example, the initial state description consists of a New Jersey corporation with common and preferred stock and two classes of bonds outstanding, and one identified stockholder, Phellis, who owns 250 shares of the common stock. This is only slightly more complicated than the simple example discussed earlier in the text. The several event descriptions in the case are also only slight variations of our earlier examples.[96] When the *Phellis*

---

[95] 257 U.S. at 165–68.

[96] There is a transfer of "all the assets and good will of the New Jersey com-

case is written out in full in the TAXMAN system and expanded in full, it produces only a moderately complex network.[97]

Assuming now that the full description is expanded and stored in the data base, let us look at the process of applying the analysis mechanisms to it. If we query the system first with (GOAL (B-REORGANIZATION ?A ?C ?T) ABSTRACT), where A is taken to be the acquiring corporation, C is taken to be the acquired corporation, and T is taken to be the time at which the reorganization is complete, the system will search for a Type B reorganization, at any time, with either Delaware or New Jersey as the acquiring corporation. The search for (B-REORGANIZATION DELAWARE NEW-JERSEY ?T) will fail, since Delaware never acquires any stock of New Jersey. In terms of the order of search described earlier, the failure occurs in searching for (CONTROL DELAWARE NEW-JERSEY ?T); and within the CONTROL theorem, the failure occurs in searching for (STOCKHOLDER DELAWARE NEW-JERSEY ?T). The search for (B-REORGANIZATION NEW-JERSEY DELAWARE ?T) will also fail, but for a more complex reason. Here the system finds (CONTROL NEW-JERSEY DELAWARE PHE32), and then finds the transfers of stock that have preceded this establishment of control. The result is an acquisition structure as follows:

(EXCHANGE

    ((TRANS DELAWARE PHE29 DELAWARE NEW-JERSEY PHE30)

    (TRANS DELAWARE PHE31 DELAWARE NEW-JERSEY PHE32))

    ((TRANS NEW-JERSEY PHE26 NEW-JERSEY DELAWARE PHE28)))

PHE29 and PHE31 here represent the debenture stock and the common stock, respectively, that were newly issued by Delaware

---

pany . . . at a valuation of $120,000,000"; the fact that the New Jersey company receives "$59,661,700 par value in debenture stock of the [Delaware] company . . . and $58,854,200 par value of the common stock of the [Delaware] company"; a redemption of the 5 percent mortgage bonds with cash; and a redemption of the preferred stock and the 30-year bonds with debenture stock. Finally, there is the precise example used earlier as an illustration of the description mechanisms of TAXMAN: the fact that "$58,854,200 par value of the common stock of the [Delaware] company . . . [is] immediately distributed among the common stockholders of the [New Jersey] company as a dividend, paying them two shares of the [Delaware] stock for each share they held in the [New Jersey] company."

[97] There is a list of 14 higher-level event descriptions, and there are approximately 50 internally generated symbols, all with the mnemonic prefix PHE, which represent the new classes of stocks and bonds, the ownership interests that are transferred, etc.

and then transferred to New Jersey. Curiously enough, the system has succeeded in matching a portion of the B-REORGANIZA-TION pattern to the description of the *Phellis* case: it has found an "acquisition" of Delaware stock by New Jersey, which is followed by a situation in which New Jersey "controls" Delaware. But PHE26 then turns out to represent the assets of Delaware, and thus in checking the "solely for voting stock" requirement of the Type B reorganization, the system discovers that the transfer is not even made in exchange for "stock," let alone "voting stock." Hence the search to match the full pattern of the B-REORGANIZATION concept ultimately fails, as it should.

Suppose we now query the system with (GOAL (C-RE-ORGANIZATION ?A ?C ?T) ABSTRACT).[98] When the C-REORGANIZATION pattern is matched to the description of the *Phellis* case, the system finds the acquisition structure

(EXCHANGE

    ((TRANS NEW-JERSEY PHE26 NEW-JERSEY DEL-AWARE PHE28))
    ((TRANS DELAWARE PHE29 DELAWARE NEW-JERSEY PHE30)
    (TRANS DELAWARE PHE31 DELAWARE NEW-JERSEY PHE32)))

and proceeds to apply the additional constraints of the statutory definition. It checks first to determine that PHE26 is "substantially all of the properties" of the New Jersey corporation, which it is. Then it examines what is exchanged for these properties: PHE29, which turns out to be the Delaware debenture stock, and PHE31, which turns out to be the Delaware common stock. If both of these are voting stocks,[99] the C-REORGANIZA-TION program succeeds, and returns: (C-REORGANIZATION DELAWARE NEW-JERSEY PHE28).

The concept of a Type D reorganization [100] cannot presently

---

[98] A Type C reorganization is defined as "the acquisition by one corporation, in exchange solely for all or part of its voting stock (or in exchange solely for all or part of the voting stock of a corporation which is in control of the acquiring corporation), of substantially all of the properties of another corporation . . . ." I.R.C. § 368(a)(1)(C).

[99] Although the report of *Phellis* contains no mention of the voting rights of these securities, it is quite likely that the debenture stock is nonvoting, thus preventing the transaction from qualifying as a Type C reorganization under the current statute. For purposes of the illustration, however, I have stipulated that both of these stocks are voting stocks. A more realistic approach would require the expansion of the concepts of "common stock" and "debenture stock" to a more concrete level, *see* pp. 883–84 & note 107 *infra*.

[100] The definition is "a transfer by a corporation of all or a part of its assets to

be fully implemented in the TAXMAN system, since there are no facilities for representing the distributions that would qualify under sections 354, 355, or 356.[101] Nevertheless, we can implement the structural core of the remainder of the concept: the transfer of property to a corporation which the transferor then controls. When this core concept is matched against the description of the *Phellis* case, the system finds:

((TRANS NEW-JERSEY PHE26 NEW-JERSEY DELA-
WARE PHE28))

and

((CONTROL NEW-JERSEY DELAWARE PHE32)
(CONTROL NEW-JERSEY DELAWARE PHE33)
(CONTROL NEW-JERSEY DELAWARE PHE36))

Restricted to this partial fragment of the concept, then, the system determines that a Type D reorganization has occurred, and returns: (D-REORGANIZATION NEW-JERSEY DELA-WARE PHE28).

This example illustrates the fact that the various reorganization patterns can be matched up to a case description network in multiple ways.[102] The existence of these partial matches and multiple matches suggests some of the ways in which the concepts of corporate reorganization law can be manipulated in the planning of a corporate transaction, and some of the ways in which ambiguities can arise in the analysis of a corporate reorganization case. It is potentially a very powerful feature of the TAXMAN system that it can identify and display these partial and multiple matches automatically.

V. Feasible Extensions

One of the main purposes behind the work on TAXMAN was the expectation that some of the techniques developed here could eventually prove useful in automating the more mundane

---

another corporation if immediately after the transfer the transferor, or one or more of its shareholders (including persons who were shareholders immediately before the transfer), or any combination thereof, is in control of the corporation to which the assets are transferred; but only if, in pursuance of the plan, stock or securities of the corporation to which the assets are transferred are distributed in a transaction which qualifies under section 354, 355, or 356." I.R.C. § 368(a)(1)(D).

[101] *See* p. 845 & notes 26–30 *supra*.

[102] The same three TRANS propositions appear in both the C-REORGANIZATION pattern and the partial B-REORGANIZATION pattern, but with their order within the EXCHANGE structure reversed in the two situations. In the partial B-REORGANIZATION pattern, the CONTROL structure appears in association with the acquisition of stock; whereas in the D-REORGANIZATION pattern, the same CONTROL structure appears in association with the transfer of assets.

aspects of legal research and analysis. Clearly the TAXMAN system in its present form does not yet provide a very useful tool for the practicing tax lawyer. The coverage of the system is much too limited, and even with a broader coverage of the tax law, the necessity of writing state descriptions and event descriptions in sequential order, and doing so in an obscure programming language, would render the system inaccessible to most potential users. Nevertheless, viewed as a simple pilot program rather than a full-scale applications program, the TAXMAN system does suggest a number of extensions which should eventually prove to be of practical significance. In this Part, I will describe some of these extensions and sketch briefly the directions in which future work in this area might proceed. Then, assuming that these extensions are feasible, I will outline how a more sophisticated version of the TAXMAN program might function within a system for computer-aided legal research, and compare such a system with the legal research systems on the market today.

The coverage of the system could be extended in many instances simply by a straightforward application of the basic techniques analyzed throughout this Article. One important area for further work would be the treatment of distributions and exchanges pursuant to a statutory reorganization. The major defect of the D-REORGANIZATION concept discussed in Part IV resulted from the inability of the current TAXMAN system to analyze the distributions that would qualify under sections 354, 355, or 356. An extended version of the system should be able to represent at least part of these nonrecognition rules [103] and at

---

[103] *See* note 26 *supra.* The basic structure of the nonrecognition rule could be represented, certainly, since it has some similarities to the basic conceptual structures we have already examined in Part III, *supra.* For example, the general rule of § 354(a)(1) reads: "No gain or loss shall be recognized if stock or securities in a corporation a party to a reorganization are, in pursuance of the plan of reorganization, exchanged solely for stock or securities in such corporation or in another corporation a party to the reorganization." Here, the core of the concept is a simple exchange structure, which would cause very few difficulties for the TAXMAN system, and the more important problems would then arise in representing the concepts that are attached to this conceptual core. *See generally* BITTKER, *supra* note 18, ¶¶ 14.30–.34. The definition of a "party to the reorganization" in § 368(b) would not be too difficult to implement, since it is built up out of a number of definite descriptions extracted from the components of the reorganization concept itself. *See* BITTKER, *supra* note 18, ¶ 14.32(1); Treas. Reg. § 1.368-2(f) (1976). *But see* Groman v. Commissioner, 302 U.S. 82 (1937); Helvering v. Bashford, 302 U.S. 454 (1938). The concepts of "stock" and "securities" are not defined in the statute, but it is possible to articulate some of the rules governing the application of these concepts, as these have emerged from the cases. *See* BITTKER, *supra* note 18, ¶ 14.31; Treas. Reg. § 1.354-1(e) (1960); cases cited note 32 *supra*; Neville Coke & Chem. Co. v. Commissioner, 148 F.2d 599 (3d Cir.), *cert. denied,* 326

least part of the associated basis rules.[104] More ambitiously, an extended version of the system should be able to represent some of the rules for distributions generally, even outside the reorganization context.[105] An extension of the analysis mechanisms in these directions would require a comparable extension of the description mechanisms: the system would have to expand the concepts of stocks and bonds, as suggested earlier,[106] and provide a formalism for describing various hybrid securities; [107] it would

---

U.S. 726 (1945); Carlberg v. United States, 281 F.2d 507 (8th Cir. 1960). Not all the components of the general nonrecognition rule could be handled in a straightforward fashion, however. The concept of an exchange being made "in pursuance of the plan of reorganization" is not well defined at all, and it is further complicated by its involvement in the problems of "creeping acquisitions," *see* pp. 873–76 & notes 87–88 *supra*, "business purpose," *see* pp. 843–48 *supra*, and "step transactions," *see* pp. 848–49 *supra*. *See* BITTKER, *supra* note 25, ¶¶ 14.32(1), .50, .51; Manning, *"In Pursuance of the Plan of Reorganization": The Scope of the Reorganization Provisions of the Internal Revenue Code*, 72 HARV. L. REV. 881 (1959); Treas. Reg. §§ 1.368–1(c) (1960), –2(g) (1976), –3(a) (1962).

[104] *See* p. 844 *supra*. The general rule of § 358(a) is quite mechanical: "the basis of the [nonrecognition] property . . . received [is] the same as that of the property exchanged, decreased by the fair market value of any other property [and] any money received by the taxpayer, . . . and increased by . . . the amount of gain to the taxpayer which was recognized on such exchange . . . ." Thus, assuming that that nonrecognition rules could be represented well enough to determine "the amount of gain . . . recognized," the representation of the basis rules would be a simple matter. Further rules prescribing the allocation of basis when several different stocks and securities are exchanged could also be represented quite easily. *See* Treas. Reg. § 1.358–2 (1960).

[105] *See* pp. 843–44 *supra*. The rules for corporate distributions have some of the same characteristics that were observed in note 103 *supra*: some, employing relatively precise tests, could be handled in the TAXMAN system in a straightforward fashion, but others, involving vague or ill-defined concepts, might require a fundamental modification of the TAXMAN paradigm. For example, the rules for identifying "stock redemptions" include the simple mechanical tests of a "substantially disproportionate" distribution, § 302(b)(2), as well as the vague standard of a redemption "not essentially equivalent to a dividend," § 302(b)(1). The new stock dividend rules of § 305 specify certain distributions which are taxable, § 305(b) (3)–(5), but also require an inquiry into whether or not a distribution "has the result of the receipt of property by some shareholders, and an increase in the proportionate interests of other shareholders," § 305(b)(2). The general dividend rule, § 316(a), requires a determination of the corporation's "earnings and profits," which can be computed in most instances from the complex rule of § 312 and Treas. Reg. § 1.312 (1960), but which is nowhere given a comprehensive statutory definition. *See generally* BITTKER, *supra* note 18, ¶¶ 7.01–.04, 7.60–.63, 9.20–.24.

[106] *See* p. 861 *supra*.

[107] This would be necessary, for example, to implement the rules governing the exchange of "stock or securities" under § 354(a), *see* note 103 *supra*, and to implement the rules governing "stock dividends" in § 305, *see* note 105 *supra*. The general approach here would be to develop descriptions of the possible components of a security interest: the voting rights, the priorities upon liquidation, the dividend provisions, etc. These components could then be combined in various combinations

also have to provide a better formalism for corporate account-
ing [108] and for some of the economic consequences of the transactions.[109] But once this expanded factual network is developed,
a good many of the rules and concepts governing corporate distributions generally, and reorganization exchanges specifically,
could be represented in abstraction theorems not dissimilar to
those of the current version of TAXMAN.[110] These extensions
would not be trivial, of course, but they would not seem to require
any major conceptual breakthroughs.[111]

A number of techniques are also available to overcome the
rigidities of the current system. I have mentioned some of the
difficulties that arise from the requirement that event descriptions
be written out in a strict sequential order.[112] An extended version
of the TAXMAN system should have built into it a more sophisticated model of temporal relationships and a method of
manipulating these relationships by means of higher-level descriptions.[113] More generally, an extended version of TAXMAN

---

to produce, *e.g.*, "convertible subordinated debentures," § 279(b), "hermaphrodite
convertible preferred stock," Rev. Rul. 70–108, 1970–1 C.B. 78, or whatever.

[108] This would be necessary to implement any of the rules concerning "earnings
and profits" of §§ 312 and 316(a), *see* note 105 *supra*, and in a number of other
contexts.

[109] A very simple economic model would suffice to represent the concept of
"gain" or "loss" and to implement the basis rules of § 358, *see* note 104 supra.
More complex models would be required to represent the economic differences between the ownership of various classes of securities, as in note 107 *supra*. Finally,
for a fuller understanding of the "purposes" and "motivations" behind the various
reorganization patterns, and an understanding of the divergences between "form"
and "substance," it would be necessary for the TAXMAN system to have available
a means of describing both the tax and the nontax benefits to the participants in
any corporate transaction. The development of these economic models would not
be a simple task, but once developed they would play an important role in an
extended version of TAXMAN.

[110] The proposals in notes 103–105 *supra* would, in effect, treat the DISTRIB-
UTE concept as an analysis mechanism and implement it as an abstraction theorem;
whereas the previous discussion of corporate distributions, pp. 868–70 *supra*, treated
the DISTRIBUTE concept as a description mechanism and implemented it as an
expansion theorem.

[111] There are two caveats to this statement. The first has already been indicated in notes 103–105 *supra*: some of the concepts and rules of corporate reorganization law may elude the current methods of semantic information processing.
The second caveat is that although it may be possible in principle to describe the
factual situations and conceptual structures that occur in this area of the law, the
programming effort could conceivably become bogged down in the complexity of
the details. My own judgment, however, is that a large portion of corporate
reorganization law could be incorporated into an extended version of TAXMAN
before either of these limits is reached.

[112] *See* note 92 *supra*.

[113] The current version of TAXMAN represents "time" as a simple linear list.
The natural generalization would use an unordered set of "time points," which could

should permit a more flexible use of description and analysis mechanisms of all kinds.[114] A still more radical variation would shift the operation of the entire system from an "analysis" mode to a "planning" mode. The current system is designed to produce a legal analysis of a given sequence of events. In a planning mode, by contrast, the system would construct a sequence of events so as to satisfy a given legal analysis.[115] Although this is not a trivial problem, it is one that has been solved in other contexts.[116] In

then be given a partial ordering by relationships such as "before" and "after"; and a corresponding set of "time intervals," which could be connected to each other by expressions such as "*A* occurs during *B*," and "*B* overlaps with *C*." It should be possible in this system to express incomplete knowledge, or even to express inconsistent knowledge, about these temporal relationships. For an example, see Bruce, *A Model for Temporal References and Its Application in a Question Answering Program*, 3 ARTIFICIAL INTELLIGENCE 1 (1975).

[114] One rigidity of the current system is the requirement that a case be described in full, and then expanded in full, before any analysis mechanisms can be applied. A more flexible system would accept a partial description, produce only a partial expansion, and attempt with this to do a partial analysis. The analysis mechanisms would then generate, if necessary, an additional expansion, or request from the user an additional piece of the description.

The problem here could be characterized as a *store vs. recompute* decision: Is it preferable to expand all factual descriptions at once, and thus "store" in computer memory everything that can be said about a given situation? Or is it preferable to leave the descriptions in an unexpanded form, as they are received, and then "recompute" the lower-level information every time an analysis mechanism actually needs it? Any response to this issue, however, requires a response to a large number of other issues about the efficient representation of conceptual information in computer data structures, and this leads quickly to most of the currently active areas of research in semantic information processing. For a discussion of the "design issues" that must be faced in constructing any representation of conceptual knowledge, see Moore & Newell, *How Can MERLIN Understand?*, in KNOWLEDGE AND COGNITION 201 (L. Gregg ed. 1974); Bobrow, *Dimensions of Representation*, in REPRESENTATION AND UNDERSTANDING 1 (D. Bobrow & A. Collins eds. 1975). Some of these issues have been briefly mentioned earlier in this Article. *See, e.g.*, the discussion of control structures, note 62 *supra*; abstraction theorems and procedural representations, note 63 *supra*; expansion theorems, note 65 *supra*; and references cited therein.

[115] These two models are of course not entirely distinct, and each can appear as a component of the other. Obviously the planning mode requires the use of the analysis mode to determine the legal consequences of various alternative plans, but the analysis mode may often require the use of the planning mode as well. In the corporate tax area, for example, the arguments concerning the proper legal characterization of a given transaction may be strongly influenced by a consideration of the alternative ways in which the transaction could have been carried out. This can be seen in many of the cases involving the "business purpose" doctrine, *see* pp. 847–48 *supra*, and the "step transaction" doctrine, *see* pp. 848–49 *supra*.

[116] A close analogy can be seen in the problem of chemical synthesis, where computer programs have been written to construct a sequence of chemical reactions from commercially available compounds that will produce a desired organic molecule, such as vitamin A. *See* Sridharan, *Search Strategies for the Task of Organic Chemical Synthesis*, PROCEEDINGS OF THE 3RD INT'L JOINT CONF. ON ARTIFICIAL

general, if the conceptual structures in a problem domain are reasonably well understood and reasonably well defined, it is a manageable task to devise a computer program to search heuristically for an appropriate "plan." [117]

Finally, let us look briefly at the problem of natural language understanding. The important point here is that the type of programming language in which TAXMAN is written is intended to function as part of a larger system for natural language processing, and thus it would be possible, though not at all easy, to write programs that could translate automatically from the description and analysis mechanisms of TAXMAN into a simplified form of English, and vice versa. The best example of a program of this sort is found in the work of Winograd, cited earlier.[118] Winograd's system conducts a dialogue in English about a simple world of blocks — small yellow cubes, large red boxes, tall green pyramids, etc. — which can be moved around and stacked on a table top. The system has three main components which interact with each other: a component for *inference*, which maintains the basic model of the block world, and is written in the same language as TAXMAN;[119] a component for *syntax*, which contains a basic grammar of English;[120] and

---

INTELLIGENCE 95 (1973). Other examples include constructing proofs of simple mathematical theorems, *see, e.g.*, Bledsoe, Boyer, & Henneman, *supra* note 15, and building towers and other structures in a world of children's blocks, *see, e.g.*, Fahlman, *A Planning System for Robot Construction Tasks*, 5 ARTIFICIAL INTELLIGENCE 1, 26–29 (1974).

[117] In TAXMAN, for example, it should be possible to reproduce some of the formal manipulations that were seen in Helvering v. Elkhorn Coal Co., 95 F.2d 732 (4th Cir.), *cert. denied*, 305 U.S. 605 (1938); *see* pp. 848–49 *supra*. Given the initial state description in that case, and a description of the desired end result, an extended version of the TAXMAN system should be able to notice that the Type C reorganization almost works, except for the problem of "substantially all properties," and then with this information generate the sequence of Type D, Type C, and Type B reorganizations that would be, formally, tax-free. This proposal for generating a "plan" would, in effect, treat the REORGANIZATION concept as a description mechanism, and implement it as an expansion theorem; whereas the previous discussion of corporate reorganization, *see* pp. 872–76 *supra*, treated the REORGANIZATION concept as an analysis mechanism, and implemented it as an abstraction theorem. The planning mode can thus be viewed as a process of positing, hypothetically, a higher-level description that we would like to have applied to our case, and then generating the lower-level expansions which would make that hypothetical description come true, consistent with the other assertions already present in the data base. On the dual representation of such concepts, compare note 110 *supra*.

[118] *See* notes 12, 63, 66–68, 80 *supra*.

[119] Winograd, *supra* note 12, at 23–27, 108–26.

[120] *Id.* at 16–23, 46–108. The syntactic component is based on Halliday, *Notes on Transitivity and Theme in English*, 3 J. LINGUISTICS 37 (1967), 4 J. LINGUISTICS 179 (1968); Halliday, *Functional Diversity in Language as Seen from a Considera-*

a component for *semantics*, which mediates between the other two components.[121] Winograd's system operates by translating an English sentence, usually a question or a command, into the internal representation of the block world model, generating an appropriate response within this model, and then translating this response back into English.[122] In the long run, a program of this

tion of Modality and Mood in English, 6 FOUNDATIONS OF LANGUAGE 322 (1970).

[121] Winograd, *supra* note 12, at 28–34, 126–69. Winograd provides the following introductory account of the role of the semantic component in his system: "There has never been a clear definition of what the field of 'semantics' should cover, but attempts to program computers to understand natural language have clarified what a semantic theory has to do, and how it must connect with the syntactic and logical aspects of language. In practical terms, we need a transducer that can work with a syntactic analyzer, and produce data which is acceptable to a logical deductive system. Given a syntactic parser with a grammar of English, and a deductive system with a base of knowledge about particular subjects, the role of semantics is to fill the gap between them." *Id.* at 28. In many ways the semantic component is the key to the success of Winograd's system, and the reader is advised to consult the complete work for an understanding of how it operates.

[122] The following dialogue is typical. The system has been requested earlier to "stack up both of the red blocks and either a green cube or a pyramid," and it has done so, in the process removing a small pyramid from the top of a red cube so that it could use that cube to complete the stack as specified. The following exchange then occurs (with queries to the system given in lower case, and responses in upper case):

Had you touched any pyramid before you put the green one on the little cube?
YES, THE GREEN ONE.
When did you pick it up?
WHILE I WAS STACKING UP THE RED CUBE, A LARGE RED BLOCK AND A LARGE GREEN CUBE.
Why?
TO GET RID OF IT.
Why did you do that?
TO CLEAR OFF THE RED CUBE.
Why did you clear off that cube?
TO PUT IT ON A LARGE GREEN CUBE.
Why did you do that?
TO STACK UP THE RED CUBE, A LARGE RED BLOCK AND A LARGE GREEN CUBE.
Why did you do that?
BECAUSE YOU ASKED ME TO.
How did you do it?
BY PUTTING A LARGE RED BLOCK ON THE TABLE; THEN LETTING GO OF IT; THEN PUTTING A LARGE GREEN CUBE ON IT; THEN LETTING GO OF THAT CUBE; THEN PUTTING THE RED CUBE ON THAT CUBE; THEN LETTING GO OF THAT CUBE.
How many objects did you touch while you were doing it?
FOUR OF THEM.
What did the red cube support before you started to clean it off?
THE GREEN PYRAMID.
There were five blocks to the left of the box then.

sort could be developed for use with the TAXMAN system; but in the short run, the attempt would probably by stymied by the problem of complexity. Even in its very restricted current version, the TAXMAN system is more complex than the block world model, mainly because of the complexity of the higher-level concepts of "distributions" and "reorganizations." A future version of TAXMAN, extended in coverage and flexibility as suggested above, would greatly exceed the capacity of the current programs for the syntactic and semantic components of natural language. I consider it more important, then, to develop the other feasible extensions first, and to restrict communications with the computer for the time being to a high-level programming language, as in the current system. It should later be possible to return successfully to the design of a natural language processor for corporate reorganization law.

How might the extended version of TAXMAN described in the preceding paragraphs function within a system for computer-aided legal research? The basic idea would be to develop and maintain a data base consisting of (1) a large number of factual descriptions, taken from reported cases, revenue rulings, treasury regulation hypothticals, etc.; (2) a wide variety of legal concepts and legal rules, taken from the Code, the Regulations, and other sources; and (3) for each factual description in the data base, the set of all possible legal characterizations of these facts in terms of the stored concepts and rules. If the system is sophisticated enough, it should be possible to store and analyze each factual description in the same way that the case of *United States v. Phellis* was stored and analyzed, but with greater descriptive flexibility, and with some form of natural language input. The system could then be used in several ways. It could be used simply as a device to retrieve the factual situations which match certain patterns of interest, or which satisfy certain fragments of a legal concept or a legal rule. It could be used to develop a suggested analysis of a new case: the user could describe the new case to the system and then generate a range of applicable higher-level concepts. Finally, the system could be used in a planning mode: the user could describe an initial situation and a desired end result and then generate a number of possible transaction patterns with the desired tax consequences.

It may be instructive to compare this imagined system with the systems for computer-aided legal research and analysis which are currently available. First, there are a number of systems in

NO, ONLY FOUR OF THEM: THE RED CUBE, TWO LARGE GREEN CUBES AND A LARGE RED BLOCK. . . .

Id. at 13–14.

operation today which maintain a data base of statutes and decided cases and retrieve this information in response to an appropriate query.[123] But the form in which these materials are
stored, and the techniques for retrieval, are quite different from
those of the proposed extension of TAXMAN. The existing
retrieval systems generally store the full text of a legal document
and retrieve it by key-words, or combinations of key-words,
which in its most primitive form amounts simply to requesting,
e.g., "all cases in which the word 'jurisdiction' appears." [124] Although this type of retrieval can be very useful in many circumstances, it is confined to looking only at what might be called
the "surface statistics" of legal language. By contrast, the extended version of TAXMAN would store a representation of the
underlying conceptual structure of a statute or a case and retrieve
this structure by a sophisticated pattern-matching operation.[125]

---

[123] The two most prominent systems in this country are LEXIS, developed by
Mead Data Central, Inc., and WESTLAW, a service recently offered by the West
Publishing Co. Other important legal retrieval systems include LTE, an early
system developed by the Air Force; JURIS, developed by the Justice Department;
QUIC/LAW, developed at Queen's University in Canada; DATUM, developed at
the University of Montreal; UNIDATA in Switzerland; CREDOC in Belgium;
and CRIDON in France. *See generally,* J. SPROWL, A MANUAL FOR COMPUTER-
ASSISTED LEGAL RESEARCH (Am. Bar Foundation, 1976); AMERICAN BAR ASS'N,
AUTOMATED LAW RESEARCH (1973); C. TAPPER, COMPUTERS AND THE LAW (1973).

[124] A typical example of the retrieval process in the LEXIS system is given in
Harrington, *What's Happening in Computer-Assisted Legal Research?*, 60 A.B.A.J.
924, 930–31 (1974). Harrington poses the problem of finding a case in the United
States Supreme Court which addresses the following question: "If the United
States appears in a probate court to assert a claim against a decedent's estate, does
it thereby waive its immunity against being sued in a state court so that the
fiduciary can assert a counterclaim greater than the amount of the original claim
asserted by the United States?" The first request to the LEXIS system is to
search for all cases in which the phrase *United States* occurs within ten words of
either the word *counterclaim* or the word *crossclaim*. The computer locates 25
cases which satisfy this request, and the researcher specifies further that the case
should also contain the phrase *state court*. This time the computer locates 19 cases,
and the researcher specifies further that the word *jurisdiction* be found within seven
words of the phrase *state court*. The computer locates only one case which satis-
fies this last request and the researcher displays it on the screen. It is United
States v. Shaw, 309 U.S. 495 (1940), which happens to be precisely on point. The
researcher can then "Shepardize" *Shaw* automatically by searching for all subsequent cases in which its citation appears. The use of the West Publishing Co.
WESTLAW system is similar, except that the data base consists of West headnotes
rather than the full text of the opinions. *See* J. SPROWL, *supra* note 123, at 55–78.

[125] As a simple illustration of the difference between these two approaches,
suppose we wish to locate a case in which there occurs a single transaction fitting
the general pattern of a Type C and a Type D reorganization, and fitting the
pattern of a Type B reorganization except for the "solely for voting stock" requirement. In an extended version of TAXMAN, this specification could easily be
expressed, and the system would retrieve *United States v. Phellis*, among others.

It would therefore be substantially more powerful and flexible than the systems for legal information retrieval on the market today.[126]

The second approach to computer-aided legal research today is based upon the methods of computer-assisted instruction (CAI). The computer poses questions designed to elicit the essential facts of a case, and then, depending on the information received, either suggests a tentative legal analysis or poses an additional factual question.[127] There are parallels here, of course, to the way an extended version of TAXMAN might develop the description and analysis of a case. But note the rigid structure of these CAI-based systems: the user faces a series of pre-

---

But this search request could not even be formulated in the existing legal retrieval systems, nor is it likely that any other request could be formulated which could retrieve with precision the factual pattern of *Phellis*. The difficulty in locating *Phellis* itself is that the statutory reorganizaion provisions were inapplicable to it, and the opinion contains no mention of them. Even confining the search to cases that postdate the reorganization statutes, the existing retrieval systems would still encounter difficulties. The most efficient way to search for a Type C reorganization, for example, is to search for the statutory section number "368(a)(1)(C)," and its predecessor in the 1939 Code, "112(g)(1)(C)." Thus a researcher might request a search for 368(a)(1)(B) AND 368(a)(1)(C) AND 368(a)(1)(D), and then a search for 112(g)(1)(B) AND 112(g)(1)(C) AND 112(g)(1)(D). But the system would then retrieve *any* case in which these three statutory sections were mentioned, whether applicable or not, and *no* case which failed to discuss all three; there would be no way to specify to the system that the three reorganization patterns should fit the same basic transaction, or that the Type B reorganization pattern should only be partially applicable. For example, had it been decided under the 1939 or the 1954 statute, one case that would be retrieved with this request is Helvering v. Elkhorn Coal Co., 95 F.2d 732 (4th Cir. 1938), *see* pp. 848–49 *supra*, where the three reorganization patterns apply to sequential transactions, rather than a single transaction. Similar illustrations could be constructed for most other kinds of retrieval problems in the corporate tax area.

[126] A similar conclusion is advanced by P. SLAYTON, ELECTRONIC LEGAL RETRIEVAL (Report prepared for Canadian Dep't of Communications, 1974). *See also* P. Slayton, Radical Computer Use in Law (Draft Report prepared for the Canadian Dep't of Communications, June 1974).

[127] This approach has not yet been extensively developed as an aid to practicing attorneys, but one experimental project has produced a client interviewing system for use by the Cook County Legal Assistance Foundation in Chicago. *See* Chatterton & McCoy, *Computer-Assisted Legal Services*, LAW & COMPUTER TECH., Nov. 1968, at 2; *Discovery of Jurimetrics Projects*, 15 JURIMETRICS J. 56 (1974). The CAI approach has been used more extensively as an educational tool, with the computer posing questions and hypothetical cases to a law student and evaluating the responses. *See, e.g.,* Maggs & Morgan, *Computer-Based Legal Education at the University of Illinois: A Report of Two Years' Experience*, 27 J. LEGAL ED. 138 (1975). For a thorough survey of computer-assisted instruction generally, see R. LEVIEN, THE EMERGING TECHNOLOGY: INSTRUCTIONAL USES OF THE COMPUTER IN HIGHER EDUCATION (1972); for a sharp critique, see A. OETTINGER & S. MARKS, RUN, COMPUTER, RUN: THE MYTHOLOGY OF EDUCATIONAL INNOVATION (1969).

programmed questions and usually responds in a strict multiple-choice format; the author of the program faces the tedious task of anticipating all possible responses and programming explicitly every logical branch. In the extended version of TAXMAN, by contrast, the most important and difficult work is done at the start, when the description and analysis mechanisms are designed to capture the basic conceptual structure of the problem domain. Once these basic conceptual structures are written, the "analysis" and "planning" modes of the system can then be programmed more easily, in a uniform and systematic way. For the user of the system this permits a much greater flexibility in the interactive process, and for the author of the program it requires much less concern about the specific details of the interaction. In general, then, the TAXMAN approach appears to have much greater long-range potential than the CAI approach as a technique for computer-aided legal research, either for the law student or for the practicing attorney.[128]

But the important question remains: Just how feasible is this extended version of TAXMAN? The answer depends both on the characteristics of the problem domain in which we wish to have the extended system operate and on the expected advances in semantic information processing in the next few years. In order for the current paradigm to be applicable, as we have seen, it is necessary to develop an adequate model of the lower-level factual situations that we expect to occur [129] and an adequate representation of the higher-level legal concepts in the relevant area of the law.[130] The taxation of corporate reorganizations is an excellent problem domain in both of these respects. It appears

---

[128] The position taken here is similar to that of Carbonell and his associates, who have done the pioneering work on the application of artificial intelligence techniques to computer-assisted instruction. *See, e.g.*, Carbonell, *AI in CAI: An Artificial-Intelligence Approach to Computer-Assisted Instruction*, 11 IEEE TRANSACTIONS ON MAN-MACHINE SYSTEMS 190 (1970); Brown & Burton, *Multiple Representations of Knowledge for Tutorial Reasoning*, in REPRESENTATION AND UNDERSTANDING 311 (D. Bobrow & A. Collins eds. 1975). Carbonell's views on the relative merits of the traditional CAI systems and the more experimental AI systems are well-balanced: " . . . we are not advocating the complete elimination of [traditional CAI]. It will have its role for some time to come. We see it convenient for cases in which the subject matter is very diversified and the interactions with the students are planned to be brief. In those cases, the development of complex semantic networks is not justified. When discussion in depth is desired, when the student should have some initiative, when detailed anticipation is unwanted, then [CAI] systems are to be preferred. On the other hand, when teaching sequences are extremely simple, perhaps trivial, one should consider doing away with the computer, and using other devices or techniques more related to the task." Carbonell, *supra*, at 201.

[129] *See* pp. 883–84 & notes 106–109 *supra*.

[130] *See* pp. 882–83 & notes 103–105 *supra*.

that a large number of important and interesting problems can be handled here well before we reach the apparent limits of the TAXMAN paradigm.[131] It is a risky business predicting future advances in computer science, but based upon a knowledge of both the law of corporate reorganizations and the current work in semantic information processing, I would be willing to hazard a guess: if a substantial amount of resources was committed to the project, a sophisticated prototype system of demonstrable utility to a corporate tax lawyer could be developed within approximately ten years.

VI. Conclusion

In this Article I have shown how the current paradigm of semantic information processing can be applied to a particular area of the law, and I have indicated how this approach could lead to several practical applications. But the theoretical purpose behind the work on TAXMAN has not yet been addressed. I suggested that the work should provide a tool for the development of our theories about legal reasoning, enabling us to acquire a more precise understanding of the structure and dynamics of legal concepts. The suggestion was that we view the TAXMAN system as a formal model of the concepts of corporate reorganization law and assess its adequacies and inadequacies in this respect. For this purpose, however, it should be clear by now that there are serious deficiencies in even the extended version of TAXMAN. The most important deficiencies appeared in Part I, where it was emphasized that the "continuity of interest," "business purpose," and "step transaction" doctrines were developed in opposition to the mechanical manipulation of abstract statutory rules, and that they seemed to have a different structure from the concepts that have so far been successfully implemented in TAXMAN.[132] A possible explanation of these deficiencies was suggested at the close of Part II, where it was noted that the TAXMAN system was statically equivalent to the higher-order predicate calculus, even though the programming language in which it was written added to this static representation a certain dynamic power and flexibility.[133] In general, then, the detailed analysis of the TAXMAN system has tended to support what

---

[131] *See* note 111 *supra.*

[132] *See* pp. 846–50 *supra.* A similar observation occurred in the discussion of the feasibile extensions in Part V: although it appeared that a great many of the rules and concepts of corporate reorganization law could be added to an extended version of TAXMAN, this claim could not be made for all such rules and concepts. *See* pp. 882–84 & notes 103–11 *supra.*

[133] *See* pp. 861–62 *supra. See also* note 103 *supra.*

should surely be a lawyer's intuition: that the current TAXMAN paradigm fails to capture many of the significant facts about the structure of legal concepts and the process of legal reasoning.

I do not believe, however, that this is the final word on the subject. A systematic exploration of the limitations of the current TAXMAN paradigm would, I believe, lead us to a modified paradigm which would correct some of these limitations and permit us to say something about the structure and dynamics of even the more vaguely defined concepts of corporate reorganization law.[134] Although we would ultimately come to the conclusion, not unlike the lawyer's intuition, that nothing as complex as legal reasoning could ever be represented in a computer program, I believe it would be possible to sketch out a formal computer model somewhat more realistic than the current version of TAXMAN. And this, after all, is the task of greatest theoretical interest. Even if our formalisms will always be inadequate in one or more respects, the process of constructing and modifying these formalisms, if carefully done, should itself be a source of insight and understanding.

---

[134] I will pursue this analysis in detail in a future article.

THE DECLINE OF LAW AS AN AUTONOMOUS
DISCIPLINE: 1962–1987

*Richard A. Posner**

Being of a skeptical cast of mind, I at first declined the editors' invitation to contribute to this issue commemorating the hundredth anniversary of the founding of the *Harvard Law Review*. That the *Review* is 100 years old has no significance. Even the fact that I live in a house that is eighty-two years old has greater significance: it has implications for problems of maintenance and repair, and it tells one something about the architectural and structural features of the house. But as a journal has no natural life span, the fact that it is 100 years old should interest only people who have a superstitious veneration for round numbers. The reason the *Harvard Law Review* is 100 years old is that it was started 100 years ago; the law reviews of all the major law schools are still being published, and if they had been started 100 years ago they too would be 100 years old.

What is true, however, and an apt subject for anniversary reflections, is that the *Harvard Law Review*, for reasons outside the control of the able students who run it, may have reached the peak of its influence — may, indeed, have started its journey down the mountain. One factor is the democratization of legal teaching and research — a leveling process as a result of which the Harvard Law School is now but one of a half-dozen or so law schools of roughly equal quality, rather than the unquestioned leader of legal education that it once was. Another factor — the one that will concern me in this Essay — is the changes in the legal system and legal thought that began in the early 1960s. Until then the autonomy of legal thought was the relatively secure, though periodically contested, premise of legal education and scholarship. It is no longer. I am particularly conscious of this change because I was educated toward the end of an era in which law — the attack of the legal realists having been blunted — was confidently regarded as an autonomous discipline, and because the law school I attended epitomized this conception (I graduated from the Harvard Law School in 1962); yet much of my professional energy since has been devoted to opposing this conception. I shall try to explain what the conception was, why it has been (as I think) dethroned, and what the implications are for the legal system, for legal

* Judge, United States Court of Appeals for the Seventh Circuit; Senior Lecturer, University of Chicago Law School.

The author wishes to acknowledge the research assistance of Paul Eberhardt, and the very helpful comments of Paul Bator, Frank Easterbrook, Philip Elman, Edward Levi, Richard Porter, Geoffrey Stone, and Cass Sunstein on a previous draft.

education and scholarship, and, incidentally, for the next century of the *Harvard Law Review.*

I. LAW AS AN AUTONOMOUS DISCIPLINE

The idea that law is an autonomous discipline, by which I mean a subject properly entrusted to persons trained in law and in nothing else, was originally a political idea. The judges of England used it to fend off royal interference with their decisions,[1] and lawyers from time immemorial have used it to protect their monopoly of representing people in legal matters. Langdell in the 1870s made it an academic idea. He said that the principles of law could be inferred from judicial opinions, so that the relevant training for students of the law was in reading and comparing opinions and the relevant knowledge was the knowledge of what those opinions contained.[2] He thought that this procedure was scientific, but it was not, not in the modern sense at any rate. It was a form of Platonism; just as Plato had regarded particular chairs as manifestations of or approximations to the concept of a chair, Langdell regarded particular decisions on contract law as manifestations of or approximations to the legal concept of contract.

This perverse or at best incomplete way of thinking about law was promptly assailed by Holmes, who pointed out that law is a tool for achieving social ends, so that to understand law requires an understanding of social conditions.[3] Holmes thought the future of legal studies belonged to the economist and statistician rather than the "black-letter" man.[4] But because the economist and the statistician — not to mention the philosopher, the sociologist, the political scientist, the historian, the psychologist, the linguist, and the anthropologist (notably excepting Henry Maine)[5] — were not much interested in law, Holmes's assault on Langdell did not undermine the autonomy of the

---

[1] In the words of Sir Edward Coke:

then the King said, that he thought the law was founded upon reason, and that he and others had reason, as well as the Judges: to which it was answered by me, that true it was, that God had endowed his Majesty with excellent science, and great endowments of nature; but His Majesty was not learned in the laws of his realm of England, and causes which concern the life, or inheritance, or goods, or fortunes of his subjects, are not to be decided by natural reason but by the artificial reason and judgment of law, which law is an act which requires long study and experience, before that a man can attain to the cognizance of it: and that the law was the golden met-wand and measure to try the causes of the subjects; and which protected his Majesty in safety and peace . . . .

Prohibitions Del Roy, 6 Coke Rep. 280, 282 (1608).

[2] *See, e.g.,* C. LANGDELL, A SELECTION OF CASES ON THE LAW OF CONTRACTS viii (2d ed. 1879). For a superb description of his method see Grey, *Langdell's Orthodoxy,* 45 U. PITT. L. REV. 1 (1983).

[3] *See* O.W. HOLMES, JR., THE COMMON LAW (1881).

[4] *See* Holmes, *The Path of the Law,* 10 HARV. L. REV. 457, 469 (1897).

[5] *See* H. MAINE, ANCIENT LAW (1861).

law as a discipline. Holmes himself was steeped in the philosophical thought, both ethical and epistemological, of the late nineteenth century, in particular Social Darwinism and Charles Peirce's pragmatism. However, the lesson suggested by his career, as by the careers of such other notable legal thinkers as Benjamin Cardozo, Louis Brandeis, Roscoe Pound, John Wigmore, Felix Frankfurter, Karl Llewellyn, Learned Hand, Jerome Frank, Henry Hart, and Lon Fuller, was that a legal thinker should be cultivated, broadly educated, and intellectually well-rounded (rather than merely proficient in the doctrinal analytics taught by Langdell and his successors) — not that any of the keys to understanding law were held by disciplines other than law.

Such was the atmosphere of the Harvard Law School when I was a student. With a handful of exceptions (such as Donald Turner in antitrust),[6] the faculty believed, or at least appeared to believe, that the only thing law students needed to study was authoritative legal texts — judicial and administrative opinions, statutes, and rules — and that the only essential preparation for a legal scholar was the knowledge of what was in those texts, and the power of logical discrimination and argumentation that came from close and critical study of them. The difference from Langdell's day — a difference that was the legacy of Holmes and the legal realists — was that law now was recognized to be a deliberate instrument of social control, so that one had to know something about society to be able to understand law, criticize it, and improve it. The "something," however, was what any intelligent person with a good general education and some common sense knew; or could pick up from the legal texts themselves (viewed as windows on social custom); or, failing these sources of insight, would acquire naturally in a few years of practicing law: a set of basic ethical and political values, some knowledge of institutions, some acquaintance with the workings of the economy.

You may think that the next thing to be said about this faith in law's autonomy as a discipline is that it was a complacent faith; but if so you are wrong. It was empirically supported. In 1965 it reasonably appeared that any deficiencies in the legal system could be rectified by lawyers trained and operating in the tradition of autonomy. For in a period of twenty-five years, lawyers had, it seemed, with little help from other disciplines, reformed the procedural system of the federal courts[7] (and by force of example, were well on their way to reforming the procedural systems of the state courts); had corrected the profound epistemological error that had led the Supreme

---

[6] See, e.g., Turner, The Definition of Agreement Under the Sherman Act: Conscious Parallelism and Refusals to Deal, 75 HARV. L. REV. 655 (1962).

[7] See the Federal Rules of Civil Procedure enacted in 1938.

Court to claim authority to create a general federal common law in diversity of citizenship cases;[8] had brought commercial law into harmony with modern commercial practices through the Uniform Commercial Code; had (under considerable political pressure, to be sure) saved the Supreme Court by abandoning "liberty of contract" as a substantive constitutional right; had completed (or at least brought much nearer to completion) the work of the Civil War by outlawing racial segregation in public schools and other government institutions both state and federal; had in the second flag salute case[9] resurrected the Constitution as a charter of civil liberties; had systematized and regularized the administrative process[10] and used that process as the foundation for creating imaginative new systems of legal regulation of labor relations and the securities markets; had taken substantial steps to civilize criminal procedure;[11] had overcome the courts' traditional hostility to statutes; had tidied up the common law through the American Law Institute's Restatements; had rethought substantive criminal law in the ALI's Model Penal Code; had eliminated a number of arbitrary barriers to legal liability (such as the privity limitation in products liability); had come to terms with the New Deal; and were well on their way to dismantling the remaining archaic, formalistic, or dysfunctional rules of law, such as the intricate rules governing the liability of landowners to persons injured because of conditions on the land.[12] In hindsight some of these achievements can be questioned, and there were always some doubters, but on the whole the lawyer's traditional faith in the autonomy of his discipline seemed well founded in 1960.

Buttressing this faith was the apparent inability of other disciplines to generate significant insights about law. For example, until the publication in 1961 of articles by Ronald Coase[13] and Guido Calabresi,[14] economics seemed to have rather little to say about law outside

---

[8] See Erie R.R. v. Tompkins, 304 U.S. 64 (1938) (overruling Swift v. Tyson, 41 U.S. (16 Pet.) 1 (1842)).

[9] See West Va. State Bd. of Educ. v. Barnette, 319 U.S. 624 (1943).

[10] See Administrative Procedure Act, ch. 324, 60 Stat. 237 (1946) (current version at 5 U.S.C. §§ 551–559, 701–706, 3105, 3344 (1982)).

[11] See, e.g., Gideon v. Wainwright, 372 U.S. 335 (1963) (applying the sixth amendment's guarantee of assistance of counsel to the states); Mapp v. Ohio, 367 U.S. 643 (1961) (applying the fourth amendment exclusionary rule to the states); Brown v. Allen, 344 U.S. 443 (1953) (holding that federal habeas corpus relief for a state prisoner is not barred simply because certiorari to review his conviction directly has been denied); Brown v. Mississippi, 297 U.S. 278 (1936) (excluding coerced confession on due process grounds).

[12] See, e.g., Rowland v. Christian, 69 Cal. 2d 108, 443 P.2d 561 (1968) (replacing the "ancient" set of "rigid" common law classifications with one general duty to act reasonably toward all who enter upon one's land).

[13] See Coase, The Problem of Social Cost, 3 J.L. & ECON. 1 (1961).

[14] See Calabresi, Some Thoughts on Risk Distribution and the Law of Torts, 70 YALE L.J. 499 (1961).

the antitrust field (though in retrospect it is hard to understand how Henry Simons' work on the economics of taxation[15] could have been ignored). Even in the field of antitrust there were grounds for skepticism. Antitrust was then the domain of the field of economics known as "industrial organization" — at the time a "soft" field, unlikely to impress lawyers with its rigor, for the very good reason that it was not rigorous.[16] In particular, economists had made little progress toward understanding oligopoly, which was thought to be the central problem of antitrust economics. Hence it was possible for Professor Bok (as he then was) to write an article in 1960 debunking the pretensions of economists to be able to guide the application of the antimerger law.[17] Yet then as now economics was understood to have greater relevance to law than other fields had. Ethical and political philosophy were in a slump, and virtually the only relevance that the then-dominant analytical or linguistic philosophy was thought to have to law was in the age-old debate between positivists and natural lawyers over the question, "What is law?" (a question that has little practical significance if, indeed, it is a meaningful question at all).

An additional reason for the prevailing faith in the autonomy of law was the remarkable political consensus of the late 1950s and early 1960s. Since 1940, and especially since 1952, there had been little ideological difference between the major parties. At least in the academy, the radical right had been discredited, first by its isolationism and then by its racism, and the radical left had been squashed by the Cold War. Secular, humanistic, patriotic, and centrist, the American intellectual scene in the late 1950s and early 1960s was remarkably free from ideological strife. In such a period it was natural to think of law not in political but in technical terms, as a form of "social engineering" with the lawyers as the engineers. Just as society had left the design of bridges to civil engineers, so it could leave the design of its legal institutions to lawyers. If civil engineers disagreed fun-

---

[15] See H. SIMONS, PERSONAL INCOME TAXATION (1938); see also W. BLUM & H. KALVEN, JR., THE UNEASY CASE FOR PROGRESSIVE TAXATION xiv–xvii (1953) (discussing Simons' work and reaction to it).

[16] See Posner, The Chicago School of Antitrust Analysis, 127 U. PA. L. REV. 925, 928–29 (1979) (discussing, among other works, E. MASON, ECONOMIC CONCENTRATION AND THE MONOPOLY PROBLEM (1957)). The rigorous analysis of monopoly and competition by Aaron Director, George Stigler, and others was just beginning to be published and was not yet well known. For early examples, see Bork, Vertical Integration and the Sherman Act: The Legal History of an Economic Misconception, 22 U. CHI. L. REV. 157 (1954); Director & Levi, Law and the Future: Trade Regulation, 51 NW. U.L. REV. 281 (1956); McGee, Predatory Price Cutting: The Standard Oil (N.J.) Case, 1 J.L. & ECON. 137 (1958); Stigler, A Theory of Oligopoly, 72 J. POL. ECON. 44 (1964); Telser, Why Should Manufacturers Want Fair Trade?, 3 J.L. & ECON. 86 (1961).

[17] See Bok, Section 7 of the Clayton Act and the Merging of Law and Economics, 74 HARV. L. REV. 226, 228, 239–47, 349 (1960).

damentally about wind resistance, society could not safely leave the design of bridges entirely to them; similarly, if lawyers disagreed about the aims and nature and consequences of law, society could not leave the design of legal institutions to them. But in the period of which I am writing there was little such disagreement and therefore little opposition to the lawyers' claim to have an autonomous discipline. And although in some ultimate sense law, unlike civil engineering, is unavoidably political, this fact is unlikely to be noticed, let alone to have practical significance, at a time when the entire respectable band of the professional spectrum agrees on the basic political questions that are important to law. With political differences not infecting legal analysis, the law appeared to be a technical and objective discipline.

It had not always been thus. The legal realists of the 1920s and 1930s believed quite the opposite and mounted a powerful attack on legal doctrines, practices, and institutions. They believed that much of law reflected a politically motivated hostility by judges and the legal profession generally toward state and federal social welfare legislation, administrative agencies, labor unions, radicals, and proposals to change common law doctrines.[18] By the 1950s, however, when many of the changes advocated by the legal realists had been adopted and many of the leading realists had been coopted into the judiciary and into the drafting of uniform laws and other mainstream legal activities, it was widely believed that the law had been restored to a position of political neutrality.

II. The Decline of Law's Autonomy

The supports for the faith in law's autonomy as a discipline have been kicked away in the last quarter century. First, the political consensus associated with the "end of ideology"[19] has shattered. The spectrum of political opinion in law schools, which in 1960 occupied a narrow band between mild liberalism and mild conservatism, today runs from Marxism, feminism, and left-wing nihilism and anarchism on the left to economic and political libertarianism and Christian fundamentalism on the right. Even if we lop off the extremes, a broad middle area remains, running from, say, Ronald Dworkin on the left to Robert Bork on the right — both entirely respectable, "establishment" figures who, however, are so distant ideologically from one another that there is no common ground of discourse between

---

[18] For an authoritative collection of readings on legal realism, see D. Hutchinson, History of American Legal Thought II: The American "Legal Realists" (1984) (unpublished manuscript, University of Chicago Law School).

[19] *See* D. Bell, The End of Ideology: On the Exhaustion of Political Ideas in the Fifties (1960).

them.[20] We now know that if we give a legal problem to two equally distinguished legal thinkers chosen at random we may get completely incompatible solutions; so evidently we cannot rely on legal knowledge alone to provide definitive solutions to legal problems.

The shattering of the political consensus would not matter if American law were confined to nonpolitical issues; chemistry has not ceased to be an autonomous discipline just because there is more political diversity among chemists today than there was thirty years ago. But far from being so confined, many fields of law today are deeply entangled with political questions. In part, this entanglement is due to the aggressiveness with which the Supreme Court has created constitutional rights in politically controversial areas, such as abortion (and other matters involving sex), reapportionment, political patronage, and school and prison conditions. In part, it is due to the expansion of government generally, which has brought more and more subjects, often intensely political ones, into the courts — subjects such as poverty, campaign financing, environmental protection, and the plight of disabled people. Moreover, the Supreme Court has pioneered an aggressive style of judicial activism that, imitated by state courts and by lower federal courts in diversity cases, has led to politically controversial extensions of rights in such nonfederal fields as tort and contract law. There are still politically uncontroversial fields of law, such as trusts and taxation (the latter a field where statutory detail leaves little room for judicial discretion), but fewer than in the 1950s.

Coinciding with the decline of political consensus has been a second development: a boom in disciplines that are complementary to law, particularly economics and philosophy. Economics not only has become more rigorous since the 1950s, but it has branched out from market to nonmarket behavior,[21] thus taking in the subject matter of most interest to legal thinkers. It has also become more empirical. Not only is there today a well-developed economic theory of crime, but economists have measured the effects of punishment on the crime rate more rigorously than other social scientists, or lawyers, have ever done.[22] There is an economics of accidents and accident law, of the family and family law, of property rights and property law, of finance and corporations, even of free speech and the first amendment, and so on through almost the whole law school curriculum. In several

---

[20] *See* Dworkin, *Reagan's Justice*, N.Y. REV. BOOKS, Nov. 8, 1984, at 27. There are methodological as well as political differences between Bork and Dworkin; but the motivation for Dworkin's attack on Bork, which begins with speculation that Reagan might appoint Bork to the Supreme Court, is unmistakably political.

[21] *See* G. BECKER, THE ECONOMIC APPROACH TO HUMAN BEHAVIOR (1976); Hirshleifer, *The Expanding Domain of Economics*, 75 AM. ECON. REV., Dec. 1985, at 53 (special issue commemorating the American Economic Association's centennial).

[22] *See* D. PYLE, THE ECONOMICS OF CRIME AND LAW ENFORCEMENT chs. 3–4 (1983).

important fields — antitrust, commercial law (including bankruptcy), corporations and securities regulation, regulated industries, and taxation — the economic perspective either is already dominant or will soon be, when the older professors and practitioners retire. In other important fields, such as torts, property law, environmental law, and labor law, the economic approach is making rapid strides. In still others, such as criminal law and family law, the traditionalists retain the upper hand — but for how long, who can say?[23]

Philosophy has also made notable progress in areas related to law. The revival of interest in moral and political philosophy, a revival that owes much to the work of John Rawls, has generated philosophical perspectives on a variety of issues of great importance to law, including capital punishment; abortion, obscenity, and women's rights; the rights of the poor; and the role of corrective justice and distributive justice in the theory and practice of law.[24] Developments in Continental philosophy and in literary theory (for present purposes best regarded as a specialized branch of epistemology) have exposed a deep vein of profound skepticism about the possibility of authoritative interpretation of texts.[25] This skepticism has fueled, along with political radicalism and sheer infantilism,[26] the contemporary movement in legal scholarship known as "critical legal studies." The combined impact of radicalism and philosophy on constitutional law scholarship has been especially dramatic, some might say disastrous.[27] Lacking real intellectual autonomy, law may be too open to incursions from other fields of thought.

The theory of public choice, a hybrid of economics and political science, is beginning to be used in the analysis of law;[28] so, too, are game theory,[29] statistical theory (particularly in relation to the law of evidence),[30] empirical statistics (as in discrimination and antitrust

---

[23] For a recent summary of the economic approach to law, see R. POSNER, ECONOMIC ANALYSIS OF LAW (3d ed. 1986).

[24] See J. RAWLS, A THEORY OF JUSTICE (1971). For an up-to-date set of readings, see J. FEINBERG & H. GROSS, PHILOSOPHY OF LAW (3d ed. 1986).

[25] See, e.g., T. EAGLETON, LITERARY THEORY: AN INTRODUCTION ch. 4 (1983).

[26] See, e.g., Freeman & Schlegel, Sex, Power and Silliness: An Essay on Ackerman's Reconstructing American Law, 6 CARDOZO L. REV. 847 (1985); Gabel & Kennedy, Roll Over Beethoven, 36 STAN. L. REV. 1 (1984). For a broader sense of the field, see Critical Legal Studies Symposium, 36 STAN. L. REV. 1 (1984).

[27] The rejection of the possibility of objective constitutional interpretation is illustrated by Brest, Interpretation and Interest, 34 STAN. L. REV. 765 (1982), and the rejection of rejectionism is illustrated by Grey, The Constitution as Scripture, 37 STAN. L. REV. 1 (1984).

[28] See, e.g., Easterbrook, Ways of Criticizing the Court, 95 HARV. L. REV. 802 (1982); Spitzer, Multicriteria Choice Processes: An Application of Public Choice Theory to Bakke, the FCC, and the Courts, 88 YALE L.J. 717 (1979).

[29] See, e.g., C. GOETZ, CASES AND MATERIALS ON LAW AND ECONOMICS 8–20 (1984); Birmingham, Legal and Moral Duty in Game Theory: Common Law Contract and Chinese Analogies, 18 BUFF. L. REV. 99 (1969).

[30] See, e.g., Kaye, The Limits of the Preponderance of the Evidence Standard: Justifiably

cases),[31] rational but not economic social theory,[32] and even literary criticism.[33] Legal history has become more rigorous and more professional. Some fields that had once seemed to promise important applications to law, such as psychology, linguistics, and sociology, have not made much recent progress toward improving our understanding of law. Nevertheless, the overall progress of disciplines other than law in illuminating law has been striking and cannot but undermine the lawyer's (especially the academic lawyer's) faith in the autonomy of his discipline.

Third, confidence in the ability of lawyers on their own to put right the major problems of the legal system has collapsed. Some of the supposed triumphs of the 1930s through 1950s have been revalued and no longer seem so triumphant; this is true, for example, of the Federal Rules of Civil Procedure and of the Administrative Procedure Act (and of the trial and administrative processes generally).[34] This reason is related to the second: the decline of lawyers' self-confidence is due partly to the rise of other disciplines to positions where they can rival the law's claim to privileged insight into its subject matter. More important than any revaluation of the older legal achievements, however, is a series of confidence-shattering events since the early 1960s. All sorts of reforms adopted in this period, reforms engineered by lawyers, appear to have miscarried. These include a bankruptcy code that has led to a large and unanticipated increase in the number of bankruptcy filings;[35] a runaway expansion of tort liability that may be destroying the institution of liability insurance,[36] coupled with the

---

Naked Statistical Evidence and Multiple Causation, 1982 AM. B. FOUND. RES. J. 487; Kaye, *The Laws of Probability and the Law of the Land*, 47 U. CHI. L. REV. 34 (1979).

[31] *See* D. BARNES & J. CONLEY, STATISTICAL EVIDENCE IN LITIGATION (1986).

[32] *See* Sunstein, *Legal Interference With Private Preferences*, U. CHI. L. REV. (forthcoming 1986).

[33] *See, e.g., Symposium: Law and Literature*, 60 TEX. L. REV. 373 (1982); Papke, *Neo-Marxists, Nietzscheans, and New Critics: The Voices of the Contemporary Law and Literature Discourse*, 1985 AM. B. FOUND. RES. J. 883 (reviewing J. WHITE, WHEN WORDS LOSE THEIR MEANING (1984)); Posner, *Law and Literature*, 72 VA. L. REV. 1351 (1986)).

[34] These codes have been criticized for encouraging excessive and even predatory discovery, fomenting litigation, being too pro-plaintiff, and taking to long to join issue and eliminate groundless claims. See, for example, Brazil, *Views from the Front Lines: Observations by Chicago Lawyers About the System of Civil Discovery*, 1980 AM. B. FOUND. RES. J. 217; Stewart, *The Reformation of American Administrative Law*, 88 HARV. L. REV. 1667, 1681–88 (1975); Brazil, *The Adversary Character of Civil Discovery: A Critique and Proposals for Change*, 31 VAND. L. REV. 1295 (1978); Miller, *The Adversary System: Dinosaur or Phoenix*, 69 MINN. L. REV. 1 (1984); Resnik, *Failing Faith: Adjudicatory Procedure in Decline*, 53 U. CHI. L. REV. 494 (1986), and references cited therein.

[35] *See* Boyes & Faith, *Some Effects of the Bankruptcy Reform Act of 1978*, 29 J.L. & ECON 139 (1986); Shepard, *Personal Failures and the Bankruptcy Reform Act of 1978*, 27 J.L. & ECON. 419 (1984).

[36] *See, e.g.*, REPORT OF THE TORT POLICY WORKING GROUP ON THE CAUSES, EXTENT AND POLICY IMPLICATIONS OF THE CURRENT CRISIS IN INSURANCE AVAILABILITY AND AFFORDA-

disappointing results (and lethal side-effects) of the no-fault automobile compensation movement;[37] a no-fault divorce movement that has boomeranged against the women's movement that urged its adoption;[38] the creation of a system of environmental regulation at once incredibly complex and either perverse or ineffective in much of its operation;[39] the destruction of certainty in the field of conflict-of-laws (especially in accident cases) as a result of the replacement of mechanical rules (such as the rule of *lex loci delicti*) by "interest analysis" and its many variants;[40] the rather hapless blundering of the federal courts into immensely contentious, analytically insoluble ethical-political questions such as capital punishment, prison conditions (how comfortable must they be?), sex and the family, and political patronage; the accidental growth of the class-action lawsuit, through a seemingly minor amendment to rule 23 of the Federal Rules of Civil Procedure, into what many observers believe is an engine for coercing the settlement of cases that have no real merit yet expose defendants to astronomical potential liabilities;[41] the flood of one-way attorney's-

---

BILITY (GPO Feb. 1986); *Sorting Out the Liability Debate*, NEWSWEEK, May 12, 1986, at 60; *Sky-High Damage Suits*, U.S. NEWS & WORLD REP., Jan. 27, 1986, at 35; *Sorry, Your Policy is Cancelled*, TIME, Mar. 24, 1986, at 16. For a discussion of the capacity of lawyers to resolve the fundamental issues of tort policy, see Posner, *Can Lawyers Solve the Problems of the Tort System?*, 73 CALIF. L. REV. 747 (1985).

[37] *See, e.g.,* 1979 Nev. Stat. 1513 (repealing Nevada's no-fault statute); Karcher, *No More No-Fault: Beyond the Rhetoric Toward True Reform of the New Jersey Automobile Insurance System*, 8 SETON HALL LEGIS. J. 173 (1984); AUTOMOBILE NO-FAULT INSURANCE: A STUDY BY THE SPECIAL COMMITTEE ON AUTOMOBILE INSURANCE LEGISLATION 26–39 (Am. Bar Ass'n Feb. 1978); Comment, *Michigan No-Fault: The Rise and Fall of Socialized Negligence*, 56 U. DET. J. URB. L. 99 (1978). For an account of the unfortunate side-effects of no-fault auto insurance (including an increased rate of fatal accidents), see Landes, *Insurance, Liability, and Accidents: A Theoretical and Empirical Investigation of the Effect of No-Fault Accidents*, 25 J.L. & ECON. 49, 50 (1982).

[38] "The major economic result of the divorce law revolution is the systematic impoverishment of divorced women and their children." L. WEITZMAN, THE DIVORCE REVOLUTION: THE UNEXPECTED SOCIAL AND ECONOMIC CONSEQUENCES FOR WOMEN AND CHILDREN IN AMERICAN xiv (1985); *see* Becker, *Cut the Divorce Rate With Marriage Contracts*, BUS. WEEK, Dec. 23, 1985, at 12; Fineman, *Implementing Equality: Ideology, Contradiction and Social Change: A Study of Rhetoric and Results in the Regulation of the Consequences of Divorce*, 1983 WIS. L. REV. 789.

[39] *See, e.g.,* R. CRANDALL, CONTROLLING INDUSTRIAL POLLUTION: THE ECONOMICS AND POLITICS OF CLEAN AIR (1983); Ackerman & Stewart, *Reforming Environmental Law*, 37 STAN. L. REV. 1333 (1985); Crandall, Keeler & Lave, *The Cost of Automobile Safety and Emissions Regulation to the Consumer: Some Preliminary Results*, 72 AM. ECON. REV. 324 (1982); Pashigian, *The Effect of Environmental Regulation on Optimal Plant Size and Factor Shares*, 27 J.L. & ECON. 1 (1984).

[40] *See, e.g.,* Brilmayer, *Governmental Interest Analysis: A House Without Foundations*, 46 OHIO ST. L.J. 459 (1985); Reese, *American Trends in Private International Law: Academic and Judicial Manipulation of Choice of Law Rules in Tort Cases*, 33 VAND. L. REV. 717, 734–37 (1980).

[41] *See, e.g.,* *Free World Foreign Cars, Inc. v. Alfa Romeo, S.p.A.*, 55 F.R.D. 26, 30

fee-shifting statutes, which overencourage litigation;[42] and the creation of an intricate code of federal criminal procedure (requiring for
example a three-volume treatise on search and seizure)[43] in the name
of the Constitution, and the wholesale imposition of the code on state
criminal proceedings through the doctrine of incorporation.

In part as a result of these developments, the last quarter century
has witnessed an astonishing rise in the amount of litigation in the
country (including a ten fold increase in the number of cases filed
annually in the federal courts of appeals),[44] to which the legal profession has responded with all the imagination of a traffic engineer whose
only answer to highway congestion is to build more highways, or of
a political establishment whose only answer to increased demands for
government services is to print more money. Rather than raising court
fees to dampen demand for court services, the powers who administer
the judicial systems of this country (lawyers all) have lowered them
in real terms. Our society's response to more litigation — dubious
though much of that litigation is — has been more judges, more
lawyers, more subsidies to litigation, more bureaucrats, and more law
clerks and other judicial adjuncts.[45] Responding at last to a sense
that the overload of the courts has become critical, lawyers and judges
are now busy proposing reforms (collectively referred to as "alternative
dispute resolution") that raise substantial questions both of efficacy
and legality.[46] The fundamental reason this litigation explosion has
gone unchecked is that nothing in a conventional legal education —
nothing gleaned from a close reading of judicial opinions, statutes,
and rules — equips a person to notice, let alone to measure, explain,
temper, and adjust to, an increase in the demand for judicial services.
Whatever the reasons, the performance of the legal profession in
responding to the challenges of the past quarter century has undermined confidence that reform of the system can be left to lawyers.

The weakening of the traditional supports of faith in the law's
autonomy as a discipline is not the only reason (or set of reasons) for
the decline of that faith. Another reason, which is purely internal to
the enterprise of academic law, is the same one that led composers to
write atonal music and that led English poets eventually to tire of the
heroic couplet. When a technique is perfected, the most imaginative

(S.D.N.Y. 1972); AMERICAN COLLEGE OF TRIAL LAWYERS, REPORT AND RECOMMENDATIONS
OF THE SPECIAL COMMITTEE ON RULE 23 OF THE FEDERAL RULES OF CIVIL PROCEDURE
(1972).
   [42] See R. POSNER, supra note 23, at 542.
   [43] See W. LaFAVE, SEARCH AND SEIZURE (1978).
   [44] See R. POSNER, THE FEDERAL COURTS: CRISIS AND REFORM 61 (1985) (tab. 3.1); ADMIN.
OFFICE OF THE U.S. COURTS, FEDERAL JUDICIAL WORKLOAD STATISTICS 2 (Mar. 1986).
   [45] See R. POSNER, supra note 44, at 94–112.
   [46] See Posner, The Summary Jury Trial and Other Methods of Alternative Dispute Resolution:
Some Cautionary Observations, 53 U. CHI. L. REV. 366 (1986).

practitioners get restless.[47] They want to be innovators rather than
imitators, and this desire requires that they strike out in a new direction. By 1960 most of the changes on the theme of the law's autonomy
had been rung. Holmes and Cardozo between them had said most of
the important things; Henry Hart, Jr. and Albert Sacks in their de-
servedly renowned book on the legal process,[48] and Edward Levi in
his classic *Introduction to Legal Reasoning*,[49] had completed the ed-
ifice of what might be termed classical legal thought. Of course, with
law in continuous flux there were (and are) always new cases, new
doctrines, even entire new fields to which to apply the techniques of
legal reasoning in the autonomous tradition, often with splendid results, as in the opinions of Judge Henry Friendly. Nevertheless, after
a while this was bound to seem, at least in the higher reaches of the
academy, and whether rightly or wrongly, work for followers rather
than leaders.[50] Because of this perception, and also because of the
growth of other disciplines, in the 1960s a new type of legal scholarship began to emerge in the leading law schools — the conscious
application of other disciplines, such as political and moral philosophy
and economics, to traditional legal problems. A notable example
besides those already mentioned is Frank Michelman's article on just
compensation, which used both philosophy and economics to examine
legal doctrine in a more scientific spirit than had been traditional.[51]
Between a Barton Leach and a Frank Michelman in property law, as
between a Warren Seavey and a Guido Calabresi in tort law, yawned
a chasm.

A related reason for the decline of faith in law as an autonomous
discipline is the continuing rise in the prestige and authority of scientific and other exact modes of inquiry in general, that is, apart from
any direct application they might have to legal analysis. Advances in
medical science, space and weapons technology, computers, mathematics and statistics, cosmology, biology, economics, linguistics, and

---

[47] *See* T.S. ELIOT, "Milton II," in ON POETRY AND POETS 146, 150 (1957).

[48] *See* H.M. HART, JR. & A. SACKS, THE LEGAL PROCESS: BASIC PROBLEMS IN THE
MAKING AND APPLICATION OF LAW (tent. ed. 1958).

[49] E. LEVI, AN INTRODUCTION TO LEGAL REASONING (1949).

[50] For disparagement of doctrinal analysis by influential legal academics, see H. PACKER &
T. EHRLICH, NEW DIRECTIONS IN LEGAL EDUCATION 32 (1972); Wellington, *Alumni Weekend*,
25 YALE L. REP., Winter 1978–1979, at 4, 7–8. Even though I have criticized the disparagement
of doctrinal analysis, *see* R. POSNER, *supra* note 44, at 330–34, some practitioners of such
analysis are so defensive that they perceive my unwillingness to agree that doctrinal analysis is
the be-all and end-all of legal scholarship as an implicit denial that it deserves any important
place in legal scholarship at all. *See, e.g.,* Redish, *The Federal Courts, Judicial Restraint, and
the Importance of Analyzing Legal Doctrine,* 85 COLUM. L. REV. 1378 (1985). The issue is not
the indispensability of doctrinal analysis (which of course need not be so narrowly conceived as
it was by Langdell and the other nineteenth-century formalists) but rather its sufficiency.

[51] *See* Michelman, *Property, Utility, and Fairness: Comments on the Ethical Foundations
of "Just Compensation" Law,* 80 HARV. L. REV. 1165 (1967).

many other areas of scientific and technological endeavor are making traditional legal doctrinal analysis — the heart of legal thinking when law is conceived as an autonomous discipline — seem to many younger scholars old-fashioned, passé, tired. Fields in similar plight, such as literary criticism, have not hesitated to borrow from trendier, arguably more rigorous fields; in retrospect it is obvious that academic law would do the same thing. Although the classic works of traditional legal scholarship can still be read with profit and admiration, it is no longer easy for academic lawyers who want to be considered on the "cutting edge" of legal thought to imagine writing in the same vein. This point is distinct from my previous one, that the genre has been perfected (which is not to say completed). A purely verbal, purely lawyer's scholarship, in which the categories of analysis are the same as, or very close to, those used by the judges or legislators whose work is being analyzed — a scholarship moreover in which political consensus is assumed and the insights of other disciplines ignored — does not fit comfortably into today's scholarly *Zeitgeist*.

The last cause of the decline of faith in the law's autonomy that I shall consider is the increasing importance of statutes and of the Constitution, compared to common law, as sources of law. The particular skill honed by legal education and cultivated by legal scholars is that of extracting a legal doctrine from a series of cases and fitting it together with other doctrines similarly derived. It is a particularly valuable skill in dealing with common law, that is, judge-made law. Now it is true that much statutory and more constitutional law is common law in a practical sense, because after a while a statutory or constitutional provision becomes so encrusted with interpretive decisions that the original text almost disappears, and the analyst's principal task becomes that of interpreting the decisions. This description is dramatically true of the antitrust laws, the first, fourth, sixth, and eighth amendments to the Constitution, the due process and equal protection clauses, and much else besides. Nevertheless, a body of case law building upon a statute or upon the Constitution can never free itself entirely from its roots, because ultimately its legitimacy depends, at least in part, on fidelity to the original written instrument, in a way that common law doctrines do not. Moreover, new statutes are continually passed which must be interpreted, and for this interpretive task there is no crutch of case law.

The growing importance of statutes and the Constitution as sources of law would be of no significance to my present inquiry if lawyers had good tools for interpreting legislative texts; but, sad to say, we do not. This fact was obscured in Hart and Sacks's influential treatment of statutory interpretation by certain assumptions whose arbitrariness was not perceived at the time. Writing in the wake of the New Deal, of which they heartily approved, Hart and Sacks implicitly treated the legislature (including the original constitutional convention and the ratifying state legislatures) as a single mind, an intelligent and far-seeing mind, and moreover a mind that both was dedicated to serving the public interest and had a conception of the public interest identical to that of the judges who would be called on to interpret the legislation (the last point was an aspect of the political consensus that existed when they wrote).[52] This conception of the legislature made the task of statutory interpretation no more problematic than interpreting a contract — indeed, less problematic, because it had always been recognized that the parties to a contract might have different objectives and also different understandings of just what they had agreed to.

Since Hart and Sacks wrote, a large number of factors have combined to inflict a mortal blow on the comfortable view of statutory interpretation they espoused. Chief among these factors have been the breakdown of political consensus; the growth of social choice theory on the foundation of Arrow's impossibility theorem;[53] the rediscovery of interest groups by economists and political scientists on both the left and the right; the criticisms of the "public-interestedness" of legislation by the conservative and deregulation movements; the debunking of the "canons of statutory construction";[54] and the attacks made by Continental philosophers and their American followers on the objectivity of interpretation.

The inherently problematic character of statutory interpretation is well illustrated by the Supreme Court's unanimous — and at first blush dry, technical, unexceptional, and unexceptionable — decision in *Leo Sheep Co. v. United States.*[55] In 1862 Congress granted land to the Union Pacific Railroad as a means of subsidizing the construction of a transcontinental railroad. The grant was not limited to the right of way but included land on both sides of the right of way. This land was divided into "checkerboard" sections, each of 640 acres, the odd-numbered sections of which were given to the railroad, while the even-numbered ones were retained by the government. The idea behind this arrangement was that because the construction of the railroad would increase the value of the adjacent lands, the government could reap a direct benefit from its grant to the Union Pacific by retaining some of the land. The *Leo Sheep* case arose more than a century after the land grant. Land owned by the petitioners in the

---

[52] *See* 2 H.M. HART & A. SACKS, *supra* note 48, at 1414–15. For criticism of this view see R. POSNER, cited above in note 44, at 288–89.

[53] Arrow's theorem, brutally simplified, is that voting is not a reliable method of aggregating the voters' preferences. For an application of the theorem to Supreme Court decisionmaking, see Easterbrook, cited above in note 28, at 813–31.

[54] *See* R. POSNER, *supra* note 44, at 276–86.

[55] 440 U.S. 668 (1979). Justice White did not participate in the decision.

case, successors in interest to the Union Pacific, blocked access to a government-owned reservoir from the south and east. The government wanted to run an access road over the petitioners' land to connect the reservoir area (which was used for recreation) to a county road. The issue in the case was whether Congress had implicitly reserved (for there was no express reservation) an easement of access when it granted the land to the Union Pacific back in 1862. The Court held that it had not.

The Court begins its analysis by noting that the 1862 statute contained several specific reservations to the checkerboard grant, such as a reservation of mineral rights, and comments that "given the existence of such explicit exceptions, this Court has in the past refused to add to this list by divining some 'implicit' congressional intent."[56] Although the Court does not explain why the existence of explicit exceptions should negate an implicit exception, it must have been alluding to the well-known canon of statutory construction that *expressio unius est exclusio alterius* — the expression of one thing is the exclusion of another. Recent Supreme Court decisions sometimes approve the canon, but more often reject it.[57] The doctrine should be rejected. Congress may want to create an exception to a general grant without wanting to prevent the courts from recognizing additional exceptions in keeping with the spirit of the statute.

Next, the Court turns to the government's argument that all the government wants is an easement of necessity, and that, because such an easement would be implied in any private conveyance of real estate, it should also be implied in a public one.[58] The Court rejects the argument on a number of grounds. First, it states that "whatever right of passage a private landowner might have, it is not at all clear that it would include the right to construct a road for public access to a recreational area."[59] To say that a proposition "is not at all clear" is not to say it is false; but the Court may think these are equivalents, because it moves immediately to its second ground: that "the easement is not actually a matter of necessity in this case because the Government has the power of eminent domain."[60] There is, however, a big

---

[56] *Id.* at 679.

[57] *Compare* TVA v. Hill, 437 U.S. 153, 188 (1978) (applying the canon *expressio unius est exclusio alterius*), and Note, *Intent, Clear Statements, and the Common Law: Statutory Interpretation in the Supreme Court,* 95 HARV. L. REV. 892, 896–98 (1982) (discussing the canon), *with* Herman & MacLean v. Huddleston, 459 U.S. 375, 387 n.23 (1983) (rejecting the canon), Standefer v. United States, 447 U.S. 10, 20 n.12 (1980) (same), *and* Transamerica Mortgage Advisors, Inc. v. Lewis, 444 U.S. 11, 29 n.6 (1979) (same).

[58] For example, if you sell the land that surrounds your house but retain the house, you retain by implication a right of access to the house.

[59] *Leo Sheep,* 440 U.S. at 679 (footnote omitted).

[60] *Id.* at 679–80.

difference, not remarked upon by the Court, between having a "free" right of access and having to pay the fair market value of the right of access.

The Court then points out that some states do not recognize easements of necessity in favor of the government and that others have abolished the doctrine in favor of giving all owners of surrounded lands the power of eminent domain; the court makes no effort, however, to connect these apparently recent developments with the Congress of 1862. Next, the Court remarks unexpectedly that the application of the doctrine of easements of necessity is

> ultimately of little significance. The pertinent inquiry in this case is the intent of Congress when it granted land to the Union Pacific in 1862. The 1862 Act specifically listed reservations to the grant, and we do not find the tenuous relevance of the common-law doctrine of ways of necessity sufficient to overcome the inference prompted by the omission of any reference to the reserved right asserted by the Government in this case.[61]

This argument is just *expressio unius est exclusio alterius* again. The Court then remarks, "It is possible that Congress gave the problem of access little thought; but it is at least as likely that the thought which was given focused on negotiation, reciprocity considerations, and the power of eminent domain as obvious devices for ameliorating disputes."[62] Yet suppose these two possibilities *are* equally likely; what is the inference to be drawn?

Next, the Court confronts an objection based on "the familiar canon of construction that, when grants to federal lands are at issue, any doubts 'are resolved for the Government, not against it'"[63] but dispenses with it by noting that "this Court long ago declined to apply this canon in its full vigor to grants under the railroad Acts."[64] In support of this proposition the Court quotes from two old decisions[65] but neglects to mention *United States v. Union Pacific Railroad*,[66] in which the Court in 1957 had applied the canon to the very statute involved in *Leo Sheep*.[67]

Notice that apart from its repeated allusions to the canon *expressio unius est exclusio alterius*, the Court spends all of its time batting down the government's arguments rather than constructing an affirmative case — until at the very end of the opinion it says, "we are

---

[61] *Id.* at 680–81.
[62] *Id.* at 681 (footnote omitted).
[63] *Id.* at 682 (quoting Andrus v. Charlestone Stone Prod. Co., 436 U.S. 604, 617 (1978)).
[64] *Id.*
[65] *See id.* at 682–83 (quoting United States v. Denver & Rio Grande R. Co., 150 U.S. 1, 14 (1893), and Winona & St. Peter R.R. Co. v. Barney, 113 U.S. 618 (1885)).
[66] 353 U.S. 112 (1957).
[67] *See id.* at 116.

unwilling to upset settled expectations to accommodate some ill-defined power to construct public thoroughfares without compensation."[68] This is a good argument, but it has nothing to do with the intent of Congress in 1862. The truth is that no one knows how Congress would have resolved the issue of the case had that issue been brought to its attention in 1862.

Unfortunately, such indeterminacy is a frequent problem in interpreting statutory and constitutional provisions, especially old ones. With the aging of the Constitution and the expansion of statutory law relative to common law, lawyers and judges are increasingly engaged in a form of inquiry — the interpretation of unclear texts — for which conventional legal training, with its emphasis on the analysis of judge-made doctrine, does not prepare them well. And, unfortunately, the arguments from economics, social choice, and interpretive theory ("hermeneutics") that have undermined the lawyer's naive faith in the easy interpretability of statutory and constitutional provisions have put nothing in its place. The skeptics have not succeeded either in creating widely accepted alternative methods of interpretation or in persuading the profession that we should forget about interpretation — that we should call what we do "construction" and mean it literally. The more diffident that academic lawyers become in defending the objectivity of their interpretations of statutes and the Constitution, the less confidence they will have about even attempting this traditional form of legal scholarship.

III. Suggestions and Prognoses

I hope the reader will not think that by describing the decline over the past twenty-five years of law as an autonomous discipline, I am predicting or would welcome the disappearance of traditional legal thought and scholarship. As an appellate judge, I am both a consumer and producer of doctrinal analysis. I do think, though, that the law was too parochial twenty-five years ago and that despite all the false starts and silly fads that have marred its reaching out to other fields, the growth of interdisciplinary legal analysis has been a good thing, which ought to (and will) continue. Disinterested legal-doctrinal analysis of the traditional kind remains the indispensable core of legal thought, and there is no surfeit of such analysis today. I daresay that many legal scholars who today are breathing the heady fumes of deconstruction, structuralism, moral philosophy, and the theory of the second best would be better employed studying the origins of the *Enelow-Ettelson* doctrine or synthesizing the law of insurance. Never-

---

[68] *Id.* at 687–88 (footnote omitted).

theless it seems unlikely that we shall soon (if ever) return to a serene belief in the law's autonomy.

Recognition that the law is increasingly an interdisciplinary field has many implications, several of which I shall mention, but without trying to elaborate on them:

1. Economists, statisticians, and other social scientists should have a far more prominent role in efforts at legal reform than has been traditional — such as the effort of the Sentencing Commission (whose research director and two of whose members, I am happy to say, are social scientists rather than lawyers) to revise federal sentencing, and efforts in process or to come to revise the Federal Rules of Civil Procedure, the Bankruptcy Code, the tax code, and tort law.

2. The type of "advocacy" scholarship in which political sallies are concealed in formalistic legal discourse — a staple of modern law review writing — should be replaced by a more candid literature on the political merits of contested legal doctrines. In this literature, as yet almost unknown, the author would acknowledge the point at which authoritative legal materials run out, and justify the leap of faith necessary to bridge the gap between those materials and his conclusion.

3. A related point is that we need a new style of judicial opinion writing (really a return to an older style), in which formalistic crutches — such as the canons of statutory construction and the pretense of deterministic precedent — that exaggerate the autonomous elements in legal reasoning are replaced by a more candid engagement with the realistic premises of decision.[69] Judicial decisionmaking must also become more receptive to the insights of social science. Lawyers and judges must overcome the prevalent (and disgraceful) math-block that afflicts the legal profession.

4. The law schools need to encourage the branch of academic law that I call "Legal Theory," viewed as an endeavor distinct from doctrinal analysis, clinical education, and the other traditional, practice-

---

[69] Candor is illustrated by National Society of Professional Engineers v. United States, 435 U.S. 679, 687 (1978) (Stevens, J.) ("§ 1 of the Sherman Act . . . cannot mean what it says"); Jacobellis v. Ohio, 378 U.S. 184, 197 (1964) (Stewart, J., concurring) ("I know it when I see it"); Brown v. Allen, 344 U.S. 443, 540 (1953) (Jackson, J., concurring in the result) ("We are not final because we are infallible, but we are infallible only because we are final."); Olmstead v. United States, 277 U.S. 438, 470 (1928) (Holmes, J., dissenting) ("We have to choose . . . . "); Hynes v. New York Central Railroad Co., 231 N.Y. 229, 131 N.E. 898 (1921) (Cardozo, J.). Judge Cardozo stated in *Hynes*:

> Rules appropriate to spheres which are conceived of as separate and distinct cannot both be enforced when the spheres become concentric. There must then be readjustment or collision. In one sense, and that a highly technical and artificial one, the diver at the end of the springboard is an intruder on the adjoining lands. In another sense, and one that realists will accept more readily, he is still on public waters in the exercise of public rights.

Id. at 236, 131 N.E. at 900.

oriented branches of legal training and scholarship. By Legal Theory, I mean the study of the law not as a means of acquiring conventional professional competence but "from the outside," using the methods of scientific and humanistic inquiry to enlarge our knowledge of the legal system. There should be departments of law, where students can pursue doctoral programs in Legal Theory, or alternatively programs that meld college, law school, and doctoral training in another discipline into an integrated course of study taking less than the minimum of ten years after high school that such a program would currently require. Three years of college, two years of law school, and three years of doctoral study should, if these stages of training are integrated, equip a student to contribute creatively to the understanding and improvement of the legal system of the twenty-first century. I hope I will not be understood to be suggesting either that instruction and research in Legal Theory replace doctrinal analysis, or that Legal Theory be equated with, or even be thought to include, the advocacy of new constitutional rights.

   5. And what of the law reviews? What is to be the second century of the *Harvard Law Review*? The student-edited law review is a fine vehicle for the publication of doctrinal analysis written by students, professors of law, and practitioners. The best law students, who staff the law reviews (though this is changing at some law schools),[70] are sufficiently adept at doctrinal analysis to be able to make intelligent selections among submitted works of such analysis, to edit them helpfully, and to write useful doctrinal scholarship of their own. And doctrinal analysis will always be the mainstay of legal scholarship.

   However, as the rise of faculty-edited law journals in the past three decades attests,[71] the focus of scholarly publication at the academic frontier is gradually shifting from student-edited to faculty-edited, faculty-refereed journals. More scholars are coming to realize that law reviews are not well-equipped to select, and through editing to improve, articles outside of the core of legal doctrinal analysis, which, important though it is, no longer exhausts the domain of legal scholarship. For years to come, the authors of nontraditional articles will continue to seek publication of much of their work in the traditional law reviews in order to reach a wide audience and to take advantage of the quick turnaround time of the reviews compared to that of most faculty-edited journals. Moreover, some law reviews may be able to compete effectively with the faculty-edited reviews by

---

[70] Traditionally, the best student-edited journals were staffed by the best exam-takers, but some law reviews are now abandoning (or diluting) that criterion in favor of others — and some in favor of purely voluntary membership.

[71] This trend is illustrated by the *Journal of Law and Economics*, the *Supreme Court Review*, *Law & Society Review*, the *Journal of Legal Studies*, the *American Bar Foundation Research Journal*.

making greater use of referees (though this process will increase turnaround time) and, more important, by using a student's prelegal training (for example, graduate study in economics or philosophy), as well as grades or performance in a writing competition, as a criterion of selection, promotion, or assignment. Nevertheless, the faculty-edited journals may one day control the commanding heights of advanced legal scholarship.[72] If so, then quite apart from the leveling trend I mentioned at the outset, the next century will not belong to the *Harvard Law Review* in quite the way the last century has.

---

[72] *See* Cramton, *"The Most Remarkable Institution": The American Law Review*, 36 J. LEGAL EDUC. 1 (1986).

Artificial Intelligence and Law: Stepping Stones to a Model of Legal Reasoning

Edwina L. Rissland†

This Comment discusses developments in the twenty-year-old interdisciplinary field of Artificial Intelligence (AI) and law. This field is important for both AI and law because it is directed at improving our understanding and modeling of legal reasoning.

The AI and law projects discussed here are landmarks in this field.[1] A unifying theme of the projects is the goal to understand and model legal argument, a keystone of an overarching goal to understand and model legal reasoning. These goals require that we know first how to represent several types of knowledge, such as cases, rules, and arguments; second, how to reason with them, such as to manipulate precedents, to apply and make inferences with rules, and to tailor arguments to facts; and third, how to use them ultimately in a computer program that can perform tasks in legal reasoning and argumentation, such as analogizing favorable cases and distinguishing contrary ones, anticipating parries in adversarial argument, and creating artful hypotheticals.

The projects constitute a coherent set of studies about key topics in AI and law: (1) reasoning with rules; (2) handling open-textured legal concepts; (3) reasoning with cases and hypotheticals; (4) integrating reasoning with rules and reasoning with cases; and (5) representing legal knowledge. The limitations of techniques for handling the first topic are addressed by the second, and the third topic addresses critical issues not covered at all by work on the first. The fourth integrates work on the first three, and the fifth provides underpinnings needed for all of them. The projects are some of the major accomplishments in AI and law, especially

† Associate Professor, Department of Computer and Information Science, University of Massachusetts at Amherst and Lecturer on Law, Harvard Law School. I am grateful to my colleagues and students, in particular, Kevin Ashley, David Blank, Martha Minow, Oliver Selfridge, and David Skalak for numerous discussions in the preparation of this manuscript, and to the National Science Foundation, the Defense Advanced Research Projects Agency of the Department of Defense, and GTE Laboratories for their support.

1. For one of the earliest discussions of AI and law, see Buchanan & Headrick, *Some Speculation About Artificial Intelligence and Legal Reasoning*, 23 Stan. L. Rev. 40 (1970). *See also* Gardner, *Law Applications*, in The Encyclopedia of Artificial Intelligence 456 (S. Shapiro ed. 1989) (providing general overview of AI and law). For a representative collection of current work, see The Second International Conference on Artificial Intelligence and Law: Proceedings of the Conference (1989) [hereinafter ICAIL-89].

those seeking to understand and model legal argument, and they exemplify and illustrate the progress, concerns, and style of its research.

I. BACKGROUND ON ARTIFICIAL INTELLIGENCE

A. What is Artificial Intelligence?

AI is the study of cognitive processes using the conceptual frameworks and tools of computer science.[2] As a distinct subfield of computer science, AI had its beginnings in the mid-fifties.[3] In 1968 Marvin Minsky, one of the founders of AI, said it well: AI is "the science of making machines do things that would require intelligence if done by man."[4] Thus, all manner of intelligent behavior is in the realm of AI, including playing chess,[5] solving calculus problems,[6] making mathematical discoveries,[7] understanding short stories,[8] learning new concepts,[9] interpreting visual scenes,[10] diagnosing diseases,[11] and reasoning by analogy.[12] Any discussion of AI must

---

2. For additional background, see E. CHARNIAK & D. MCDERMOTT, INTRODUCTION TO ARTIFICIAL INTELLIGENCE (1985); 1-4 HANDBOOK OF ARTIFICIAL INTELLIGENCE (A. Barr, P. Cohen & E. Feigenbaum eds. 1981-89); G. LUGER & W. STUBBLEFIELD, ARTIFICIAL INTELLIGENCE AND THE DESIGN OF EXPERT SYSTEMS (1989); THE ENCYCLOPEDIA OF ARTIFICIAL INTELLIGENCE, supra note 1; P. WINSTON, ARTIFICIAL INTELLIGENCE (2d ed. 1984).

3. A summer conference held at Dartmouth College in 1956 is perhaps the most convenient landmark to denote its beginning. See P. MCCORDUCK, MACHINES WHO THINK 93-114 (1979) (describing history surrounding the Dartmouth Conference and its lasting effects in AI community).

4. SEMANTIC INFORMATION PROCESSING v (M. Minsky ed. 1968).

5. See, e.g., Newborn & Kopec, Results of The Nineteenth ACM North American Computer Chess Championship, 32 COMM. ACM 1225 (1989) (describing several games).

6. Research on symbolic mathematics began with James Slagle's SAINT, a program which solved 52 out of 54 problems selected from MIT freshman calculus final examinations. See Slagle, A Heuristic Program That Solves Symbolic Integration Problems in Freshman Calculus, in COMPUTERS AND THOUGHT 191 (E. Feigenbaum & J. Feldman eds. 1963). The next project was Joel Moses's program SIN. See Moses, Symbolic Integration: The Stormy Decade, 14 COMM. ACM 548 (1971). Further research on symbolic mathematics has led to the development of systems such as MIT's MACSYMA, "a large, interactive computer system designed to assist mathematicians, scientists, and engineers in solving mathematical problems." 2 HANDBOOK OF ARTIFICIAL INTELLIGENCE, supra note 2, at 143. Commercial versions of such programs are now available for personal computers. Wayner, Symbolic Math on the Mac, BYTE, Jan. 1989, at 239.

7. A program that modeled the process of discovery in mathematics was Doug Lenat's AM. Using a knowledge base containing fundamental concepts and rules of thumb, AM was able to "discover" such mathematical concepts as "divisor" and "prime." R. DAVIS & D. LENAT, KNOWLEDGE-BASED SYSTEMS IN ARTIFICIAL INTELLIGENCE 1-225 (1982); AM, in 3 HANDBOOK OF ARTIFICIAL INTELLIGENCE, supra note 2, at 438.

8. See, e.g., R. SCHANK & R. ABELSON, SCRIPTS, PLANS, GOALS, AND UNDERSTANDING: AN INQUIRY INTO HUMAN KNOWLEDGE STRUCTURES (1977) (discussing theory for story understanding); INSIDE COMPUTER UNDERSTANDING: FIVE PROGRAMS PLUS MINIATURES (R. Schank & C. Riesbeck eds. 1981). For general collections of work on natural language processing, see READINGS IN NATURAL LANGUAGE PROCESSING (B. Grosz, K. Jones & B. Webber eds. 1986); STRATEGIES FOR NATURAL LANGUAGE PROCESSING (W. Lehnert & M. Ringle eds. 1982).

9. See, e.g., 1-2 MACHINE LEARNING: AN ARTIFICIAL INTELLIGENCE APPROACH (R. Michalski, J. Carbonell & T. Mitchell eds. 1983, 1986).

10. See, e.g., READINGS IN COMPUTER VISION: ISSUES, PROBLEMS, PRINCIPLES, AND PARADIGMS (M. Fischler & O. Firschein eds. 1987).

11. See, e.g., RULE-BASED EXPERT SYSTEMS, THE MYCIN EXPERIMENTS OF THE STANFORD HEURISTIC PROGRAMMING PROJECT (B. Buchanan & E. Shortliffe eds. 1984) [hereinafter Buchanan & Shortliffe] (thorough discussion of MYCIN diagnostic system for bacterial infections).

12. See, e.g., Gentner, Structure-Mapping: A Theoretical Framework for Analogy, 7 COGNITIVE

note that tasks involving "common sense" reasoning or perception, such as language understanding, are by far the most difficult for AI.[13] More technical tasks, like solving calculus problems or playing chess, are usually much easier. That is because the latter can be framed in well-defined terms[14] and come from totally black-and-white domains, while the former cannot and do not. What distinguishes the AI approach from other studies of cognition and knowledge, such as psychology or philosophy, is its insistence on grounding the analysis in computational terms—preferably in a successfully running computer program that embodies the analysis.[15]

AI is pursued for at least two reasons: to understand the workings of human intelligence[16] and to create useful computer programs and computers that can perform intelligently. Most workers in the field of AI pursue these goals simultaneously. For instance, in the course of designing a computer program for commercial purposes like making credit card approval decisions, the program designer needs to examine how experienced people make such decisions, since they are usually the best, and often the only, source of information about how the job is done.[17] Likewise, in engaging in AI for the sake of understanding or modeling cognition, it is far

SCI. 155 (1983). Reasoning by analogy was the subject of one of the earliest programs in AI. Evans, *A Program for the Solution of a Class of Geometric-Analogy Intelligence-Test Questions*, in SEMANTIC INFORMATION PROCESSING *supra* note 4, at 271.

13. *See, e.g.*, E. CHARNIAK, TOWARD A MODEL OF CHILDREN'S STORY COMPREHENSION 271-74 (MIT AI Lab Technical Report No. 266, 1972) (even understanding "simple" children's stories can be quite messy).

14. For instance, the rules of chess completely define the game. Furthermore, in the case of games, solutions can be found using high-powered, specialized "search" techniques. This is how highly successful chess programs, such as Deep Thought, work. Deep Thought can examine 720,000 chess positions per second. *See* Newborn, & Kopec, *supra* note 5, at 1225. However, it is quite a different matter whether such programs work in the same way human chess experts do and whether they can shed light upon human thought processes. *See* Chase & Simon, *The Mind's Eye in Chess*, in VISUAL INFORMATION PROCESSING 215, 278 (W. Chase ed. 1973).

15. *See* D. DENNETT, BRAINSTORMS: PHILOSOPHICAL ESSAYS ON MIND AND PSYCHOLOGY 112 (1978); MIND DESIGN (J. Haugeland ed. 1981).

16. For two interesting theories of human cognition, see M. MINSKY, THE SOCIETY OF MIND (1986); A. NEWELL, UNIFIED THEORY OF COGNITION (forthcoming 1990).

17. Even if psychological validity is not usually paramount, it is often helpful. The MYCIN Project illustrates this point. The goal of the MYCIN Project was to build a system that could diagnose bacterial blood infections at an expert level. Although the goal was not to model closely the diagnostic behavior of expert physicians, observations of medical experts were critical during the early phases of the project stage, when the AI researchers (known as "knowledge engineers") gathered, structured, and encoded the experts' medical knowledge for use by the program. Later, having the program operate in a comprehensible manner was critical for debugging and refining it. *See generally* Buchanan & Shortliffe, *supra* note 11. It is usually the case that if there is no point of contact between the program's processing style and the human's, the program behavior appears inscrutable, impeding its development. Some similarity between the program's and the experts' processing also enhances one's belief in the correctness of the output of the program; sometimes this is so because it is easier for the program to explain its own reasoning in the user's terms. With respect to the issue of capturing the style of expert reasoning, a chess playing program like Deep Thought is an extreme case of a high performance program where there is no claim to cognitive validity. *See* Newborn & Kopec, *supra* note 5. There was no attempt to make Deep Thought think like a grand master. *See* Leithauser, *Kasparov Beats Deep Thought*, N.Y. Times, Jan. 14, 1990, § 6 (Magazine), at 33, 74 (discussion of grand master Kasparov's thoughts on ramifications of some of these issues).

more satisfying to exhibit a running program: to some degree success is a working computational model.[18]

In the context of law, these twin rationales translate into the twin goals of understanding certain key aspects of legal reasoning and building computational tools useful for legal practice, teaching, or research. An example of the former is the development of an AI model for reasoning based upon the doctrine of precedent. The process of developing an AI model causes one to learn about legal reasoning. Modeling involves elucidating key ingredients of precedent-based reasoning, such as making assessments of the relevance of precedents to new situations, distinguishing contrary cases, and drawing connections between relevant cases; then describing them in detail and building a program to execute them.

An example of the second, more applications-oriented goal, is construction of a set of computational tools (a lawyer's workbench, so to speak) to assist in the preparation of a brief. These may include functions to assist in gathering relevant precedents from data bases, sorting them according to their doctrinal approaches, and "Shepardizing" them. Building a practical system, like one to assist with writing a brief, requires developing analytical models. Typically, satisfaction with an analytical model increases if it offers insights leading to the practical advances.

The desire to develop a model of legal reasoning is not new. Certainly key aspects of legal reasoning, such as the analysis of precedent, have been the subject of many discussions.[19] However, for the most part, previous studies have not provided the level of detail required of an AI model; that is, they have not provided enough detail to indicate how they could be implemented as a computer program.[20] In AI, one is forced to be detailed. For instance, law has been described as "reasoning by example."[21] This may be an appropriate level of description for some purposes, but for AI, it leaves too many questions unanswered. To take advantage of invaluable

---

18. Actually building a program is quite different from speculating about it. Programming makes abundantly clear the weaknesses or difficulties of the model. Cf. McDermott, *Artificial Intelligence Meets Natural Stupidity*, in MIND DESIGN, *supra* note 15, at 143, 156–59 (highlighting risk of theorizing about implementation without actually implementing).

19. *See, e.g.*, B. CARDOZO, THE NATURE OF THE JUDICIAL PROCESS (1921); E. LEVI, AN INTRODUCTION TO LEGAL REASONING (1949); K. LLEWELLYN, THE BRAMBLE BUSH (1930); K. LLEWELLYN, THE CASE LAW SYSTEM IN AMERICA (1989); Radin, *Case Law and Stare Decisis: Concerning Präjudizienrecht in Amerika*, 33 COLUM. L. REV. 199 (1933).

20. Although this was obviously not their purpose, some discussions have come remarkably close. For instance, some of the analyses done by Llewellyn and Radin capture the spirit of the sort of description desired in AI. *See, e.g.*, K. LLEWELLYN, *supra* note 19, at 50 n.1 (describing doctrine of precedent, particularly concerning broad and narrow reading of rule of case); Radin, *supra* note 19, at 206–09 (describing concept evolution in law). Radin's description is uncannily similar to an algorithm, called the "candidate elimination algorithm," used in machine learning. *See* 3 HANDBOOK OF ARTIFICIAL INTELLIGENCE, *supra* note 2, at 385–91. For a comparison of this algorithm and Radin's analysis, see Rissland & Collins, *The Law as Learning System*, in PROCEEDINGS OF THE FOURTH ANNUAL CONFERENCE OF THE COGNITIVE SCIENCE SOCIETY 500, 501 (1986) (examining evolution of concept of "inherently dangerous" from Radin).

21. E. LEVI, *supra* note 19, at 1.

insights offered by legal scholars about legal reasoning, an AI researcher needs to specify both how the reasoning is to happen and what information and methods are required.

The AI approach forces one to be relentlessly analytic and specific. It advocates that one use ideas and methods of computer science to develop conceptual and computational frameworks.

B. *AI and Law: A Fruitful Synergy*

The law offers abundant opportunities for developing analytic and computational AI models. Law also has unique characteristics that make it a particularly challenging field for AI:

1. Legal reasoning is multi-modal, rich and varied: it includes reasoning with cases, rules, statutes and principles;
2. Case law has an explicit style and standard of reasoning and justification: stare decisis.
3. Specialized legal knowledge, such as cases and statutory rules, is well-documented and available from many sources, including case reporters, treatises, restatements, statutes, commercial summaries, and scholarly commentaries.
4. The law is self-aware and self-critical, and has an established tradition of examining its processes and assumptions. There is lively debate between proponents of competing jurisprudential schools.
5. The character of answers in the law is different from those in many other disciplines: answers are much more a matter of degree than clear-cut yes-or-no and they can change over time.
6. The knowledge used in legal reasoning is diverse, ranging from common sense to specialized legal knowledge, and it varies greatly in structure, character, and use.

These observations suggest the possibility of fruitful synergy between law and AI, and have implications for AI approaches. That the law is multi-modal means that an AI program will need to know about several modes of reasoning and how to use them in concert. That the law has an explicit, accepted style of reasoning gives the researcher a definite reasoning style to incorporate into a model and to use to analyze legal reasoning. However, some of the modes of reasoning, such as reasoning with cases, are very different from those used most widely in AI, and AI researchers have become interested in these only recently.

That the law is well-documented, self-aware, and self-critical makes it more accessible to AI researchers. If there were no repositories of legal knowledge and no tradition of trying to describe and criticize the goals and methods of legal reasoning, an AI researcher would have to start from scratch in trying to understand legal reasoning and to elucidate the knowledge involved. By no means is this to say that all the spadework has been done—the philosophical descriptions of legal reasoning are vague for AI purposes, and there is a lot more to legal knowledge than the "book knowledge" of traditional legal materials. Still, an AI study of the law has been provided with a good beginning, an epistemological leg up.

That what counts as an "answer" in the law is not clearcut is also different from other disciplines. In law there is usually no unique right answer; rather there are reasonable alternative answers, more a matter of degree than of extremes. The answers are highly contextual, depend on goals and points of view, and change as the law evolves. Even the rule-based aspects of legal reasoning cannot be modeled with purely deductive methods. This also means that, unfortunately, there is never the comfort of a *quod erat demonstrandum* at the end of a reasoning episode to sanction it as sound and beyond reproach, as there is in mathematics. From the legal point of view, this is no real deficit—it's a feature and not a bug, to use the computer scientists' phrase—since it allows law to accommodate to changes in circumstance and purpose. But, computationally, the nature of legal answers adds complexity and difficulty as well as richness and flexibility.

These observations all suggest that the law is an exceedingly challenging domain for AI. Research in AI and law will impel AI in new directions and thus benefit AI. In turn, law will also benefit from AI, both analytically and practically. As an analytical medium, AI forces meticulous attention to details and precise testing of theoretical ideas. This, in turn, facilitates the unmasking of flaws, furthers the understanding of assumptions, and leads to proposals for refinements. AI focuses a spotlight on issues of knowledge and process to a degree not found in noncomputational approaches, which often assume that some key task, like analogical reasoning, will be accomplished magically without a hint as to how,[22] or with too many critical details left. underspecified.[23] The practi-

---

22. The philosopher Dan Dennett calls this the problem of a "loan of intelligence" or the hidden homunculus. *See* D. DENNETT, *supra* note 15, at 12. In an AI model, some process, somewhere, must actually do the work or else as Dennett puts it, the theory is "in the red." *Id.* A great danger is in "designing a system whose stipulated capacities are miraculous." *Id.* at 112; *see also* McDermott, *supra* note 18, at 143.
23. Some of Dworkin's models are intriguing in this regard, such as his model of hard cases. *See, e.g.,* R. DWORKIN, TAKING RIGHTS SERIOUSLY (1977). He argues that there may not really be any "hard" cases since one can use a set of relatively weighted principles to resolve certain "hard" questions, which arise because the on point cases are in conflict or there is a tie in the principles. The principles and weights are generated from a collection of relevant precedents. Dworkin omits the details of how to decide which precedents to use and how to induce principles from them. He is not necessarily wrong, but it would be instructive to extract a more detailed description of how his model works. By declining to instruct further on how to develop the weighting system, Dworkin has simply moved the problem of analysis back one step. Regarding the assignment of relative weights, he has walked headlong into the "credit assignment" quagmire, well known to workers in machine learning, where the problem is to assign credit or blame for the overall success or failure of a problem solution to an individual step or aspect of it. For instance, is the credit for a win or the blame for a loss in a game of checkers to be given to the penultimate move of a game, the first move, or some intermediate move or moves? How can one tell which features or principles "caused" a case to be resolved for one party or the other? *See* Minsky, *Steps Toward Artificial Intelligence*, in COMPUTERS AND THOUGHT, *supra* note 6, at 432 (1963); Samuel, *Some Studies in Machine Learning Using the Game of Check-*

cal benefits to law from AI are intelligent computational tools. The relationship between AI and law is truly synergistic.

C. Some Desiderata for AI and Law Programs

Given the special characteristics of law described above, we can enumerate several goals that we would like an ideal AI and law program to achieve. It should be able, among other things, to:

1. Reason with cases (both real and hypothetical) and analogies;
2. Reason with rules;
3. Combine several modes of reasoning;
4. Handle ill-defined and open-textured concepts;
5. Formulate arguments and explanations;
6. Handle exceptions to and conflicts among items of knowledge, like rules;
7. Accommodate changes in the base of legal knowledge, particularly legal concepts, and handle non-monotonicity, that is, changes in which previous truths no longer hold as more becomes known;[24]
8. Model common sense knowledge;
9. Model knowledge of intent and belief;
10. Perform some aspects of natural language understanding.

We are a long way from such an ideal. There is, however, activity on all of these important fronts, and impressive progress on a few.

In fact, one can today speculate about which of these desiderata can be expected now, in the near future, someday, or probably never. Presently, AI is actively pushing back the boundaries on case-based reasoning (goal 1), has well-understood methodologies in rule-based reasoning (goal 2), and is exploring multi-paradigm reasoning (goal 3). Reasoning with open-textured predicates (goal 4) has had an admirable first cut, but it will require further contributions from other AI specialties like case-based reasoning (CBR)[25] and machine learning.[26] Major contributions

---

ers, in 3 IBM J. Res. & Dev. 211 (1959).

24. For instance, the overturning of established doctrine with a new precedent.

25. "Case-based reasoning" is the process by which a program uses previous cases (e.g., precedents, experiences, problem-solving episodes, detailed solutions, plans) to solve a new case. There are two kinds of CBR: (1) "problem-solving CBR," in which the emphasis is on generating a solution to a new problem (case) by reusing and modifying old solutions; and (2) "interpretive CBR," in which the emphasis is on generating an interpretation of a new case by comparing and analogizing it with interpretations made in past cases. For both varieties, the key issues are the structure and content of case memory, indexing mechanisms for retrieving cases from memory, and metrics for assessing similarity or relevancy of retrieved cases. The sort of precedent-based reasoning done in the law is a paradigm for the second type of CBR. *See generally* PROCEEDINGS: WORKSHOP ON CASE-BASED REASONING (J. Kolodner ed. 1989) (good sampling of current research); Kolodner, Rissland & Waltz, *Case-Based Reasoning from DARPA: Machine Learning Program Plan*, in PROCEEDINGS: CASE-BASED REASONING WORKSHOP 1 (1989) (sponsored by Defense Advanced Research Projects Agency; sets forth major classes of CBR, ingredients of CBR, and outstanding research issues).

26. "Machine learning" is the ability of a program to change itself, particularly its knowledge, so that it can perform better.

have been made to precedent-based argumentation,[27] and progress is being made on explanation (goal 5). Thus one can be optimistic that someday AI will be able to deal with many of the key goals for an AI and law program in at least a rudimentary manner. I would go so far as to say that the first five desiderata are attainable now or in the near future.

The next two desiderata—handling exceptions and conflict (goal 6) and accommodating to change in the base of knowledge (goal 7)—presently are being addressed broadly in AI, particularly in machine learning. It is reasonable to expect AI programs to be able to handle gradual change soon, but not abrupt or rapid change.[28] Non-monotonicity is being vigorously explored by an active cohort of researchers, primarily using approaches grounded in sophisticated logics. Thus, these two desiderata might be met someday.

As for the last three desiderata, I am much less optimistic. Modeling common sense reasoning, knowledge of intent and belief, and natural language capabilities are by far the hardest tasks. With regard to language, some capabilities like interactive dialogue and understanding of short summaries can be achieved in narrowly circumscribed domains; fuller capabilities are far off.[29] Widely applicable general "solutions" are very distant. Some, like the understanding of written appellate opinions—the ultimate fantasy—I expect never to see.[30]

II. SIGNIFICANT STEPS TOWARD A MODEL OF LEGAL ARGUMENT

This Section discusses several landmark projects in AI and law that provide significant steps toward the long range goal of understanding and modeling legal reasoning, particularly legal argument. They address: (1) reasoning with rules: (2) reasoning with open-textured concepts; (3) reasoning with cases, hypotheticals, and precedent-citing argumentation; (4) mixed paradigm reasoning with rules and cases; and (5) deep models of legal knowledge.

---

27. *See infra* Section II.C.

28. Changes of the type involved in "normal science," to use Kuhn's term, are amenable to techniques from machine learning. In contrast, the types of change involved in a Kuhnian "paradigm shift" are probably not, at least in the sense of the system on its own recognizing the need for a shift and carrying it out through the creation of novel concepts. *See* T. KUHN, THE STRUCTURE OF SCIENTIFIC REVOLUTIONS 10, 66 (2d ed. 1970); *see also* E. LEVI, *supra* note 19, at 8, 9 (describing change in law).

29. *See generally*, Lehnert, *Knowledge-Based Natural Language Understanding*, in EXPLORING ARTIFICIAL INTELLIGENCE: SURVEY TALKS FROM THE NATIONAL CONFERENCES ON ARTIFICIAL INTELLIGENCE 83 (1988).

30. This is not so much because of any special difficulties with opinions, but because understanding text is just plain hard. *See supra* notes 13, 29. Legal opinions use specialized vocabulary and conventions, so they might be harder because these considerations require extra processing; on the other hand, the extra constraints these considerations impose might make legal opinions more amenable to computational analysis.

A. *Reasoning with Rules*

One of the earliest steps toward a model of legal reasoning was the use of expert systems[31] to model certain rule-based aspects of law.[32] This step reflects the development of AI: Rule-based expert systems were the first type of AI system to become widely available and employed beyond the AI research community.[33] Furthermore, their underlying computational mechanisms are conceptually clear and they have many computational strengths. While from the legal standpoint there is a variety of opinions as to the validity, usefulness, and status of rules, and there are acknowledged difficulties in representing them,[34] it is still quite natural to take some body of legal rules and embed them in a standard rule-based computational framework.

In the rule-based approach, a rule is encoded in a simple, stylized if-then format: If certain conditions are known to hold, then take the stated action or draw the stated conclusion.[35] Rule-based systems work by chaining these rules together.[36]

---

31. An "expert system" is a special-purpose computer program, which can be said to be expert in a narrow problem area. Typically, such a program uses rules to represent its knowledge and to reason. *See, e.g.,* P. HARMON & D. KING, EXPERT SYSTEMS (1985); D. WATERMAN, A GUIDE TO EXPERT SYSTEMS (1986); B. BUCHANAN & R. SMITH, *Fundamentals of Expert Systems,* in 4 HANDBOOK OF ARTIFICIAL INTELLIGENCE, *supra* note 2, at 149.

32. An even earlier effort related to rule-based aspects of law was Layman Allen's work on "normalization." His emphasis was on eliminating syntactic ambiguity in statutes and legal documents rather than on using computational programs to reason with them. *See* Allen, *Symbolic Logic: A Razor-Edged Tool for Drafting and Interpreting Legal Documents,* 66 YALE L.J. 833 (1957). Of course, if certain ambiguities, for instance those about the scope of logical connectives and the meaning of words like "if," "except," and "unless," were eliminated from legal sources, encoding legal rules for use by an expert system would be easier and less open to debate. Allen & Saxon, *Some Problems in Designing Expert Systems to Aid Legal Reasoning,* in THE SECOND INTERNATIONAL CONFERENCE ON ARTIFICIAL INTELLIGENCE AND LAW: PROCEEDINGS OF THE CONFERENCE 94 (1987) [hereinafter ICAIL-87] (discussing 48 alternative interpretations of structure of proposed limitations on exclusionary rule).

33. For example, the expert system DENDRAL has been widely used by organic chemists, *see* R. LINDSAY, B. BUCHANAN, E. FEIGENBAUM & J. LEDERBERG, APPLICATIONS OF ARTIFICIAL INTELLIGENCE FOR ORGANIC CHEMISTRY: THE DENDRAL PROJECT (1980); sources cited *supra* note 31.

34. Besides "syntactic" difficulties, *see* Allen, *supra* note 32, there are "semantic" difficulties such as the presence of conflicting rules, imprecise terms, and incompleteness. *See* Berman & Hafner, *Obstacles to the Development of Logic-Based Models of Legal Reasoning,* in COMPUTER POWER AND LEGAL LANGUAGE 183 (C. Walter ed. 1988) (discussing difficulties with logic-based approaches); Berman, *Cutting Legal Loops,* in ICAIL-89, *supra* note 1, at 251 (discussing definitional circularity, recursion, and self-referencing in statutes).

35. For instance, Rule 1, concerning "responsibility for use of the product," from the case settlement system of Waterman and Peterson states, "IF the use of [the product] at the time of the plaintiff's loss is foreseeable and (that use is reasonable-and-proper or that use is an emergency or (there is a description by the defendant of that use and that description is improper) or there is not a description by the defendant of that use) THEN assert the defendant is responsible for the use of the product." D. WATERMAN & M. PETERSON, MODELS OF LEGAL DECISION MAKING 37 (Institute for Civil Justice of The Rand Corporation Memo R-2717-ICJ 1981) (parentheses used to denote scope and distribution of logical connectives; thus, here there are two principal antecedents, second of which can be satisfied in alternative ways).

36. The systems can work either "forward" by reasoning from facts to a desired conclusion supported by them, or "backward" from a desired conclusion to find facts supporting it. Forward chaining simply is the repeated application of the logical inference rule *modus ponens:* If one has a rule "If A then B" and the fact A, conclude the fact B. Alternatively, in backward chaining, to establish the

The rule-based approach is particularly useful because in many domains much of an expert's knowledge is amenable to expression in if-then rules, many of which are "heuristic."[37] Heuristics are typically an expert's individual synthesis of past problem solving, and they capture methods for making educated hunches. Expert systems provide a straightforward way to harness heuristic expertise, expressed as rules.

The first uses of the expert systems approach in law were those of Donald Waterman and Mark Peterson at the RAND Corporation's Center for Civil Justice.[38] In their systems, rules were used to encode statements of doctrine as well as legal expertise, cast as rules of thumb.[39] Their work, done while expert systems approaches were beginning to be widely applied, is representative of both what can be accomplished in law with the expert systems methodology and also of the difficulties inherent in such an approach. Waterman and Peterson investigated how the expert systems approach fared as a practical tool in legal applications, and demonstrated it as a methodology for modeling legal expertise.[40]

The problem area of one of their systems, called LDS (for Legal Decision-making System), was assessing the "worth" of a products liability case for settlement purposes. The program, using rule-based models for strict liability, comparative negligence, and calculation of damages, was able to compute the worth of a case, to capture chains of inferences supporting a conclusion like negligence, and to model certain aspects of settlement negotiation. The project demonstrated the applicability of rule-based techniques for legal applications.

Perhaps their system's greatest weaknesses were that it glossed over difficulties inherent in reasoning with imprecise terms and it underplayed the adversarial nature of legal reasoning. For instance, LDS asked the user whether the use of the product was "foreseeable."[41] This is a notoriously subtle question, whose answer is open to interpretation and is entirely contextual. One can argue that coming to a conclusion about the foreseeability of use is at the heart of reasoning in the negligence area,

---

fact B, one looks for such a rule and verifies that one has information to satisfy its precondition, A; if A were not satisfied, one then would look for rules establishing A, and so on until the necessary factual basis were reached and the desired conclusion logically supported. *See* W. SALMON, LOGIC (2d ed. 1973); sources cited *supra* note 31.

37. A "heuristic" is a rule of thumb, a bit of encapsulated wisdom. Much problem-solving behavior is guided by heuristic rules of thumb, such as "If it is fourth down and long yardage is required, then punt," or "If you need to get your citations in correct law journal form, then ask a law journal editor." Heuristics are methods that past experience has shown to be "good" or "wise" things to do; they do not necessarily guarantee a solution, as might algorithms or mathematical theorems, and occasionally they might even produce wrong answers or lead in counter-productive directions. The word "heuristic" stems from the Greek for invention or discovery. The mathematician George Polya discussed heuristic reasoning and the use of heuristics in mathematical reasoning and problem solving. *See* G. POLYA, HOW TO SOLVE IT (1973).

38. *See generally* D. WATERMAN & M. PETERSON, *supra* note 35.

39. *See, e.g., supra* note 35 (example of one of their rules).

40. *See* D. WATERMAN & M. PETERSON, *supra* note 35, at 13-15.

41. *Id.* at 45.

and that by asking the user to make such an interpretive call, the system has given away the whole game. LDS also illustrates another general problem with the rule-based approach: it does not give enough prominence to the adversarial nature of legal reasoning, where the opposing sides seek to establish different, and often contradictory, conclusions. Perhaps more fundamentally, the rule-based approach assumes that the set of rules has no inherent difficulties, like ambiguities, gaps, and conflicts. To make a rule-based system work, the programmer must usually eliminate these problems and make the rules appear more consistent and complete than they are.

Although oversimplified, the system built by Waterman and Peterson was a landmark in unknown territory. It is unfair to condemn it for failing to solve all the hard problems of modeling legal reasoning. To their credit, Waterman and Peterson confront these criticisms head-on in their own critiques. For instance, they address both the difficulty in handling imprecise legal predicates and the need for subtler reasoning with such concepts.[42]

Today, expert systems are one of the most important approaches used and there are many additional examples of current applications. Two recent efforts in Britain are particularly noteworthy. The first is the Latent Damage System by Richard Susskind and Phillip Capper, which addresses a problem area concerning the 1986 British Latent Damage Act.[43] Their system addresses the complex legal issues relating to time periods within which claimants may start proceedings when the damage or suffered loss was "latent."[44] Besides providing a useful application in an intricate body of law, this work is also interesting in the way in which Susskind explains the project in terms of analytic jurisprudence.[45]

The second effort is a group of projects of the Logic Programming Group at Imperial College, University of London, one of which modeled the recent 1981 British Nationality Act.[46] A major goal of this project was to test the suitability of rule-based approaches for representing large, complicated statutes. The process of modeling the statute with rules helped the programmers uncover problems specific to the Act, such as undefined legal predicates and loopholes in the Act, as well as a variety of general problems in the rule-based approach concerning the formalization of negation, the use of defaults and counterfactuals, the representation of com-

---

42. *See id.* at 26. Waterman, a pioneer in machine learning, understood how learning issues were also critical to expert systems. He was well ahead of his time and his early death in 1987 was a great loss.

43. Latent Damage Act, 1986.

44. P. CAPPER & R. SUSSKIND, LATENT DAMAGE LAW—THE EXPERT SYSTEM (1988). The book contains diskettes for installing and running the system on a machine like the IBM PC or XT.

45. *See* R. SUSSKIND, EXPERT SYSTEMS IN LAW (1987).

46. British Nationality Act, 1981. *See* Sergot, Sadri, Kowalski, Kriwaczck, Hammond & Cory, *The British Nationality Act as a Logic Program*, 29 COMM. ACM 370 (1986) [hereinafter Sergot].

mon sense knowledge, and the use of administrative discretion in statutes, each of which poses technically interesting problems for AI.[47]

Although rule-based techniques are but one component in a full model of legal argument, they can be satisfyingly powerful from the perspective of building useful applications. There are abundant examples of applications, many motivated by a need for practical, labor-saving tools in the trenches, where expert resources are terribly strained.[48] Given the availability of inexpensive expert systems development tools and rule-based programming languages, such application systems will continue to proliferate; anyone having access to such tools can write one.[49] In summary, rule-based techniques have demonstrated utility for frequently performed analyses on stereotypical cases in stable, well-developed bodies of law.[50]

B. *Reasoning with Open-Textured Concepts*

Whether there are run-of-the-mill cases amenable to straightforward rule-based analysis is a question with a long jurisprudential history. This brings us to understanding the limitations of rule-based reasoning and the special problems inherent in legal concepts. Anne Gardner's work both elucidates the limitations of rule-based approaches and also points the way toward the use of case-based techniques.[51] Gardner investigated the adequacy of rule-based approaches through the framework of "hard/easy questions."[52] In the hard/easy paradigm, a question is considered "easy" if the legal experts agree as to its analysis or outcome; otherwise, it is "hard." Hard questions typically arise in conjunction with "open-textured" legal concepts.[53] To implement this distinction in a program,

---

47. *See, e.g.*, Sergot, *supra* note 46, at 379 (defining "negation as failure" as the conclusion that something is false if all known ways of showing it true fail); *id.* at 382 ("counterfactual conditionals" as in the statutory phrase "became a British citizen by descent or would have done so but for . . . ."); *id.* at 382 (discretion as in the phrase "If . . . the Secretary of State sees fit"); Berman, *supra* note 34; Berman & Hafner, *supra* note 34.

48. *See, e.g.*, Grady & Patil, *An Expert System for Screening Employee Pension Plans for the Internal Revenue Service*, in ICAIL-87, *supra* note 32, at 137 (describing Internal Revenue Service project to process employee pension plans); Pethe, Rippey & Kale, *A Specialized Expert System for Judicial Decision Support*, in ICAIL-89, *supra* note 1, at 190-94 (system for processing claims under The Federal Black Lung Benefits Act); Weiner, *CACE: Computer-Assisted Case Evaluation in the Brooklyn District Attorney's Office*, in ICAIL-89, *supra* note 1, at 215-23 (describing system for post-arrest/pre-trial processing of drug busts by police).

49. *See, e.g.*, Wiehl, *Computers Assuming New Roles at Law Firms*, N.Y. Times, Jan. 20, 1989, at B4, col. 3; Blodgett, *Artificial Intelligence Comes of Age*, 73 A.B.A. J. 68 (1987).

50. For example, Paul Brest has commented that constitutional law would be "wildly unsuited for an expert system because the principles are vague . . . . Expert systems are best for areas of law that are rule-bound." Blodgett, *supra* note 49, at 70 (quoting Brest).

51. *See generally* A. GARDNER, AN ARTIFICIAL INTELLIGENCE APPROACH TO LEGAL REASONING (1987). Gardner holds a J.D. from Stanford and practiced law before returning to Stanford to obtain a Ph.D. in computer science.

52. For a discussion of this framework, see Hart, *Positivism and the Separation of Law and Morals*, 71 HARV. L. REV. 593 (1958), *reprinted in* H.L.A. HART, ESSAYS IN JURISPRUDENCE AND PHILOSOPHY (1983); R. DWORKIN, *supra* note 23, at 81.

53. For a discussion of "open textured" legal concepts, see H.L.A. HART, THE CONCEPT OF LAW 121-32 (1961).

several specifics must be provided, such as who are the experts to be used, what counts as a disagreement among them, and how to tell if a disagreement exists. From a practical standpoint, if one could sift the easy from the hard, one could employ rule-based techniques, for instance, to solve the easy questions, and attack the hard questions with other methods.[54]

Gardner built a computational model for the hard/easy paradigm and for reasoning with open-textured legal concepts. The problem area of her program was classic offer-and-acceptance law, and its task was to analyze issue-spotter questions, taken from sources such as bar exams and Gilbert's Law Summaries. The program analyzed what the legal questions were, spotted which were hard, and answered the easy ones. Gardner required that her program be computationally reasonable; it should not take an unduly hard computation to decide which questions are easy and hard, or else nothing much would have been gained, at least computationally, if not theoretically.

In Gardner's model, hard questions arise from problems with rules in two ways: either the rules relevant to the domain, such as those from the Restatement of Contracts,[55] are incomplete, circular, or contradictory; or the legal predicates used in the rules are indeterminate and their interpretation cannot be resolved.[56] When there is a mixture in the disposition of cases used to resolve these problems, Gardner's program categorizes the problem as hard. Typically it is not possible to handle indeterminate concepts because, as Gardner puts it, the rules "run out;" that is, a needed rule's premise uses an undefined term.[57]

Gardner's approach to these problems was to give her program a rich body of knowledge and several powerful heuristics. Her program's knowledge included (1) Restatement-like rules for the doctrine of offer and acceptance,[58] (2) a "network" to represent various states in which parties

---

54. This is of course not the only way to model the hard/easy problem; for instance, case-based techniques could be used for both types of questions. However, given that rule-based methods are well-understood, Gardner's approach is quite natural.

55. RESTATEMENT (SECOND) OF CONTRACTS (1981).

56. Note that a typical rule-based approach to handling difficulties with the rule set is to resolve conflicts by hand before encoding the rules in the program. Of course, one cannot always eliminate conflicts in the rule set because even the experts disagree. For example, Gardner's program has pairs of conflicting rules about a rejection that revokes a previous acceptance of an offer, and about simultaneous acceptance and proposal to modify the contract. See A. GARDNER, supra note 51, at 134. Gardner deliberately leaves conflicting rules in her system because she wants her model to be able to handle the fact that legal experts, and thus their rules, can be in conflict. See id. at 3-4. A typical rule-based way to finesse problems with open-textured legal predicates is either simply to ask the user to make the judgment or engage in what might be called "definitional backchaining:" write rules whose pre-conditions specify whether a legal predicate obtains, and then write rules defining what those pre-conditions mean, and so on. See Sergot, supra note 46, at 378 (implementing this approach); D. WATERMAN & M. PETERSON, supra note 35, at 45 (suggesting this approach).

57. A. GARDNER, supra note 51, at 33-34 (discussing problem of inadequacy of rules). This brings the traditional rule-based technique (of backward chaining) to a complete standstill before an adequate definitional basis is reached and application of the ambiguous term can be resolved.

58. For example, her program uses about twenty rules covering contract doctrines such as offer and acceptance. See id. at 133.

could be in offer and acceptance situations, and transitions between these states,[59] (3) relevant common sense knowledge,[60] and (4) prototypical fact patterns (exemplars) for certain key concepts.[61] The exemplars serve as simplified precedents in that their classifications have already been determined and are used to interpret new cases. For convenience in this discussion, the rules, network, and common sense knowledge will be called as a group the "non-exemplar" knowledge.

Gardner's program tries to answer a question by first using the non-exemplar knowledge, and then, if that fails, by using the exemplars, which function as prototypical clear cases. If an answer can be derived with non-exemplar knowledge, the validity of the answer is checked against relevant exemplars.[62] Thus, her program uses exemplars both in a primary way to derive an answer, and in a secondary way to check the validity of an answer. In any case, if there is a mix in the disposition of relevant exemplars, the question is considered hard.[63]

Gardner took the skeleton of an idea from legal philosophy and provided it with computational flesh. Obviously, hers is not the only model that one can propose for the hard/easy paradigm, but it is a computationally disciplined one. By examining the model's computational underpinnings and assumptions, one can learn something about the hard/easy distinction.[64] Her work raises interesting questions about the use and content

59. For example, there can be an offer pending, and an acceptance will enable one to make a transition to the state of being in a contractual relationship. See id. at 123-25; id. at § 6.2.
60. For instance, that a telegram is a kind of document, which in turn is a kind of inanimate object, which in turn is a kind of physical object. See id. at 90-91. See generally id. at 85-117 (very detailed presentation of representation issues).
61. For example, her program has two prototypical fact patterns for the legal predicate "produces a manifestation with content:" making an utterance with some content, and sending a document with some content. See id. at 156-57.
62. The determination of hard/easy cases is made as follows. If a problem such as the application of a legal predicate to the current facts can be (tentatively) answered using the program's non-exemplar domain knowledge, primarily rule-like in character, and if there are no opposing case exemplars, then the question is deemed easy and its answer is the one derived. If the case exemplars used to check the tentative answer all point the opposite way, then the question is also considered easy but the answer is that supported by the case exemplars. If, on the other hand, there is a mixture in the disposition of the case exemplars, then the question is flagged as hard and the program does not attempt to provide an answer. If a (tentative) answer cannot be derived with the domain rules because, for example, a predicate cannot be resolved, but all the relevant cases point the same way and thus can be used to posit and support an answer, then the question is considered easy and the answer is that indicated by the case exemplars. On the other hand, if an answer cannot be derived using the domain rules and there is a mixture in the cases, then the question is also deemed hard. See id. at 54-55, 160-61 (abbreviated descriptions of her program's algorithm).
63. One might ask, why not go to the cases right off? My interpretation is that the reasoning involving the other knowledge, the rules, the transition network, and the common sense knowledge, provides a means by which to index relevant cases. Furthermore, even in the easy cases, one would need to derive the answer by some means, and in her model this is attempted with the rule-guided reasoning, which would need to be done at some point anyway. Alternatively, one could omit looking at the rules altogether and just consider cases. Of course, one would need to say which cases to consider and what exactly to do with them. See infra Section II.C (discussing work of Ashley).
64. For instance, too many questions might be categorized as "hard" in this model since there is very often a mixture in the disposition of the cases. Perhaps one needs to be more discriminating in the use of cases.

of cases, and about which cases to include in a decision maker's case base.[65]

While Gardner's work certainly addresses some of the shortcomings of purely rule-based models, her program still falls short with regard to reasoning with cases. Some of the core features of precedent-based argumentation, such as determining relevancy and drawing analogies, are beyond the scope of her program; these issues are the focus of the next set of projects to be explored here. Nonetheless, Gardner's research provides an exceptionally important step toward the goal of understanding and modeling legal argumentation.

C. Precedent-Based Reasoning with Cases and Hypotheticals

The next landmark AI project was Kevin Ashley's, which was done in this author's research group at the University of Massachusetts.[66] Ashley developed a program called HYPO to model certain aspects of case-based reasoning as exemplified by appellate-style argumentation with precedents. The problem area of this project was trade secret law. The task was to produce elements of precedent-based argument. The HYPO project focused solely on reasoning with cases, and was the first project—not only in AI and law, but also in AI in general—to attack squarely the problem of reasoning with cases and hypotheticals in a precedent-based manner.

HYPO performs as follows: Given a fact situation, HYPO analyzes it according to its model of trade secret law and then retrieves relevant cases from its knowledge base of cases. It then determines which relevant cases are most on point, or potentially so, for whose point of view, and from which analytic approach. HYPO then generates the skeleton of an argument. In such an argument snippet, HYPO first argues for side one (plaintiff or defendant) by making a legal point and citing its best, most on point cases; then it argues for side two by responding with a counterpoint, citing a most on point case supporting side two's point of view or also by distinguishing the current facts from side one's cases; and finally, HYPO argues again for side one with a rebuttal of side two's position, which may include distinguishing side two's cases and strengthening the

---

65. For instance, in Gardner's program cases are prototypical fact patterns rather than actual cases. What about using real fact patterns instead, or in addition? Which ones? How should the program's memory of cases be organized? Are certain cases to be preferred to others?

66. See generally K. ASHLEY, MODELING LEGAL ARGUMENT: REASONING WITH CASES AND HYPOTHETICALS (forthcoming 1990) (originally completed as Ph.D. dissertation, Department of Computer and Information Science of the University of Massachusetts, Amherst, February, 1988, under this author's direction); Ashley & Rissland, A Case-Based Approach To Modeling Legal Expertise, IEEE EXPERT, Fall 1988, at 70-77 (short overview and example). Ashley holds a J.D. from Harvard Law School and practiced as a litigator with White & Case in New York before returning to study computer science at the University of Massachusetts.

relationship of side one's analysis to the current facts.[67] At various points in the argument, HYPO may generate and employ hypotheticals—for instance, to refute a claim when no actual counter-example case exists in HYPO's knowledge base of cases.[68]

HYPO is able to: assess relevancy of cases; decide for each side which relevant cases are most on point and which of these are best to cite in argument; analogize and distinguish cases; generate and reason with hypotheticals; cite various types of counterexamples to a point; and construct the skeleton of a case-citing argument. HYPO does not in any way attempt to bring in policy-level concerns or argumentation; rather, it sticks to arguing with cases, on their facts, in a technical way. HYPO also does not include other aspects of legal reasoning, such as reasoning with rules.

A key feature of HYPO is a kind of case index, called a "dimension," which it uses to retrieve and analyze cases. Dimensions represent important legal factors. They encode the knowledge that the presence of certain facts enables a case to be addressed from a certain point of view.[69] A dimension enables HYPO to retrieve a set of cases that support the same analytic approach and to compare and assess the relative strength of the cases within this group.[70]

HYPO uses dimensions to define concepts like "relevant," "most on point" and "best" cases.[71] In HYPO, a case is considered "relevant" if it shares at least one dimension with the fact situation. HYPO ranks cases according to how on point they are by examining the overlap between the set of dimensions present in the fact situation and the sets of dimensions present in the cases. If the overlapping set of dimensions of one case, B, is contained within that of another case, A, then A is defined as more on point than B, the rationale being that A has more lines of analysis in common with the fact situation than does B.[72]

---

67. For several examples, see K. ASHLEY, *supra* note 66; Ashley & Rissland, *supra* note 66, at 74-76.

68. K. ASHLEY, *supra* note 66.

69. For instance, in HYPO's domain of trade secret misappropriation law, knowing facts about the relative costs incurred by the plaintiff and defendant in developing their putative secrets into a product enables one to make arguments about the gain of competitive advantage, and knowing facts about the disclosures made by the plaintiff enables one to make arguments about how well the plaintiff kept his knowledge secret. *See, e.g.*, Gilburne & Johnston, *Trade Secret Protection for Software Generally and in the Mass Market*, 3 COMPUTER L.J. 211 (1982). For further explanation and examples, see K. ASHLEY, *supra* note 66; Rissland, Valcarce & Ashley, *Explaining and Arguing with Examples*, in PROCEEDINGS OF THE NATIONAL CONFERENCE ON ARTIFICIAL INTELLIGENCE 288, 291-93 (1984).

70. In HYPO, for instance, the greater the disparity between the development costs of plaintiff and defendant, the easier it is to argue that, all other things being equal, the defendant gained an unfair competitive advantage through misappropriation of plaintiff's trade secret. Thus, for example, since there is a case in which the plaintiff prevails with a ratio of two to one for plaintiff's to defendant's costs, *see* Telex Corp. v. IBM Corp., 367 F. Supp. 258 (N.D. Okla. 1973), then a new case with a ratio of four to one would represent an even stronger position for the plaintiff in HYPO.

71. *See* K. ASHLEY, *supra* note 66.

72. So, for instance, suppose the dimensions that apply to the current fact situation (CFS) are W, X, Y, and Z. Suppose Case A shares X, Y, and Z with CFS, and Case B shares just X and Y. Then

By then taking into account which cases support or cut against a party, their relative strength along shared dimensions, and the dimensions not shared, HYPO is able to analogize, distinguish, and otherwise manipulate cases to construct snippets of precedent-citing argument. For instance, to distinguish a case that the opposing party, say the plaintiff, has cited as controlling the outcome of the current fact situation, HYPO looks at the cited case for the existence of dimensions unshared with the current situation. HYPO then argues, for the defendant, that the presence or absence in the current factual setting of these dimensions diminishes the applicability of the cited case; in other words, these are differences that really make a difference.[73]

To summarize, the HYPO project models some of the key ingredients of reasoning with precedents. The model provides computational definitions of relevant cases, on point cases, and best cases to cite.[74] Because of the precision of HYPO's model, a researcher can examine specific details and assumptions.[75] By providing an analysis and computational model for reasoning with cases, perhaps the most vital aspect of legal reasoning, Ashley's work is a giant step toward the goal of understanding legal argumentation.

An earlier effort addressing some of the same concerns as HYPO was the work of Thorne McCarty on legal argument.[76] One of McCarty's longstanding goals has been the construction of knowledge representation mechanisms with which to model certain aspects of legal argumentation. For instance, McCarty has proposed a mechanism called "prototypes and deformations" to model certain aspects of appellate argument. He has used it to examine the sort of situation in which one incrementally steps from a desirable precedent to the current case, through a sequence of intermediate real and hypothetical cases, in order either to construct an argument by analogy for the result one desires, or else to show the inconsistency of the result argued for by one's opponent.[77] His model requires a

---

Case A is more on point than Case B because the set that B shares with CFS is a subset of the set that A shares. Suppose there is a third relevant case, Case C, sharing dimensions W and X with CFS; Case C is neither more nor less on point than A or B. Both Case A and Case C are most on point cases since each shares maximally with respect to a subset of dimensions.

73.   For instance, if the case cited by the plaintiff is very strong on a pro-plaintiff dimension not present in the current case, the defendant can argue that that particular dimension is responsible for the pro-plaintiff outcome. If, in addition, the defendant can point to a different case, the same in all respects to the plaintiff's cited case except for that one dimension, in which the defendant prevailed, then the assignment of credit for the outcome in the plaintiff's case to the missing dimension is all the more convincing.

74.   For instance, the best cases for a side to cite are defined as those most on point cases for that side that share at least one applicable dimension favoring that side.

75.   For instance, an alternative way to measure relevancy is to minimize the sets of dimensions not shared. One could then swap this alternative definition for relevancy in the HYPO model and observe the repercussions.

76.   See generally McCarty, *Reflections on TAXMAN: An Experiment in Artificial Intelligence and Legal Reasoning*, 90 HARV. L. REV. 837 (1977).

77.   See McCarty & Sridharan, *The Representation of an Evolving System of Legal Concepts: II*

great deal of attention to details concerning the representation of cases and their constituent parts.[78] Thus, although some of McCarty's research is clearly tied to that on cases, hypotheticals, and argument, the bulk of his work is more aptly grouped with efforts on developing "deep models" of legal knowledge, which concentrate more on developing highly detailed models of knowledge than the other projects discussed thus far, and will be discussed briefly later.[79]

One of the shared concerns of McCarty and this author is the use of hypotheticals in legal arguments and development of computational methods to generate them.[80] For example, HYPO uses hypotheticals to fulfill the need for counter-examples to refute another's position when real cases cannot be found or to show the sensitivity of a given fact to the interpretation of a case.[81] It uses its internal mechanisms, like dimensions, to generate hypotheticals, for instance by adding, deleting, or changing a fact affecting a dimension.[82]

The conceptual framework provided by such AI models can also be used to analyze expert use of hypotheticals in Socratic law school dialogues, advocacy, judical opinion, and appellate oral argument.[83] Improvements of advocacy and pedagogical skills are two potential benefits from these analyses. Another is increased understanding of the development of legal concepts and theories. For instance, a good hypothetical provides a way to test the validity of a theory: it provides a *gedanken* experiment. This is especially valuable when there are very few real cases. Hypotheticals play a special role in case-based reasoning, and increased understanding of them would contribute to our goal of modeling legal reasoning.

Another contribution to understanding the case-based aspects of legal reasoning would be to understand how new arguments could be generated by modification of old arguments, without starting "from scratch" from a statement and analysis of the facts, proceeding through an analysis of rele-

---

Prototypes and Deformations, PROCEEDINGS OF THE SEVENTH INTERNATIONAL JOINT CONFERENCE ON ARTIFICIAL INTELLIGENCE 246 (1981) (discussion of prototypes and deformations); L. McCARTY & N. SRIDHARAN, A COMPUTATIONAL THEORY OF LEGAL ARGUMENT (Laboratory for Computer Science Research, Rutgers University, New Brunswick, N.J. Technical Report No. LRP-TR-13, 1981) (presenting example from Justice Pitney's opinion and Justice Brandeis' dissent in landmark tax case Eisner v. Macomber, 252 U.S. 189 (1920)).

78.   McCarty & Sridharan, *supra* note 77.

79.   *See infra* Section II.E.

80.   *See, e.g.*, McCarty & Sridharan, *supra* note 77; L. McCARTY & N. SRIDHARAN, *supra* note 77; Rissland, *Examples in the Legal Domain: Hypotheticals in Contract Law*, in PROCEEDINGS OF THE FOURTH ANNUAL CONFERENCE OF THE COGNITIVE SCIENCE SOCIETY 96 (1982).

81.   *See* K. ASHLEY, *supra* note 66; Rissland & Ashley, *Hypotheticals as Heuristic Device*, PROCEEDINGS OF THE FIFTH NATIONAL CONFERENCE ON ARTIFICIAL INTELLIGENCE 289 (1986).

82.   For instance, one can make a trade secret misappropriation case incrementally weaker or stronger by variation of a key fact, like the relative competitive advantage gained by the defendant or the number of disclosures made by the plaintiff. *See, e.g.*, *supra* notes 69-70.

83.   *See, e.g.*, Rissland, *Argument Moves and Hypotheticals*, in COMPUTING POWER AND LEGAL REASONING 129 (C. Walter ed. 1985) (examples of hypotheticals in Socratic teaching); Rissland & Ashley, *supra* note 81, at 290-91 (examples in context of advocacy); McCarty & Sridharan, *supra* note 77 (examples in context of judicial opinion).

vant precedents, and culminating in an argument, as HYPO describes. Of course, a model to describe this alternative approach would require representation and manipulation of a knowledge base of arguments. This is the subject of the on-going research.[84] Another step would be to explore more fully the relationship between relevance and analogy.[85]

However, just as Waterman and Peterson artificially confined themselves to reasoning with rules, others, like Ashley, considered only reasoning with cases. From the long range perspective of developing an all-encompassing model for legal reasoning, both approaches leave something out, since many areas of the law are neither purely case-based nor purely rule-based. Both types of reasoning are clearly needed in statutory areas, where, despite the drafters' best efforts, there are always legal terms and rules whose meaning and scope are not totally fixed and for which one must look to cases for interpretation. The next major step toward a model of legal reasoning is development of approaches to combine reasoning with cases and reasoning with rules.

D. *Reasoning with Rules and Cases*

Reasoning in a statutory area like tax law is typical of mixed paradigm reasoning. For instance, consider the subsection of tax law governing the deductibility of expenses for a so-called home office. The tax code includes requirements that the office be used regularly and exclusively, and that it is the principal place of business or a place where one meets or deals with clients.[86] However, nowhere in the tax code are the requirements for what constitutes "regular" or "exclusive" use, etc., set forth. All such terms have been the subject of numerous cases,[87] and to determine whether they apply to a new situation, one must typically examine precedents and create precedent-based arguments or subarguments to justify the interpretation. Of course, the argumentation must be tied back to the requirements and structure of the statute.

Methods for accomplishing hybrid rule-based and case-based reasoning go beyond those needed for pure case-based and or rule-based reasoning in isolation. For instance, suppose that one had a rule with three preconditions for the awarding of a certain benefit: "In order to receive bene-

---

84. *See, e.g.*, Branting, *Representing and Reusing Explanations of Legal Precedents*, in ICAIL-89, *supra* note 1, at 103 (developing model of how past arguments can be modified for re-use in new case).

85. *See* K. BELLAIRS, CONTEXTUAL RELEVANCE IN ANALOGICAL REASONING: A MODEL OF LEGAL ARGUMENT (submitted to the University of Minnesota, 1989) (Ph.D. thesis) (how relevance can be defined in terms of analogy). This work continues the examination begun by Ashley of what it means for one case to be relevant to another. It draws on work such as Gentner's, *supra* note 12, which views analogy as a mapping between structured objects like legal concepts and cases.

86. I.R.C. § 280A(c)(1) (1988).

87. For example, cases examining "exclusive use" include Frankel v. Commissioner, 82 T.C. 318 (1984), Baie v. Commissioner, 74 T.C. 105 (1980), and Chauls v. Commissioner, 41 T.C.M. (CCH) 234 (1980).

fit B, one must satisfy requirements R1, R2, and R3." Suppose that R1 and R2 are clearly satisfied. To argue for receiving the benefit, one has several strategies to consider. For instance, one can try to find on point precedents addressing the interpretation of antecedent R3, and then argue that, in fact, the facts actually do satisfy R3 and thus the rule. Alternatively, one can try to find on point precedents in which only the first two requirements were met and the benefit was awarded nonetheless, and then argue that the first two are sufficient by themselves. These are examples of "near miss" strategies. To carry them out requires not only the use of both the rule and the cases, but also that both types of reasoning be done in concert. It is not good enough to confine one's attention to the cases; the case-based aspects must speak to the rule. Similarly, one gets nowhere using the rules alone, since the rules "run out." Figuring out how to coordinate the reasoning activities of the rule-based and case-based aspects is a question of "control."[88]

Gardner's research suggests one model for integrating rule-based and case-based reasoning: use cases when reasoning with rules comes to an impasse, and also use cases to validate the conclusions reached using rules.[89] In this approach, case-based reasoning is subjugated to rule-based reasoning. Of course, selecting the dominant mode of reasoning should really depend on the context or circumstances: sometimes the rules should drive the reasoning, and sometimes the cases.

A different approach for an AI program would be to have independent processes—one for case-based tasks, one for rule-based tasks—where each works from its own point of view independently. Later, an executive process would integrate the results. Metaphorically, this is like sending off associates to do specific tasks, such as library work on case law or statutory law, and having the senior associate integrate the information and the reasoning.

For a computational model, one must spell out when and how the processes interact. In particular, how should the associate processes communicate their results with one another? Should they wait until they are done with their individual tasks before communicating? Should they share intermediate results and insights?

One AI model for integrating the work of the associate processes would be the following: each process could have access to a common blackboard, on which it could write anything interesting or useful it learns, and from which it could read any piece of information it found to be interesting or useful. In this model, the processes reason largely independently of each other, and yet they can capitalize opportunistically on each other's results.

---

88. "Control" refers to issues concerning how a program is organized, how its parts interact, and, in general, how it decides what to do next.
89. *See supra* Section II.B.

This is in fact the approach taken in so called "blackboard" systems.[90] Of course, many more details must be specified before an actual AI and law program could be built using this framework.[91]

In the same spirit, but slightly simpler, is the so-called "agenda-based" model in which, at any given moment, an individual process is in control as it tries to accomplish its assigned task.[92] As the process performs its assignment, it makes note of other tasks it would find necessary, interesting, or useful to be accomplished by another process or itself. As a task is being worked on, other tasks are proposed for consideration.[93] Specifically, the tasks spawned are added to an overall "wish list" of things to do. Since computational resources are limited, this list (the agenda) is ordered according to some standard, such as interest, novelty, or importance. The task with the highest ranking is selected from the agenda and is worked on next. Heuristic rules, like strategies for dealing with near misses, are used to specify what sort of tasks should be proposed and how they should be ordered.[94]

Blackboard and agenda-based systems behave in a dynamic, opportunistic way, sometimes working from one approach, sometimes from another, and deciding which task is best to do as it proceeds. The methods that a system uses to manage the posting and execution of proposed tasks largely define its overall style of reasoning.[95]

Research on hybrid reasoners is currently underway at several sites. Two using an agenda-based approach are the PROLEXS Project at the Vrije Universiteit in Amsterdam in the area of Dutch landlord-tenant law,[96] and the CABARET (for CAse-BAsed REasoning Tool) project of this author's group at the University of Massachusetts in statutory areas,

---

90. See Nii, *Blackboard Systems*, in 4 HANDBOOK OF AI, *supra* note 2, at 3. The blackboard model was first used in the 1970's in the HEARSAY II project for understanding continuous speech (this has nothing to do with the hearsay rule in evidence). *See, e.g.,* Erman, Hayes-Roth, Lesser & Reddy, *The HEARSAY-II Speech-Understanding System: Integrating Knowledge To Resolve Uncertainty,* 12 COMPUTING SURVEYS 213 (1980).

91. For example, one would need to determine which "knowledge sources," as the rule-based and case-based associates would be called, have access to what information on the blackboard. For instances, can some access more information than others? What is the relative import of their results?

92. The program AM used an agenda. *See generally* R. DAVIS & D. LENAT, *supra* note 7.

93. For instance, in our benefits rule example, the first task of applying the benefit rule would spawn several near-miss tasks concerning the third antecedent, R3, such as finding cases to show R3 is satisfied or not needed.

94. The overall behavior of agenda-based systems is to work in a "best first" manner. Since the decisions as to what counts as "best" are often based on evaluative heuristics, and at any given moment the tasks on the agenda represent alternatives, agenda-based systems perform "heuristic best first search."

95. The management scheme can be used to bias the system to behave in a certain way. For instance, one can bias the system always to look at rule-based tasks in preference to case-based ones.

96. *See, e.g.,* Oskamp, *Knowledge Representation and Legal Expert Systems,* in ADVANCED TOPICS OF LAW AND INFORMATION TECHNOLOGY 195 (G. Vandenberghe ed. 1989); Oskamp, Walker, Schrickx & van den Berg, *PROLEXS Divide and Rule: A Legal Application,* in ICAIL-89, *supra* note 1, at 54.

such as the home office deduction.[97] There is a rising tide of interest in such systems throughout AI.

CABARET contains full-fledged rule-based and case-based reasoners, each with its own dedicated "monitoring" process, which harvests observations and describes them in terms understandable by the agenda-based controller. The controller, in turn, applies heuristics to these observations to propose and order tasks.[98] For instance, the rule-based monitor would post the observation that a near-miss situation had obtained with regard to antecedent R3 of our benefits example, and this would trigger near-miss heuristics. CABARET currently uses approximately thirty heuristics, grouped into ten or so categories, such as ways to begin reasoning, to check on reasoning, to respond to failures in reasoning, to respond to near misses, to broaden rules and concepts, and to narrow rules and concepts.[99] These were developed through observations of experts as well as from legal sources.[100]

E. Deep Models of Legal Knowledge

The goal of research on deep models is to allow an AI program to reason about ingredients of its own legal and general knowledge by representing this knowledge in great detail.[101] Types of knowledge used in deep models include knowledge about temporal and spatial relations, quantity, common sense taxonomies, relations among individuals and beliefs. This topic is often addressed under the rubric of "deep models" and is very much related to fundamental problems concerning common sense reasoning. The motivating assumption is that the richer the representation, both in scope and detail, the better the reasoning. The need to use deeper models of knowledge will ultimately forge a link between the other research

---

97. See supra text accompanying notes 85–87; Rissland & Skalak, Interpreting Statutory Predicates, in ICAIL-89, supra note 1, at 46; Rissland & Skalak, Combining Case-Based and Rule-Based Reasoning: A Heuristic Approach, in 1 PROCEEDINGS OF THE ELEVENTH INTERNATIONAL JOINT CONFERENCE ON ARTIFICIAL INTELLIGENCE 524 (1989) [hereinafter Rissland & Skalak, A Heuristic Approach].
98. For some of the computational details, see Rissland & Skalak, A Heuristic Approach, supra note 97.
99. Id. at 526.
100. See, e.g., W. TWINING & D. MIERS, HOW TO DO THINGS WITH RULES (2d ed. 1982) (discussing various problems, examples, and approaches for reasoning with statutes and rules).
101. By contrast, in most of the systems discussed in this Comment, perhaps with the exception of Gardner's system, there is no method by which the program may reason about such knowledge explicitly. While questions of time and number come up, for instance, in HYPO's reasoning about disclosure events, see supra notes 69, 82, HYPO cannot reason explicitly about time or numeracy as topics in their own right. However, note that since HYPO knows that 10,000 disclosures is a far worse number of disclosures from the plaintiff's point of view than two would be, in a sense HYPO implicitly knows the difference between big and small numbers. One might even say that since, with respect to the dimensions about disclosures, fact situations with the same number of disclosures are treated as being the same (all other things aside), HYPO could be said to know what 2 or 10,000 means. However, numbers and their absolute magnitudes are not topics HYPO can reason about in an explicit way. If HYPO were redesigned so that it used a deep model containing information about numbers it would be able to do so.

discussed in this Comment and that research seeking to develop rich representation schemes for legal knowledge.

Work on representation of legal knowledge is exemplified by the research projects of Thorne McCarty[102] and Tom Gordon.[103] Deep models stand in contrast to situations where one simply uses representation items to encode domain knowledge, but cannot reason further about their meaning. If one were to employ deep knowledge in a system like HYPO, for instance, one would represent in much more detail information about such things as disclosure events, companies, time periods of employment and product development, obligations of employers and employees, and products. For instance, in a deep model an AI researcher could reify a relation such as employer-employee at a deeper level, perhaps in terms of relations of permission or obligation, so that the program could reason about the employer-employee relation as a topic in itself.[104]

III. CONCLUSIONS

Obviously, I cannot do justice to the number and variety of projects in AI and law in this Comment. However, I hope my discussion gives some idea of the richness and variety of current projects.

I foresee the continuation of work on rule-based, case-based, mixed paradigm, hypothetical reasoning, and argument, and predict it will be extended by results concerning deep models of representation, sophisticated control regimes, and machine learning. These lines of research eventually will merge and culminate in an extensive theory of legal argumentation. In time, more and more of the desiderata for AI models of legal reasoning will be incorporated into running AI systems. One can expect some research systems, like HYPO, to have an impact on practical systems, just as Waterman and Peterson's did.[105] What was first a research idea will find its way into practical systems.[106]

---

102. *See, e.g.*, McCarty, *Permissions and Obligations*, 1 PROCEEDINGS OF THE EIGHTH INTERNATIONAL JOINT CONFERENCE ON ARTIFICIAL INTELLIGENCE 287 (1983) (using "permissions" and "obligations" to represent certain relations between parties in case); *cf.* Hohfeld, *Some Fundamental Legal Conceptions as Applied in Legal Reasoning*, 23 YALE L.J. 16 (1913) (developing similar relationship-type structures). The need for representing such deontic relationships in his scheme required McCarty to develop a great deal of logical apparatus, which has been the focus of his work for many years. Of late, McCarty has been coming back to some of his primary concerns: development of a comprehensive representational theory for legal knowledge and ultimately, legal argument. *See, e.g.*, McCarty, *A Language for Legal Discourse I. Basic Features*, in ICAIL-89, *supra* note 1, at 180.
103. *See* Gordon, *Issue Spotting in a System for Searching Interpretation Spaces*, in ICAIL-89, *supra* note 1, at 157 (1989); Gordon, *OBLOG-2: A Hybrid Knowledge Representation System for Defeasible Reasoning*, in ICAIL-87, *supra* note 32.
104. Hohfeld, *supra* note 102.
105. *See supra* Section II.A.
106. For instance, I predict that work on case-based reasoning will lead to practical tools for creating and managing case data bases of individual practitioners and firms, which can then be used in preparation of new cases. A beneficial side-effect of such CBR tools, and of course, of traditional expert systems, will be the capturing and preservation of a firm's "institutional memory" and its use to leverage new or inexperienced attorneys in the areas of the firm's expertise to higher levels of

I have tried to show how AI and law researchers are pursuing their twin goals of analytic and practical advances, and how past and ongoing research can be viewed as a coherent attempt to model legal reasoning, particularly argumentation. Even though we may be a long way from some vision of the ideal legal reasoning AI program, and in fact may never be able to achieve certain aspects of human expertise, we can already accomplish very interesting and useful projects. We can use the fine lens of AI to explicate the process of legal reasoning, for instance the creation of case-based arguments; to shed light on questions in legal philosophy, such as the nature of open-textured predicates; and to provide practical, even socially beneficial, applications, such as expert systems in certain administrative areas. The insistence on using computational methods in the AI approach provides a useful discipline for considering longstanding issues in legal reasoning.

Although I have not discussed it here, this body of research can also be fruitfully applied to the law school curriculum. For instance, we can provide our law students with environments in which to examine their own legal knowledge.[107] The conceptual framework of AI can also provide a way to describe our own expertise, such as posing of artful hypotheticals, and show students how they may also possibly acquire it. AI provides a set of tools, based on detailed models of representation and process.

By this discussion, I hope both to encourage those wishing to attempt AI-style projects, and also to reassure those unsure of whether we should. For instance, some might be concerned that the use of AI models will somehow trivialize legal reasoning by making it seem too simple, undermine the importance of lawyers and judges by relegating them to the role of mere users of systems which do all of the interesting reasoning, or dehumanize us by describing intelligent behavior in well-defined terms. I think AI research shows just the opposite: The more we understand human reasoning, the more we marvel at its richness and flexibility, the more questions we ask as we try to understand its workings, and the more we require of a computer program exhibiting intelligence.

Legal reasoning is complex. Our current AI models, albeit too simple, are but steps to more subtle and complete models, and at each step we understand more. There will always be a need for human lawyers and judges. The goal is to assist, not to replace. Demystification of some of the

---

performance, at the very least by keeping them from asking "obvious" questions and making "silly" mistakes.

107. For example, one can use currently available commercial expert systems shells to allow students to build their own small applications and then to experiment with them. The very exercise of developing a rule base forces students to develop a theory of the application area and to think about general issues regarding the validity and appropriateness of using rule-based approaches. For instance, developing rule sets for consumer tort law or offer-and-acceptance law requires understanding of the specifics of the law as well as general issues about rules and legal predicates and problematic aspects of them. *See supra* Sections II.A-B.

most precious qualities of human intelligence is not to be feared; understanding does not destroy or diminish that which is understood. We should not be afraid to know how we know.

Of course, use of AI techniques, whether in basic research or straightforward applications, requires detailed knowledge of their underlying assumptions, simplifications, strengths, and weaknesses. Successful projects require not only thorough knowledge of both AI and the law, but also a willingness to try new approaches without knowing exactly where they will lead, or whether or not they will achieve exactly the desired result. In short, work in AI and law is no different from work in other fields: you cannot get anywhere without trying; and one invariably learns from trying.

In seeking to understand and model legal reasoning, AI will be challenged and enriched. By engaging in AI endeavors, the law will be challenged and enriched too; it will better understand its own modes of reasonings, including the knowledge and assumptions underlying them, and it will benefit from practical computational tools and models. The relationship between AI and law is a true synergy, the shared specialty of AI and law adding value to both.

Artificial Intelligence and Law 1, 3–44, 1992.
© 1992 *Kluwer Academic Publishers. Printed in the Netherlands*

Arguments and Cases:
An Inevitable Intertwining[1]

DAVID B. SKALAK AND EDWINA L. RISSLAND

Dept. of Computer Science, University of Massachusetts. Amherst. Massachusetts 01003, U.S.A
Skalak@cs.umass.edu.Rissland@cs.umass.edu

(Received 16 November 1991, accepted 14 February 1992)

Abstract. We discuss several aspects of legal arguments, primarily arguments about the meaning of statutes. First, we discuss how the requirements of argument guide the specification and selection of supporting cases and how an existing case base influences argument formation. Second, we present our evolving taxonomy of patterns of actual legal argument. This taxonomy builds upon our much earlier work on 'argument moves' and also on our more recent analysis of how cases are used to support arguments for the interpretation of legal statutes. Third, we show how the theory of argument used by CABARET, a hybrid case-based/rule-based reasoner, can support many of the argument patterns in our taxonomy.

Key words: argument, case-based reasoning, mixed paradigm, statutory interpretation

1. Introduction

Good supporting cases make good arguments. Selecting the best cases possible is crucially important to advancing one's interests, especially in an adversarial domain such as law that requires advocates to support their positions with previous cases. Deciding precisely what constitutes a good, better, or best case requires addressing a variety of theoretical and pragmatic questions.

In this article, we raise and address issues of case selection in the context of statutory interpretation, which we view as argument about the application of a stated legal rule to a new problem situation. Some of the central concerns of statutory interpretation are addressed by our attempt to provide a computational model for selecting the cases that can be used to argue for a particular interpretation of a legal rule. For instance, we distinguish reasoning about the necessity and sufficiency of the antecedents in a rule from reasoning about the meaning of the words used therein. As an example of the former, argument over the status of the antecedents in a rule, consider an advocate whose client has satisfied all but one of a rule's prerequisites, but who nonetheless wants to receive a benefit provided by the rule. The advocate must argue, ideally with the aid of supporting

---

[1] This work was supported in part by the National Science Foundation, contract IRI-890841, the Air Force Office of Sponsored Research under contract 90–0359, the Office of Naval Research under a University Research Initiative Grant, contract N00014-87-K-0238, and a grant from GTE Laboratories, Inc., Waltham, Mass.

4   DAVID B. SKALAK AND EDWINA L. RISSLAND

cases, that the unsatisfied prerequisite is not strictly necessary to satisfy the rule's requirements. On the other hand, statutory interpretation often takes the form of argument about the meaning of a rule's individual terms. For example, 'Is taxpayer's home office his "principal place of business," as that term is used in Section 280A(c)(1)(A) of the Internal Revenue Code?' Arguments about the status of rules, the necessity and sufficiency of their conditions, the presence or absence of tacit exceptions and requirements, and the scope and meaning of ingredient terms is the heart of statutory interpretation. These and related issues have been considered in depth by legal philosophers from a spectrum of jurisprudential positions, such as Llewellyn, Hart, Fuller, Twining and Miers [Llewellyn, 1989], [Hart, 1958], [Fuller, 1958], [Twining & Miers, 1982]. Their treatments have provided us with such classic examples of statutory ambiguity as Hart's 'No vehicles in the park' and 'Take off your hat when entering a church.'

To put the matter simply, the best case for your argument about the meaning of a legal rule is a case that is available to you, that is similar to yours, and that went your way. Providing computational definitions of 'similar' and 'went your way' is one theme of this article. In trying to locate such cases, one must temper a specification of the ideal supporting case with the cases that are actually present in a case library. The characterization of the best case that can be found is a mixture of 'case-base-dependent' and 'case-base-independent' influences. Varying the proportions of the mixture yields a continuum of possible approaches to how to find cases that support a legal rule interpretation.

Although neither extreme approach is pursued in its pure form in legal practice, it may be instructive to observe that each approach is manifested in the way attorneys sometimes work. Consider the task of writing a legal brief. At one extreme, one could specify the ideal case independently of what cases are in the case base and then try to find that ideal case. (In the absence of an actual precedent meeting one's specifications, one could create a hypothetical case that makes the point.) One would specify 'top down' the features the ideal case must have and perhaps, must not have,[2] and which features may be ignored.[3] This case-base-independent approach is at work when a senior litigator leaves space in a brief for supporting citations for well-established propositions of law, and then directs her associates to go to the library to fill in the placeholders with citations to actual cases.[4]

At the other extreme approach, case-base dependence, one can determine what the best cases are through exhaustive examination of the case base, choosing cases according to some construction of 'best.' This is a case-driven, 'bottom-up', approach to best case

---

[2] In effect, this approach attempts to reduce the problems of partial matching of cases to the simpler one of a complete match. The problems of partial matching intrude on this attempt to require 'complete matches,' however. If one specifies only those features that the ideal case is required to have, one must state also whether additional features must be absent or can simply be ignored.

[3] Treatment of any unspecified or unanticipated features implicitly entails a decision whether — and to what extent – to adopt the closed world assumption. See also [Gibbons, 1991].

[4] This specification-driven approach may be used to plan a sequence of 'deformations' of a current fact situation to yield a series of hypotheticals. See [McCarty & Sridharan, 1982]. The current case may be linked with an ideal case in such a 'connect-the-dots' manner. Of course, planning the intermediate hypothetical case points involves subtleties from each of the aspects of legal argument we will enumerate. For example, 'How much will the court tolerate in the way of deformations?' would be an important jurisprudential question.

selection. A best case is best only relative to the cases actually present in the case base. The case-base-dependent approach is evident in brief writing when the legal propositions advanced are actually derived from generalizations of the common law contained in the cases. In particular, the dependence of argument on the constituents of the case base is clear where argument is restricted to cases from a given jurisdiction, time period or court.

Of course, brief-writing, like many other argument tasks, is usually a mixture of both approaches. Empty placeholders for string cites to cases stating well-accepted propositions of law may be left for routine completion, but more tenuous and arguable propositions often must be derived bottom-up from relevant cases.

Selecting the best cases to use in an argument actually requires confronting a variety of aspects of legal argument: precedential aspects, rhetorical aspects, doctrinal aspects and jurisprudential aspects.

- Precedential aspects of argument include an analysis of the current problem (the 'current fact situation'), cases from the current case base and their inter-connections, the range of possible hypothetical variations on cases, and approaches to determining case similarity.
- Rhetorical aspects include persuasive strategies, such as the short-term strategy of how to argue the current fact situation, the repertoire of available argument techniques and forms, and any long range strategy of how to argue future cases addressing the same issue.
- Doctrinal considerations include the legal claim at issue and its elements, the recognized factors in the domain, and any evidence of doctrinal drift.
- Lastly, jurisprudential aspects include a model of what constitutes a *bona fide* argument, a model of the adherence required to decided cases ('*stare decisis*'), a theory of the relative pedigree or importance of cases, and a recognition of the varying procedural postures of precedents.

In this article, we will limit our attention to precedential aspects of legal argument, particularly on collecting, organizing, and implementing detailed argument patterns for using cases to support rule interpretation.

1.1 ORGANIZATION OF THE ARTICLE

We explore in this article how case-base-independent and case-base-dependent approaches influence each other. We provide a theoretical framework for combining them and present an empirical collection of argument patterns, observed in practice, and show how the two approaches manifest themselves in the patterns. We have applied this framework in CABARET, a domain-independent architecture that heuristically combines rule-based and case-based reasoning [Rissland & Skalak, 1991].

The desire to understand legal argument, particularly precedential aspects of statutory law, has motivated much of our work on CABARET. While we usually have viewed CABARET as a primary example of a 'hybrid' or 'mixed paradigm' reasoning shell – integrating the rule-based and case-based reasoning 'paradigms' – the system is also a study of how to use available cases and rules to formulate arguments. Ultimately, both views of CABARET fundamentally concern the issue of program control: how the program decides what to do when.

We make several related points in this article.

1. A computational model of case-based legal argument must account for the complex control problems involved in simultaneously selecting cases and making arguments based on them.

2. Legal argument in practice often takes stereotypical forms, and we present a partial list of argument patterns found in legal practice.

3. These stereotypical forms may provide a partial solution to the problems of point (1) by providing top-down direction as to what types of cases to look for next and how to argue with them once found.

4. Primitive argument techniques already incorporated in CABARET are useful for implementing such stereotypical argument forms, even though CABARET's current implementation does not necessarily produce output in the form of the patterns we inventory.

We anticipate that such stereotypical patterns of argument could be used to extend CABARET and support the control core of a new hybrid architecture.

We interleave these points by organizing the paper in the following way. We complete Section 1 with a a brief survey of previous work on computational legal argument. Section 2 is a general introductory discussion of how 'specification-driven' (top-down, case-base-independent) and 'case-driven' (bottom-up, case-base-dependent) considerations influence argument. Our view is that these influences are intertwined, with each providing feedback to the other.

In Section 3 we provide some background on CABARET and its current domain of the so-called 'home office deduction' [Rissland & Skalak, 1991]. In Section 4, we present our partial inventory of argument patterns found in actual legal practice; we provide several examples of each. Section 5 describes CABARET's implemented approach to argument-generation in some detail, but the general point is that CABARET uses a control strategy incorporating both top-down and bottom-up processing to generate skeletal legal arguments. We conclude Section 5 with an example of a straightforward argument generated by CABARET.

In Section 6 we discuss work slated for the immediate future. There we demonstrate how some of the less straightforward argument forms discussed in Section 4 could be implemented using CABARET's framework. Section 7 retraces our steps in an attempt to remind ourselves where we have been and where we would like to go in future work.

1.2 PREVIOUS WORK ON COMPUTATIONAL LEGAL ARGUMENT

Past work in artificial intelligence (AI) and in law has addressed the precedential, rhetorical, doctrinal and jurisprudential aspects of legal arguments.[5] Precedential aspects have been addressed by a growing community of AI-and-law researchers, including [Ashley, 1990, 1991; Ashley & Rissland, 1988a], [Branting, 1989, 1991], [Bellairs, 1989],

[Berman & Hafner, 1991], [Gardner, 1987], [Goldman, Dyer & Flowers, 1987], [McCarty & Sridharan, 1982], [Stucky & Gidley, 1990] and ourselves [Rissland et al., 1984, 1985; Rissland & Skalak, 1991; Skalak & Rissland, 1991].

Much of the present work builds upon the model of case-based reasoning of the HYPO program by Ashley and developed in a series of papers by Rissland and Ashley. Cases in HYPO are represented at two levels: *factual features*, which represent the input description of a case; and *factual predicates*, which are derived features computed from the factual features. The second level is often called the 'interpretation frame' level [Ashley, 1990]. Cases are contained in a case knowledge base (*CKB*), which is an unstructured memory. Indices for retrieving cases from the CKB are called *dimensions* [Rissland, Valcarce and Ashley, 1984], [Ashley, 1990]. Dimensions capture the observation that cases are usually analyzed and argued about using a set of important domain-specific factors, and that a case's strength or weakness with respect to each factor can be assessed. In effect, dimensions are the thread of argument running through a 'line of cases' that addresses a particular issue in a similar way. Dimension-based analysis draws on both general knowledge of the domain and past, specific cases to which the factor applied. Each dimension has a set of prerequisites that determine its applicability – these encode the facts necessary for mounting an argument with respect to this dimension – and a means for comparing cases along it. In HYPO, the metric for assessing case relevancy ('on-pointness') is based on the intersection between the sets of dimensions applicable to the problem case and those applicable to a case from the CKB. Intuitively, the larger this overlap, the more on-point a precedent is. However, HYPO does not rely merely on the number of dimensions in this intersection. HYPO partially orders cases according to the precise subset of dimensions in common with the problem case into a 'claim lattice' [Ashley & Rissland, 1988a], [Ashley, 1990]. Construction of this partial order gives HYPO the ability to recognize the lines of cases bearing on a specific subset of relevant dimensions: they are linear suborderings within the claim lattice partial ordering. For a detailed exposition of HYPO's model of case-based reasoning and its implementation, see [Ashley, 1990].

The CABARET system incorporated into a hybrid architecture a case-based reasoner that uses many of the same data structures developed in HYPO (e.g., case, interpretation-frame, dimension and claim lattice) and also takes some of its procedural mechanisms from HYPO (e.g., initial analysis of the input case resulting in an interpretation frame, indexing of cases by dimensions, and sorting of cases by similarity into a lattice.)

In our own past work, the second author has compiled a collection of strategic argument moves, such as 'bolstering,' 'obfuscating,' 'red herring,' and 'slippery slope'

[5.] Some of these aspects really deserve more attention than research has given them, however. For instance, how the argument made in the current fact situation affects and is affected by long range strategic goals has not been addressed by computational approaches to argument, as far as we know. Strategic considerations would be especially important for a specialist litigating several cases in one area of law. Existing work might be extended to this end, however. For instance, McCarty and Sridharan's work on prototypes and deformations [McCarty & Sridharan, 1982] may be used to plot a sequence of cases. HYPO [Ashley, 1990] could be used to answer long range planning questions such as, "If this case were decided for the claimant, how will that affect the complexion of our backlogged cases in light of the resulting case base?".

[Rissland, 1985]. The current article builds on that foundation by identifying additional argument forms actually used by practitioners and providing explicit computational mechanisms for effecting some of them. In recent work, [Rissland & Skalak, 1991; Skalak & Rissland, 1991], we have attempted to tease statutory argument into a tiered set of 'strategies' and 'moves,' which are ultimately implemented through combinations of generic argument 'primitives,' such as analogizing and distinguishing.

Branting has provided an alternative framework for integrating cases and rules, particularly to improve case matching through rule-based reasoning. Branting's program embodying this framework ('GREBE') uses a detailed semantic network representation of each of the case arguments in his case base. This article takes a wider, more taxonomic perspective for argument that does not assume the presence of detailed relational representations for case opinions. Similarly, Bellairs's extensive work on analogical reasoning in the law assumes a relatively strong domain theory, where 'significant relationships between the facts [of problem situations and of case situations] are known.' [Bellairs, 1989, p.50]. Berman and Hafner have argued that the procedural posture of a case is a crucial aspect of reasoning with precedents and must be incorporated into a model of legal argument. Goldman, Dyer and Flowers have emphasized memory organization and case representation in their research modeling aspects of contract law. Stucky and Gidley point out that pragmatic considerations for legal argument have been overlooked in current models. See generally [Rissland, 1990] and [Stucky, 1986] for overviews of computational legal argument. Stucky also argues for a top-down and bottom-up control strategy for argument creation.

Other AI models of legal argument have been put forth in seminal work by McCarty and by Gardner. McCarty's longstanding work on legal knowledge representation models legal concepts as 'prototypes plus deformations,' which are logical templates incorporating necessary conditions for a concept, a set of examples inside or outside the concept class, and a collection of transformations that map one example to another. Gardner's approach to legal reasoning and her program have influenced the design of our CABARET program in several ways. First, Gardner used several simple heuristics to determine when a case was 'hard,' such as a failure to establish a result using rules only, or a conflict between rules or between cases. Second, her program made use of positive and negative[6] examples of predicates used in the rules, (although the examples were abstract fact patterns, rather than particular cases). Third, Gardner's work incorporated both reasoning with rules and reasoning with these abstract examples. On the other hand, the implementation of Gardner's model did not create arguments, and all of the cases in CABARET's case base would be 'hard' according to the characterization used by her model and program.

---

[6] The terms 'positive' and 'negative' are used in the sense given by machine learning. A positive example of a concept is a member of that concept class; a negative example is not a member of the class. In the legal examples we will give, the relevant concept is often implicit: the category defined by the result desired by the advocate. For example, if the advocate argues to receive a deduction for an office in a home, then the category is 'deductible home office expenses.' See [Skalak, 1989] for a discussion of models of classification applied to the law.

The literature on jurisprudential aspects of argument is vast, and since we concentrate on other aspects of argument, we point arbitrarily to a few of our favorite sources: [Levi, 1949], [Llewellyn, 1989] and [Twining & Miers, 1982]. [Kennedy, 1989] presents a taxonomy of argument types at a level of abstraction higher than that of our classification. [Perelman & Olbrechts-Tyteca, 1969] and [Toulmin, 1958] are classic and encompassing works on argument generally. Several researchers have used Toulmin's analysis as a basis for their own work [Marshall, 1989; Storrs, 1991].

1.3 PREVIOUS WORK ON COMPUTATIONAL ARGUMENT IN GENERAL

While our focus in this article is the task of creating legal arguments, many AI researchers have made contributions to the computational theory of argument applied to a variety of task domains, including [Alvarado, 1990, 1991] (editorial comprehension), [August & McNamee, 1991] (editorial comprehension), [Birnbaum, Flowers & McGuire, 1980; McGuire, Birnbaum & Flowers, 1981; Flowers, McGuire & Birnbaum, 1982; Birnbaum, 1982, 1985] (argument understanding and response), and [Wu & Lytinen, 1991] (advertisement comprehension). While Clark [1988] and Sycara [1985, 1987, 1989, 1991] have not aimed their models at the legal domain, each has made contributions to the theory of case-based argument. Clark has presented a formal, logic model of argument that represents background domain knowledge as sets of arguments for or against a problem hypothesis. Models for argument in a distributed, multi-agent setting have been presented by Sycara, in which arguments are constructed with both case-based and decision-theoretic, utility-based support.

Of this work on argument outside the legal domain, that of Birnbaum, Flowers and McGuire is closest to our own approach. Their research recognized that argument creation requires a mixture of bottom-up and top-down control and tried to identify higher-level argument structures ('molecules' in their terminology) and tactics. However, this line of research apparently recognized only two higher-level argument forms. The tactics they suggest are more abstract than our argument moves, and appear tantamount to such strategies as attacking the 'warrant' and attacking the 'backing' of a claim, to use Toulmin's classic terminology [Toulmin, 1958].

2. Intertwining case specification and argument

While one can hypothesize about the ideal case for an argument independently of an existing case corpus, the cases that are actually available temper this vision.[7] To a lesser extent, what hypothetical cases are reasonable also constrains argument.[8] We maintain

---

[7.] We assume that the 'available' cases are contained in a 'case base.'

[8.] Much of the past work of our research group has focussed on hypotheticals and the important role accorded them in case-based reasoning [Rissland & Ashley, 1986], [Ashley, 1990]. Nonetheless, in legal argument one cannot rely on hypotheticals for authoritative statements of existing law. One can use them, however, to illustrate a point, poke holes in an argument, or show the ramifications of a line of reasoning. We shall treat 'cases' as including hypotheticals.

that computational argument with cases requires at least two types of processes: 'specification-driven' and 'case-driven'.

2.1 TWO ROUTES TO THE THE IDEAL CASE

By 'specification-driven' we mean that the arguer specifies what the ideal case for his situation might be, independently of what cases exist in the case base. By 'case-driven' we mean that the arguer creates and defines arguments according to what cases actually exist and are available to him.

In the law, it is certainly the case that both specification-driven and case-driven approaches are at work. The doctrine of *stare decisis* trivially requires that an advocate must at a minimum be case-driven. Cases must be cited and used according to the modes permitted by the prevailing institutional interpretation of the doctrine of precedent. On the other hand, an arguer is also driven by the need to establish certain goals, for instance, that some requirement of a relevant legal rule has been satisfied. The needs of argument define the desiderata for the perfect case. Thus, an arguer – computer system or human litigator – must interleave at least these specification-driven and case-driven processes. One can start from either vantage point but feedback will be given and direction exerted by the other.[9]

A system that uses a bottom-up approach is HYPO [Ashley, 1990], where case selection is driven by cases in the case base. In HYPO, a 'best case' for a user is a 'most on-point' case that is decided for his point of view (his side), and shares a factor with the current fact situation that is favorable to his point of view [Ashley, 1989]. A 'most on-point' case is maximal in the ordering of cases by similarity to the problem situation. HYPO does have a specification-driven aspect in that it limits the factors on which the similarity ordering is based to those that are present in the current situation. To that extent, a best case is implicitly specified (top-down) as one possessing the same applicable dimensions as the problem. But primarily HYPO works bottom up from the available case base by percolating best cases from the case base towards the upper levels of the similarity ordering, which contain the cases maximally similar to the current fact situation.

In a new tutoring system based on HYPO, Ashley and Aleven are re-implementing case-based argument terms such as 'best case' and 'most on-point case' as defined and manipulable object relations, rather than as the output of a particular procedure [Ashley & Aleven, 1991]. This change in representation from HYPO is designed to enable their system to function top-down: to retrieve argument fragments from a specification of the relations that must be present between the cases involved.

A mixture of case-driven and specification-driven approaches is evident in the way CABARET works. CABARET uses a tiered framework of argument strategies, moves and primitives, which sets up retrieval specifications for precedents to be used in

---

[9.] For a description of how lawyers alternate between constructing a theory of a case and assessing its emerging facts, see [Gibbons, 1991] and [Morris, 1937].

argument. CABARET's framework lays out specifications for potentially useful classes of cases and ways to use them in argument. After retrieving cases with the required characteristics, the system's case-based reasoning module, which is modelled closely after HYPO, sorts those cases, compares them, and selects the cases to use. Thus, the argument moves and strategies in this framework specify what the ideal case would be for a particular argument strategy-move combination. The cases actually found then determine which of the specific moves can be used to implement the argument strategies given the limitations of the current case base. Details of CABARET's tiered argument framework are given in Section 5.

The need to mix specification-driven and case-driven approaches is present in domains outside the law as well. For instance, in developing computer programs, specifying the program and developing concrete code are intertwined [Swartout & Balzer, 1982]. Mathematics interleaves deductive reasoning and reasoning with examples [Polya, 1973; Lakatos, 1976; Rissland et al., 1984]. We believe the interplay of reasoning with cases with other modes of reasoning is ubiquitous.

This interplay can be viewed as a special kind of theory formation. In mounting an argument, writing a proof, designing a computer program, one is putting forth a theory of how things are, or ought to be; this theory is tempered by actual examples of what is. In the case where the examples function as counterexamples to the posited theory, the tempering can be quite severe.

3. Background on CABARET and the home office deduction

CABARET is a mixed paradigm reasoner that combines case-based and rule-based reasoning. The model of case-based reasoning used is based upon HYPO; the rule-based reasoning used involves the standard forward and backward inference methods. CABARET couples these two styles of reasoning with control heuristics that post to an agenda tasks for each of the reasoners to perform. Some of these heuristics encode various techniques used in statutory argument. For instance, if after attempting to satisfy the antecedents of a rule, one finds that only one of the rule's antecedents is unsatisfied, then one can try to argue that the missing condition is not necessary. This argument would be supported by the case-based task of finding and reasoning with cases where there was a similar 'near miss' but where the result of the rule was obtained nevertheless.

CABARET has several components, including a case-based reasoning module and a rule-based reasoning module, and for each, a dedicated monitoring process that makes observations on the progress and achievements of the individual reasoners. These observations are recorded in a 'control description' language that is also used to encode the control heuristics. The control module applies these heuristics, which are encoded as rules, to the observations to determine the next tasks to be posted to the agenda. A full description of CABARET's architecture and a detailed discussion of the control heuristics is provided in [Rissland & Skalak, 1991].

One of the domains in which the CABARET shell is currently instantiated is an area of U.S. Federal income tax law referred to as the 'home office deduction.' The home

257

office deduction domain is governed primarily by Section 280A of the Internal Revenue
Code, and we have focused on Section 280A(c)(1), which contains the heart of the
statute:

> [A deduction may be taken for] any item to the extent such item is alloca-
> ble to a portion of the dwelling unit which is EXCLUSIVELY USED on a
> REGULAR basis –
>
> (A) [as] the PRINCIPAL PLACE OF BUSINESS for any trade or
> business of the taxpayer,
>
> (B) as a place of business which is used by patients, clients, or cus-
> tomers in MEETING OR DEALING with the taxpayer in the normal
> course of his trade or business, or
>
> (C) in the case of a SEPARATE STRUCTURE which is not attached
> to the dwelling unit, in connection with the taxpayer's trade or business.
>
> In the case of an employee, the preceding sentence shall apply only if the
> exclusive use referred to in the preceding sentence is for the CONVE-
> NIENCE OF HIS EMPLOYER.
>
> *[capitalization supplied]*

The home office deduction deals with the circumstances under which taxpayers may
legitimately deduct on a U.S. Federal income tax return expenses relating to an office
maintained at the taxpayer's residence. We have supplied capitalization to certain terms
in the statute to emphasize their role as *statutory predicates*, important words or phrases
on which the meaning of the statute turns.

CABARET's case base in the home office deduction domain currently contains representations of 23 actually litigated tax cases. In addition, there are 6 hypothetical cases in
the case base. To give the flavor of this area, several examples of litigated cases follow.

• The case of David Weissman, *Weissman v. Commissioner*, 751 F.2d 512 (2d Cir. 1984)
  who was a professor of philosophy at City College in New York City. Although he was
  provided with a shared office at City College, it was not 'a safe place to leave teaching,
  writing, or research materials and equipment,' [Court of Appeals Opinion, p.513,
  quoting the lower Tax Court opinion.] In his 10-room apartment, Professor Weissman
  maintained a home office, consisting of two rooms and adjoining bathroom. He estimated working between 64 and 75 hours each week, and spent 80% of that time
  writing and researching in his home office. The Internal Revenue Service challenged
  Professor Weissman's deduction of $1540 of rent and other expenses relating to his
  home office. The IRS claimed that Weissman's home office did not satisfy the requirements of the statute, in particular that it was not his principal place of business and that
  it was not for the convenience of his employer, City College. On appeal of a decision
  against Weissman, the Court of Appeals for the Second Circuit determined that in
  these circumstances, the home office could be considered Weissman's principal place
  of business, especially where most of his work was done at home and a home office
  was necessitated by the lack of suitable workspace on campus. Under *Drucker*, below,

Weissman also satisfied the convenience of employer requirement for the deduction.

- The case of Earnest Drucker, *Drucker v. Commissioner*, 715 F.2d 67 (2d Cir. 1983), who was a violinist with the Metropolitan Opera Orchestra, concerns the 'convenience of employer' requirement for employees (among other requirements of Section 280A). Drucker was not provided with a practice room at Lincoln Center (or elsewhere, for that matter). Drucker and others in the orchestra therefore maintained home practice studios. Practice was absolutely necessary to the fulfillment of the musicians' responsibilities. The Second Circuit held that the home practice areas were for the convenience of the Met, since they relieved the Met from providing the necessary practice space for the musicians to do their jobs.

- The case of Yolanda Baie, *Baie v. Commissioner*, 74 T.C. 105 (1980), a woman who operated a foodstand (the 'Gay Dog') near her residence in Los Angeles, also addresses the 'principal place of business' requirement. Appearing for herself in Tax Court (and apparently doing an excellent job), Ms. Baie argued that – since she used her kitchen for preparing food, particularly hot dogs for her stand – her kitchen (and not the stand) was her principal place of business. In denying the deduction, the court used the 'focal point test', which looked to the 'focal point' of the taxpayer's activities, which was determined to be the Gay Dog itself.

We return in Sections 5 and 6 to discuss CABARET's approach to modeling argument. As a prelude to that discussion, we first consider some of the typical forms that legal argument actually takes, with a view to determining the types of cases that are required to drive them.

4. Recognized forms of legal argument: a partial inventory

Legal argument often takes stereotypical forms. The law student or legal scholar who has read the usual large volume of legal cases can often recognize immediately the overall form of an argument. Some easily-recognized forms include 'slippery slope arguments', 'balancing arguments' and 'make weight' arguments. Occasionally these arguments involve the creation of hypothetical cases, if real cases are not available to meet the requirements of the argument form. Slippery slope arguments, for example, require a sequence of hypothetical cases. Some of the argument forms we inventory apparently have not been named (or previously characterized). We ask the reader's indulgence where we have supplied our own neologisms.

We begin to make our inventory a taxonomy by considering the following dimensions on which arguments may be placed, which are based in part on the cases used in support:

- whether the cited case is a favorable (positive) example or an unfavorable (negative) example for the advocate making the argument;
- whether the cited case is a strong one or a weak one for the arguer;
- whether the argument is used offensively, to establish a result, or defensively, to respond to an opponent's case citation;
- whether a single case or a set of cases is used to complete the argument; and
- if more than one case is used, whether the set of cases is ordered in some way.

It will be useful to have certain additional terminology at our disposal. In this paper we use the term *disposition* to refer to the outcome of a case on the ultimate result argued for, regardless of whether that result was supported by a rule in issue. The disposition of a personal income tax case might be whether a desired deduction was allowed or denied, for example. When we want to refer explicitly to the conclusion warranted by a specific rule, we will refer to the rule's *consequent*. Finally, we will refer to the *status* of a rule with respect to a precedent and mean whether the rule's preconditions were or could be satisfied under a strict application of the rule to the precedent's facts.

We use the word 'rule' to encompass a legal statute, a regulation or other rule promulgated pursuant to a statute, a common law rule derived from a group of cases, or the rule of the case stating a rule of law implicit in a single case. In general, we also intend that 'rule' include rules of thumb that are heuristically gleaned and applied by experts in order to characterize the law in a particular domain. 'Teachers often have difficulty satisfying the principal place of business requirement of the home office deduction,' is an example.

The distinction between 'disposition' and 'consequent' can be subtle and an anticipatory example may be helpful. Consider a rule in the Internal Revenue Code (the 'Code') that entitles one to a deduction of a particular kind, for example, a deduction for certain travel expenses under Section 162. The consequent of the rule may be expressed as 'taxpayer is entitled to a travel expense deduction.' The ultimate disposition desired by the taxpayer is that he is entitled to a travel deduction by law, regardless of whether it is sanctioned by this particular Code rule or by some other justification (e.g., another Code rule or even a Supreme Court case holding that a social policy is more important than strict compliance with Section 162). The taxpayer aims to argue his way into the concept class 'taxpayer entitled to a travel expense deduction' named in the Code rule, by any warrant available. Due to the presence of alternative ways of arguing for a desired result, establishing a particular rule consequent may not be a *necessary* condition for obtaining the desired case disposition.

This distinction between rule consequent and disposition can cut against taxpayer's case for a deduction, of course. There may be impediments to his legitimately receiving the deduction, notwithstanding the satisfaction of the Code section (e.g., a more powerful controlling statute with an opposite result, or a case invalidating the rule on constitutional grounds). Thus, establishing the rule consequent is not always a *sufficient* condition for obtaining the desired case disposition. This conflict between a rule result and other norms dealing with the rule consequent can be the source of 'hard' questions as that term is used in jurisprudence (see, e.g., [Gardner, 1987]).

We will press on with examples of the forms of argument with reference to the following hypothetical situation:

SITUATION: Alice, a single parent of two young children, is a junior faculty member at an urban law school. To obtain affordable housing and decent schooling for her children she lives in a suburban community located 25 miles from her office. Crowded highways extend the one-way trip commuting time to approximately one hour during rush hours from the half hour trip at other times. Given the lengthy commute and her parenting responsibilities, Alice asked her dean whether she could spend two days a week working at home since she is able to do much of her research by accessing on-line legal databases from home. She ensured she would be available for faculty, committee, and student meetings. Her dean agreed and asked whether, given enormous space constraints, she would mind sharing her office with another junior faculty member. Alice readily accepted that arrangement. The evidence shows that it became difficult for Alice to conduct her research while at the school. Sharing an office interferes with her concentration and the library does not provide adequate computing facilities. The evidence also shows that several other junior faculty members have been required to share offices.

Alice converted a bedroom into a study. She uses the study mostly for her work as law professor except on rare occasions when she has house guests who sleep on a couch in the study. She also uses the study for some personal correspondence and paying her bills. Alice claimed a deduction for the costs attributable to her new study. The Commissioner of the Internal Revenue Service ('Commissioner') assessed a tax deficiency, which the Tax Court sustained. Alice has appealed.

In the following sections, we describe each argument form, give an example of its use in Alice's case and finally provide an instance of its use taken from an actual judicial opinion. A suggestive illustration is also provided for most forms.

4.1 ARGUMENTS INVOLVING THE CURRENT FACT SITUATION AND A SINGLE CASE

The following arguments typically involve reasoning with the current fact situation and one other case. If one thinks of these argument forms as procedures, their inputs are the current fact situation and another case, and the output is an argument or some data structure from which an argument in natural language can be prepared.

4.1.1 Straightforward argument. We suppose that a lawyer's first impulse is to analogize cases that have the desired disposition on the particular point in issue and were decided in what would be his favor. Also, he would be prepared to distinguish cases that were decided oppositely both as to the point he is trying to establish and as to ultimate disposition of the case. *Analogizing* and *distinguishing* are the fundamental processes of straightforward argument. Each process typically entails taking the current fact situation and analogizing it to or distinguishing it from a single case at a time.

EXAMPLE: In the hypothetical situation given, Alice may analogize the *Weissman* case described in Section 3: 'This case is governed by the *Weissman* case. In *Weissman*, a faculty member was prevented from working on campus by practical considerations, such as an inadequate on-campus office and inappropriateness of the library facilities, and the principal place of business of the taxpayer was found to be the home office. The deduction was allowed in *Weissman* and so should it be in my case.

The Commissioner of the IRS might distinguish *Weissman*: '*Weissman* is distinguishable from Alice's case in that (1) the home office is not for the convenience of Alice's

employer, whereas Weissman satisfied the statute's convenience-of-employer requirement; (2) she only uses it 40% of the time, whereas Weissman used his office 80% of his
working time; and (3) Alice's use of the home office is not exclusively related to her
faculty position, whereas Weissman performed no other business in the home office.'

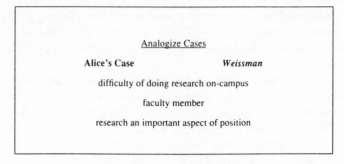

Fig. 1: Common features that may be used to form an analogy between Alice's case and *Weissman*.

Distinguish Cases

Alice's Case	Weissman
40% of working time at home	80% of working time at home
personal convenience	convenience of employer
some personal use	exclusively business use

Fig. 2: Contrasting features that may be used to distinguish Alice's case and *Weissman*.

There are many ways to make an analogy between Alice's case and *Weissman*. For
example, one can draw analogies via shared ground-level features (e.g., both Alice and
Weissman were provided with shared campus offices), important derived, domain-level
factors (e.g., both spent a substantial amount of time in their respective home office), the
taxonomic class of the parties (e.g., both Alice and Weissman are faculty members), or
shared functionality (e.g., the home office supports research).

The implicit model of analogy used by HYPO relies on intersections of domain factors
present in the two cases being compared. HYPO's model makes a distinction between the
ground-level features at which problem cases are input and derived features, 'factual
predicates,' that are used as prerequisites for the presence of important domain factors.

CABARET extends HYPO's model of analogy in several small ways. Term hierarchies are used in CABARET to store domain knowledge that is not conveniently represented as rules or as cases. Under certain conditions CABARET's control heuristics

direct its case-based reasoning component to search these taxonomic hierarchies so that cases involving related terms in the hierarchy can be retrieved. CABARET also expands HYPO's claim lattice datatype; it was re-implemented in CABARET's case-based reasoning component to admit other similarity metrics, to use an improved case sorting algorithm, and to associate a lattice for each predicate in a rule.

Also, to find analogous or dissimilar cases, CABARET can apply case similarity metrics other than HYPO's 'maximize overlap' metric. For instance, CABARET can use the 'minimize differences' metric that minimizes the set of factors that are present in either case but not in the other.

In addition, CABARET also applies control rules that heuristically change from one similarity metric to another. These control heuristics examine the similarity ordering of cases created using one metric and, if various anomalies are found in the lattice reflecting that ordering, the system will apply another similarity metric in an attempt to ameliorate the anomaly. Example anomalies include (1) a trivial similarity ordering consisting of one node, (2) a surfeit of most-on-point cases, and (3) an approximately equal distribution of outcomes of the most-on-point cases between the two sides in a litigation.

EXAMPLE: An actual example of straightforward legal argument is one that HYPO has successfully re-created. This example is taken from [Ashley, 1988] and is discussed in detail there and in [Ashley, 1990]. The example is useful in that it applies both analogizing and distinguishing as straightforward tactics. In this case, which deals with misappropriation of trade secrets regarding a rivet-making machine, *USM Corp. v. Marson Fastener Corp.*, 379 Mass. 90 (1979), ('USM'), the primary issue was whether the plaintiff had taken adequate measures to protect its trade secrets. The Massachusetts court set out the relevant factors explicitly, quoting Kubik, Inc. v. Hull, 56 Mich. App. 335, 356 (1974):

Relevant factors to be considered include (1) the existence or absence of an express *agreement restricting disclosure*, (2) the nature and extent of *security precautions* taken by the possessor to prevent acquisition of the information by unauthorized third parties, (3) the circumstances under which the information was disclosed . . . to [any] employee to the extent that they give rise to a reasonable inference that further disclosure, without the consent of the possessor, is prohibited, and (4) the degree to which the information has been placed in the public domain or rendered 'readily ascertainable' by the third parties through patent applications or unrestricted product marketing.

USM, at 98. [*Underlining* supplied].

The court then treats each factor in turn, citing analogous cases and sometimes distinguishing contrary cases. With respect to the first factor, for example, the presence of agreements restricting disclosure, *Eastern Marble* is analogous and the court sets up the analogy by using the 'see' citation signal:[10]

USM required . . . personnel . . . to sign nondisclosure agreements . . . [S]pecificity [of the agreement] is not required to put employees on notice that their work involves access to trade secrets and confidential information. *See Eastern Marble Prods. Corp. v. Roman Marble, Inc.*, 372 Mass. 835, 840 (1977) [and other cases].

USM, at 99.

With respect to the second factor, security precautions, the court in USM simultane-

---

[10.] See [Ashley & Rissland, 1987].

ously analogizes a favorable case and distinguishes an unfavorable case by using the introductory case citation form 'compare <case1> with <case2>.' The major issue for the court with respect to security precautions was that USM provided tours of its operations:

The fact that USM conducted escorted tours...does not militate against a finding that USM denied public access to the USM machine. *Compare Plant Indus., Inc v. Coleman.* 287 F.Supp 636, 643 (C.D. Cal. 1968) (tours by women's clubs and customer's representatives do not constitute failure to maintain secrecy)...*with Motorola. Inc. v. Fairchild Camera & Instrument Corp.* 366 F.Supp. 1173. 1186 (D. Ariz. 1973) (security inadequate where competitors toured plant. operated 'secret' machine and 'observed its 'secret' process in a separate microscope placed there for this purpose')...

USM. at 100-101.

Straightforward arguments are sufficiently common that a system of stylized citation signals has evolved to flag the types of comparisons (analogize, distinguish) that are made between cases [BlueBook, 1986]. See [Ashley & Rissland, 1987] for a discussion of the use of citation signals in case-based argument.

Although analogy is an area of intense AI research, we treat 'analogizing' and 'distinguishing as primitive procedures in this article. We recognize that analogizing and distinguishing may nonetheless be implemented in a variety of ways that stem from different theories of analogy, such as structure-mapping [Gentner, 1983; Falkenhainer, Forbus & Gentner, 1989], constraint-mapping [Holyoak & Thagard, 1989], transformational and derivational analogy [Carbonell, 1983, 1986] and mapping of corresponding features [Winston, 1980, 1982].

4.1.2 Make-weight argument. A make-weight argument cites cases, facts or factors that are not necessary to reach the conclusion desired, but merely provide additional support. often of a less probative sort. See Figure 3.This style is a weak version of what has been called 'bolstering' [Rissland, 1985] and 'strengthening' [Rissland & Ashley, 1986]. Legitimate strengthening or bolstering involves adding or deleting facts or improving the value of a 'focal slot' that determines a dimension's strength [Ashley, 1990].

EXAMPLE: To use a make-weight argument, the Commissioner, after distinguishing *Weissman*, might cite *Henry C. Smith*, 40 B.T.A. 1038 (1939) aff'd per curiam. 113 F.2d 114 (2d Cir. 1940) (denying child care expenses as a ordinary and necessary

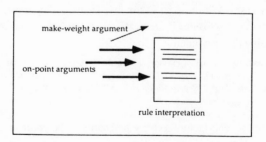

Fig. 3: A make-weight argument is a weak argument that does not squarely address the issue at hand.

business expenses) and argue: 'Furthermore, taxpayer implicitly attempts to convert the personal expenses of child care into ordinary business expenses.' This line of attack does not deal directly with the satisfaction of the home office provision, but merely attempts to darken Alice's case with the shadow of a tax shibboleth that personal expenses are not deductible.

One does not usually set out to create a make-weight argument: one relies on an opponent to characterize an argument disparagingly as merely 'make-weight'.

4.2 ARGUMENTS INVOLVING THE CURRENT FACT SITUATION AND A SET OF TWO OR MORE CASES

The following arguments involve reasoning with the current fact situation and a set of cases or a representative of a set of cases.

4.2.1 Turkey, chicken and fish or 'double negative' argument. This convoluted argument takes the following form: the case at bar is so *unlike* the cases where a rule's conditions were held *not* to have been established that the rule *should* apply to the current case. The argument may be used more generally to claim that an instance is within some category, whether or not that category is implicitly defined by a rule consequent. This slightly expanded form of the argument maintains that something is so unlike negative examples of a category – unlike things outside the category – that it should be considered as a positive example – as within the category. See Figure 4.

EXAMPLE: The name 'turkey, chicken and fish' stems from a hypothetical example in which a turkey farmer in Delaware tries to receive an entitlement reserved by a Federal Department of Agriculture regulation for chicken farmers. If the only cases denying the entitlement dealt with fish farmers, then the turkey farmer could argue that his turkey farms are so unlike fish farms that the FDA regulation should apply to his turkey business as well. Cf. *Frigaliment Importing Co. v. B.N.S. Int'l Sales Corp.*, 190 F.Supp. 116 (1980) (Friendly) (dealing with the definition of a 'chicken').

This fairly weak form of argument may be effective where the set of on-point cases is small and contains instances only of egregious attempts to crawl within the ambit of a statute that is inapplicable on its face (the fish cases in the example). In this setting, the advocate then claims that – unlike those flawed cases – his (turkey) claim is reasonable and comes within the statute. The advocate might support this line by appealing to a legislative history that revealed, for example, that when the regulation was promulgated, 'chicken farm' was merely a compromise term to clearly omit the (weak lobby) fish farmers, and should be construed to include all (strong lobby) fowl farms.

EXAMPLE: Alice may use this argument form to claim: 'The precedents where the home office deduction was denied involved situations where the home office was used almost 100% of the time for *personal* purposes. Business use was *de minimis* there. My own situation is not one of these abusive situations where the claim of a home office was merely a facade, which led Congress to tighten the requirements. In my own case, the personal use was infrequent and minor. A deduction should not be denied in my case, which is clearly distinguishable from those egregious precedents.'

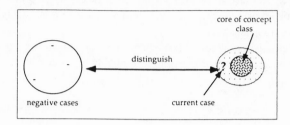

Fig. 4: The turkey, chicken and fish strategy distinguishes negative cases to argue that the current case is within the penumbra of the concept class of cases implicitly defined by the rule interpretation.

EXAMPLE: *Landreth Timber Co. v. Landreth*, 471 U.S. 681, 105 S.Ct. 2297, 85 L.Ed. 2d 692 (1985), uses a variation on this argument form. The issue in *Landreth* was whether the sale of all the stock of a company was held to be a 'security' subject to the antifraud provisions of the Federal securities laws. The definition of a security is given in the Securities Act of 1933 (15 U.S.C. §77b(1)): 'The term "security" means any note, stock, treasury stock, bond, debenture ... investment contract ... or, in general, any interest or instrument commonly known as a "security" ....' In *Landreth*, the Court stated that different tests might be used for (a) the prototypical case of an instrument that was called 'stock' on its face and possessed the usual characteristics of stock and (b) other enumerated items. Previous Supreme Court cases had applied tests looking to the 'economic reality' of various financial instruments in the 'security' determination. *Landreth*, however, looked to the face of the security, which was clearly that of stock. In arguing in dicta that a formal test may be used for things that are labeled 'stock' and an economic reality test may be used for other enumerated items, the Court applied a chicken, turkey and fish argument variant. The case of an instrument entitled 'Stock' (the 'turkey') is so unlike the other enumerated categories of security where the economic substance of the transaction has to be evaluated (the 'fish'), that the instrument should be considered stock (a 'chicken').

Statutes that contain enumerated lists by way of definition often present opportunities for arguing with turkey, chicken and fish.

4.2.2 'Throw the dog a bone' or 'gratuitous' argument. A gratuitous argument is similar to the foregoing double-negative argument in that it applies primarily in a setting where one is trying to broaden a rule by distinguishing a negative case. Here, however, the negative case is a hypothetical one that clearly does not satisfy the rule. A weak example (the 'bone'), whose negative classification is conceded, is retrieved or concocted and the arguer proceeds to show how the current situation is a stronger example than the artificial weak one. In practice, use of this argument may be advisable in a 'defensive' position where one perceives a case is weak.

EXAMPLE: In Alice's case, the Commissioner could argue that to allow Alice to claim a home office deduction would permit almost any single parent who does 'office' work to make a deal with the employer which would permit the employee to deduct expenses which for most other taxpayers are non-deductible personal expenses under Section 262, thereby eviscerating the intent of Congress when it enacted Section 280A. The taxpayer would then reply, 'Your honor, I agree with the Treasury that one cannot permit any taxpayer who has an office and does some work at home to claim a home office deduction. Such a result would clearly undermine Congress's intent in passing Section 280A. But we are not asking for anything resembling the judicial invalidation of Section 280A. We are not advocating making the deduction available to a worker with ideal working conditions at their office and who spends only 10% of their time in their home office to deduct personal living expenses. We are only arguing that the deduction be available where the taxpayer spends a significant amount of her time working at home because of overcrowding at her employer's office.'

In this example, Alice throws a gratuitous bone to the court in admitting that she would not be entitled to a deduction had she spent only 10% of her time working at home when an ideal office was available to her elsewhere.

4.2.3 Straw man argument. Straw man arguments are familiar to students of law. The term is used disparagingly by an opposing counsel, a judge, or a commentator to describe an argument with an allegedly obvious flaw. One does not deliberately set out to create a straw man argument. Various sorts of disingenuous or exaggerating arguments may be characterized as straw men arguments, but the term at least encompasses the creation of a hypothetical case that is analogized by one side to the current situation, but which is easily distinguished from the current problem. See Figure 5.

EXAMPLE: In the home office area, if the Commissioner were to seek disallowance on the ground that the study was not used 'exclusively' for business purposes the taxpayer might create the following straw man. 'Your honor, the statute cannot mean what the Commissioner says it means. Certainly, Congress did not intend that someone otherwise entitled to a deduction for a home office should lose the deduction merely because they write a single personal check at a desk that is otherwise used entirely for business.' To which the Commissioner might appropriately respond, 'Your honor, the taxpayer has raised a total straw man. We're not talking about the writing of a single check. We're talking about the use for house guests, for personal correspondence and for handling personal financial transactions. Taxpayer does not satisfy the statutory requirement of exclusive use.'

EXAMPLE: In *Schneckloth v. Bustamonte*, 412 U.S. 218, 93 S.Ct. 2041 (1973), a leading constitutional case on the definition of voluntary 'consent' to search, Justice Marshall, in dissent, said on the issue of the allocation of the burden of proof (at 285–286),

[Under one view, t]he question then is a simple one: must the Government show that the subject knew of his rights, or must the subject show that he lacked such knowledge?

I think that any fair allocation of the burden would require that it be placed on the prosecution. On this question. the Court indulges in what might be called the 'straw man' method of adjudication. The Court responds to this suggestion by overinflating the burden. [The Court wrote in part 'For it would be thoroughly impractical to impose on the normal consent search the detailed requirements of an effective warning.'] And. when it is suggested that the *prosecution's* burden could be easily satisfied if the police informed the subject of his rights. the Court responds by refusing to require the *police* to make a 'detailed' inquiry. Ante. at 245. If the Court candidly faced the real question of allocating the burden of proof. neither of these maneuvers would be available to it.

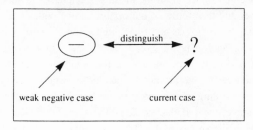

Fig. 5: A straw man argument often sets up a weak analogy that is easily distinguished by an opponent.

4.3 ARGUMENTS INVOLVING THE CURRENT FACT SITUATION AND A SEQUENCE OF CASES

The following argument forms involve not simply a set of cases, but an ordered sequence of them.

4.3.1 Slippery Slope. This form of argument may be familiar to students of the law almost to the point of banality.[11] An advocate suggests a sequence of cases. real or hypothetical. whose starting point is the current situation and whose endpoint is an untenable application of the rule or predicate in question. The difficulty of making a principled distinction among the cases in the sequence supports the argument that the interpretation of the rule or predicate in issue must be limited to the precedent and not expanded to the current fact situation. See Figure 6.

EXAMPLE: The Commissioner may pose: 'Consider your honor, a sequence of cases before you – all similar to Alice's case, but where the percentage of total work time the home office decreases: not the 80% found in *Weissman*, but the 40% in the current case. then 25%. 10%...How little use will be conceded? This court must stem the flow of home office litigation and require at least 80% of work be done in the home.'

[11.] One of the authors attended a first-year law school class in which this form of argument was invoked on a daily basis.

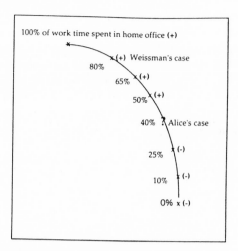

100% of work time spent in home office (+)

x(+) Weissman's case
80%

x(+)
65%

x(+)
50%

40% Alice's case

x (-)
25%

x (-)
10%

0% x (-)

Fig. 6: A slippery slope argument suggests that the lessening of a threshold will lead to further decreases, until clearly negative cases are illegitimately included as positive examples.

EXAMPLE: In [Ely, 1975, p.1501], John Ely mimics a jurist questioning an attorney about a series of hypotheticals: 'I understand that you would protect sound-trucks. But what about a hospital zone? What about the middle of the night? Surely you wouldn't let a mayoral candidate aim a bullhorn at your window at three in the morning. Surely you have to balance, or employ a clear and present danger test, at *some* point.'

Finally, a slippery slope argument provided a light moment during oral argument before the Supreme Court in the *State of Texas v. Gregory Lee Johnson*, 491 U.S. 397 (1989), in response to the contention by counsel for Texas that a Texas statute proscribed the burning of an American flag. A member of the Court asked if burning a flag with 48 stars would be reachable by the Texas law. Texas counsel thought that it would. The Justice then asked if burning a flag with 47 stars was proscribed. When Texas counsel admitted that it would not be, the Justice observed, 'So, all you have to do is take one star out of a – out of the flag, and it's okay.'

4.3.2 Reductio[12] Loop. This argument form is the same as the slippery slope except that it leads to the conclusion that a case residing on what was assumed to be unimpeachable ground ('further up the slope') is questioned as well. One way to perform a *reductio* loop is to show how the supposedly unimpeachable case can be linked to the current fact situation, which in turn slides farther down the slope to the *reductio* case. The conclusion is that the allegedly unimpeachable case is as suspect as the *reductio* case and the current fact situation, since the difference among all of these cases is just a matter of degree. The

---

[12] A 'reductio ad absurdum' argument is 'the method of disproving an argument by showing that it leads to an absurd consequence.' Black's Law Dictionary (5th Edition).

reductio argument might be used to subvert the effect of an established ruling in a precedent relied upon by opposing counsel. See Figure 7.

EXAMPLE: As an example of a *reductio* argument, the Commissioner might argue that the taxpayer's claim in this case shows the problems that inhere in decisions like *Weissman*. 'Your honor, once you allow an employee who has an office provided by her employer to claim that her principal place of business is the home then one can not draw a defensible line – a line that is both fair to all taxpayers and capable of efficient administration. Therefore, *Weissman* should not be followed in this court [or it should be reversed].'

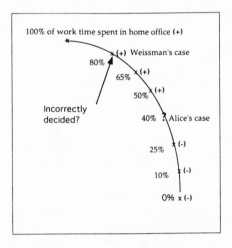

Fig. 7: The *reductio* argument is similar to a slippery slope argument, but questions a previous decision near the top of the slippery slope. *Weissman* is questioned as incorrectly decided in view of its slippery consequences for Alice's case and others.

EXAMPLE: In *Commissioner v. Flowers*, 326 U.S. 465 (1945), a taxpayer who lived in Jackson, Mississippi, but who worked for days at a time at the headquarters of his railroad employer in Mobile, Alabama, attempted to deduct meals and hotel expenses while in Mobile. In dissenting from a decision in which the deduction was denied, Justice Rutledge wrote (at 478–479),

Congress gave the deduction for traveling away from home on business. The commuter's case, rightly confined, does not fall in this class. One who lives in an adjacent suburb or city and by usual modes of commutation can work within a distance permitting the daily journey and return, with time for the day's work and a period at home, clearly can be excluded from the deduction on the basis of the section's terms equally with its obvious purpose. But that is not true if 'commuter' is to swallow up the deduction by the same sort of construction which makes 'home' mean 'business headquarters' of one's employer. If the line may be extended somewhat to cover doubtful cases, it need not be lengthened to infinity or to cover cases as far removed from the prevailing connotation of commuter as this one. Including it pushes 'commuting' too far, even for these times of rapid transit.

The thrust of J. Rutledge's reasoning is that the majority's position will support an improper *reductio* argument. Rutledge argues that the 'top of the slope' prototype of a 'commuter' is weakened when decisions are made to deny the travel deduction in cases that are far removed – far down the slope – from that prototype are justified as 'commuting expenses'.

4.4 MISCELLANEOUS ARGUMENT FORMS

4.4.1 Hedging argument. Suppose that the advocate wants to argue in his brief that an apparently unfavorable rule does not apply or does not control the decision in the current case, but if the rule *is* found to be dispositive, the desired result follows nevertheless. This form of argument can be seen in legal briefs, where an attorney will hedge his rhetorical bet. See Figure 8.

EXAMPLE: The Commissioner may argue 'Your honor, we have established in the immediately preceding argument (the *reductio* argument) that the rule of *Weissman* should not apply because it is bad law. But if *Weissman* does apply, then Alice's case is distinguishable because of her smaller percentage use and her non-exclusive use. In addition, Weissman created a home office partly due to concerns for his safety.'

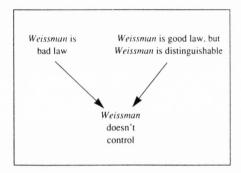

Fig. 8: A hedging argument can use a forked argument that the result in *Weissman* should not control the disposition in the current case.

4.4.2 Weighing or balancing argument. Perhaps the form of argument seen most by law students is the 'weighing' argument. Weighing arguments pre-suppose the identification of domain-important factors that are somehow 'weighed' against each other. Compare [Rissland, Valcarce & Ashley, 1984; Ashley, 1990] (arguing for a least-commitment, implicit weighting scheme). A closely related and possibly co-extensive form of argument is the 'balancing' argument, where one attempts to place policies supporting two legal ideas or ideals 'in balance'. In the typical application of this form of argument, the competing policies never balance (equally) and the balance arm dips in favor of the weightier policies.

EXAMPLE: To invoke a weighing or balancing argument, the Commissioner might argue, 'Your honor, this case requires you to balance the policy of preventing taxpayers from deducting purely personal expenses against the policy of only taxing net income. income earned after the expenses incurred to produce that income. Where the taxpayer who is an employee has NO office provided by the employer then the balance tips in the taxpayer's favor. But where the employer does provide an office, then the balance shifts the other way. To balance these policies in this case in favor of the taxpayer would erode the tax base and create inequities between those taxpayers who can do a considerable amount of their employer's work at home and those who just work there on evenings and weekends.'

EXAMPLE: In *Bob Jones University v. U.S.*, 461 U.S. 574 (1983), dealing with whether schools that use racially discriminatory admissions standards can qualify as tax-exempt organizations. Justice Powell, concurring in part and concurring in the judgment, argued (at 610–611),

Congress. of course. may find that some organizations do not warrant tax-exempt status. In this case I agree with the Court that Congress has determined that the policy against racial discrimination in education should override the countervailing interest in permitting unorthodox private behavior.

I would like to emphasize. however. that the balancing of these substantial interests is for *Congress* to perform.

Professor Henkin described the balancing process in First Amendment cases:

The Court will hold the scales. attribute different weights to different communications (taking account of content. form. and context) and to values affected by the communication. will determine the level of tolerance imposed on government by the first amendment. and read the balance. [Henkin. 1968. p.81]

Henkin goes on to say, parenthetically, however,

(I use the metaphor of balancing but the point is the same however one describes the scope and limits of the amendment. or the judicial process in determining them.) [Henkin. 1968. p.81]

As Henkin observes. in practice this form of analysis provides a metaphor more than a rhetorical method. Legal opinions, which frequently invoke metaphorical language appealing to the 'physical mass' of competing factors, rarely – if ever – provide a scale that can gauge the 'weight' of these factors. And so the weighing argument often smacks of contrivance. Its role in actual use may be to dress up in objective clothing a decision made on other, unstated grounds. Often, the arguer presses his thumb on the scale: the words chosen to state the opposing claims are an immediate key as to which side possesses greater credence in the author's eyes. In a comment dealing with the means of deciding flag desecration cases under the first amendment. John Ely shores up this view:

The categorizers were right: where messages are proscribed because they are dangerous. balancing tests inevitably become intertwined with the ideological predispositions of those doing the balancing – or if not that. at least with the relative confidence or paranoia of the age in which they are doing it – and we must build barriers as secure as words are able to make them. [Ely. 1975, p. 1501]

Balancing or weighing arguments thus provide a familiar framework for stating legal problems. rather than suggesting an adversarial approach for their resolutions.

In this section we have given a partial taxonomy of legal argument forms as they are applied in legal practice. The next section changes pace to discuss a distinct computational implementation of some of the argument terms and methods in our CABARET system. The reader may see connections between CABARET and the argument forms just presented in this Section. In Section 6 we make explicit these connections between the argument forms and the computational model we are about to present in Section 5.

5. Argument strategies and moves in CABARET

In this section, we describe a model of legal argument implemented in CABARET that involves three components: **argument strategies, argument moves,** and **argument primitives.** The facet of legal argument on which we concentrate is how to apply cases to argue for an interpretation of a term used in a legal rule. We define the term 'rule' quite expansively to include not only a statute and a supporting regulation, but also a blackletter rule of law induced from a group of cases, such as a rule from the Restatement of Contracts, or a 'rule of a case,' a rule-like statement capturing the holding of a single case.

CABARET's argument strategies, moves and primitives may be seen as inhabiting a hierarchy of argument techniques (Figure 9):

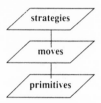

Fig. 9: The hierarchy of argument strategies, moves and primitives.

In the following sections we discuss each of the three levels of argument techniques, starting with argument strategies.

5.1   ARGUMENT STRATEGIES

How one argues about a rule depends on one's point of view. For instance, with respect to a deduction against gross income, a taxpayer would likely take a *pro* (in the sense of 'in favor of') position whereas the IRS may protect the tax revenues of the nation by adopting a *con* strategy. In our model, the pro or con point of view is the initial determinant of how one argues.

Suppose that the IRS has challenged a home office deduction on the grounds that the taxpayer did not meet the 'use on a regular basis' requirement, but the IRS admits that the other requirements of Section 280A(c)(1) have been met. The task confronting the taxpayer is to extend the rule so that it covers a situation – the taxpayer's – which is outside the strict scope of the rule as construed by the IRS. Taxpayer's task can be captured in the following rule of thumb:

If a rule's conditions are not met and the arguer wants the rule to succeed, then broaden the rule.

On the other hand, the IRS has adopted the contrary point of view ('con'): against allowing the home office deduction. The IRS would argue that the rule is to be strictly applied. To bolster that contention, it would attempt to find cases interpreting that section that confirm that the rule's conclusion – the deduction – should not follow in this situation. The parallel heuristic from the IRS's point of view is:

If a rule's conditions are not met and the arguer wants the rule to fail, then confirm the miss.

In section 5.2 we discuss how certain precedents can be used to support rule broadening and rule miss confirmation. The two points of view and the two possibilities that a rule's conditions are met or are not met by a fact situation suggest a 2 × 2 matrix of top-level **argument strategies** for the interpretation of a rule (Table I).

Table I. A matrix of argument strategies.

Point of View/ Rule Conditions	Point of View = Pro	Point of View = Con
Rule Conditions Met	Confirm the Hit	Discredit the Rule
Rule Conditions Not Met	Broaden the Rule	Confirm the Miss

Each of the individual cells represents a strategy useful in circumstances that depend on the arguer's goal and a strict interpretation of the rule:

- **broadening** is used to argue that a rule applies to a situation where strict application indicates it does not, or to argue for membership in the concept class implied by the rule consequent, irrespective of the rule;
- **discrediting** is used to argue that a rule does not apply to a situation where strict application indicates it does;
- **confirming a hit** is used to argue that a rule does apply to a situation just as strict application indicates;
- **confirming a miss** is used to argue that a rule does not apply to a situation just as strict application of the rule indicates it does not.

This presentation of argument strategies is directed at appellate argument. The model assumes that a determination has been made whether a rule's conditions have strictly been met. This determination may have been given by administrative interpretation (as by the IRS) or by a lower court's interpretation (as by the Tax Court). Alternatively, on questions of first impression, the arguer may make a hypothetical assumption regarding whether a rule's conditions have been met and 'play out' the arguments using the resulting strategies.

In this approach to statutory argument, each of the argument strategies is effected through a set of *argument moves*,[13] which are described in the next subsection.

5.2 ARGUMENT MOVES

An arguer can carry out a chosen argument strategy in several ways. While the choice of strategy looks in part to the current fact situation, the choice of move looks also to the available precedents. For each of the four argument strategies, there are four possible moves in turn. Each move depends on two factors: (1) the disposition of a precedent – whether or not the precedent held for the ultimate desired result; and (2) the status of the rule with respect to the precedent – whether or not the rule's conditions were satisfied by the facts of that precedent. We give some informal examples of possible argument moves and then provide a systematic treatment.

Consider again the example of a home office deduction claim that is challenged on the basis of taxpayer's failure to meet the 'regular use'[14] requirement of the statute. On the basis of available precedents, a taxpayer could attempt to carry out an argument for broadening the home office rule in several ways. She can argue, for example:

1. that the unmet condition actually has been satisfied: that the allegedly missing condition has been met in fact and thus the rule should apply. A useful precedent would be a case in which (a) the regular-use condition and all other rule conditions have been satisfied, (b) the home office deduction conclusion was therefore established, and (c) the taxpayer's situation is similar – especially with respect to the regularity of home office use. Or

2. that the unmet condition is not necessary: that the result of the rule follows without meeting the condition with which she is having difficulty. A good precedent would be a case in which the regular-use condition was not met but where the home office deduction was granted nonetheless. Or

3. that her case is so *unlike* the cases where the rule's conditions have *not* been established that the rule's conditions should be interpreted as being met in this situation. Useful precedents would be a group of cases that did not satisfy the regular-use condition and were not granted the deduction, but that were markedly different from cases that did satisfy the regular-use requirement, and distinguishable from the current situation.

Choices (1) and (2) are variations of arguments based on precedents with the desired disposition: the taxpayer in the retrieved cases was allowed the deduction. The arguer would draw analogies with these favorably disposed cases to justify why the desired dis-

---

[13]. In a recent article, [Gordon, 1991] refers briefly to 'argument moves' as analogs of three roles for cases identified by Ashley: 'cited cases', 'distinguished cases' and 'counter-examples'. We reserve the term 'argument moves' for specific, active tactics that an advocate can use to support his stance. The term was also previously used by Rissland [1985] and Ashley and Aleven [1991].

[14]. No well-formulated test for 'use on a regular basis' has been applied by the courts. The 'frequency and repetitive nature' of the business use appear to be the most important considerations. See [Knobbe, 1986] for a description for practitioners of the home office deduction.

position should be reached in his situation as well. In (1), the arguer works with a precedent where the rule applied and in (2), with one where it did not. Choice (3) provides one way to use a case offensively that has been decided in favor of the opposing point of view.

In (1), the arguer uses the precedent to establish an unmet condition in her current case in order to argue for the consequent of the rule. The more her facts support the unmet condition relative to the precedent's, the better her argument.[15] ('Since the other taxpayer met the requirement and I am at least as well situated as he. I also meet the requirement.')

In (2), one argues directly for the disposition by soft pedaling or denying outright the necessity of meeting the unmet rule precondition. Thus. in (2) the arguer will analogize the current case and the precedent to justify the deduction. She might go further to argue that the rule is invalid on its face, as opposed to incorrectly applied to this particular situation. The better the match between the unmet condition in the current fact situation and in the precedent, the easier the argument. ('Since the other taxpayer was allowed the deduction even though he failed the same alleged requirement, so it should be allowed in my case.')

Choice (3) might be used in light of precedents whose outcome is the opposite to that desired: the deduction was not allowed and just as in the current case, a condition was deemed unmet. The arguer would distinguish those cases: that they should not govern her case because her case is much stronger than those cases. She would need to argue by 'double negative' that the desired disposition should be reached in her case. ('Since I am so unlike those cases where the deduction was disallowed. I should be allowed the deduction.')

More difficult to make even than (3) would be an argument using a precedent with an undesired disposition despite the fact that the rule conditions were met. To use such a case, one would have to both distinguish the negative disposition and make use of its positive aspect concerning rule satisfaction. This strategy is tricky: it tries to make a silk purse out of a sow's ear. Besides, an obvious counterattack exists. The opponent could use such a precedent to argue that the standard is even stricter than the rule specifies. In fact, the opposition may well rely on this precedent in the first place and the advocate would have to respond to it. It is in this defensive role that an advocate may be forced to reply with such delicate arguments.

Typically, one's first line of argument is to analogize cases with the disposition that one desires for the current fact situation. However, since the only relevant precedents might have been decided oppositely, argument moves are needed to use them to build offensive arguments. And as suggested in the last paragraph, since one's opponent is sure to cite cases with unfavorable outcomes, it is also necessary to respond defensively to cases with unfavorable dispositions by distinguishing them.

Argument choices (1), (2) and (3) are particular instances of a scheme of argument moves developed for the CABARET system. We now place these three choices in a

---

[15]. The stereotypical form of this argument is supported by cases that hold on the predicate in question and whose supporting criterial facts can be matched. analogized or favorably compared. See [Branting, 1991].

larger plan of argument moves and tie all such moves into the broad argument strategies presented in Section 5.1.

First consider the broadening argument strategy. In general there are two possibilities for the disposition of a relevant precedent and two possibilities for the success of strict application of the rule to it, yielding four possible types of precedents to be dealt with. These four possibilities provide the setting for the argument moves for broadening, which are listed in Table II.

Table II: Argument Moves for Broadening. (*Cell numbers in braces are included for reference only.*)

Disposition of Precedent/ Rule Consequent is established in Precedent	Precedent has Desired Disposition	Precedent doesn't have Desired Disposition
Yes	Analogize Case {1}	Distinguish Case {3} Disposition and Analogize Rule Consequent
No	Analogize Case {2} Disposition (and Distinguish Rule Consequent)	Distinguish Case {4}

A word as to terminology in Table II: 'Analogize Case Disposition' means to draw analogies between the precedent and the current situation of any sort to argue that the outcome of the two cases should be the same. 'Analogize Rule Consequent' means to draw analogies between two cases using features related to the rule's preconditions, in order to argue that the rule should hold – or fail to hold – in both cases. 'Analogize Case' means to do both: 'Analogize Case Disposition' and 'Rule Consequent' Analogize. 'Distinguish Case', 'Distinguish Case Disposition', and 'Distinguish Rule Consequent' are parallel to their three 'analogize' counterparts, except that distinctions between cases are exploited, not similarities.

Distinguishing moves are applied in the two situations for broadening where the retrieved cases have the wrong disposition. These moves are contained in cells {3} and {4} in Table II. There, the precedent may have a different factual complexion or a different status with respect to the strict application of the rule. Hence, an advocate may need to distinguish a case decided 'for the other side' with respect to the precedent's disposition, the result of strict rule interpretation in that situation, or both.

The broadening table also summarizes how to carry out the argument strategy to confirm a hit, that is, to confirm that a rule's preconditions are satisfied. That these strategies share moves makes sense in that the argument moves do not depend on the application of the rule to the current problem situation, but depend only on the retrieved precedents. The difference between being in a broadening mode and in a confirming mode depends only on the application of the rule to the current problem.

In confirming a hit, one would prefer to analogize a similar case with the right disposition where the rule's conditions were satisfied. However, depending on the cases that are available to an arguer, he may have to rely on cases that have unfavorable dispositions or reflect unfavorable strict interpretations under the rule. Various other argument moves to confirm a hit are available as with broadening. With a merely confirmatory strategy, however, it is less incumbent upon the arguer to use precedents that are in any way unfavorable. There is no need to stretch arguments very far when the received rule interpretation favors one's own side.

The remaining two argument strategies, discredit and confirm a miss, also can be effected through similar argument moves. These two strategies also share a table of argument moves, which is presented in Table III.

Table III: Argument Moves for Discredit a Rule and Confirm a Miss. (*Cell numbers in braces are included for reference only.*)

Disposition of Precedent/ Rule Consequent established in Precedent	Precedent has Desired Disposition	Precedent doesn't have Desired Disposition
Yes	Analogize Case {1} Disposition and Distinguish Rule Consequent	Distinguish Case {3}
No	Analogize Case {2}	Distinguish Case {4} Disposition and Analogize Rule Consequent

The tables for all the argument moves use the same generic argument tasks of analogizing and distinguishing, which for convenience we therefore call 'primitive' argument tasks. These primitives are considered briefly in the next section.

5.3 ARGUMENT PRIMITIVES

So far in our discussion of argument moves we have made a simplifying assumption: that there is no difference between similarly disposed cases aside from their status with respect to a rule. However, in order to carry out the details of analogizing and distinguishing cases, an arguer must give close consideration to the facts of the available precedents, the current fact situation, and the degree of match between an available case and the current fact situation. These are central concerns of case-based argument. The selection of a strategy, and then of a move, focuses attention on how the rules constrain the use of case-based reasoning to argue case similarity and difference. We now address some of the case-based concerns of how distinguishing and analogizing are implemented.

In performing moves that require analogies, an arguer would usually rely on 'best' cases in the sense defined by Ashley [1990]. Best cases are most on-point cases for which there is no 'trumping counterexample,' which in turn is defined as a 'case with the opposite outcome that contains all of the cited case's similarities and then some'[16] [Ashley, 1989]. Relying on cases other than best cases can be rhetorically dangerous. Features present in a precedent but not in the current fact situation permit a counterargument: that the result was obtained in the precedent due to the presence of those other mitigating or contributing factors [Ashley, 1987]. The use of best cases to implement a strategy, such as broadening, forestalls a contrary argument about credit assignment. For instance in our taxpayer example, careful selection of the precedents on which the taxpayer relies can hinder a counterargument in which the taxpayer's adversary could 'distinguish away' taxpayer's case citations. Given a choice of ways to pursue an argument strategy, an

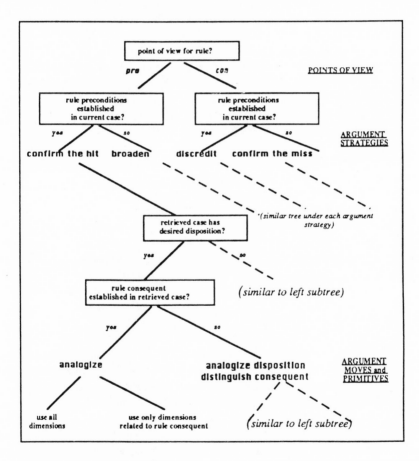

Fig. 10. Decision tree fragment showing points of view, argument strategies, argument moves and primitives.

[16] A best case must also share some factor with the problem that affimatively favors one's own side. [Ashley, 1989].

arguer chooses a specific tactical move based on the cases actually available. But given a variance in the closeness of match of these cases with the current case, some moves might be better than others, but no one case or move may be clearly best.

When no best cases or even favorably disposed cases are available, the arguer might usefully employ hypothetical cases [Rissland & Ashley, 1986; Ashley, 1990], but in strict precedent-based domains hypotheticals lack the pedigree of genuine precedents.

One way to implement this theory of strategies, moves and primitives is to form arguments in a top-down manner. In this way, the entire sequence of choices of strategies, moves, and generic argument tasks can be shown in a decision tree whose branch points involve point of view, status of the current fact situation with respect to the rule, disposition of available precedents, status of precedents with respect to the rule, and degree of match of precedents with the current fact situation. Figure 10 shows a portion of the decision tree, in particular that fragment relevant to the confirm-a-hit strategy. Although the figure includes only two leaves below the choice of argument move, there may be many ways to effect the moves. The means chosen will involve consideration of the details of the cases. In this top-down approach, the degree of case match is only considered after the choice of move.

In the next subsection we give an example of an argument generated by CABARET by applying its implemented strategies, moves and primitives.

5.4 ARGUMENT GENERATION IN CABARET

The current implementation of CABARET generates argument skeletons that report the processing of the system to suggest lines of possible attack. Figure 11 gives an example. A complete argument could be based on such a skeleton. A correspondence can be seen between portions of the argument on one hand and the argument strategies, moves and primitives and the control heuristics that invoke them, on the other. For example, the first sub-argument for the *Weissman* case in Figure 11 corresponds to the rule-based-near-miss control rule, the broadening argument strategy, and a straightforward 'analogize case strategy' (as in cell {1} of Table I). The other pieces of the argument in Figure 11 are direct reflections of other tasks performed by CABARET.

The argument skeleton can be seen as a direct reporting of its controlled processing. This transparency (to use a hackneyed phrase) may be a feature or a bug. That arguments may be outlined simply by reporting the processing of the system emphasizes the primary role of argument techniques in controlling what tasks CABARET creates and performs. On the other hand, one of the points of this article is the simple one that creating arguments in a task domain that is guided by both rules and precedents presents a complex control problem. As Golding and Rosenbloom [1991] point out, CABARET presents all the evidence that it acquires to support a user's viewpoint, but it is important to note that part of that evidence is gathered in response to the failure of one reasoner or the other to achieve its goals alone. CABARET would profit from an ability to plan arguments and to prune arguments that are weak. The first of these potential extensions to CABARET is the subject of the next section.

```
;;; ARGUMENT for the WEISSMAN case with respect to the predicate
;;; PRINCIPAL-PLACE-OF-BUSINESS:
;;; =================================================
```

While the rule PRINCIPAL-PLACE-OF-BUSINESS-RULE did not fire and the consequent of the rule, PRINCIPAL-PLACE-OF-BUSINESS, WAS NOT established, we may appeal to the following arguments to support a claim for the predicate PRINCIPAL-PLACE-OF-BUSINESS:

(1.) Note that only one conjunct of that rule,
((WEISSMAN PRIMARY-RESPONSIBILITY-IN-HOME-OFFICE T)), was missing.
   For cases where that domain rule did fire and the result of the case was our own, consider the following cases as analogies:
ADAMS, DRUCKER, FRANKEL, JUNIORXCHAMBER, MEIERS, SCOTT,....

. . .

To analogize DRUCKER and WEISSMAN, consider the following factors possessed by them in common:
   there was evidence as to the frequency of usage of the home office by the taxpayer,
   the home office was necessary to perform the taxpayer's duties....

(2.) Looking at case-based analysis,.... dimensional analysis on the WEISSMAN case yields for the predicate PRINCIPAL-PLACE-OF-BUSINESS:
   The APPLICABLE factors are: income was derived from activities in the home office;
there was evidence as to the relative use of the home office and other work places;...
   The NEAR MISS factors are: the home office was the location where the primary responsibilities were discharged.

The UNSATISFIED factors are: NONE.

For a pure COMMON LAW argument, the best cases to cite with respect to the predicate PRINCIPAL-PLACE-OF-BUSINESS are: BELLS MEIERS WEISSMAN_EMR
To analogize BELLS and WEISSMAN, consider the following factors in common:....

(3.) The best cases for the OPPOSING side with respect to the predicate PRINCIPAL-PLACE-OF-BUSINESS are: BAIE CRISTO HONAN LOPKOFF POMARANTZ.

To distinguish BAIE from WEISSMAN, consider the following factors that were present in WEISSMAN but not in BAIE:
there was evidence as to the frequency of usage of the home office by the taxpayer;
there was evidence as to the relative use of the home office and other work places;
the home office was physically separated from the living area . . .

On the other hand, also consider the following factors that were present in BAIE but not in WEISSMAN: . . .

Fig. 11: Excerpts from CABARET's argument for the *Principal Place of Business predicate*[17].

[17]. This Figure also appeared in [Rissland & Skalak, 1991], which discusses CABARET's implementation at a more detailed level than this article.

6. Future work: connect CABARET with the argument forms

6.1 USING ARGUMENT FORMS TO CONTROL PROCESSING

Argument moves and argument strategies are closely tied to the stereotypical argument forms. We revisit some of the argument forms described in Section 4 and briefly explain how the model of argument strategies and moves presented above can account for many of them. However, the stereotypical argument forms presented in Section 4 have not been implemented in CABARET, with the exception of straightforward arguments. We do envision several possible ways they may be used to direct the computation of arguments in the CABARET framework.

First, they may be used as control plans provided by the user in a top-down fashion. For instance, a user could direct the system to provide a slippery slope argument with respect to the exclusive use predicate of Section 280A(c)(1). The program would then create tasks to fill in a slippery slope argument frame. Such a template (Figure 12) would include slots for the predicate at issue, the dimension along which the predicate will be monotonically varied, the features that must be kept approximately constant from case to case, the case at the top of the slope (whose disposition is acknowledged), a list of cases with the appropriate disposition that vary along the dimension specified, and a foot-of-the-slope case whose decision is arguably untenable:

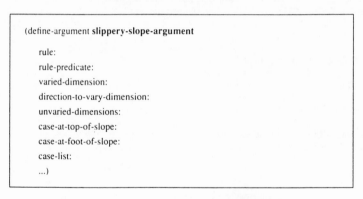

Fig. 12: A hypothetical definition of a template for the slippery-slope argument.

We envision one such template for each argument form. But each template may have different instantiations, of course. Using a slippery-slope argument for one dimension of the exclusive-use predicate does not preclude using slippery-slope on another predicate. (The repetition may be tedious as a matter of rhetorical presentation, however.)

Argument forms can be used as control plans to coordinate processing. Using control plans may serve to coordinate knowledge sources explicitly, flexibly and transparently (see [Cohen, 1987]). In particular, using argument forms as top-down plans would ameliorate at least two deficiencies in CABARET's current implementation. (1) There is minimal coordination of knowledge sources in CABARET. The system proposes tasks that are useful in a given context, but has no knowledge of how to coordinate a sequence of tasks. (2) The selection of which task to execute next is done through an *ad hoc* numerical assessment of priority, rather than in a way that does not attempt to capture a complex control context in a single number.

The second application for the argument forms is to use them in a bottom-up fashion. During CABARET's normal processing, cases and relationships are discovered that can fill slots of the various argument templates. In this way, the system could opportunistically pursue arguments not envisioned at the outset of the run.

For example, suppose CABARET has already created a satisfactory argument (by some standard) with respect to the home office statutory predicate 'principal place of business' based on cases A through F. (See Figure 13.) If CABARET unearths a favorable case G that is the only case that shares a particular dimension with the current problem case (and that dimension is a factor with respect to principal place of business), then G may provide the foundation for a make-weight argument. Since G shares only a single dimension with the current case, it does not provide a very strong analogy. However, if it is the only case that shares that one dimension with the problem case, it may nonetheless be cited as a favorable case without fear of an opponent's responding with a 'trumping' case that is more on-point but has the opposite outcome [Ashley, 1990].

Such a case would be a leaf node that appears in level 1 of a 'claim lattice', the partial ordering of cases by similarity originally developed in HYPO [Ashley, 1990]. See Fig. 13.

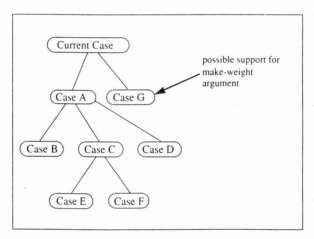

Fig. 13: The skeleton of a claim lattice for a hypothetical Current Case. If Case G shares a single dimension with Current Case, it may be a candidate for the basis for an additional, make-weight argument.

Consider another example of how argument forms can be used to control a system's processing from the bottom up. Suppose a number of cases (A-F) are most on-point, but they share few dimensions in common with the current fact situation (and each shares a different small subset of dimensions with it). Suppose further that cases A to F have been decided in favor of the opposing viewpoint. A claim lattice based on this configuration of cases would be shallow, with a large branching factor at the first level (Figure 14). In this situation the control template representing the argument form 'turkey, chicken and fish' may be opportunistically invoked. For at this point the system would have the means to argue that the Current Case (the 'turkey') is sufficiently dissimilar from the oppositely decided cases A to F (the 'fish') – because the Current Case shares only a couple of dimensions in common with each of them – that the Current Case should be decided consistently with the desired viewpoint (i.e., should be considered a 'chicken').

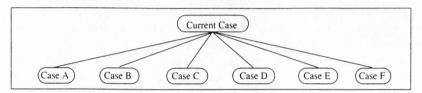

Fig. 14: Another possible claim lattice for a hypothetical Current Case. Case A to F are most on-point cases but may fail nonetheless to have many dimensions in common with Current Case.

We have argued in this article that the demands of argument require the use of (something such as) argument forms to control top-down and bottom-up processing. The argument forms could coordinate both specification-driven aspects of argument in which one attempts to find cases fitting specified criteria, with the precedent-driven aspects of argument, in which cases that have been unearthed by whatever means can be arranged to form a coherent argument.

6.2 HOW THE CURRENT FRAMEWORK OF STRATEGIES AND MOVES SUPPORTS ARGUMENT
   FORMS

Regardless of how argument forms might be implemented to direct processing, the thrust of this section is that the argument strategies and moves as described in Section 5 (a) provide examples of certain forms of arguments (e.g., straightforward, double-negative, hedging, make-weight), and (b) provide the means to create more complicated forms of argument (e.g., slippery slope, *reductio*). An attempt to place an argument forms plane in Figure 9 would require links both to the strategies and moves planes in that figure. We now discuss some of these links between the stereotypical forms of legal argument found in practice and the three-tiered model of argument previously developed for CABARET.

Straightforward argument. Analogizing favorable cases and distinguishing unfavorable ones are the basis of many straightforward arguments. These tactics are captured in the analogize case and distinguish case moves on the main diagonal of the Broaden/Confirm a Hit Table (Table II). Similarly, analogize case and distinguish case – counterdiagonal argument moves of the Discredit/Confirm a Miss Table (Table III) – also represent straightforward methods to argue that rule should not have fired. In these moves, cases that have the appropriate outcome for the kind of move that's being made (favorable for analogy, opposite for distinguishing) are compared or contrasted. No additional qualification is required to account for unfavorable aspects of such cases, as in some of the hedging arguments below.

Of course, the term 'straightforward' argument is somewhat misleading. Analogizing and distinguishing are straightforward only within the context of this argument taxonomy, where they are distinguished from more complex forms of argument involving several cases or favorable pieces of unfavorable cases. Analogy and distinguishing are complex moves in themselves. They depend on a complex assessment of the features that are relevant to the comparison and of how relative similarity of cases is determined once the appropriate features have been identified [Ashley, 1987].

Turkey, chicken and fish argument.   Recall that this form of argument uses negative cases to establish a positive result. For instance, one might use a case where a statute was held not satisfied to establish a positive result – that the statute's requirements are satisfied in the current case. One way to accomplish this rhetorical feat is to establish striking differences between the negative cases and the current fact situation, and argue that the point of the statute is to exclude the 'obviously egregious' negative cases. Closely similar cases – such as one's own – are within the penumbra of cases to which the statute applies.

The move in cell {4} of the Broaden/Confirm a Hit Table (Table II), is designed to use this strategy to expand the scope of a rule. One argues that the cases where the rule did not fire are so easily distinguished from the present case that the rule should apply to the present case.

Note that this use of the distinguishing move in cell {4} is an offensive[18] use of the move – a move to establish a particular interpretation. This argument form thus provides an unusual role for distinguishing. The usual role for distinguishing is a defensive response to the precedents cited by an opposing side. HYPO, for example, applies distinguishing in this role only, as a response to a case cited in a previous ply of a 3-ply point-counterpoint-rebuttal argument [Ashley, 1990].

Make-weight argument.   A simple make-weight argument may be required if for example (a) the application of a controlling rule is clearly in one's favor or (b) if one has advanced other strong arguments. In the first situation, an advocate will have adopted either of the main diagonal strategies – confirm the hit or confirm the miss – of the Argument Strategies Table (Table I). In that setting, the weight of interpretation is presumably on the arguer's side since the initial interpretation of the statute has favored his case. As for (b), the example given in Figure 13 of using a case alone on a branch provides an example of a situation that CABARET can identify to yield a make-weight argument.

---

[18]. 'Offensive' is used as an antonym to 'defensive,' but we grant that other constructions of 'offensive' may be appropriate in this context.

By contrast to the confirming strategies, broadening and discrediting require arguing against an initial interpretation. There, the onus is upon the advocate who attempts to change the previously accorded interpretation. Lightweight make-weight arguments are usually inappropriate in these situations, where one is trying to overturn a previously established interpretation. However, an opponent may disparagingly refer to an opponent's argument as make-weight.

Straw man argument. One form of straw man argument uses a weak, irrelevant, or inappropriate example allegedly to bolster an opponent's position. Since we assume that an advocate does not deliberately set out to create a straw man argument (except possibly on rare occasions where a flamboyant straw man is created for its theatrical effect on a jury), we shall not examine how straw man arguments are reflected in the argument taxonomy. It should be clear, however, that straw man arguments may be the target of a distinguishing move in cell {3} of the Discredit Table, Table III. To discredit or limit the application of a rule, one may distinguish such a weak, hypothetical case to which the rule allegedly would apply. As we have noted, distinguishing may be applied to weak or to strong examples and so is not limited to defeating straw man arguments.

Hedging argument. As outlined in Section 4, a hedging argument argues that rule or case A controls a situation and yields a favorable outcome, but even if rule or case B controls, the outcome is still favorable. Presumably one's opponent would argue that rule or case B controls and the result is favorable to himself. A hedging argument offers two paths, both of which lead to a favorable result.

Two such paths are reflected in some of the more complex moves in the Broadening Table. For example, when an advocate is presented with a precedent whose overall result is favorable, but whose holding on a rule in issue is unfavorable, Cell {2} suggests using a combination of analogizing and distinguishing. The precedent is effectively split into two aspects. As to the features of the case that lead to a failure of the rule to fire, the precedent should be distinguished, if one is trying to argue for the rule's firing. However, as to the ultimate disposition, the move requires analogizing the aspects that lead to that favorable outcome. These two moves together reflect an attempt to hedge one's argument. The distinguishing part of the move argues that the precedent does not control the interpretation of the predicate in issue. But even if that precedent is deemed by the court to be controlling, the second half of the move argues by analogy for the favorable overall disposition of the current case.

Weighing argument. Rather than residing in any of the argument tables presented above, weighing arguments inhere in the model of case-based reasoning assumed by CABARET, which was originally implemented in HYPO [Ashley, 1990]. HYPO used important domain factors called 'dimensions' to index, retrieve and compare cases. Numerical weights were not used by HYPO, and the importance of dimensions depended on the argument context, in particular the cases that are retrieved from the case base for support. The same is true of the weighing arguments that appear in many legal opinions. A court may list the various competing factors that are taken into account in deciding some issue, but numbers never enter the picture. The HYPO model does specify that dimensions (and values along dimensions) are considered to be favorable to one party or the other. So when cases are retrieved and sorted according to the dimensions present that are relevant to the current fact situation, the 'weight' of a set of dimensions depends on the relative similarity of the cases retrieved to the problem situation and the outcomes of those cases. Favorable and unfavorable dimensions are implicitly weighed, just as legal opinions may purport to weigh competing factors without the intervention of any quantitative aspects. See [Ashley & Rissland, 1988b] for an in-depth discussion of the implications of weighting.

7. Summary

Creating arguments is hard. It is hard for humans and it is hard for computer programs (Section 1). It is difficult for both of them partly due to this task's control problems: how does one decide what to do and when to do it? In particular, control decisions must resolve competing 'specification-driven' and 'case-driven' influences. To argue with cases effectively, one has to arrive at an idea of the overall form of the argument one would like to make, the legal categories that must be addressed and the kinds of precedents that would be useful. In those determinations one is constrained all the while by the precedents (and the rules) that can be unearthed (Section 2).

We have tried to elucidate some of the difficulties of creating arguments by presenting two sets of related ideas. The first set of ideas stems from the observation that legal argument often comes in stereotypical forms and that these forms can be placed in a taxonomy (Section 4). The other set of ideas arises out of the computational model implemented in CABARET of how to use cases to interpret terms in legal rules (Sections 3 and 5). The model distills aspects of statutory argument into three parts: assuming argument strategies, making argument moves, and implementing primitive argument techniques. The connection between the two sets of ideas is that this model appears to contain the vocabulary and methods necessary to implement actual legal argument forms (Section 6). Finally, we envision that these implemented forms could be applied as control devices to combine the top-down and bottom-up facets of case-based argument formation.

Acknowledgements

In a review of a previous draft of this article, Donald Berman provided many of the Alice examples of argument styles in the home office deduction area. We are grateful to him for expanding beyond recognition his role as reviewer. The rule-based reasoner and many of the other software tools used by CABARET were written by Dan Suthers. Elizabeth Gene and Tony Reish also programmed elements of CABARET. We thank Scott Anderson, Timur Friedman and an anonymous reviewer for their comments on a draft of this article.

References

Alvarado, S.J. 1990. *Understanding Editorial Text: A Computer Model of Argument Comprehension*. Boston, MA: Kluwer Academic Publishers.

Alvarado, S.J. 1991. Interrelationships Between Reasoning and Planning in One-Sided Arguments. *Working Notes, AAAI Spring Symposium Series: Argument and Belief*. Palo Alto, CA.

Ashley, K.D. 1987. Distinguishing – A Reasoner's Wedge. *Proceedings, Ninth Annual Cognitive Science Society Conference*. Seattle, WA.

Ashley, K.D. 1988. *Modelling Legal Argument: Reasoning with Case and Hypotheticals*. Ph.D. Thesis, Department of Computer and Information Science, University of Massachusetts, Amherst, MA.

Ashley, K.D. 1989. Toward a Computational Theory of Arguing with Precedents: Accommodating Multiple Interpretations of Cases. *The Second International Conference on Artificial Intelligence and Law*, 93–102. Vancouver, BC. Association for Computing Machinery.

Ashley, K.D. 1990 . *Modelling Legal Argument: Reasoning with Cases and Hypotheticals*. Cambridge, MA: M.I.T. Press.

Ashley, K.D. 1991 . Toward an Intelligent Case-Based Tutorial Program for Teaching Students to Argue with Cases. *Working Notes, AAAI Spring Symposium Series: Argument and Belief*. Palo Alto, CA.

Ashley, K.D. & Aleven, V. 1991 . A Computational Approach to Explaining Case-Based Concepts of Relevance in a Tutorial Context. *Proceedings, Case-Based Reasoning Workshop 1991*, 257–268. Washington, DC. Morgan Kaufmann.

Ashley, K.D. & Rissland, E.L. 1986 . Towards Modelling Legal Argument. In A.A. Martino & F.S. Natali (Eds.), *Automated Analysis of Legal Texts. Logic, Informatics. Law* (pp. 19–30). Elsevier (North-Holland).

Ashley, K.D. & Rissland, E.L. 1987 . But, See, Accord: Generating Blue Book Citations in HYPO. *Proceedings, First International Conference on Artificial Intelligence and Law*, 67–74. Northeastern University, Boston, MA. Association for Computing Machinery.

Ashley, K.D. & Rissland, E.L. 1988a . A Case-Based Approach to Modelling legal Expertise. *IEEE Expert*, 3(3), 70–77.

Ashley, K.D. & Rissland, E.L. 1988 . Waiting on Weighting: A Symbolic Least Commitment Approach. *Proceedings, Seventh National Conference on Artificial Intelligence*, 239–244. Minneapolis, MN. American Association for Artificial Intelligence.

August, S.E. & McNamee, L.P. 1991 . ARIEL: A Model of Analogy Understanding in Arguments. *Working Notes, AAAI Spring Symposium Series: Argument and Belief*. Palo Alto, CA.

Bellairs, K. 1989 . *Contextual Relevance in Analogical Reasoning: A Model of Legal Argument*. Ph.D. Thesis, University of Minnesota, St. Paul, MN.

Berman, D. & Hafner, C. 1991 . Incorporating Procedural Context into a Model of Case-Based Legal Reasoning. *Proceedings of the Third International Conference on Artificial Intelligence and Law*, 12–20. Oxford, England. Association for Computing Machinery.

Birnbaum, L. 1982 . Argument Molecules: A Functional Representation of Argument Structure. *AAAI-82. Proceedings of the National Conference on Artificial Intelligence*. Pittsburgh, PA. American Association for Artificial Intelligence.

Birnbaum, L. 1985 . A Short Note on Opportunistic Planning and Memory in Arguments. *Proceedings, Ninth International Joint Conference on Artificial Intelligence*, 281–283. Los Angeles, CA. American Association for Artificial Intelligence.

Birnbaum, L., Flowers, M. & McGuire, R. 1980 . Towards an AI Model of Argumentation. *AAAI-80. Proceedings of the National Conference on Artificial Intelligence*. Palo Alto, CA. American Association for Artificial Intelligence.

BlueBook. 1986 . *A Uniform System of Citation* (14th ed.). Cambridge, MA: Harvard Law Review Association.

Branting, L.K. 1989. Integrating Generalizations with Exemplar-Based Reasoning. *The Second DARPA Case-Based Reasoning Workshop*. Pensacola Beach, FL. Morgan Kaufmann.

Branting, L.K. 1990. *Integrating Rules and Precedents for Classification and Explanation: Automating Legal Analysis*. Ph.D. Thesis, University of Texas, Austin, TX. Available as Artificial Intelligence Laboratory Technical Report AI90-46.

Branting, L.K. 1991 . Building Explanations from Rules and Structured Cases. *International Journal of Man-Machine Studies*, vol. 34(6), 797-838.

Carbonell, J.G. 1983 . Learning by Analogy: Formulating and Generalizing Plans from Past Experience. In

R.S. Michalski, J.G. Carbonell & T.M. Mitchell (Eds.), *Machine Learning: An Artificial Intelligence Approach* (pp. 137–162). Los Altos, CA: Morgan Kaufmann.

Carbonell, J.G. 1986. Derivational Analogy: A Theory of Reconstructive Problem Solving and Expertise Acquisition. In R.S. Michalski, J.G. Carbonell & T.M. Mitchell (Eds.), *Machine Learning: An Artificial Intelligence Approach* (pp. 371–392). Los Altos, CA: Morgan Kaufmann.

Clark, P. 1988. Representing Arguments as Background Knowledge for the Justification of Case-Based Inferences. *Proceedings, Case-Based Reasoning Workshop, AAAI-88*. Minneapolis-St. Paul, MN.

Cohen, P.R. 1987. The Control of Reasoning under Uncertainty. *The Knowledge Engineering Review*, 2, 5–25.

Ely, J.H. 1975. Comment, Flag Desecration: A Case Study in the Roles of Categorizational Balancing in First Amendment Analysis. *Harvard Law Review*, 88, 7(May), 1482.

Falkenhainer, B., Forbus, K. & Gentner, D. 1989. The Structure-Mapping Engine: Algorithm and Examples. *Artificial Intelligence*, 41, 1 (November), 1–63.

Flowers, M., McGuire, R. & Birnbaum, L. 1982. Adversary Arguments and the Logic of Personal Attacks. In W. Lehnert & M. Ringle (Eds.), *Strategies for Natural Language Processing* (pp. 275-294). Hillsdale, NJ: Lawrence Erlbaum.

Fuller, L.L. 1958. Positivism and Fidelity to Law: A Reply to Professor Hart. *Harvard Law Review*, 71, 630–672.

Gardner, A. vdl. 1987. *An Artificial Intelligence Approach to Legal Reasoning*. Cambridge, MA: M.I.T. Press.

Gentner, D. 1983. Structure-Mapping: A Theoretical Framework for Analogy. *Cognitive Science*, 7, 155–170.

Gibbons, H. 1991. *The Death of Jeffrey Stapleton: An Exploration of Legal Reasoning*. (In Press).

Golding, A.R. & Rosenbloom, P.S. 1991. Improving Rule-Based Systems through Case-Based Reasoning. *Proceedings, Ninth National Conference on Artificial Intelligence*, Anaheim, CA. American Association for Artificial Intelligence.

Goldman, S.R., Dyer, M.G. & Flowers, M. 1987. Precedent-based Legal Reasoning and Knowledge Acquisition in Contract Law. *Proceedings of the First International Conference on Artificial Intelligence and Law*. Boston, MA. Association for Computing Machinery.

Gordon, T.F. 1991. An Abductive Theory of Legal Issues. *International Journal of Man-Machine Studies*, 35, 95–118.

Hart, H.L.A. 1958. Positivism and the Separation of Law and Morals. *Harvard Law Review*, 71, 593-629.

Henkin, L. 1968. The Supreme Court, 1967 Term – Forward: On Drawing Lines. *Harvard Law Review*, 82, 63.

Holyoak, K.J. & Thagard, P. 1989. Analogical Mapping by Constraint Satisfaction. *Cognitive Science*, 13 (July–September, 1989), 295–355.

Kennedy, D. 1982. The Stages of the Decline of the Public/Private Distinction. Draft, Prepared as a comment for a seminar on 'The Public/Private Distinction' sponsored by the University of Pennsylvania Law Review on January 23, 1982.

Kennedy, D. 1989. *A Semiotics of Legal Argument*. Draft manuscript.

Knobbe, K.G. 1986. *Hobby and Home Office Deductions – Sections 183 and 280A*. Edited by L.L. Silverstein, Tax Management Portfolio, vol. 241–4th. Washington, DC: Tax Management, Inc.

Lakatos, I. 1976. *Proofs and Refutations*. London: Cambridge University Press.

Levi, E.H. 1949. *An Introduction to Legal Reasoning*. Chicago, IL: University of Chicago Press.

Llewellyn, K.N. 1989. *The Case Law System in America*. Chicago, IL: University of Chicago Press.

Marshall, C.C. 1989. Representing the Structure of Legal Argument. *Proceedings, Second International Conference on Artificial Intelligence and Law*. Vancouver, BC. Association for Computing Machinery.

McCarty, L.T. & Sridharan, N.S. 1982. *A Computational Theory of Legal Argument* (LRP-TR-13). Laboratory for Computer Science Research, Rutgers University.

McGuire, R., Birnbaum, L. & Flowers, M. 1981. Opportunistic Processing in Arguments. *Proceedings, Seventh International Joint Conference on Artificial Intelligence*, 58–60, Vancouver, BC. International Joint Conferences on Artificial Intelligence.

Morris, C. 1937. *How Lawyers Think* (Swallow Paperbooks ed.). Cambridge, MA: Harvard.

Perelman, C. & Olbrechts-Tyteca, L. 1969. *The New Rhetoric: A Treatise on Argumentation*. Notre Dame, Indiana: University of Notre Dame Press.

Polya, G. 1973. *How to Solve It* (Second Ed.). Princeton, NJ: Princeton University Press.

Rissland, E.L. 1990. Artificial Intelligence and Law: Stepping Stones to a Model of Legal Reasoning. *Yale Law Journal*, 99(8), 1957–1982.

Rissland, E.L. 1985. Argument Moves and Hypotheticals. In C. Walter (Ed.), *Computing Power and Legal Reasoning*, St. Paul, MN: West Publishing Co.

Rissland, E.L. & Ashley, K.D. 1986. Hypotheticals as Henristic Device. Proceedings, Fifth National Conference on Artificial Intelligence, 289–297. Philadelphia, PA. American Association for Artificial Intelligence.

Rissland, E.L & Skalak, D.B. 1989. Combining Case-Based and Rule-Based Reasoning: A Heuristic Approach. *Proceedings of the Eleventh International Joint Conference on Artificial Intelligence*, 524–530. Detroit, MI. International Joint Conferences on Artificial Intelligence.

Rissland, E.L. & Skalak, D. B. 1991. CABARET: Rule Interpretation in a Hybrid Architecture. *International Journal of Man-Machine Studies* 34(6):839–887.

Rissland, E.L., Valcarce, E.M. & Ashley, K.D. 1984. Explaining and Arguing with Examples. *AAAI-84. Proceedings of The National Conference on Artificial Intelligence*. Austin, TX. American Association for Artificial Intelligence.

Skalak, D.B. 1989. Taking Advantage of Models for Legal Classification. *Proceedings, Second International Conference on Artificial Intelligence and Law*, 234–241. Vancouver, BC. Association for Computing Machinery.

Skalak, D.B. & Rissland, E.L. 1991. Argument Moves in a Rule-Guided Domain. *Proceedings, Third International Conference on Artificial Intelligence and Law*, 1–11. Oxford, England. Association for Computing Machinery.

Storrs, G. 1991. Extensions to Toulmin Form for Capturing Real Arguments. *Working Notes. AAAI Spring Symposium Series: Argument and Belief*. Palo Alto, CA.

Stucky, B.K. 1986. *Understanding Legal Argument*. Counselor Project Technical Report 13. Department of Computer Science, University of Massachusetts. Amherst, MA.

Stucky, B.K. & Gidley, J.M. 1990. Legal Argument with Counterplans. *Workshop Notes. Artificial Intelligence and Legal Reasoning Workshop. AAAI-90*. Boston, MA.

Swartout, W. & Balzer, R. 1982. On the Inevitable Intertwining of Specification and Programming. *Communications of the ACM*, 25(7), July.

Sycara, K.P. 1985. Arguments of Persuasion in Labour Mediation. *Proceedings, Ninth International Joint Conference on Artificial Intelligence*, 294–296. Los Angeles, CA. International Joint Conferences on Artificial Intelligence.

Sycara, K.P. 1987. *Resolving Adversarial Conflicts: An Approach Integrating Case-Based and Analytic Methods*. Ph.D. Thesis. School of Information and Computer Science, Georgia Institute of Technology. Atlanta, GA.

Sycara, K.P. 1989. Argumentation: Planning Other Agents' Plans. *Proceedings, Eleventh International Joint Conference on Artificial Intelligence*, 517–523. Detroit, MI. International Joint Conferences on Artificial Intelligence.

Sycara, K.P. 1991. Pursuing Persuasive Argumentation. *Working Notes. AAAI Spring Symposium Series: Argument and Belief*. Palo Alto, CA.

Toulmin, S. 1958. *The Uses of Argument*. Cambridge, England: Cambridge University Press.

Twining, W. & Miers, D. 1982. *How To Do Things With Rules* (Second Ed.). London: Weidenfeld and Nicolson.

Winston, P.H. 1980. Learning and Reasoning by Analogy. *Communications of the ACM*, 23(12).

Winston, P.H. 1982. Learning New Principles from Precedents and Exercises. *Artificial Intelligence*, 19, 321–350.

Wu, H.J.P. & Lytinen, S.L. 1991. Attitude and Coherence Reasoning in Persuasive Discourse, *Working Notes. AAAI Spring Symposium Series: Argument and Belief*. Palo Alto, CA.

A Theory of Preliminary Fact Investigation*

*Peter Tillers** and David Schum****

* We blame no one except ourselves for any errors in our Article, but we are grateful for the comments and suggestions made by William Twining, Robert Thompson, Paul Shupack, Bernard Robertson, John Jackson, Ward Edwards, Terence Connolly, David Carlson, Terence Anderson, and Ronald Allen. We are also grateful for having been allowed to present and discuss the ideas in this Article at various institutions and conferences, including the University of Southern California Law Center (Apr. 12, 1988), Flaschner Judicial Institute (May 12, 1988), Oxford University Law Faculty Seminar (May 30, 1988), University College London Seminar (June 11, 1988), University of Southern California 28th Annual Bayesianism Conference (Feb. 15-17, 1989), Boston College Law School (Oct. 27, 1989), Cardozo School of Law Evidence Workshop (Jan. 25, 1990), International Conference on Forensic Statistics at the University of Edinburgh (Apr. 2, 1990), and George Mason University Law School Faculty Seminar (Oct. 2, 1990). The research reported in this Article was supported by National Science Foundation Grants SES-8704377 and SES-9007693 to George Mason University.

** Professor of Law and Director, International Seminar on Evidence in Litigation, Benjamin N. Cardozo School of Law, Yeshiva University.
*** Professor of Information Technology and Operations Research/ Applied Statistics, George Mason University.

291

INTRODUCTION

Anon., "Just imagine!" (date unknown)

How do human beings *know*? And how can human beings make
sure that they know the truth? These are old questions.[1] How-

---

[1] *See, e.g.*, PLATO, *Thaetetus*, in THE COLLECTED DIALOGUES OF PLATO (E.
Hamilton & H. Cairns eds. 1961).

ever, their shape has changed, or so many people think. Until very recently — roughly until the middle of the twentieth century — many observers believed that the question of the foundations of human knowledge is an unanswerable philosophical riddle.[2] Today, however, there are signs of a shift in the attitude toward epistemological issues. A diverse group of theorists views the riddle of human knowledge as a practical problem that admits of answers.[3] These epistemological optimists would reject the wry suggestion that "cognitive science" is an oxymoron; they believe that a science of the mind is possible.[4] Indeed, some of these optimists are hyperoptimists. In recent years "neural networks" have become one of the hottest topics in the field of computer

---

[2] *See, e.g.*, L. WITTGENSTEIN, ON CERTAINTY (G. Anscombe & G. von Wright eds. 1969) (notes made by Wittgenstein in 1950-51). A more recent example of epistemological skepticism is N. GOODMAN, FACT, FICTION, AND FORECAST (2d ed. 1965). Another contemporary example may be Thomas Kuhn's theory of the evolution of scientific theory, which seems to have relativizing and possibly skeptical implications. *See* T. KUHN, THE STRUCTURE OF SCIENTIFIC REVOLUTIONS (1962). Epistemological skepticism, of course, has a long history. *See, e.g.*, D. HUME, ENQUIRY INTO THE HUMAN UNDERSTANDING (1748). *See generally* Popkin, *Skepticism*, in 7 THE ENCYCLOPEDIA OF PHILOSOPHY (1967) (providing historical overview).

Of course, even though some philosophers may have despaired at explaining how and why people know, people went on knowing anyway. They unravelled some of the mysteries of the atom, they developed the periodic table of the elements, they predicted weather, and the like.

[3] *See, e.g.*, A. GOLDMAN, EPISTEMOLOGY AND COGNITION (1986); *see also infra* notes 4-5.

[4] *See, e.g.*, Z. PYLYSHYN, COMPUTATION AND COGNITION xi (1984) (stating: "there is another, much more exciting possibility: the prospect that cognitive science is a genuine scientific domain like the domains of chemistry, biology, economics, or geology").

Only some of the theorists alluded to in this Article are professionally employed solely as "cognitive scientists." One of them is Paul Thagard, mentioned at *infra* note 5. The others have various kinds of professional titles. For example, Alvin Goldman, *supra* note 3, holds a professorship in philosophy. Zenon Pylyshyn, *supra*, holds a professorship in psychology and computer science and is the director of a center for cognitive science. Paul Churchland, *infra* note 5, is a professor of philosophy and a faculty member of a cognitive science department. Whatever their nominal fields, however, these theorists are students of cognitive science. *See* Z. PYLYSHYN, *supra*; A. GOLDMAN, *supra* note 3; and P. THAGARD and P. CHURCHLAND, *infra* note 5. The diverse professional backgrounds of these epistemological optimists is not surprising. Their work blends elements of psychology (cognitive science), philosophy (epistemology), mathematics (logic), and computer science (artificial intelligence and computer logic).

logic and artificial intelligence. Some students of cognitive science believe that "neurocomputational" logic may allow them to model and mimic the operations of the brain, and not just understand them.[5]

We share the view that real progress in understanding human knowledge is now possible. In one respect, however, we part ways with the more enthusiastic advocates of artificial intelligence, neural networks, computational models of the mind, and the like. We believe that imagination plays an essential role in all human knowledge, and we believe that no model of the mind, no matter how esoteric or subtle, can duplicate, much less replace, the imaginative activities of the human mind. Despite our skepticism about machine-minds, however, we think it is important to use logic to map the operations of the mind. Logic portrays human thought in an orderly way. Logical pictures of possible ways of thinking can facilitate orderly and imaginative reasoning about facts.

Fact investigation in litigation is hard to do well.[6] One of the causes of investigative failure is conceptual failure; effective investigation requires good thinking. This Article describes a device for ordering thought during preliminary fact investigation: a network of twelve systems for marshalling evidence. Although this network is not a machine that somehow churns out good investigative decisions all by itself, it is a useful tool for the analysis of investigative problems. The network of evidence marshalling strategies described in this Article facilitates good thinking about problems of evidence in the early stages of fact investigation in litigation.

In Part I of the Article we provide a bird's-eye view of our theory. We identify twelve separate systems or strategies for mar-

[5] *See, e.g.*, P. CHURCHLAND, A NEUROCOMPUTATIONAL PERSPECTIVE: THE NATURE OF MIND AND THE STRUCTURE OF SCIENCE (1989); P. THAGARD, COMPUTATIONAL PHILOSOPHY OF SCIENCE (1988).

[6] There is a substantial body of literature on fact investigation. The quality of this literature is uneven, but some of it is quite good. *See, e.g.*, T. ANDERSON & W. TWINING, ANALYSIS OF EVIDENCE (rev. ed. 1987) (forthcoming Little, Brown & Co. 1991); M. BERGER, J. MITCHELL & R. CLARK, PRETRIAL ADVOCACY: PLANNING, ANALYSIS AND STRATEGY (1988); D. BINDER & P. BERGMAN, FACT INVESTIGATION: FROM HYPOTHESIS TO PROOF (1984); E. IMWINKELRIED & T. BLUMOFF, PRETRIAL DISCOVERY: STRATEGY & TACTICS (1986-1988 & Supp. 1990); *see also* Brazil, *The Adversary Character of Civil Discovery: A Critique and Proposals for Change*, 31 VAND. L. REV. 1295 (1978).

shalling evidence. We provide in Part I a brief description of each of these methods of marshalling evidence, and we suggest how these various marshalling strategies can influence each other. A diagram depicts the entire theory as a network of linked marshalling operations.[7]

In Part II we describe several of the marshalling strategies in more detail. In particular, we discuss how factual hypotheses are constructed, refined, and also "coarsened."[8] We pay close attention to the impact of evidentiary trifles, or details, on the formation of factual hypotheses and conjectures.[9] Evidentiary details support and suggest various possibilities, and a detail combined with one or more other details may suggest and support yet further possibilities. Since different combinations of details suggest and support different possibilities, arranging and combing evidentiary trifles in various ways may be a useful heuristic exercise. However, even a small number of details can be combined in many different ways. Shuffling details in a random fashion to see what they suggest is inefficient. Therefore, we describe several systematic procedures for combining details and for flushing out the possibilities that different combinations of details might suggest or support.[10]

In Part II we also discuss strategies for eliminating hypotheses and possibilities, but strategies for generating factual hypotheses and conjectures remain our primary concern. Although shuffling combinations of details is a useful strategy for generating hypotheses, it is not always sufficient. Imagination and conjecture play an essential role in effective fact investigation.[11] While most of our methods for flushing possibilities out of details and combinations of details require the use of imagination, not all of the strategies involve fancy or conjecture. For example, we describe a strategy of marshalling evidence by "possibilities." This strategy involves imaginative reasoning but not conjecture because marshalling by possibilities supposes that every possibility must be directly supported by the evidence.[12] It is often useful — and it may be essential — however, to entertain possibilities that go past or "outrun" the available evidence. Hence, some of the "abduc-

---

[7] *See infra* Figure 2 and accompanying text.

[8] *See infra* text accompanying notes 123-38.

[9] *See infra* text accompanying notes 123-34.

[10] *See infra* text accompanying Figures 5-9.

[11] *See infra* text accompanying notes 141-49.

[12] *See infra* Section I(C)(8).

tive" marshalling strategies we describe generate hypotheses that are not directly supported by evidence.[13] For example, we discuss the role of stories in hypothesis formation.[14] Stories, or "scenarios," combine elements of fact and fancy.

The Article concludes with some general observations about the nature of our theory. We argue that our network of evidence marshalling systems, though complex, is "user-friendly" at least in principle.[15] The intellectual processes and operations we describe do not have a "transcendental" character or origin, but are "natural" to ordinary thinking human beings. It is true that the workings of our network of marshalling systems can be very intricate: the twelve marshalling systems can interact in complex ways, and users of our network may be forced to pay attention to several marshalling operations simultaneously. The obstacles to the use of our marshalling systems are no greater than those presently faced by real-world investigators, however, who must already walk and chew gum at the same time. The purpose of our theory is to facilitate the management of already complex tasks.

Our final observations concern the computer-generated diagrams and devices that we use to depict the network of evidence marshalling operations. We argue that our computer-generated visual representations serve a theoretical purpose as well as a practical one. These representations are metaphors. The fact that they are user-friendly — the fact that they make complex strategies for organizing evidence more understandable and intelligible — is some evidence of the validity of our theory. Our theory is a map of the mind. If it is a good map, it will enable us to think more clearly.

I. Outline of Theory

A. The Place of Preliminary Fact Investigation in the Life Cycle of Litigation

The traditional centerpiece of American legal scholarship in evidence is the trial. Wigmore's mammoth treatise on the law of

---

[13] *See infra* Section II (B)(1).

[14] *See infra* text accompanying notes 154-62.

[15] Although we have not yet developed a user-friendly technology for implementing the network in real-time, real-world situations, we believe the development of such user-friendly systems is possible. We have developed computer based prototypes of our evidence marshalling systems. *See infra* text accompanying notes 51-53, 171.

evidence[16] devotes little attention to the pretrial process. As its title suggests, its focus is on the legal rules governing the admissibility and presentation of evidence at trial.[17] The focus of Wigmore's contemporaries and successors was much the same; scholars such as Edmund Morgan, Charles McCormick, and John Maguire talked about the trial, and little if at all about evidentiary processes before trial.[18]

Things are not much different today.[19] Contemporary casebooks, legal treatises, and "hornbooks" on evidence typically pay little attention to evidentiary processes before trial.[20] The new evidence scholarship has not significantly diminished the traditional emphasis on the trial. Although the new evidence scholarship focuses more on proof and less on the admissibility of evidence at trial,[21] the work of the new evidence scholars focuses on the process of proof at trial,[22] and only little is said about evi-

---

[16] J. WIGMORE, A TREATISE ON THE ANGLO-AMERICAN SYSTEM OF EVIDENCE IN TRIALS AT COMMON LAW (3d ed. 1940).

[17] Wigmore's treatise on the logic of proof, however, devotes substantial attention to fact investigation. *See* J. WIGMORE, THE PRINCIPLES OF JUDICIAL PROOF §§ 156-58 (1913) [hereafter J. WIGMORE, JUDICIAL PROOF]. Until recently, however, Wigmore's work on the logic of proof had little effect on the work of other evidence scholars. *See* W. TWINING, THEORIES OF EVIDENCE: BENTHAM AND WIGMORE 112-13 (1985).

[18] *See, e.g.*, J. MAGUIRE, EVIDENCE: COMMON SENSE AND COMMON LAW (1947); C. McCORMICK, HANDBOOK OF THE LAW OF EVIDENCE (1954); E. MORGAN, BASIC PROBLEMS OF STATE AND FEDERAL EVIDENCE (5th ed. 1976).

[19] There is, however, one important exception. Clinical education has emerged as an important force in American legal education. Although clinical courses in litigation tend to emphasize trial practice, a substantial number of clinical offerings deal with pretrial practice and preparation. Even in these courses, however, systematic study of the logic of evidentiary processes is often absent. The emphasis instead is on the "touchie-feelie" aspects of fact investigation and case preparation (*e.g.*, the personal and social dynamics of witness interviews). In recent years, however, clinicians have generated literature in a rather different, more analytic vein. *See, e.g.*, D. BINDER & P. BERGMAN and E. IMWINKELRIED & T. BLUMOFF, *supra* note 6.

[20] *See, e.g.*, L. LETWIN, EVIDENCE LAW: COMMENTARY, PROBLEMS AND CASES (1986); G. LILLY, AN INTRODUCTION TO THE LAW OF EVIDENCE (2d ed. 1987); J. WEINSTEIN & M. BERGER, WEINSTEIN'S EVIDENCE MANUAL (1987); G. WEISSENBERGER, FEDERAL EVIDENCE (Student Edition) (1987).

[21] Lempert, *The New Evidence Scholarship: Analyzing the Process of Proof*, 66 B.U.L. REV. 439, 439-40 (1986).

[22] For example, the extensive debate about Dr. Cohen's "conjunction paradox" has always addressed that supposed paradox in the context of a trial. *See* Allen, *A Reconceptualization of Civil Trials*, 66 B.U.L. REV. 401, 405-07 (1986).

dentiary processes before trial.[23]

There are good practical reasons to bemoan this emphasis on the trial,[24] but there are also theoretical disadvantages. When a case goes to trial — particularly when a case is submitted to the trier of fact — the factual issues in the case have been determined with a relative degree of specificity, and the evidence to be considered by the decision maker is known. If theorists view the trial as the paradigmatic setting for problems of evidence, inference, and proof, they are likely to focus on a type of inferential analysis that we call "relational analysis."[25] This is because in the sort of trial setting we have described, the most obvious responsibility of the trier of fact is to determine how strongly known evidence supports the factual contentions that the parties and the court have identified and formulated.[26] As this Article demonstrates, however, the process of proof in litigation involves forms of analysis

---

[23] There are some exceptions. *See, e.g.,* Jackson, *Theories of Truth Finding in Criminal Procedure: An Evolutionary Approach,* 10 CARDOZO L. REV. 475 (1988); Schum, *Probability and the Processes of Discovery, Proof, and Choice,* 66 B.U.L. REV. 825 (1986). *Cf. supra* note 6 (listing some scholarly works on fact investigation).

[24] For example, litigators spend far more time preparing cases than trying them. Pretrial preparation undoubtedly has a major impact on the outcomes of the relatively few cases that are tried. Pretrial fact investigation in criminal cases raises a wide variety of constitutional issues and careful analysis of the evidentiary dimensions of those problems would be helpful. *See infra* text accompanying notes 35-43.

The preoccupation with the trial cannot be justified by the important insight that proof and admissibility requirements at trial influence and shape pretrial activity. Although the trial does cast a backward shadow, pretrial processes and activities also cast a shadow into the future. While some features of trials may be invariant, many are not, and actors such as lawyers and police detectives know that the character of their pretrial investigation and preparation will influence the structure of any subsequent trial, including the character of the evidence presented at any such trial. Hence, the requirements for effective pretrial investigation and preparation cannot be "read off" directly or simply from the general rules and principles regulating admissibility and proof at trial. The expected structure and characteristics of a trial naturally influence pretrial activity. Yet, decision makers in litigation expect that the structure and characteristics of a trial in any particular case will be affected by pretrial proceedings and events, including the decisions that participants such as lawyers make before trial.

[25] Tillers & Schum, *Charting New Territory in Judicial Proof: Beyond Wigmore,* 9 CARDOZO L. REV. 907 (1988).

[26] Jury instructions, of course, tell the jury that this is one of its primary responsibilities. *See, e.g.,* 1 CALIFORNIA JURY INSTRUCTIONS: CRIMINAL (CALJIC) 2.20 (5th ed. 1988).

other than relational analysis. For example, the process of proof involves the formation and differentiation of factual hypotheses[27] and the acquisition of new evidence. Cognitive processes of this sort can and do take place during a trial,[28] but many of them are far more palpable in the pretrial process than at the trial itself.[29] Hence, fact investigation is a field of study that offers important insights into the nature of inference and proof in litigation.[30]

When we began our research, we hoped to examine marshalling processes throughout the life cycle of inferential problems in litigation.[31] Figure 1 is a representation of what we imagined a full-scale life cycle might include.

---

[27] *See infra* Section II(A).

[28] For example, although the factual issues in a case may have been determined by the court by the start of trial (*e.g.*, in a pretrial conference), the issues as defined may still be relatively diffuse, and the lawyers at the trial may attempt to formulate them more precisely. Similarly, lawyers at a trial will frequently be faced with the decision whether to acquire additional evidence (*e.g.*, by cross-examining a witness about matters on which the witness has not been questioned before).

[29] This is partly, but not entirely, because: (1) in the early stages of litigation factual issues are typically less stable (*i.e.*, more dynamic, more likely to change) than they are at the trial; (2) the factual issues "in the case" are ordinarily less precisely defined in early phases of litigation than in later phases; and (3) at the outset of a lawsuit the quantity of the pertinent evidence and information is typically far more meager than it is by the time of trial.

[30] Some law teachers may think that fact investigation is the wrong horse to ride in the pursuit of theoretical objectives. To judge by the their choice of subject matter in the typical course in civil procedure, many civil procedure teachers seem to think of fact investigation as a nuts-and-bolts topic that is bereft of any theoretical significance. However, the view that fact investigation lacks theoretical charm is mistaken. While it is true that fact investigation involves tedious and pedestrian work — very often a great deal of it — it is not true that fact investigation in litigation is a simple intellectual activity; it is an immensely complex activity that implicates the highest reaches of human thought. In particular, imagination plays a crucial role in the initial stages of the process of judicial proof. This fact alone makes fact investigation a worthy object of study. *See infra* Sections II(B) and II(C)(2).

[31] We sketched our research objectives in Tillers & Schum, *supra* note 25. For an unduly defensive comment on our sketch, see W. TWINING, RETHINKING EVIDENCE: EXPLORATORY ESSAYS 319 (1990). In defending Wigmore's evidence marshalling strategy against a nonexistent attack, however, Twining glosses over the difference between a marshalling strategy that is compatible with other evidence marshalling strategies and methods of organizing evidence and devices that portray other evidence marshalling strategies. *Id.* For example, while it is true that Wigmore's

FIGURE 1

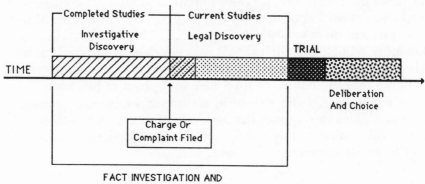

FACT INVESTIGATION AND
OTHER PRETRIAL ACTIVITIES

This life cycle includes investigation, legal discovery and other pretrial preparation, the trial, and deliberation and choice by the trier of fact.[32] Very soon after we began our work, however, we realized that the full life cycle of the process of judicial proof involves a far larger number of types of marshalling and inferential activity than Figure 1 shows.[33] We therefore chose to limit the scope of our project and decided that a good place to begin a study of the process of judicial proof was at the beginning. Hence, instead of trying to tackle the entire process of proof, we use this Article to examine only the initial pretrial evidentiary processes.[34] We refer to these initial phases of the process of

---

"chart method" is compatible with the use of scenarios, the chart method does not portray the structure, formation, and evaluation of stories.

[32] *See* Schum, *supra* note 23, at 830-46.

[33] We did not foresee that preliminary fact investigation alone involves at least the twelve marshalling systems described in this Article. Figure 1, *supra*, offers, at best, only a hint of this complexity.

[34] It follows that our theory is not a complete theory of evidentiary processes in litigation, let alone a complete theory of empirical knowledge. For example, this Article does not examine the impact of resource limitations on the acquisition of human knowledge. Moreover, we do not consider how human beings might try to calculate the relative utility of divergent lines of real-world investigative activity. Furthermore, our Article does not examine how social, legal, or similar stipulations about initial assumptions affect the enterprise of finding out the "truth" about matters of fact. Nonetheless, our theory adds to an understanding of proof. Any comprehensive theory of judicial proof must take the history of any stage of proof into account. Moreover, the evidence marshalling strategies used in investigation also play a role in proceedings such as trials.

proof as "preliminary fact investigation."

A theory describing strategies for marshalling evidence in preliminary investigation may be valuable for a variety of reasons. First, if our theory holds any water, it ought to interest actors such as trial lawyers, who must marshal and analyze evidence. Moreover, a good theory of evidence marshalling during investigation may be beneficial for the society at large. A central function of litigation is the adjudication of factual disputes.[35] The reliability of factual adjudication is a matter of considerable importance from the standpoint of almost any perspective on litigation, whether from a moral,[36] social,[37] ideological,[38] or economic[39] perspective, or from the point of view of fields of law

---

[35] *Cf.* Rose v. Clark, 478 U.S. 570, 577 (1986)("the central purpose of a criminal trial is to decide the factual question of the defendant's guilt or innocence," quoting Delaware v. Van Arsdall, 475 U.S. 673, 681 (1986)).

[36] *See, e.g.*, Frankel, *The Search for the Truth: An Umpireal View*, 123 U. PA. L. REV. 1031 (1975) (criticizing existing adversary system for placing too low a premium on truth); Zuckerman, *Law, Fact or Justice?*, 66 B.U.L. REV. 487, 498-508 (1986) (emphasizing importance of accurate fact finding in each case). Even Professor Laurence Tribe, who stresses the moral, symbolic, and expressive functions of litigation and modes of proof in litigation, does not deny that factual truth is important. *See* Tribe, *Trial by Mathematics: Precision and Ritual in the Legal Process*, 84 HARV. L. REV. 1329, 1376 (1971) (stating: "It would be a terrible mistake to forget that a typical lawsuit is only *in part an objective search for the historical truth*") (emphasis added).

[37] Professor Charles Nesson emphasizes the importance of the "social acceptability" of verdicts but, like Tribe, *supra* note 36, he does not deny that truth is important. *See* Nesson, *The Evidence or the Event? On Judicial Proof and the Acceptability of Verdicts*, 98 HARV. L. REV. 1357, 1359 (1985)("Through trials, society *seeks* not only *to discover the truth* about a past event, but also to forge a link between crime and punishment") (emphasis added). Nesson suggests that there must be compromises between the value of truth and other values, but his argument assumes that truth is an important value. *Id.* at 1390-92.

[38] The ideal of the rule of law puts a premium on accurate fact finding. *See* Tillers, *Introduction, Symposium on Probability and Inference in the Law of Evidence*, 66 B.U.L. REV. 381, 381-82 (1986) [hereafter Tillers, *Introduction*]. Professor Kenneth Graham apparently does not share this view. *See* Graham, *Book Review, "There'll Always be an England": The Instrumental Ideology of Evidence*, 85 MICH. L. REV. 1204, 1232-34 (1987) (viewing ideal of law as an ideology and demanding "fairness" rather than accuracy in litigation). But see the rejoinders to Graham in Tillers, *Prejudice, Politics, and Proof*, 86 MICH. L. REV. 768, 773-74 (1988) and Twining, *Book Review, Hot Air in the Redwoods, a Sequel to the Wind in the Willows*, 86 MICH. L. REV. 1523, 1544-45 (1988).

[39] Tillers, *Introduction, supra* note 38, at 381.

such as the law of evidence[40] and constitutional law.[41] (There are dissenters, but they are few).[42] A theory about the logical and cognitive dimensions of fact investigation is germane to a concern about the reliability of adjudication because the manner in which actors in litigation marshal and analyze evidence affects litigation outcomes.[43]

While the practical significance of a valid theory of fact investigation may be substantial, the theoretical significance of the topic of fact investigation is no less important. Although we have said that our Article is about preliminary fact investigation, we might as easily have said that it is about "investigative discovery."[44] The

---

[40] The law of evidence has always put special emphasis on the reliability of fact finding. *See, e.g.*, FED. R. EVID. 102 ("to the end that the truth may be ascertained").

[41] *See, e.g.*, Perry v. Leeke, 109 S. Ct. 594, 601 (1989) (holding that in interest of trial's truth-seeking function, defendant-witness had no right to consult with attorney between direct and cross-examinations); Rose v. Clark, 478 U.S. 570, 579 (1986) (stating: "The thrust of many constitutional rules governing the conduct of criminal trials is to ensure that those trials lead to fair and correct judgments") *In re* Winship, 397 U.S. 358, 364 (1970) (reasonable doubt standard necessary in criminal cases because "[i]t is critical that the moral force of the criminal law not be diluted by a standard of proof that leaves people in doubt whether innocent men are being condemned"); Tehar v. Shott, 382 U.S. 406, 416 (1965).

[42] *See, e.g.*, Graham, *supra* note 38, at 1232-34 (1987); Weyrauch, *Law as Mask—Legal Ritual and Relevance*, 66 CALIF. L. REV. 699, 710 (1978) ("The rules of relevancy, in short, have little to do with logic, reason, daily experience, common knowledge, and proper courtroom atmosphere. They are, rather, the product of deep-seated and largely unconscious value choices.").

Professor John Langbein has argued that rules of evidence were introduced into English criminal trials only to serve the interests of lawyers, not to advance the search for the truth. *See* Langbein, *The Criminal Trial before the Lawyers*, 45 U. CHI. L. REV. 263 (1978). *Cf.* Brilmayer, *Wobble, or the Death of Error*, 59 S. CAL. L. REV. 363 (1986) (apparently arguing that idea of legal error is an incoherent if not illusory concept).

[43] Although many factors affect the accuracy of fact finding in litigation, the analytical and marshalling techniques used by decision makers do so as well.

[44] Preliminary fact investigation and investigative discovery overlap because investigative discovery tends to play an important role in the early stages of the life cycle of the process of proof in litigation. We use the phrase "investigative discovery" to distinguish it from the type of "discovery" authorized by Federal Rules of Civil Procedure 26-37. We refer to the latter type of discovery as "legal discovery." Investigative discovery may take place during legal discovery. Although investigative discovery is ordinarily most prominent during the earliest stages of litigation, it can and

function of proof is to provide an answer. Any answer, however, requires a question. Figuring out how to ask a good question is as important as figuring out how to answer a question.[45] In studying preliminary fact investigation, we are essentially studying a process of questioning.

Asking appropriate questions is partly an art; it requires imagination. Yet, just as imagination alone cannot produce a great work of art, imagination alone cannot generate useful questions. Mental discipline is required to produce either a great overture in a symphony or a productive question during fact investigation. The network of evidence marshalling strategies described in this Article constitutes a theory of the economics of questioning. Our theory speaks to the efficiency of the questioning process; it speaks to the effective and disciplined deployment of cognitive resources during the process of inquiry.[46]

---

does occur during other stages as well. Legal discovery, however, is not always investigative discovery; legal discovery can serve other purposes.

[45] A good answer to a bad question is worthless.

[46] Some observers believe that theories of mental processes (such as those involved in inference) are either descriptive or prescriptive. However, our theory of discovery and questioning neither describes how investigators actually think nor how investigators should think. Indeed, our theory does not even purvey conditional imperatives such as "If you wish to ask useful and productive questions, think this way or that way." Nonetheless, our theory is not an illegitimate hybrid. The range of possible types of theories of mental processes is not exhausted by the dichotomy between descriptive theories and prescriptive theories (or by the somewhat less common trichotomy between descriptive, prescriptive, and normative theories). This is because mental processes have two peculiar qualities. First, some mental processes are in the nature of standards. These standards, which "really exist," cannot be trapped either by a purely descriptive theory or by a purely prescriptive theory. *See* Tillers, *Mapping Inferential Domains*, 66 B.U.L. REV. 883, 932-33 (1986). *Cf.* 1 D. SCHUM, EVIDENCE AND INFERENCE FOR THE INTELLIGENCE ANALYST 376 (1987) (accepting distinction between cognitive performance and cognitive competence). Second, since it is not possible to demonstrate that natural standards of cognitive performance are defective, Cohen, *Can Human Irrationality Be Experimentally Demonstrated?*, 4 BEHAV. & BRAIN SCI. 317 (1981); Tillers, *supra*, at 933, there is no objective basis for claiming that any general way of thinking is better than another general way of thinking.

Although we do not see our theory as a purely normative theory of fact investigation, we do think that our theory describes strategies that can improve cognitive performance. However, given our conviction that the practical value of our theory to any individual must stand or fall at the bar of that individual's subjective judgment, it follows that our theory is nothing more than a tool, to be used by an individual as she sees fit. Hence, we

The question of the nature of discovery processes, of course, arises in contexts other than forensic proof and investigation; the issue has engaged the attention of philosophers and other people for generations.[47] It is therefore possible that a better understanding of the nature of investigative discovery in litigation has general implications. While it may be true that lawyers and judges use an "artificiall reason"[48] to interpret legal rules and principles, it probably is not true that lawyers, judges, and other participants in the process of litigation do use or should use entirely idiosyncratic mental and logical operations when addressing factual issues. Differences in methods of assessing evidence in legal contexts and in nonlegal contexts such as medicine and science may stem from contextual and situational factors and from the characteristics of specialized bodies of knowledge about particular types of phenomena. They do not necessarily stem from any fundamental differences in methods of analyzing problems of evidence and inference.

B. General Structure of Theory

Our theory consists of twelve linked systems for marshalling evidence. This entire network of systems is represented in Figure 2.

---

characterize our theory not as a descriptive theory, nor as a prescriptive theory, but as a theory of the possible. We describe a set of procedures that a rational person could use and might choose to use.

[47] *See, e.g.*, F. BACON, *The New Organon*, in THE NEW ORGANON AND RELATED WRITINGS 3 (F. Anderson ed. 1960); N. HANSON, PATTERNS OF DISCOVERY (1965); A. KOESTLER, THE ACT OF CREATION (1964); T. KUHN, *supra* note 2; P. LANGLEY, H. SIMON, G. BRADSHAW & J.M. ZYTKOW, SCIENTIFIC DISCOVERY: COMPUTATIONAL EXPLORATIONS OF THE CREATIVE PROCESS (1987); K. POPPER, THE LOGIC OF SCIENTIFIC DISCOVERY (1959); B. RUSSELL, HUMAN KNOWLEDGE: ITS SCOPE AND LIMITS (1948); I. SCHEFFLER, THE ANATOMY OF INQUIRY (1963); Hempel, *Fundamentals of Concept Formation in Empirical Science*, 2:7, INT'L ENCYLOPEDIA UNIFIED SCI. 1 (1952).

[48] COKE, COKE ON LITTLETON *62a ("Not . . . understood of eurie unlearned mans reason, but of artificiall and legall reason").

FIGURE 2

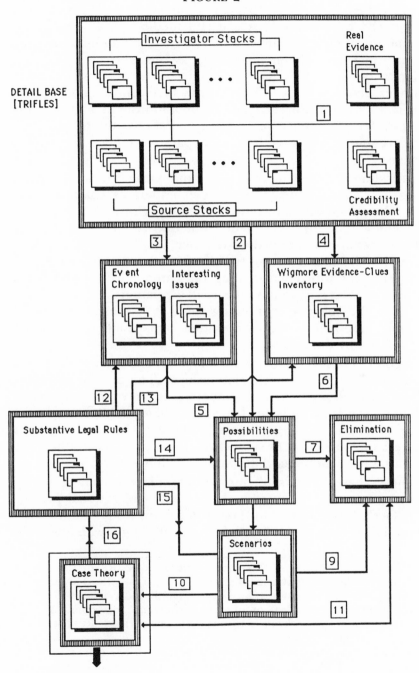

Figure 2 resembles an influence diagram. This resemblance is entirely deliberate. The concept of an influence diagram, first introduced by Howard,[49] is a useful method of describing the operations of complex networks. The nodes in an influence diagram, which typically appear either as boxes, circles, or ovals, refer to operations or functions. The arcs, or lines, represent linkages between nodes. Hence, arcs that connect nodes show the relations of different types of operations. In Figure 2 the nodes refer to evidence marshalling operations and the arcs indicate avenues of influence between separate evidence marshalling systems.[50]

In addition to showing operations and linkages between operations, our network diagram has two important characteristics. First, the operations shown there can be performed in any order (providing that the movement from one set of operations to another set of operations does not take a path for which there is no arc). The spatial arrangement of nodes or arcs conveys no suggestion of which marshalling operation must be the initial operation. More generally, the spatial relationships among the nodes in the network say nothing about the necessary or appropriate temporal order of the evidence marshalling operations symbolized by the nodes.

Second, our network diagram, unlike some influence diagrams, does not represent causal relationships. The arcs between the nodes, or evidence marshalling operations, only indicate avenues of influence; they indicate that marshalling schemes may influence other marshalling schemes. These avenues of influence express the possibility of subjective conceptual links, rather than of causal links, between different marshalling strategies.

These characteristics of our network diagram reflect several basic propositions about the characteristics of rational preliminary fact investigation. Our first proposition is that an investigation relating to matters of fact can rationally begin with any of the

---

49 Howard & Matheson, *Influence Diagrams*, in 2 READINGS ON THE PRINCIPLES AND APPLICATIONS OF DECISION ANALYSIS (R. Howard & J. Matheson eds. 1983); Howard, *Knowledge Maps*, 35 MGMT. SCI. 903 (1989). There is now a great deal of interest in influence diagrams. *See, e.g.*, Shachter, *Evaluating Influence Diagrams*, 34 OPERATIONS RESEARCH 871 (1986).

50 An influence diagram is an acyclical graph. In our diagram acyclical movement is possible. Hence, we will refer to the diagram in Figure 2 as the "network diagram."

marshalling systems symbolized by the nodes. The choice of where analysis starts depends on the nature of the problem and the judgment of the investigator. Second, we propose that the sequence of marshalling strategies is not objectively or causally determined, and we therefore believe that analysis can move from any given marshalling strategy along any of the arcs leading to other marshalling strategies. Thus, the order in which marshalling strategies should be used depends on the investigator's view of the nature of the problem she faces. Finally, since the arcs in the network diagram represent only possible avenues of influence, the design and contents of the network diagram do not imply that an investigator must use all of the marshalling schemes represented in the diagram. We believe that a rational investigator may make little or no use of a variety of the marshalling operations that we have identified. These three judgments taken together reflect our more global judgment that our theory is a device for mapping the mind rather than the world. Unlike the world, the mind is not determined by law-like principles.

The network diagram in Figure 2 also suggests how research on evidence marshalling strategies can combine theoretical analysis and technological considerations. While Figure 2 represents our analysis of marshalling strategies and the manner in which they may affect each other, it also reflects our attempt to use computer technology to facilitate the use of our theory in real-world settings. We have developed computer-implemented prototypes of each of the twelve evidence marshalling strategies in our theory, and we have developed a computer-based method of exhibiting the linkages among these prototypes of evidence marshalling strategies. The resulting network of linked evidence marshalling systems emulates a complex system of evidence marshalling operations.

Our attempt to construct computer prototypes of evidence marshalling systems is more than a gimmick; there is an intimate relationship between our work on theoretical issues and our work on technological issues. We will explain more of how and why this is so after we describe our theory in more detail.[51] We will make two general claims now. The first is that our theoretical analysis determines which prototypes need to be constructed. In addition, however, we claim that our computer-based prototypes are metaphors that illuminate and illustrate elements of our the-

---

[51] *See infra* CONCLUSION.

ory of evidence marshalling.[52] In particular, our computer prototypes of evidence marshalling strategies use the metaphor of a
stack of cards.[53] In our discussion of the marshalling of details,[54]
we illustrate how evidence marshalling strategies can be captured
with this metaphor.

C. Basic Characteristics of Individual Marshalling Systems

Our network of twelve marshalling systems can be broken
down into subgroups. The first subgroup is comprised of four of
these separate marshalling systems which together form a basic
detail or information base. Two of the systems in this subgroup
allow the marshalling of evidence from and about investigators
and other sources such as witnesses. A third system concerns real
or tangible evidence and structuring an analysis of the authenticity of such evidence. The fourth system concerns marshalling evidence about the competence and credibility of witnesses.

The second major subgroup is comprised of three systems concerned with the marshalling of combinations of details. One of
these systems facilitates the formation of event chronologies;
another marshals thought and evidence about issues of interest
that arise during investigation; and a third marshals evidence on
the basis of the order in which events occur and evidence of those
events appears.

The third major subgroup also contains three systems. These
systems are concerned primarily with the marshalling of possibilities and scenarios. One allows for the marshalling of evidence on
the basis of hypotheses, or possibilities, at various levels of refinement as they emerge during investigation. Another allows marshalling of evidence to eliminate possibilities in a systematic way.
The last system in the subgroup facilitates the construction of stories and scenarios, which serve to suggest new evidence and
possibilities.

The eleventh and twelfth systems can be classified under a
fourth subgroup centered around marshalling evidence on the
basis of legal doctrine. The eleventh system consists of a base of

---

[52] *See id.*

[53] This metaphor is taken from the software system we used in the
construction of our prototypes of evidence marshalling strategies. That
system is the "Hypercard" system developed by Apple Computer
Corporation.

[54] *See infra* Section I(C)(5).

legal rules and principles. The twelfth, and final, system allows for marshalling of evidence on the basis of the elements, or points, of these legal theories.

1. Marshalling Details

The first four marshalling systems concern details. Details, or small parcels of data, ordinarily accumulate very rapidly during an investigation. Since few investigators can match the ability of Sherlock Holmes to remember "trifles,"[55] the recording of details for later use is important.

There are practical and logistical difficulties in recording large quantities of information. The computer-based system we have constructed allows large numbers of trifles to be recorded and stored in a compact form. The storing of details, however, also involves theoretical difficulties. The first difficulty is caused by the fact that the world is full of trifles. Even if we had the most powerful computer in the world, we could not record all the trifles that come to our attention. Moreover, even if we could record every trifle, we would not want to do so. (For one thing, we would not want to expend the resources necessary to do so.) Hence, in any investigation it is necessary to decide which details are worth recording and preserving and which are not.

Determining the relevance of details during an investigation is difficult. Investigators face a dynamic environment and they lack clairvoyance. Consequently, a detail that seems irrelevant at Time "x" may become highly relevant at Time "x + 1."[56] Unfortunately, we know of no method of recording that will preserve all significant details and discard the rest. There are methods of marshalling, however, that may improve the chances that important details will be preserved. Moreover, there are methods of storing details on the basis of important differences in their evidential character. We examine some of these methods next.

2. Marshalling by Actors

The first two systems in our detail base organize evidence in

---

[55] A. DOYLE, *The Boscombe Valley Mystery*, in THE COMPLETE SHERLOCK HOLMES 202, 214 (1981) (Holmes remarking that his method "is founded upon the observation of trifles").

[56] This is why we call the set of recorded details the "detail base." We avoid the more conventional label "knowledge base" because the details in an investigator's base may or may not supply knowledge.

relationship to "actors." In our usage, actors are people who are sources of information. The domain of actor-based marshalling is wide because all details acquired during an investigation originate with or pass through people.

The first actor-based evidence marshalling system makes it possible for investigators to identify the actors who are the sources of specific items of information and to identify the details that originated or passed through particular actors. The second actor-based marshalling system makes it possible to identify the details that contain information about actors. In other words, one marshalling system records details from actors and the other records details about actors.[57]

These two actor-based marshalling systems have a variety of advantages and uses. It may be of some theoretical, as well as practical, significance that trial lawyers routinely marshal evidence on the basis of people, frequently recording the identities of people having information and the type of information that such individuals have.[58] Lawyers are particularly likely to make this type of record when a trial is near. This is because they need to know which people should be called as witnesses. However, lawyers also make such records earlier in the life of a lawsuit. They do so, for example, because they need to know which people might have to be questioned again for further information about particular matters.

In making records about potential witnesses and about people who are potential sources of evidence, lawyers also routinely record details about these sources of information. Thus, matters such as age, occupation, employment history, and other matters will be recorded. Among the reasons for this sort of record-keeping, of course, is the lawyer's concern with the credibility of his potential witnesses. There are other reasons for this sort of record-keeping, some of which are mundane and some of which are not. Among the mundane, for example, is the lawyer's need to be able to locate people when she wishes to speak with them or subpoena them. Yet some of the reasons why lawyers preserve

---

[57] Our computer prototype of these two marshalling systems allows the user to obtain either kind of actor-based details with ease. One "button" produces on-screen the details provided by an actor, another produces the details about an actor.

[58] *See, e.g.*, Brosnahan, *Are You Going Through Life without a Trial Notebook?*, CASE & COMMENT, Nov.-Dec. 1990, at 9, 11 (recommending that lawyers follow this common practice).

details about actors are less mundane. For example, as already noted, lawyers may think that information about actors is important because they may think that the credibility of actors is an important consideration even during investigation.

There may be another reason why the preservation of details about actors is an important method of marshalling evidence. The importance of stories during the trial process is well-documented.[59] As we shall later show, stories, or scenarios, are also important during investigation.[60] In almost every lawsuit the matter, or matters, in controversy involve actions by human beings. Consequently, the scenarios that investigators construct must also involve actions by human beings. As we shall later show, the construction of useful stories for investigative purposes is not an automatic act. Story telling involves imagination and, in a legal context where the truth of a story is a matter of considerable concern, effective story telling, or scenario construction, may involve a considerable amount of intellectual labor. Consequently, a system that marshals evidence about "actors" may facilitate the process of scenario construction.

Actor-based marshalling can facilitate the construction of scenarios in several different ways. Most obviously, an efficient method for preserving and recalling information about actors involved in a scenario makes it easier to flesh out the scenario, and the ability to retrieve details about people can speed and improve the initial decision of whether a person should be made an actor in a particular story. In addition, an actor-based detail base can aid in the construction of complex scenarios where actors interact. For example, actor-based marshalling may facilitate the process of telling the story of each individual actor which, in turn, may lead to the combination of those stories into a larger story.[61]

3. Marshalling Real Evidence

Another method of marshalling evidence seems so natural that it may not seem to require comment: the process of segregating evidence that has a tangible form. Lawyers and other investiga-

---

[59] *See infra* notes 83, 85-86.

[60] *See infra* Section II(C)(2).

[61] In short, it will sometimes happen that the best way to construct a useful story is to move from parts to wholes rather than from a global story to its pieces.

tors routinely separate evidence on this basis. Here again, the reasons for doing so are both conceptual and logistical. Conceptually, real and testimonial evidence impart information in different ways and thus require different analytical treatment. This assumption, which plays an important role in the law of evidence,[62] is well-founded. Although the assessment of real evidence does involve inference — it is not true that real evidence speaks entirely by or for itself — it is also true that human sources and nonhuman sources of information are fundamentally different and the special characteristics of human sources require a different and special mode of inferential reasoning.

In the case of real evidence, the structure of the inferential process required is simpler than in the case of testimonial evidence.[63] The use of real evidence generally involves the question of its authenticity: it must be determined whether the thing in question is what it appears to be or what its proponent says it is. Attention will not focus, however, on the question of whether the tangible thing in question is "sincere" or whether it is "biased." Consequently, it is logistically useful to segregate evidence that does not involve these sorts of issues.[64]

4.   Marshalling for Credibility

In our discussion of actor-based marshalling we have noted the importance of marshalling details about the credibility of human sources of information.[65] Although one of the actor-based marshalling systems is a technique for gathering details about human

---

[62] The law of evidence draws a distinction between "real" and testimonial evidence. *See* 1A J. WIGMORE, WIGMORE ON EVIDENCE § 24 (P. Tillers rev. 1983). Wigmore coined the neologism "autopic proference" to refer to evidence that presents itself directly to the senses. *Id.*

[63] This is not to say that assessing the properties of tangible things is easy. If it were, we would not need sciences such as physics and chemistry.

[64] It is, of course, true that testimonial evidence will often be necessary to lend meaning to the tangible evidence in the case. Often it is also true that the decision maker's attention will focus not on the information that can be obtained from a tangible thing if it is what its proponent claims but, rather, on the question of whether a witness is believable when she claims that a tangible thing is such-and-such. All of this, however, does not denigrate the conclusion that if certain testimony about the authenticity of a tangible thing is believed, the assessment of the tangible thing lacks forms of inferential reasoning that are involved when the believability of a human source is drawn into question.

[65] *See supra* text accompanying notes 57-61.

sources of information, however, the resulting collection of evidence is just a list of details. Such a list does not organize details in a way that fully displays their significance for credibility issues. One of the authors of this Article, David Schum, has described a method for organizing evidence and thought about questions of credibility.[66] Although that analysis will not be restated here, we do note that Schum's analysis of credibility has many affinities with the way the law of evidence views problems of credibility. For example, in both Schum's schema and the law's, veracity, objectivity, and observational accuracy of a human source are important factors bearing on the probative value of testimonial evidence.[67] It is clearly useful to organize details on the basis of their potential bearing on matters such as sincerity, bias, and memory.

5. Marshalling by Arranging and Combining Details

A major purpose of marshalling strategies in investigation — at least in the preliminary phases of investigation — is the stimulation of useful questions or hypotheses. Marshalling schemes interest us to the extent that they perform this heuristic function. On some occasions a single detail provokes or stimulates a question or hypothesis. For example, X has died of a gunshot wound and one detail at the scene of the crime is a small quantity of a narcotic substance. This single datum will likely provoke the formation of the relatively diffuse hypothesis that X was killed by someone who was somehow involved with narcotics. In addition, details can also provoke the formation of relatively discrete hypotheses. For example, the information that X's body has a firearm wound and that Y's recently-fired revolver was found at the scene of the crime is likely to provoke the hypothesis that Y killed X with his revolver.

While single details can provoke the formation of hypotheses, so too can combinations of details. When details accumulate,

---

[66] Schum's theory of credibility assessment, which is part of his more general theory of multistage or "cascaded" inference, appears in a variety of journals and books. A recent formulation of his theory of credibility is found in Schum, *Knowledge, Credibility, and Probability*, 2 J. BEHAV. DECISION MAKING 39 (1989).

[67] *See, e.g.*, 3A J. WIGMORE, WIGMORE ON EVIDENCE § 922 (J. Chadbourn rev. 1970) (impeachment for lack of veracity); *id.* §§ 948-53, 966-69 (impeachment for bias and interest); *id.* §§ 931-38 (impeachment for organic incapacity).

however, there are both practical and conceptual difficulties. A practical difficulty is keeping track of the vast number of details that typically accumulate even during a brief investigation.. For example, in the simulation on which this Article rests we accumulated thousands of details. In addition to the practical difficulty of preserving large numbers of details, there is the conceptual or analytical problem of combining details in an order that will stimulate the formation of useful questions and hypotheses.

A method based on the procedure used in our computer prototype may substantially alleviate many of the practical problems of recording details for later use. As noted earlier, the computer prototype uses a method of storage that resembles a stack of cards.[68] The prototype permits a user to enter details on each card within each of the stacks for each of the four detail marshalling methods that we have just described. Questions and ideas can also be recorded on each of these cards. The underlying Hypercard system[69] on which these stacks are built makes it easy for a user to navigate through and between these various stacks with relative ease. If there is merit to the theories of evidence marshalling on which these four types of stacks rest, a method of recording data based on the prototype computer-based marshalling system we have designed should enhance the ability of users to ask productive questions on the basis of the available details.

The ability to navigate among the four stacks, however, does not resolve the issue of how details should be combined in order to enhance the efficiency of the process of questioning. Even with the assistance of a computer, it is neither practicable nor enlightening to consider every possible combination of details. Even when the number of details is relatively small, it would take aeons to consider every possible combination.[70] Moreover, long before anyone could finish considering all possible combinations of details, there would almost certainly be new details to consider. Hence, we need a more efficient method for arranging and combining details. We need a strategy for combining details that omits a variety of combinations, but does so without obliterating an excessive number of potentially useful combinations and arrangements. As shown immediately below, the arcs numbered

---

68 *See supra* text accompanying note 53; *supra* note 57.

69 *See supra* note 53 (explaining Hypercard system).

70 If there are just 50 details, there are 2^{50}-1 combinations. This is roughly 1,000,000,000,000,000 combinations.

3 and 4 in Figure 2 lead us to methods of combining details that may be productive.

6. Marshalling Details for Interesting Issues and Temporal Inventorying of Evidence

Details may provoke the formulation of hypotheses and questions that we call "interesting issues." These issues are relatively granular hypotheses that are derivative of more general hypotheses. For example, the general hypothesis that a murder was committed in some fashion may, and often does, provoke a variety of more discrete hypotheses or questions that bear on the general question of the *modus operandi*. One such general hypothesis might be that a murder was committed in one way or another. This hypothesis may provoke the "interesting issues" of why an attempt was made to remove blood stains from the scene of the crime and who attempted to do so. It is plainly useful to record these sorts of subsidiary queries.

It is also useful to "time-stamp" evidence. To gauge the significance of evidence, it is often necessary to know if it postdates, accompanies, or predates the hypothesized event.[71] Time-stamping evidence — organizing and arranging it on the basis of the order of its appearance in time in relation to possible events in the world — is important because evidence is not just evidence. It is also an event in time. The temporal locus of evidence in time is a matter of some importance because, as an event in time, evidence stands in a causal relationship with other events in the

---

[71] Wigmore distinguished among evidence that predates, accompanies, and postdates a fact in issue. He called these three classes: prospectant, concomitant, and restrospectant. J. WIGMORE, JUDICIAL PROOF, *supra* note 17, at §§ 55, 83, 138; *see also* 1A J. WIGMORE, WIGMORE ON EVIDENCE, *supra* note 62, § 43, at 1140-42. Some observers may think that Wigmore's tripartite temporal classification of evidence is merely quaint. This sort of reaction to Wigmore's tripartite temporal classification of evidence, however, may be another example of the tendency of some of Wigmore's most important theoretical work to suffer the fate of a lead balloon. W. TWINING, *supra* note 17, at 164-66. Indeed, the words Wigmore used to discuss the temporal sorting of evidence, *e.g.*, "progress chart of indications," are not elegant. Yet, buried in Wigmore's ungainly language is the important insight that dating the appearance of evidence can serve an important heuristic function. *See* J. WIGMORE, THE SCIENCE OF JUDICIAL PROOF § 4, app. 5, at 998-1003 (3d ed. 1937) (discussing value of temporal classification of evidence in investigation) [hereafter J. WIGMORE, SCIENCE OF JUDICIAL PROOF].

world. Consequently, identification of the temporal locus of evidence — dating its appearance in the world — facilitates investigation of the causal relationships between evidence, on the one
hand, and hypotheses about events of legal significance, on the
other. In some cases, time-stamping evidence promotes a kind of
reasoning known as retroduction.[72] An investigator using this
kind of reasoning will suppose, for example, that the murder in
issue in the case did in fact take place and then attempt to predict
the evidence that would likely appear after such a murder. On
this basis, he might predict in a particular case that the defendant
would have referred to the murder in later conversations with his
close friends.[73] The major difference between the retroductive
reasoning used in scenario analysis and the reasoning in this connection is that scenario analysis focuses on causal relations among
events,[74] whereas time-stamping evidence promotes retroductive
reasoning about the causal relations between (possible) events
and evidence.

One might argue that temporal marshalling of evidence does
not merit a separate node in the influence diagram. The node
representing evidence marshalling with scenarios already
describes a procedure for thinking about temporal and causal
relationships among events. Wigmore's method of temporal marshalling differs from marshalling by scenarios, however, because
Wigmore's method of time-stamping evidence has an "eliminative" element.[75] Wigmore argued that a complete temporal audit
of evidence — which he called a "progress chart of indications"
— can indicate when a case is "completely" prepared.[76] In his
view a case is completely prepared when all alternative possibilities are eliminated and only one remains.[77] The basis for this process of elimination appears to be a form of causal reasoning about
the relationship between evidence-events and issue-events.
Hence, in Wigmore's view it is possible, at least on some occasions, to use this type of reasoning to establish conclusively that
only one hypothesis is possible. Wigmore undoubtedly overstated

---

[72] We discuss retroductive reasoning *infra* in Section II(B)(2).

[73] This type of reasoning is structurally similar to the retroductive
process in scenario analysis discussed *infra* in Section II(B)(2).

[74] *See infra* Section I(C)(7).

[75] *See generally* J. WIGMORE, SCIENCE OF JUDICIAL PROOF, *supra* note 71,
§ 4, app. 5, at 998-1003 (explaining "progress chart").

[76] *Id.*

[77] *Id.*

his case when he said that it is possible to reach the conclusion that a case has been "completely prepared." Causal reasoning can never conclusively exclude alternative causal explanations.[78]

7. Event Chronologies and Scenarios

One way of arranging details is by the temporal order of the events they seem to indicate. This method of arranging and marshalling details is familiar to many lawyers. The practice of constructing "time lines" is a common method of pretrial preparation.[79] This method of marshalling evidence is useful because it often stimulates fruitful questions. For example, event chronologies may disclose "gaps." By constructing time lines an investigator may discover the existence of time intervals about which there are no details and it may be apparent to the investigator that some events in that interval may be important. Similarly, an event chronology may reveal that there is some information about an interval of time, but it is not enough or it is not the right kind.[80]

While event chronologies, or time lines, are heuristically valuable in their catalyzing questions about a case, they also have limitations. A symptom of these limitations is "clutter." When numerous events are packed into an event chronology, the usual effect is that the event chronology appears cluttered.[81] The primary reason for the cluttered appearance of event chronologies is that many of the events entered on a temporal axis have no appar-

---

[78] Wigmore appears to have good company, however. For example, Dr. L. Jonathan Cohen has argued that the weight of evidence is a function of the number of evidential tests that a possibility or hypothesis has surmounted. In Cohen's opinion, conclusive proof of a hypothesis is possible and it is achieved when a hypothesis has surmounted every imaginable evidential test. *See* L. COHEN, AN INTRODUCTION TO THE PHILOSOPHY OF INDUCTION AND PROBABILITY 37-38 (1989). Cohen's thesis is much like Wigmore's. It is possible, however, to reach the conclusion that the preparation for a case is effectively and practically complete. For example, it may be hard to imagine additional evidential tests.

[79] *See* D. BINDER & P. BERGMAN, *supra* note 6, chs. 4, 14.

[80] In Part II we examine in more detail some of the possible uses and forms of event chronologies.

[81] The clutter effect is not solely or even largely attributable to the density of the events in a time line. As we explain *infra* in Part II(C)(1), there are devices that can reduce the apparent density of events in an event chronology.

ent relationship with each other. In this situation, an event chronology may muddle as well as clarify the process of inquiry.

Our reason for the limitations of event chronologies also suggests the cure. If simple temporal sequences are often unilluminating or confusing because of the lack of any apparent connections between the events recorded in an event chronology, one remedy is the construction of scenarios,[82] or "stories."[83] Unlike a simple event chronology, a scenario describes a sequence of events that are causally related. This type of temporal marshalling gives scenarios a measure of intelligibility that time lines do not have.

Powerful theoretical considerations speak in favor of story telling as an evidence marshalling technique. For example, Kant made the ontological argument that states of the world are necessarily part of a spatio-temporal order.[84] This view implies that all of the issues in every lawsuit concern causally related events. Moreover, there is strong empirical evidence that stories are both a common natural information processing technique and an effective technique for storing and recalling large amounts of information.[85] It is also noteworthy that trial lawyers often consciously tell stories in trials.[86] Some lawyers may view stories only as rhetorical devices, yet others realize that story telling makes evidence

---

[82] There is an extensive body of literature on scenario analysis. A good introduction is D. VON WINTERFELDT & W. EDWARDS, DECISION ANALYSIS AND BEHAVIORAL RESEARCH 163-72 (1986).

[83] In recent years there has been growing interest in the role of stories in trials. *See, e.g.*, Bennett, *Storytelling in Criminal Trials: A Model of Social Judgment*, 64 SPEECH 1 (1978); Bennett, *Rhetorical Transformation of Evidence in Criminal Trials: Creating Grounds for Legal Judgment*, 65 SPEECH 311 (1979). An overview is provided in W. TWINING, *Lawyers' Stories*, in RETHINKING EVIDENCE: EXPLORATORY ESSAYS 219-61 (1990); *see also* Tillers, *supra* note 46, at 916-27; *cf.* Allen, *supra* note 22, at 426-28 (conceptualizing trials as presenting and evaluating plaintiff's story and defendant's story, rather than merely plaintiff's allegations and defendant's denials).

[84] I. KANT, KRITIK DER REINEN VERNUNFT (2d ed. 1787).

[85] *See, e.g.*, W. BENNETT & M. FELDMAN, RECONSTRUCTING REALITY IN THE COURTROOM 3-18 (1981); R. HASTIE, S. PENROD & N. PENNINGTON, INSIDE THE JURY 22-23, 163-65, 234 (1983); Pennington & Hastie, *Explanation-Based Decision Making*, in PROGRAM OF THE NINTH ANNUAL COGNITIVE SCIENCE SOCIETY 682, 682 (1987).

[86] *See, e.g.*, W. TWINING, *supra* note 83, at 224 (classic example of forensic story telling); *cf.* Snadaker, *Storytelling in Opening Statements: Framing the Argumentation of the Trial*, 10 AM. J. TRIAL ADVOCACY 15 (1986) (role of stories in lawyer's opening statement).

more intelligible to the trier of fact. Hence, the importance of stories in inferential contexts has been recognized in many different quarters. If we have something to add to the argument that story telling is important, it is the claim that stories are important in investigative processes as well as in deliberative processes.

There are many different kinds of stories. The kinds of stories we have in mind — scenarios[87] — contain a mixture of evidence and conjecture. In a forensic context stories ordinarily must incorporate evidentiary elements as well as a dose of fancy. In a forensic context stories are constructed because of an interest in actual states of the world; their purpose is to facilitate the accurate assessment of matters of fact. If a story has no evidentiary foundations, there is ordinarily little reason to think that the story is a plausible one. Scenarios are very complex hypotheses about a temporal sequence of events in the "real world." These hypotheses are useful only if they have a basis in evidence. In the absence of evidentiary indicators and constraints, an infinite number of possible scenarios of equal dignity can be constructed. Yet, in the absence of all evidence, no scenario that describes a possible sequence of events can be deemed more or less plausible than any other scenario describing another possible sequence of events.

While useful scenarios rest on evidence, they are not limited to the possibilities directly disclosed by the evidence. Any scenario must have an element of fancy. A scenario is a hypothesis about connections between events; it contains a theory or explanation of how things are connected in time. When a scenario is constructed for forensic purposes, it serves as a gap-filler. Scenarios fill gaps precisely because they incorporate, or are, theories that specify relationships between events in time. Hence, story telling is more than just another method of organizing details. Story telling is a method of marshalling that explicitly mixes evidence with the construction of theories about the behavior of sectors of the cosmos over time.

The conjectural dimension of a story serves a number of important purposes. The conjectural or hypothesized parts of a story serve as indicators of potentially relevant evidence. A story having conjectural components suggests the importance of evidence bearing on the conjectural portions of the story. For example, if an investigator conjectures that a suspect purchased a gun at a

---

[87] For present purposes we equate "stories" with "scenarios."

store before he shot the victim, an investigator would also have to guess that evidence showing such a purchase might be useful. In addition, a clearly told story practically forces an investigator or decision maker to focus on the relative merits of competing visions and theories of the workings of natural processes and human beings. The construction of an intelligible scenario makes a story teller's causal theories explicit. Hence, a story, if clearly articulated, invites and facilitates rumination about the adequacy of the causal theory that underlies the story. For example, if an investigator conjectures that a suspect killed the victim to get revenge for the mistreatment of the suspect's dog, questions are likely to be raised about whether this is the way the mind of the suspect could have worked.[88]

Although we believe that event chronologies may spur and facilitate the formation of stories, we believe that the link between event chronologies and stories is indirect rather than direct.[89] We believe that the interaction of time lines and stories is mediated by other marshalling strategies, including marshalling according to "possibilities." The term "possibilities" refers to hypotheses that are directly[90] indicated or suggested by evidence. We believe that stories can emerge out of "possibilities" but not out of time lines.[91] We discuss the marshalling of possibilities next.

8.   Possibilities Marshalling

When taken at face value, evidence often seems to indicate a variety of possibilities. A trace of cocaine is found at the scene of an apparent murder. This evidence indicates the possibility that the perpetrator of the murder (if there was a murder) was a user or peddler of cocaine. A gun is also found near the dead body.

---

[88] *See infra* text accompanying Figures 17 & 18 in Section II(C)(2) (discussing devices and procedures that facilitate formation, assessment, and comparison of stories).

[89] The absence of an arc linking the story node and the event chronology node in Figure 2 signifies that there is no direct interaction between the operation of marshalling evidence by forming time lines and marshalling evidence by telling stories.

[90] To be sure, a possibility requires an inference from evidence. Our point is that a possibility never outruns evidence.

[91] One may have the "experience" of seeing a scenario emerge out of an event chronology. However, we believe that when an event chronology inspires a scenario it does so because an event chronology suggests possibilities, which then become the basis of a scenario.

This evidence may indicate the possibility that the murderer (if there was a murderer) used a gun to kill the victim, and it may indicate the alternative possibility that the dead person committed suicide by shooting herself. As noted earlier,[92] however, evidentiary details can be combined in various ways. Examination of various combinations of evidentiary details is a useful technique for stimulating the formation of further possibilities and hypotheses. For example, the evidence of the cocaine and the gun taken together may suggest the possibility that the killer shot the victim to get the victim's cocaine. The examination of such a possibility may suggest a scenario. For example, the possibility that the killer shot the victim to get the victim's cocaine may induce an investigator to conjecture that the killer and the victim had dealings with each other in the past.

It is also important to assess the possibilities that the available evidence seems to suggest. A useful way of doing so is to imagine further possibilities that are compatible with the possibilities already recognized. When this is done, the extent to which existing evidence supports different sets of possibilities at various levels of refinement can be considered. Moreover, identification of hypotheses lacking extensive evidentiary support can serve as a guide for additional investigation or inquiry. We describe this sort of possibilities analysis at some length in Part II of this Article. There we describe a "possibilities tree" and some other graphic representations that may facilitate both the formation and assessment of possibilities.[93]

While orderly thinking about the relationship between possibilities and evidentiary details can clearly be useful and productive, the strategy of marshalling details on the basis of possibilities also has its limitations. As we suggested before,[94] when details multiply the number of possibilities increases rapidly. This fact alone places limits on a strategy that aims to "exhaust the possibilities." In addition, there is a further complication: a single possibilities tree, supported by a relatively small collection of evidence can contain a vast number of possibilities.[95] Ordinarily it is neither feasible nor desirable to examine all the possibilities that a collection of details suggests. Hence, it is essential to prune

---

[92] *See supra* Section I(C)(5).
[93] *See infra* Sections II(B)(1)-(2).
[94] *See supra* note 70 and accompanying text.
[95] *See infra* Figures 8 & 9 together with accompanying text in Section II(A).

some of the possibilities from the possibilities tree that we describe in Section II(B).

There are at least two methods for pruning a possibilities tree of some of its branches. First, since combinations of possibilities tend to suggest possible scenarios, one way of pruning a possibilities tree (as well as making it grow new branches) is to construct scenarios that incorporate some of the possibilities suggested by the evidence. Once such scenarios are constructed and their plausibility assessed, they may be used to reconsider the possibilities that evidence suggests. In some situations, this reassessment will cause an investigator to jettison a variety of possibilities.

Another method of reducing possibilities is to engage in a process we call "elimination." This approach subjects possibilities to evidential tests. The use of evidential tests involves an analytic process known as retroductive reasoning.[96] When an investigator uses eliminative reasoning to extinguish possibilities, he thinks retroductively because he makes predictions or guesses about the evidence that would exist if a particular possibility is, in fact, true. After making this prediction, or guess, he then attempts to determine whether these items of evidence actually exist. The nature of this process of evidential testing is described in detail by Dr. Cohen.[97] He argues that the strength of a hypothesis, (in our usage here, a "possibility") is a function of the number of evidential tests that it is able to pass. The greater the number of evidential tests that a hypothesis passes, the greater is our confidence in that hypothesis.[98]

Of course, neither of these two methods for eliminating possibilities, scenario analysis and eliminative reasoning, guarantees that an investigator will be able to cope with a number of possibilities so large as to cause mental stupefaction. If an investigator entertains so many possibilities that they cause only bewilderment, the investigator will not be able to use marshalling methods such as story telling and eliminative reasoning to reduce a cognitively unmanageable number of possibilities to manageable proportions. Nonetheless, methods such as scenario analysis

---

[96] *See infra* Section II(B)(2).

[97] L. COHEN, THE PROBABLE AND THE PROVABLE, pt. III (1977).

[98] *Id.* at ch. 13. Some critics have argued that Dr. Cohen's theories of inference and probability are incoherent. *See, e.g.*, Williams, *The Mathematics of Proof*, pts. I & II, 1979 CRIM. L. REV. 297, 340. However, these critics have made a category mistake: they fail to appreciate the difference between enumerative and eliminative inference.

and eliminative reasoning do have the capacity to make a relatively (but not wholly) unmanageable number of possibilities relatively more manageable. The fact that an investigator can make no headway if he entertains a stupefying number of possibilities only demonstrates that the network of marshalling strategies described does not capture all of the processes involved in investigation.[99]

The importance of cognitive manageability is obvious. Yet, although it is advantageous to have fewer possibilities rather than more, this kind of simplicity is not the only important cognitive value. For example, marshalling by scenarios may expand as well as reduce the number of recognizable possibilities, but an investigator may rationally embrace story telling as a marshalling strategy even when it multiplies possibilities. Similarly, when an investigator suspects that possibilities having no present relevance may become significant later, he should hesitate to abandon them completely and irrevocably. Thus, intricacy and complexity in matters such as possibilities are only one factor in a theory of the economics of questioning. The benefits of entertaining, considering, and recording possibilities and details must be weighed against the costs of doing so. Thus, while cognitive parsimony is important, it does not follow that an efficient strategy for marshalling evidence is one that reduces possibilities and details to a small number.[100]

---

[99] At this point we have no recourse except to refer to these undescribed processes as "intuitive" or "tacit" methods of dissecting, organizing, and assembling evidence.

[100] We can make the point found in the text by drawing an analogy between a parsimonious strategy for understanding natural processes and a parsimonious strategy for assessing evidence. A parsimonious theory of nature (*e.g.*, special relativity theory) does not achieve parsimony by obliterating the complexity of natural processes. Rather, it is a parsimonious strategy for explaining complex natural processes. To be sure, the analogy is imperfect because a theory of evidence marshalling is a map of the mind rather than the world, and the subject matter of our theory — including matters such as "possibilities" and "details" — exists only in our heads. It does not follow, however, that investigators should capitalize on this kind of subjectivity of the subject matter of our theory by randomly eliminating — thinking away, as it were — including matters such as possibilities and details. If that were a rational strategy, every investigator would eliminate details and possibilities until only one was left. This *reductio ad absurdum* demonstrates that whatever the subjectivity of inferential processes and strategies may mean, it does not mean that they impose no constraints or limitations on cognitive processes concerning the existence of

9. Legal Marshalling

We claim that substantive legal rules are important heuristic devices. Our claim may sound odd; if asked to explain the importance of substantive law, people are more likely to refer to the impact of substantive law on conduct than to its impact on the process of inquiry and discovery. Nonetheless, substantive legal rules really are important heuristic devices. Yet, the reason for the heuristic importance of substantive law for investigative and evidentiary processes is special. The other evidence marshalling strategies considered in this Article have innate heuristic charm and power. The same cannot be said of the strategy of marshalling evidence on the basis of substantive law. Substantive legal rules have heuristic significance because they are *authoritative*. If substantive legal rules were not authoritative, participants in litigation would not necessarily want to use them to organize evidence.[101] However, judges and jurors are required to follow the

matters of fact. This Article devotes considerable attention to processes and strategies that can multiply details and hypotheses.

[101] The distinctive character of legal marshalling raises several interesting questions. One of them is whether there are comparable marshalling strategies in nonlegal contexts. For example, do some marshalling strategies in medical investigation owe their existence to social conventions rather than to the inherent "fertility" of the marshalling strategy in question? Questions of this sort raise the further question of the universality of the marshalling strategies described in the Article. *See supra* text accompanying notes 62-63; *infra* note 103.

Another interesting question is whether legal marshalling is entirely different from other evidence marshalling strategies described in this Article. Although the "nonlegal" marshalling strategies described in this Article have innate heuristic charm, the structure of the legal process sometimes encourages or requires the use of specific marshalling strategies. For example, there are legal rules that prescribe certain methods of impeachment and proscribe others. Legal rules of this sort might result in the use of marshalling strategies that would not otherwise have been employed. As our study of investigation brings us closer to the trial, the question of the extent to which marshalling strategies have their roots in social and legal conventions will become more acute. As the trial draws nigh, pretrial activities of lawyers focus more on the preparation for the tasks they must perform in the trial. For example, a lawyer facing a jury trial knows that the trial judge will instruct the jurors to determine whether the evidence in the case shows that the parties having the burden of proof on specified claims and defenses have met their burden of proof. The trial lawyer's expectation that these instructions will be given may influence the way that the lawyer marshals evidence when preparing for trial. For example, she may want to focus more than she otherwise would on matters

applicable substantive rules when making decisions in a lawsuit. The substantive legal rules function as "decision rules" that specify the conditions under which the decision maker ought to grant or deny redress.[102] The obligatory character of these rules lends them heuristic significance. For example, any person trying a lawsuit must take substantive legal rules into account when marshalling and presenting evidence; it is possible that the judge and jurors will abide by the rules that the substantive law tells them to use when reaching a decision in the case.

Although it is apparent that substantive legal rules about matters such as "battery," "nuisance," "larceny," and "manslaughter" have important implications for marshalling evidence in pretrial investigation as well as at trial,[103] the question of precisely how substantive law influences fact investigation remains to be answered. Unfortunately, we cannot give the full answer to this question here. We are reasonably sure that the substantive legal framework of legal disputes dictates the use of a wide variety of evidence marshalling strategies,[104] and we have neither the

---

such as the range and force of her evidence and less than she otherwise would on matters such as "story telling."

[102] The jurisprudentially-minded reader may regard this perspective on substantive legal rules as both unduly crabbed and unduly expansive — unduly crabbed because it ignores the possibility of substantive legal rules that do not themselves specify the conditions of liability or nonliability; and unduly expansive because it ignores the possibility of procedural preconditions for judicial recognition of a claim or defense. Neither slight is intended here. It is enough for our purposes that *some* substantive rules specify at least *some* conditions (under some circumstances) for the award or denial of judicial relief.

[103] Although most trial lawyers do not need to be told that marshalling evidence on the basis of legal theories is important, there are several reasons why some discussion of this method of marshalling evidence is warranted. First, of course, many people who are not schooled in the arts of litigation and pretrial preparation have not even thought about legal marshalling, and it may be necessary to convince them that legal marshalling is important. Second, our discussion of legal marshalling may reveal specific methods of legal marshalling that even meticulous trial lawyers may not yet appreciate. Third, systematic analysis of legal marshalling raises important questions about the relationship between reasoning about evidence and reasoning about law. Finally, since legal doctrines are not implicated in many inferential processes (*e.g.*, those in astrophysics), analysis of legal marshalling makes it possible to examine the question of the extent to which the network of evidence marshalling systems described in this Article is context-specific rather than general.

[104] There is more than a little reason to believe that legal reasoning and

time nor the resources to examine all of these law-related marshalling strategies. We have given some thought to a strategy that involves the decomposition of legal concepts, however. This strategy requires that concepts such as "murder" and "battery" be broken down into their constituents, or "elements." For example, "negligence" might be broken down into the elements of "duty of care," "breach," "proximate cause," and "damages."[105] In our network diagram the decomposition of legal rules and concepts into elements is symbolized by the node called "substantive legal rules."[106]

The enumeration of the elements of a legal claim or defense may suggest various methods of organizing evidence. For example, the procedure of explicitly articulating the elements of a legal claim such as "conspiracy" may inspire the formation of possible scenarios which, if shown to be true, would support that claim. Similarly, an investigator, again proceeding in a retroductive mode, may ponder the elements of legal rules in the abstract and then speculate about the possible combinations of facts and events that would instantiate those generic, abstract elements. In that case, she might then examine the detail base to see whether the evidence already available supports the elements of the claims or defenses she is considering, or she may engage in further

---

argument take a variety of forms. *See infra* note 116. If there are various types of legal reasoning and argument, there is likely to be a corresponding diversity in law-related, evidence marshalling strategies. Each distinctive method of legal reasoning may assign a distinctive role to facts and evidence and may therefore require distinctive forms of evidence marshalling. We do not attempt to provide a comprehensive account of the varieties of legal reasoning and the evidence marshalling schemes that various species of legal reasoning might entail. However, we do allude to the distinctive evidentiary heuristics that two specific types of legal argument might generate. *See infra* notes 113-16 and accompanying text; *cf.* Tillers, *The Value of Evidence in Law*, 39 No. IRE. LEG. Q. 167 (1988).

[105] This list of elements highlights the fact that the appropriate breakdown of a legal concept may be uncertain. This is not an insignificant fact. Uncertainty about the definition of a legal claim or defense complicates the task of marshalling evidence.

[106] *See supra* Figure 2. Not all legal doctrines and rules fall into the category of "substantive" rules; there are also "procedural" rules. We are certain that marshalling evidence on the basis of procedural rules is as important as marshalling evidence on the basis of substantive rules. We have not yet examined how the process of relating evidence to procedural rules works, however. We propose to do so in the next phase of our research.

investigation to see if evidence supporting those claims or defenses can be found.

These examples of the retroductive use of the elements of legal concepts have special pertinence to the initial stages of litigation and investigation. In pretrial phases of litigation it is often very uncertain whether a possible legal basis for relief or for denial of relief will survive to the time of any trial or whether it will die an early death for lack of evidence. In the face of such uncertainty, an investigator might find it useful to imagine scenarios and possibilities that might substantiate the legal grounds for relief or defense that he can imagine asserting at some eventual trial. In some situations, however, it might make sense for the investigator to work the other way around — to emphasize not fine evidentiary details, but gross legal categories. For example, if an investigator has few details and the meager evidence available to him does not point specifically to particular elements of substantive legal rules, he may wish to rely on his "gut sense" of what legal rules are likely to be important "down the road" to guide his investigation of the case. In some circumstances, this approach may be an efficient strategy for hypothesizing interesting possibilities and for ruling out others.

The law-related marshalling strategies just mentioned center largely on problems that involve uncertainty about the future. However, there is another type of uncertainty associated with substantive legal rules and doctrines: to some extent, legal principles, rules, and doctrines are always vague and fuzzy. The vagueness and imprecision of legal rules might be thought to pose only a problem of theories and strategies of legal argument and legal reasoning. In fact, however, the imprecision of legal rules has important implications for evidence marshalling strategies as well. In addition, the fuzziness of substantive legal doctrine has important implications for the way that investigators and lawyers must grapple with the uncertainties associated with the dynamic character of investigation and litigation: an investigator's or lawyer's appreciation of the fuzziness of substantive legal rules can have a profound impact on the nature and extent of her uncertainty about future developments in the case.

In assessing the impact of "doctrinal fuzziness" on investigation, it is important to understand the ways in which legal rules may be "fuzzy." In an earlier article we suggested that the concept of an "equivalence class" may be a useful device for describing the relationship between legal doctrines and factual hypotheses.[107] Our use of this concept rests on a distinction between the elements of a legal rule,[108] on the one hand, and factual hypotheses on the other. Although it is sometimes said that a party having the burden of proving a claim or defense has the burden of proving the elements of "negligence," "waiver," and similar matters, this is a loose way of talking. Like a number of legal experts,[109] we prefer to say that a party having the burden of proving the elements of a claim or defense has the burden of proving legally material facts.

There is a difference between the elements of a legal rule and the facts that establish those elements in a particular case. The elements of a legal rule — *e.g.*, "causation" or "failure to warn" — have a generic character. The elements of legal concepts such as "negligence" do not require proof of a unique set of factual circumstances; they can be satisfied by proof of a great variety of acts and events. Hence, particular acts and events instantiate rather than constitute the elements of legal claims and defenses. When the relationship between the elements of a legal theory and facts is understood this way, it is possible to use the concept of an equivalence class to describe the relationship between legal doctrines and hypotheses about states of the world.

The concept of an equivalence class originates in mathemat-

---

107 Tillers & Schum, *supra* note 25, at 956-59.

108 There are at least two ways in which substantive legal rules may be fuzzy. First, the definition of a legal doctrine such as "conspiracy" may be in doubt. It may not be clear, for example, whether or not an "overt act" is one of the elements of "conspiracy." Although the implications of this type of fuzziness for evidence marshalling strategies during investigation are fairly apparent — *e.g.*, an investigator faces the choice of gathering or not gathering evidence pertaining to an "overt act" — the other type of fuzziness is more interesting. The meaning of a legal concept or category may be elastic. This type of fuzziness more clearly and directly implicates the question of the relationship between concepts and facts as well as the question of the implications of fuzzy decision rules for preparatory investigative activity.

109 For example, Wigmore's analysis of the notion of "materiality" presupposes a distinction between the elements of a legal theory and the "historical" or factual events that satisfy those elements. 1 J. WIGMORE, *supra* note 62, § 2, at 15-19; *see also* H.L.A. HART, THE CONCEPT OF LAW 123 (1963) ("Particular fact-situations do not await us already marked off from each other, and labelled as instances of the general rule, the application of which is in question; nor can the rule itself step forward to claim its own instances."); A. ZUCKERMAN, THE PRINCIPLES OF CRIMINAL EVIDENCE ch. 2 (1989).

ics.[110] Formally stated, an equivalence class is the class of all outcomes that have the property that they correspond with the occurrence of some "event." The word "event" in this definition is a term of art referring not to a unique event but to a set of general conditions or circumstances embodied in a "reference class." Hence, informally stated, an equivalence class is the collection of all particular instances that satisfy the requirements of a general rule.[111] In the case of legal concepts, the number of instances in an equivalence class is practically infinite. For example, the number of factual circumstances ("outcomes") that satisfy the requirements of a general concept ("reference class") such as "manslaughter" or "waiver" is enormous. The concept of an equivalence class is a useful device for describing the impact of uncertainty in legal doctrine on other evidence marshalling strategies, and the concept of an equivalence class also brings into relief different possible strategies for reducing or coping with the uncertainty of legal rules.

One of the difficulties any investigator or lawyer faces before trial is the problem of marshalling evidence when legal doctrines are vague and uncertain. In the parlance of mathematics, such an investigator confronts fuzzy (legal) reference classes. When the definition of a reference class is fuzzy[112] or vague, there is a measure of uncertainty about the membership of any particular entity in the reference class. Moreover, if the definition of a reference class is completely vague, it is impossible to determine whether any particular event falls within or without the reference class; *i.e.*,

---

110 MILLINGTON & MILLINGTON, DICTIONARY OF MATHEMATICS 84 (1966).

111 For example, in a game of cards there are a number of different outcomes of a card deal that satisfy, or fit within, the reference class "full house." Similarly, a legal concept such as "manslaughter" may be instantiated by a variety of factual circumstances. In the parlance of statisticians, the event "murder" can be made to occur by numerous particular states of the world. (The intersection between the language of probabilists and the language of lawyers can be confusing. In the eyes of a lawyer an "event" such as "murder" is a particular, specific state of the world whereas for a probabilist an "event" such as "murder" is more akin to a general concept. The probabilist would refer to a particular as an "outcome." A lawyer might speak of a particular murder as an instance of the general idea of murder).

112 There is a well-known theory of fuzzy probability. *See* Zadeh, *Fuzzy Sets*, 8 INFO. & CONTROL 338 (1965). In using the word "fuzzy" in this Article we are not suggesting that fuzzy probability theory is useful in the analysis of fuzzy legal reasoning. At this time we take no position on this question.

if the definition of an "event," taken in its probabilistic sense, is completely fuzzy, it is impossible to determine whether any particular state of the world makes that "event" occur.[113]

Legal concepts such as "murder" are often vague.[114] When a legal concept is vague, there must also be uncertainty about whether a particular act or situation is an example or instance of the concept. This proposition may be rephrased in terms of the equivalence class concept: if a legal reference class such as "murder" is fuzzy, there must be uncertainty about which "outcomes" make an "event" such as "murder" occur. Stated otherwise, if the event "murder" has an ambiguous definition, there will always be uncertainty about whether any particular state of affairs does or does not constitute, or instantiate, murder.

If we visualize the relationship between legal reasoning and factual issues in litigation against this conceptual background, it seems natural to think that when the ambiguity of a legal concept (*e.g.*, "undue influence") impedes or hinders an attempt to use a legal concept to marshall evidence, the proper remedy is to clarify the legal reference class. This way of grappling with the unsettling effects of uncertainty in the law on the marshalling of evidence is a top-down process — the uncertainty in the law is addressed before the law is used to marshal evidence. Yet, once the relationship between fuzzy legal concepts and particular instances is formulated in these terms — as a top-down process — almost any lawyer trained in the common law tradition will recognize that this is not the only possible way that generic legal concepts and specific instances are related. She will see that legal reasoning involving fuzzy legal doctrines may work in reverse. That is, instead of trying to clarify a legal concept before applying it to particular situations, a judge or lawyer may examine particular situations (*e.g.*, in prior cases) that admittedly or apparently constitute instances of a particular legal concept, such as "murder," and try to use those instances to formulate or reformulate the definition of the concept.[115]

In noting the differences between top-down and bottom-up

---

[113] For example, if the reference class "justice" means anything and everything, there is no way to decide whether any particular state of affairs in the world is or is not an example of "justice."

[114] Indeed, all legal concepts are vague to some degree.

[115] Perhaps a bottom-up process, rather than a top-down process, is the one that legal theorists such as Edward Levi favored. *See* E. LEVI, AN INTRODUCTION TO LEGAL REASONING (1949).

responses to legal uncertainty, we do not answer the question of which of these two general approaches is the appropriate one or which of them is more often used. Moreover, our distinction between two types of responses to legal uncertainty is not intended to be an exhaustive taxonomy of modes of reasoning that address uncertainty in the law.[116] Our objective is to describe an heuristic strategy that people such as investigators and lawyers can use to organize their thinking about a case. We have accomplished something important if we have shown that the concept of an equivalence class facilitates analysis of the evidentiary and investigative implications of top-down and bottom-up approaches to legal uncertainty. Moreover, our analysis of the implications of two types of responses to legal uncertainty ought to suggest that careful study of the relationship between facts and other types of legal responses is warranted. The question of the evidentiary implications of different modes of legal reasoning is an important topic.

II.   GRANULAR ANALYSIS OF MARSHALLING SYSTEMS

In the previous Part of the Article, we surveyed some of the heuristic functions of legal marshalling. We have not yet expressly considered a form of legal marshalling that involves a "case theory." A case theory is an unusually complex method of marshalling evidence, because a case theory incorporates several distinct marshalling techniques. Before examining the notion of a case theory,[117] we will first consider in more detail several marshalling strategies that are embedded in, and intrinsic to, case theories.

Our study concerns factual proof in litigation. Many general discussions of evidentiary processes in litigation focus on analysis of the impact available and known evidence has on an identifiable

---

116 Theories of legal reasoning abound. *See, e.g.,* S. BURTON, AN INTRODUCTION TO LAW AND LEGAL REASONING (1985) (legal argument has a definable logical structure but specific conclusions are not logically determined); N. MACCORMICK, LEGAL REASONING AND LEGAL THEORY (1978) (arguing for possibility of deductive legal argument); Ross, *Tû-Tû,* 70 HARV. L. REV. 812, 818 (1957) (arguing that legal concepts are "nothing at all . . . merely . . . empty word[s] . . . semantic reference[s]" for particular states of affairs); Simpson, *The Analysis of Legal Concepts,* 80 L.Q. REV. 535 (1964) (criticizing Ross); *see also* Tillers, *supra* note 104 (arguing that there can be "evidence" for interpretation of law).

117 *See infra* Section II(C)(3).

and identified factual hypotheses. This type of analysis, which we call "relational analysis,"[118] is not the primary focus here.[119] In preliminary fact investigation the investigator knows that she does not yet have all of the relevant evidence that she may later acquire. Ordinarily she has not yet identified the factual issues to her satisfaction. Moreover, the task of assessing the force of evidence is relatively less prominent during investigation than at trial.[120] Our detailed analysis of marshalling strategies begins with a discussion of the formation and specification of issues and hypotheses. The framing of hypotheses is particularly important in exploratory investigation.

A. *Determining Possibilities and Framing Issues*

When a lawyer or other actor in litigation first encounters information suggestive of a possible lawsuit, he may anticipate having problems of proof if litigation ensues. If the lawyer does think ahead about such possible problems, however, he is likely to have only a fairly vague sense of what those problems may turn out to be. The potential proof problems he sees ahead are likely to be ill-defined.[121]

The poor definition of the problems that an investigator faces at the outset of an investigation raises a variety of interesting and important issues. For example, how do and how should actors in litigation cope with fuzzy problems during investigation? Why is it important to make factual issues specific? And if it is important to frame problems of evidence, inference, and proof in a discrete and specific way by the time a trial eventuates, is it important to be specific long before trial, in the early stages of investigation? If so, how is that to be done in an efficient manner?

Imagine yourself a detective in a metropolitan police force in

---

118 *See* Tillers & Schum, *supra* note 25, at 943.

119 Indeed, in this Article we have no discussion of methods for gauging the degree of the probative force of evidence on material facts in issue.

120 It cannot be said, however, that assessments of the force of evidence are immaterial during investigation. Decisions about the direction of an investigation are, and should be, affected by assessments of the strength of available and expected evidence.

121 This consequence is partly, but not entirely, a function of the limited amount of information available to the lawyer at the outset. There is not yet enough information, either factual or legal, to give the problem a more precise structure or definition.

the United States.[122] On December 8, 1987, you learn that the body of a white male has been found in a garage attached to a home in Falls Church, Virginia. You learn that the body was found lying on a floor between two cars and that the hood of one car was open. You have been told that there were deep lacerations in the head of the deceased.

How might you think about this information?

You might entertain the hypothesis that the deceased — whom we shall call Mark Vincent — died as a result of someone's criminal act. Given the limited and ambiguous nature of the information available to you, however, you might also entertain other hypotheses. You might, for example, entertain the hypotheses that Mark Vincent's death was accidental, that Mark Vincent died as a result of natural causes, or that he committed suicide.

These hypotheses are relatively diffuse, vague, coarse, or undifferentiated. The evidence does not seem to suggest any hypotheses about the precise sort of criminal act that might have caused Mark Vincent's death. Alternatively, if you are willing to speculate that a homicide took place, the evidence does not seem to support any guesses about the grade of any homicide that might have been committed. Similarly, if the evidence suggests the possibility of a suicide, the evidence does not seem to suggest how Mark Vincent might have done himself in.

Glenn Shafer has suggested a way of thinking about conjectures and hypotheses that are suggested by evidence.[123] He refers to different sets of possible hypotheses, or outcomes, as "frames of discernment."[124] In Shafer's terminology, the set of conjectures we have ascribed to you — our hypothetical police detective — is a frame of discernment. Your frame — the frame of our hypothetical police investigator — consists of all the hypotheses about Mark Vincent's death that you happen to entertain.[125]

---

[122] This example and other examples in this Article are drawn from an extended simulation conducted by the authors. The full details of the simulation are given in D. SCHUM & P. TILLERS, MARSHALLING EVIDENCE THROUGHOUT THE PROCESS OF FACT-INVESTIGATION: A SIMULATION (pts. 1-4) (1989) (copy on file with U.C. Davis Law Review).

[123] G. SHAFER, A MATHEMATICAL THEORY OF EVIDENCE (1976).

[124] *Id.* at 114-40, 172-95, 274-86.

[125] Glenn Shafer emphasizes the importance of the "construction" of probability arguments and he has emphasized how, from a formal point of view, it makes quite a difference how one formulates the possibilities or, in fancier parlance, how one partitions the "sample space" or, to say the same

We shall refer to your first frame as F_1 and we stipulate that it consists of the possible outcomes (1) death by natural causes, (2) death by accident, (3) death by suicide, and (4) death by criminal act. This frame may be represented thus:

F_1 = {natural causes, accident, suicide, criminal act}

Now suppose that you, the detective, acquire some additional morsels of information. You have some evidence that Mark Vincent's sister, Marsha Vincent, was in the residence adjacent to the garage on the day of Mark Vincent's death. Under these circumstances you might entertain a slightly different set of tentative hypotheses, conjectures, or possibilities. (Expressed in terms of probability theory, you might now partition the sample space in a different way.) Your new list of possibilities, which constitute another frame of discernment F_2, might now look like this:

F_2 = {natural causes, accident, suicide,
        Marsha did it, someone else did it}

This frame is somewhat more specific and somewhat more differentiated because the hypothesis of death by criminal act has been divided into two hypotheses, one of which focuses on a particular person, Marsha Vincent.

It is of course possible that the police detective has a different set of conjectures. He might rule out death by natural causes. If so, his collection of hypotheses might look like this:

F_3 = {accident, suicide, criminal act}

The possibilities in this frame are as coarse as in the first frame. However, the frame now contains fewer possibilities.

Shafer speaks of these sets of possible outcomes as frames of discernment because he maintains that differences in the possibilities or hypotheses a person entertains generate differences in the way that information and data are partitioned. As different questions or hypotheses are asked or put, the available evidence sorts itself out, or is sorted out, in different ways.

Shafer's insight that there is a relationship between the structure of hypotheses and evidence is very important. The notion of a frame of discernment implies that the relevance of evidence depends on the nature of the hypotheses or conjectures "in the case." It illustrates the familiar and common sense point that the

---

thing, how one specifies the possible outcomes to which probabilities are to be assigned. *See, e.g.,* Shafer, *The Construction of Probability Arguments,* 66 B.U.L. Rev. 799 (1986).

pertinence and relevance of information is in part a function of
the question or questions that one asks or wishes to answer. This
basic insight is crucial. Unlike most probabilistic perspectives on
evidence and inference, Shafer's theory speaks to the process of
inquiry.[126] This is because Shafer examines the formation of factual hypotheses, not just the question of how existing factual
issues are to be resolved.[127]

Shafer makes a variety of useful observations about the influence of evidence on the formation of factual hypotheses. Shafer
observes that hypotheses, conjectures, and "possibilities" vary in
their degree of differentiation. Some hypotheses are relatively
coarse or diffuse while other hypotheses are relatively differentiated and specific.[128] The fact that the specificity of hypotheses
can vary has two important implications. First, since the relevance of evidence is a function of the nature of the hypotheses or
conjectures posited, the relevance of evidence varies as the specificity of the hypotheses varies.[129] Second, the relative specificity
of a frame of possibilities is a function of the available evidence.
Shafer maintains that as evidence accumulates, a frame and the
possibilities within it tend to become more specific.[130] Shafer
illustrates this point with "The Case of the Missing Cookie."[131]

Sally and Billy are two children. One morning their mother
notices that there is only one cookie left in the cookie jar. Later
that morning she notices that the cookie is no longer there. She

---

[126] However, Shafer's theory perhaps does not speak to "investigation,"
which connotes the process of gathering evidence as well as the process of
deciding what evidence to gather.

[127] Both traditional and modern evidence scholarship focuses on the
relevance and probative force of evidence on already-specified issues. At a
theoretical level, this produces an emphasis on "relational analysis." *See
supra* notes 25, 26 and accompanying text.

[128] *See, e.g.*, G. SHAFER, *supra* note 123, ch. 6; *cf.* Shafer, *supra* note 125, at
809-15 (illustrating how more inclusive likelihood ratios are generated as
more evidentiary details are taken into account).

[129] This thesis pervades the entire argument made by Shafer in G.
SHAFER, *supra* note 123. The thesis that the relevance of evidence is a
function of the possibilities discerned is perhaps stated most directly in *id.*
ch. 6.

[130] *See, e.g., id.* at 36 ("It should not be thought that the 'possibilities' that
comprise . . . [a set of possibilities] will be determined and meaningful
independently of our knowledge. Quite to the contrary: [the set] . . . will
acquire its meaning from what we know or think we know . . . .").

[131] G. SHAFER, THE PROBLEM OF DEPENDENT EVIDENCE 5 (Sch. of
Business, Univ. of Kansas, Working Paper No. 164, 1984).

shouts, "Who took the last cookie?" Billy answers, "I saw Sally take it." The mother rushes to Sally's room and finds cookie crumbs there. This evidence suggests that Sally was the miscreant, but it does not convince the mother of Sally's guilt. Hence, Sally's mother entertains two possibilities, "Sally Did It" and "Sally Didn't Do It." In Shafer's terminology these two possibilities make out a "frame" and they may be represented in the following way:

$$F_A = \{\text{Sally Did It, Sally Didn't Do It}\}$$

As the mother ponders these alternative possibilities, it seems to her that two separate pieces of evidence support the possibility "Sally Did It;" Billy's accusation does so, but so does the cookie crumb evidence. Hence, even if Billy is being untruthful and did not see Sally take the cookie, the cookie crumb evidence still supports the hypothesis that Sally took the cookie. As the mother ponders further, however, it occurs to her that it is possible that Billy ate the cookie and planted the cookie crumbs in Sally's room.

Shafer argues that the way the mother originally framed the possibilities is no longer satisfactory. The mother originally believed that two pieces of evidence point to Sally as the miscreant. However, if it is possible that Billy planted the cookie crumbs, the possibility that Billy was being untruthful affects the probative value of the cookie crumb evidence as well as the probative value of Billy's accusation.[132] Given this relationship between the two pieces of evidence, it is necessary for the mother to reformulate or restructure the problem of the missing cookie. Shafer argues that if she wants to think about the problem clearly, she must construct a new and more refined frame that takes into account the possibility that Billy planted the cookie crumbs.[133] Figure 3 describes the possibilities she now sees.

---

[132] Stated in the parlance of probability theory, the difficulty is that the two pieces of evidence are not independent with respect to the possibilities in Frame F_A.

[133] G. SHAFER, *supra* note 131.

FIGURE 3

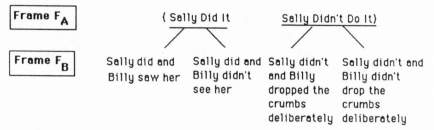

The new frame F_B is more refined, less coarse, and more differentiated than frame F_A. Yet, Frame F_A can be differentiated in various ways. Moreover, it may be differentiated to a greater degree. For example, if Sally's and Billy's mother notices that there are other children in the house — friends of Billy and Sally who have come over to play — she may wish to consider a variety of new hypotheses about the reason for the missing cookie. For example, she may decide that it is possible that neither Sally nor Billy took the missing cookie. It is possible that Sally joined with one, or more, of the visiting children in taking the missing cookie, and that Billy and a visitor, or visitors, acted in concert. It may now also occur to the mother that Billy and Sally might have acted in concert. She might entertain this possibility, together with the possibility that Sally acted alone and the possibility that Billy acted alone. This new set of possibilities, greater in number and more differentiated than those in F_B, is represented in Figure 4.

FIGURE 4

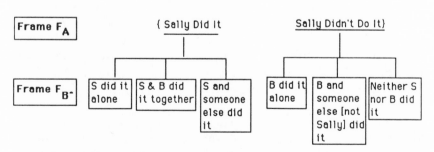

Notice that $F_{B^{\wedge}}$, like F_B, is consistent with F_A. Moreover, $F_{B^{\wedge}}$ and F_B, we have supposed, were formed after F_A was formed. However, the process can also work in reverse; a relatively richer frame such as F_B can be abandoned (because, for example, it is discovered that Billy was not in a position to plant cookies in

Sally's room), thus restoring the primacy of a more general frame, such as F_A.

There are multiple messages in "The Case of the Missing Cookie." First, the specificity of frames can vary. Second, the specificity of a frame is related to the nature of the available evidence. Third, frames can be refined and made more specific. Fourth, the frames can be made more specific in different ways. Another possible lesson is that the frames can be coarsened as well as refined. These propositions shed a great deal of light on investigative strategy.

Shafer's argument about how the mother in the cookie case refines her possibilities suggests that extremely coarse hypotheses are generally of little value to an investigator. For example, suppose that the frame concerning Mark Vincent's death consists of the possibilities: (1) Mark Vincent died unfairly, and (2) Mark Vincent did not die unfairly. The possibilities in this frame are not sharp; they are relatively undifferentiated. They are also of little value to an investigator because they do not serve to sort out potentially interesting items of evidence in any very specific or discrete way. Indeed, the possibilities in the frame are so coarse that they give little if any indication of what sort of evidence might serve to confirm or repudiate them. We might say that this frame does not serve to partition any evidence we might happen to acquire.[134] Hence, this frame of coarse possibilities gives almost no guidance or instruction to an investigator.

Specific hypotheses, by contrast, are excellent indicators of important evidence. Specific hypotheses focus attention on particular types and items of evidence. Their specificity is suggestive of the specific items of evidence that are relevant to the assessment of the hypotheses under consideration. For example, suppose that you — the police detective — seriously entertain the hypothesis that Marsha Vincent deliberately stabbed Mark Vincent in the head with a screwdriver at 3:01 a.m. in the garage

---

[134] Shafer's general thesis about the importance of frames of discernment in the construction of probability arguments is related to the debate about the alleged theory-dependence of evidence. Shafer's point of view, however, is not the same as those who argue that evidence is a function of theory. While Shafer agrees that the significance of evidence is related to the hypotheses under consideration, Shafer also believes that evidence shapes hypotheses. *See supra* note 130. Shafer's unique contribution consists of his detailed and precise account of how evidence may influence the formation of hypotheses.

because she became angry about his animosity toward Harriet Jones. This hypothesis or possibility is highly differentiated or particularized. It is also suggestive of the types of evidence that might be of interest to you. For example, it suggests that (1) an interview with Harriet Jones might produce highly significant evidence, (2) you might wish to ask Marsha about her feelings toward Harriet, (3) you should attempt to establish that Marsha was home before 3:01 a.m., and so on.

The highly specific hypothesis also imparts a very different lesson. It demonstrates that specificity in conjectures and hypotheses is not always a virtue. Even if highly differentiated and specific hypotheses indicate more precisely how they may be verified or disconfirmed, it does not follow that investigators should always formulate highly differentiated hypotheses. As the Mark Vincent problem suggests, highly differentiated hypotheses may be of little value if they "outrun" the available evidence.[135] For example, there is little if anything in the evidence recited earlier that supports the conjecture that the homicide (if one took place) was committed at 3:01 a.m. rather than at 3:02 a.m. The precision of this conjecture outruns the evidence.[136] A rational investigator

---

[135] However, in our view — if perhaps not in Shafer's — hypotheses that outrun the evidence, that is that contain conjectures not directly supported by the evidence, sometimes do have heuristic value. *See infra* notes 141, 148-49.

[136] The problem of excessive specificity is not overcome if the detective decides to construct, not one or two differentiated homicide hypotheses, but a mass of differentiated homicide hypotheses that exhaust (pretty much, at least) every possible way that a homicide might have occurred (assuming that a homicide occurred). Suppose the detective uses only two variables — the time of the killing and the identity of the killer — to construct a (relatively) exhaustive set of differentiated homicide hypotheses. It is easy to see that the detective would have to formulate an enormous number of distinct homicide hypotheses. For example, if the detective limited herself to one 24-hour period and distinguished homicide hypotheses on the basis of the minute when the death occurred, she would generate 1440 distinct homicide possibilities. Moreover, if the detective assumed that anyone in the Washington, D.C., metropolitan area might have been the killer, the number of distinct homicide hypotheses would be vastly greater. If the adult population in the D.C. area were 3,000,000, the number of distinct homicide hypotheses would have to equal 1440 x 3,000,000, or more than four billion hypotheses. Hence, it seems clear that differentiated sets of hypotheses and conjectures are not always better than coarser and more diffuse hypotheses.

will sometimes decide not to refine her hypotheses, but to make them more coarse and diffuse.

The difficulty with constructing differentiated hypotheses that outstrip the evidence is partly economic. It would be much, much too expensive and time-consuming to give equal dignity to all of the discrete hypotheses that could be imagined by an investigator who feels free to invent possibilities without any reference to the available evidence. The costs associated with simply inventing and recording such possibilities — not to speak of the costs associated with actually gathering evidence about all of them — would very quickly exceed the gross world product.[137]

The difficulty posed by rampant multiplication of distinct homicide hypotheses, however, is not entirely economic; it also violates the virtue of cognitive parsimony. One objective of formulating conjectures and hypotheses is to facilitate analysis of possible courses of investigation (and, ultimately, possible courses of proof activity at trial). In the investigative situation we have just hypothesized, one can imagine little reason for the particular method used to generate specific hypotheses. For example, there is no apparent reason to distinguish homicide conjectures on the basis of the exact minute they might have been committed. For all that appears, distinctions on the basis of hours or days would have served equally well. Hence, there is no particular reason to think that differentiating homicide hypotheses on the basis of the minute of the killing or on the basis of the identity of the killer will produce any cognitive benefits; ruder distinctions, it appears, would do as well. Indeed, given the available evidence, the variable of the identity of the killer might well be omitted altogether.[138] In short, the precision of the possibilities is excessive and spurious and the frame it generates is cognitively unparsimonious.

If it is true that one cause of waste of cognitive resources is the absence of evidential support for possibilities, what is an investi-

---

[137] Our theory of investigative discovery does not address the relationship of real-world resources and investigation. Our focus is on cognitive parsimony and productivity. We may address more traditional forms of economic analysis in the next phase of our research.

[138] Adverse resource implications result from this analytical failure but one of the causes of the resource difficulties is of a cognitive, analytical sort. That is, not only is the amount of investigation required enormous, but the mental structuring of the problem, which gives rise to the demands on resources, is itself not efficient or parsimonious.

gator to do when the evidence available to him fails to suggest any possibilities except hopelessly coarse ones? It is safe to say that the concept of frames of discernment offers little if any help to an investigator in this situation. This does not mean that the refinement of possibilities is of no value during exploratory investigation. Even small collections of details may suggest relatively differentiated possibilities, and Shafer's procedure has considerable heuristic value when some possibilities begin to emerge from the evidence at hand.

The Case of the Missing Cookie illustrates Shafer's thesis that evidence serves to refine hypotheses. By this he means that evidence itself suggests various possibilities and evidence gets incorporated in hypotheses. This is why we say that Shafer refuses to permit possibilities to outrun the evidence. Shafer describes a procedure for incorporating evidence into hypotheses.[139] To illustrate how Shafer's technique works we will now add a few details to the detective's information base.

Suppose, first, that the detective searched Mark's body, the garage, and the adjacent house, and she did not find Mark Vincent's wallet. Suppose, further, that evidence suggests that Mark Vincent and Marsha Vincent stopped to cash a check for $200 shortly before Mark and Marsha went home the night before Mark's death. This new information suggests a new possibility: Mark's death occurred in the course of a robbery. If we take F_3 as the basic frame, this new possibility of robbery generates a new frame, which we shall call $F_{3.1}$. Figure 5 shows the relationship of this new frame to the basic frame F_3.

FIGURE 5

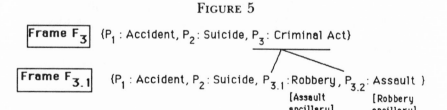

Now add some more information to the pot. Specifically, after a further search Mark's wallet is found in a bush directly adjacent to the garage in which Mark's body was found. There is no money in it, however, and even though it is known that Mark usu-

---

139 G. SHAFER, *supra* note 123, ch. 6.

ally carried credit cards, there are also no credit cards in the wallet. Moreover, the search uncovers an Anacin box in the vicinity of Mark's body. The Anacin box may contain traces of cocaine. Furthermore, the investigator discovers that Mark Vincent had been seeing a woman called Monica Carlson, the wife of Richard Carlson, and that Richard Carlson's van had been seen in the vicinity of Mark's house the night of Mark's death. Finally, the investigator discovers that Mark and Marsha, who were brother and sister, were joint owners of a computer company.

This new information again suggests the possibility of a robbery, but this time it may also suggest the possibility that the robbery was ancillary to an assault, motivated either by Carlson's possible jealousy, by a sour narcotics deal, or by the desire of Marsha to harm Mark to get his share of the computer company for herself. If we add these possibilities to the pot, we get this sort of picture:

FIGURE 6

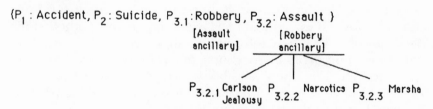

In addition, the facts recited suggest another possible variation on frame F_3. It is possible that there was an assault on Mark Vincent, but no robbery. If so, the new frame now may look like this:

FIGURE 7

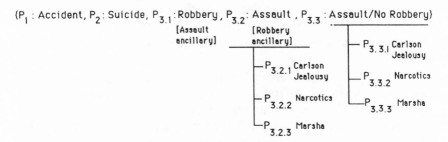

(P_1 : Accident, P_2 : Suicide, $P_{3.1}$: Robbery, $P_{3.2}$: Assault , $P_{3.3}$: Assault/No Robbery)

It is now becoming apparent, we trust, that the process of refining frames of possibilities may generate disadvantages as well as advantages. We have already described why disadvantages may accrue if an investigator allows her hypotheses to outstrip the available evidence. The tactic of refining possibilities, however, can cause difficulty even if all of the possibilities are suggested by the available evidence. The illustrations we have given of the process of refinement show that possibilities are extracted by a branching, tree-like procedure. Figure 8 shows one abstraction of the refinement process.

FIGURE 8

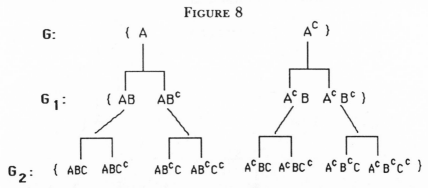

The initial frame G shows two possibilities, $\{A, A^c\}$. (Read A^c as "not A.") These possibilities are embellished in frame G_1 because the occurrence or nonoccurrence of B is now considered. Thus, one possibility now is AB^c, A happened and B did not happen. In Frame G_2 the possibilities are further embellished by consideration of the occurrence C.

There is an entailment relationship among these three levels of refinement. For example, ABC → AB → A. (Read "→" as "implies.") That is to say, if A and B and C happened, then A and B necessarily happened, and if A and B happened, then A necessarily happened. This logical point is quite important for present purposes because it means that all of the possibilities in the lower frames are compatible with the possibilities in the higher frames; there is no contradiction between the possibilities in the different frames.

The compatibility of lower frames with frames higher up means that possibilities can easily be expanded without limit and without fear of producing any contradiction with the initial frame. The refinement process shown in Figure 8 is just a special case of the process of producing compatible refinements. If S is the universe of all possibilities, frame G is simply a partition of all of these possibilities in terms of $\{A, A^c\}$; frame G_1 is just another partition of S when $\{B, B^c\}$ are considered; and frame G_2 results when $\{C, C^c\}$ are considered. In addition, new frames can be generated at will, and to any level, simply by increasing the number of single events in joint events (*i.e.*, A & B & C & D & . . . N), together with the complements of those single events. Moreover, different sets of compatible refinements can be generated by selecting joint events consisting of different single events. For example, Figure 9 shows another set of refinements, different from those in Figure 8, but also compatible with frame G.

FIGURE 9

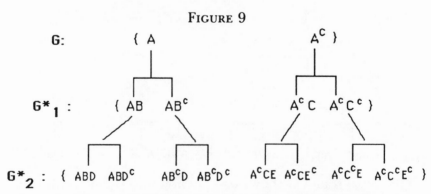

We need not describe this tree-like refinement process any further. It is evident that the refinement strategy can generate a vast number of possibilities and that it can do so even without the possibilities outstripping the evidence. While it is possible that a real-world investigator who is attempting to make sense of the information available to her might make conscious use of only a

possibilities strategy, it is very unlikely that the possibilities marshalling strategy can fully explain how any real-world investigator conducts a real-world investigation. Since the possibilities strategy is a tree-like hierarchical process, the number of possibilities directly indicated by evidence can multiply rapidly. Indeed, if the possibilities branch out symmetrically, the number of possibilities increases exponentially at each additional level of branches. Consequently, if the tree metaphor correctly describes the manner in which evidence generates possibilities, the strategy of refining possibilities can generate millions or billions of possibilities even if there has been only little investigation and the number of details collected is small.

Ordinarily it is not useful to formulate millions or billions of possibilities. There are, of course, considerable logistical problems and resource allocation problems associated with any investigative process that generates this many possibilities for serious consideration and investigation. Another kind of cost may be associated with numerous possibilities: even if an investigator has all the time and resources in the world at her command, she will not wish to scan all refined possibilities that the evidence suggests. It is not cognitively fruitful to consider all the possibilities suggested by the evidence.

It is fair to infer that any real-world investigator — particularly a mortal investigator having limited resources — must and will prune the possibilities tree of many of its limbs and branches. If an investigator prunes branches from a possibility tree, however, while leaving others intact, it is clear that some sort of cognitive process apart from possibilities analysis is at work in her brain, telling her that some possibilities should be eliminated and others retained. Something is telling the investigator that some possibilities are interesting while others are not. If this process of selective pruning of possibilities is effable rather than ineffable, it follows that the investigator who prunes possibilities trees is using one or more marshalling strategies that, although making an imprint on Shaferean marshalling, are not captured, or portrayed, by Shaferean formalizations.

The remainder of this Part of the Article will examine in detail several of the other marshalling strategies that may interact with the Shaferean possibilities marshalling strategy that we have just described. Yet, instead of emphasizing how various marshalling strategies can reduce the number of possibilities, we will generally emphasize how marshalling strategies can expand the number of possibilities to be considered.[140]

B. Possibilities and Imaginative Reasoning

1. Possibilities and Abduction

A marshalling system based on Shaferean possibilities tends to emphasize the importance of framing hypotheses that incorporate the possibilities disclosed and supported by available evidence. In this Part of the Article we view the relationship between hypotheses and evidence in a rather different way: we stress the importance of having hypotheses, conjectures, and possibilities that outstrip and outrun the available evidence. The Shaferean perspective is rooted in common sense; there are clearly risks in forming hypotheses that outstrip the available evidence. However, there are also grave dangers if possibilities analysis is the only strategy used to marshall evidence.[141] The Shaferean perspective on hypothesis formation, by stressing the isomorphism between evidence and hypothesis, understates the importance of invention in hypothesis formation.

Among the most important contributions made by the cantankerous American theorist Charles Saunders Peirce were his discus-

---

[140] It is true that it is unfruitful to form and consider an excessive number of possibilities, but it is also true that multiplication of possibilities is sometimes a cognitively productive strategy. Much depends on the nature of the possibilities that are "in the picture" because not all possibilities are equally valuable in generating further evidence.

[141] By suggesting that other marshalling strategies (e.g., scenario analysis) influence possibilities structuring, we are not making an imperialistic claim that other methods of structuring are superior to possibilities analysis. The marshalling strategies we are about to discuss complement rather than displace possibilities analysis. Hence, while it is true that scenario analysis and other formalizations capture features of investigation that elude Shaferean analysis, it is also true that Shaferean analysis captures features of investigation that elude other forms of analysis and structuring. Moreover, we are not just trying to be charitable to Glenn Shafer. A central theoretical underpinning for our entire research project is the thesis that a variety of logics is necessary to portray the process of judicial proof. *See* D. SCHUM, *Research on the Marshalling of Evidence and Structuring of Argument*, in OPERATIONS RESEARCH AND ARTIFICIAL INTELLIGENCE: THE INTEGRATION OF PROBLEM SOLVING STRATEGIES (D. Brown ed.) (forthcoming); *see also* Tillers, *supra* note 46, at 887-91. Hence, the discussion below of matters such as scenario analysis is as much designed to vindicate the general thesis of the importance of using a variety of logics as to vindicate the value of any specific marshalling strategy such as scenario analysis.

sions of the nature of imaginative and creative processes.[142] In Peirce's day it was fashionable to say that scientific investigation involves two types of reasoning processes, deduction and induction.[143] Peirce's contemporaries — many of whom were steeped in Mill's theory of scientific method — generally portrayed both deductive and inductive reasoning as rule-based processes.[144] While Peirce did not deny that rule-based inductive reasoning is important in scientific investigation, he did insist that imaginative reasoning — a type of reasoning that produces outcomes that are not determined by pre-existing rules — also plays a crucial role. According to Peirce, imaginative reasoning cannot be subsumed under deduction or induction, but rather is a third category of reasoning, distinct from both deduction and induction. He called this third form of reasoning abduction.[145]

The concept of abduction is a useful device for thinking about the relationship between possibilities and scenarios, and it also helps to explain why possibilities analysis cannot always stand alone. Return to the Mark Vincent hypothetical. Recall that one collection of the evidence in the case supports the possibilities, captured in Frame 3.3, which look like this:

---

[142] *See, e.g.*, PEIRCE, COLLECTED PAPERS OF CHARLES SAUNDERS PEIRCE (C. Hartshorne, P. Weiss & A. Burke eds. 1931-58).

[143] *See, e.g.*, A. SIDGWICK, FALLACIES: A VIEW OF LOGIC FROM THE PRACTICAL SIDE 212 (1883).

[144] *See* J. MILL, A SYSTEM OF LOGIC—RATIOCINATIVE AND INDUCTIVE (8th ed. reprint Longmans Green & Co. 1952). See discussions of Mill's theory in A. BURKS, CHANCE, CAUSE, REASON: AN INQUIRY INTO THE NATURE OF SCIENTIFIC EVIDENCE 102 (1977); J. CARNEY & R. SCHEER, FUNDAMENTALS OF LOGIC 355-56 (2d ed. 1974); L. COHEN, A PREFACE TO LOGIC 20-21 (1944); M. POLANYI, PERSONAL KNOWLEDGE 167, 270-71 (1958); I. SCHEFFLER, *supra* note 62, at 22-24, 76, 79, 295-97, 304-05.

[145] *See* N. RESCHER, PEIRCE'S PHILOSOPHY OF SCIENCE 41-51 (1978); THE SIGN OF THREE: DUPIN, HOLMES, PEIRCE (U. ECO & T. Sebrok eds. 1983).

FIGURE 7

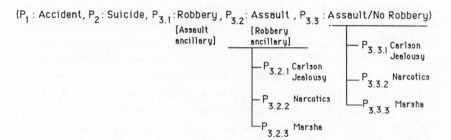

In verbal terms, the possibilities portrayed in the above diagram are the following:

1. Mark Vincent was killed as a result of an assault that was incidental to a robbery. The evidence of Vincent's empty wallet supports this possibility.

2. Mark Vincent was killed incidental to an assault that was made to look like a robbery. The evidence that a person was at the scene of the crime after the ambulance removed the body and that the wallet was not found before the ambulance removed the body supports this possibility.

3. Mark Vincent was killed during an assault. Mark Vincent lost the empty wallet at some other time or was robbed at another time by another person.

Now consider Figure 10.

FIGURE 10

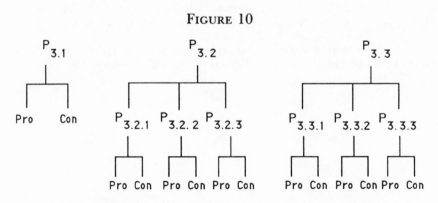

The diagram in Figure 10 captures one crucial ingredient of Shaferean possibilities analysis. The terms "pro" and "con" rep-

348

resent evidence that bears on each possibility suggested by the evidence. For each possibility, however, there is always "pro" evidence. This is because, in Shafer's scheme, a possibility is always embedded in the evidence; the only possibilities he recognizes are those that the evidence discloses. In reality, however, people attempting to assess the significance of evidence frequently construct or invent possibilities that the evidence itself does not suggest or manifest. The possibility P_n in the square below the question mark in Figure 11 represents such a possibility.

FIGURE 11

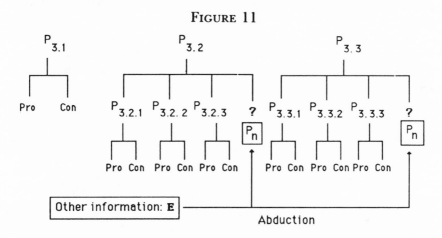

The extraction of the new possibility P_n is an example of abduction. Figure 11 arrays all the evidence that favors and disfavors the possibilities in frames of discernment such as frame 3.3. Yet, as Figure 11 illustrates, after the evidence is arrayed pro and con on identified possibilities, it often happens that there remains a body of evidence or details that neither favors or disfavors any of the possibilities that have been previously identified. In Figure 11 this "unconnected" body of evidence is represented by the symbol E. In the face of E an investigator may well invent a new possibility, P_n. E is evidence in search of an hypothesis. The invention of a hypothesis P_n to explain E is a form of abduction. Since possibility P_n is not directly shown by the evidence E, we can say that the investigator manufactures hypothesis P_n.

2. Possibilities and Retroduction

We have just seen that abductive reasoning may be applied to possibilities. In addition, possibilities may figure in another type of reasoning that Peirce called "retroduction."[146] There is a close relationship between abductive and retroductive reasoning. When an investigator thinks abductively, he invents possibilities. When an investigator thinks about possibilities retroductively, he reverses the process. Instead of hypothesizing possibilities to explain otherwise mystifying evidence, he imagines the evidence that a possibility might generate; instead of asking what possibilities are suggested by the evidence, he asks what evidence is suggested by the possibilities. When thinking retroductively the investigator would ask the following type of question: "If a given possibility (hypothesis) is true, what sort of evidence should I expect to find?"[147]

Retroductive thinking about the relationship between evidence and possibilities is hypothesis-driven. Abductive reasoning, by contrast, is evidence-driven. Figure 12 represents the basic nature of abduction.

FIGURE 12

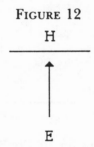

The arrow in Figure 12 indicates the direction in which reasoning moves. It moves from evidence E to hypothesis H; that is, H is inferred from E. However, the direction of the reasoning process can be reversed. In abduction a body of evidence supports an inference about a hypothesis, but when the direction of the reasoning process is reversed, H, a hypothesis, is the basis for an inference about E, evidence. Figure 13 represents this reverse reasoning.

---

[146] N. RESCHER, *supra* note 145, at 65-72.

[147] For example, he might ask, "Suppose it is true that Jimmy Hoffa was killed at Fidel Castro's order. If this is what led to Hoffa's death, what sort of evidence should I expect to see?"

FIGURE 13

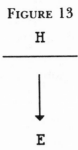

While abduction is bottom-up reasoning, retroduction is top-down reasoning. In abduction we have evidence in search of a hypothesis, and in retroduction we have a hypothesis searching for evidence. Retroduction, properly so-called, results when top-down reasoning follows on bottom-up reasoning. We have pictured this reasoning process as one that involves the steps shown in Figure 14.

In this schema, we suppose that an investigator (1) begins with a given set of hypotheses H_1 through H_n, (2) discovers that there is an body of evidence E that cannot be arrayed against these existing hypotheses, (3) infers a new hypothesis from E that may explain H_{n+1}, and (4) infers new evidence (in addition to E) from H_{n+1}.

When retroductive reasoning is applied to evidence and possibilities, one or more hypotheses — "possibilities," in Shafer's terminology — are taken as true. Additional hypotheses, or possibilities, are then extracted, or "deduced," from the possibilities that are assumed to be true. The derivative hypotheses or possibilities become indicators of potentially relevant evidence. They indicate, or point to, the potential significance of evidence that either favors or disfavors the deduced possibilities. For example, consider possibility $P_{3.2.1}$ (see Figure 7), the possibility that Mark Vincent was assaulted by Richard Carlson, the jealous husband of Monica Carlson. If retroductive reasoning is employed, the investigator might ask, "If $P_{3.2.1}$ is true, what other possibilities and evidence would we expect to have?" If she asks this question, the investigator might conclude that there may be witnesses who will say that they saw Mark and Monica together in circumstances consistent with the possibility of a romantic interest between Mark and Monica.

The concepts of abduction and retroduction serve to clarify our thesis that possibilities analysis does not stand alone and that it is

FIGURE 14

A. Abduction: Generating A New Possibility

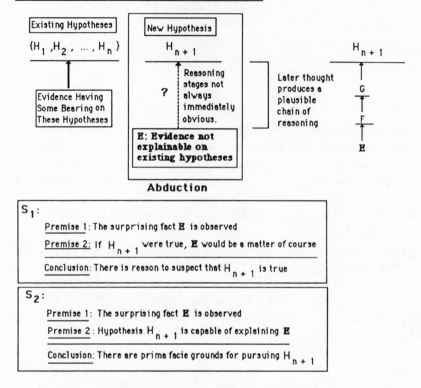

Abduction

S_1:

    Premise 1: The surprising fact **E** is observed

    <u>Premise 2:</u> If H_{n+1} were true, **E** would be a matter of course

    Conclusion: There is reason to suspect that H_{n+1} is true

S_2:

    Premise 1: The surprising fact **E** is observed

    Premise 2: Hypothesis H_{n+1} is capable of explaining **E**

    Conclusion: There are prima facie grounds for pursuing H_{n+1}

B. Retroduction And Hypothesis Testing

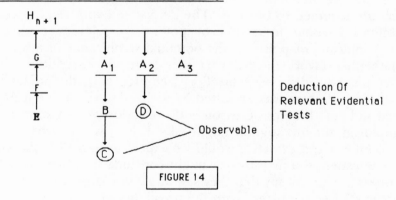

FIGURE 14

subject to the influence of other evidence marshalling techniques. Indeed, the illustrations we have given of the potential impact of abduction and retroduction on possibilities analysis understate the potential impact of abductive and retroductive reasoning. For example, in our discussion of abduction we assumed that abduction only enters the picture when a portion of the available evidence cannot be arrayed (pro and con) against existing possibilities.[148] Hence, we assumed that existing possibilities are simply present or given. However, it is of course possible that the existing possibilities were themselves obtained by abduction. Indeed, it might be said that no possibility exists in the absence of abduction. For example, the formation of the hypothesis that Mark Vincent was killed as a result of a robbery is a possibility manufactured by the investigator. Although this possibility is supported by the evidence, it is nevertheless a hypothesis that the investigator formulates and invents.[149]

Our earlier illustrations also understated the potential impact of retroductive reasoning on possibilities analysis. Any assessment of the force of evidence on known possibilities inescapably involves retroduction. Even if a body of evidence can be arrayed pro and con against existing possibilities, it is always possible to invent a new possibility having evidential implications and consequences. Hence, whether or not existing possibilities are satisfactory cannot be determined without a determination of whether there are yet other plausible possibilities that can also explain the available evidence. For example, if all the available evidence could be arrayed pro and con against the hypothesis that Mark Vincent was killed as a result of a robbery, it might still be necessary to consider the additional possibility that Mark Vincent was killed as a result of a drug deal gone sour. It might turn out that the sour drug deal hypothesis is superior to the robbery hypothesis even though all of the available evidence is pertinent to the robbery hypothesis.

These considerations are a partial vindication of our general thesis that it cannot be assumed that any single evidence marshalling system operates without being influenced by any other

---

[148] *See supra* text accompanying Figures 10 & 11.

[149] *Cf.* G. SHAFER, *supra* note 123, at 285 (although the assessment of evidence within a frame is a disciplined activity, "[t]he construction of a frame of discernment is a creative act, and we choose among frames of discernment, in the first instance at least, by asking not which is truer but which is more beautiful and more useful").

scheme of evidence marshalling. If this general point is granted, however, the exact nature of the connection between possibilities analysis and other evidence marshalling strategies remains to be determined and described. Hence, we now focus on the possible relationships between possibilities analysis and several other forms of evidence marshalling.

C. *Event Chronologies, Scenarios, Possibilities*

1. Marshalling by Time: Event Chronologies

The construction of a hierarchy of possibilities takes into account the order in which evidence was discovered. Yet, the order in which events are believed to have occurred is also a matter of considerable importance. An investigator who acquires details may feel a need not only to record the time at which the evidence was received (which is not the same as time-stamping the order in which possibilities were imagined), but also to time-stamp the events that the evidence may show. One reason for the importance of the effort to temporally order the events possibly shown by the evidence is plain: one of the investigator's ultimate objectives may be to demonstrate that certain events or acts-in-time took place or that a certain sequence of events or acts took place.[150] Consequently, as we mentioned in Part I, one step an investigator may take is to construct a "time line." We refer to a time line as an "event chronology." Figure 15 is an example of a simple event chronology.

---

[150] Many, perhaps most, legal rules specifying grounds for liability and defense imply a need for a certain sequence of events. For example, killing is first degree murder only if the killing was premeditated, and killing is murder only if death occurred as a result of the act designed to cause death.

FIGURE 15

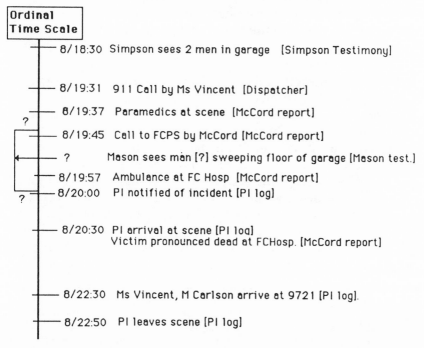

An event chronology can serve various useful functions. One of its functions hinges on the inconclusive character of evidence. Since evidence is always inconclusive, it is never certain that the reported order of events conforms to the actual order of events. An event chronology is a useful device for marshalling various items of evidence that bear on the question of the temporal locus of a particular event. The evidence suggesting a particular temporal locus of an event can be arrayed against a point or an interval on a time line.

Assuming that an investigator has some confidence that the reported order of events conforms with the actual order of events, an event chronology also serves the obvious function of arranging significant events in a temporal order. As noted earlier,[151] one obvious reason for arranging events temporally is the expectation that at any trial someone — judge or jury — must

---

[151] *See supra* note 150 and accompanying text.

make decisions about events and acts that took place in time. Moreover, the order in which events and acts occur may be of enormous significance. In a murder case, for example, it may make all the difference whether the accused purchased a gun before or after the victim was shot, and in a conspiracy case it may make a difference whether the alleged conspirators became acquainted with each other before or after the alleged conspiracy.

Although a time line of events can be useful, it is not always simple to assemble a useful one. In the course of an investigation an investigator may receive reports of a great many events. The multitude of such reports can generate two kinds of difficulties. The first difficulty is that the number or distribution of reported events may make it difficult to display them clearly. For example, a great many events and acts may have taken place in one relatively short interval of time (*e.g.*, twenty seconds). The result may be great "event density" in one interval of time, while relatively few events and acts are reported as having occurred in other comparable intervals in the event chronology. It is not easy to display events clearly when they are distributed unevenly over time.[152]

Event density is not the only cause of clutter in an event chro-

---

[152] Suppose that an attempt is made to depict a sequence of events graphically. If some time intervals are filled with many events, several unfortunate things can happen. First, the time line may be unintelligible because too many events are packed too closely together in some intervals of the time line. Alternatively, if the size of the time line is expanded to create more space between densely packed events, the expanded diagram may be physically unwieldy and it may not be possible to "take in" the entire time line in one glance. There appears to be a third remedy, however: keep the physical dimensions of lightly peppered intervals small and expand the size only of densely-packed intervals. Yet, this remedy also exacts a cost. For example, since the graphic dimensions of time intervals do not correspond to their true dimensions, the diagram may impede an observer's ability to grasp temporal relationships accurately. (For example, it may matter whether a price of a commodity was raised shortly after or long after an alleged price-fixing agreement was made.) Moreover, as new reports of events are gathered, events may have to be recorded on time segments that were not expanded.

While no remedy for the practical difficulties generated by differentials in event density is without cost, computer-based technology can alleviate such difficulties. For example, it would not be difficult for an artful software programmer to design a program that allows a user to expand a densely packed segment of a graphic event chronology at the push of a button. This would allow a user both to scan the events already recorded in a densely-packed interval more easily and record additional events in that interval. *See* D. SCHUM & P. TILLERS, *supra* note 122, pt. 3, at 65-68.

nology. The intrinsic nature of an event chronology creates a second source of clutter. If an investigator receives reports of numerous events and attempts to record every such event, the resulting event chronology will appear cluttered even in the absence of event density because many of the events recorded by the investigator will have no apparent connection with each other and many of the recorded acts and events will have no apparent significance. The consequence is that such an event chronology may impede rather than improve comprehension.[153]

The existence of this second type of clutter reflects the fact that an event chronology is not a scenario. An event chronology merely lists the order of events and acts but establishes no links or connections between the acts and events shown in the chronology. The absence of links between events may produce clutter and impede comprehension even if all the events recorded are significant ones. For example, Event A, a significant event, may be connected with Events F and J, but not with Events B, C, D, and E, which fall between A and F, or with Events G, H, and I, which fall between F and J.[154] The importance of being able to see connections between events suggests that one of the purposes of an event chronology is the development of a scenario. A scenario, unlike an event chronology, purveys a theory about events and acts in time; a theory that explains events establishes connections among them. Hence, a scenario lends a measure of intelligibility and coherence to temporally-ordered events and, by doing that, it also makes it easier for an observer to grasp, store, and recall the events in question.

---

[153] One seemingly obvious remedy for this type of clutter is a prohibition against the recording of insignificant events and acts; only salient, important, or significant events should be recorded. Although easily stated, however, this mandate is less easily implemented. The unanswered question, of course, is when an act or event is important enough to be recorded.

[154] For example, the following events take place in the following order (A) Peter Plaintiff hits David Defendant, (B) Shopkeeper closes his drug store for the day, (C) David Defendant goes to Shopkeeper's drug store, (D) David Defendant's wife Martha Marks takes a sleeping pill, (E) Peter Plaintiff hits Martha Marks, (F) Shopkeeper unlocks his closed drugstore, (G) David Defendant screams in anguish, (H) David Defendant takes a pain killer, and (I) Peter Plaintiff suffers an attack of strychnine poisoning. All of these events may be significant but their arrangement is unilluminating. They can be arranged in a more meaningful way. For example, (A), (B), (C), (E) and (C), (D), (E), (G), (I) are some possible arrangements that are more illuminating.

If it is granted that an event chronology facilitates the development of scenarios and that scenarios make an event chronology more intelligible to an observer, it remains to be established how an event chronology should be constructed in order to facilitate the construction of scenarios. This, like every similar question about the relationship between marshalling strategies, presents something of a chicken and egg problem: without knowing what the probable scenario is, we cannot be sure how to construct an event chronology, and without some type of an event chronology, we may find it hard to construct a scenario.

Part of the answer to this dilemma must be simply that the investigator must rely on her intuitions in deciding which events are likely to be significant.[155] However, we have more substantial and useful advice to give about the design of event chronologies. One piece of advice is that investigators consider constructing event chronologies around actors. Figure 16 shows how such an event chronology might look.

---

[155] The first step is always the hardest; any initial effort to marshal evidence is practically by definition unstructured. However, beginnings are made and some beginnings are well made. This suggests that nature, accident, intuition, biology, and matters of that sort can work to give the investigator some confidence (for reasons he cannot explain) that one type of marshalling strategy is the right one to use at the outset and that it is appropriate to use it in this or that particular way. In a report on the research described here, we invoke chaos theory in an effort to describe the meandering character of investigative activity and to explain how meandering sometimes becomes productive. *See* D. SCHUM & P. TILLERS, *supra* note 122, pt. 3, at 158-61. Our recourse to chaos theory, however, is a recourse to a simile. Although chaos theory may provide comfort and reassurance, it yields no specific prescriptions for marshalling evidence in the face of intellectual and cognitive confusion.

FIGURE 16

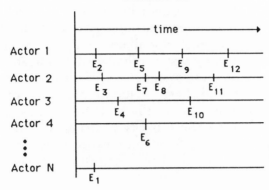

While our advice to construct event chronologies around actors partially begs the question of how an investigator is to decide whether an actor is or is not a significant player, our advice does not beg the somewhat different question of the appropriate design of an event chronology when an investigator's ignorance is great but not complete. An investigator may always surmise that the issues in any eventual trial will implicate hypotheses about human actions; lawsuits always involve hypotheses about the conduct of human beings. Consequently, an investigator may reasonably surmise that regardless of the nature of the central issues in a case, a party involved in a trial will have to construct and present a coherent and plausible story about the activities of one or more people. Hence, lacking any particular reason to use any particular marshalling strategy or to use a particular marshalling strategy in a particular way, an investigator may be well-advised to begin the project of constructing an overall scenario by assembling mini-scenarios about particular individuals, with the expectation that she may later be able to piece together those mini-scenarios to make out the larger story that she, or someone else, will eventually want to tell at trial. One additional reason to take this course is that most investigators already have a reservoir of background information about the behavior of human beings. This reservoir of information allows them to make plausible guesses, even when little specific information is available, about how actors might have acted and interacted.[156]

In the discussion of scenarios found immediately below we offer more advice about the design and uses of event chronologies. The reason we can do so — the reason why the chicken-and-

---

[156] Tillers, *supra* note 46, at 927-32.

egg problem does not stop us — is that it is not sensible to assume that an investigator cannot have a sense of the possible uses and purposes of an event chronology before she has used another marshalling strategy. Not all knowledge is explicit; some is tacit.[157] The marshalling systems that we describe are heuristic devices. Any users of these systems must and will capitalize on the knowledge they already have, including their tacit knowledge. Indeed, it may be permissible to think of the network described here as a device that has the capacity to bring to consciousness and make explicit the methods and procedures that people already tacitly and naturally use when they engage in fact investigation.[158]

2. Marshalling by Time: Scenarios

We have already explained that a scenario constitutes an explanation of a sequence of events in time.[159] We also noted that a scenario also serves as a "gap filler."[160] A scenario performs this service precisely because a scenario is an explanation or a theory. That is, there is more to a scenario than the events it explains; there is also the explanation or theory that it contains. This theory is a theory of how things and events are related in time and a theory of this sort — a scenario — allows the person constructing it to posit events and acts for which there is no evidence. It is this conjectural or fanciful ingredient that legitimates use of the loose phrase "story telling" to refer to the process of scenario construction. As we explained in Part I,[161] however, a story used for forensic purposes cannot be entirely fanciful. We are ultimately concerned about the truth of a matter or matters of fact. Hence, if a scenario has elements of fancy, it must be a mixture of fact and fancy — we are interested only in plausible stories. Figure 17 represents a scenario containing a mixture of fact and fancy.

---

157 *See, e.g.*, I. ROCK, THE LOGIC OF PERCEPTION 11 (1983) (noting that "child who erroneously refers to 'sheeps' evidences [implicit] knowledge of the rule that plural nouns add an 's'" though child has never seen or heard the word). In a more philosophical vein, see M. POLANYI, THE TACIT DIMENSION (1958).

158 Making tacit cognitive processes explicit is not necessarily a useless exercise. The explicit formulation of tacit standards can change the "outputs" of cognitive processes. *See* Tillers, *supra* note 46, at 933.

159 *See supra* text accompanying notes 82-83, 154.

160 *See supra* text accompanying notes 79-80, 87-88.

161 *See supra* text accompanying note 87.

FIGURE 17

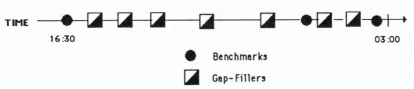

The partially shaded squares in Figure 17 represent "gap fillers." For example, if an investigator has good evidence that Abel intended to go to Stop & Shop (a supermarket) but there is no other evidence whether he actually did so, we may "fill the gap" in our story by guessing that he did go to the supermarket. Hence, gap fillers are hypothesized events representing the fanciful or conjectural components of a scenario.[162] By contrast, the black circles in Figure 17 represent "benchmark events." Benchmark events are the stable components of the scenario; they are the scaffolding on which the conjectural parts of the scenario can be hung.

Although some events may be treated as benchmarks, the question of whether an event is or is not a benchmark does not always, if ever, have a secure answer. If benchmark events are ever "stable," they are only relatively so. An event that was taken to be a benchmark may later seem less (or more) "solid," and the initial judgment that an event is a benchmark may be questioned and revised later. Hence, the question of whether an event is a benchmark may be the subject of conscious, and continuing deliberation. An investigator may wonder which events should serve as the basis for additional conjectures.

The strength of the evidence pointing to the existence of an event is one factor that influences the decision whether or not to treat an event as a benchmark. The reason for this is plain: since our ultimate interest is in the truth of some matter of fact, we do not want to build the fanciful parts of our stories on rungs that

---

[162] Of course, it is true that the evidence of Abel's intent may be taken as evidence of Abel's action as well as of his intent. While true, this point is immaterial. A scenario shows that the reasoning that takes us from evidence of intent to the conclusion of the act involves causal and temporal reasoning, *i.e.*, hypotheses about workings of space-time sectors, including, of course, the workings of persons in space and time. That is to say, an important component of the argument that leads from evidence of intent to action is a theory of how things, events, persons, and actions are related in a spatio-temporal framework.

may fall out from under our feet. We want to choose rungs that we think will hold up. The importance of identifying benchmarks for possible scenarios suggests that one of the functions of an event chronology is to facilitate assessments of the strength of the evidence supporting an event recorded on the event chronology. We have already noted that an event chronology permits an investigator to juxtapose events and the evidence that points to the occurrence of those events. This juxtaposition improves an investigator's ability to determine how strongly evidence supports the hypothesis that an event occurred, and it aids the investigator in making the decision whether to accord a hypothesized event benchmark status. In short, an event chronology stimulates the formation of scenarios not only by the manner in which it displays the temporal order of possible events, but also by the way it displays the probability that the events recorded conform to actual events. It follows that a well-supported event in an event chronology may become a benchmark event in a scenario. The manner in which this transposition might take place is illustrated by the diagrams in Figure 18.

FIGURE 18

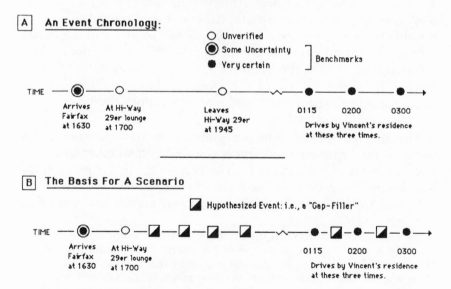

3.   Legal Marshalling & Case Theories

The use of a case theory as an evidence marshalling strategy is closely related to the use of elements of substantive legal rules to marshal evidence.[163] Like marshalling by legal rules, a case theory implicates substantive[164] legal doctrines. However, a case theory is more than a method for marshalling thought about legal doctrines. A case theory is a method of relating legal doctrines to evidence and hypotheses about facts.

A lawyer might say that a theory of the case relates factual issues to the elements of the legal claims and defenses that are (thought to be) "in" the case. Indeed, our imaginary lawyer might go one step further by saying that a case theory describes the relationship between the material factual issues in the case and the evidence that is relevant to each material factual issue.[165] When viewed in these terms, a case theory collapses several distinct marshalling strategies into one. In formulating his case theory the lawyer will consider the elements of legal rules, material factual hypotheses, and, in our terms, "details," "possibilities," or other matters of this sort. While we use rather different language to explain what a case theory is, our account of a case theory is very much like our imaginary lawyer's. Moreover, our formulation of a case theory also suggests that a case theory combines, or integrates, several distinct methods of marshalling. It is as if several different methods of marshalling are drawn up into a case theory.

In our terms (*i.e.*, in terms of the equivalence class concept) a case theory incorporates those substantive legal rules whose joint satisfaction through a scenario constitutes instantiation of a case theory. In other words, a case theory prescribes a theoretical

---

[163] We have already discussed the use of substantive legal rules to marshall evidence. *See supra* Section I(C)(9). As already explained, legal marshalling may involve the decomposition of legal rules into their elements. Marshalling by case theories, which we discuss here, is closely related to marshalling by "substantive legal rules." However, there are also some important differences. *See* discussion at text accompanying *infra* notes 165-67.

[164] We have not yet considered the implications of procedural and evidentiary rules for evidence marshalling. We plan to do so in the next stage of our research.

[165] This way of formulating a case theory conflates analysis of the elements of legal rules with analysis of the legal materiality of factual hypotheses. It is interesting to note that the blurring of this real distinction can enhance the efficiency of a decision maker's ability to array available evidence against pertinent factual issues. This gain in cognitive efficiency will sometimes occur precisely because it is sometimes cognitively fruitful and efficient to suppress explicit analysis of the validity of a definition of a legal claim or legal defense.

equivalence class consisting of scenarios in which all of the substantive legal rules in the theory are instantiated by the evidential foundations of those scenarios. This interpretation of the notion of a "case theory" involves several methods of marshalling evidence. First, since a case theory is a theory about the relationship between legal doctrines and evidence, a case theory involves the decomposition of legal doctrines into elements. Second, since a case theory is a theory of how facts establish or satisfy the elements of legal doctrines, a case theory incorporates a hypothesis that specifies the particular states of the world (factual situations) that instantiate the elements of legal rules. (We might think of this as reasoning that addresses the relationship between abstract legal principles and concrete factual situations.) Third, since a case theory posits instantiation of elements of legal rules by particular facts whose existence is uncertain, a case theory necessarily incorporates factual hypotheses, and since a factual hypothesis is always embedded in a scenario,[166] a case theory inevitably incorporates a scenario. Finally, since a case theory has value only if there is evidential support for the theory, a case theory incorporates or reflects methods of marshalling such as the marshalling of details, marshalling by possibilities, marshalling for credibility, and the marshalling of real evidence.[167]

CONCLUSION

A. Integration and Coordination of Marshalling Strategies

We have shown that marshalling strategies taken individually have the capacity to generate very complex webs of arguments and extremely intricate arrangements of details.[168] In view of this, one may question whether any natural person has the capacity to use a single marshalling strategy effectively. The use of a

---

[166] This is because "facts" always occur in a temporal order and hypothetical facts are part of a hypothetical temporal order, which is nothing other than a scenario.

[167] In summary, a case theory contains (at least): (1) a theory of the elements of a legal rule; (2) a theory of how these elements may be instantiated in facts (*i.e.*, which facts are instances of an element); (3) a scenario containing hypotheses (events) that constitutes such instantiations; and (4) a theory or theories about how evidence supports such hypotheses.

[168] Only a few details are necessary to produce enormously complex argument structures and arrangements of details. Recall that there are $2^{100}-1$ combinations of 100 details. Now note that each combination of details can be used to form one or more arguments that have various steps.

case theory to organize investigation makes this question more acute because at least several different methods of marshalling are embedded in any case theory.[169] Hence, if it is true that the use of a case theory to marshal and organize evidence "works," this fact has important implications for the feasibility of coordinating marshalling strategies.

We have devoted a substantial amount of discussion to several marshalling strategies. In some of those discussions, we have alluded to the problem of coordinating marshalling strategies. For example, our discussion of the relationship between scenarios and event chronologies suggests that an intelligent investigator may want to skip back and forth between different marshalling strategies. Thus, when an investigator attempts to construct a scenario, he may also want to think — at the same time — of an event chronology. Moreover, to make good use of the event chronology, he may also want to think, again roughly at the same time, about the evidence that is arrayed against the events shown in the event chronology.[170] The job of coordinating and integrating marshalling strategies forces an investigator to do more than merely walk and chew gum at the same time. Indeed, the mental operations required for such coordination are extraordinarily complex. Their complexity raises the question whether it is possible to use a network of marshalling strategies such as ours to any practical advantage.

Our answer to this question is by way of confession and avoidance. The confession is that it is true that the mental processes described by our network of marshalling strategies are extraordinarily complex, and it is true that it may be impossible for any human being to keep all of these systems and all of their details and refinements in her head at the same time. The plea by way of avoidance is twofold. First, it is likely that human beings, unaided by our theory, are also required to keep different kinds of mental processes in their heads at the same time. The question, therefore, is not whether anyone can keep everything in one's head at the same time. Rather, the question is how one can better keep in

---

169 Indeed, we might say that the very purpose of a case theory is to integrate distinct marshalling strategies.

170 This need for thinking in different modes need not stop there. For example, while constructing a scenario and also thinking about an event chronology and also ruminating about the evidence supporting the events in the event chronology, an investigator may also want to be thinking — at the same time! — about the elements of legal claims and defenses.

one's head the various things that one would like to keep in her head.

Second, one of the purposes of our computer system is precisely to improve the ability of people to keep many things in their heads. It is a fact that people's ability to recall all pertinent details and to think of everything pertinent is limited. We cannot, and do not, promise that our scheme for marshalling evidence will enable people to recall everything and to conjure up every argument and consideration simultaneously. To the extent that our work addresses the marshalling of evidence in real-world contexts, our aim is only to improve people's ability to remember and think about various things at the same time.

The problem of coordinating and integrating marshalling strategies is nothing more than a problem of juxtaposing ideas in an orderly and meaningful way. There are several reasons for believing that natural persons have the capacity to coordinate and integrate contrived marshalling strategies. First, people already have an enormous capacity to juxtapose ideas. It is noteworthy that many of the marshalling strategies we describe are ones that some lawyers already use. Second, our theory is itself a system or procedure designed for juxtaposing ideas; that is, our theory is a tool or device that can be used, and is meant to be used, to juxtapose diverse ideas.[171] Third, there is good reason to think that the orderly and meaningful juxtaposition of ideas greatly increases the capacity of human beings to remember details while keeping them in order. Hence, if our method of sorting evidence and organizing thought about evidence is orderly and meaningful, there is reason to think it can improve the ability of people to keep their thinking about details straight.

Consider the schematic representation in Figure 19 of how a lawyer might visualize a particular case theory.

---

[171] The theoretical significance of our work on computer prototypes of evidence marshalling systems may now be more apparent. Our prototypes allow users to shift back and forth between different marshalling strategies and they allow users to view, almost simultaneously, linked portions of different marshalling strategies. These prototypes thus illustrate the importance of the juxtaposition of ideas. However, they also do more. They illustrate the particular types of juxtaposition that are helpful and in this way they suggest some basic properties of human thinking about facts and evidence. In particular, our effort to portray the nature of a case theory suggests, first, the epistemological importance of juxtaposing local and global perspectives, *see infra* Section B, and, second, the epistemological importance and implications of metaphors, *see infra* Section C.

FIGURE 19

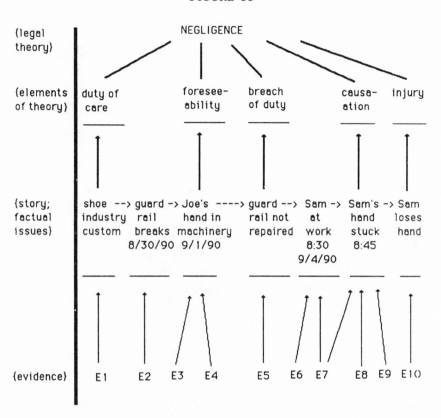

It seems to us that a case theory such as the one depicted in Figure 19 "works;" that is, we think that this way of structuring thought about a case may be an effective and intelligible way of keeping in mind a variety of matters and details at the same time. Moreover, it seems to us that when a case theory such as the one schematized in Figure 19 does work, it does so because a case theory is an orderly and meaningful way of arranging evidence. Both the overall structure and the lattices within the structure make sense.

Intuition suggests that meaningful arrangements of information, as opposed to random arrangements, improve memory and retrieval. For example, people can apparently better remember sequences of letters or numbers when those letters or numbers are meaningfully arranged than when they are randomly arranged. Moreover, empirical research by Pennington, Hastie, and Penrod strongly suggests that a "story model" allows people to retrieve details with great efficiency.[172]

B. Parts and Wholes in Inference

One of the lessons we relearned from our work on computer prototypes is that people need to be able both to recall details and to "see the whole picture;" effective marshalling of evidence requires both a local and a global juxtaposition of ideas. The importance of both these perspectives, however, raises a basic logical problem. We can refer to this problem as the problem of the relationship between parts and wholes.

The problem of parts and wholes — the problem of the relationship between synthetic and granular perspectives on evidence — assumes various guises. One example of this problem also illustrates why a synthetic perspective on problems of investigation and proof is essential. As we noted earlier,[173] the task of coordinating marshalling strategies closely parallels the project of making effective use of a single marshalling strategy. When a marshalling strategy is actually applied, it can produce an intricate network of arguments. In graphic form a complex of arguments based on a marshalling system takes the form of a network of arcs and nodes. This network can resemble a spider web. A person attempting to assess the significance of a collection of evidence may sense the importance of the details but she may have a hard time keeping all of those details in mind when she is trying to assess the overall impact of her fine-grained analyses.

We have discussed various strategies that may enhance the ability of people to remember and retrieve details. While those strategies seem sensible and effective, the premise that any one of them can work is not free of difficulty. A chicken-and-egg problem inheres in the use of any particular strategy that we recommend. We have said that uninhibited use of any marshalling strategy can produce excessive complexity, and we have suggested that an investigator should refer to other marshalling strategies to prune away such excessive noise and complexity. The chicken-and-egg difficulty is that those other marshalling strategies are themselves intricate and an investigator's ability to use them as shearing devices depends on her ability to remember their details. But how is she supposed to do that without resort-

---

172 *See* R. HASTIE, S. PENROD & N. PENNINGTON, *supra* note 85, at 22-23, 163-65, 234; Pennington & Hastie, *supra* note 85.

173 *See supra* text accompanying note 168.

ing to yet some other marshalling strategy, which then again presents her with the same problem?

We believe that a global perspective is necessary to make this otherwise inexplicable process work. The workings of any network of marshalling systems are inexplicable without the supposition that people have the capacity to regulate the detailed workings of individual marshalling strategies by some sort of global, synthetic perspective. In an earlier work one of the authors of this Article wrote:

> It is tempting to think that what happens (and should happen) [in fact finding] is that a trier of fact — any trier of fact — engages in a sequential process in which there is a repeated reciprocal interaction between a general vision of the evidence as a whole and a general vision of its parts, a process in which each vision is progressively revised and checked by the other but in which neither can be supposed, in principle, to be entirely independent of the other.[174]

We still think that the general sentiment expressed here is correct. From a logical point of view, however, the ability of people to shift back and forth between local and global perspectives does not solve the chicken-and-egg problem. While local perspectives may have to rest on global ones, global perspectives must rest on granular details. We end where we began.

The logical intractability of the question of the temporal relationship between local and global perspectives leaves us no alternative except the supposition that the logical problem is answered by psychology. On another occasion one of the authors wrote: "While, as a logical matter, it seems, at least to us, that the interaction of parts and wholes, and their interdependence, are inescapable, it is not true, physically considered, that this logical interdependence continues indefinitely . . . ."[175] The same kind of answer must be given to the question of the temporal relationship between wholes and parts during the beginnings of the process of inference and proof. Logically speaking, neither global analysis nor granular analysis can start first, but "physically considered" — psychologically speaking — one or the other must have some sort of priority at any given moment in time. By the same token, despite the fact that it is hard to keep a granular and a global perspective in mind at the same time, and despite the fact that one or another must have some kind of priority at any partic-

---

[174] 1A J. WIGMORE, *supra* note 62, § 37.7, at 1084.
[175] *Id.*

ular time, it must also be true that both perspectives are somehow at work at the same time, no matter how mysterious this proposition may seem. This proposition, however, is not really all that mysterious. We only need to posit that marshalling processes, even artificial ones such as ours, are partly psychological. When any marshalling process is explicitly at work, tacit marshalling processes are also work. Those tacit processes remain in the background, but they are working nonetheless.

C. *Personal Meaning, Metaphorical Translation, and Theoretical Validity*

We have often been asked whether our theory of evidence marshalling is a descriptive or a prescriptive theory. Our answer is that it is neither. Our theory is of a third kind: it is an heuristic theory. We reject the thesis that a theory about evidence and inference must be either descriptive or prescriptive.[176] This has been and this remains our answer to questions about the character and purpose of our theory of evidence marshalling. We also recognize that this answer is incomplete, however. There must be a link between any heuristic theory and natural mental processes. Without such a link, an heuristic theory cannot serve as a device that illuminates natural thought.

Our work on computer prototypes of evidence marshalling systems suggests the nature of the link between our theory and natural mental processes. We have said that our computer prototypes and our diagrams serve as metaphors.[177] If we are right in thinking that our prototypes and diagrams are effective metaphors, our diagrammatic devices appeal to the natural imagination. By doing so they translate our theoretical constructs into natural and familiar ways of thinking. Hence, our computer prototypes and diagrams are far more than gimmicks or mere rhetorical devices. The link between our heuristic theory and natural thought is by way of metaphor.[178] Metaphors serve to translate our theory into

---

[176] *See supra* note 46; *infra* notes 180-81.

[177] *See* Tillers, *supra* note 46; text accompanying *supra* notes 46-47.

[178] Lon Fuller made a similar claim in L. FULLER, LEGAL FICTIONS 113-21 (1967). There Fuller discussed Hans Vaihinger's theory of fictions and why "New Experiences Are Converted into the Terms of Those Already Familiar." *Id.* at 113. Fuller shared Vaihinger's view that "human thought must always proceed by analogy, and . . . analogies must always be taken

natural language and thought.[179] If we are unable to find metaphors that translate our theory into received ways of thinking and imagining, our theory must suffer the fate of being either a descriptive theory or a prescriptive theory. This fate would not be a happy one since neither one of these types of theories can guide people in the investigation of real-world factual problems.[180]

If it is true that metaphor is the link between heuristic theory and natural imagination and thought, we have obviated certain objections to our theory, but new questions about the validity of our theory emerge. For example, suppose our metaphors are not popular. Must we admit the invalidity of our theory if the intended consumers of our theory do not find our theory "user-friendly?" Are we required to take the inability or unwillingness of our audience to make any sense or use of our theory as evidence that our theory is defective?

Although we have not yet attempted to formulate comprehensive responses to these questions, we see a good possibility that the answers to them might be "no." This possibility occurred to the authors as they reflected on the way that they initially tackled

---

from an existing stock of experience." *Id.* Fuller says, "*A metaphorical element taints all our concepts.*" *Id.* at 115. (emphasis in original)

While Fuller believed that fictions and metaphors are essential, he also believed that they do harm as well as good. He asserted that analogies, metaphors, and fictions must "*drop out of the final reckoning,*" *id.* at 117 (emphasis in original), after they have done their job of making new concepts familiar. The "hypostatization" of concepts — the use of fiction after it has done its job of making a new concept familiar — is the "original sin of human reasoning." *Id.* at 118.

While we do not doubt that metaphors can be harmful as well as beneficial, it is probable that a theory having an heuristic character cannot wholly abandon metaphors and analogies. A novel mathematical concept was Fuller's paradigmatic example of an unfamiliar concept. *See id.* An heuristic theory, however, is a special kind of beast. Its purpose is to shed light on natural and familiar mental processes rather than to replace them with novel conceptual operations. Since an heuristic theory cannot replace existing, familiar thinking, metaphor would seem to be always necessary.

[179] We are indebted to Richard Weisberg for this thought. *Cf.* J. WHITE, JUSTICE AS TRANSLATION 36 (1990) (one learns language by learning from it the meaning of what we already know how to say).

[180] A purely descriptive theory — one that merely describes existing mental processes — cannot improve inferential performance. A purely prescriptive theory of inference — one that mandates the replacement of natural inference with ideal inference — cannot be used by real-world human beings. *See* Tillers, *supra* note 46, at 932-36.

the project of investigating investigation. One of the authors is something of an expert on probability theory. He is also adept at figuring the probabilities of various outcomes in card games. By contrast, the other author is singularly inept both in card games and at calculating probabilities. It is probably not a matter of chance that the author who is familiar with card games was drawn to computer prototypes that are based on the metaphor of a stack of cards. This author saw a card game metaphor as the appropriate metaphor for describing both the underlying structure of all evidence marshalling systems and the nature of the relationships between evidence marshalling systems. It is probably also not fortuitous that this same author has devoted a great deal of attention to combinations of "possibilities," shuffling them in various ways, like a pack of cards. The other author, by contrast, entertained no hypotheses or images that even remotely resembled the structure of a card game when he first tackled the topic of investigation. He thought about matters such as stories and the fuzziness of legal language, but in no event about card games.

This difference in the way that we as co-authors initially tackled the problem of investigation shows that different metaphors have different appeal for different people. Does this suggest that the epistemological validity of different techniques of marshalling evidence varies with the person? Perhaps. Yet, our own experience learning and understanding each other's metaphors demonstrates that metaphors that are initially unfamiliar and unappealing may, in time, become appealing and powerful. Hence, it is possible that our metaphors and images will have general appeal. If they do, this may be some evidence that our heuristic theory of evidence marshalling has interpersonal force and theoretical validity.[181]

---

[181] The criteria of the validity of any heuristic theory are perforce rather different from the criteria of the validity of a mathematical theory or of a theory in the sciences. The reason lies in the subject matter of an heuristic theory. An heuristic theory is a map of the mind. It is a logical map of the mind. But it is not just a picture of logic. The picture must also appeal to the mind; the mind must say, "That's the way it is!"

THE CURVATURE OF CONSTITUTIONAL SPACE:
WHAT LAWYERS CAN LEARN FROM MODERN PHYSICS

*Laurence H. Tribe**

Twentieth-century physics revolutionized our understanding of the physical world. Relativity theory replaced a view of the universe as made up of isolated objects acting upon one another at a distance with a model in which space itself was curved and changed by the presence and movement of objects. Quantum physics undermined the confidence of scientists in their ability to observe and understand a phenomenon without fundamentally altering it in the process. Professor Tribe uses these paradigm shifts in physics to illustrate the need for a revised constitutional jurisprudence. He argues that judges and lawyers need to recognize the profound impact that the law has in shaping the social background. This background is too often taken as given. Judges, in particular, cannot simply reach in and resolve disputes between individuals without permanently altering the legal and social space. The very act of judging alters the context and relationships being judged. Professor Tribe concludes that, while perspectives resembling those of modern physics have been integrated into some of the most important constitutional cases decided during the twentieth century, the current Supreme Court shows an unfortunate tendency toward relying too often on visions of society and knowledge that have long been rejected as overly formal and sterile.

I. INTRODUCTION

Although my topic is the constitutional lessons of general relativity and quantum physics, I do not address the subject because I am determined to bring science or mathematics into law; I still believe what I wrote in the 1970's about the perils of that enterprise.[1] Nor

---

* Tyler Professor of Constitutional Law, Harvard Law School. I am grateful to Rob Fisher, Michael Dorf, Kenneth Chesebro, Gene Sperling, and Barack Obama for their analytic and research assistance and to Professor Gerald Holton (Harvard Physics Department) for his helpful comments. This essay builds upon the 43d Annual Cardozo Lecture I gave before the Association of the Bar of the City of New York on May 11, 1989, 44 RECORD OF THE ASS'N OF THE BAR OF THE CITY OF NEW YORK 575 (1989).

[1] *See infra* note 2.

do I wish to suggest that there exists an epistemological hierarchy with the law perched on a lower rung looking up to its superiors for guidance. Rather, my conjecture is that the metaphors and intuitions that guide physicists can enrich our comprehension of social and legal issues. I borrow metaphors from physics tentatively; my purpose is to explore the heuristic ramifications for the law; my criterion of appraisal is whether the concepts we might draw from physics promote illuminating questions and directions. I press forward in this endeavor because I believe that reflection upon certain developments in physics can help us hold on to and refine some of our deeper insights into the pervasive and profound role law plays in shaping our society and our lives.

In the same spirit, I continue to maintain my previous objection to any form of dogmatism that closes down discourse about fundamental values within the law.[2] To search the sciences for authoritative answers to legal questions, or any questions for that matter, is misguided. The formalist philosophy which views science as a "collection" of the "proven" or even of the "provable" is based upon an inappropriate reification. The better vision of science is as a continual and, above all, critical exploration of fruitful insights; the better metaphor is that of a journey. Science is not so much about proving as it is about *im*proving. To look to the natural sciences for authority — that is, for certainty — is to look for what is not there.[3]

This look beyond law in order to understand law is necessary because our formal methods of reasoning about legal problems in general, and constitutional problems in particular, have not always kept pace with widely shared perceptions of what makes sense in thinking and talking about the state, about courts, and about the role of both in society. How we think about these institutions has been fundamentally influenced by new insights into the operation of the physical world. Michel Foucault speaks of "an epistemological space specific to a particular period";[4] he suggests that tacit positive rules of discourse cut across and condition different disciplines in any given

---

[2] I still believe that attempts to reduce human issues to cost-benefit equations, as people in the law and economics movement sometimes do, are bound to be distorting. *See* Tribe, *Policy Science: Analysis or Ideology?*, 2 PHIL. & PUB. AFF. 66 (1972); *see also* Tribe, *Constitutional Calculus: Equal Justice or Economic Efficiency?*, 98 HARV. L. REV. 592 (1985); Tribe, *Seven Deadly Sins of Straining the Constitution Through a Pseudo-Scientific Sieve*, 36 HASTINGS L.J. 155 (1984); Tribe, *Technology Assessment and the Fourth Discontinuity: The Limits of Instrumental Rationality*, 46 S. CAL. L. REV. 617 (1973); Tribe, *Trial by Mathematics: Precision and Ritual in the Legal Process*, 84 HARV. L. REV. 1329 (1971); Tribe, *Ways Not To Think About Plastic Trees: New Foundations for Environmental Law*, 83 YALE L.J. 1315 (1974).

[3] For essays on relevant aspects of the philosophy of science, see CRITICISM AND THE GROWTH OF KNOWLEDGE (I. Lakatos & A. Musgrave eds. 1970).

[4] M. FOUCAULT, THE ORDER OF THINGS: AN ARCHAEOLOGY OF HUMAN SCIENCES at xi (1970).

period. Interdisciplinary comparison brings greater awareness of pre-
conceptions, and it is the unearthing of such tacit knowledge that
often creates the possibility of choice and intellectual progress. Although our intuitive understanding about the relationships among law,
the state, and society has evolved, our vocabulary has lagged behind
our intuitions: the language in which we still tend to ask legal questions and express legal doctrine has yet to reflect the shift in our
perceptions. The result has been to make it easier for courts and
lawyers to couch their analyses of many areas in terms that are deeply
out of sync with that shift in underlying perceptions.

Thus, while some aspects of Supreme Court jurisprudence, as I
will try to show, have become reasonably congruent with this shift,
other aspects of that jurisprudence either have never become so or
have fallen perceptibly behind our shared insights. In order to illustrate that failure, this essay will discuss some of the work of the
Burger and Rehnquist Courts. Beyond this, the essay will argue that
the central conceptual shifts represented in modern physics provide
useful new ways of thinking and talking about law, legal argument
and legal practice.

I am hardly the first to use science to speak of law. Early in our
nation's history it was commonplace, for example, to say that the
1787 Constitution was Newtonian in design, with its carefully coun-
terpoised forces and counterforces, its checks and balances, structured
like a "machine that would go of itself" to meet the crises of the
future.[5] Later, as the country grew and the pace of social change
quickened, and after Darwin's theory of evolution gained acceptance,
many thinkers — Justice Holmes, for example, and Woodrow Wilson
— saw in the Constitution organic aspects of a living, evolving thing.[6]

---

[5] See M. KAMMEN, A MACHINE THAT WOULD GO OF ITSELF: THE CONSTITUTION IN
AMERICAN CULTURE (1986). In a trenchant essay, Brian Koukoutchos observes:

After the close of the sixteenth century, a reaction set in against the mystical tradition in
the form of a mechanistic view of the universe. If the former paradigm drew upon Plato,
the latter one traced its lineage to Archimedes. . . . The Framers — an apt sobriquet
for a mechanistic age — naturally thought and expressed themselves according to the
prevailing paradigm of their time. . . . It was the legacy of Newton's *Principia* that
"[a]ll mechanics acquired, for a while, the charm of complexity controlled."

Koukoutchos, *Constitutional Kinetics: The Independent Counsel Case and the Separation of
Powers*, 23 WAKE FOREST L. REV. 635, 641–42 (1988) (footnote omitted) (quoting G. WILLS,
INVENTING AMERICA: JEFFERSON'S DECLARATION OF INDEPENDENCE 98 (1978)). In another
recent paper, Professor A.E. Dick Howard discusses the influences of clocks, "gadgets," and
mechanical metaphors on the founding fathers. He raises the question, "to what extent does
the ordering of the constitutional system assume a Newtonian universe — a self-regulating
mechanism . . . ?" A.E. Dick Howard, The Mechanical Conception of the Constitution 24
(paper presented at Colloque International: *1789 et l'Invention de la Constitution*, Association
Francaise de Science Politique, Mar. 2–4, 1989) (available at the Harvard Law School Library).

[6] As Holmes put it: "However much we may codify the law into a series of seemingly self-
sufficient propositions, those propositions will be but a phase in a continuous growth." O.W.
HOLMES, THE COMMON LAW 32 (1881). Biological and evolutionary metaphors are prominent

However interesting these metaphors may be, I want to borrow from science not possible images for describing particular legal institutions from the *outside*, but a language for engaging in legal analysis itself. I hope to shed light not on the nature of the Constitution as a thing but on the character and structure of constitutional analysis as a process.

II. THE CONSTITUTIONAL LESSONS OF MODERN PHYSICS

The Newtonian physics of two centuries ago took the view that objects acted on each other across the expanse of a neutral, undifferentiated space in an objective and knowable manner, according to simple physical laws that seemed to explain observed reality without requiring much further reflection about the basic structure of the universe.[7] As in a game of marbles, objects might collide with one another, but they could not alter the field of play.[8]

Since the 1920's, physics has been guided by two key shifts away from this view. On the grand scale, the general theory of relativity has demonstrated, among other things, that the physical universe, as seen through a telescope, can be explained only by realizing that objects like stars and planets *change* the space around them — they literally "warp" it — so that their effect is both complex and interactive.[9] On the subatomic scale, quantum theory has demonstrated

---

in Holmes' work: "Just as the clavicle in the cat only tells of the existence of some earlier creature to which a collarbone was useful, precedents survive in the law long after the use they once served is at an end and the reason for them has been forgotten." *Id.* at 31. On Holmes, see Veilleux, *The Scientific Model in Law*, 75 GEO. L.J. 1967, 1977 (1987). On evolutionary theories in the law, see *id.* at 1977 n.57. Woodrow Wilson perhaps put it best: "the Constitution of the United States is not a mere lawyers' document: it is a vehicle of life, and its spirit is always the spirit of the age." W. WILSON, CONSTITUTIONAL GOVERNMENT IN THE UNITED STATES 69 (1911). *See also* Tribe, *The Idea of the Constitution: A Metaphor-morphosis*, 37 J. LEGAL EDUC. 170 (1987).

[7] "Newtonian scientific thought was based fundamentally on metaphysical assumptions involving God, absolute space, absolute time, and absolute laws." M. KLINE, MATHEMATICS AND THE SEARCH FOR KNOWLEDGE 165 (1985); *see also* THREE HUNDRED YEARS OF GRAVITATION 4 (S. Hawking & W. Israel eds. 1987).

[8] In more technical terms, Einstein describes some of the assumptions of pre-relativity physics:

> In the first place, it is assumed that one can move an ideal rigid body in an arbitrary manner. In the second place, it is assumed that the behaviour of ideal rigid bodies towards orientation is independent of the material bodies and their changes of position, in the sense that if two intervals can once be brought into coincidence, they can always and everywhere be brought into coincidence.

A. EINSTEIN, THE MEANING OF RELATIVITY 4–5 (5th ed. 1956).

[9] As Einstein states: "Our world is not Euclidean. The geometrical nature of our world is shaped by masses and their velocities." A. EINSTEIN & L. INFELD, THE EVOLUTION OF PHYSICS: FROM EARLY CONCEPTS TO RELATIVITY AND QUANTA 237 (1938). *See infra* section II.A.

that the universe cannot be observed as though the natural world at the end of the microscope were unaffected by the eye looking into the lens — the very process of observation and analysis can fundamentally alter the things being observed, and can change how they will behave thereafter.[10]

The insights that general relativity and quantum theory have to offer for our purposes require no mastery of technical detail, but do require familiarity with several fairly simple but fundamental concepts. This section offers a brief explication of each of these theories and then examines how their insights might help us arrive at a paradigm[11] of legal reasoning and constitutional analysis to address some of our current difficulties.

A. General Relativity Theory

1. Curved Physical Space. — In popular culture, the phrase "general relativity" has an almost mystical quality,[12] but as a historical matter its effect was largely demystifying. The theory emerged from an attempt to improve on Newton's theory of gravity.[13] In Newton's theory, gravity is a discrete physical force, in which the greater the mass of an object, the more strongly it "pulls" on other objects.[14] For example, the earth exerts a stronger pull on an object placed on its surface than that which the object experiences on the surface of the moon, which explains why the astronauts get to bounce so high when they are on the moon, and how Alan Shepard managed to set a galactic record in 1971 for driving a golf ball — by his account "miles and miles and miles" — with a six-iron attached to a sampling rod. Although Newton developed a precise formula for calculating this

---

[10] *See infra* section II.B.

[11] My approach is obviously inspired to some extent by Thomas Kuhn's vision of paradigmatic discourse found in his seminal work, T. KUHN, THE STRUCTURE OF SCIENTIFIC REVOLUTIONS (2d ed. 1970). I do not, however, rely on the specific structure of Kuhn's "paradigm" paradigm, which has been properly criticized on a number of different levels. *See, e.g.*, Lakatos, *Falsification and the Methodology of Scientific Research Programmes* in CRITICISM AND THE GROWTH OF KNOWLEDGE, *supra* note 3, at 91.

[12] As Paul Davies writes:

Over fifty years ago something strange happened in physical science. Bizarre and stunning new ideas about space and time, mind and matter, erupted among the scientific community. . . . Physicists began to realize that their discoveries demanded a radical reformulation of the most fundamental aspects of reality. They learned to approach their subject in totally unexpected and novel ways that seemed to turn commonsense on its head and find closer accord with mysticism than materialism.

P. DAVIES, GOD AND THE NEW PHYSICS at vii (1983).

[13] Einstein states: "The general theory of relativity attempts to formulate physical laws for all CS [co-ordinate systems]. The fundamental problem of the theory is that of gravitation. The theory makes the first serious effort, since Newton's time, to reformulate the law of gravitation." A. EINSTEIN & L. INFELD, *supra* note 9, at 235.

[14] *See* M. KLINE, *supra* note 7, at 112.

pull,[15] the formula left one huge mystery unexplained: if the sun and planets pull on each other with varying strengths depending on where they happen to be in relation to one another, those bodies must have some way of detecting one another's location. But how? Who or what "tells" the earth where, and how big, the sun is?[16] The only available answers always seemed oddly mystical — as though each atom of the earth were connected to each atom of the sun by an invisible but heavy "rope" of gravity, to each atom of the moon by an equally invisible "string," and to each atom of the distant planets by mere "threads." In this picture, as the planets orbited the sun, the tendrils of this odd "force" called gravity forever shifted; but how such a "force" could act instantaneously and across the vast distances of empty space, between objects that could have no possible "awareness" of one another's existence, or mass, remained a complete puzzle.[17]

General relativity reformulated the theory of gravity from the ground up. In Einstein's view, the planets did not move in reaction to the pull or beckon of some invisible connection to another mass. He posited instead that space itself is bent and shaped by the masses within it,[18] causing masses to move through space and time according to that shape, guided not by invisible forces but by the very curvature of the space around them — much as a marble tossed into a bowl would spin around in accord with the curvature of the bowl itself.[19]

---

[15] $F = Gm_1m_2/d^2$ (The masses of the attracting objects are m_1 and m_2; d is the distance between them; and G is the universal gravitational constant.)

[16] Newton expressed his dissatisfaction in a letter to Richard Bentley:

> That one body may act upon another at a distance through a vacuum without the mediation of anything else, by and through which their action and force may be conveyed from one to another, is to me so great an absurdity that, I believe, no man who has in philosophic matters a competent faculty of thinking could ever fall into it.

M. KLINE, *supra* note 7, at 121.

[17] Kline states:

> Newton made many statements about gravity in the three editions of his *Mathematical Principles* . . . . Just how gravitation could reach out 93 million miles and pull the earth toward the sun seemed inexplicable to him, and he framed no hypotheses concerning it. He hoped that others would study the nature of this force. People did try to explain it in terms of pressure exerted by some intervening medium and by other processes, all of which proved unsatisfactory.

Id. at 122.

[18] George Gamow explains: "The great idea, which was included by Einstein in the foundation of his general theory of curved space, consists of the assumption that *the physical space becomes curved in the neighborhood of large masses*; the bigger the mass the larger the curvature." G. GAMOW, ONE TWO THREE . . . INFINITY 106 (1961) (emphasis in original).

[19] Hawking notes:

> Einstein made the revolutionary suggestion that gravity is not a force like other forces, but is a consequence of the fact that space-time is not flat, as had been previously assumed: it is curved, or "warped," by the distribution of mass and energy in it. Bodies like the earth are not made to move on curved orbits by a force called gravity; instead, they follow the nearest thing to a straight path in a curved space, which is called a geodesic.

S. HAWKING, A BRIEF HISTORY OF TIME: FROM THE BIG BANG TO BLACK HOLES 29 (1988).

In a curved space the shortest distance between two points is a line that curves along with space itself. In a sense, the planets couldn't care less where the sun is, and aren't connected to it by rope-like gravitational "threads"; they need no marching orders since the paths along which they travel are determined by the geometry of the space around them. So the problem of "action at a distance" is solved by a paradigm-shift — from a paradigm in which space was seen as absolute and uniform, and simply part of the background,[20] to a paradigm in which space is seen as relative and not uniform at all, and just as much a part of the foreground as the objects within it.

2. *Curving Legal "Space."* — Newton's conception of space as empty, unstructured background parallels the legal paradigm in which state power, including judicial power, stands apart from the neutral, "natural" order of things. In the realm of physics, Einstein trenchantly criticized the world view in which

> space as such is assigned a role in the system of physics that distinguishes it from all other elements of physical description. It plays a determining role in all processes, without in its turn being influenced by them. Though such a theory is logically possible, it is on the other hand rather unsatisfactory. Newton had been fully aware of this deficiency, but he had also clearly understood that no other path was open to physics in his time.[21]

In Einstein's view, space is not the neutral "stage" upon which the play is acted, but rather is merely one actor among others, all of whom interact in the unfolding of the story. Einstein's brilliance was to recognize that in comprehending physical reality the "background" could not be abstracted from the "foreground." In the paradigm inspired by Einstein, "[s]pace and time are now dynamic quantities: when a body moves, or a force acts, it affects the *curvature* of space and time — and in turn the structure of space-time affects the way in which bodies move and forces act."[22]

A parallel conception in the legal universe would hold that, just as space cannot extricate itself from the unfolding story of physical reality, so also the law cannot extract itself from social structures; it cannot "step back," establish an "Archimedean" reference point of detached neutrality, and selectively reach in, as though from the outside, to make fine-tuned adjustments to highly particularized con-

---

[20] Karl Popper nicely describes the Kantian interpretation of Newtonian space and time: "space and time themselves are neither things nor events: they cannot even be observed: they are more elusive. They are a kind of framework for things and events: something like a system of pigeon-holes, or a filing system, for observations." K. POPPER, *Kant's Critique and Cosmology*, in CONJECTURES AND REFUTATIONS: THE GROWTH OF SCIENTIFIC KNOWLEDGE 175, 179 (rev. 4th ed. 1972).

[21] A. EINSTEIN, *supra* note 8, at 140.

[22] S. HAWKING, *supra* note 19, at 33 (emphasis added).

flicts. Each legal decision restructures the law itself, as well as the social setting in which law operates, because, like all human activity, the law is inevitably embroiled in the dialectical process whereby society is constantly recreating itself.

To provide an initial view of how useful the "curved space" metaphor might be in law, we need look no further than two of the most controversial cases that the Supreme Court decided this year.

(a) Child Abuse. — The first case concerns the tragic life of young Joshua DeShaney. Joshua was the infant son of a father who repeatedly beat him severely.[23] Despite the various warnings the social service agencies received about his father's violence, no one came to Joshua's rescue.[24] Joshua now lies in an almost vegetative state, well beyond the powers even of modern science to fully revive.[25] He lies there, forever alone in his own world, because, while the social services authorities of Winnebago County, Wisconsin dutifully recorded the awful things they knew were happening to poor Joshua and kept meticulous, bureaucratically rational records of the child's injuries, they did not lift a finger to help him.[26]

After Joshua was beaten and permanently injured by his father, Joshua's guardian sued the social workers and other local officials who had allowed those terrible beatings to occur, on the theory that their failure to act deprived him of his liberty in violation of the due process clause of the fourteenth amendment,[27] and that Joshua was therefore entitled to recover damages under the civil rights statutes.[28] The Supreme Court held in *DeShaney v. Winnebago County* that there was no violation of the fourteenth amendment, and thus no basis for recovery under the statutes enacted in the wake of the Civil War to enforce that amendment.[29]

The Court spoke movingly of what it called the "undeniably tragic" facts of the case,[30] but proceeded to say:

> nothing in the language of the Due Process Clause . . . requires the State to protect the life, liberty and property of its citizens against invasion by private actors. The Clause is phrased as a limitation on the State's power to act, not as a guarantee of certain minimal levels of safety and security.[31]

---

[23] *See* DeShaney v. Winnebago County Dep't of Social Servs., 109 S. Ct. 998, 1002 (1989).

[24] *See id.* at 1001–02.

[25] *See* DeShaney v. Winnebago County Dep't of Social Servs., 812 F.2d 298, 300 (7th Cir. 1987).

[26] *See DeShaney*, 109 S. Ct. at 1010 (Brennan, J., dissenting).

[27] *See* 109 S. Ct. at 1001.

[28] 42 U.S.C. §§ 1983, 1985, 1988 (1982); *see* DeShaney v. DeShaney, No. 85-C-310, slip op. at 1 (E.D. Wis. June 20, 1986).

[29] *See* 109 S. Ct. at 1001.

[30] *See id.*

[31] *Id.* at 1003.

Near the close of the majority opinion, written by Chief Justice
Rehnquist, the Court paused to note:

> Judges and lawyers, like other humans, are moved by natural sym-
> pathy in a case like this to find a way for Joshua and his mother to
> receive adequate compensation for the grievous harm inflicted upon
> them. But before yielding to that impulse, it is well to remember
> once again that the harm was inflicted not by the State of Wisconsin,
> but by Joshua's father. The most that can be said of the state func-
> tionaries in this case is that they stood by and did nothing when
> suspicious circumstances dictated a more active role for them.[32]

The Court went on to say, in defense of the officials, that

> had they moved too soon to take custody of the son away from the
> father, they would likely have been met with charges of improperly
> intruding into the parent-child relationship, charges based on the same
> Due Process Clause that forms the basis for the present charge of
> failure to provide adequate protection.[33]

Justice Blackmun, in a bitter dissent, chided the majority for pur-
porting "to be the dispassionate oracle of the law, unmoved by 'natural
sympathy.'"[34] He compared the Rehnquist Court to "the antebellum
judges who denied relief to fugitive slaves."[35] He had little sympathy
for the Court's claim that "its decision, however harsh, is compelled
by existing legal doctrine."[36] In his view, the question was "an open
one."[37] He argued that the fourteenth amendment precedents could
"be read more broadly or narrowly depending upon how one chooses
to read them."[38] He wrote that, faced with such a choice, *he* "would
adopt a 'sympathetic' reading, one which comports with dictates of
fundamental justice and recognizes that compassion need not be exiled
from the province of judging."[39]

My purpose here is not to take any position on who has the better
of the argument. My distress centers neither on the majority's result,
nor on the notion that the majority was too hard-hearted — too
unwilling to allow reason to be tempered with mercy. Indeed, I would
reject the idea that the majority's mode of analysis really *had* "reason"
on its side, or that the dissenters came out where they did principally
because they allowed themselves to feel more sympathy for Joshua.
My trouble is with the majority's quite primitive vision of the state

---

[32] *Id.* at 1007.
[33] *Id.*
[34] *Id.* at 1012 (Blackmun, J., dissenting).
[35] *Id.*
[36] *Id.*
[37] *Id.*
[38] *Id.*
[39] *Id.*

of Wisconsin as some sort of distinct object, a kind of machine that
must be understood to act upon a pre-political, natural order of private
life. From the majority's perspective, the state of Wisconsin operates
as a thing, its arms exerting force from a safe distance upon a sometimes unpleasant natural world, in which the abuse of children is an
unfortunate, yet external, ante-legal and pre-political fact of our society.[40] Courts, as passive and detached observers, may reach in to
offer a helping hand only when another arm of the state has reached
out and shattered this natural, pre-political order by itself directly
harming a young child.

Within the majority's stilted pre-modern paradigm,[41] there is no
hint that the hand of the observing state may itself have played a
major role in shaping the world it observes. Thus when the Supreme
Court majority looked out at one of the most defenseless persons in
the universe we know — an abused child — it did not inquire whether
the hand of the state may have altered an already political landscape
in a way that encouraged such child-beating to go uncorrected. The
majority's question in *DeShaney* was simply, "did the State of Wisconsin beat up that child?" and not, "did the law of Wisconsin, taken
in its entirety, warp the legal landscape so that it in effect deflected
the assistance otherwise available to Joshua DeShaney?"

Only Justice Brennan's dissent bothered to ask whether the state
of Wisconsin — by establishing a child welfare system specifically to
help children like Joshua, by creating a system for investigating reported instances of child abuse, and by outlawing private intrusions
into a home where a child seems imperiled — effectively *channeled*
all reports of such abuse, and all actions in response to such reports,
to specific agencies. In this way, the state invited citizens and others
"to depend on local departments of social services . . . to protect
children from abuse."[42] The dissenters, in what I would praise as an

---

[40] In my book, L. TRIBE, CONSTITUTIONAL CHOICES (1985), I argue that there is a psychological and ideological predilection to perceive the existence of a private sphere — albeit
circumscribed by law and by the state — in which actions are autonomous: "Many of us . . .
cling to such institutions as freedom of contract and private property, viewing them as a natural,
'given' part of the legal landscape which provides a background for our private, consensual
transactions." *Id.* at 264.

[41] I use the term "modern" to capture the movement in both the sciences and the arts. In
a discussion of cubism, Eugene Lunn states:

> While the symbolists and impressionists had exploited metaphor and color to aestheticize
> reality, the cubists more directly assaulted the notion of art as leading an independent
> hermetic existence insulated from the outer visible world. At the same time, they sought
> to show through such means as incorporating 'found objects' (e.g., news pages, pieces of
> cord or of wood) that art is not a window into the 'external' world but an aspect of
> 'reality' itself.

E. LUNN, MARXISM AND MODERNISM: AN HISTORICAL STUDY OF LUKACS, BRECHT, BENJA-
MIN, AND ADORNO 49 (1982).

[42] 109 S. Ct. at 1010 (Brennan, J., joined by Marshall and Blackmun, JJ., dissenting).

admirably post-Newtonian insight, concluded that it belied reality to
contend that the state had done *nothing* with respect to Joshua. On
the contrary, Wisconsin's child-protection program "actively intervened in Joshua's life" and "effectively confined [him] within the walls
of Randy DeShaney's violent home until such time as DSS took action
to remove him."[43] "Conceivably, . . . children like Joshua are made
worse off," the dissenters reasoned, "by the existence of this program
when the persons and entities charged with carrying it out fail to do
their jobs."[44]

Justice Brennan relied heavily on *Youngberg v. Romeo*[45] and *Estelle v. Gamble*[46] — cases holding that the due process clause requires
that persons institutionalized by the state be provided with services
sufficient to meet basic needs. (In *Youngberg* the institution was a
psychiatric hospital; in *Estelle*, it was a prison.) Justice Brennan read
these cases "to stand for the . . . generous proposition that, if a State
cuts off private sources of aid and then itself refuses to aid, it cannot
wash its hands of the harm that results from its inaction."[47] From
there he found the *DeShaney* case but a small jump away.

But *Youngberg* and *Estelle*, like two will-o'-the-wisps, seem to have
lured Justice Brennan away from the perhaps deeper insights offered
by *Boddie v. Connecticut*.[48] In *Boddie*, an indigent couple could not
obtain a divorce because they could not afford the filing fee. The
Court held:

> given the basic position of the marriage relationship in this society's
> hierarchy of values and the concomitant state monopolization of the
> means for legally dissolving this relationship, due process does prohibit
> a State from denying, solely because of inability to pay, access to its
> courts to individuals who seek judicial dissolution of their marriages.[49]

Of course, Justice Brennan did cite *Boddie* — for the proposition
that "the monopolization of a particular path of relief may impose
upon the State certain positive duties."[50] He labeled it as "instructive"

---

[43] *Id.* at 1011.

[44] *Id.*

[45] 457 U.S. 307 (1982).

[46] 429 U.S. 97 (1976).

[47] 109 S. Ct. at 1009. *See also* RESTATEMENT (SECOND) OF TORTS § 324 (1965) (stating
that one who comes to the aid of a person and then leaves that person in a worse position is
liable for that person's injury); Black v. New York, N.H. & H.R.R., 193 Mass. 448, 79 N.E.
797 (1907) (holding defendant liable for leaving intoxicated plaintiff in a dangerous position after
helping him off a train); Zelenko v. Gimbel Bros., 158 Misc. 904, 287 N.Y.S. 134 (Sup. Ct.,
Special Term 1935) (holding defendant liable for rendering insufficient medical aid when defendant's action cut off plaintiff's intestate from other sources of aid), *aff'd*, 247 A.D. 867, 287
N.Y.S 136 (1936).

[48] 401 U.S. 371 (1971).

[49] *Id.* at 374.

[50] 109 S. Ct. at 1009.

and included it within a class of cases that "signal that a state's prior
actions may be decisive in analyzing the constitutional significance of
its inaction."[51] Justice Brennan portrayed *Boddie* as a close parallel
to *Youngberg* and *Estelle*: "I . . . would locate the DeShaneys' claims
within the framework of cases like *Youngberg* and *Estelle*, and more
generally, *Boddie* . . . ."[52]

Yet there is a fundamental distinction to be made between *Youngberg* and *Estelle* on the one hand, and *Boddie* on the other. In both
Youngberg and *Estelle*, it was the state's institutionalization of a *particular individual* that had isolated that person from alternative means
of fulfilling his or her basic needs. In *Boddie*, however, there had
been no previous state action directed at the particular individual. It
was the legal structure itself — combined, to be sure, with the economic and social circumstances of the individual — that had isolated
the person from the fulfillment of an important need.

Boddie, instead of focusing in a Newtonian way on the isolated
forces acting on particular individuals, introduced the curved space
of a post-Newtonian world in which the focus broadens to encompass
the larger geometry of the "space" in which the relevant events and
persons interact. If the law creates a state monopoly over the fulfillment of certain needs (dissolution of a failed marriage, protection from
a violent parent) and thereby renders some, but not all, individuals
particularly vulnerable, can the very act of creating this legal *structure*
constitute state action violative of due process? Has the creation of a
state monopoly over the fulfillment of a category of needs warped
legal space itself in a cognizable fashion? *Boddie* answers "yes," at
least where the state's interest in preserving that legal structure in-
violate is insufficient to "override the interest" of the plaintiff.[53]

Although Justice Brennan stressed *Youngberg* and *Estelle*, the spirit
of his argument seems to derive from *Boddie*. From a post-Newtonian
perspective, *Boddie* is the more dramatic case and provides the
stronger parallel to *DeShaney*. As in *Boddie*, the governmental act
in *DeShaney* that isolated Joshua — that is, the establishment of a
legal structure that narrowly channeled all information and action in
regard to child abuse — was not a force directed at Joshua personally;
his isolation was a result of the simple juxtaposition of Wisconsin law
and his personal situation. And, again as in *Boddie*, it was the
monopoly created by the legal structure in *DeShaney* that made the
plaintiff peculiarly vulnerable.[54]

---

[51] *Id.* at 1010.

[52] *Id.*

[53] 401 U.S. at 381.

[54] A similar analysis helps shed light on the Supreme Court's less distressing but still quite
primitive 5–4 decision in National Collegiate Athletic Association v. Tarkanian, 109 S. Ct. 454
(1988). There, the Court reasoned that the NCAA was not a "state actor" suable under 42

We may all be engulfed by, and dependent upon, the structure of the law, but we are not all rendered equally vulnerable by it. If the special dependence upon the law and its omissions that is experienced by the most vulnerable among us could be dismissed as irrelevant because it was not directly created by any state force targeting such individuals, their heightened dependence might be seen as legally immaterial. But if the systemic vulnerability of some — battered children are perhaps prime examples — is instead regarded as centrally relevant to how the law's shape should be understood, then one is more likely at least to ask whether the legal system's very failure to do more for such persons might not work an unconstitutional deprivation of their rights. The Newtonian judge, viewing those whose fate she determines as though from a removed, objective vantage point, can easily absolve the state of responsibility for their plight. But her post-Newtonian judicial counterpart, viewing the perspectives of those whom her ruling affects as no less legitimate than her own, and asking what social space the body of legal rules helps to define, may find it more difficult to distance the state from the helplessness of the most vulnerable.

The approach I am suggesting here need not lend itself to, nor embrace, an ideology of paternalism. A post-Newtonian heuristic does not force answers upon us; rather, it pushes us to more probing questions. It is not a cry for "all power to the judges," but rather a plea for circumspection and questioning in assessing how the distribution and direction of all public powers — including those of judges — define the legal space through which we all move, and in whose recesses some of us are lost. It may well be that those who are most likely to be lost are those for whom this plea would make the greatest difference. For it is the most vulnerable, the most forgotten, whose perspective is least akin to that of the lawmaker or judge or bureaucrat and whose fate is most forcefully determined by the law's overall design — by its least visible, most deeply embedded gaps and deflec-

---

U.S.C. § 1983 by the University of Nevada's basketball coach, Jerry Tarkanian, who had been suspended by the University of Nevada in direct compliance with the NCAA's rules and recommendations. The Newtonian lines of force pointed from the state university to the coach. There was a powerful argument that the NCAA action was procedurally unfair and that it decisively shaped the action of the state university, but only the four dissenters saw in that joint relationship a basis for treating the NCAA as part of the state structure. The fact that the majority opinion was written by Justice Stevens and that "conservative" Justices White and O'Connor (as well as Justices Brennan and Marshall) saw the space warp through more modern eyes illustrates the fact that the Newton-Einstein dichotomy need not be congruent with a simple conservative-liberal division. Justice Stevens, observing for the majority that the traditional state action case is one where the state lurks in the background, says "the mirror image presented in this case requires us to step through an analytical looking glass to resolve it." 109 S. Ct. at 462. When Justice Stevens and his four brethren step through, they ignore the way the mirror bends what they can see.

tions. By another route we arrive at philosopher John Rawls' conclusion that the fundamental fairness of a society is best judged by an examination of its treatment of the least advantaged.[55]

The fact that Justice Brennan's arguments were the impassioned words only of a dissent in *DeShaney* unfortunately reflects the reality that the still-reigning paradigm of constitutional law stands in sharp contrast to most contemporary modes of social thought.

(b) Abortion. — Perhaps an even more dramatic illustration of the persistence or resurgence of the pre-modern paradigm in law is the perspective expressed by my colleague Charles Fried, who served as Solicitor General during the Reagan years, when he returned to the Supreme Court on behalf of the Bush Administration to urge the Court to overturn *Roe v. Wade.*[56] In his argument in *Webster v. Reproductive Health Services,*[57] Mr. Fried was asked by Justice O'Connor:

> Do you think that the state has the right to, if . . . we had a serious overpopulation problem, . . . require women to have abortions after so many children?

Mr. Fried answered:

> I surely do not. That would be quite a different matter.

Justice O'Connor pressed on:

> What do you rest that on?

Mr. Fried responded:

> Because unlike abortion . . . , that would involve not preventing an operation but violently taking hands on, laying hands on a woman and submitting her to an operation . . . .[58]

In drawing his distinction between a forced abortion and a forced pregnancy, Mr. Fried implicitly invoked the notion that, when the state makes abortion a crime, it is not *intervening* in the natural order of things but is simply requiring people to let "nature" take its course. It is as though the state were not genuinely "acting" at all.

Whatever one's position on a woman's "right to choose" in reproductive matters, it seems extraordinarily difficult to justify the constitutional distinction pressed by Charles Fried in *Webster* between the state's power to *require* an abortion in certain circumstances and the state's power to *forbid* one. One could as well define "natural" in a way that allowed a woman who desires an abortion, and a doctor

---

[55] *See* J. RAWLS, A THEORY OF JUSTICE (1971).
[56] 410 U.S. 113 (1973).
[57] 109 S. Ct. 3040 (1989).
[58] N.Y. Times, Apr. 27, 1989, at B12, col. 5.

who has the skills and equipment to perform one, to engage in a transaction undisturbed by the state.[59]

To be sure, even if a woman were still deemed to have a fundamental right to make her own choice regarding the continuation or termination of a pregnancy, the state *might* be said to have a compelling justification that offsets her right from the moment of conception, in the case where the woman's choice is to *terminate* the pregnancy but not in the case where her choice is to *continue* it. But any such view collapses the woman's "right to make her own choice" into a pseudo-right to "choose" in only one direction. In what would this asymmetry be grounded? Once the state reaches the threshold of eliminating the woman's choice by taking control over a woman's womb from the point of conception, there remains no logical demarcation — no hierarchy of "natural" and "artificial" — that would preclude the declaration at some future time of compelling state interests supporting mandatory abortions.

I have elsewhere observed that the state makes women and men unequal before the law by automatically translating biology into social destiny, thereby denying women power over both their bodies and their futures.[60] This manipulable concept of a "natural" social order, providing a backdrop to state action, is often employed to negate the state's role in and responsibility for creating and reinforcing power relations.[61] The Court's willingness to uphold laws whose apparent

---

[59] It would be hard to say what the "natural" outcome of the Davis couple's divorce dispute over seven frozen "pre-embryos" (fertilized ova) would have been. *See* Davis v. Davis, 1989 Tenn. App. LEXIS 641 (No. E-14496 Sept. 21, 1989) (granting Mrs. Davis "temporary custody" of the pre-embryos for purposes of implantation).

[60] *See* L. TRIBE, *supra* note 40, at 243. Of course, treating nature as social destiny can also disadvantage men — as shown in Michael H. v. Gerald D., 109 S. Ct. 2333 (1989), where a plurality of the Court, led by Justice Scalia, rejected a California man's claim that he had a constitutionally protected "liberty" interest in protecting his parental relationship with a daughter whom he had fathered with a woman who was then married to another man. *Michael H.* again reflects the view that the Constitution is satisfied so long as the law merely "mirrors" and thereby reinforces what is "natural" — such as marital fidelity and continuation of female pregnancy. Indeed, the plurality offers the revealing remark that "California law, like nature itself, makes no provision for dual fatherhood." *Id.* at 2339. For an argument that equal protection might be better suited than due process to the task of challenging traditional practices, see Sunstein, *Sexual Orientation and the Constitution: A Note on the Relationship Between Due Process and Equal Protection,* 55 U. CHI. L. REV. 1161, 1170–79 (1988).

[61] In *Constitutional Choices,* I propose another example of the manipulation of the "natural" in discussing the vanishing procedural rights of the dispossessed

> when creditors are invited by law to seize and sell, without a whisper of official involvement, the items for which such creditors claim not to have been paid. This practice was held by the Court in *Flagg Brothers, Inc. v. Brooks* to be immune from constitutional scrutiny . . . essentially on the ground that this is what creditors would 'naturally' tend to do in the economic jungle: authorizing creditors to do what they would do anyway, the *Flagg* Court reasoned, mirrors economic reality accurately enough to free the state from any responsibility at all — and thus to render inapplicable the protections afforded by the Fourteenth Amendment.

L. TRIBE, *supra* note 40, at 242 (footnotes omitted).

injustice is thought simply to reflect the world's own cruelty — to
women, to the poor, or to both — seems most vivid in the abortion
funding cases, which upheld bans on federally funded abortions for
those otherwise unable to pay for them.[62] If we can define social
problems as within the "natural" order, then we can quietly blame a
god or, as Social Darwinism did, biology. But perhaps "[t]he fault,
dear Brutus, is not in our stars, [b]ut in ourselves."[63]

In *Webster*, the Supreme Court went further than it had in the
abortion funding cases: *Webster* upheld a ban even on *privately* fi-
nanced abortions in a public facility, under a statute that defined the
concept of "public facility" broadly enough to include essentially the
only hospital in a large part of the state of Missouri — a hospital that
was privately owned but happened to be located in a space rented
from the government.[64] This was predictable not solely because the
Court's composition has shifted rightward since *Roe v. Wade*, but also
because, having won abortion rights in the name of personal privacy
on the basis of a distinctly Newtonian vision of separate spheres of
private life and public power, women have been poorly situated ever
since either to demand public funds for the exercise of such "privacy"
rights or to resist governmental actions that deliberately cement the
"wall of separation" between the public sphere and the supposedly
private choice to terminate a pregnancy.

The *Roe v. Wade* opinion ignored the way in which laws regulating
pregnant women may shape the entire pattern of relationships among
men, women, and children. It conceptualized abortion not in terms
of the intensely *public* question of the subordination of women to men
through the exploitation of pregnancy, but in terms of the purportedly
private question of how women might make intimately personal decisions about their bodies and their lives. That vision described a
part of the truth, but only what might be called the Newtonian part.

The mode of thought that, I believe, led Mr. Fried to draw the
distinction he did, and that gives it considerable appeal, is one that
regards the state as a kind of "thing" which the Constitution both
confines within its public, political sphere, and fences out of certain

---

[62] *See* Harris v. McRae, 448 U.S. 297 (1980); Poelker v. Doe, 432 U.S. 519 (1977); Maher
v. Roe, 432 U.S. 464 (1977).

[63] W. SHAKESPEARE, JULIUS CAESAR, act I, scene 2, ll. 140–41, at 110 (A. Humphreys ed.
1984).

[64] *See* 109 S. Ct. at 3053. Although I gave the Cardozo Lecture several months prior to the
Webster decision, in rewriting this paragraph I had to change little but the tenses of the verbs.
The role played by *DeShaney* in the *Webster* plurality opinion is also noteworthy. *See, e.g.,*
id. at 3050 (quoting *DeShaney* for the proposition that "the Due Process Clauses generally confer
no affirmative right to governmental aid, even where such aid may be necessary to secure . . .
interests of which the government itself may not deprive the individual." 109 S. Ct. at 1003).
I mention these things less from the pride of a prognosticator than as a modest corroboration
of the framework I am presenting.

pre-political private spheres of personal property or individual liberty. Carried to its limit, this physicalist conception of the state suggests that, whether by deploying carrots or by wielding sticks, as long as the state keeps its hands to itself, any change in social parameters simply constitutes a different menu of outcomes within which private citizens remain free to make their own choices. On this view, only the extreme situation in which the state literally grabs someone and drags her off to a jail cell or to a surgical ward would implicate the Constitution. Given the typical rhetoric of those who would reify the state, it is both sad and ironic that it is precisely this objectification which leaves personal freedom at its most vulnerable. For it is the lack of recognition that a change in the surrounding legal setting can constitute state action that most threatens the sphere of personal choice. And it is a "curved space" perspective on how law operates that leads one to focus less on the visible lines of legal force and more on how those lines are bent and directed by the law's geometry.

B. Quantum Theory

1. Altering the Physical World in the Process of Observing It. — A second advance over Newtonian physics — quantum theory — also offers significant heuristic insights for legal analysis. One of the most familiar postulates of quantum theory is the Heisenberg Uncertainty Principle, which exploded the assumption that, by taking enough care and remaining sufficiently uncoupled from the system, one could detect, with any desired degree of precision, the behavior of all objects in the universe. According to Heisenberg, the more accurately you measure where a particle is, the less accurately you are able to measure where it's going.[65] This effect grows more and more pronounced as you try to measure ever smaller things.

To see how the Heisenberg Uncertainty Principle works, imagine first a really *big* hypothetical "particle" — say, a basketball. Assume the ball is at rest, and you want to figure out where it is in relation to some fixed point — say, the floor directly beneath the basket. One obvious approach would be just to *look* at the ball — you might see that it is sitting on the rim exactly 10 feet above that fixed point. Where does the Uncertainty Principle come in? The answer is that our *viewing* the ball, in the sense of measuring its position, necessarily changes where it is. How can that be? Surely it's impossible to move a basketball just by looking at it.

---

[65] For a brief but illuminating account of Heisenberg's Principle, see S. HAWKING, cited above in note 19, at 54. Hawking states: "The uncertainty principle signaled an end to Laplace's dream of a theory of science, a model of the universe that would be completely deterministic: one certainly cannot predict future events exactly if one cannot even measure the present state of the universe precisely!" *Id.* at 55.

The problem is that, for the ball to be visible, at least a little light must shine on it, and reflect off it. True, the light particles individually seem ephemeral. But when they bounce off the ball they still move it a little — although the movement usually is too small to detect with the naked eye. Of course, if light particles had the momentum of moving marbles, the movement would be obvious. And if you could tell where the basketball was located only by hitting it with light particles that had the momentum of moving basketballs, the process of finding its location would inevitably cause quite a change in velocity

That is precisely the situation at the subatomic level, the province of quantum theory. Because light particles, which physicists call photons, can easily act on the tiny electrons, using a light beam to figure out the precise location of an electron at an instant in time would significantly disturb its velocity.[66] This tradeoff is the result of the Uncertainty Principle at work. For this reason, the principle is sometimes put in terms of a relationship between the observer and the observed: the more you try to learn about an object's position, the less you can know about its velocity, and vice versa. In any case, the act of observing always affects what is observed.

The Heisenberg Principle may be applied successfully beyond the micro-level of quantum mechanics. It relies generally on two premises: first, that any observation necessarily requires intervention into the system being studied; and second, that we can never be certain that the intervention did not itself change the system in some unknown way. Consider this example:[67] You have a very ill friend in the next room at a hospital. You want to find out how she is faring. (This corresponds to the "black box" of nature — the unknown contents of which we are attempting to fathom.) You call to her, "How are you doing?" (This corresponds to the "experiment" — the question we ask of nature — the inevitable intervention into the system.) She replies, "Fine." But the effort kills her. (The word "fine" corresponds to the "outcome" or "observation" of the "experiment.") Clearly, the outcome

---

[66] In more technical terms, Heisenberg states:

The position of the electron will be known with an accuracy given by the wave length of the gamma ray. The electron may have been practically at rest before the observation. But in the act of observation at least one light quantum of the gamma ray must have passed the microscope and must first have been deflected by the electron. Therefore, the electron has been pushed by the light quantum, it has changed its momentum and its velocity, and one can show that the uncertainty of this change is just big enough to guarantee the validity of the uncertainty relations.

W. HEISENBERG, PHYSICS AND PHILOSOPHY: THE REVOLUTION IN MODERN SCIENCE 47–48 (1958).

[67] For this example I am indebted to Professor Robert Fisher, a former economist who is now a law student at Harvard. Professor Fisher is reluctant to take credit for the example's originality.

is sadly misleading — the very process of observation changed the system under study.

The deeper philosophical insight underlying the Heisenberg Principle is, of course, that the observer is never really separate from the system being studied, even though the contrary presumption might occasionally be a useful abstraction. In some disciplines the importance of this insight is obvious. For example, no culture can ever be studied in its "pristine" state since the very presence of an anthropologist is bound to have a significant impact on the way of life of the people being studied.[68]

Applications of the Heisenberg Principle within the social sciences are not limited to such circumstances. For example, in the heyday of "scientific management," an experiment was conducted at General Electric's Hawthorne plant to see if improved lighting would lead to greater labor productivity. The experimenters found that it did. Just to be sure of their results, however, they also turned the lights down for a while. To their surprise, productivity increased yet again. As a recent article stated: "just about anything done to the Hawthorne workers increased productivity. They liked the attention."[69]

Although quantum theory arose to deal with very small phenomena, whereas general relativity seeks to explain very large phenomena, these key revolutions appear to be connected in important ways. Contemporary physicists like Stephen Hawking and Steven Weinberg are trying to unify general relativity — the very big — and quantum theory — the very small — by studying black holes and exploring what the universe was like in the infinitesimal fractions of a second following the "Big Bang" that marked its creation. They aim to explain the basic forces of the universe in a "Unified Field Theory." Physicists ultimately hope to arrive at what they have termed a "Theory of Everything."[70]

For our more modest purposes we should note a conceptual link between these two revolutions in physics. Both general relativity and quantum theory deny the possibility of isolation. Modern physics is dynamic as opposed to static — in the sense that it recognizes the

---

[68] *See generally* J. CLIFFORD, THE PREDICAMENT OF CULTURE (1988); J. CLIFFORD & G. MARCUS, WRITING CULTURE (1986); G. MARCUS & M. FISHER, ANTHROPOLOGY AS CULTURAL CRITIQUE (1986).

[69] *Management Brief: To MBA or Not To MBA*, ECONOMIST, July 8, 1989, at 66.

[70] Hawking explains:

The quest for such a theory is known as "the unification of physics." Einstein spent most of his later years unsuccessfully searching for a unified theory, but the time was not ripe: there were partial theories for gravity and the electromagnetic force, but very little was known about the nuclear forces. Moreover, Einstein refused to believe in the reality of quantum mechanics, despite the important role he had played in its development. Yet it seems that the uncertainty principle is a fundamental feature of the universe we live in.

S. HAWKING, *supra* note 19, at 155–56.

importance of interaction between background and foreground,[71] between subject and object, between observer and the phenomena observed. As we have noted, it is this recognition of *pervasive interaction* that is now quite commonplace in many disciplines besides physics.[72] It is this recognition that I think has come to affect our ordinary understanding of the legal world — so deeply as to make some of what the Court says in a case like *DeShaney*, and much of what the Justice Department argued in a case like *Webster*, appear quite counterintuitive to many of us, even if we have a hard time saying exactly *why*. As I have said, our formal conceptions of constitutional law have yet to catch up with our intuitions. Like Moliere's gentleman who had been speaking prose all his life but did not know it, we have become physicists behind our backs.

   2. *Altering the Legal World in the Process of "Observing" It.* — If law is, in fact, best understood through some such post-Newtonian framework, then courts do not have the luxury of deciding who did what to whom, measuring that conduct against pre-existing norms, awarding appropriate relief, and then proceeding as though the relief granted or withheld were all that ultimately mattered. Instead, courts must take account of how the very process of legal "observation" (i.e., judging) shapes both the judges themselves and the materials being judged. The results courts announce — the ways they view the legal terrain and what they say about it — will in turn have continuing effects that reshape the nature of what the courts initially undertook to review, even beyond anything they directly order anyone to do or refrain from doing. The law is thus not simply a backdrop against which action may be viewed — even a "backdrop" that may be "curved" by the acting objects themselves — but is itself an integral part of that action. As Clifford Geertz puts it: "The state enacts an image of order that — a model for its beholders, in and of itself — orders society."[73]

   The case of *Wooley v. Maynard*[74] well illustrates how the process of observation alters the thing observed. In *Wooley*, two Jehovah's Witnesses, George and Maxine Maynard, sought declaratory and injunctive relief under 42 U.S.C. § 1983 against the enforcement of a state statute that forbade obscuring the state motto, "Live Free or Die," on New Hampshire license plates.[75] The Maynards objected to being forced to display this statement on the ground that it was

---

[71] There is a fine chapter (Ch. III) on *Figure and Ground* in Douglas Hofstadter's Pulitzer Prize winning book GÖDEL, ESCHER, BACH: AN ETERNAL GOLDEN BRAID 64–81 (1979).

[72] Anthropology and history are two examples.

[73] C. GEERTZ, LOCAL KNOWLEDGE: FURTHER ESSAYS IN INTERPRETIVE ANTHROPOLOGY 30 (1983).

[74] 430 U.S. 705 (1977).

[75] *See id.* at 707.

contrary to their religious and political beliefs.[76] The district court had held that covering over the motto was constitutionally protected expression.[77] The Supreme Court did not reach the symbolic speech issue, upon which the district court had relied, and instead focused on "the proposition that the right of freedom of thought protected by the First Amendment against state action includes both the right to speak freely and the right to refrain from speaking at all."[78] The majority held that the state may not "constitutionally require an individual to participate in the dissemination of an ideological message by displaying it on his private property in a manner and for the express purpose that it be observed and read by the public."[79]

The *Wooley* Court implicitly regarded itself as occupying an Archimedean reference point — a removed observation post from which all could be safely viewed. How else can one understand the Court's description of the Maynards' request for license plates without the state motto as "hardly consistent with [their] stated intent to communicate affirmative opposition to the motto"?[80] The Court assumed that, if the Maynards were trying to *say* something by covering over the motto, they would want to continue to keep it covered. Their request for the "expurgated" plates was thus seen by the Court as inconsistent with their defense of symbolic expression.

For this analysis to make sense, the Court had to ignore its own existence and the impact of its own statements on the situation before it. For might not the Maynards *change* what they wanted to express if they went from a world in which they were coerced to advertise the state motto (the pre-judgment situation) to a world in which they are no longer required to do so (the post-judgment situation which they have requested)? Any subsequent display by the Maynards of license plates *without* the state motto would surely be symbolic expression — especially if one focuses on the fact that the Maynards would have one of the small number of New Hampshire automobiles (barring the few legal exceptions) not displaying the state motto. In fact, the very existence of the controversy may have made the Maynards public figures in New Hampshire. In such a scenario, their display of license plates without the state's motto may well be understood by many as a symbolic expression. Indeed, why go to jail, as Mr. Maynard did, over a symbol if *not* as a symbol?

In cases such as this — perhaps in all cases — social meaning can be understood only from a post-Newtonian perspective. The Court, the Maynards and the rest of society are interlocked in a complex grid

---

[76] *See id.* at 707–09.
[77] *See id.* at 713.
[78] *Id.* at 714.
[79] *Id.* at 713.
[80] *Id.* at 713 n.10.

of meanings, linking message to context, context to judicial and other state actions, and state action back to message. The law, as it develops, constantly alters the warp and woof of the relevant epistemological space. The Court cannot delete its own existence from its analysis and still arrive at sensible results.

A post-Newtonian perspective obviously cannot dictate the conclusions a court must reach, but it can suggest the questions it should ask. Nor need the post-Newtonian view tilt those questions toward supposedly "liberal" outcomes. For example, a post-Newtonian might well note, as Justice Rehnquist did in his dissent in *Wooley*, that the very existence of the challenged New Hampshire law in a sense *protected* free speech rights. For it was well known that people had no choice about whether the state motto was to appear on their license plates.[81] Hence, to have the state motto on one's plates in no way implied any particular feelings or beliefs on the part of the owner of the car.[82] Why, then, did the Court see any first amendment problem at all? The majority did not really offer an explanation.

Ironically, by requiring the state to give people the option whether or not to have its motto displayed on their license plates, the *Wooley* Court forced people into a symbolic expression. Once they had been given the choice as a matter of law, it would have become well-known that there was indeed such an option. Hence, whether or not one displays the motto in a post-*Wooley* world will come to be seen as a personal statement. All car owners *must* then express themselves one way or the other. This forced symbolic expression may itself be problematic, given the Court's statement that the first amendment "includes both the right to speak freely and the right to refrain from speaking at all."[83] An adequate constitutional analysis cannot ignore the impact on social meaning of the Court's own action.

Similar insights provided by a post-Newtonian paradigm become even more poignant in the constitutional analysis of laws requiring children at school to salute the flag and to pledge allegiance.[84] When it is known by all that such a salute and pledge are required, the actual performance by any one individual is unlikely to be perceived by others as an expression intended by that person to convey anything about the individual's views. On the other hand, once one introduces — whether by statute or by Supreme Court decree — such options as leaving the room, or remaining silent and motionless, an expression of views is in a sense coerced. Only making the pledge mandatory at one extreme — or eliminating it altogether, at the other extreme — can remove that effect. It does not follow that the Court's "opt-out"

---

[81] *See id.* at 721 (Rehnquist, J., dissenting).
[82] *See id.* at 722.
[83] 430 U.S. at 714.
[84] *See* West Virginia State Bd. of Educ. v. Barnette, 319 U.S. 624 (1943).

solution was inappropriate — either in its flag pledge case, or in *Wooley*. But it *does* follow that, in assessing any judicial solution, a post-Newtonian would feel constrained at least to consider how the judiciary's own action would necessarily alter the social reality under adjudication, by changing the meanings of the various acts or omissions at issue.

So too, when the Court observes and describes the legal phenomena at issue in cases like *DeShaney* and *Webster*, we sense, among other things, that it is not simply taking measurements and making a record of something that is already "out there." Rather, it is bending and changing the legal and social landscape so that, after such cases are decided, people will be guided by assumptions and premises and patterns that differ from those that shaped their behavior before those cases were decided.

Thus it is the picture of the court as a largely passive observer, and of the state as a subject exerting force from a safe distance upon the natural world regarded as an external and pre-political object, that, for most of us, is false to our sense of reality. And it is this picture that I think can be usefully dissolved, and then helpfully refocused, from the perspective of twentieth-century physics.

III. Changing Legal Paradigms

Lawyers and judges have incorporated post-Newtonian insights into some areas of law, but those insights still have a tentative foothold in the culture of accepted legal argument and analysis. As I seek to show in what follows, perhaps the earliest dramatic break with the Newtonian vision of a pre-political and pre-legal background came with the demise of *Lochner v. New York*[85] in the early twentieth century. Later, in *Shelley v. Kraemer*[86] and in a series of first amendment cases beginning with *New York Times v. Sullivan*,[87] the Supreme Court extended what might be understood as post-Newtonian conceptions into other areas of the law. However, as the Court's decisions in *Pasadena City Board of Education v. Spangler*[88] and *Milliken v. Bradley*[89] suggest, the pre-modern paradigm still reigns in much of legal analysis (notably also in some law and economics scholarship[90])

---

[85] 198 U.S. 45 (1905).

[86] 334 U.S. 1 (1948). *See* L. TRIBE, *supra* note 40, ch. 16.

[87] 376 U.S. 254 (1964).

[88] 427 U.S. 424 (1976).

[89] 433 U.S. 267 (1977).

[90] Insights and images traceable to physics may already have played a significant role in shaping law and economics scholarship. Neoclassical economics, upon which much of law and economics draws, assumes, like Newtonian physics, a fixed background: the structure of markets and the motivations of consumers. It then attempts to predict the behavior of markets and consumers without considering how they might fundamentally alter each other in the process of

and appears to have undergone a revival under the Burger and Rehnquist Courts.

A. *The Delayed Demise of* Lochner v. New York

During the early twentieth century, lawyers began to question
whether the background of social and economic relations that legislation sought to change might not itself be part of what the law had
wrought. Many observers were unpersuaded by the reasoning of
judicial decisions from the 1890's to the 1930's that treated "property"
and "contract" as categories somehow preexisting the artifice of law.
It was the formal rejection of such treatment that finally ended the
now infamous *Lochner* era in 1937. The Supreme Court accommo-
dated its doctrine to the growing belief that the "brooding omnipres-
ence" of the common law was not a fact of nature, but an artifact of
politics and government and of judge-made rules. In essence, the
post-*Lochner* Court acknowledged that the property interests available

---

interacting. The neoclassical economic assumption that people are rational optimizers is also
akin to the Newtonian postulate that objects in the physical world act on one another according
to simple, observable laws.

This parallel is no accident. Economist Phil Mirowski has unearthed a link between neoclassical economics and pre-modern physics. He argues:

> in the final analysis, however coy and ambivalent neoclassicals may appear to be about
> their physics metaphor, it cannot seriously be repudiated or relinquished, because there
> is nothing else that can hold the neoclassical research program together. In the absence
> of the metaphor of utility as nineteenth-century potential energy, there is no alternative
> theory of value, no heuristic guide to research, no principle upon which to base mathe-
> matical formalism.

P. Mirowski, More Heat Than Light 287 (1989) (unpublished manuscript) (on file at the Harvard
Law School Library) (emphasis omitted). Mirowski goes on to argue that neoclassical economics
borrowed not only its metaphor from nineteenth-century physics, but its legitimacy as well, *see
id.* at 280 — a dangerous loan, indeed, to the extent that new ways of seeing the physical world
can subvert the claim that economics has finally become scientific. *See id.*

Once we are aware of underlying analytical presumptions that may have been incorporated
into at least some versions of the law and economics method, we can consider alternative
metaphors from modern physics that may lead us to ask more fruitful legal questions. As I
argued in my article, *Constitutional Calculus: Equal Justice or Economic Efficiency*, cited above
in note 2, the law and economics school often proceeds as if unaware that constitutional choices
affect, and hence require consideration of, the way in which a polity wishes to constitute itself:
"A court not only chooses *how* to achieve preexisting ends, but also affects *what* those ends are
to be and *who* we are to become." *Id.* at 595 (emphasis in original).

In contrast, some of the best law and economics scholarship, perhaps influenced by post-
Newtonian concepts, evokes the warped space notion of general relativity as well as the Hei-
senbergian view of joint causation and nondeterminism. Whether pre- or post-Newtonian,
physics metaphors and concepts have filtered into the development of law and economics but
have, thus far, done relatively little to dislodge the persistent notion (reminiscent of neoclassical
economics) that the preferences of economic actors are given, rather than shaped by the markets
within which those actors' choices are made. *See* Tribe, *Policy Science: Analysis or Ideology?,
supra* note 2; Tribe, *Constitutional Calculus: Equal Justice or Economic Efficiency, supra* note
2.

for people to use as contractual bargaining chips had all along been largely the reflections of prior social choices, expressed through law, about the acquisition and allocation of control over human and material resources, and that a law banning certain employer-employee bargains as unfairly exploitative was therefore no more an affront to the "natural order of things" than were the legal understandings making such one-sided bargains possible in the first place.[91] It is no coincidence that *Erie R.R. Co. v. Tompkins*,[92] which in 1938 ended the *Swift v. Tyson*[93] era in which federal courts had felt free to follow their own views of general common law, was decided within a year of the watershed decision in *West Coast Hotel v. Parrish*,[94] which upheld laws restricting the "liberty of contract" between employers and employees.

In many other areas of law, the Supreme Court has similarly come to recognize that the state cannot be understood as some sort of robot-like thing that one can observe walking about, a machine whose arms — and it's instructive that we still speak of the "arms of the state" — sometimes reach out and grab a Joshua DeShaney, sometimes reach out and perform surgery on an unwilling woman, sometimes interfere with free exchanges between businesses and consumers.

B. The Tentative Emergence of a Post-Newtonian Paradigm

If we are to conduct constitutional discourse through conversation truer to contemporary sensibilities — abandoning the prism of Newtonian physics and its legal analogies — then we must consistently speak of the state not as a thing but as a set of rules, principles, and conceptions that interact with a background which is in part a product of prior political actions. And we must talk of the events and people involved without pretending they are pre-political; they too are in part shaped by political and legal interactions.

The Supreme Court recognized as much in *Shelley v. Kraemer*,[95] when it held that the common law of Missouri violated the fourteenth amendment insofar as that state's common law made racially restrictive covenants, but not other restraints on the alienation of land, judicially enforceable. Notwithstanding the absence of any racist decision by any particular state actor, what was crucial in *Shelley* was the *geometry* of the state's common law: it drew a line between those

---

[91] *See* L. TRIBE, AMERICAN CONSTITUTIONAL LAW ch. 8 (2d ed. 1988) (describing the rise and fall of Lochnerism); *see also* Sunstein, *Lochner's Legacy*, 87 COLUM. L. REV. 873 (1987) (suggesting that *Lochner* represents a constitutional requirement of neutrality toward preexisting entitlements, a view that persists in the law to this day).
[92] 304 U.S. 64 (1938).
[93] 41 U.S. (16 Pet.) 1 (1842).
[94] 300 U.S. 379 (1937).
[95] 334 U.S. 1 (1948).

restraints on land sales that courts would enforce and those that they
would not enforce, and knowingly put racially restrictive covenants
on the enforceable side of that line.

A similar understanding of the "geometry" of law was at work in
New York Times v. Sullivan,[96] in *NAACP v. Claiborne Hardware
Co.*,[97] and in *Hustler Magazine v. Falwell*.[98] In each of those decisions, the Supreme Court held that first amendment principles were
violated not by some state official's act of censorship but by the *overall
shape* of the state's body of judge-made rules for awarding damages
to people allegedly injured by speeches or publications. The fact that
the "chilling effect" upon the speech involved in those cases was caused
not by any discrete act of a government official, but by the fabric of
legal rules developed in a given jurisdiction over time, has not prevented the Supreme Court from perceiving that this fabric of rules
might violate the first amendment.

In fact, the Supreme Court's entire development of the "chilling
effect" doctrine over the past several decades[99] itself reflects a judicial
recognition that widespread private behavior, in the form of self-
censorship, can be directly traceable not only to particular enforcement
actions by specific state officials but to the very existence of a set of
rules or lines that the state stands ready to enforce or to draw. A
primitive conception of the state as a mechanism that operates only
through exerting direct vectors of force in particular cases could not
possibly account for this doctrine. A retreat from the Supreme Court's
once vigorous concern with this "chilling" of protected speech might
well reflect a partial throwback to a more primitive paradigm.

The paradigm-shift toward a mode of thought that stresses both
the geometry of the legal landscape and the interaction between the
legal observer and the phenomenon observed thus has deep roots in
existing practices and ways of thinking about law. It also accounts
for many of the most powerful and salutary insights of contemporary
legal analysis. We need not return to the more primitive and simplistic
paradigm in which the universe is seen as an empty and apolitical
space across whose vast reaches legal actors hurl their thunderbolts
of force at distant and discrete objects.

C. Judicial Retrogression[100]

We are not doomed to do so — but we sometimes do. Consider
the 1976 case of *Pasadena City Board of Education v. Spangler*.[101]

---

[96] 376 U.S. 254 (1964).

[97] 458 U.S. 886 (1982).

[98] 485 U.S. 46 (1988).

[99] *See* L. TRIBE, *supra* note 91, at 861–86.

[100] This section is heavily influenced by Gene Sperling's excellent Note, *Judicial Right
Declaration and Entrenched Discrimination*, 94 YALE L.J. 1741 (1985).

[101] 427 U.S. 424 (1976).

That case appears to concern two fairly simple linear relationships: to what extent a federal district court may control a school board, and to what extent a school board may control the movements of the families who live in the school district.

In *Spangler*, the district court had found a history of official segregation and had ordered that, as part of the remedy, there should be "no school in the District . . . with a majority of any minority students."[102] The Supreme Court held that the district court could not "require annual reassignment of pupils in order to accommodate changing demographic residential patterns in Pasadena from year to year."[103] The Court's reasoning contains no hint that the Supreme Court itself might have played some role in encouraging or sanctioning such resegregation.[104] Rather than influencing events themselves, the Supreme Court appears only to be recognizing inherent weaknesses in both linear relationships: in a free society, school boards cannot order parents not to move, no matter how much we may dislike white flight.[105] And, in light of this weak link, district courts should not be able to order school boards to do what is beyond their power.

This perspective of *Spangler* ignores the fact that the legal landscape that creates the perception that white flight is inherently private and beyond the scope of the law has itself been explicitly shaped by Supreme Court decisions. In the parlance of our hypothetical quantum theory experiment, this perspective ignores the disruption caused by viewing a basketball with a basketball. The "inherently private" perspective of *Spangler* is based on several assumptions — every one of them the result of specific Supreme Court decisions.

The first assumption is that parents have the right not to send their children to public schools. Much resegregation is caused not by parents changing their place of residence, but by parents taking their children out of public school systems that are attempting to integrate and putting those children in private schools. The expectation that parents may "of course" do that if they wish is not inherent, but is the specific result of the Supreme Court's 1925 decision in *Pierce v. Society of Sisters*,[106] where the Court held — based on no explicit constitutional clause (although I think correctly) — that no state has

---

[102] *Id.* at 428.

[103] *Id.* at 433.

[104] The closest the Court came to recognizing even the possibility that the Court played a role in this resegregation is its statement: "The District Court rejected petitioners' assertion that the movement was caused by so-called 'white flight' traceable to the decree itself." *Id.* at 435. In his dissent, Justice Marshall made as much as he could of the Court's intimation "that it would view this case differently if the demographic changes were themselves a product of the desegregation order." *Id.* at 444 n.2 (Marshall, J., dissenting).

[105] The Court states: "in *Swann* the Court cautioned that 'it must be recognized that there are limits' beyond which a court may not go in seeking to dismantle a dual school system." 427 U.S. at 434 (quoting Swann v. Charlotte-Mecklenburg Bd. of Educ., 402 U.S. 1, 28 (1971)).

[106] 268 U.S. 510 (1925).

"any general power . . . to standardize its children by forcing them to accept instruction from public [school] teachers only."[107]

The second assumption is that school boards and school districts are the parties responsible for ensuring that school systems desegregate. This school board focus creates the perception that white flight is an insoluble problem. Yet, although Supreme Court decisions in 1955 and 1971 created the expectation that school boards must be the primary remedial agents,[108] the fourteenth amendment speaks to the *state* as a single entity. In theory, interstate flight could occur even with a *state-as-a-whole* perspective, but the perception of futility that surrounds judicial efforts to deal with white flight was largely created by the Supreme Court's own focus on school boards as opposed to states.

The third assumption is that suburban school boards cannot be required to participate in integration remedies unless a fairly specific interdistrict segregative impact can be shown. The result is an "inherent right" to keep one's children in white, affluent classes by moving to a suburban school district. But that "right" traces to the 1974 *Milliken v. Bradley*[109] decision, whose compartmentalization of states into school districts, while an outgrowth of the second assumption, is hardly inherent in the natural geometry of the world. As Justice White said in his *Milliken* dissent, "[t]he Court draws the remedial line at the Detroit school district boundary, even though . . . the *State* denies equal protection of the laws when its public agencies, acting in its behalf, invidiously discriminate. *The State's default* is 'the condition that offends the Constitution.'"[110]

Thus, while *Spangler*, like *DeShaney*, appears to be a case in which the Supreme Court is simply recognizing the limits of judicial power to affect private behavior, in fact the case illustrates the profound ways in which judicial power has helped to shape the legal and social landscape so that a white parent who wants to *resist* desegregation feels not a gravitational pull to accept racial integration as inevitable, but instead a pull to follow her worst instincts and flee. For the judiciary has shaped the legal landscape so that there are enormous obstacles for parents who want desegregated schools, and no comparable obstacles for those who do not. Ironically, as parents follow the gravitational pull created in large part by how these Supreme Court cases have tilted the playing field, this very movement is used as proof of the limits of the law in affecting private behavior in matters of social importance.

---

[107] *Id.* at 535.

[108] *See* Swann v. Charlotte-Mecklenburg Bd. of Educ., 402 U.S. 1, 16 (1971); Brown v. Board of Educ., 349 U.S. 294, 299 (1955).

[109] 418 U.S. 717 (1974).

[110] *Id.* at 771-72 (White, J., dissenting) (emphasis added).

Even in the extreme case of remedial impotence, what a court says and does can shape the political dialogue in profound ways. Justice Powell's busing opinions — saying that the law has severe limits in sensitive social contexts[111] — and Justice Scalia's 1989 Holmes Lecture at Harvard[112] — arguing that arriving at a clear and uniformly applied rule of law is often more important than "getting it right" — both implicitly rest on the view that the only real effect of the law is the linear, direct force it exerts in isolated cases. Yet the differences between the 1954 to 1973 period and the post-*Milliken* period show that the law has a much richer, more pervasive and powerful effect on our lives.

By 1964, less than two percent of southern schools were desegregated.[113] The direct force of the law had been almost a total failure. Yet *Brown v. Board of Education*'s mere declaration of rights profoundly affected the political dialogue in America.[114] One reason was that this declaration of rights had in itself dramatically altered the country's perspective as to which group had law and order on its side.[115] During the Montgomery bus boycotts and throughout the civil rights movement, *Brown* put the force of legal morality behind the demonstrators.[116] And, because most Americans believe in law and respect individual rights, the then unavoidable perception of a right-remedy gap fueled the political dialogue — with Martin Luther King using *Brown* to help propel the passage of major civil rights legislation.[117]

---

[111] *See, e.g.*, Keyes v. School Dist. No. 1, Denver, Colo., 413 U.S. 189, 249–50 (1973) (Powell, J., concurring in part and dissenting in part).

[112] Address by Justice Antonin Scalia, Oliver Wendell Holmes Annual Lecture (Feb. 14, 1989) (on file at the Harvard Law School Library).

[113] *See* R. KLUGER, SIMPLE JUSTICE 758 (1977).

[114] Brown v. Board of Educ., 347 U.S. 483 (1954). As Gene Sperling observed:

> The declaration in *Brown I*, that state-maintained school segregation is unconstitutional, instantaneously created a wide discrepancy between constitutional ideals and reality for black school children. In the years between *Brown* and *Swann v. Charlotte-Mecklenberg*, this disturbing gap prompted civil rights advocates to push continually for judicial remedies that would truly realize the rights articulated in *Brown I*.

Note, *supra* note 100, at 1743 (footnote omitted). The central argument in *Brown* is in accord with the theme of this article. As I put it in *American Constitutional Law*:

> The most obvious rationale for the holding in *Brown I* is also the most persuasive. Racial separation by force of law conveys strong social stigma and perpetuates both the stereotypes of racial inferiority and the circumstances on which such stereotypes feed. Its social meaning *is* that the minority race is inferior.

L. TRIBE, *supra* note 91, § 16-15, at 1477.

[115] Gene Sperling put it well: "Whereas *Plessy v. Ferguson* had frozen the anti-caste claims of blacks, *Brown* fanned an already-sparked fire by placing the legal and moral weight of the Constitution behind the black leadership who sought to dismantle the southern caste system." Note, *supra* note 100, at 1745 (footnotes omitted).

[116] *See id.* at 1744–45.

[117] *See id.* at 1745–46.

In the Detroit interdistrict busing case, *Milliken v. Bradley*, the Court confronted a new generation of complex remedial issues.[118] This time, however, the Court sought to close any possibility of a right-remedy gap by simply narrowing the definition of the violation until it fit the very limited intradistrict remedy the Court was willing to mandate.[119] Even if it would have had no impact on judicial *remedies*, a judicial proclamation that inner city ghettoization was constitutionally infirm might have avoided legitimating this nation-wide travesty.[120] Had the Court exerted the one thing it clearly can control — its rights-declaration powers — to recognize the role of law and of state action in creating ghettoization, the Court could at least have created positive social and political tension, the sort of tension that makes kids grow up thinking something is wrong, instead of inevitable, about ghettoization. Black leaders could have relied on such a positive tension in 1984, a decade after *Milliken*, to stress, as Martin Luther King did in 1964, how much had been promised and how little delivered. Invariably, the recognition of such tensions has its costs as well as its benefits: too many right-remedy gaps may mock the law and spawn disillusion and cynicism rather than inspire polit-ical effort. At a minimum, it seems crucial to focus on how a court's observations about legal responsibility might alter the reality that the court is addressing — both negatively *and* positively.

Frederick Douglass was far ahead of his time when he recognized the positive value of a right-remedy tension in his speech denouncing the Supreme Court's 1883 invalidation of the 1875 Civil Rights Act.[121] Douglass admitted that the Act probably could not have been enforced

---

[118] As Sperling described the situation:

At the trial in *Milliken v. Bradley*, Judge Roth was forced to confront the limitations of focusing only on particular school boards when defining both the violation and the remedy. Roth realized that where a network of state policies had created a condition of inner-city racial containment, any remedy *within* the contained area would *perpetuate* rather than eliminate the discriminatory violation. Holding the state of Michigan ulti-mately responsible, Roth contemplated a busing remedy reaching into fifty-four white school districts surrounding the Detroit inner-city area.

Id. at 1750 (footnotes omitted) (emphasis in original).

[119] As Sperling explains:

with no remedial decree before it, the Court could have spoken purely in terms of the right involved. Instead, the Court carefully defined an intra-district, local school-board-oriented violation that allowed for matching intra-district remedies at the expense of exploring the deeper causes and potential cures for racial containment in the inner cities.

Id. at 1751 (footnotes omitted).

[120] When courts view a fragment of the state (e.g., a local school district) as the party remedially responsible for segregation, flight from or racial isolation of that district denies possibilities of meaningful remedies while allowing for judicial denial of the continuation of constitutional harm. When courts view the state as a whole as responsible, white flight and racial containment, however troublesome as remedial obstacles, would not obscure the judicial recognition and societal perception of constitutional tension.

Id. at 1754 (footnotes omitted).

[121] *See id.* at 1764.

in the America of the 1880's, but he reminded his listeners that the Civil Rights Act, "like all advanced legislation, was a banner on the outer wall of American liberty, a noble moral standard. . . . There are tongues," he said,

> in trees, books, in the running brooks, — sermons in stones. This law, though dead, did speak. . . . It told the American people that they were all equal before the law. . . . The Supreme Court has hauled down this flag of liberty in open day . . . . It is a concession to race pride, selfishness and meanness . . . .[122]

Thus did Frederick Douglass, a former slave, recognize a half-century before Heisenberg that the act of observation changes the reality observed — in law no less than in nature.

Justice Jackson made a similar point in his impassioned dissent from the Supreme Court's decision in *Korematsu v. United States*, which upheld a conviction of an American citizen of Japanese descent for violating one of the infamous "military exclusion" orders applicable to thousands of similarly situated citizens of Japanese ancestry on the West Coast.[123] Quoting Justice Cardozo from *The Nature of the Judicial Process* to the effect that a principle, once judicially pronounced, tends to "expand itself to the limit of its logic,"[124] Justice Jackson argued that, when a military commander oversteps the Constitution's bounds,

> it is an incident. But if we review and approve, that passing incident becomes [constitutional] doctrine . . . , [where] it has a generative power of its own, and all that it creates will be in its own image. . . . [O]nce a judicial opinion rationalizes . . . [race-based exclusion] to show that it conforms to the Constitution, or rather rationalizes the Constitution to show that the Constitution sanctions such an order, . . . [t]he principle of racial discrimination . . . lies about like a loaded weapon . . . .[125]

What Frederick Douglass, Benjamin Cardozo, and Robert Jackson all recognized, each in his own context, is the profoundly flawed character of the notion that there exists a natural, pre-political and pre-legal state of things — such as the "natural" separation of the races, or the "natural" flight of whites to the suburbs, or the "natural" condition of a pregnancy continuing to its conclusion despite a woman's wish to end it — and that the process of making and interpreting law has no effect on that "natural" background. But in what sense *is* it "natural" that a woman must continue to remain pregnant, even

---

[122] *Id.* (quoting 4 P. FONER, THE LIFE AND WRITINGS OF FREDERICK DOUGLASS 401 (1955)).

[123] Korematsu v. United States, 323 U.S. 214 (1944).

[124] B. CARDOZO, THE NATURE OF THE JUDICIAL PROCESS 51 (1921).

[125] *Korematsu*, 323 U.S. at 246 (Jackson, J., dissenting).

against her will, when there is a doctor willing to perform a surgical procedure that will terminate her pregnancy? When there is a pharmaceutical firm willing to produce RU-486, which will prevent the implantation of the embryo in the wall of her placenta? If these things seem "natural," is it not only by virtue of an entire background of legal arrangements — including the licensing and regulation of physicians and the control of new drugs by the FDA? This means that the transmutation from biology to destiny is mediated not by an inexorable order of nature, but by a set of prior legal observations that have changed the very universe being observed.

Thus, if an activist Supreme Court should begin losing the traditionalists' respect for precedent, that, too, would be a kind of throwback. For, in a sense, the doctrine of stare decisis represents essentially a judicial recognition that, when courts make observations about the legal landscape, they may so deeply alter the terrain itself that future decisions must take sensitive account of how expectations have been built upon such prior judicial decisions.[126] However old and venerable the notion of stare decisis might be, its incorporation into legal reasoning might best be understood as a recognition of the operation in our law of a principle analogous to Heisenberg's.

I am not suggesting that a post-Newtonian viewpoint would always or even usually provide us with different constitutional doctrines; as I have said, it cannot yield determinate *answers* to constitutional problems. What I am suggesting is that, by taking seriously insights and perspectives parallel to those of contemporary physics, we might avoid regressing in the kinds of questions we ask. It is for this reason that I have focused less on "better" outcomes in the cases I have explored than on the questions that I believe might better have been asked.

The inquiries pursued in Justice Brennan's dissent in *DeShaney*, probing the state's role in shaping a legal environment which isolated the abused Joshua, were indeed post-Newtonian in spirit. Similar questions should be asked in the abortion context. Whether one is talking about a criminal prohibition (as in *Roe*), a decision to expel certain abortions from public facilities (as in *Webster*), or a decision not to fund certain abortions (as in *Harris v. McRae*), the relevant question is not, "did the state physically force pregnancy upon the woman?" The question is whether the state's combination of acts and omissions, rules, funding decisions and the like, so shaped the legal landscape in which women decide matters bearing on their reproductive lives as to violate the Constitution's postulates of liberty and equality.

---

[126] *See* Schauer, *Precedent*, 39 STAN. L. REV. 571 (1987).

D. Institutional Limits

Once one puts questions in this form, there are, of course, important institutional considerations to be kept constantly in mind about the limits of appropriate judicial intervention. For example, in the context of ghettoization, I suggested above that the Court should be much more willing than it has thus far been to recognize governmental responsibility for the racially separationist consequences of neutrally motivated acts — as in cases like *Washington v. Davis*,[127] for instance, where a verbal skills test produced a largely black ghetto ringed by a largely white police force; or in cases like *City of Memphis v. Greene*,[128] where a decision about re-routing traffic forced black people to circumnavigate a largely white and wealthy suburb.

But this need not imply that it would be appropriate for a court, lacking the remedial authority and flexibility of Congress acting under section 5 of the fourteenth amendment, to rectify each of these situations in an ordinary lawsuit — for a court to require the redesign of selection methods for police in Washington, D.C., for example, or the re-routing of roads and road-building plans so as to minimize the adverse impact on racial minorities.

In the 1987 case of *McCleskey v. Kemp*,[129] the Supreme Court refused to award any relief to a black man sentenced to death for killing someone who was white. The statistical evidence before the Court was overwhelming that the race of the victim makes an enormous difference in the probability of any given defendant's being executed.[130] Recognizing that little short of a radical overhaul in the structure of the criminal justice system, and perhaps in the structure of our society as a whole, could eliminate this tragic link between the victim's race and the system's response, the Court let the sentence of death stand in the case before it. As in the police selection case and in the road re-routing case, it is not at all clear that the Supreme Court's bottom line could realistically have been different.

But saying this is very different from announcing from the bench, as the Court unfortunately did in each of those cases, that the government bears no responsibility for the plight of the blacks who did not do well on the verbal test in *Washington v. Davis*, or for the devaluation of the lives of black citizens whose attackers may expect to be punished less severely than the attackers of white citizens in *McCleskey*. To announce that government bears no responsibility for these problems is to *legitimate* government's actions, and to relieve

---

[127] 426 U.S. 229 (1976).
[128] 451 U.S. 100 (1981).
[129] 481 U.S. 279 (1987).
[130] *See id.* at 286–87.

both governmental and nongovernmental actors of responsibility for solving these problems in institutionally appropriate ways.[131]

In an article bristling with what I have here called post-Newtonian insights, Randall Kennedy expresses concern over "the manner in which the *McCleskey* majority articulated and defended its decision," which he argues displayed "an egregious disregard for the sensibilities of black Americans."[132] Kennedy asks us to focus on the impact of that decision upon the black community:

> I am . . . concerned with the plight of black communities whose welfare is slighted by criminal justice systems that respond more forcefully to the killing of whites than the killing of blacks. . . .
> . . . I argue that even in the absence of discriminatory purpose, the unjustified racial disparities that characterize capital sentencing in Georgia should be viewed as giving rise to a constitutional violation: the failure of Georgia to provide to its black residents the equal protection of the laws.[133]

The constitutional violation Kennedy identifies is all but invisible unless one takes a post-Newtonian perspective. "At issue" for Kennedy "is the legal significance of discrete, isolated decisions that are susceptible to a non-racial explanation when considered individually, but reveal a pattern clearly shaped by racial sentiment when considered en masse."[134] The post-Newtonian view readily exposes the injury caused by systematic violation and exacerbated by Newtonian judicial blindness.

E. Choosing Legal Paradigms

Implicit throughout my discussion of scientific and legal paradigms have been two criteria for choosing among competing paradigms. The first is empirical — which paradigm best explains the available "data"? Although the mathematics needed to work it all out is complex, Einstein's theory is not only simpler in basic conception and more elegant in design than Newton's; it makes better predictions about a

---

[131] *See* L. TRIBE, *supra* note 91, at 16–17, 34–42, 101–02, 340–50, 1336–37, 1351, 1502–14; *see also* Sager, *Fair Measure: The Legal Status of Underenforced Constitutional Norms*, 91 HARV. L. REV. 1212 (1978).

[132] Kennedy, McCleskey v. Kemp: *Race, Capital Punishment, and the Supreme Court*, 101 HARV. L. REV. 1388, 1417 (1988).

[133] *Id.* at 1394–95.

[134] *Id.* at 1406. It is not clear that anyone could be found with standing to demand a remedy absent Kennedy's "community-oriented" perspective. *See id.* at 1422–23. Nor is it clear that the limits of an article III court make this perspective, or the remedies it might entail, entirely appropriate.

number of real-world phenomena[135] — including the degree to which a star's light ray that passes in the sun's vicinity appears to be *deflected* by the sun's mass when visible during a solar eclipse.[136] Similarly, I have tried to suggest that the post-Newtonian legal paradigm fits better our modern intuitions about the state, the courts, and law.

A second criterion for choosing among competing paradigms might be called the "progressivity" of the paradigm — the resilience and usefulness of the paradigm in a new context.[137] A progressive paradigm adapts in a constructive fashion to new "data" — new situations and problems; a "degenerative" paradigm must be revised in an ad hoc fashion to handle these new facts or contexts.[138]

Consider Newtonian physics. Its major limitation was that it did not yield a consistent and principled account of events[139] — an explanation that worked independent of the kinds of changes in surrounding conditions that scientists have increasingly agreed should make no difference to the operation of basic physical laws. The most

---

[135] As Hawking explains:

For example, very accurate observations of the planet Mercury revealed a small difference between its motion and the predictions of Newton's theory of gravity. Einstein's general theory of relativity predicted a slightly different motion from Newton's theory. The fact that Einstein's predictions matched what was seen, while Newton's did not, was one of the crucial confirmations of the new theory.

S. HAWKING, *supra* note 19, at 10.

[136] Gamow describes the famous experiment:

The light rays from two stars SI and SII located (at the moment of observation) at opposite sides of the sun disk converge into a theodolite, which measures the angle between them. The experiment is then repeated later when the sun is out of the way, and the two angles are compared. If they are different we have proof that the mass of the sun changes the curvature of the space around it, deflecting the rays of light from their original paths. Such an experiment was originally suggested by Einstein to test his theory. . . .

. . . [T]he test was actually made in 1919 by a British astronomical expedition to the Principe Islands (West Africa), from which the total solar eclipse of that year could best be observed. The difference of angular distances between the two stars with and without the sun between them was found to be 1.61" (plus or minus) 0.30" as compared with 1.75 predicted by Einstein's theory. Similar results were obtained by various expeditions at later dates.

G. GAMOW, *supra* note 18, at 108.

[137] *See* Lakatos, *supra* note 11, at 116–22.

[138] *See id.*

[139] As Imre Lakatos explains:

Einstein's theory is not better than Newton's *because* Newton's theory was 'refuted' but Einstein's was not: there are many known 'anomalies' to Einsteinian theory. Einstein's theory is better than — that is, represents progress compared with — Newton's theory *anno 1916* (that is, Newton's laws of dynamics, law of gravitation, the known set of initial conditions; 'minus' the list of known anomalies such as Mercury's perihelion) *because* it explained everything that Newton's theory had successfully explained, and it explained also *to some extent* some known anomalies and, in addition, forbade events like transmission of light along straight lines near large masses about which Newton's theory had said nothing but which had been permitted by other well-corroborated scientific theories of the day; moreover, *at least some* of the unexpected excess Einsteinian content was in fact *corroborated* (for instance, by the eclipse experiments).

Id. at 124 (emphasis in original).

fundamental of the so-called "equivalence principles" that Newton's theories were too primitive to yield is the principle that the basic laws of science should be the same for a body that is undergoing uniform acceleration as they are for a body that is at rest in a uniform gravitational field.[140] You who feel as though you and anything you happen to drop are being pulled toward the floor by the "force" of gravity, would feel exactly the same "pull" if the entire earth vanished and the building you happened to be occupying were accelerating quite rapidly in the direction you *used* to call "up" — so that the building would be going about 65 miles per hour after the first three seconds, about 130 miles per hour three seconds later, about 200 miles per hour after another three seconds, and so on, and you were in fact continuously being pressed against the floor with a force equal to the earth's gravitational field — one "g," or "gravity."

To understand how much more coherently and consistently Einstein's paradigm can deal with this equivalence between acceleration and gravity, imagine that somebody just outside the room in which you sit as you read this were to shine a laser beam through a small opening located where the wall to your left meets the ceiling, shooting it horizontally across the room.[141] Where would it hit the wall to the right? If the building you occupy were rapidly accelerating in deep space, and if there were a device on the wall to the right to measure it *very* accurately, you would find that the laser beam hits *not* where the wall meets the ceiling, but slightly *below* that point. And if you could trace the path of the laser beam across the room, you would notice it *not* zipping perfectly across the ceiling, but dropping toward the floor in a very slight arc. The reason is clear: as the beam crosses the room, the room continues to speed up, leaving the beam further and further behind as it crosses.

A Newtonian would be satisfied with that discrete explanation. But an Einsteinian would say that the acceleration of the room creates "g" forces that *warp* the space in the room, and the light beam is *bent* by this curved space. Why is that a better explanation? Because with it, an Einsteinian would not be in the least surprised to find, if you performed the laser beam experiment on earth in your room right

---

[140] Einstein states:

> The ratio of the masses of two bodies is defined in mechanics in two ways which differ from each other fundamentally; in the first place, as the reciprocal ratio of the accelerations which the same motive force imparts to them (inert mass), and in the second place, as the ratio of the forces which act upon them in the same gravitational field (gravitational mass). The equality of these two masses, so differently defined, is a fact which is confirmed by experiments of very high accuracy (experiments of Eötvös), and classical mechanics offers no explanation for this equality.

A. EINSTEIN, *supra* note 8, at 56.

[141] Einstein explores the following "idealized experiment" in A. EINSTEIN & L. INFELD, *supra* note 9, at 218–22.

now, that the beam would drop in an arc in *precisely* the same way. Having said that the earth's mass warps the space in your room exactly as the acceleration of the room in deep space would, she would *expect* the effect on the light beam to be identical.

But the Newtonian would be totally mystified to learn that, even on earth, the laser beam curves downward. To account for the curve, he would probably suggest that the beam should be thought of as a stream of water particles, and he would start making special assumptions about the "weight" of individual "particles" of light that are contained in it, and about how the "gravity" of the earth pulled these particles toward the floor. By contrast, Einstein's approach provides a more consistent explanation for why the physical universe is the way it is, and yields a set of physical laws that would work equally well for earthbound creatures and for astronauts accelerating away from earth. Thus an Einsteinian is spared the fate of being forced to rewrite his laws in an ad hoc way to address each new context.[142] The Einsteinian paradigm is, in this way, more progressive than the Newtonian paradigm.

Back down on earth, in the constitutional realm, it is equally important to avoid that fate. The most basic substantive principles affecting the kinds of things that government may do in its dealings with people should not depend on accidents of form and appearance — like the accident of whether the government exerts pressure through a single administrative regulation instead of through a series of judicial rulings, or by imposing a fine on those who *do* something instead of offering a benefit only to those who agree *not* to do it.[143]

I believe that, in law just as in physics, the goal of freeing constitutional analysis from such entirely artificial distinctions is best achieved if we think of law, and of governmental action, as changing the social landscape and redirecting the "geometry" of human interactions, instead of regarding government as a physical entity that, through the "forces" exerted by its component parts, tugs and pulls at people who are "out there" in a "state of nature". In this way, the post-Newtonian legal paradigm is more progressive than the Newtonian paradigm. Whether in the child abuse context of *DeShaney*, in the abortion context of *Webster*, in the symbolic speech setting of *Wooley*, or in the resegregation setting of *Spangler*, we are more likely

---

[142] Einstein states:

The possibility of explaining the numerical equality of inertia and gravitation by the unity of their nature gives to the general theory of relativity, according to my conviction, such a superiority over the conceptions of classical mechanics, that all the difficulties encountered must be considered as small in comparison with this progress.

A. EINSTEIN, *supra* note 8, at 58.

[143] For a splendid article seemingly animated in large part by the desire to avoid just such dependence, see Sullivan, *Unconstitutional Conditions*, 102 HARV. L. REV. 1415 (1989).

to put better questions if we focus on how collective political action has reconstituted the relevant "social space" than if we simply ask who is laying hands on whom.

IV. CONCLUSION

A corollary of responsible modernism is to admit that we can *see* more than we can *do*.[144] But this does not mean that we should lie about what we see. Those lies sap the creative tension that fuels progress. Thus, as we consider whether judicial opinions or other governmental measures unconstitutionally tilt the legal landscape in favor of some groups and against others, it is crucial not to ignore the *social meaning* of whatever the state has done.[145]

To understand such meaning in a way that fully acknowledges the interconnectedness of legal events — and to recognize, as modern physics has, the interdependence between the process of observing and what is observed — is to avoid the parochial fallacy of looking at the legal universe only through the eyes of those in power.[146] It requires abandoning any notion that the "objective" picture of the legal universe is the one seen from the vantage point of those who make legal decisions.[147] Difficult as it is to view the world from someone else's perspective, not to make the effort is to ignore what science learned

---

[144] *See supra* pp. 13–14 (discussing *DeShaney* and paternalism).

[145] Clifford Geertz put this idea most succinctly: "[T]his prejudice . . . that the dramaturgy of power is external to its workings, must be put aside." C. GEERTZ, NEGARA: THE THEATRE STATE IN NINETEENTH-CENTURY BALI 136 (1980). In a more extended passage, Geertz writes:

What our concept of public power obscures, that of the Balinese exposes; and vice versa. . . . [I]t is there, in exposing the symbolic dimensions of state power. . . . Such study restores our sense of the ordering force of display, regard, and drama.

Each of the leading notions of what the state 'is' that has developed in the West since the sixteenth century — monopolist of violence within a territory, executive committee of the ruling class, delegated agent of popular will, pragmatic device for conciliating interests — has had its own sort of difficulty assimilating the fact that this force exists. None has produced a workable account of its nature. Those dimensions of authority not easily reducible to a command-and-obedience conception of political life have been left to drift in an indefinite world of excrescences, mysteries, fictions and decorations. And the connection between what Begehot called the dignified parts of government and the efficient ones has been systematically misconceived.

This misconception, most simply put, is that the office of the dignified parts is to serve the efficient, that they are artifices, more or less cunning, more or less illusional, designed to facilitate the prosier aims of rule. . . .

. . . [I]n all these views, the semiotic aspects of the state . . . remain so much mummery. They exaggerate might, conceal exploitation, inflate authority, or moralize procedure. The one thing they do not do is actuate anything.

Id. at 121–23.

[146] One could interpret John Rawls' "veil of ignorance" as essentially capturing this insight into the nature of justice — that "fairness" requires looking at things from the perspective of those on the bottom of the social ladder. *See* J. RAWLS, *supra* note 55, at 136–42.

[147] See Minow, *When Difference Has Its Home: Group Homes for the Mentally Retarded, Equal Protection and Legal Treatment of Difference*, 22 HARV. C.R.-C.L. L. REV. 111 (1987).

long ago. How strange that physics should have to reteach the Golden Rule.

Among the consequences of adhering more consistently to this post-Newtonian perspective might well be a reduced tendency to blame the state's victims for the harm done when the state sets them apart — as though their view of what government has done or failed to do is to be discounted in light of their supposedly limited or distorted perspective. The late nineteenth-century Supreme Court did just that in *Plessy v. Ferguson*,[148] when it indicated that forced separation by race merely tracks nature's law; if such separation makes blacks feel stigmatized, it's all in the construction *they* put upon it.[149] Justice O'Connor, in an otherwise sensitive examination of a city's official celebration of a nativity scene at Christmas, fell into a similar trap when she said that no "objective" observer would take that display as an endorsement of Christianity or as a put down of non-Christians.[150]

Discerning the social meaning of a challenged practice — of a legal space shaped by certain acts juxtaposed with certain omissions — entails inquiry into how the practice affects the human geometry of the situation. Such inquiry in turn demands less an effort to uncover the hidden levers, gears or forces that translate governmental actions into objective effects, than an attempt to feel the contours of the world government has built — and to sense what those contours *mean* for those who might be trapped or excluded by them.

So too with discerning the operative effect of an incomplete social welfare program. Just as the path of a beam of starlight passing near the sun is best understood not as responding to a hidden tug but as moving along the shortest distance between two points in a space bent by the sun's very mass, so the citizens who might have come to Joshua DeShaney's aid but for the assumption that the state's elaborate welfare program would do so are best understood not as reacting to a muffled signal or a gentle push but as following the path of least resistance laid out by the very presence and structure of the state's program. And the judicial declaration that Joshua's fate is not the state's fault but the natural result of private action, operates not simply as a passive *observation* about who caused injury to whom, but as an *action* that may entrench all the more deeply the geometry of public indifference that will shape the lives of Joshuas yet unborn.

---

[148] 163 U.S. 537 (1896).

[149] *See id.* at 551.

[150] *See* Lynch v. Donnelly, 465 U.S. 668, 692–93 (1984). *But see* County of Allegheny v. ACLU Greater Pittsburgh Chapter, 109 S. Ct. 3086 (1989) (holding that the creche display, when viewed in its overall context, violates the establishment clause since the creche carried a patently Christian message and nothing in the setting detracted from that message); *id.* at 3117–24 (O'Connor, J., concurring).

Acknowledgments

Cohen, Morris Raphael. "Law and Scientific Method." *American Law School Review* 6 (1928): 231–39.

Kaplow, Louis. "Rules Versus Standards: An Economic Analysis." *Duke Law Journal* 42 (1992): 557–629. Copyright 1992. Reprinted with the permission of the *Duke Law Journal.*

Landes, William M. and Richard A. Posner. "Legal Precedent: A Theoretical and Empirical Analysis." *Journal of Law and Economics* 19 (1976): 249–307. Reprinted with the permission of the University of Chicago, publisher. Copyright 1976 University of Chicago.

McCarty, L. Thorne. "Reflections on *Taxman*: An Experiment in Artificial Intelligence and Legal Reasoning." *Harvard Law Review* 90 (1977): 837–93. Copyright 1977 by the Harvard Law Review Association.

Posner, Richard A. "The Decline of Law as an Autonomous Discipline: 1962–1987." *Harvard Law Review* 100 (1987): 761–80. Copyright 1987 by the Harvard Law Review Association.

Rissland, Edwina L. "Artificial Intelligence and Law: Stepping Stones to a Model of Legal Reasoning." *Yale Law Journal* 99 (1990): 1957–81. Reprinted by permission of the Yale Law Journal Company and Fred B. Rothman and Company.

Skalak, David B. and Edwina L. Rissland. "Arguments and Cases: An Inevitable Intertwining." *Artificial Intelligence and Law* 1 (1992): 3–44. Reprinted with the permission of Kluwer Academic Publishers.

Tillers, Peter and David Schum. "A Theory of Preliminary Fact Investigation." *University of California, Davis, Law Review* 24 (1991): 931–1012. Reprinted with permission. Copyright 1991 by the Regents of the University of California.

Tribe, Laurence H. "The Curvature of Constitutional Space: What Lawyers Can Learn from Modern Physics." *Harvard Law Review* 103 (1989): 1–39. Copyright 1989 by the Harvard Law Review Association.